Levine & Shefner's
Fundamentals of Sensation and Perception

LEVINE & SHEFNER'S
Fundamentals of Sensation and Perception

Third Edition

Michael W. Levine

Department of Psychology, University of Illinois at Chicago

OXFORD
UNIVERSITY PRESS

OXFORD

UNIVERSITY PRESS

Great Clarendon Street, Oxford ox2 6DP
Oxford University Press is a department of the University of Oxford.
It furthers the University's objective of excellence in research, scholarship,
and education by publishing worldwide in

Oxford New York

Auckland Cape Town Dar es Salaam Hong Kong Karachi
Kuala Lumpur Madrid Melbourne Mexico City Nairobi
New Delhi Shanghai Taipei Toronto

With offices in

Argentina Austria Brazil Chile Czech Republic France Greece
Guatemala Hungary Italy Japan Poland Portugal Singapore
South Korea Switzerland Thailand Turkey Ukraine Vietnam

Oxford is a registered trade mark of Oxford University Press
in the UK and in certain other countries

Published in the United States
by Oxford University Press Inc., New York

A catalogue record for this book is available from the British Library

Library of Congress Cataloging in Publication Data
(Data applied for)

ISBN-13: 978-0-19-852466-3
ISBN-10: 0-19-852466-8

7 9 10 8 6

Typeset by J&L Composition, Filey, N. Yorks
Printed in Great Britain
on acid-free paper by
Antony Rowe Ltd., Chippenham, Wiltshire

Preface

Rationale

When Jeremy Shefner and I set out to write the first edition of this book, we faced a problem. In our courses in the psychology of sensation and perception, each of us tried to integrate what we knew about the physiology of sensory systems with the classical perceptual problems commonly discussed in psychology courses. Within this framework, students generally found the physiology sections of the course both interesting and useful in understanding the cognitive aspects of perception. Finding a textbook to accompany the lectures, however, proved to be a difficult task. The existing books discussed the cognitive aspects of perception with little reference to their physiological bases. The first edition of this book was our attempt to integrate these two complementary ways of studying perceptual processes.

What happens to information about the physical stimulus as our sensory systems produce complicated perceptions of the world around us? In following this pathway, you will get a general idea of how anatomy and physiology allow us to extract the information upon which our perceptions are built. Perception is a very complex field, however, with many phenomena that cannot now be explained physiologically. As far as possible you will see explanations at the physiological, psychophysical, and cognitive levels. While this text is an introduction to the subject, material is presented in enough depth, and with enough reference to current research methods, that it can also serve the more advanced student who is becoming more involved in the field.

Features

In a few ways, this book is different from other texts. Knowing about these features will help you get the most from this book.

Boxes

Often there are topics of interest and relevance to the subject at hand that are more advanced or specialized than the rest of the text. For example, in some cases a few equations could help to make a point but would only confuse any reader who is not familiar with mathematics. In many places, demonstrations make the material clearer. Often, there are interesting details that are not essential for the 'big picture', but should be offered to the reader with more than a 'passing' interest. Such material is segregated into **boxes**. The boxes in this book have been written to follow from the text at a particular point. To lead you to them at just that point (if you wish) there is a **hyperlink**— like the underlined terms on a web page. I couldn't figure out how to 'hide' boxes in a book until you click, so the hyperlinks just sit there and the boxes are elsewhere. When you hit a bold underlined reference to a **BOX** and read it; the **hyperlink** will remind you where you left off in your reading..

Demonstrations

Many of the figures, particularly in Chapters 9 through 14, are intended to demonstrate a perceptual effect or illusion. In most cases, you can just look at the figure and say, 'Oh yes, that looks like . . . (whatever).' In some cases, a little more effort is required—looking at the figure from a greater distance, turning it upside down, or covering parts of it with a sheet of paper. Please take the trouble to do these things, for they will demonstrate the effect, and make it real for you.

Stereograms

Stereograms (three-dimensional pictures) are among the demonstrations that will require a bit of work on your part. The perceptual effect of a three-dimensional scene justifies the effort you may make.

Printing stereograms in a book poses a special problem that is usually solved by one of two methods. One is direct and requires no extra equipment from the reader but is hard for many people to see; the other is easy for almost anyone to see, but requires having a small mirror, which often is not handy. (A more recent third method, the 'magic eye', is not suitable for the kinds of stereogram demonstrations needed here.)

Stereograms consist of two pictures: one is to be seen by your right eye, and the other by your left. The small differences between the images in these two pictures (or frames) correspond to the differences in points of view of two eyes; these differences lead to a strong perception of depth (see Chapter 11). In the direct-viewing method, the frames are printed side by side; the reader must then manage to look at each one with one eye (see Box P1). In the mirror-viewing method, the frame on the right is printed as a mirror image of how it should appear to the right eye. A small mirror held between the two frames allows the left eye to view the left frame directly, while the right eye sees the right frame reflected in the mirror. Tilting the mirror makes it easy to position the images so that they overlap.

These methods are combined in this book so that the stereograms can either be viewed directly or seen with the aid of a mirror. To our knowledge, this was the first book in which the reader is offered such an option; when you encounter stereograms in other books, you have to view them in the way the book says, or they will not work (unless by chance the right frame is mirror-symmetric). In all the stereograms in this book, the right-hand frame is mirror-symmetric about its middle; it therefore looks the same whether viewed directly or in a mirror, and so the stereogram can be viewed by either method. The following box explains how to view the stereograms using each method. **BOX P1**

Box P1 Viewing the stereograms

Before attempting to view a stereogram, check that you are not stereoblind—that is, that you use both of your eyes and fuse the images to give a three-dimensional perception. A simple test for stereoscopic vision is illustrated in Fig. P1. Stare at a spot on a wall across the room (for example, the star in the figure). Bring your two hands in front of your face, about 1 foot in front of your eyes, with the pointer fingers aiming at each other. When the two fingers are about to touch (about half an inch apart), you should see what is shown on the top part of Fig. P1(b): the star (that you are focused on) should be sharp; in front of it, and blurred, should be a sausage-like blimp floating between your two fingers. If you focus on your fingers, the blimp vanishes, the fingers become sharp, and the star should split into two blurry stars (Fig. P1b, bottom). If you see either of the pictures shown in Fig. P1(b) you are not stereoblind, and should be able to see three-dimensional stereograms (unless you also have double vision all the time). You should be able to achieve the stereo effects by one of the methods described below—direct and mirror, practicing on the stereogram in Fig. P2.

If you are stereoblind, you will see a single set of fingers (as in Fig. P1b, bottom) *and* a single star (as in Fig. P1b, top) *at the same time*. If you close one eye, there will be no change in the image; if you close the other, the star will jump to a different position relative to your fingers. If you are stereoblind, you will not see the three-dimensional effect in the stereograms, and will have to trust what the book says you would have seen. BOX P1

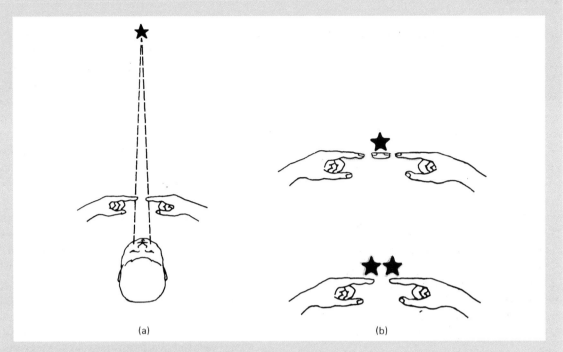

Fig. P1 Method for testing for stereoblindness. (a) Top view of subject. (b) Two ways the fingers and star should look to a normal (not stereoblind) person.

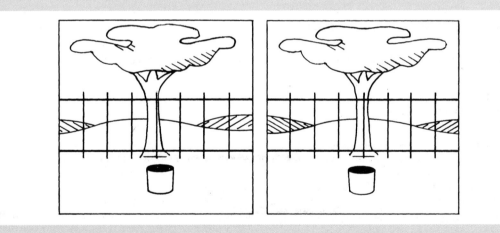

Fig. P2 Practice stereogram. The can should appear in front of the fence, and the tree behind it. It may be viewed by either the direct or the mirror method.

Direct method

The direct method requires no special equipment, but takes a bit of concentration. The idea is to look at the left frame with your left eye and the right frame with your right eye; the two images get superimposed in your brain and fuse into a single three-dimensional scene. The technique is shown in Fig. P3. (If you are familiar with the 'magic eye' three-dimensional pictures that were popular a few years ago, this will be old hat to you.) Just look at the two frames directly, and concentrate on making the

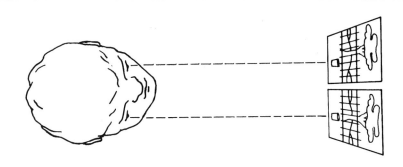

Fig. P3 Direct method of viewing strereograms: top view

double images superimpose. Even when they do, it may take an extra moment or two for the three-dimensional effect to become obvious.

To view a stereogram by this method, you have to have your eyes looking apart, rather than converging. When you look at something close, like this book, your eyes automatically point inward so that both are aimed at the same point. They diverge when you look into the distance. Therefore you should relax your eyes as much as possible, as if you were looking into the distance, even though the book is still close to your eyes.

There are several tricks that can help you view stereograms by this method:

1. If you are nearsighted, and wear glasses to see in the distance (*not* for reading), take off the glasses. You will then have to focus for distance to see the book, and your eyes will diverge (see Chapter 3). If you wear reading glasses you should keep them on.

2. Focus for infinity by staring across the room, then try not to change focus as you bring the book into your field of view. Squinting may help.

3. When your eyes start to diverge, you will see a pair of images of the stereogram, with the left frame of one image superimposed on the right frame of the other. Use the frames as a guide, and concentrate on bringing the corners into register. If one image is displaced upward relative to the other (instead of side to side) tilt your head slightly one way or the other. Tilting will also help you to identify the two images you are trying to bring together.

4. If both of your eyes keep trying to look at the same frame, you can erect a barricade between them. Use a piece of paper and hold it between your nose and the division of the frames, like the mirror in Fig. P4.

The barricade should prevent your left eye from seeing the right frame, and vice versa. Then you have only two images to try to bring together.

5. You can help diverge your eyes slightly by pressing gently at the inside corners. Place your fingers on the sides of your nose, and press very gently into the corners of your eyes (do *not* do this if you have any kind of eye infection, glaucoma, or other eye ailments).

Mirror method

Some people simply cannot see stereograms by the direct method, either because they cannot manage to diverge their eyes while seeing close up, or because their eyes are set too closely together in their heads. If you could not see the stereogram in Fig. P2 by the direct method, you should try the mirror method.

You will need a small hand mirror. The best is the rectangular kind that drugstores sell 'for pocket or purse', about 3 or 4 inches square. The mirror built into a makeup kit will do, although the kit itself can get in the way. A shiny, smooth piece of metal can also work, but the image in it is not likely to be as good as that produced by a real mirror.

Place one edge of the mirror along the space between the frames of the stereogram, with the shiny side to the right (see Fig. P4). Bring your head down to the mirror, so that it divides your field of view; your left eye can look directly at the left frame, but cannot see the right frame because the view is blocked by the dull back of the mirror. Your right eye can see the right frame directly or reflected in the mirror, but cannot see the left frame.

Concentrate on the left frame, and change the tilt of the mirror until the right frame seen by the right eye (reflected in the mirror) lines up with it. As with the di-

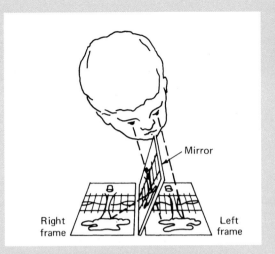

Right frame

Left frame

Mirror

Fig. P4 Mirror method of viewing stereograms

rect method, concentrate on aligning the corners of the frames. If there is a vertical misalignment, the mirror is not straight along the division between the frames. Left-to-right misalignment can be corrected by tilting the mirror or sliding it from left to right. The three-dimensional effect should appear moments after you align the two frames.

Demonstration programs

A CD-ROM is packaged with this book. The CD has a program that is compatible with PC-style computers running Windows NT or Windows 95 (or above). It won't sound very good on your stereo!

To install the demonstrations from the CD, place the CD in the drive and click the CD drive in 'My Computer' or 'Explorer'. Double click on the 'Setup' icon, a blue-screened computer with a box of diskettes standing before it. The installation program will ask you to confirm where you want to install the program; the default is to create a directory called 'SensPerc' on your 'C' drive [C:\Programs\SensPerc\], but you can specify any directory you like. The program icon, also called 'SensPerc', will be placed in the group of your choice or can be added to your 'start' listings or shortcuts. The icon for SensPerc is a red book. (Or is it? Take a closer look . . .) **BOX P2**

When you start SensPerc (by clicking its icon, or through the 'run' window), you will see a panel

Box P2 Installing the demonstration program from your CD

There are a few technical details about the program that you may have to consider. First, two of the demonstrations have to produce fine gradations of hue: in Chapter 8 (which produces color-balanced displays to demonstrate an effect called equiluminance) and Chapter 14 (color). Even for black and white, finer gradations can be obtained when more colors are available (this is true for the 'See your own CSF' demonstration in Chapter 9).

Now, in order to create all these nice colors on your screen, Windows needs access to what is called a 'palette'; even though your monitor is set up to produce at least 256 different levels of strength of each of the three color guns (which multiplies to $256 \times 256 \times 256 = 16\ 777\ 216$ different colors), Windows can only keep track of a limited number of them. If your system is set up in the usual 20th-century way, it has a 256-color palette, so you can only show 256 of those colors (and there are some restrictions on *which* 256 colors). This is also called '8-bit color', because it takes 8 bits (1 byte) to count 256 items. But you can probably set your system for higher color resolution: 16 bits, called 'high color', gives you 65 536 colors. The highest resolution, 24 bits ('true color'), allows the full 16 777 216 colors; only the 'See your own CSF' demonstration makes use of that resolution. You can change to these higher resolutions (if your hardware supports them) by clicking 'Settings' on the **'Start'** menu; then choose 'Control Panel', and in that window select 'Display'; select the 'Settings' tab, and you will see a drop-down menu for colors near the lower left.

The rest of the demonstrations don't need these higher color resolutions. Those that do will prompt you when you start them, suggesting you quit the program and change resolution. If you do not (or your hardware doesn't support higher resolution), you can run the demonstrations, but the features that depend on high resolution will be disabled. The images will not really be right, and controls that would have let you make adjustments will not be available.

This program was designed for a screen with a 'desktop' of 640 by 480 pixels. If you have a larger desktop, all the demonstrations will be smaller than intended; you may wish to reset your system settings before running these demonstrations. You can change your settings exactly as you changed color resolution: click on 'Settings' from the **'Start'** menu. Choose 'Control Panel' and then 'Display'. The screen resolution is controlled by a slide bar at the lower right.

The sounds that accompany the program are produced from 'wav' files. You can control the sound level from the volume control of your system. To see the volume control, double click on the little yellow loudspeaker icon (it is usually at the extreme lower right of the screen, next to the time, on the task bar). A panel will appear with sliders for controlling the volume of various sound functions. The leftmost part ('Volume Control') affects all the sounds on your computer (clicking 'Mute all' turns off all sound). The next one to the right is labeled 'Wave'; this is the one that controls the sounds made by SensPerc. Slide the level bar higher to make the sounds louder, lower to make them softer. The horizontal balance near the top determines whether the sound comes from the left, right, or both speakers. You can adjust the sound while SensPerc is running; the Chapter 1 'Instructions' program takes you through these settings (as well as color and size), and will play test sounds to help you make the sound adjustments.

Note that unless you have checked the 'Select' box at the bottom of the 'Wave' section, SensPerc will produce no sounds at all. You may wish to turn off the sound if you are in a room where sound would annoy others. Some of the modules of SensPerc allow you to turn off certain sounds by clicking a 'Silence' button: The main panel 'Silence' button stops the background tone and the beep each time a choice menu appears (but does not affect the sounds of the demonstrations); the demonstrations of cell responses (Chapters 5, 7, and 14) have a box to defeat the 'victory' music you get when you 'let the computer choose' a cell type and guess it correctly; and the Chapter 16 animation of traveling waves allows you to silence the accompanying tones. Note that checking 'silence' will not interrupt a sound once it has begun, but will preclude future sounds.

like that in an elevator, except that, instead of floors, the buttons select chapters of the text. 'Chapter 1' gives an overview of some of the common features of the demonstrations and how to use them. It also has details on system setup, as discussed in the Box P2. For many chapters, there is a single demonstration or set of demonstrations, but some chapters will pop up a menu of two or more different options. Some of the demonstrations are animations, in which color and motion make it easier to grasp a concept. Others are demonstrations of perceptual effects that require color or motion. In Chapter 12, you are asked to adjust the size or color of an object to match another; you can then measure how much you were fooled by an illusion. Of particular interest are the demonstrations in Chapter 8 in which the color must be balanced to your own particular visual system—obviously, that could not be done with pre-printed figures. Some are simple color figures, which are presented on your computer screen rather than being reduced onto a corner of a color plate in the book. Since these figures are included on the disk, which is needed for the moving demonstrations, the color figures are not reproduced in the book itself.

Please use the CD in conjunction with the book. You will find references to these demonstrations throughout the text, with more specific instructions relevant to the use of each. I believe your understanding and enjoyment of the material will be greatly facilitated by running the demonstrations.

Suggested readings

At the end of each chapter, you will find a list of readings that you might wish to pursue. For the most part, these readings take you a little deeper into the subject, but they are generally not at a very technical level. A brief description of each indicates roughly what to expect. You may wish to consult the readings for extra information, or to help you understand material that was not clear.

Appendix

Many students in a perception course have little experience with science, and find graphical representation and mathematics unfamiliar. There is an appendix at the back of the book that should help refresh your memory of graphs, equations, logarithms, and trigonometric functions. There is also a brief overview of neural function.

Glossdex

Books usually have indexes so that you can find the pages on which particular topics are discussed. They often also have glossaries, where you can find the definitions of terms. Here, these functions are merged in a 'glossdex'. Each word in the glossdex has a brief definition (unless it is a common term that requires none), followed by a list of the pages on which it is discussed in the text. Usually, the first page reference will be in bold type and will refer to the place where the term was introduced. When a term is first introduced, it is printed in italics and defined in the text.

A glossdex is better than a separate index and glossary because it saves looking up each item twice. Looking up a word in a glossary locates its definition, but then it is necessary to go to the index to find the pages where more can be learned about it. Looking up words in an index

does not indicate exactly which meaning of the term is indexed by the reference given and may lead you to the wrong subject. In a glossdex you can find the meaning and the references in one place.

References

The references give the complete citation to all of the published works cited in this book (over 1400 of them!). At the end of each reference—{in curly brackets like these}—is listed the number(s) of the chapter(s) in which the work is mentioned or discussed. Any figure(s) based on the article is indicated in **bold**. You will also find listings '*see*' or '*see also*' that point you to articles to which the person contributed but was not the first author.

Changes from the previous editions

There are a number of ways in which this edition differs from the first two editions of this text. First, of course, there have been many advances in the nearly 10 years between editions, and most of the chapters have been extensively revised and updated. Some developments that seemed very exciting in 1980 have proven less fruitful than expected, and these topics have been pared down to a more appropriate size. In a few cases, beliefs current when the earlier editions went to press have proven misguided, and corrections have been made. Topics that were not generally discussed have since taken a dominant position in our thinking and have been added to the newer editions. I can only imagine what topics may be deemed important if a fourth edition is prepared at some future date.

One particular branch of research has undergone a veritable explosion in the last decade: the investigation of the role and functioning of visual areas of the cortex. Not long ago, we knew of cell types and a structural pattern in primary visual cortex but only made vague statements that the information must be processed in 'higher' centers. We have now identified putative roles for many higher centers. In addition, we see parallel processing systems (identifiable at the lowest levels, but not always noticed in earlier research) within the cortical pathways. We are beginning to appreciate the ways in which these parallel systems interact and can hope one day to understand how a percept may emerge from the interplay of these regions. This explosion of information and understanding so expanded the material about higher centers that what had originally been a single chapter, 'Higher visual centers', was split into two: 'the primary visual areas of the brain' and 'Architecture of vision in the cortex'. In this edition, I add more material about how these neural networks relate to the actual extraction of a visual percept (Chapter 10).

The first edition of this text treated only two sensory systems: vision and audition. While these are still the primary emphases, the second edition added two new chapters discussing other sensory systems. Chapter 19 treats the 'body' senses—the senses of body position, touch, and temperature. Closely related to these is an important though sometimes unpleasant sense: the sense of pain. Chapter 20 adds the 'chemical' senses—taste and smell. While these additions were not intended to make this book an encyclopedia of sensory and perceptual processes, they did repair some serious omissions.

The biggest changes between the second and third editions are to be found in Chapters 8 and 10. Thinking about the parallel pathways in the visual cortex was just beginning to change when the second edition was being prepared; in this edition, I take a longer perspective on these 'higher' visual areas. Advances in technology that allow imaging of the living brain and its activity in a perceiving human subject have changed our outlook dramatically. Similarly, the ideas of interacting neural networks, enhanced by computer capabilities that allow researchers to confirm capabilities of such networks that they had only hy-

pothesized before, have led to new ways of thinking about how perception occurs.

Instructors who used the second edition and are now preparing a syllabus using the third will notice a minor change: the chapter numbers are different. That is because the background chapter (formerly Chapter 3) about basic neurophysiology has been removed. This information, which is not normally part of a sensation and perception course, has been abbreviated and placed in the Appendix.

A major innovation for the third edition is the accompanying CD that allows you to see moving, color figures. I hope you will take advantage of these demonstrations (they sure took a lot of work to create!), and they will serve to make your learning easier and—dare I hope it?—fun.

There is one other change for the third edition: the first two editions were written and revised by two of us: Jeremy Shefner and myself. But Dr Shefner's interests have changed, and he stepped back from this edition, so I am pressing on alone.

Chicago   *M.W.L*
January 2000

Summary of contents

Contents

Chapter 1

Introduction

Nemo Psychologus
Nisi Physiologus

THE words above are those of the 19th-century psychologist J. Müller; they mean 'one is not a psychologist who is not also a physiologist'. The sentiment is more valid today than it was a century ago and becomes even more true with each decade. Psychology is the science of the mind, and we are finally reaching a stage at which we can hope to relate the understanding of the mind to the physiological organ of which it is a manifestation: the brain.

The study of sensation and perception is central to psychology. The sensory systems were among the first investigated by the pioneers of this science. Through the years, perception has remained a major focus of psychology, as it is the area in which the goal of understanding how the nervous system relates to behavior is most nearly realized. In this area, more than in many others, Müller's statement is undeniable.

That statement is a guiding philosophy for this book. A person cannot understand the process of perception while ignoring the known physiology of the sensory systems that underlie the perceptual process. We are not yet in a position to provide a physiological explanation for perception, but we can deduce (from the physiology of sensation) what some of the relevant principles will be.

Sensation and perception

There are two aspects to the study of our senses: sensation and perception. For our purposes, draw the following distinction between them. *Sensation* refers to the process of detecting a stimulus (or some aspect of it) in the environment. It is the necessary collection of information about the world from which perceptions will be made. The organs of sensation are the eyes, ears, nose, tongue, skin, whiskers (in some animals), and so forth. The study of sensation is generally the study of how these organs function, often on a physiological scale.

Perception refers to the way in which we interpret the information that is gathered (and processed) by the senses. In short, you sense the stimulus but you perceive what it is. Here you enter the realm of another branch of psychology: cognitive psychology. The word *cognitive* (from the Latin for 'getting to know') refers to the processes by which we generate a representation of the world as we recognize it, think about it, and remember it. Perception includes the more cognitive processing by which you develop an internal model of what is 'out there' in the world beyond your body. But it is based on sensations, and can be no more accurate than the information provided by your sensory systems.

You know the world from the energy your senses can intercept. Sound and light can travel considerable distances, and so may carry information about objects or events quite distant from you. Molecules emitted by an odorant travel shorter distances, while the mechanical energy of pressure on the skin tells you about your immediate vicinity. Light is shaped and formed by objects it encounters; it therefore reveals more about the things around you than about the light source itself. Other forms of energy are more directly tied to their actual sources.

But the energy 'out there' is of little direct use to you. It must be channeled to the receptors specific to it. Light is focused on the retinae of your eyes to generate a useful image. Sound is channeled through the outer parts of your ears to the sensitive inner parts. Molecules are dissolved in fluids and brought in contact with receptors in your nose or on your tongue. You usually play an active role in this process: you turn your head and aim your eyes; you turn your head, and perhaps hold a hand cupped behind an ear; you sniff at the air, savor your food, and caress with your hands.

And you perceive. You make the most reasonable interpretations you can, given the information of your senses. *Given the information of your senses.* If your senses are fooled, you cannot help but be fooled. Have you ever seen a crime movie in which the robbers fool the security guards by placing a still picture in front of the CCTV camera monitoring the area? The robbers use a picture that is the exact view the camera normally scans, so the monitors display an empty room. Behind the picture, in the real room, the robbers are free to do their thing, while the guards, lacking the information that the room is occupied, are unaware of the deception.

The guards depended on the TV monitor as an extension of their senses, but your senses can be fooled directly. In Chapter 12, you will see optical illusions that appear to be quite different from what they really are. Lines that are identical can be made to seem different in size. Gray patches that are identical can be made to look like, well, day and night. You can gauge just how much you are fooled by trying to match sizes or shades in the

demonstrations associated with Chapter 12 on the CD-ROM accompanying this book.

Optical illusions also occur in nature. Have you ever noticed that the moon looks larger at the horizon than overhead? It is not really larger; your visual system is simply applying principles that do not quite work for the moon (see Chapter 12).

Optical illusions are amusing, but similar principles are essential in the arts. A painter who wishes to create an impression of depth on a canvas, or an architect who wants a building to look taller than it is, applies the rules outlined in Chapter 12 (see Fig. 1.1). The mimes who really seem to be carrying a huge sheet of glass are applying the principles of Chapter 10.

It is not only by intent that your senses are fooled. Have you ever walked down a dark alley in a bad neighborhood at night? How easy it is to see every shadow as a threatening, armed person! A conscientious lifeguard hears 'help!' in every sudden cry. Perception is grounded in sensation, but it is far from a straightforward process.

In this book you will learn about sensory processes; although we do not have a complete understanding of how these systems function, with a few guesses here and there, a reasonable picture can be created. You will read about what has been learned of the cognitive processes by which perceptions are created from the sensory input; less is known of the physiology of perception, so these principles are not as well related to the workings of the nervous system.

Students sometimes ask what these topics (particularly the more biological aspects of sensation) have to do with psychology. Biopsychologists reply that the science of psychology seeks to explain, understand, or even modify behavior, behavior being the response of an organism to the environment. There are stimuli in the world, and organisms or people perform actions based on their perceptions of the stimuli—with guidance from their past experiences (memory), and perhaps some innate predilections. How can you understand the response to the stimulus without first understanding the subject's perception of it?

Fig. 1.1 Two examples of how architects use perceptual principles to enhance buildings. (a) By making the windows successively smaller on higher stories, this building in New York City seems taller than it actually is. The architect exploited the depth cues of texture and linear perspective (see Chapter 12). (b) This building in Chicago presents a facade that is wholly false. Look again at the fancy doors, the imposing stairs, and arched entrance: this is a painting on a blank stone wall! (The entrance is around the side, to the left.) An artist has made use of several of the cues discussed in Chapter 12 to give the impression of a real, three-dimensional structure. This technique is known as *trompe l'oeil*, French for 'trick the eye'.

There is another reason for our attention to the sensory processes: the sensory systems are parts of the nervous system that are relatively easily identified and that have relatively comprehensible purposes. If we can understand the functioning of a bit of tissue such as the retina in the eye (which is, in fact, central nervous tissue), we can hope to apply the same principles in deciphering the workings of the less well-defined, associative parts of the brain. Our attention to the physiology of sensation is useful not only in understanding the sensory process, but also as a guide toward realizing Müller's dream of providing an understanding of behavior at the physiological level.

Overview

The goal of this book is to present some of what is now known of how we perceive the world. Physiological explanations for the phenomena of perception are emphasized, for they tend to be the most satisfactory ones. Nevertheless, our present understanding of brain function is still rather rudimentary. We must not neglect the more cognitive aspects of the perceptual process, for which a physiological explanation lies in the future.

This book places a heavier emphasis on vision

than on audition and the other perceptual systems. The visual system and the perception of visual stimuli are presented in some detail to develop the principles of sensation and perception. Many of the same principles apply in other sensory systems, and you should be able to see similarities between them. The emphasis here is not because there are not interesting perceptual aspects to audition, touch, or smell, but because visual phenomena are more familiar, and are directly presentable on the pages of a book.

Organization

You will first find some background material in Chapter 2. This chapter introduces the principles and methodology of psychophysics. This material is general to the study of sensory processes, and will be drawn on in later chapters.

The visual system is the topic of Chapters 3–14. For the most part, the sensory and physiological aspects are covered in the earlier chapters (3–8), and the more cognitive aspects in later ones (9–13). Chapter 14, on color vision, represents a fusion of physiological and cognitive topics.

The material on the auditory system (Chapters 15–18) is similarly organized. The first two chapters concentrate on sensory processing and physiology, while the last two are more concerned with cognitive aspects.

The other senses are divided into two main groups. Chapter 19 deals with the body senses: somesthesis, temperature, and pain. These are the senses that tell us about our bodies, relaying information from peripheral receptors via the spinal cord to the brain. Finally, Chapter 20 considers the chemical senses: taste and smell.

Chapter 2
Psychophysics

PSYCHOPHYSICS is the oldest field of the science of psychology. It stems from attempts in the 19th century to measure and quantify sensation. Psychophysics and the study of sensation and perception thus stand at the very base of the family tree of psychology.

The 'father of psychophysics' was G. T. Fechner, who coined the term *psychophysics* (*psycho* = of the mind, *physics* = tangible or measurable) and devised the classical methods of psychophysics. Fechner was a mathematician, philosopher, and scientist who hoped to derive the relationship between a physical stimulus and the psychological perception of it. Modern psychophysics continues to quantify the relationship between stimulus and sensation, usually for the purpose of divining the processes underlying perception.

The basic methods are generally simple and straightforward, although particular experiments are often ingeniously devised to demonstrate specific points. The methods depend on the experimenter's knowledge of two things: a physical stimulus, and the response made by a subject to whom it is presented. The stimulus may be varied along any number of different dimensions. If it is a light, for example, it could vary in wavelength, size, shape, or any number of other dimensions; if it is a sound, it could vary in frequency, intensity, duration, etc. The response to the stimulus may be a verbal report ('yes, I see it', 'no, I saw nothing', or 'these two look alike'),[1] or a mechanical response (press *button A* when you see *stimulus 1, button B* for *stimulus 2*, and so forth). Human subjects make ver-

bal responses, but both humans and animals can be taught to press buttons.

Classical psychophysics

Thresholds

Much of the early work in psychophysics was devoted to finding out how well a person (or animal) could detect a stimulus. It was a search for the ultimate capability of the sensory system, the minimal quantity that could be detected. This minimum is called the *threshold* (the Latin equivalent, *limen*, is often used). Threshold means just what it implies: a boundary at which one crosses from not detecting to detecting.

The concept of the threshold underlies most of classical psychophysics. If an intense light is visible and an extremely weak light is not, increasing the intensity of the invisible light eventually leads to a point at which it becomes visible; that point is the threshold.

Given the notion that there is a threshold to be measured, there are numerous ways to proceed. The most straightforward was suggested in the

---

[1] This chapter refers to detecting a stimulus as 'seeing' it, although psychophysics can be applied to any sensory system (and even some non-sensory systems, as in detecting 'happiness' 'well-being', or 'value'). The use of visual system terms is purely a convenience to avoid using the word 'detectable' again and again.

preceding paragraph: begin with an undetectable stimulus, and gradually increase the intensity until the subject detects it. This method, probing until the threshold is reached, is called the *method of limits*. A hypothetical method of limits experiment is shown in Table 2.1. Stimulus intensity (it could be light, sound, force of pressure against the skin, or any number of possible stimuli) is shown along the side; the subject's response to each stimulus is listed under 'trial 1' ('Y' means 'yes, I see it'; 'N' means 'no, I didn't see a thing when you said I should have'). As each stimulus was presented, the subject responded negatively, although the stimulus strength was becoming progressively greater. Finally, when the sixth stimulus (S6) was given, the subject responded 'yes'. There was no need to continue, for if S6 was visible, surely S7, which is stronger still, would be detected. The threshold must lie between S5 and S6.

Repeat the experiment, however, and the result is not necessarily the same. Responses to a second trial are shown in the next column of Table 2.1; this time the subject failed to detect S6, S7, and even S8. Continue to repeat the experiment, and the threshold varies from trial to trial. It seems that the same stimulus the subject saw on one trial is invisible on another. There is no fixed threshold; we can only ask how detectable a stimulus is. Strong stimuli such as S9 and S10 are always seen; weak stimuli such as S4 are never seen. Stimuli in between are seen some percentage of the time: stimulus S8 was seen in three of four trials, or 75%; stimulus S6 was seen in only one of the four trials, or 25%. The percentage detection for each stimulus is shown in the last column of Table 2.1.

The ideal threshold was postulated to be a stimulus strength such that stimuli weaker than it would never be seen, and stimuli stronger than it would always be seen. In that case, a plot of percentage detection versus intensity would be represented by an abrupt change, or 'step' function, as shown in Figure 2.1(a). The result of the experiment shown in Table 2.1, however, does not look like a step. The percentage detection values from the last column in Table 2.1 are plotted as a func-

tion of intensity in Fig. 2.1(b). The circles can be fitted with a smooth S-shaped curve called an *ogive*, as shown. A curve of percentage detection versus intensity is called a *psychometric function*, and is generally an ogive.

One possible interpretation of the psychometric function is that the threshold has a slightly different value from trial to trial. This could happen either because the threshold is actually changing, or because there is a variable amount of extraneous, apparent stimulus added to the real stimulus (this is called *noise*). In any case, whatever the threshold is at a given moment, stimuli greater than threshold evoke a 'yes' response, and stimuli less than it evoke a 'no'. Clearly, the threshold is rarely above S9 or below

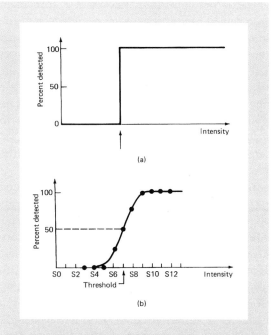

Fig. 2.1 Percentage of detection as a function of stimulus intensities. (a) Result to be expected if there were a perfect threshold for detection. (b) Psychometric function of the kind generally obtained. Circles are the hypothetical data of Table 2.1.

Box 2.1 Understanding the psychometric function

The discussion indicates that the psychometric function represents the probability of the threshold being at each intensity or lower. That is, the psychometric function is the integral of the probability function describing the distribution of the threshold.* Assume that the distribution of the threshold is a normal probability distribution, as shown by the bell-shaped curve in Fig. 2.2(a). Integration of the normal distribution gives the cumulative probability function shown in Fig.

2.2(b). This function is similar to the ogives found for psychometric functions. The psychometric function can be interpreted to mean that the threshold takes on values distributed according to a normal probability distribution, with its peak at the 50% point on the psychometric function. However, this is still an approximation, as better fits are often obtained with a function called the *Weibull function*.

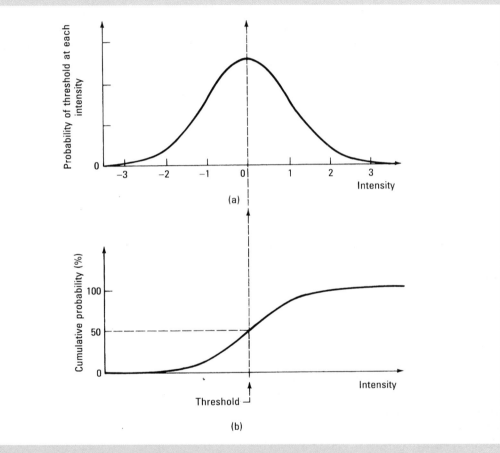

(a)

(b)

Fig. 2.2 Interpretation of the psychometric function as a variable threshold. (a) A normal distribution representing the probability that the threshold will be at a particular intensity. (b) The psychometric function that would be obtained by integrating the curve in (a). Half the area of the curve in (a) is to the left of the vertical dashed line.

* The integral represents the area under the probability curve, from −∞ to x. It is the sum of all the probabilities of obtaining each value up to some particular value, x. In other words, it is the probability of obtaining a value x or less. The integral of any probability distribution from −∞ to ∞ is 1.0—it is guaranteed to take **some** value.

Table 2.1 Hypothetical responses to stimuli presented in four ascending trials and percentage of detection of each stimulus based on these results

Stimulus	Trial 1	Trial 2	Trial 3	Trial 4	Pecentage Detection
S1	N	N	N	N	0
S2	N	N	N	N	0
S3	N	N	N	N	0
S4	N	N	N	N	0
S5	N	N	N	N	0
S6	Y	N	N	N	25
S7		N	Y	N	50
S8		N		Y	75
S9		Y			100
S10					100
S11					100
S12					100

S4; it is usually around S7. It is usual to define the threshold stimulus as that stimulus intensity corresponding to 50% detection on the psychometric function; however, other criteria may also be used. <u>BOX 2.1</u>

In the method of limits, the subject is a passive observer who does nothing but respond 'yes' or 'no' as stimuli are presented. There is a variant of this method in which the subject is an active participant; it is called the *method of adjustment*, in which the subject has control of the stimulus intensity. When the stimulus is invisible, the subject presses a button that causes the succeeding stimulus to be stronger; when it is visible, pressing a different button causes the stimulus to be weaker next time. In this way, the subject 'tracks' the threshold, wavering from just above to just below threshold. This is a rapid way to obtain threshold measurements, and is particularly useful when threshold is changing, such as during a period of dark adaptation (see Chapter 6).

Now think again about the original hypothetical experiment. On each trial a slightly different threshold was measured. Suppose that S1 represented a more intense stimulus. In this case, the subject would probably say 'no' to stimuli that previously elicited a 'yes'. If a series started with a

stimulus less intense than S1, the subject would probably say 'yes' at a lower intensity. There is a tendency to place the threshold according to how far down the list you think it should go, as well as whether the stimulus can actually be detected. It is good practice to start each series with a different first stimulus to avoid this effect, but the general objection still applies.

The experiments described, in which stimuli progressively increase in intensity until threshold is crossed, are called *ascending series*. Obviously, the opposite is possible: begin with a clearly detectable stimulus, and gradually decrease intensity until the subject first responds, 'No, I don't see it.' This is called a *descending series*. The descending series suffers from the same drawback as the ascending series: the initial intensity at which the series begins can influence the point at which the subject reports threshold.

The problems associated with the method of limits are partly caused by the fact that at any point the subject knows how intense a stimulus to expect next. As the series of presentations progresses, the expected intensity changes, and the subject knows that succeeding stimuli will be either successively weaker or successively stronger. A second method of classical psychophysics is specifically designed to overcome this problem: it is called the *method of constant stimuli*. The order of presentation of the stimuli in any given trial is random, so the subject has no way of anticipating the intensity. It is not the stimuli that are constant, it is what the subject *expects* that does not change from trial to trial.

If the experiment of Table 2.1 were being run by the method of constant stimuli, you might present S6, then S2, then S1, then S8, and so forth, until each of the intensities was presented a sufficient number of times (say 50). At each presentation of each stimulus, the subject would respond 'yes' or 'no', and you would record each response. Ultimately, you would completely fill out a table such as the one in Table 2.1, and compute the percentage detection for each stimulus. Note that every stimulus must be presented as many times as

the others; in the method of limits, the stimuli beyond threshold could be omitted. BOX 2.2

The result of an experiment by the method of constant stimuli is a psychometric function like the one in Fig. 2.1(b). The threshold can be 'read off' from this function. This method overcomes some of the problems associated with the method of limits, but both suffer from vulnerability to the subjective whims of the observer. When a subject is asked to say 'yes, I see it', or 'no, I don't', the experimenter has little control over the *criterion* applied in deciding whether a stimulus was actually present. One subject might refuse to say 'yes' unless the stimulus was obvious, while another might be willing to claim seeing at the slightest hint. Worse, the same subject may alter the criteria used during the course of an experiment.

Box 2.2 Demonstration—a threshold experiment

You can perform a threshold detection experiment with the demonstration program on the CD accompanying this book. To do so, start the **SensPerc** program that you have presumably already installed from the CD. (If you have not, do so; instructions may be found in the *Preface*, with details in Box P2.) When you click the Chapter 2 button 'Psychophysics', a drop-down menu will offer the choice of 'Threshold experiment' or 'Signal Detection Theory'. Select 'Threshold experiment'; you will see a screen with a blue explanatory box (use the scroll bar on the right to see the rest of the text). When you clear the text (click 'OK' in the black window at the upper right), stimuli will appear in the black window. A graph like Figure 2.1(b) is at the upper left.

Before running the experiment, you need to set a range of stimuli appropriate for you and your viewing conditions; otherwise, you might say 'yes' to all of them or 'no' to all of them. This pre-test is called a 'pilot experiment'. Each time you click on 'present stimulus', a box will appear inside the black window. Your task is to decide whether the inside of the box was black or a gray lighter than black. Be honest: if you say you saw grays that you didn't, you won't see the stimuli in the experiment, but if you wait until the gray is obviously light, you will never miss a stimulus.

When you have found an appropriate range, the exper-

iment begins. The procedure is just as it was for the pilot experiment, except that the computer randomly chooses one of six possible grays ranging from black to slightly lighter than the one you saw in the pilot experiment. Each time you respond, your response is recorded, so the percentage of times you claimed to see each gray can be displayed on the graph at the upper left.

The graph at the lower left displays the same information on normal probability coordinates. This coordinate system is explained in the Appendix. When at least three valid points are plotted on these coordinates, a straight line is fitted to the points. If the line has a positive slope, it is shown in blue and drawn as an ogive on the upper graph. Click the '?' in the upper right of each graph for more information about the graphs.

Be patient! You will need to run a large number of trials before the data begin to look neat as in Fig. 2.1(b). Even then, it will not be a beautiful fit. (I know when students have cheated on a lab because their 'data' look too good!) After you have enough valid points to define the ogive, you will be able to watch it shift subtly as you run more and more trials.

There is another classical method that removes the choice of criterion from the subject: the *method of forced choice*. The subject is presented with two or more alternatives, and must pick one even if she thinks she never saw the stimulus. For example, the stimulus might appear in either of two windows; after the presentation, the subject must respond by stating which window it was. If the subject does not know, then she must guess. The question is not *whether*, but *which*.

Consider another hypothetical experiment using the same set of stimuli as shown in Table 2.1 and Fig. 2.1(b). A stimulus light will appear in either the right or left window of a display, with both the stimulus intensity and location varying randomly from presentation to presentation. After each flash, the subject must respond 'left' or 'right'; depending on where it actually was, the answer is either right or wrong. The percentage correct is recorded for each stimulus level, and plotted as a psychometric function. <u>BOX 2.3</u>

The results of this experiment are shown in Fig 2.3. Two features distinguish this psychometric function from that in Fig. 2.1(b). First, there is 100% accuracy for stimulus values that were not detected 100% of the time in experiment 1. This method often gives a lower threshold than either the method of constant stimuli or the method of limits. That is because in forced choice the subject must make a response; in the other methods the response can simply be 'no' if the subject is unsure.

Box 2.3 Demonstration—a forced choice experiment

The same program that let you test your threshold with a constant stimulus paradigm can run a forced choice experiment. Select the '2 Alternative Forced Choice' dot from the panel at the lower right. Now when you click 'Present stimulus', two boxes will appear in the black area; one will be black and the other gray. Your task is to choose whether the gray was the left or the right box. (The computer will switch sides at random; a window below the choice buttons will tell you if you chose correctly or incorrectly on each trial.) The data from this experiment will appear as red squares in the graph at the upper left. You can switch back and forth between 'Constant Stimuli' and '2 Alternative Forced Choice' without erasing the previous results from either. As in the constant stimuli experiment, you will need to run a large number of trials before the results become as neat as in Fig. 2.3.

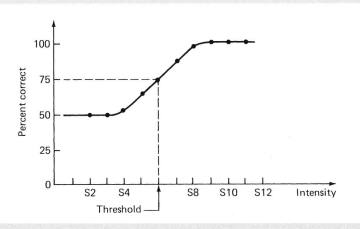

Fig. 2.3 Psychometric function resulting from a hypothetical experiment in which the subject is required to choose which window a stimulus was in.

Many of the responses may be guesses, but most subjects are surprised to learn (after the experiment) that while they thought they were just guessing they were getting many more correct than would be expected by chance.

The second difference is that the psychometric function derived from the forced choice experiment does not fall to 0% for weak stimuli; it levels off at 50%. This is obvious if you think about the consequences of guessing. When the stimuli are intense, there is no question of whether to say 'left' or 'right', and the score is 100% (right side of Fig. 2.3). When the stimuli are weaker, more mistakes are made. If the stimulus is actually invisible, there is nothing to do but make a pure guess. In saying 'left' or 'right', there is a 50:50 chance of being correct (the stimulus is in either one or the other). There may be runs of luck (just as there will be runs of straight heads in tossing a coin), but after enough trials the expected result is that the subject will get half right when the stimulus is not visible.

Since 50% is the score expected for an invisible stimulus, it cannot be taken as the threshold. Figure 2.3 shows that the psychometric function is an ogive going from 50 to 100%. Threshold must be between these limits; the point analogous to threshold on the previous curve is at 75%. (Because of this difference in range, the data must be converted to a 0–100 range before they can be plotted on the lower graph. Click the '?' button on the lower graph in the demonstration program for a further explanation.)

The fact that the psychometric curve has its range limited between 50 and 100% makes it harder to measure threshold, especially as the probability of getting *exactly* 50% by guessing is small unless the number of trials is extremely large. It would be nice to improve matters by making it difficult to do so well by guessing. We can do this by increasing the number of possible responses. In the hypothetical forced choice experiment just described, there were only two choices the subject could make; this is called a *two-alternative forced choice* paradigm, or *2AFC*. Why not in-

crease the number of alternatives to three, four, or more (3AFC, 4AFC, and so forth)? Consider a 4AFC experiment: the subject's task is to state in which of four windows the stimulus appeared. The probability of guessing correctly when the stimulus is invisible is 1 in 4, or 25%. The psychometric function thus runs from 25 to 100%, and threshold is defined as 62.5%. The curve is stretched to a wider range, so it is easier to determine threshold.

The more alternatives there are, the lower the expected score for guessing, but also the greater the chance of the subject becoming confused or missing the stimulus because it is difficult to attend to so many windows at once. Imagine trying to say which of 50 windows had the stimulus! As a result, the best performance is less than 100% when there are too many alternatives. As a general rule of thumb, 4AFC is about optimal for stretching the psychometric function, but since vision is the only sense in which several alternatives can be presented simultaneously, most experiments in other sensory systems use 2AFC.

Before leaving this discussion of the classical methods for measuring thresholds, it is worth noting that these methods can be, and have been, used to measure the sensory capabilities of animals. It is important to know whether animals' sensory systems are similar to those of humans, as sensory physiology must be done on animals. The ways in which these methods have been applied to animal work also serve as good examples of the use of psychophysics.

Blough (1955) used the method of adjustment to track the threshold of a pigeon that had been exposed to a bright light. Pigeons were trained to peck at one key when a light appeared in a window, and another key when there was no light. Pecking the correct key a number of times resulted in a food reward. The experiment was arranged so that pecking the key that meant 'light present' caused the light to become weaker, while pecking the key that meant 'no light' caused it to become more intense (the method of adjustment). The setting of the light was always either just above or just below threshold, so threshold could be deduced from the average of several runs.

The method of constant stimuli has been applied by a number of workers to the problem of defining fishes' ability to detect colored lights (Otis *et al.*, 1957; Northmore & Muntz, 1974; Shefner & Levine, 1976). All of these workers used a classical conditioning procedure: the fish received electric shocks after the presentation of light. When it is shocked, a fish misses a breath, a wholly involuntary response. When light and shock have been paired often enough, light alone causes the involuntary gasp (this is exactly like Pavlov training dogs to salivate at a sound). Once the fish are trained, they are presented with the test stimuli. If the test light evokes a gasp, the fish must have seen it (the gasp is its way of saying 'yes'); if there is no gasp, it did not see the stimulus.

The 4AFC method has been used successfully with many animals from pigeons to monkeys. An example is the comparison of the capabilities of human and monkey visual systems for detection of flickering of a light (DeValois *et al.*, 1974). A monkey was trained to press the one panel in an array of four that was different from the other three. Correct selection gave the monkey a squirt of grape juice, which monkeys rather like. Once the monkey learned the task, all the panels were illuminated with steady lights except the one with the intermittent test light in it; if the monkey chose that panel, it presumably could see the flicker (or guessed correctly). The procedure was repeated over and over, with different panels chosen and different rates of flicker, so that a psychometric function could be drawn and threshold deduced.

Differential sensitivity

So far the only problem considered has been detection—can a subject see that a stimulus is present? The threshold for detection is the *absolute threshold* (sometimes abbreviated *RL*, for *Reiz limen*, a German/Latin concatenation). But absolute threshold is only one possible kind of threshold; one could also ask whether the subject can detect a difference between two stimuli. The threshold for detection of differences is called the *difference threshold* (or *differential threshold*); it is often abbreviated *DL*, for *difference limen*, or *jnd* for *just noticeable difference*. In a sense, the RL is a special case of the DL—it is the detection of the difference from zero.

The jnd is the amount of change in a stimulus necessary for it to be perceived as different. It is the difference between a test stimulus and a standard comparison stimulus. Denote the intensity of the standard stimulus by I_0, and the intensity of the test stimulus by I_t; the question is whether the subject can detect a difference of $(I_t - I_0)$ at the level I_0. It is usual to avoid having to write '$I_t - I_0$' by calling the difference 'delta I', written ΔI (Δ is the Greek letter *delta*, which is generally used in mathematics to indicate a difference). That is, $\Delta I \equiv (Ic - I_0)$. Here, ΔI is the difference between test and standard (but ΔI is usually used to indicate the *threshold* difference between test and standard—that is, the jnd).

The measurement of jnd can be made by any of the classical methods. You could ask the subject whether a difference is visible, and, by making the difference greater or smaller, obtain the jnd by the method of limits. Alternatively, you could ask whether there is a noticeable difference, and present various random pairings of standard stimuli and test stimuli according to the method of constant stimuli. You could use the forced choice method by presenting the test and standard stimuli and asking which is brighter, or by presenting several (identical) standard stimuli and one test stimulus and asking the subject to pick out the one that is different.

The result of a series of presentations is a psychometric function, like the ones in Fig. 2.1(b) or 2.3, except that the abscissa is ΔI instead of I. From the psychometric function a threshold value, the DL, can be deduced; this DL is the ΔI appropriate to the I_0 used. If a different I_0 had been taken, a different psychometric function would have been generated, and a different ΔI derived.

By measuring ΔI for a large number of I_0, you can develop a function that describes how the jnd changes for different levels of stimulation. If

I_0 is some value of intensity of light, or sound, or weight, or pressure against the skin, increases in I_0 really would represent increases in the amount of stimulation. Variables of this type are called *prothetic continua*; they are variables in which a larger numerical value indicates a greater amount. But not all dimensions of a stimulus represent a change in amount of stimulation, however; some represent changes in the quality. It is also possible to ask how big a change is needed along a qualitative dimension. For example, how large a difference in frequency of sound is needed to produce a noticeable pitch difference, and how large a difference in wavelength of light to produce a noticeable color difference? Increasing the frequency of sound makes the pitch higher, but one would not consider a higher-pitched tone to be somehow 'greater' than a low tone; similarly, a long-wavelength light (which appears red) is not 'more' of something than a short-wavelength light (which appears blue). Variables that do not imply a change in quantity are called *metathetic continua*. It is interesting and valid to ask how our frequency discrimination changes with pitch, or how well we can discriminate various similar colors, but it is not the same as asking how well we can discriminate at different levels of stimulation. The remainder of this discussion will be concerned with prothetic continua only.

The pioneering work on the relationship between ΔI and I_0 for prothetic continua was done by E. H. Weber in the 1830s. Weber found that the increment in stimulation required for a jnd was proportional to the size of the standard stimulus. That is,

$$\Delta I = k\, I_0,$$

where k is a constant less than 1. This can be rewritten in the somewhat more familiar form

$$\Delta I/I_0 = k,$$

which simply says that the jnd is a constant fraction of the comparison stimulus.

Weber's law is a precise formulation that says the bigger the stimulus, the bigger the increment needed for a change to be detectable. This should not be a surprise; stars that are invisible in the day are bright against the black night sky, $50 enriches a pauper, but far more is needed to change the net worth of a millionaire.

To understand Weber's law, it is easiest to consider an example. Weber found that the constant k (also known as the *Weber fraction*) for detection of additional weight on the finger is about 1/30. In other words, given two weights to compare, if one is exactly 1 lb, it will be just possible to detect a difference if the second is 1/30 lb heavier, or about 1.033 lb. If the original weight were 2.0 lb, the DL would be approximately 0.067 lb; you could just discriminate between a 2.000 lb weight and a 2.067 lb weight. If you tried to discriminate between a 2.000 lb weight and a 2.033 lb weight (the same *difference* discriminated in the first case) you could not, for 0.033 is less than the DL for an I_0 of 2 lb. Given a 3 lb weight, the next heavier weight that could be discriminated would be about 3.100 lb; given a 6 lb weight, a 6.200 lb weight would be just noticeably different. The larger the standard weight, the larger the increment required. **<u>BOX 2.4</u>**

Box 2.4 The Weber fraction

The value of the Weber fraction, k, while constant over a reasonable range of stimulus strengths, is not the same for all sensory systems. In fact, the value of k in a given sensory modality can depend on how it is measured; for example, the Weber fraction for weights would be quite different if the weights were tested by placing one in each hand, rather than one after the other in the same hand. Similarly, the Weber fraction for brightness would depend on the size of the light tested, and how long the subject is allowed to look at each light.

Magnitude of sensation

Weber's law takes us away from threshold stimulation, and we can now ask a rather different question: given a stimulus large enough to be clearly detectable, how large does it seem to be? Psychophysicists refer to this as the problem of *scaling*, which means measuring the psychological effect.

The first attempt to define the magnitude of sensation was done without actually making a measurement. Fechner, who devised the classical methods of psychophysics, used Weber's result to derive a theoretical relationship between stimulus magnitude and sensation. In fact, he was responsible for first stating Weber's law as a mathematical relationship, and is probably more responsible than Weber for bringing the latter's work to light (for this reason, Weber's law is sometimes referred to as the Weber–Fechner law).

Fechner did not believe it possible to measure sensation directly, but saw the jnds of Weber's law as a potential scale for sensation. He made a bold assumption: all jnds, being barely perceptible (by definition), are perceived as being equal changes in sensation. That is, the jnds are the measure of sensation; the perceived magnitude of any stimulus is in proportion to the number of jnds it is above absolute threshold.

Figure 2.4 shows how the magnitude of sensation would be related to stimulus intensity according to Fechner. The Weber fraction is taken to

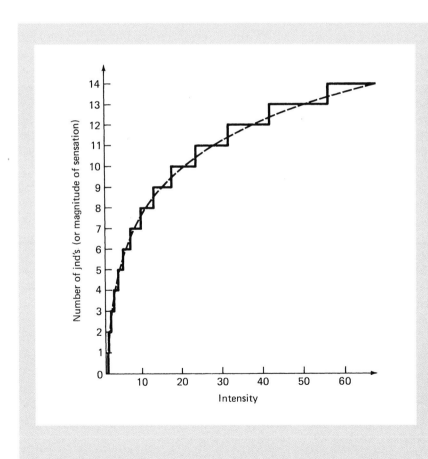

Fig. 2.4 Fechner's derivation of how the apparent magnitude of the stimulus should relate to actual intensity, on the assumption that apparent magnitude is proportional to the number of just noticeable differences (jnds). The dashed curve is a log function.

be one-third (the approximate value for tasting differences in the saltiness of water). If the threshold stimulus is assigned the value 1, from threshold to 1 jnd above threshold is one-third of a unit in the abscissa. At that point there is a 1 jnd increase in the ordinate, representing a 'unit' change in sensation. From that point, the next jnd is at 1.77; the change in the abscissa is just slightly larger than the first step, while the ordinate again increases by one unit. At larger values of I_0, the horizontal steps become longer. For example, at $I = 10$, $\Delta I = 3.33$ ($3.33 = 1/3$ of 10), which is larger than the first four steps put together. Since the vertical change is the same for each step, as the steps become wider, the climb becomes less steep. This is evident in Figure 2.4.

Fechner used this argument to derive the form of the relationship between stimulus magnitude and sensation. Of course, the relationship is not a series of steps, but a smooth curve like the dashed curve drawn through the steps. The mathematical form of the curve that fits this shape is a logarithmic relationship (derived by integrating Weber's law); this is called Fechner's *log law*. It states that the magnitude of sensation (S) is proportional to the logarithm of the stimulus magnitude (I):

$$S = c \times log\ (I)$$

Here, c is a constant of proportionality that can be directly related to the Weber fraction for the given sensory dimension.

Fechner's law says that the sensation grows according to the logarithm of the stimulus. Put another way, constant *differences* in sensation are given by the same *ratios* of stimulation ($S_2 - S_1$ corresponds to $c \log I_2 - c \log I_1$, and subtraction of logarithms corresponds to division—see the Appendix). It is an extension of Weber's law (from which it is of course derived): the apparent difference between a 1 lb weight and a 3 lb weight is the same as the apparent difference between a 20 lb weight and a 60 lb weight.

Fechner's law should not be too surprising; you know that increments appear smaller against large backgrounds. The moon is sometimes visible in the day, but does not appear to be nearly as bright as it does at night. When you turn on a 50–100–150 three-way light, the biggest change comes when the light is turned on in a dark room; there is a noticeable increase when going from 50 to 100 watts (W), but practically no difference between the medium and high ranges (100–150 W). The differences in light are all about the same—it is the compression of sensation with increased stimulation that makes the later increments seem smaller.

Fechner's law states that the apparent increment in sensation declines with increasing levels of stimulation (see Fig. 2.4). It also means larger changes in stimulus are required for the same sensory effect at higher intensities. To go from the first to the third jnd in Fig. 2.4 (a difference of 2 jnds) requires a change in intensity from 1.33 to 2.37. This is a change of barely more than 1 intensity unit. But to go from the 10th to the 12th jnd (also a difference of 2 jnds) requires a change in stimulation from 17.76 to 31.57, a difference of nearly 14 units. Notice, however, that the *ratios* of the changes are the same:

$$\frac{(2.37 - 1.33)}{1.33} = \frac{(31.57 - 17.76)}{17.76} = 0.78.$$

In vision, the ratio of the change in light to the level of the background light is generally known as *contrast* (this particular definition is the *Weber contrast*; you will encounter a slightly different definition of contrast in Chapter 9). What this relationship means, then, is that the sensory effect is the same when the contrast is the same. In essence, that is why a photograph looks the same whether it is viewed in dim light or bright: the contrast is a function of the photo, not the illumination. Each bit of the photo reflects a given percentage of the incident light, so the ratio of light reflected from any two points is the same in any illumination.

What this means is that sensation grows less rapidly than the stimulus, and that large changes at high intensities are sometimes less noticeable than small changes at low intensities. The logarithm function proposed by Fechner has this 'compressive' property. The curve relating sensation to stimulation in Fig. 2.4 bends over and becomes less steep at high levels of stimulation. The logarithmic relationship was long believed to represent a truth, and even today some workers are attempting to find the way in which receptors 'take the logarithms' of stimuli. The logarithm function is not the only curve that becomes less steep at high levels, however, and there is evidence that it may not be the correct one.

In the 1800s, J. A. F. Plateau measured the relationship of stimulus and sensation by asking artists to mix the shade of gray that lay exactly halfway between two given shades of gray, one light and one dark. He found a scale that implied ratios of sensation were related to ratios of stimulation, and proposed what is called a *power law*:

$$S = k \times I^n.$$

where S is sensation, k is a constant, I is intensity, and n is an exponent to which the intensity is raised.

The power law was largely forgotten until the 1950s, when it was resurrected by S. S. Stevens (1956, 1957). Stevens took issue with Fechner's fundamental assumption that all jnds are perceptually equal. Stevens said that even if 1 lb is the jnd for a 30 lb weight, and 0.1 lb is the jnd for a 3 lb weight, the observer somehow *feels* that the 1 lb jnd is larger than the 0.1 lb jnd.

Stevens proposed that equal physical ratios are psychologically equal; the mathematical relationship that satisfies this rule is the power law suggested by Plateau. Stevens also measured the relationship of stimulus and sensation by a method so simple it eluded investigators for 100 years: he *asked* the subjects how intense the stimulus appeared. This is called *direct scaling*.

As an example, suppose a subject is presented with 10 intensities of light, and asked to assign a number to each one according to its relative brightness. This is called *magnitude estimation*, for the subject is being asked to estimate the magnitude of each stimulus. A standard light of a physical intensity defined as 'one unit',[2] is presented to the subject, who is instructed to assign it a 'brightness' rating of 1. Each of the other lights is then rated by the subject according to its relative brightness compared to the standard (several times each, so an average rating can be obtained), and the value of the rating is plotted. Figure 2.5(a) shows the result of this hypothetical experiment. The 1-unit stimulus is rated 1, the 2-unit light is rated 1.4, and the 16-unit light is rated 4. The smooth curve drawn to fit the 'data' shows the property expected from Fechner's law: it becomes less steep as intensity increases. The smooth curve drawn, however, is not a logarithmic function; it is a power function: $S = I^{1/2} = \sqrt{I}$. This can be demonstrated by replotting this graph on log–log coordinates, as in Figure 2.5(b). Log–log coordinates (see Appendix) plot the logarithm of the estimated magnitude versus the logarithm of the intensity. The logarithmic scale has the property of making ratios into differences. The logarithmic transform of intensity implies ratio changes in intensity; the logarithmic transform of magnitude implies ratios of sensation. This was the defining characteristic of the power function as stated earlier, that ratios of stimulation lead to ratios of sensation.

A straight line on log–log coordinates indicates a power function. This is the result Stevens obtained when he performed magnitude estimation experiments on brightness, loudness, weight, odor, and a number of other sensory stimuli. The exponents were different for different types of stimuli, but they all appeared as straight lines on log–log coordinates, indicating power functions (Stevens, 1962). The slopes of the lines obtained represent the exponents of the power functions, as explained in the Appendix.

There is a second method Stevens used to demonstrate power functions. It is called *magni-

---

[2] For our purposes, it does not matter what units are used to measure the light. In fact, strictly speaking, 'intensity' is misused throughout this chapter; technically, 'intensity' refers to the light emitted by a point source. It is just easier to write this discussion by misusing the term in its colloquial sense of amount of light per unit area of a luminous source. For the correct terminology, see Chapter 3.

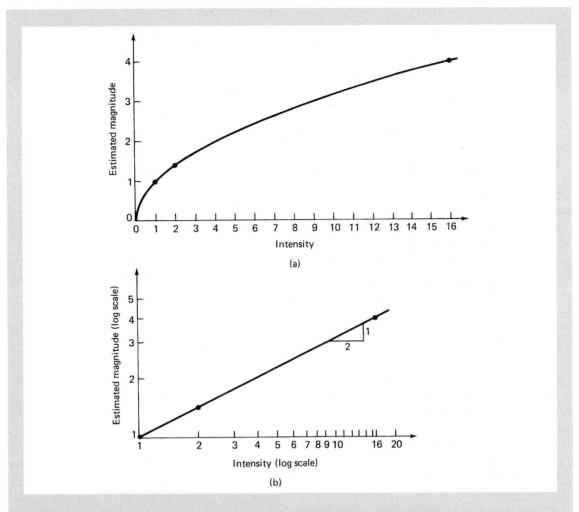

Fig. 2.5 Hypothetical estimates of magnitude of stimulus as a function of actual intensity, assuming a power function. (a) Three 'data' points plotted on linear scales. (b) The same data plotted on log–log coordinates (see Appendix); they fall along a straight line with a slope of one-half.

tude production and is the inverse of magnitude estimation. Instead of being given a stimulus and asked to produce a number representing its intensity, the subject was given a knob controlling the intensity and asked to turn it until the stimulus intensity was some multiple of the standard intensity (this is just like what Plateau asked artists to do when he first discovered the power law). Subjects are quite consistent; the method of

magnitude production gives results comparable to those derived by the method of magnitude estimation.

The fact that different types of stimuli effective for different senses all gave power functions enabled Stevens to test the consistency of his data. He did this with a procedure called *cross-modal matching* (referring to two senses, or modalities). The subject first was tested in two different sensory

Box 2.5 The 'catch' in the cross-modal match

The assertion that a power law will give the result of a straight-line log–log plot in cross-modal matching is relatively easy to show. For each modality, there is a power function; indicate the modalities as 1 and 2, and subscript all the variables to indicate which modality they refer to. The conditions for which a match is made occur when the sensation in modality 1 is the 'same' as that in modality 2, i.e. $S_1 = S_2$. Now write out the power law for each:

$$S_1 = k_1 I_1^{n_1} = S_2 = k_2 I_2^{n_2}$$

or

$$k_1 I_1^{n_1} = k_2 I_2^{n_2}.$$

Taking the logarithm of both sides gives

$$\log(k_1) + \log(I_1^{n_1}) = \log(k_2) + \log(I_2^{n_2})$$

or, rearranging terms and expanding the logarithms of the exponentials,

$$n_1 \log(I_1) = n_2 \log(I_2) + \log(k_2) - \log(k_1)$$

so

$$\log(I_1) = n_2/n_1 \log(I_2) + 1/n_1 \log(k_2/k_1).$$

(Don't you love reading stuff that has so many equations peppered in it?) The graph is of $\log(I_1)$ versus $\log(I_2)$, so the ordinate is $y = \log(I_1)$ and the abscissa is $x = \log(I_2)$. Substitution gives

$$y = (n_1/n_2)x + 1/n_1 \log(k_2/k_1),$$

which is the equation of a straight line with a slope of n_2/n_1. (Remember: $y = m x + b$.)

Ekman (1964), however, has shown that the results of cross-modal matching would be the same even if Fechner's log law were correct. Ekman's derivation is virtually the same as that shown in the preceding paragraph, but each S is defined by a logarithm:

$$S_1 = c_1 \log(I_1) = c_2 \log(I_2).$$

There is no need to take logarithms of each side; simply rearrange terms:

$$\log(I_1) = c_2/c_1 \log(I_2).$$

As before, substitute $x = \log(I_2)$ and $y = \log(I_1)$. Again, a straight line results for the cross-modal match.

Ekman's argument is more damaging than simply demonstrating that the cross-modal match does not prove there is a power law. It may be carried a step further: the very process of magnitude estimation (or magnitude production) may itself be considered a cross-modal match in which one modality is perception of the number system (Attneave, 1962). There is reason to believe that numbers are perceived in a compressed fashion (Schneider et al., 1974). For example, perception of the values of money (expressed by numbers) behaves similarly to the perception of light or sound. Is $5 a lot of money? It is a big price increase for a candy bar, but irrelevant to the price of a computer. If numbers are treated as still another sensory input, magnitude estimation is really nothing more than cross-modal matching against the sense of numerosity. By Ekman's argument, a straight-line log–log plot must result, regardless of whether the sensory stimulus is transformed according to a log law or a power law. Thus Stevens has not demonstrated that the power law is more appropriate than the log law (Rushton, 1961b).

This does not imply that the power law is wrong. Various lines of evidence have implicated a power function rather than a logarithmic function (Easter, 1968a; Levine & Abramov, 1975; Schneider et al., 1974; Zeng & Shannon, 1994), and the argument in the previous paragraph does not *disqualify* a power function. There is still controversy over which formulation may be correct. It is even likely that both the power function and the logarithmic function are valid. Wasserman et al. (1979) have argued that a logarithmic function seems most appropriate when responses must be made at the instant a stimulus appears, but a power function is obtained when the subject is allowed to consider the stimulus for a longer period of time.

Perhaps the relationship is neither a power function nor a logarithmic one. After all, why must a physiological system produce a mathematically neat and concise function? The various operations and relationships could effectively produce a function similar to a logarithmic or power function. But one important feature is shared by both: the relationship between stimulus and sensation is a downward curve, so larger increments are needed to produce similar effects at higher stimulus levels.

modalities so that the exponent for each could be estimated. This could be done by either magnitude estimation or magnitude production. The subject was then asked to match stimuli of one type by producing an equivalently intense stimulus of the other type. The instruction was 'turn this knob until the sound you hear is as loud as the light in front of you is bright'. Believe it or not, subjects can do this without becoming confused.

The data produced by the cross-modal match are intensities in one modality that match intensities in the other. They are plotted on log–log coordinates. If the power law is a correct description of the sensation/stimulation functions in each modality, the resultant plot must be a straight line whose slope is the ratio of the exponents found for each modality. This is the result Stevens obtained. **BOX 2.5**

Static invariances

There is another question related to the perception of differences; that of how stimulus parameters can be changed in tandem in order that two quite different stimuli can be judged the same. Testing the jnd determined what minimal change of one parameter, such as intensity, could be made so that the difference would be detectable. But how might one parameter be changed so that it will compensate for changes in another? If the correct compensation is made, the subject may judge that the two stimuli are the same in some way (although in most cases it is still possible to discriminate between them).

There are two classes of static invariances to consider. In the first class, the total energy is held constant, but the way it is delivered changes; the subject makes judgments of intensity. In the second class, there is no attempt to equalize energy; the subject judges whether the stimuli are alike in a particular quality. In a way, these two classes parallel the distinction between prothetic and metathetic continua.

As an example of the first class of invariances, consider a circular spot of light of a particular wavelength. The total energy in that stimulus depends on three things: (1) the *intensity* of the light (technically, the *radiance*)—that is, how much light is issuing from the stimulus per unit area; (2) the *area* of the stimulus; and (3) the *duration* of the stimulus (how long it is present). The total energy delivered within the stimulus is the product of these three numbers. Now take them two at a time.

First, suppose that the duration is constant; all test flashes last the same amount of time. The total energy depends on the product of area and radiance. A subject can be tested with spots of different areas, and asked (for each area) what radiance results in sensations of equal 'brightness'. Usually, the brightness chosen is the threshold, so the question is what radiance is necessary to reach absolute threshold for each spot's diameter (Fig. 2.6).

For small spots, the radiance required is inversely proportional to the area; this is known as *Ricco's law*. Simply put, it requires half as much radiance to see a spot that is twice as large in area (1.4 times the diameter). Notice, however, that because the total energy is proportional to area times radiance, the same total energy is present in both cases. The threshold energy is the same, regardless of whether all the light is condensed into a small intense spot, or is spread out into a larger but less intense disc. This does *not* mean the subject cannot tell the difference between a large dim spot and a small intense one, only that the two are equivalently detectable.

Ricco's law implies a trade-off between area and radiance; however, it only applies for sufficiently small areas. When the spots become too large, additional area gives no additional advantage for detection (see Fig. 2.6). Beyond this point, the radiance remains the same despite increases in area (and the total energy required increases as area increases). This means that there is a trade-off between area and radiance, but only so long as the energy falls within some limited area. This area, within which Ricco's law applies, is called *Ricco's area*, or the *summing area*. It is assumed that signals arising within that area sum together to give a signal that ultimately reaches threshold, but beyond

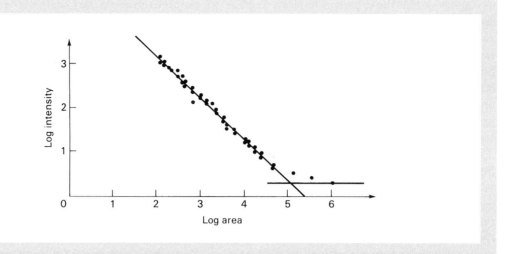

Fig. 2.6 Log radiance needed to reach threshold as a function of log area of the test spot. The slanted line declines with a slope of –1, indicating a trade-off between area and radiance (Ricco's law). The horizontal line indicates a failure of the relationship for large areas. Data are from Graham, C. H. and N. R. Bartlett (1939). The relation of size of stimulus and intensity in the human eye. II. Intensity thresholds for red and violet light. *J. Exp. Psychol.* 24: 514–587.

some distance the signals no longer affect that area.

Now choose a particular stimulus size, and vary the duration of the stimulus. Rather than asking the threshold radiance for each of several areas, ask the threshold radiance for each of several durations of stimulus flash. The result is analogous to Ricco's law: the threshold radiance is inversely related to the flash duration. As the total energy in the flash is the product of duration and radiance, this means that the same total energy is required to reach threshold, regardless of how it is distributed in time. An extremely brief flash of high radiance is just as detectable as a longer flash of lower radiance. This relationship is called *Bloch's law*. Like Ricco's law, Bloch's law has an upper limit, usually about 0.1 s (Graham, 1965). Once this *critical duration* has been reached, there is no further advantage to increasing the time in which the stimulus is present. This implies that the visual system sums lights over a relatively limited period of time.

The auditory system also sums energy it receives. There is no good spatial analog of Ricco's law, for the ears do not detect the size of a sound source, but there is an analog of Bloch's law (it has apparently never been given a specific name). Garner (1947) has shown that there is a trade-off between the intensity and duration of threshold tones, indicating summation of signals in time.

The second class of static invariances is qualitative; that is, the invariances are not concerned with the distribution of energy in stimuli, but with finding physically different stimuli that are the same in a particular qualitative way. If the quality in question is 'brightness', we are simply asking what the capabilities of the system are as a function of another variable. For example, we could ask how the absolute threshold for lights varies as wavelength (color) changes, or how the absolute threshold for sound varies as the frequency (pitch) changes. Each of these examples examines the capability of the visual or auditory system.

There are other static invariances that do not simply reflect the capability of the system. For example, the color (hue) of a light is generally associated with its wavelength, while its energy

Box 2.6 Seeing the Bezold–Brücke hue shift

The Bezold–Brücke hue shift can be demonstrated by placing a frosted white light bulb in front of a white wall. Look at the combination through a piece of red filter; presumably, the light from the bulb and the light from the wall are the same except that the light from the bulb is more intense. It should be apparent that the bulb appears yellow compared with the red of the wall.

determines the *luminance* (brightness). It would seem that for a light of a particular wavelength, changing the energy should simply make it brighter or dimmer but not affect the hue. This turns out not to be true. When energy is increased, the colors generally change slightly. A red light made brighter also becomes yellower; violet lights become bluer. This is called the *Bezold–Brücke hue shift*. To maintain the same hue when the energy changes, the wavelength must be changed. The Bezold–Brücke hue shift is not easy to explain (and not all color theoreticians agree on one explanation), but is a complication to be aware of when reading about color in Chapter 14. <u>BOX 2.6</u>

An effect similar to the Bezold–Brücke hue shift is found in audition. It is a common simplification to say that the frequency of vibration of a sound wave determines the pitch of sound, while intensity (amplitude of vibration) determines the loudness. If, however, a sound of a particular frequency has its intensity increased, the pitch changes slightly. A low-frequency (low-pitched hum) tone seems even lower (more basso) when the intensity increases. There is also a shift of high frequencies, such that high-frequency tones seem even higher-pitched when made more intense. To maintain the same pitch when intensity increases, the frequency must be changed. More will be said of these phenomena in Chapter 17 (and there is a demonstration of this effect on the CD accompanying this book). For now, remember that the *physical* attributes of a sound (frequency and intensity) must not be confused with the *psychological* attributes (pitch and loudness).

Signal detection theory

In modern psychophysics, the concept of the threshold has fallen into some disrepute. It is still useful for defining the capabilities of a sensory system, but the idea that there is an actual threshold or limen does not seem to be a satisfactory model for the way in which a subject determines whether or not there is a stimulus present. Many workers now prefer the concept of *detectability* of a stimulus, a term that avoids all the decision criteria and vagaries of attention, and concentrates on the capabilities of the sensory system.

There is a kind of shortcoming in classical psychophysics: all the data are concerned with whether the subject sees a stimulus when it is actually there; there is no consideration of performance in trials in which there is no stimulus. In those cases, the subject could also be right by correctly saying 'no' when there was nothing, or wrong by incorrectly saying a stimulus was seen when in fact it was not there (a 'false alarm'). Signal detection theory, adapted from a theory developed to analyze communication systems, was intended to overcome these shortcomings (Swets *et al.*, 1961).

Signal detection theory assumes that there is noise in the sensory system. Noise means just what it seems to: something that interferes with 'hearing' what you are intended to hear. For instance, if your radio develops static, the static is a noise that makes it harder for you to hear the programs. The noise referred to by signal detection theory, like static, is an ever-varying level of

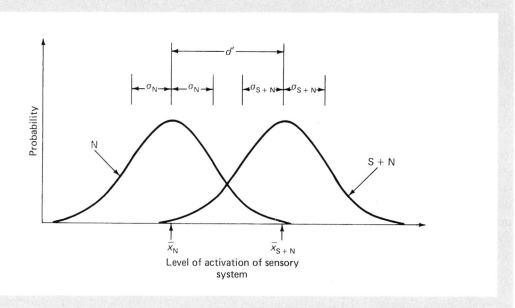

Fig. 2.7 Hypothetical activations of a sensory system from noise in the absence of a signal (N) or a signal with the superimposed noise (S + N). The means of each distribution are indicated on the abscissa (x_N) and x_{S+N}), and the difference between the means at the top (d'). Standard deviations of each are shown (σ_N and σ_{S+N}).

neural activity exactly like the nervous system's responses to the stimulus. There is a background level of activity in the nervous system, and sensory signals are superimposed on this activity. Noise in this sense is present in vision and the other senses, as well as in audition.

Noise varies at random. The activation of the sensory system during a period when a stimulus could have been (but in fact was not) present could be large, small, or in between; it is assumed that the distribution of the noise is a normal distribution, as shown by the bell-shaped curve on the left in Fig. 2.7 (marked N). The curve is centered about the *mean* (average) value of the noise, indicated by $\bar{x}_N$. The variability of the noise (how much it tends to change) is given by a measure called its standard deviation, indicated by σ_N.

N is the distribution of activation in the sensory channel in the absence of any stimulus. The stimu-

---

Box 2.7 Signal detection theory—on the CD

Signal detection theory is a 'Chapter 2' topic on the CD accompanying this book. You will probably find the discussion in this section much easier to understand if you follow along with the demonstration program.

Click the Chapter 2 button 'Psychophysics', and select 'Signal Detection Theory' from the drop-down menu. You

will see a screen with several smaller windows. On the upper left is a color version of Fig. 2.7, and that is what you should concentrate on for now. The means and standard deviations shown in Fig. 2.7 are not marked on the program figure, but you can see the distribution of N (outlined in blue) and of S + N (outlined in light green).

lus, when it is present, simply adds some amount of activity to the noise to give the activation caused by stimulus plus noise. Activation of the sensory system when the stimulus is present will thus be given by a distribution like that of the noise distribution, but shifted to a higher mean by the amount it is activated by the stimulus. This is shown in Fig. 2.7 as the curve marked S + N. **BOX 2.7**

The observer's task in a detection experiment is to say whether the activation during a given trial was just noise, or stimulus plus noise, that is, the observer must decide whether what was sensed was part of the distribution N or part of the distribution S + N. How well this can be done is determined by how far apart the two distributions are relative to their variability. If the difference is small, the two are almost completely overlapped, and any particular activation could almost equally well have come from either. If the difference is large (compared with the variability), there will be two quite distinct distributions; the one for N will include only small values of activation, and the one for S + N will include only large values of activation. The observer's choice is simple: if there is a large activation, choose S + N; if there is a small activation, choose N. The distance between the two distributions thus determines the *detectability*, or how well the subject can discriminate. Detectability is labeled d', and is expressed in units of the standard deviation of the distributions. The larger the value of d', the more 'detectable' the signal is. Signal detection theory provides a way to measure the d' for the presumed distributions of N and S + N. In a way, d' is analogous to t in testing the statistical significance of the difference between two distributions.

Consider a case in which d' is moderate, as in Fig. 2.8, or the initial setting of the program. How might a subject decide whether a given activation was from N or S + N? An observer will set a *criterion*; that is, choose a particular value of activation and say, 'All values greater than this I shall call "stimulus", and all values less than this I shall call "noise". ' Performance will depend on what criterion is chosen. For example, if it is essential to spot every stimulus that was given, you might set a lax criterion (marked *A* in Fig. 2.8). Very few stimuli will be presented that will not be spotted, but at the expense of making many false alarms. In fact, 'stimulus present' will be said on a large majority of the trials, whether it is there or not. This is the way pilots might react to blips on the radar that could represent another plane with which they might collide. Better to pay attention and plan to get out of the way, than to say, 'Probably not, let's just see what happens.'

On the other hand, the subject might feel it more important to avoid making false alarms, and set a criterion that is quite strict (such as *B* in Fig. 2.8). With a strict criterion, the subject will rarely claim to have seen something that is not there, but will similarly miss many actual presentations. This might be the tactic of the person watching the early warning radar: better to be sure the blips on the screen are enemy missiles than to start a nuclear holocaust over a flight of sparrows.

The actual strategies of observers are likely to be somewhere between these extremes. An 'ideal' observer will set the criterion so that most responses are correct. Consider the performance of a subject who sets the criterion at *C* in Fig. 2.8 (this is also the initial setting of the demonstration program; criterion is indicated by a light blue vertical line). This subject will correctly identify the stimulus the majority of times that it is presented, for more than half of the distribution of S + N is above the criterion; these correct identifications are called '**hits**'. This subject will correctly reject the noise a majority of the times that no signal is presented, for more than half of the N distribution lies below the criterion (**correct rejections**).

There will inevitably be two kinds of errors: when there is no signal but the level of activation is above the criterion level, there will be a '**false alarm**' (the probability of this is represented by the gray area in the upper plot of Fig. 2.8, and shaded red in the demonstration). When the stimulus is actually presented but the activation is below the criterion (the probability of this happening is represented by the gray area in the lower

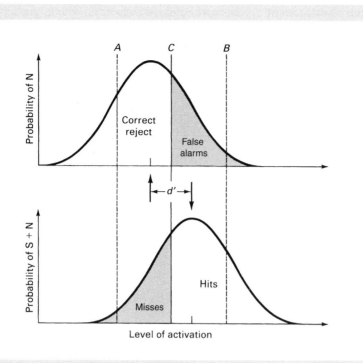

Fig. 2.8 Noise and signal + noise distributions, with three possible decision criteria (*A*, *B*, and *C*) discussed in the text. The shaded areas represent the proportions of misses and false alarms to be expected if criterion *C* is used.

plot of Fig. 2.8, and shaded black in the demonstration) the subject will say nothing is seen even though the stimulus is present. This is referred to as a '**miss**'.

The effect of differences in criterion can be seen by plotting the probability of 'hits' (the white area in the lower plot of Fig. 2.8, visible under the light green curve in the demonstration) *versus* the probability of false alarms (the shaded area in the upper plot of Fig. 2.8, red in the demonstration). This can be done for each criterion level tried. This plot, shown in Fig. 2.9, is called an *ROC curve* (for 'receiver operating characteristic'—remember that signal detection theory was originally derived from communication engineering). The ROC curve is shown on the upper right of the demonstration. The point corresponding to the situation in the upper left is marked and highlighted in light green. You can also see the percentages of time that the signal was present and the subject would

say 'yes' (the 'hits' area) or 'no' (the 'miss' area) in the table at the lower left. The percentages of 'correct rejections' and 'false alarms' are also given in the table, in numbers color-coded to the corresponding parts of the curves in the upper left. Note that the hits (in green) and the false alarms (red) are the coordinates of the point plotted in the ROC curve on the upper right. The middle criterion shown in Fig. 2.8, at *C*, would lead to the point on the ROC curve in the upper left quadrant. The percentage of stimuli correctly hit should be over 50%, while the percentage of noise presentations incorrectly called a stimulus (false alarms) should be under 50%.

As the criterion changes, the probabilities of hits and false alarms both change. If the criterion is lax (at *A* in Fig. 2.8), the probability of hits is high, close to unity. The probability of false alarms is also fairly high, as the subject says 'yes' almost every time that the stimulus is *not* present.

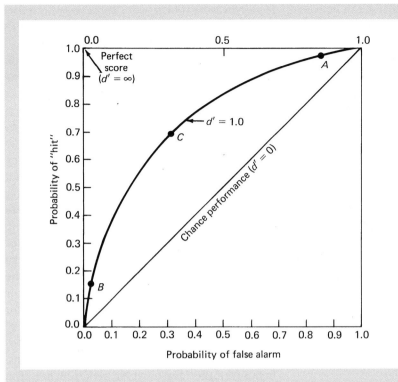

Fig. 2.9 ROC curve expected for the noise and signal + noise curves in Fig. 2.7. The points corresponding to criteria A, B, and C are indicated, as are the diagonal line corresponding to chance performance ($d' = 0$) and the point of perfect detection ($d' = \infty$).

The subject with closed eyes who just said 'yes' every time would plot a point in the upper right-hand corner, never missing a stimulus, but also making a false alarm every time there was no stimulus. You can change the criterion in the demonstration by moving the slide-bar under the distributions at the upper left. Each time you move the criterion to a new value, the percentages in the table will change accordingly, and a new point (highlighted in green) will be plotted on the ROC curve at the upper right. (Depending on the speed of your computer, it may take a second or two to do the calculations and redraw the pictures.) Since the old points are not erased (they remain in red), you can see the ROC curve developing as you choose various criteria.

The subject with a high criterion does no better (Fig. 2.8, at B), almost never having a false alarm, but also missing most of the stimuli. This subject plots a point near the lower left corner of the ROC curve; both the hit rate and false alarm rate are nearly zero. The subject with closed eyes who said 'no' every time would never claim to see a stimulus that was not there, but would also never detect a stimulus that was present.

The smooth curve in Fig. 2.9 is what would be traced as the criterion changed between the extremes. The curve corresponds to a particular distance between the S + N and N distributions relative to their standard deviation—that is, to a particular d'. The value of d' is determined by the strength of the stimulus relative to the noise in the subject's nervous system. More about how to determine d' can be found in the Appendix.

You can change d' in the demonstration with the slide-bar in the red box directly under the ROC curve. Each time you change d', the ROC curve is erased, so you will have to remember what it was like for other settings. The value of d' can be seen in the window to the left of the slide-bar.

Now consider the straight line running from the lower left to upper right-hand corner (main diagonal). This line corresponds to a d' of 0, or no difference between the S + N and N distributions. Any point along the diagonal represents purely chance performance; if the observer closed his or her eyes and just said 'yes' or 'no' at random (so there is no difference between the S and S + N distributions), a point should be plotted on the diagonal. The position along the diagonal at which the point falls depends on the relative proportion of 'yes' and 'no' responses. If the response is always 'yes' or always 'no', a point will be plotted in the upper right or lower left corner, respectively. If the answer is 'yes' 50% of the time, 50% of the stimuli will be hit, making a false alarm on 50% of the noise presentations (plot in the very center of the graph). Whatever is the probability of a hit will also be the probability of a false alarm. You can see this in the demonstration by setting d' to 0 (set the slide-bar to its extreme left).

In order (reliably) to plot to the left of the diagonal, the subject must be able to detect the stimulus to some extent. As the detectability d' increases, the curve moves up and to the left. A stimulus that could never be confused with noise (perfectly detectable) would plot at the upper left corner. The upper left corner represents a perfect score: it indicates detection of every stimulus and correct rejection in every trial in which there was only noise. (Try making d' very large by setting its slide-bar to the extreme right.)

In order to trace out more than a single point on an ROC curve (corresponding to the criterion chosen by the subject), you must make the subject change criterion from experimental session to experimental session. Subjects can be 'coerced' to change their criteria and trace out a curve by a number of means. One way to manipulate this is by changing a 'payoff matrix'. Say the subject is not working for free, and that the payment is going to depend on performance. Suppose you designate payment of some amount, say a nickel, for every correctly spotted stimulus. If there is no penalty for false alarm, a clever subject can maximize the take by saying 'yes' every time, or at any rate every time there is even a possibility it was there. On the other hand, suppose there is also a nickel deduction for every false alarm; the subject who says 'yes' every time will not earn anything, unless the stimulus presentations outnumber the noise presentations. In this case, the 'ideal observer' makes out best. The more punishing the penalty for false alarms, the more care the subject must take; if there is no reward for correct answers, and only a deduction for false alarms, it would be advisable to say 'no' every time. Given these instructions, subjects trace out ROC curves such as theory predicts, although few subjects adopt as extreme criteria as are optimal. **BOX 2.8**

Box 2.8 Playing the odds

Notice that the subject's strategy for dealing with punishment depended on the probability of stimulus presentations. In fact, the optimum strategy for getting the most correct answers includes 'playing the odds'—changing the criterion to optimize likelihoods. For example, if the stimulus was presented in two-thirds of the trials, it would be a better bet to say 'yes' than 'no' when unsure. The optimum criterion is the point at which the S + N and N curves intersect (when adjusted for their relative likelihood), for above that point signal is more likely, and below that point noise is more likely.

While adjusting the criterion for optimum performance changes the relative number correct, it has no effect on d'. This may be seen in the demonstration by changing the relative frequency of S + N (a selection made in the green box below the red d' box). The total fraction correct (hits plus correct rejections) can be seen in the window in the lower center. Notice that the performance is best when the criterion is at the intersection, but the points all lie on the same ROC curve, representing the same d'.

Signal detection theory provides a way of measuring the detectability of a stimulus, regardless of the criterion employed by the subject. It avoids the notion of the threshold, but what it substitutes (detectability) is also a measure of the capabilities of the system. In fact, the area under the ROC curve gives the probability of a correct response in 2AFC, so signal detection measures can be related directly to classical psychophysics.

Suggested readings

It is hard to find a book that deals exclusively with the techniques of psychophysics. There is a book of collected readings by W. S. Cain and L. F. Marks, called *Stimulus and sensation* (Little, Brown, Boston, 1971). In it are slightly abridged versions of articles that tell the story of psychophysics, including a good general introduction to classical psychophysics by J. C. Stevens (reprinted from the *International encyclopedia of the social sciences*, D. L. Sills, ed., Vol. 13, pp. 120–126, 1968). It also includes articles on static invariances, scaling and the Weber–Fechner–Stevens laws, signal detection theory, animal psychophysics, and a classical absolute visual threshold experiment by Hecht, Shlaer, and Pirenne (1942) that is perhaps the most elegant in the literature. A second account of some of the same topics may be found in W. R. Uttal's book *The psychobiology of sensory coding* (Harper and Row, 1973). Chapter 6 includes signal detection theory, classical psychophysics, scaling, and a description of the Hecht, Shlaer, and Pirenne study.

A new book at invariances can be found in the chapter 'Spatial and temporal summation in human vision' by T. Cohn in *Vision: coding and efficiency* (C. Blakemore, ed., Cambridge University Press, Cambridge, 1990, pp. 376–385). Other chapters from that book will be recommended in later chapters of this book.

Chapter 3
Light and the eye

THE preceding chapter provided some necessary tools to address the major topics of this book. Now for the specific sensory systems, starting with the visual system. This chapter begins with some of the physical properties of the basic stimulus for vision: light. You will then learn about the general structure of the peripheral visual system, and see how the eye acts as an optical instrument.

Light

Many attributes of vision are imposed by the nature of light. Most objects are not self-luminous, but are visible because they reflect light from other sources. The reflecting properties of objects may be constant, but the light illuminating them is not. Nevertheless, it is the properties of the object, not the light source, that you wish to 'see'.

There is a limitation of light that is also useful: it generally travels in a straight line. That means you cannot see around corners, or behind opaque objects. But as you will see in Chapter 12, the occlusion of one object by another is a powerful cue to the relative distances of the objects. When light does not travel in a straight line you are fooled; think about trying to locate an object underwater.

Light can travel enormous distances, allowing you to sense a distant world. Through your visual sense, you know about objects far beyond your reach, and thus can construct cognitive maps of relatively large regions of the world around you. Since objects in that larger world may move (and you may move within the world), vision allows you to predict part of your future. For example, you see the low branch before you actually touch it with your advancing forehead.

Visible light is a form of energy called *electromagnetic radiation*. Qualitatively, it is similar to electromagnetic phenomena such as X-rays, radar, gamma rays, and radio waves. The continuum of electromagnetic radiation is shown in Fig. 3.1; obviously, visible light is only a small subset of the continuum.

You can think of light (or any type of electromagnetic radiation) in two apparently different theoretical frameworks. In the first, light is considered to be composed of individual, indivisible particles called *photons*. Photons travel in a straight line at a speed that depends only on the medium through which they are passing. In a vacuum, photons travel at a speed of approximately 3×10^8 m/s (or 186 000 miles/s); in any other medium the speed is slightly less, with the reduction depending on the density of the medium. Although photons always tend to travel in a straight line, their direction of movement may be changed as they pass from one medium to another; the bending of light rays by a lens is an example of this property.

Photons are identical in their speed of movement; however, they do differ in the energy they possess. The energy of a particular photon is related to a property called *frequency*, which will be explained below. Frequency is related to energy in

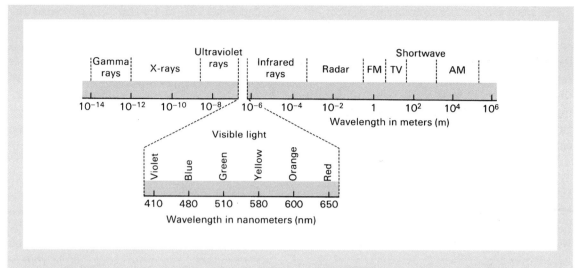

Fig. 3.1 The electromagnetic energy spectrum; the portion of the spectrum perceived as visible light is enlarged in the lower portion of the figure.

the following way: $E = hv$, where v is the frequency and h is a scaling constant called Planck's constant. Thus, the higher the frequency associated with a photon, the more energy it possesses.

Instead of thinking of light as being composed of many tiny particles, you can also conceive of it as a wave phenomenon. In this conception, light travels analogously to the way a wave travels when you drop a stone into a still pool. The water waves spread out from the stone at a constant speed. Figure 3.2 shows a schematic cross-section of a wave. It is a cyclic phenomenon; there is a regular pattern of depressions and upheavals. The wave is characterized by a property called *wavelength*, which is the distance from the beginning of one cycle to the beginning of the next cycle, or one peak to the next peak. Wavelength is generally represented by the Greek letter λ (lambda).

Frequency (the property of photons alluded to above) is the number of cycles that pass a stationary point in 1 s. Frequency and wavelength have an inverse relationship for wave phenomena; that is, $\lambda = c/v$, or $v = c/\lambda$, where v is frequency, λ is wavelength, and c is the speed of travel of the wave.

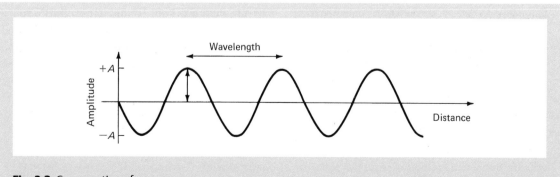

Fig. 3.2 Cross-section of a wave.

The wave and particle conceptions of light are consistent with each other because matter and energy are the same in particle physics. The existence of indivisible photons is universally accepted by contemporary physicists, and wave theory continues to be useful as a way of describing the movement of large numbers of photons. You can talk about the strength of a light using either particle theory or wave theory. When light is conceived as composed of photons, the strength of a light is related to the number of photons (also called *quanta*) present; when light is considered a wave phenomenon, the strength is related to the amplitude (or height, in Fig. 3.2) of the wave. As wavelength and frequency are inversely related to each other, the energy of a ph ton is related to its wavelength by the following expression: $E = hc/\lambda$. **BOX 3.1**

Box 3.1 Measuring light

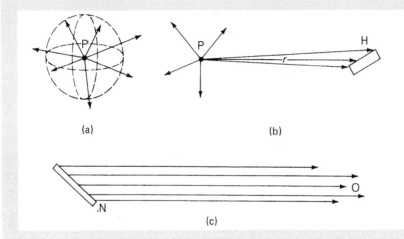

Fig 3.3
Different ways of measuring light. (a) Radiant flux from a source P. (b) Irradiance on a surface H a distance r from source P. (c) Radiance of an extended surface N in direction O.

How is light measured? Consider a light source P, as is shown in Fig. 3.3. There are many ways to measure the light coming from P. One choice you must make is whether to measure the energy coming from P or to count the number of photons. When the wavelength of the light is known, you can easily switch between measuring energy and counting photons, as the energy of a single photon is inversely related to its wavelength. For convenience, energy measures are most often used.

The next choice to be made is where the light should be measured. The *radiant flux* is a measure of all the energy coming from a light source and passing through some specified area (or falling onto a surface) in 1 s. You could measure the total radiant flux available from a source by enclosing the source in a transparent balloon, and measuring all the light passing through the balloon (Fig. 3.3a). A bigger balloon has its skin farther from the light source, but the total amount of light passing through the balloon would be the same. Since the area of the skin of the balloon grows as the square of its radius, the amount of light

passing through each unit area of skin must fall as the inverse square of the radius. That is, the flux passing through a unit area 'window' (a clear postage stamp fixed to the balloon) would fall as the inverse square of its distance from the source.

Alternatively, you might be interested in the amount of energy that reaches a surface some distance away from the light source (Fig. 3.3b). This measure is called the *irradiance*, and has units of energy per unit area. Irradiance depends on the distance between the light source and the surface, as well as the angle at which the light strikes the surface. *Radiance*, on the other hand, is a measure that depends only on the source; it is used when the light source is a surface instead of a point. Radiance is a measure of the radiant flux emerging from a surface source in a certain direction (Fig. 3.3c).

Radiant flux, irradiance, and radiance are measures of energy and are members of a class of units called *radiometric measures*. There is another class of units that measures the effectiveness of light for human vision; this is done by weighting different wavelengths according to how sensitive the human visual system is to those wavelengths. For example, suppose a light source could emit either 550 nm (which appears yellowish-green) or 650 nm light (which appears red). If it emitted the same energy at each wavelength, any radiometric measure would say the lights are equal. But your eye is more sensitive to 550 nm light than to 650 nm light, so you would judge that the 550 nm light is 'brighter' (see Chapter 4). It would be useful to have a measuring system that weights the contributions of each wavelength according to how well we see it. Light measures analogous to those of radiometry that represent the effectiveness of the light for human vision are called *photometric*

units. *Luminous flux* is analogous to radiant flux, *luminance* corresponds to radiance, and *illuminance* replaces irradiance. The weighting is determined by the average sensitivity of the human observer in normal daylight, when cones mediate vision. As you will see in Chapter 7, your relative sensitivity to wavelengths is different in very dim conditions (when only your rods are active), so a somewhat different weighting must be used for dim-light vision. The qualifier *scotopic* is added for conditions in which rods mediate vision, to distinguish those units from the usual bright-light units, called *photopic* units. When no qualifier is appended, it is understood that the units are photopic.

Optics

Light tends to travel in a straight line; however, optical instruments such as mirrors and lenses alter its direction. One of the simplest optical instru-

ments is a plane mirror, which is simply a flat, polished surface. Mirrors reflect light rays according to a simple rule illustrated in Fig. 3.4; light rays are reflected from a mirror at exactly the same angle as they approach it. From Fig. 3.4, the angle of incidence is always equal to the angle of reflection.

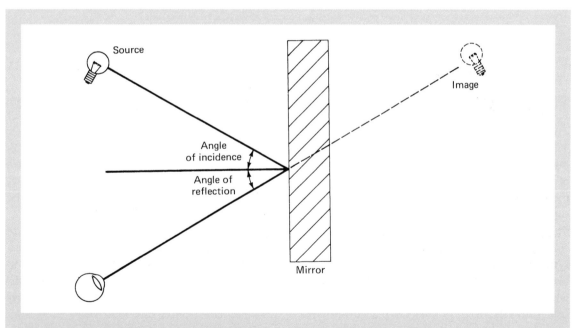

Fig. 3.4 Light rays incident on and reflected from a plane mirror. Note that the angle at which the rays approach the mirror (angle of incidence) is equal to the angle at which they are reflected away from the mirror (angle of reflection).

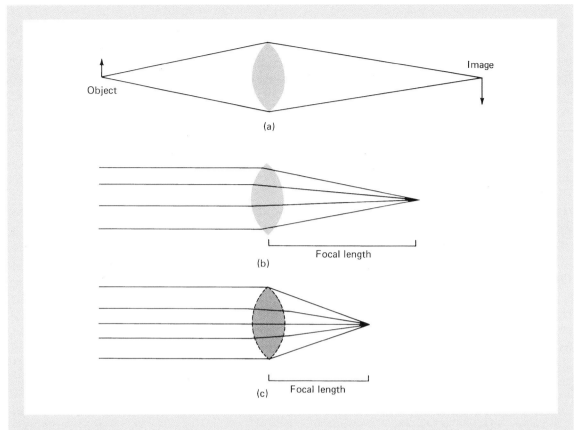

Fig. 3.5 Images produced by convex lenses. (a) Object is fairly far from lens; inverted image is produced on opposite side from object. (b) Object is at optical infinity; image is produced at focal length of the lens. (c) Lens in (b) is replaced with a stronger lens; image is moved closer to lens.

Reflection is not the only way to bend light rays; *refraction* is the process of changing the path of light using lenses. A lens is an optical instrument that can produce an *image* of an object at some distance away from that object. An image is merely a reproduction of the pattern of light rays coming from an object. Because the human visual system uses a lens to produce an image on the back of the eye, it is important to understand what a lens does. An example of a convex lens is shown in Fig. 3.5. If an object is placed fairly far away from a convex lens, the lens will produce an image of the object on the side of the lens opposite to the object. This is shown in Fig. 3.5(a), the object is an upright arrow to the left of the lens,

and the lens produces an image of that object on the right side of the lens. The strength of a lens is related to how much it can bend light rays, so that the stronger the lens, the closer the image of the object will be to it.

The measure of the strength of a lens is its *focal length*, *f*. You can determine the focal length of a lens by seeing where it will project an image of an object that is an infinite (or at least very large) distance away from the lens. Consider the light rays that emanate from a star, light years away from earth. They leave the star in all directions; however, the few that reach the earth must travel along nearly parallel paths. Thus, in general, the farther away an object is from a lens, the more nearly parallel are the light rays reaching the lens from that object.

In Fig. 3.5(b), a situation is depicted in which light rays from an object a great distance from the lens are impinging on it; as the object is far away, the rays are essentially parallel. In this example, assume that the object is a point source of light, so that the image will also be a point of light. To the left of the lens is a series of parallel light rays. To the right, the lens produces an image of the object at a distance from the lens exactly equal to the focal length. If you replace this lens with a stronger one (Fig. 3.5c), the light rays will be bent more sharply, and the image will be formed closer to the lens. Therefore, focal length is inversely related to lens strength; the shorter the focal length, the stronger the lens. Since it can be confusing for the stronger lens to be represented by a smaller number, there is a measure related to $1/f$, called the *diopter*. The strength of a lens in diopters is one over the focal length in meters. **BOX 3.2**

To understand how a lens forms an image, consider Fig. 3.6(a). An object (upright arrow) is illuminated by some source of light (not shown), and reflects light rays from its surface. Each point on the object radiates rays of light in all directions; those that strike the lens are brought into focus to create the image. Two rays from the tip of the arrow are shown; one passes through the very center of the lens, and one is exactly parallel to the main axis of the lens. The ray that passes through the center of the lens is virtually unbent, because the glass faces are nearly flat and parallel to each

other at this point, like a flat pane of glass. The ray parallel to the axis is like a ray from an infinitely distant object. It is therefore bent so that it passes through the focal point of the lens (marked 'f'). The image of that point is created where these two rays cross; all other rays from that point on the object also pass through that point on the image. Each other point on the object will project to a unique point on the image, so that a re-creation of the object is formed on the far side of the lens. Notice that the image is upside down; this is a general property of images made by convex lenses.

If you know the focal length of a given lens and the distance between the lens and an object, you can determine exactly where the lens will place an image of that object. If o is the distance between the lens and the object, i is the distance between the lens and the image, and f is the focal length of the lens, then

$$1/f = 1/i + 1/o.$$

This is the fundamental lens equation. As an example, consider the lens in Fig. 3.6(a). This lens has a focal length of 10 cm, and the arrow is placed 15 cm away from the lens. From the lens equation:

$$1/10 = 1/i + 1/15$$

or $i = 30$ cm. Therefore, an image of the arrow should be found 30 cm from the lens.

If you change the distance between the object and the lens, the placement of the image also changes. In Fig. 3.6(b), the lens is the same as in 3.6(a), but the object has been moved farther from

Box 3.2 The focal length of a lens

If you happen to have a convex lens (such as a magnifying glass), you can easily demonstrate these phenomena to yourself. Go outside on a sunny day, and place the lens so that it is about 6 inches from the ground in a direct path from the sun. Move the lens up and down to find the distance at which you see a small, bright, well-focused spot on the ground. This is the image of the sun formed by the lens. Because the sun is virtually an infinite distance away from the lens, the distance between the lens and the ground (when you have a sharp image of the sun) will be a good measure of the focal length of that lens. (**Caution: never look directly at the sun through this or any other optical instrument. The sun's rays can cause permanent eye damage or blindness.**)

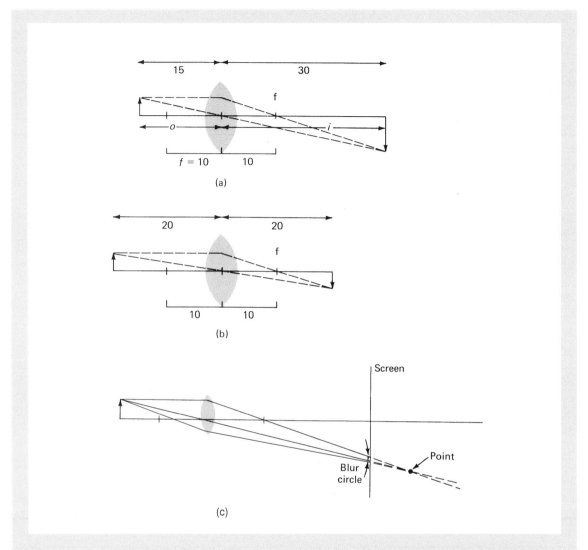

Fig. 3.6 Demonstration of the lens equation. (a) The object is 15 cm from a 10-diopter lens. (b) The object is 20 cm from the lens; critical rays have been drawn to show how the image is created. (c) Blur circle on a screen closer to the lens than the image.

the lens. The effect of this is to move the image closer to the lens: from 30 cm away in Fig. 3.6(a) to 20 cm away in 3.6(b). The image also becomes smaller, as you would expect when the object is farther away. <u>BOX 3.3</u>

The image is at a certain place in space, but we are generally concerned with the way it appears when projected onto a surface (such as a movie screen, the film in a camera, or the retina of the eye). When the image is exactly on the surface, it appears clear and sharp. When the image is either closer to the lens than the surface or farther away, the picture appears blurred—it is out of focus. This is because the light from each point in the object is not all at one point in the image. The cone of rays coming from all parts of the lens is intercepted

Box 3.3 Forming an inverted image with a lens

Take a magnifying lens (whose focal length has been determined in Box 3.2), and hold it parallel to a white wall in a dim room with one bright window. By varying the distance between the lens and the wall, you should be able to find a position at which a clear image of the outside scene is projected onto the wall. At other distances, the image is blurred. Notice that the image is inverted.

where it is still broad, and a single point on the object projects a blur circle (Fig. 3.6c)

The vertebrate eye

Structure

Figure 3.7 shows a cross-section of a human eyeball. In most of its basic characteristics, the human eye is similar to that of other vertebrates. It is roughly spherical in shape with a diameter of about 2 cm. The eye lies in a socket of the skull, and can be moved by six *extraocular muscles*, which will be described later. The wall of the eye is a tough, opaque material called the *sclera*. At the front of the eye (top of the figure) the sclera protrudes and becomes clear; this portion is called the *cornea*, and this is where light enters the eye. Because the front surface of the cornea is curved, it also acts as a lens and aids in bending light rays to form an image at the back of the eye.

Just inside the cornea is a small compartment, the *anterior chamber*, filled with a clear fluid called *aqueous humor*. At the back of the anterior chamber is the *iris*, a smooth ring of muscle with a central opening the size of which depends on the state of contraction of the iris. This central opening is the *pupil*, the black spot in the center of your eye. The area of the pupil varies as a function of the amount of light impinging on your eye, as well as being influenced by emotional states.

Box 3.4 Why the world isn't upside down

If the cornea and lens act like a convex lens forming an image on the retina, that image must be upside down. This bit of physics perplexed people in the 17th century, for the world is certainly not seen as upside down. Descartes actually peeled a window of sclera from a cow eye to demonstrate that the image really is inverted. Why is our world not inverted? Simply because the brain is wired to 'know' that cells in the lower part of the eye 'see' the upper part of the world. Actually, it may not even be prewired; you may have learned that relationship when you first started to connect the patterns of excitation in your retinae with the world 'out there'.

You can actually relearn the wiring. G. M. Stratton performed a series of experiments in the 1890s in which subjects wore eyeglasses with prisms that inverted images, making the images on the retinas right side up (see Wallach, 1987). Subjects were terribly confused at first, but soon learned to function under these new conditions. (You have learned to function under revised visual conditions too — remember how hard it was to move your hand correctly on your face seen in a mirror the first time you tried to shave or put on makeup?) But the subjects did not just learn how to move appropriately; after a few days, they *perceived* the upside-down world as looking normal. And when they removed their prisms after nearly a week, they had to relearn normal vision. This relearning was relatively rapid, however (Rossetti *et al.* 1993). It seems likely that the changes are actually due to a rewiring of the visual cortex (Sugita, 1996).

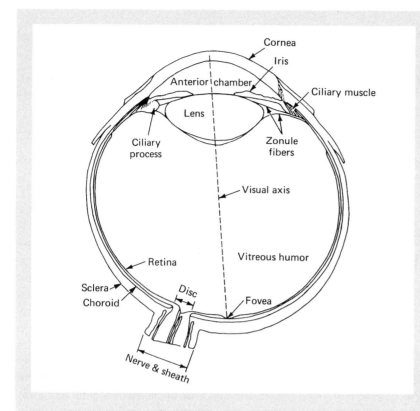

Fig. 3.7 Schematic of the human eye. Right eye, from above. From Walls, G. L. (1967). *The Vertebrate Eye and its Adaptive Radiation*. New York: Hafner. Reprinted by permission of the Cranbrook Institute of Science.

Just behind the iris lies the crystalline *lens*; its purpose is to assist the cornea in producing a focused image of the visual world in the back of the eye. The crystalline lens is convex, similar to the lenses discussed in the previous section. It is normally a clear tissue with no blood vessels in it that receives nutrition from the aqueous humor that surrounds it. (The lens sometimes becomes nearly opaque late in life; this condition is known as a *cataract*.) The lens is suspended in position by a fiber sac called the *zonule of Zinn*. This sac attaches to the *ciliary muscles*. Contraction of these muscles allows the eye to change its focus; details of this mechanism will be discussed in a later section.

Immediately behind the lens is the major chamber of the eye, which is filled with a clear viscous jelly called the *vitreous humor* (or 'glassy fluid'). The inner wall of this chamber is lined with the *retina*, a thin sheet of neural tissue. The retina is responsible for sensing the image projected by the structures at the front of the eyeball, and encoding the information as a neural signal to transmit to the brain. BOX 3.4

The retina lies against a darkly colored layer of cells called the *pigment epithelium* ('epithelium' is another word for skin); some functions of this layer will be discussed in the next chapter. Between the pigment epithelium and the tough sclera is the *choroid*, which is rich in blood vessels. The blood vessels of the choroid provide nutrition and oxygen for the pigment epithelium and deep layers of the retina. The surface layers of the retina are nourished by a second network of blood vessels that lies in the vitreous humor at the surface of the retina. BOX 3.5

Several landmarks on the back of the eye deserve mention. If you stare directly at some object in space, your eyes turn so that the image of that

---

Box 3.5 Seeing the blood vessels in your eye

It might seem that a network of blood vessels on the surface of the retina would interfere with vision, as they fall between the lens and the retina. You do not notice them in everyday vision because of an important property of the visual system: it responds only to change. The blood vessels move with the retina, and so their shadows never change. The tendency for unchanging stimuli to fade from view is called Troxler fading, which you will encounter in Chapter 11.

You can see the blood vessels in your own eye by setting up a situation in which their shadows move against the retina. Take off your glasses, if you wear them, and stare at a large uniform surface. The surface should be free of details (a blank wall is good) and not too brightly lit. Take a small penlight (the kind that clips in your pocket), and hold it near the side of your head, aiming at your eye. Shine the light against the side of your eyeball; some light will light the retina from the side. Each time your eye (or the light) moves, you will see the branching network of the blood vessels of your eye.

---

object is projected onto the central portion of your retinae. This central region is called the *macula lutea*, and is identifiable because it is yellowish in color ('*lutea*' means yellow). Within the macula lies a small indentation, or pit, called the *fovea*. The fovea is a specialized region of the retina in which the capacity for fine detail discrimination is greatest; in the next chapter you will learn some of the properties of the fovea that are responsible for this capability. The entire macula subtends about 5° of your central visual field—about the size of a large lemon held at arm's length.

The Chapter 3 module of the program on the demonstration CD that accompanies this book includes a demonstration of the higher acuity in your fovea. Start the program, and select 'Chapter 3'. From the drop-down menu, choose 'Blind spot, peripheral, and foveal vision'. You will be presented with three choice buttons at the bottom: 'Blind spot', 'Peripheral vision', and 'Foveal acuity'; select the last of these. Stare directly at the red cross; this means you are aiming your eyes such that the image of the cross is centered in your foveas. A word will flash briefly in a random position in either small or large type. Try to read the word. A moment later, it will reappear at the cross for a longer time so you can see whether you read it correctly. It will then disappear, and a warning beep will tell you the next word is about to be flashed. You should only be able to read the small type when it appears very near the red fixation cross.

Conversely, the peripheral part of your retina (the edges of your vision, far from the fovea) is poor at details and colors, even though it is certainly not blind. Your peripheral vision is particularly good at noticing motion, as demonstrated by the 'Peripheral vision' demonstration (middle button). In this demonstration, the fixation cross appears on the far left of the screen. Move as close to the screen as you comfortably can, and stare at the cross. The right side of the screen should be well to the side of your vision (it may help to center your head in front of the screen and look leftward to the cross). When you are set, click 'Begin'. A shape (of random size, color, and height on the screen) will appear at the right side of the screen. You probably won't notice it, but after a couple of seconds, it will start to pulsate in size and move along the right edge of the screen. When it does, you will clearly see that it is there, although you still will probably be unable to say what shape or color it is until you direct your eyes to the right.

Another interesting structure at the back of the eye is the *optic disc*, which is slightly to the nasal side of the retina (that is, toward the nose). It is where the axons of the retinal cells that carry visual information to the brain leave the retina and form the *optic nerve*. At the optic disc, there is a hole in the retina from which the fibers exit, so that if an object projects an image directly onto the optic disc, it will not be seen; the optic disc is therefore also called the *blind spot*. You can demonstrate this

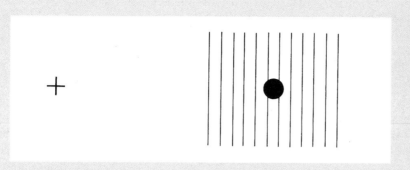

Fig. 3.8 Find your blind spot. Cover your left eye, and stare directly at the cross on the left of the figure. Take the book and slowly move it toward and away over a range of about 12–40 cm. At a particular distance, the black spot (but not the stripes) on the right of the figure should disappear; this happens when the image of the spot falls exactly on the optic disc, or blind spot. Notice that the stripes do not disappear—in fact they are seen to continue through the blind spot *even though they are not really there*. A more striking demonstration of this effect may be seen by running the 'blind spot' demonstration associated with this chapter on the CD of programs accompanying this book. You will see other examples of this 'filling in' where there is no stimulus in Chapter 10.

phenomenon on yourself by examining Fig. 3.8 as described in the legend.

An even more dramatic demonstration of the blind spot is available on the accompanying CD. Again, select the Chapter 3 and 'Blind spot, peripheral, and foveal vision', but this time select the 'Blind spot' button. You have a choice of whether to cover your right eye or left eye (left eye is the default). After selecting which eye to cover, click 'Ready'. If you choose left eye, a green cross will appear in the left part of the screen, with a flashing spot to the right (for right eye, the display is mirror-imaged). Cover the selected eye and fixate on the cross. Move toward or away from the screen until the flashing spot vanishes, meaning it is now projected on your blind spot.

Now click 'Begin'. An ellipse will move from top to bottom of the frame (its size, color, and speed are random), passing through the flashing spot (which you no longer see). If the ellipse is small, it will disappear as it crosses your blind spot, and reappear as it emerges below. If the ellipse is large, you will see it pass uninterrupted through your blind spot, even though the flashing spot remains invisible. The selection dots in the lower left let you request a new ellipse, and you can bias the size toward large or small ellipses. BOX 3.6

Box 3.6 Oops! That's *not* what the blind spot implies

The presence of a blind spot and its correspondence with the optic disc was known in the 1600s and taken as evidence that the retina was *not* the photosensitive part of the eye. As far as anatomists could then determine, the retina and the optic nerve were all the same stuff; the retina was believed to be a broadening of the optic nerve at its head. In this view, there was no lack of 'retina' at the blind spot; what was perforated was the pigment epithelium. From this, it was concluded (quite incorrectly) that the pigment epithelium was the sensitive part of the eye (Priestly, 1772).

The features you have just demonstrated from 'inside' your eyes can also be seen from the outside looking in. The other selection for Chapter 3 on the CD is called 'The normal fundus'; it is the view an ophthalmologist sees of the inside of your eye using an ophthalmoscope ('fundus' means the bottom or back of the eye). You can see the whitish optic disc with the blood vessels entering the eye and coursing over the surface of the retina. The macular area is where the blood vessels become fine and reach toward (but not into) the fovea.

Accommodation

The function of the crystalline lens is to aid in focusing an image of the visual world onto the retina. It is not the only structure that performs this function; in fact, the cornea provides as much as 70% of the total refractive power in the human eye (Westheimer, 1975). It is because of the focusing power of the cornea that people who have had their crystalline lenses surgically removed because of cataracts are still able to see with the help of glasses or contacts. The lens performs one function

that the cornea cannot, however, it is capable of changing its refractive power to focus on objects at different distances from the eye.

Consider what happens when you look at a distant object, for example, the moon. (Looking at the moon will come back to haunt you in Chapter 12.) The light rays from the moon reaching your eye are virtually parallel, as shown in Fig. 3.9(a). The cornea and lens act to bend the light rays, and produce a sharp image of the moon on your retina at the fovea. This means that the focal length of the cornea/lens combination is about equal to the distance from the lens to the retina. Now, what happens if, instead of looking at the moon, you change your gaze and stare at a thumbtack on the wall about 1 m away? Figure 3.9(b) shows what would be predicted given the focal length of the lens/cornea as derived from Fig. 3.9(a). The image of the thumbtack would not be at the retina; instead, it would be projected at a distance somewhat behind the retina. This is a direct consequence of the properties of lenses discussed earlier in this chapter; for a lens of any given focal length, as the distance between the lens and object

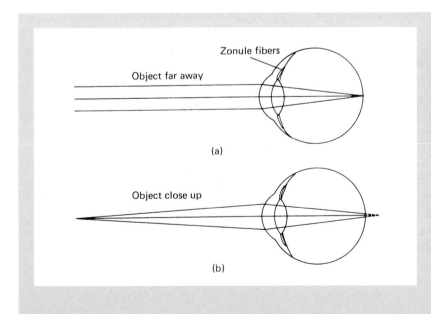

Fig. 3.9 What happens if the lens cannot change shape? (a) Eye is appropriately focused on faraway objects; (b) eye is improperly focused on a close-up object.

grows shorter, the distance between the lens and the image it projects becomes longer.

If you are under the age of 45 and have normal vision, you know that your visual system somehow compensates for the problem raised in the previous paragraph. Your eye can focus either on objects that are quite far away or on objects that are practically in front of your nose. This ability depends mainly on the fact that your lens can change its focal length to maintain the image position at the retina. When you are looking at objects a long distance away, your lens assumes a flattened shape with a minimum amount of refractive power. As the object comes closer to your eye, your lens becomes more and more rounded, increasing its refractive power (decreasing focal length) and so preventing the image of the object from moving behind your retina. This change in refractive power is called *accommodation*.

As an object moves closer to your eye, you decrease the effective focal length of your lens in order to maintain an image of the object on the retina. At a certain distance, however, your lens is maximally curved, and you cannot make any further change in its shape. Closer than this distance, your lens cannot provide sufficient accommodation, and the image is sharp *behind* your retina. At your retina, then, the image is unfocused or blurred. The closest distance for which your lens can project a sharp image of the object is called your *near point*. For very young children, the near point is about 10 cm (Brown, 1965).

The mechanism of accommodation is illustrated in Fig. 3.10. When your eye is focusing on a distant target, the zonule fibers encasing the lens and attached to the sclera are stretched tight. The stretching of the fibers flattens the lens and decreases its refractive power. This is shown in Fig. 3.10(a). When your eye focuses on a nearby object, the ciliary muscles contract. The contraction of the ciliary muscles creates a pull in the reverse direction of the stretched zonule fibers; this results in less stretching force on the sac encompassing the lens. As the stress on the lens is decreased, the lens assumes its normal shape, which is quite rounded.

In addition, the pull of the ciliary muscles squeezes the eyeball inward, slightly elongating it (Drexler *et al.*, 1998). Thus when the ciliary muscles are working hardest, the lens relaxes to assume the shape that produces the most refractive power (Fig. 3.10b), and the distance from lens to retina slightly increases.

In a normal eye, the lens is flattest when distant objects are viewed, and more rounded when close-up objects are viewed. For many of us, however, the accommodation of the lens is not sufficient to produce a focused image for objects at all distances. As one gets older, the lens becomes less amenable to having its focus changed for close-up objects (Koretz *et al.*, 1997). This decrease in accommodative ability with age is known as *presbyopia*. It is often accompanied by a general loss of accommodative power, increasing both the far point and the near point (Wang *et al.* 1994). The most noticeable consequence of presbyopia is that

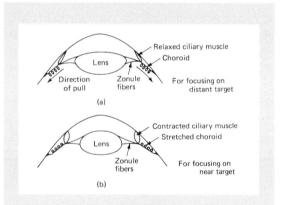

Fig. 3.10 The mechanism of accommodation. (a) Focus on a distant object; ciliary muscles are relaxed and lens ligaments are taut, causing the lens to be flattened. (b) Focus on a near object; tension on lens ligaments is reduced by contraction of ciliary muscles, and the lens assumes its normal, rounded shape. After Crouch, J. F. and J. R. McClintic. *Human Anatomy and Physiology*. Copyright © 1971 John Wiley & Sons, Inc. Reprinted by permission.

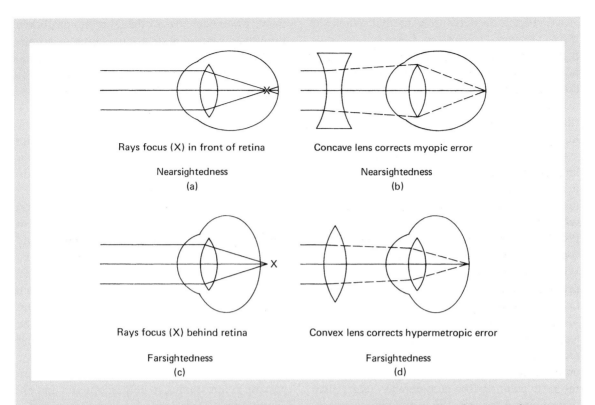

Rays focus (X) in front of retina

Nearsightedness
(a)

Concave lens corrects myopic error

Nearsightedness
(b)

Rays focus (X) behind retina

Farsightedness
(c)

Convex lens corrects hypermetropic error

Farsightedness
(d)

Fig. 3.11 Refractive states for myopic and hypermetropic eyes. (a) Uncorrected myopia; (b) corrected myopia; (c) uncorrected hypermetropia; (d) corrected hypermetropia.

the near point of the eye increases drastically, making it harder to see close objects. It is for this reason that people who had normal vision at a younger age usually need reading glasses by middle age.

Of course, many of us do not have normal, or *emmetropic*, eyes even when we are young. 'Emmetropia' sounds like a disease, but it means 'correctly focused'. Refractive errors are probably largely hereditary, although there is neural control over the shape of the developing eye (see Kolata, 1985). Visual deficits can also be the result of eye injury or eye surgery. For example, if the lens develops a cataract, so that light is diffused instead of focused, the lens must be removed. The overall focusing power of the eye is therefore severely reduced, so images would be in focus far behind the retina.

Probably the most common visual deficit in young people is *myopia*, or nearsightedness. When myopic people look at a distant object, their lenses project an image of the object somewhat in front of the retina (Fig. 3.11a). One possible reason for this inappropriate image placement is abnormal elongation of the eyeball; alternatively, either the lens or cornea may provide an abnormally large amount of refraction. As a distant object moves toward a myopic eye, the image of the object moves from a point in front of the retina back toward the retina, until the object comes into proper focus. From that distance until the object moves closer than the near point, the eye accommodates in a normal fashion. The near point of a myopic eye is shorter than for a normal eye, so that myopic individuals can focus on objects closer to their eyes than can normal individuals. Note that the entire visual range is displaced from normal. When the myopic person develops presbyopia, the near point moves back toward the far point, or most distant point on which the eye can sharply focus. Contrary to popular expectation, the farsightedness of old age does not actually cancel myopia, although the general loss of refractive power may help slightly.

Hypermetropia, or true farsightedness, is another kind of refractive error in which there is a deficit in the refractive power of the eye. When the ciliary muscles are relaxed and the lens is flattened to its maximum extent, an image of a faraway object is projected behind the retina (Fig. 3.11b); that is, either the lens is too weak, or the eyeball is too short. When looking at a distant object, the farsighted person can correct for this refractive weakness by having the ciliary muscles constantly contracted to some extent, increasing the refractive power of the lens. In this way, a farsighted person can bring distant objects into focus. However, that person will not be able to bring a close-up object into focus; the near point will be considerably longer than that of an emmetrope. When the hypermetropic person's lens stiffens with presbyopia, the near

point moves back toward the far point, until even infinitely distant objects are too close for accommodation. BOX 3.7

Control of pupil size

The pupil is the aperture of the iris, and it is controlled by the state of contraction of two muscles that comprise the iris: the sphincter and dilator muscles. The control of these muscles is antagonistic; when one muscle is excited, the other is inhibited. Contraction of the sphincter in conjunction with relaxation of the dilator causes the pupil to constrict, while relaxation of the sphincter and contraction of the dilator causes the pupil to dilate (enlarge). Increased ambient light causes constriction of the pupil to a degree dependent on the intensity of light. As the level of illumination increases, the size of the pupil decreases. Thus the pupil exerts control over the amount of light that enters the eye. BOX 3.8

The size of the pupil is often thought to be important in functioning in both bright and dim environments by restricting the light input under bright conditions, and allowing more light into the

---

Box 3.7 Eyeglass prescriptions

Myopia and hypermetropia can be corrected by lenses that cause incoming light rays to diverge (for myopia), or converge (for hypermetropia) (Fig. 3.11c and d). Another condition, *astigmatism*, results from distortion of the cornea or lens such that focus is different along different axes (for example, vertical lines might be sharp, but horizontal lines blurry). This can be compensated with a cylindrical lens.

Corrective lenses can be mounted in a frame in front of the eyes (eyeglasses), placed directly on the cornea (contact lenses), or, in the case of removal of the natural lens in cataract surgery, placed inside the sac formed by the zonule fibers in the eye. It is also possible to adjust the curvature of the cornea with a procedure called *keratotomy*, usually by shaving it with a laser.

When you visit an optometrist or ophthalmologist to have your vision checked, you are usually asked to read a chart on a distant wall. This is a test of your *acuity*, the ability to resolve fine details. The familiar chart starting with a big 'E' is called a Snellen chart; other charts require that you detect the orientation of capital Es or of the position of a gap in an interrupted circle. Acuity can also be tested with fine grating patterns (see Chapter 9). Various lenses are placed before your eyes to determine the correction needed.

Most eyeglass prescriptions have six numbers, three for each eye. The two eyes are labeled O.D. (*oculus dextra*, the right eye) and O.S. (*oculus sinister*, the left eye). The 'spherical' correction is the strength of the lens, in diopters. Positive spherical correction means a convex lens (for hypermetropia), while negative is a concave lens (for myopia) 'Cylindrical' correction is the correction for astigmatism, and 'axis' tells how to orient the axis of the cylindrical component.

Box 3.8 Other factors that control pupil size

The pupil may constrict or dilate due to factors other than the level of ambient light. Changes in pupil size are correlated with the emotional state of the subject. A number of experiments have demonstrated that visual stimuli that have positive affective connotations will produce dilation of the pupil. Hess & Polt (1960) found that women in general increased the sizes of their pupils when presented with pictures of male nudes more than when they were shown pictures of female nudes, while the pattern was reversed for men. Similarly, Fitzgerald (1968) reported that the pupils of infants dilated more to pictures of human faces than to geometric shapes; the infants also showed more pupil dilation to pictures of their mothers than to pictures of strangers. Hess (1965) has suggested that just as stimuli with positive affect cause the pupil to dilate, stimuli that have a negative emotional content will produce pupil con-

striction. Other investigators, however, have not observed this relationship (Woodmansee, 1965; Pearler & McLaughlin, 1967; Loewenfeld, 1968).

Concentrated mental activity also has an effect on pupil size. Hess & Polt (1964) found that subjects' pupils dilated when they were given arithmetic problems to solve, with the amount of dilation depending on the difficulty of the problem. Other types of intellectual tasks have also been found to have the same effect (Goldwater, 1972). Kahneman and his associates (Kahneman & Beatty, 1967; Kahneman & Pearler, 1969) have attempted to determine precisely what aspect of mental activity affects pupil size, and have concluded that the critical variable is the amount of processing that is necessary for a subject to complete a particular task.

---

eye under dim illumination. In fact, however, the pupil plays a minimal role in this regard; the pupil diameter of your eye can vary only between 2 and 8 mm, a 16-fold change in area. Such a dynamic range is minute compared with the variations of a factor of 10^9, the range of intensities over which your visual system operates.

What your pupil does do is to allow only the most optically accurate parts of the visual system to be employed, under conditions in which there is enough light for this restriction to be feasible. The edges of the human lens (or any lens, for that matter) are optically inferior to the center region; a constricted pupil restricts the passage of light to the center portion of the lens. In addition, as the pupil becomes smaller, the lens becomes less important as a refractive structure. In the limit, a pinhole aperture, the visual field would be in focus even if the lens were absent. When the pupil is small, objects that were not in sharp focus when the pupil was larger are in better focus. You can see why this is so by looking at Fig. 3.6(b) and imagining how much smaller the blur circle would be if only the rays from the center of the lens were allowed to reach the screen. The extent to which an object can be moved up and back in

front of the lens without greatly distorting the focus is called the *depth of field*. Decreasing pupil size increases depth of field, and thus allows objects at different distances from the eye to be in sharp focus simultaneously, even without changes in the shape of the lens. Photographers increase the depth of field in their photos by 'closing down' the aperture (larger *f*-stop numbers)—but when they do, they must increase the time the shutter remains open to have enough light for proper exposure.

To some extent, the change in pupil size is anticipated by the structure of the retina. The cones (more so than the rods) are 'aimed' at the center of the pupil, so that light entering the very center is more effective than light entering near the edge of the pupil. The loss of sensitivity for lights entering at the edge of the pupil is called the *Stiles–Crawford effect*. In essence, the cones 'concentrate' on the well-focused light from the center of the pupil and partially 'ignore' the light the constricted pupil would eliminate. Rods do not show nearly as strong an effect; they work in dim lighting where it is more important to gather as much light as possible than to be concerned with accurate focus or depth of field. <u>**BOX 3.9**</u>

Box 3.9 Demonstration of depth of field

Depth of field is easy to demonstrate for yourself, especially if you are either nearsighted or farsighted. Make a pinhole in a piece of paper; then take off your glasses and look through the pinhole when it is placed as close as possible to your eye. The world is in reasonable focus through the hole, even though it may be quite dim. (This is one of the reasons that squinting sometimes helps.) In fact, the first cameras were merely boxes with a pinhole in one wall and a light-sensitive substance on the opposite wall. Even without a lens, an image of the world was projected onto the far wall by the pinhole. Perhaps you used this trick to view a solar eclipse.

The extraocular muscles and eye movements

Your eye is not stationary in its socket. Its movement is mediated by the six *extraocular* muscles shown in Fig. 3.12. The muscles are arranged in three antagonistic pairs. Up and down movement of the eye is mediated mainly by the *superior* and *inferior rectus muscles*; contraction of one muscle in this pair is always coupled with relaxation in the other muscle. For example, to move the eye so that it is pointing upward, the superior rectus muscle contracts at the same time as the inferior rectus muscle relaxes. Similarly, sideways turning of the eye is mediated by the *lateral* and *medial rectus muscles*. The *superior* and *inferior oblique muscles* are important for producing rotational eye movements,

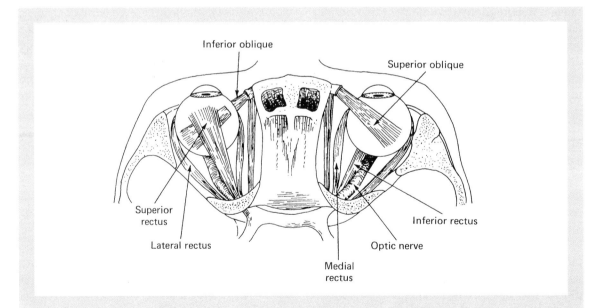

Fig. 3.12 Extraocular muscles, as seen from above. From Walls, G. L. (1967) *The Vertebrate Eye and its Adaptive Radiation*. New York: Hafner. Reprinted by permission of the Cranbrook Institute of Science.

as well as assisting the superior and inferior recti in producing vertical movements.

The extraocular muscles provide a three-dimensional gaze-control system. The lateral recti turn the eyes left and right, the superior and inferior recti turn them up and down, and the oblique recti rotate them so that the image stays horizontal when the head is slightly tipped (Tweed *et al.*, 1998). This is a fairly elaborate orchestration. There is a relatively direct, though complex, relationship between activity in the semicircular canals of the vestibular apparatus and activation of the muscles. The pattern varies across species because the eyes may be placed looking either forward or to the sides, but the end effect is quite similar (see Simpson & Graf, 1985). **BOX 3.10**

Eye movements are important for several reasons. They allow the eye to follow a moving object while maintaining an image of that object at a stationary position on the retina. In addition, eye movements allow an animal to change its direction of gaze swiftly from one part of the visual field to another, perhaps in response to the introduction of some novel stimulus. These types of eye movements involve both eyes moving in the same direction, and are called *conjugate eye movements*.

Two types of conjugate eye movements can be distinguished. Eye movements that occur in response to a moving object in the visual field are called *smooth pursuit movements*. The velocity of rotation of the eye matches the movement of the object as long as this velocity is less than about 30°/s. Smooth pursuit movements are involuntary, in the sense that you cannot produce them in the absence of a moving object.

The other major class of conjugate eye movements is *saccadic movements*, which are sudden jumps made by the eye as it changes its point of fixation. Saccades last anywhere between 20 and 50 ms and can vary in size from less than 10′ of angle to as large as 20°. Saccadic movements occur continuously while scanning the visual world, as you attend to different aspects of the stimulus array. They also occur in direct response to introduction of a novel or moving stimulus into your visual field. In such cases, the saccadic movement orients the eye so that the novel stimulus projects its image onto your foveae, as opposed to the peripheral retina where the image had previously been projected.

Conjugate eye movements involve both eyes moving in the same direction; in *disjunctive eye movements*, however, the eyes move in opposite directions. When you view a nearby object, both your eyes move inward, so that an image of the object can be projected onto the foveas of both eyes. This is called *convergence*; conversely, as an object moves away, your eyes *diverge*. If the images of the object are not in the equivalent places on the two retinae, you will experience *diplopia*, or double vision. You can demonstrate this phenomenon by

---

Box 3.10 Demonstration of vestibular control of eye movements

The relationship between the vestibular apparatus and eye movements may be demonstrated by a simple experiment. Have someone sit on a rotating chair (a desk chair is good) with his or her eyes closed, and spin the chair in one direction at a moderate speed for about 30 s. Stop the chair, and have the subject open his or her eyes. You will see the eyes move smoothly, then flick back, then move again, as if rapidly scanning a wide page of text. This pattern of movement and quick return is called *nys-* *tagmus*, and it is just what the eyes would have to do if trying to fixate a point in the world while the body was rotating. As an after-effect of the earlier motion, the subject feels as if he or she were rotating in the opposite direction (see Chapter 13 for visual movement aftereffects). The nystagmus was induced by motion, but it can also be induced by a moving visual stimulus, such as when you watch a long train move past.

trying the test for stereopsis in Box P1 (p. vi). When you focus on your fingers, you see the point at the far end of the room in duplicate. The double image (or the double image of your fingers, which you see when you focus on the far point) is an example of diplopia. Disjunctive eye movements are necessary to reduce the double images into a single image. **BOX 3.11**

Box 3.11 A very different kind of eye

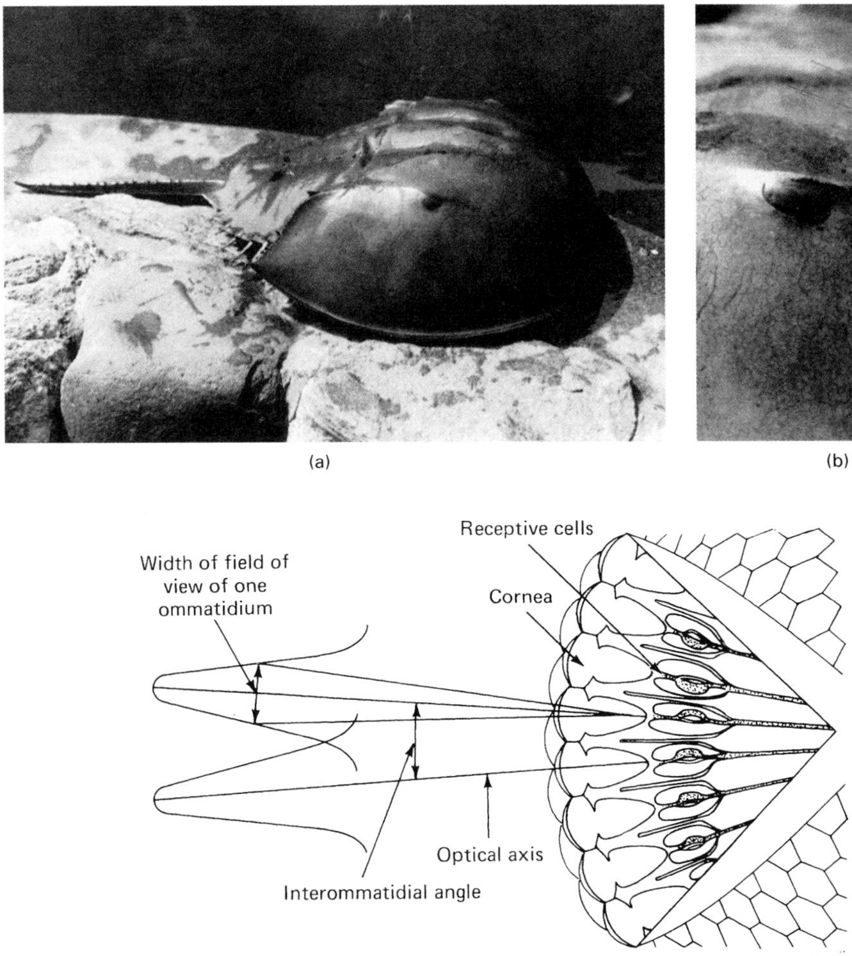

Fig. 3.13 (a) *Limulus polyphemus*, the horseshoe crab. (b) Close-up view of the lateral eye of *Limulus*. Note the slightly darker ommatidia near the center; this 'pseudopupil' is caused by viewing directly down the axes of these ommatidia. (c) Cross-section of several ommatidia.

The eyeballs of most vertebrates are remarkably similar, possessing most of the structures that you have seen in the preceding sections. Most invertebrates, however, have visual systems that are very different from the vertebrate scheme. Consider, for example, the eye of the horseshoe crab, *Limulus polyphemus*, a primitive marine animal. In contrast to vertebrate eyes that have one lens and cornea, the *Limulus* has a compound eye. As shown in Fig. 3.13, it is composed of about 800 tiny but separate facets, or *ommatidia* (Hartline *et al.*, 1956), each of which has its own lens and cornea, receptors, and optic nerve fibers that emanate from it. Each facet is oriented so that it responds to light stimuli in different areas of the visual field, with neighboring facets responding to somewhat overlapping areas. Within each ommatidium, the transparent covering of the eye acts as both a lens and a cornea to channel the light (coming from the region at which the ommatidium is pointing) to the receptor cells that lie underneath (Hartline *et al.*, 1952). The axons of these receptor cells leave the ommatidium and join the optic nerve that goes into the brain.

The eye of the *Limulus* is obviously quite different from those of humans and other vertebrates; however, there are some important parallels. After all, *Limulus*, like you, uses its eye to see. In place of the mosaic of receptors on which the vertebrate lens projects an image of the visual world, the *Limulus* has a mosaic of ommatidia. It lacks the complex inner retinal layers of our eyes, doing the processing in other ways. (The apparent simplicity of the *Limulus* eye is what attracted scientists to it in the first place. H. K. Hartline and his associates studied the properties of *Limulus* eyes in great detail; from this work, many of the basic principles that underlie human vision were first discovered. In particular, it was in *Limulus* that Hartline and his colleagues first described lateral antagonism, a main topic of Chapter 6. For his work in characterizing visual sensory processes, Hartline shared a Nobel Prize in 1967).

Suggested readings

George Wald's August 1950 *Scientific American* article entitled 'Eye and camera' (offprint #46) reprinted in *Perception: mechanisms and models*, by R. Held and W. Richards (W. H. Freeman, 1972) provides a good introduction to the comparative anatomy of animal eyes. More detailed information about light properties and the structure of the vertebrate eye can be found in Chapters 1 and 2 of *Vision and visual perception*, edited by C. H. Graham (John Wiley, 1965). Finally, for anyone who really wants to be immersed in eyes, *The vertebrate eye and its adaptive radiation*, by G. Walls (Hafner, 1967) is a classic description of the eyes of almost every vertebrate imaginable.

Chapter 4
The retina

In Chapter 3 you learned about the gross anatomy of the eye, and saw how it projects an upside down image of the visual world onto the sensitive neural retina. This chapter is an overview of how that image of light and shade is converted into a neural signal, and how that signal is encoded for transmission to the brain. In fact, this chapter does not tell the whole story; the final stage of processing and encoding is performed by the retinal ganglion cells, which are the subject of the next chapter.

The coding of the signal that the retina sends to the brain is a complicated process, and has not been fully deciphered. This chapter may seem to contain a lot of details, but actually many details have been omitted in favor of only those that are probably most pertinent to the problem at hand ('Probably', because until the process is better understood, it will be hard to judge which aspects are really the most significant). The concepts and principles introduced in this chapter will reappear in discussions of higher centers and other senses, and seem to be general principles of perceptual systems.

Pigment epithelium

Before the retina itself, consider the tissue with which the retina is closely allied, the pigment epithelium. As the name implies, it is a layer of cells that contain pigment, or coloring agent. Pigment

---

Box 4.1 Why a cat's eye shines at night

Not all animals have a dark-colored pigment epithelium. Animals that hunt at night have eyes designed to make the most use of a limited amount of light. The 'second chance' to see sparse light on the rebound is of more importance than the loss of image quality caused by scatter. Rather than having a dark layer behind the retina, these animals have a highly reflective layer called a *tapetum*. The tapetum is the reason a cat's eyes seem to glow in the dark; what you see is the light that has entered the eye, passed through the retina, bounced off the tapetum, passed through the retina again, and emerged from the eye. If the cat focuses its eye on you, you may even catch a glimpse of a blood vessel on the surface of its retina.

This kind of reflection can occur in human eyes as well. It is the explanation for the effect called 'red eye' in photography. If you take a flash photo of someone who is looking at the camera, and the flash is mounted next to the camera lens, the pupils of the subject's eyes appear to be red. The light filling the pupils is light from the flash, beamed back at the camera by the lens and cornea. It has a reddish color because the pigment of pigment epithelium absorbs long-wavelength light least efficiently, and also because the light passes through the blood vessels on the surface of the retina. This beamed-back light is what an ophthalmologist views through the ophthalmoscope when examining your retina (and what made the fundus photograph for the demonstration on the CD associated with Chapter 3).

epithelium is not neural, but is derived from the same germ cells as the retina in the developing embryo.

Pigment absorbs light, and therefore looks dark. Light absorbed by the pigment epithelium is not useful for vision, having already passed through the retina without being absorbed. If this light that failed to stimulate the retina were not absorbed by pigment epithelium, it would bounce back through the retina. It might be absorbed by the retina on the second pass, and be taken for a part of the image. On the second pass, however, it would be slightly displaced from its original position, so the image would be degraded. Some might pass through again, and strike the retina at some distant point, further confusing the image. Thus, one important function of the pigment epithelium is to prevent light from bouncing around inside the eye, an effect called *scatter*. (In this respect, pigment epithelium is the equivalent of painting the inside of a camera black.) You will see shortly that it has other important functions as well. BOX 4.1

General anatomy of the retina

The retina itself is more than just a layer of light-sensitive cells; it also performs the first stages of processing of the visual image. It comprises three major layers of cell bodies, separated by two layers of synaptic connections, called *plexiform layers* (Fig. 4.1). The layers are named according to their position relative to the center of the eyeball; layers nearest the center of the eye are referred to as *inner*, and those nearer the pigment epithelium are called *outer*.

Starting from the pigment epithelium, the cells in the outermost layer of the retina are the receptors. These are the cells that perform the task of absorbing light and transducing it into nervous energy. Light is absorbed by pigments in the recep-

tors, at which time it ceases to be light, just as the sound of a voice is no longer sound when it is transmitted through a telephone wire (you can't wiretap by placing your ear against the phone wires).

As the receptors are in the outermost layer of the retina (and, in fact, the light-absorbing pigment is in the outermost part of each receptor), light reaching the receptors must pass through all other layers of the retina (discussed in the following paragraphs). This might seem like an inefficient way to design an eyeball. Actually, the loss of light because of this 'backward' arrangement is negligible, as the retina is extremely thin (about 0.2 mm) and made of cells that are mostly water, and therefore practically invisible when immersed in the fluids of the eye. (The micrograph in Fig. 4.1a was made after treating the retina with a dye that makes the cells visible.) The slight disadvantage is more than compensated for by the advantages of having the receptors in close apposition to the pigment epithelium. Because the receptors are close, the spread of light that does bounce from the pigment epithelium is minimal. In addition, the pigment in the receptors must be replenished after absorbing light; the pigment epithelium plays a role in this replenishment.

The cell bodies of the receptors lie in a layer called the *outer nuclear layer* ('nuclear' because the nuclei of the receptors are there). The receptors terminate in a layer of synaptic connections called the *outer plexiform layer*. It is here that the receptors are presynaptic to other cells in the retina, and also postsynaptic to some of them. You will learn more about these synapses later.

The next layer of cell bodies is the *inner nuclear layer*, which actually consists of three somewhat distinct sublayers. At its outer margin are *horizontal cells*, so named because they run horizontally in the retina interconnecting distant areas. These horizontal (or *lateral*) connections provide the first stage of retinal processing of the visual image.

The bulk of the inner nuclear layer is taken up by the *bipolar cells*. Bipolar means 'having two ends'—that is, cells that interconnect two points. The bipolar cells are the links between the outer

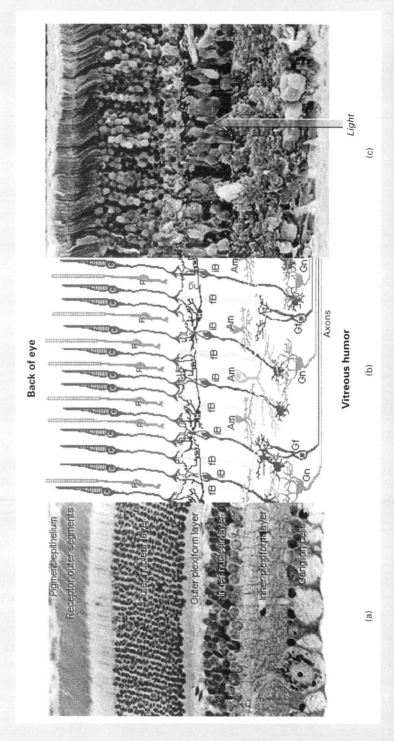

Fig. 4.1 The retina. (a) Light micrograph of a cat retina with the cell bodies made visible by treating it with a special stain. (b) Schematic showing the various cell types and some of their interconnections. This is the schematic used for the demonstration on the CD. (c) Scanning electron micrography of a cat retina. Layers of the retina are labeled in (a). Note that light enters from below, as indicated by the arrow in (c). Cell types are labeled in (b) as follows: C = cone; R = rod; H = horizontal cell; iB = invaginating (depolarizing) bipolar cell; fB = flat (hyperpolarizing) bipolar cell; Am = amacrine cell; Gn = ON-center ganglion cell; Gf = OFF-center ganglion cell. Micrographs kindly provided by E. H. Polley, Dept. of Anatomy and Cell Biology, University of Illinois at Chicago.

and inner plexiform layers, although they also participate in the processing at both ends.

Near the inner margin of the inner nuclear layer, you can see some nuclei that are slightly larger than the bulk of those in the rest of the layer. These are the *amacrine cells* (which means 'cells without axons'). The amacrine cells are the horizontal or lateral elements of the *inner plexiform layer*; their cell bodies are in the inner nuclear layer but they send a number of dendrite-like processes into the nearby plexiform layer, like an octopus sitting atop an oyster bed.

There is considerable dispute over exactly which cells should be called amacrine, how many different types of amacrine cells there are, and what their functions might be. For our purposes, they are the cells that provide the lateral interconnections required for the second stage of processing of the visual image that occurs at the inner plexiform layer. Here, the bipolar cells are presynaptic to amacrine cells and *ganglion cells*;

amacrine cells are presynaptic to other amacrine cells, to bipolar cells and to ganglion cells. The details will come later, but it is clear that many of the amacrines serve very specialized functions unrelated to lateral interconnections (MacNeil & Masland, 1998).

The inner plexiform layer varies considerably in thickness and complexity among different animals. In a comparison of this layer in a number of species, Dubin (1970) found that the thickest inner plexiform layers are in the retinas of frogs and pigeons, while it is relatively thin in humans. Moreover, the inner plexiform layer of frogs and pigeons is considerably more complex in that bipolar cells rarely synapse directly on ganglion cells; rather, bipolar cells make synapses with amacrine cells, which synapse with other amacrine cells, which ultimately lead to ganglion cells. Human and other mammalian retinas show a relatively high number of bipolar cell synapses directly to ganglion cells.

Box 4.2 Complicated connections in the retina

Although you have just read about a number of cell types and interconnections, this is actually a relatively simple picture of a retina in which information tends to flow in the direction from receptors to ganglion cells, with lateral spreading at the two plexiform layers. After all, the retina's main function should be to tell the ganglion cells about light falling on the receptors, so the ganglion cells can convey that information to the brain.

This straightforward picture has been disrupted by the discoveries of pathways by which information can also flow in the opposite direction. You will soon learn that horizontal cells not only receive information from receptors, but they also make synapses that influence the receptors. In the inner plexiform layers of the retinas of fish (Ehinger *et al.*, 1969; Dowling & Ehinger, 1975), monkeys (Dowling & Ehinger, 1975), and other mammals (Dawson & Perez, 1973; Boycott *et al.*, 1975; Dowling & Ehinger, 1978b; Fisher, 1979), there are cells that look like amacrine cells. Unlike amacrine cells, however, these cells have axons that terminate in the outer plexiform layer where they are presynaptic to horizontal cells (Dowling & Ehinger, 1978a; Dowling, 1978). These cells, which connect the two plexi-

form layers, have been named *interplexiform cells* (Gallego, 1971; for a review, see Nguyen-Legros, 1991). It is believed that the function of these backward projections is to adjust the sensitivity of the outer retina as the retina adapts to different levels of light (see Chapter 6).

More recently, Chun & Wässle (1993) reported horizontal cells that send processes into the inner plexiform layer, where they are postsynaptic, and Usai *et al.* (1991) found ganglion cells that send axon collaterals back to other retinal cells. Cells conveying information from the inner layers to the outer are *centrifugal*; that is, they conduct information from supposedly 'higher' levels backwards to earlier levels.

Another centrifugal pathway arises in the brain itself. Cells in specific areas of the brains of pigeons (Dowling & Cowan, 1966) and fish (Witkovsky, 1971) send axons that run alongside the axons of ganglion cells and end in the inner plexiform layer of the retina. This pathway enables the brain to influence the processing performed by the retina. The operation of this system is not yet well understood.

The implication of this structural complexity is that the retinas of these 'simpler' animals perform a more complex processing task than do our own retinas. Presumably, their retinas do more processing because their brains can do less. Our brains receive a more complete description of the visual world and decipher those aspects that are important. The frog's brain receives a highly processed version of the world, with the relevant information already sorted out for immediate action.

The final level of this complicated processing network is occupied by the ganglion cells. These are the only cells that communicate directly with the brain, so they provide the sole output of the retina. Ganglion cells have their dendrites in the inner plexiform layer, their cell bodies in the *ganglion cell layer* (see Fig. 4.1), and send axons across the surface of the retina (to the optic disc) to form the *optic nerve*. The optic nerves (one from each eye) each contain about one million ganglion cell axons whose ultimate destinations are in the brain. BOX 4.2

Receptors

Most vertebrate retinas contain two types of receptor cells, *rods* and *cones*. These are distinguished principally by the shape of the outermost part of each cell, the *outer segment* (which is the part that actually absorbs light and generates the initial neural signal). Rods have long cylindrical (rod-like) outer segments that are of uniform diameter for most of their length; cones have shorter, tapered (conical) outer segments that are widest near the cell body and quite narrow at the outer extremity.

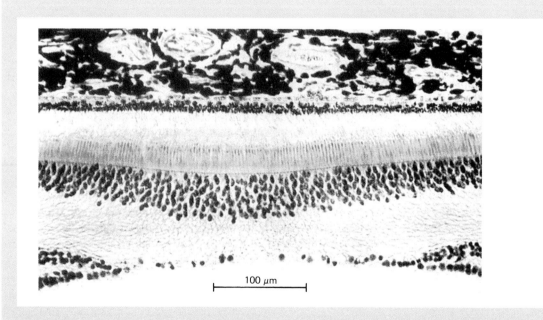

100 μm

Fig. 4.2 Section through the fovea of a monkey retina. Cell bodies have been made visible by staining with haematoxylin and eosin. From Brown, K. T., K. Watanabe, and M. Murakami (1965) The early and late receptor potential of monkey cones and rods. *Cold Spring Harbor Symp. Quant. Biol.* 30: 457–482. Reprinted by permission of the author and publisher.

In human eyes, rods and cones are not uniformly distributed in the outer layer of the retina. Along the main axis of the eye, at the very center of the retina, is the *fovea*. The retina is thinner at the fovea because the bipolar and ganglion cells serving the receptors in the fovea are off to the sides. This sweeping out from the foveal pit may be seen in Fig. 4.2. The *only* receptors in the center of the fovea are cones; there are no rods at all. The fovea is the part of the human retina that is specialized for detailed vision. When you direct your eyes to a particular object, what you are doing is turning them so that the image of that object falls on the fovea. Humans and other primates such as monkeys are the only animals to have this particular specialization. Some other animals, such as cats and birds, have specialized central regions similar to a fovea, but usually there are rods as well as cones in these regions. Many cold-blooded animals have retinas that show no specialization of this type.

Because there are no rods in the central human fovea, they must all be in the part of the retina outside the fovea. Figure 4.3 shows the distribution of rods and cones in the human eye; it represents the numbers of receptors encountered along the horizontal line that passes through the fovea. Cones are most numerous in the fovea, becoming more sparse as one moves either nasally or temporally. (Despite this difference, only about 1% of all your cones are in your foveae.) Rods are absent in the fovea, but are most dense in the region of retina to either side of it, being numerous almost all the way out to either the nasal or temporal edges, and vastly outnumbering cones outside the fovea. One other point to notice in Fig. 4.3 is that there is an interruption in both the rod and the cone curves slightly nasal of the fovea. This is an area free of any receptors—it is the optic disc or blind spot, where the optic nerve exits from the eye.

There are a number of psychophysical correlates of the distribution of rods and cones. Acuity is best in the fovea, and considerably worse outside it. (Even though vision may be mediated by cones outside the fovea, the cones of the fovea are special-

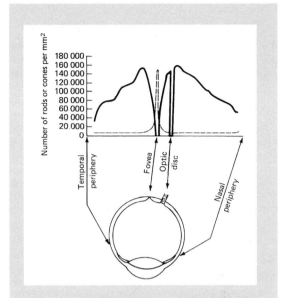

Fig. 4.3 Distribution of rods (*solid curve*) and cones (*dashed curve*) in the human retina. Data are from Østerberg (1935).

ized for better acuity.) You can demonstrate the high acuity of your fovea by looking at a picture on a color television. Stand about an arm's length from the screen. Concentrate on seeing the dots (or bars) of color that make up the picture, not on the picture itself. You should be able to see a small circular area in the very center of your gaze where individual dots are clearly seen; this is the area falling on your foveae. Outside this sharp area, which moves about as you move your eyes, the dots tend to blur together. The high acuity of your foveal vision allows you to resolve the individual dots in the areas seen by your foveae, but the rest of your retina does not have the requisite acuity. Of course, you already demonstrated your ability to read words in tiny letters presented to your fovea but not to your peripheral retina when you tried the 'Foveal acuity' demonstration in Chapter 3.

Color vision is also best in the fovea. Outside it there are fewer cones and more rods, which seem to dilute the strength of colors (Gordon & Abramov, 1977). In the far periphery, rods outnumber cones

---

Box 4.3 The specialization of rods and cones

The cones are responsible for color vision and the high acuity of foveal vision. But there is nothing special about cones *per se* to make them suited for what they do. They subserve color vision because there are cones of different types (see Chapter 14). There could be rod color vision if there were different types of rods, as there are in frogs. The high acuity of foveal cones is due in part to their thinner (rod-like!) shape than cones outside the fovea. This allows more cones to squeeze into the small area of the fovea, improving the sampling of the visual scene (if you are into computer graphics, you know an image looks better with high-resolution graphics, that is, more pixels per unit area). Equally important, there are bipolar cells serving the fovea that receive an input from a single cone (Kolb *et al.*, 1992), and these serve as the sole inputs to individual ganglion cells (Wässle *et al.*, 1990). There are thus many more ganglion cells serving the fovea than an equivalent-sized area outside the fovea.

But there are about 20 times as many rods as cones (Jonas *et al.*, 1992) — why do we have rods? Rods are better at detecting weak lights than are cones; this is due in part to the longer outer segment providing more chance for the pigment to intercept photons, but is probably due in larger part to the slower responses the shape confers. This prolongs the effect of each photon, allowing photons arriving over a period of time to add their effects (at the expense of accuracy in timing). Even more importantly, many more rods converge onto each bipolar cell, pooling the collected photons over space. This allows detection of sparsely scattered photons, but at the expense of knowing precisely where they arrived. Finally, rods seem to have been 'designed' optimally for discriminating single events from random noise (Leibovic & Moreno-Diaz, 1992).

---

by about 50 : 1, and there is little color vision at all. This was the point of the 'Peripheral vision' demonstration that you should have tried in Chapter 3. BOX 4.3

Structure of receptors

Each receptor, rod or cone, consists of two major parts. The *inner segment* consists of the cell body (with the nucleus), and an axon-like process extending into the outer plexiform layer and terminating in an enlarged portion where the synapses are made, called the *receptor terminal*. Rod terminals are ball-like endings called *spherules*; cones end in a flat foot-like process called a *pedicle*.

The outer segments of rods and cones differ in shape, but appear to be similar in that each is filled with a tightly folded membrane. Electron microscope close-ups of outer segments in Fig. 4.4 show this clearly; both rods and cones appear to be packed with sheets of membrane. There is a subtle difference between them, however. The membrane of the outer segments of cones is partly one long folded sheet, like an accordion or fan, with occasional openings to the extracellular fluid. The membranes in the outer segments of the rod consist of separate enclosed discs, like a stack of pancakes inside the membrane enclosing the outer segment (Laties & Liebman, 1970; Yoshikami *et al.*, 1974). BOX 4.4

Box 4.4 The outer segments of receptors

The inner and outer segments of rods and cones are connected by a fine filament located at one side. The filament arises from a structure in the inner segment called a *centriole*, and contains nine pairs of tubular filaments. These structures are typical of *cilia*, the fine hair-like projections

with which many single-celled organisms swim. The outer segment is a highly specialized cilium, one that does not move but instead transduces energy. The sensory portion of receptors in many other sensory systems are derived from modified cilia (Rodieck, 1973).

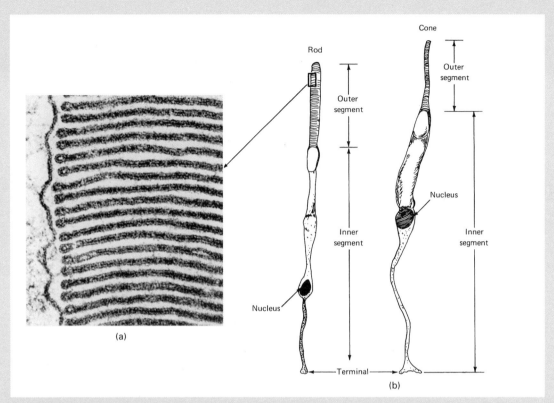

Fig. 4.4 Structure of rods and cones. (a) Electron micrograph of part of the rod outer segment. (b) Rod (*left*) and cone (*right*). Electron micrograph from Dowling, J. E. (1967) The organization of vertebrate visual receptors. In: *Molecular organization and biological function*. Edited by John M. Allen. Copyright © 1967 by John M. Allen. Reprinted by permission of Harper & Row, Publishers, Inc.

Function of receptors

The outer segment of a rod or cone is its business end, the part that actually absorbs photons and begins the process of creating a neural signal. You might say the real receptor is the outer segment. It contains molecules of pigment that absorb photons and undergo a chemical change as a result of that absorption. If light were not absorbed and its energy used to trigger this chemical change, there could be no vision.

There are two principal parts to a visual pigment molecule (more accurately, complex of molecules): the *opsin* and the *chromophore*. The opsin consists of a long chain of 364 amino acids. It is therefore a protein. This long, stringy molecule is virtually 'sewn' into the disc membrane, traversing it seven times (Bok, 1985). The chromophore nestles within the membrane, attached to this stitching (Bowmaker, 1998).

The chromophore consists of a chemical called *retinal* that is an altered form of vitamin A (*retinol*),—hence the relationship between eating vitamin A-rich foods, such as carrots, and night vision. Both retinal and retinol consist of a ring of carbon atoms decorated with some side groups, and sporting a decorated tail of nine carbon atoms. When retinal is bound to opsin it is in a

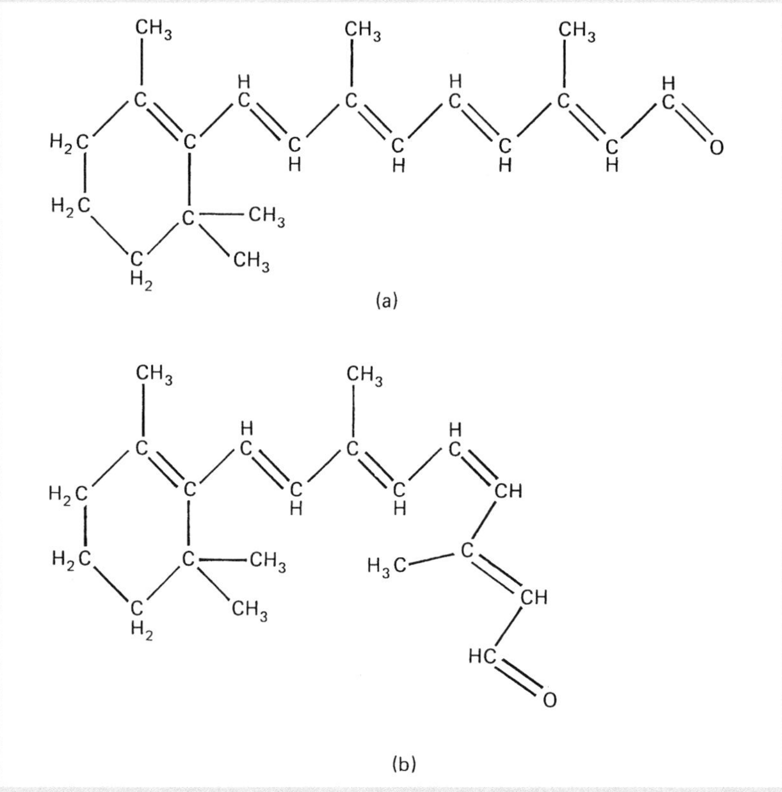

Fig. 4.5 (a) All-trans retinal; (b) 11-cis retinal.

configuration called *11-cis*; that is, there is a bend in the tail at carbon atom number 11, as shown in Fig. 4.5(b). Folded in this manner, the retinal binds to the opsin within the membrane.

When a photon is absorbed by the visual pigment, it ceases to exist as a photon and its energy is transferred to the chromophore. The chromophore then undergoes a change called *isomerization*, which is a change in the physical configuration of the molecule of retinal. Specifically, the bend at carbon atom 11 straightens out; the retinal goes from the 11-cis isomer to the *all-trans* isomer shown in Fig. 4.5(a) (stereograms showing the changes may be found in Wang *et al.*, 1994). With its tail straightened out, the retinal no longer binds to the opsin, and rapidly breaks free. The change in form of the chromophore is the first step in the process of vision.

In order for vision to continue to be possible, there must be a renewable supply of visual pigment. There are several changes the chromophore undergoes after isomerization, and a complicated set of alternative fates that could befall it. Eventually, however, it is made back into 11-cis retinal, which recombines with opsin to make new pigment. Some of the all-trans retinal is converted directly back into 11-cis by an enzyme in the outer segment (called retinal isomerase); some is converted into retinol, and is recombined with opsin by a more complicated method in which the pigment epithelium plays a role (Pepperberg *et al.*, 1978; Crouch *et al.*, 1996). <u>BOX 4.5</u>

Box 4.5 The pigment epithelium as janitor

There is another function of the pigment epithelium that requires it to be near the receptor outer segments. The receptors continuously shed the folded discs from the tips of the outer segments, and these are taken up and digested by the pigment epithelium. (Why the receptors must continuously replenish their outer segments is not understood, but they do.)

The receptors grow new discs or membrane at the innermost part of the outer segment, and the older material is pushed outward (Usukara & Obata, 1995). At first it was believed that only rods shed their discs, but it is now clear that cones also lose chunks of their outer segments (Young, 1978). Interestingly, the process of shedding occurs only at specific times of the day; cones shed their tips in the evening, and rods shed discs in the morning. The timing of shedding is partly controlled by lighting (Bassi & Powers, 1990), and can be influenced by the color of the light presented (Balkema & Bunt-Milam, 1982).

The absorption of a photon causes isomerization (within 200 femtoseconds, which is 0.000 000 0002 s; Schoenlein *et al.*, 1991), and this leads to a change in the polarization of the receptor (see Appendix). It is a slightly curious property of vertebrate photoreceptors, both rods and cones, that the response to light is hyperpolarization. In most other receptors, including the photoreceptors of most invertebrates, the response to an appropriate stimulus is depolarization. But rods and cones hyperpolarize, as if they were excited by darkness and inhibited by light. In the dark, the membrane potential is less negative than is the case for most other neurons; during a stimulus, the receptor may hyperpolarize to levels near the normal resting potential of other cells (Tomita, 1970). Thus, it may be more accurate to think of the receptors as depolarized in the dark, and repolarized in light. This really makes no difference, as the information is the same whether the signal is excitatory or inhibitory (a photographic negative has the same information as the print made from it; it just looks strange to the untrained eye). BOX 4.6

Box 4.6 The long cascade from isomerization to hyperpolarization

How does the isomerization of a pigment molecule on the disc or folded membrane of an outer segment lead to hyperpolarization of the receptor? When the first edition of this book was written, there was a tentative answer to this question. It turned out that that answer was basically wrong, although it did stimulate the research that has led to a new answer. This story is interesting not only for the explanation of how isomerization leads to hyperpolarization, but also as a glimpse at how science proceeds.

For an event on the disc membrane to affect the outer membrane of the receptor, information must get from the disc to the outer membrane. It had been observed that calcium ions are concentrated in the discs, and that adding calcium mimics some effects of light (Yoshikami & Hagins, 1971; Brown & Pinto, 1974). The 'calcium hypothesis' suggested that when rhodopsin isomerizes, it might act like an open pore in the disc and let calcium ions out. The calcium would diffuse to the outer membrane, where it could block (or close) pores that normally allow positive sodium ions to enter the cell in the dark and depolarize it.

There were some serious questions about the calcium hypothesis (Liebman & Pugh, 1979). Calcium may be sequestered in rod discs, but how is it segregated from the outer membrane in the folded membrane of cones? And why is there an effect of, and change in concentration of, a chemical called cyclic guanosine monophosphate (cGMP), a ribonucleic acid that is often a 'second messenger' at synapses (Farber *et al.*, 1978; Woodruff *et al.*, 1977)?

The answer came with the application of a technique called patch clamping to the photoreceptor. Currents were measured from microscopic patches of outer segment membrane that were exposed to various media. In both rods (Fesenko *et al.*, 1985) and cones (Haynes & Yau, 1985), a sodium gate was found that is held open by tcGMP. Matthews & Watanabe (1987) showed that this

(BOX **4.6** CONTINUED)

cGMP-operated gate has the same properties as the sodium gate closed by light. In the dark, there is ample cGMP to hold the gates open, allowing sodium ions to enter and depolarize the cell. Isomerization of the pigment by light causes a decrease in the concentration of cGMP; the gates close, blocking the sodium flow, and the cell hyperpolarizes.

How does rhodopsin cause a decrease in cGMP? There is a complicated chemical cascade similar to that found in some synapses (Lamb, 1986). The 'activated' (isomerized) rhodopsin breaks apart another molecule, variously called *G-protein* or *transducin*. Transducin molecules consist of three pieces that are bonded together. Activated rhodopsin frees one of these from the other two; the liberated piece joins another protein, *phosphodiesterase* (PDE). The PDE is thereby activated, and goes to work; its work is to break open the ring structure of cGMP, making ordinary GMP. Ordinary GMP does not open the sodium gates, so they close (until another enzyme reloops the GMP). This cascade of events allows for tremendous amplification: one photon isomerizes one rhodopsin molecule, which activates hundreds of transducin molecules. Each transducin molecule activates many PDE molecules, each of which breaks up thousands of cGMP molecules. In this way, one photon can affect enough cGMP molecules to make a significant difference in the concentration of cGMP (see the review by Yau, 1994).

Why did calcium seem to be the agent? There are three somewhat interlocked reasons. First, calcium can enter the cell through the sodium gates, but it is a tight squeeze. If a calcium ion gets in the gate, it occupies it and blocks the passage of many sodium ions (like a huge, wide-load truck slowing traffic through a tunnel). Thus, excess calcium 'clogged' the sodium gates, making them seem to be closed, as they are by light.

Second, there is a sodium/calcium exchange pump in the outer segment membrane (Yau & Nakatani, 1984). This pump allows sodium in, but throws calcium out (to make up for the calcium entering through the sodium gates). When the gates are blocked during light, the pump continues to expel calcium, so its concentration drops. This change in concentration made it look like it was being released as an internal transmitter.

Finally, calcium plays a part in light adaptation (Flaming & Brown, 1979). The concentration of calcium apparently controls the rate at which the enzyme that reloops the broken cGMP can work (Lyubarsky *et al.*, 1996). In addition, the efficiency with which the channels can be opened by cGMP depends on the calcium concentration inside the cell (Sagoo & Lagnado, 1996). 'Freezing' the calcium levels by preventing operation of the pump that would expel it during the light seems to prevent light adaptation in both rods and cones (Matthews *et al.*, 1988; Nakatani & Yau, 1988).

This all can be summarized as follows. In the dark, rhodopsin, transducin, and PDE are in their inactive states. There is a high concentration of cGMP, which holds the sodium gates open, letting sodium (and some calcium) enter and depolarize the cell. The sodium/calcium pump keeps the calcium level normal. Light isomerizes rhodopsin, which activates transducin, which activates PDE, which breaks up cGMP. Lacking cGMP, the gates close; sodium cannot enter, so the cell hyperpolarizes. Calcium also cannot enter, so the pump lowers the calcium concentration in the cell (Pugh & Lamb, 1990). Low calcium speeds the reaction that rebuilds cGMP so some gates reopen (causing an initial overshoot), and responses to flashes added to the steady light are smaller and faster than if there were no steady light (Koutalos & Yau, 1996).

The hyperpolarization of a receptor is initiated in its outer segment, and spreads through the inner segment by decremental (electrotonic) conduction. The receptor is sufficiently stubby that the slow potential is nearly full-sized at the terminal; there is no need to transmit the message by action potentials. In fact, nearly all the cells of the retina (except the ganglion cells, which project all the way to the brain) are sufficiently small that action potentials are unnecessary. As you will see when you read about the other cells in the retina, nearly all their responses are graded slow potentials transmitted by decremental conduction.

The synapses made by receptors are similar to those made by other neurons: synaptic vesicles merge with the cell membrane and release transmitter into the synaptic cleft when the cell membrane is depolarized. Receptors are depolarized in the dark, and therefore release transmitter in the dark. Since light causes hyperpolarization of the receptors, it decreases or stops the release of transmitter by the receptors (Toyoda, 1973; Kaneko & Shimazaki, 1975; Dacheux & Miller, 1976; Evans *et al.*, 1978). The information that a light is shining on a receptor is signaled by slowing the ongoing flow of transmitter.

To review: a photon of light enters the receptor, and is captured by a molecule of photopigment in the stacked or folded membranes of the outer segment. The chromophore of the photopigment isomerizes, going from the 11-cis to the all-trans form (unfolds its tail). Through a cascade of chemical events within the outer segment (see Box 4.6), channels that allow sodium ions into the receptor are closed, and the receptor hyperpolarizes. The amount of hyperpolarization depends on the number of photons absorbed. Hyperpolarization is communicated to the terminal by decremental conduction (electrotonic spread). The terminal, which had been releasing transmitter in the dark because it was in a somewhat depolarized state, slows the release of transmitter to the horizontal and bipolar cells with which it synapses in the outer plexiform layer.

Spectral sensitivity of receptors

So far, it may have seemed as if every photon impinging on a receptor gets absorbed by a molecule of photopigment in its outer segment. This is far from the case. The majority of photons pass completely through the receptor and are lost as far as vision is concerned. What determines whether a photon is likely to be absorbed or to pass clear through the receptor?

There are two factors that determine the probability of a photon being absorbed (this is the world of quantum mechanics where you cannot predict anything for a given photon, but know only the probability of outcomes). These two factors are the concentration of pigment (how many pigment molecules the photon is likely to encounter), and the match between the 'tuning' curve of the pigment molecules and the energy (wavelength) of the photon.

Here is an analogy: photons are like bullets being fired into a clump of trees; the trees are analogous to pigment molecules. What is the probability of a bullet shot at random (without aiming at a tree) embedding itself in a tree? Clearly, the more trees there are, the better the chance of hitting one; this is analogous to saying that the more pigment molecules there are (how concentrated), the higher the probability of photon capture. (Note also that a small clump of trees has a better chance of letting a bullet out the other side than a deep clump. This is analogous to outer segment length—see Bassi & Powers, 1990.) There is also a question of how well matched the bullet energies are to the type of tree. Bullet energy could refer to the muzzle velocity at which the bullet is fired, ranging from a slow air gun to a high-powered rifle. (Of course, all photons travel at the same speed, the speed of light, but they do vary in energy, which is inversely proportional to the wavelength of the light; see Chapter 3.) If the bullets travel slowly and the trees are hard, most bullets will bounce right off. Bullets that travel rapidly will pass completely through trees that are soft. When the bullet speeds are well matched to the types of trees, nearly every bullet that hits a tree will embed itself; if the speed is less well matched, only direct centered hits will result in embedding. Photons are absorbed only if their energy is appropriate to effect an isomerization.

Rather than discuss the fate of a single photon, consider the fate of a large group (a visible stimulus can contain hundreds of millions of photons). If the probability of capture of each photon is 0.01 (1 in 100), you could expect one photon to be captured from a stimulus containing 100; you would expect about 10 000 captured from a stimulus containing 1 000 000. In short, the probability in this case tells you the *percentage* of photons absorbed. You can then characterize the relative effectiveness of a visual pigment for various wavelengths of light by graphing the percentage absorbed as a function of wavelength.

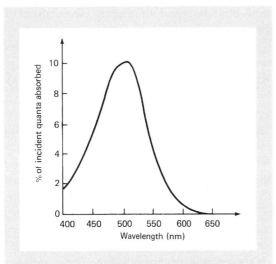

Fig. 4.6 Percentage of incident quanta absorbed by rhodopsin as a function of wavelength. Based on a nomogram presented by Ebrey, T. G. and B. Honig (1977) New wavelength-dependent visual pigment nomograms. *Vision Res.* 17: 147–151. Reprinted by permission of Pergamon Press, Ltd.

Figure 4.6 shows the percentage absorption curve for human *rhodopsin*, the pigment found in your rods. Rhodopsin most effectively absorbs photons when their wavelength is 505 nm; its ability to absorb photons of longer or shorter wavelengths is considerably less. This is the source of the name 'rhodopsin', which means 'rose-colored pigment'. It was originally called visual purple because the surviving long and short wavelengths make it appear rosy-purple when extracted and dissolved in a test tube.

Rhodopsin is the pigment in the rods of most mammals. (Many cold-blooded animals have a related pigment named *porphyropsin* in their rods.) The ability of visual pigments to absorb light is generally well matched to the average spectrum of the light normally reflected to the eye (Osorio & Bossomaier, 1992); for example, rhodopsin is matched to the light that filters through water to about 10 m in depth (Lythgoe & Partridge, 1991).

The cones do not contain rhodopsin; however,

they contain *cone pigment* (sometimes called *iodopsin*, which was the name given to the first cone pigment to be studied chemically; Wald *et al.*, 1955). In the normal (not color-blind) human retina, there are three distinct cone pigments. Each is somewhat like rhodopsin in that it is capable of absorbing light of almost any wavelength in the visible range, but the particular wavelengths to which each is most sensitive are different. Just as rhodopsin has a *peak* wavelength (505 nm), which is the light it absorbs more readily than any other, the cone pigments each have characteristic peak wavelengths. These differences are caused by subtle chemical differences in the opsins of the photopigments (Neitz *et al.*, 1991).

Each cone in your retina contains only one cone pigment (Marks *et al.*, 1964; Marks, 1965; Tomita *et al.*, 1967). There are thus three different types of cones in the human retina, distinguished from each other by the particular cone pigment each contains. As you will see in Chapter 14, it is because of these spectrally distinct types of cones that you can detect differences in color. As you have only one type of rod, rods alone cannot give information about the color of a stimulus.

Outer plexiform layer

It's time to get back to the processing done in the retina. We will follow the signal initiated by the absorption of light in the receptors as it passes through the layers of the retina. You have already seen the general anatomy of the retina; here are some details of the connections made in each of the plexiform layers, and the responses of the various cell types.

As you now know, your rods and your cones hyperpolarize in response to light absorbed by their individual outer segments. At the outer plexiform layer, information from the receptors passes to other cells in which messages from numerous receptors are mixed. This is the first stage of processing visual information. <u>BOX 4.7</u>

Box 4.7 **Communication among receptors**

As a matter of fact, the processing began before the outer plexiform layer. It is convenient to think of receptors as individual point readouts of the visual image, but each receptor is influenced by neighboring receptors as well. They send processes that come in close apposition to neighboring receptors (Scholes, 1975; Gold & Dowling, 1979), and apparently make electrical synapses with each other at these points. There is ample evidence from a number of different cold-blooded animals that the hyperpolarization of a given rod is caused in considerable measure by the photons captured by neighboring rods (Fain, 1975; Schwartz, 1976; Attwell & Wilson, 1980; Copenhagen & Owen, 1980). Coupling has also been demonstrated between cones (Richter & Simon, 1974; Tsukamoto *et al.*, 1992), and between cones and rods (Schwartz, 1975). In addition, receptors are apparently postsynaptic to horizontal cells, so they may be slightly depolarized by light in somewhat distant parts of the retina (Baylor *et al.*, 1971; Lasater & Lam, 1984).

The connections made by receptors are quite specialized. Within each receptor terminal are *invaginations*, or pockets. Processes from bipolar cells and horizontal cells fit into the invaginations and form a stylized arrangement called a *triad* (Dowling & Boycott, 1966). The central element of each triad is the dendrite of a bipolar cell; it is flanked on each side by processes from horizontal cells (Fig. 4.7). **BOX 4.8**

Horizontal cells are probably both presynaptic and postsynaptic elements in the outer plexiform layer; they contain vesicles, but are in a position that indicates receptors are presynaptic to them. Bipolar cells are apparently postsynaptic to both receptors and horizontal cells.

Although the triads are the most striking features of the outer plexiform layer, there are other contacts as well. Receptors are also presynaptic to bipolar cells that do not enter the invaginations.

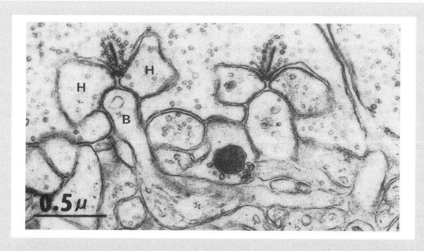

Fig. 4.7 Triads in a monkey cone. Two triads are visible, each with a synaptic ribbon surrounded by a halo of vesicles, a bipolar cell dendrite (**B**), and two horizontal cell processes (**H**). Electron micrograph from Dowling, J. E. (1965) Foveal receptors of the monkey retina: fine structure. *Science* 147: 57–59. Reprinted by permission. Copyright 1965 by the AAAS.

Box 4.8 The synaptic ribbon

The receptor is clearly a presynaptic element at the triad, as it contains synaptic vesicles and a structure called the *synaptic ribbon*, a dark double line surrounded by a halo of vesicles. The significance of the synaptic ribbon is not well known. It has been hypothesized that it serves as a temporary 'dock' to store vesicles near the active release sites (Rao-Mirotenik *et al.*, 1995). In a similar vein, Vollrath & Spiwoks-Becker (1996) depict the ribbon as a conveyor belt carrying vesicles to the membrane; they observe that the number and size of the associated vesicles depend on conditions of lighting.

These bipolar cells, called *flat bipolars* (as opposed to the *invaginating bipolars* that provide the central elements of triads) synapse at the surface of the receptor terminals. Synapses in which there is a single postsynaptic and a single presynaptic element and no specializations such as the synaptic ribbon are called *conventional* synapses. There are also conventional synapses between horizontal cells and bipolar cells. While the bipolar cells contacted by cones can be subdivided into flat and invaginating types, there are also bipolar cells exclusive for rods (they invaginate the rod spherules), and the cone bipolar cells can be further subdivided into several different subtypes. A single cone directly contacts at least eight different types of cone bipolar cell (Chun *et al.*, 1996).

The responses of the various cell types found in the outer retina can be appreciated from a simplified version of a figure first presented by Werblin & Dowling (1969) based on their recordings of cells in the retina of the mud puppy, *Necturus* (Fig. 4.8). You can see the general responses of the cells of the retina in the framework of Werblin & Dowling's classical figure, but much of what follows depends on more recent work in various animals.

The *Necturus*, an aquatic salamander, is a particularly convenient animal for intracellular studies. It is an amphibian that fails to complete its metamorphosis. All the nuclei in its cells begin mitosis and make copies of their chromosomes in preparation for a metamorphosis that never happens. *Necturus* remains water-breathing throughout its adult life, but because of the unfinished metamorphosis, its nuclei contain doubled chromosomes, and hence the cell bodies are relatively large. These large cell bodies are less difficult to impale with microelectrodes, making it possible to record responses from the cells of this retina. Werblin & Dowling took advantage of this quirk of nature to make their recordings. Improvements in technology have since made it possible to record cells from the outer retina of a number of other animals, including fish, toads, rabbits, cats, and monkeys.

A dynamic version of Fig. 4.8 can be found on the CD accompanying this book. Instead of showing the response of each cell in a matrix of plots, the simulated cells in a simplified diagram of the retina change color to indicate their state of polarization as the light flash is shone on the receptors (for more information about the simulation, see Box 4.14, p.71). Figure 4.8 is organized into four rows and two columns. Each row represents intracellular recordings of potential versus time for a particular neuron responding to stimulation of the retina by light. The records in the top tow are from a receptor (probably a rod); those in the second row are from a horizontal cell; those in the third row are from a bipolar cell; and those in the fourth row are from an amacrine cell. Each column represents the responses to a particular stimulus. The responses in the left column are to a spot of light, about 100 microns (0.1 mm) in diameter, centered on the neuron itself. The other column shows responses to *annuli* (sing., *annulus*) of light. An annulus is a common visual stimulus; the word means 'ring', and it is just that: a ring or circle of light. It allows stimulation of the area near a neuron without stimulating the area of retina in which the cell

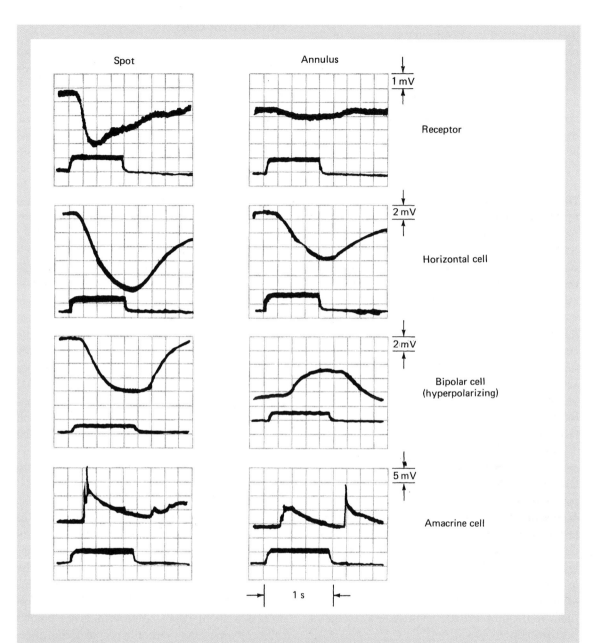

Fig. 4.8 Responses of retinal cells in *Necturus* to flashed stimuli. Responses to spots of light are shown in the left column, and responses to annuli in the right. Within each panel is the intracellular voltage as a function of time (*upper trace*) and a signal marker indicating the time the light was on (*lower trace*). *Top row*: responses of a receptor; *second row*: responses of a horizontal cell; *third row*: responses of a hyperpolarizing bipolar cell; *bottom row*: responses of an amacrine cell. Adapted from Werblin, F. S. and J. F. Dowling (1969) Organization of the retina of mudpuppy. *J. Neurophysiology*. 32: 339–355. Reprinted by permission.

itself resides. The response to a large annulus is therefore caused by lateral interconnection of the cells of the retina.[1]

In the demonstration program, the light is on a group of receptors near the left side of the diagram. There is no annulus; rather, the responses of cells near, but not in, the light may be gauged from cells that are on the right side of the diagram.

Each panel in Fig. 4.8 represents the response of a neuron to a single presentation of a stimulus. The upper trace shows the potential measured in the cell as a function of time, photographed directly from the face of an oscilloscope. (Each trace starts at the dark potential for that cell, but its position in the figure is not an indication of what that resting level was, because the position of the oscilloscope trace was arbitrarily shifted from record to record.) The lower trace in each panel is the output of a photocell that recorded the presence or absence of the stimulus light. It therefore serves as a synchronization marker, indicating exactly when the stimulus was present. Lights were on during the raised portion of this trace. The duration of the flashes was about 800 ms, or slightly less than 1 s.

The top row of the figure shows responses of a receptor; as you already know, receptors hyperpolarize when light is shone directly on them (left panel). When the light falls on neighbors (annulus, right panel), the hyperpolarization is much less; presumably this hyperpolarization is caused mainly by scattered light falling on the cell. (There may also be a contribution caused by the responses of the distant receptors; see Box 4.7, p. 61.) In the demonstration program, only those receptors actually in the illuminated region show a change in polarization.

---

[1] In practice, it is impossible to produce an annulus without a small amount of light also falling in the supposedly dark central area. This is because of scatter of light within the retina. You should bear in mind that when the theoretical stimulus is an annulus, there is actually a relatively dim illumination in the center.

Horizontal cells

The second row of the figure shows the responses of a horizontal cell. When a spot of light is shone on a horizontal cell (more accurately, on the position in the retina at which the electrode recording it is located), it hyperpolarizes. This hyperpolarization is much like the responses of the receptors presynaptic to the horizontal cell, but considerably larger (note that the scale is different from that in the upper row), and somewhat slower. In contrast to the receptors, however, the horizontal cell gives a robust response when the stimulus is an annulus.

Horizontal cells are responsive to lights across a wide area of the retina; the area of retina in which stimulation leads to response in a cell is referred to as the *receptive field* of the cell. Horizontal cells have large receptive fields; in fact, the receptive field of a horizontal cell can be considerably larger than the lateral spread of the cell itself. This is presumably because horizontal cells make electrical synapses with neighboring horizontal cells (Kaneko, 1971; Lasater, 1991; Bloomfield *et al.*, 1995). Notice that all the horizontal cells in the demonstration program hyperpolarize when the light is flashed on the left side of the figure. **BOX 4.9**

Bipolar cells

The responses of the bipolar cell shown in row 3 of Fig. 4.8 demonstrate a new and important property. The response to a spot of light (left) is hyperpolarization, much like the responses of the receptors and horizontal cells. The response of this bipolar cell to the large annulus (right panel), however, is a slight depolarization. A given bipolar cell's response can be either hyperpolarizing or depolarizing, depending on the spatial configuration of the stimulus. This cell does not simply detect light, but also discriminates between light falling directly on it (hyperpolarization) and light falling somewhat to the sides of it (depolarization). If the whole retina were flooded with light, it would attempt to hyperpolarize and depolarize at the same

Box 4.9 Different types of horizontal cells

There are several varieties of horizontal cells that can be distinguished both anatomically and physiologically. One distinction is that horizontal cell dendrites do not go indiscriminately to rods and cones. In fish, there is a division between horizontal cells that contact only rods, and those that contact only cones (Stell, 1967, 1975); these two types of horizontal cells, which are segregated into separate sublayers in the inner nuclear layer, do not interconnect directly with each other (Kaneko, 1971). In animals such as the cat, some horizontal cells have a thin 'axon' with a bulbous ending. The processes from the horizontal cell bodies contact only cones, while the processes from the axon terminal contact only rods (Kolb, 1974). The axon is sufficiently thin that there seems to be no communication between the rod-specific

soma and the cone-specific terminals (Nelson et al., 1975) (remember that horizontal cells do not fire action potentials, so conduction along the axon is decremental).

In animals with color vision, there is a further subdivision of the horizontal cells that contact cones. Cells that hyperpolarize regardless of the wavelength of the light are called *L-type* (for luminosity). There are other horizontal cells, called *C-type* (for color), that hyperpolarize for some wavelengths but depolarize for others. These are *spectrally opponent* responses, and presumably play a role in the processing of color information. Other spectrally opponent responses are discussed in Chapter 14, so you need not worry about this aspect of cell responses here.

time, and the response would be weaker than for the small spot.

The kind of organization displayed by this bipolar cell is called *spatial antagonism*; the receptive field of this cell is *concentric* (one region inside another), and referred to as *center/surround* (the center is the middle or direct region that leads to hyperpolarization, while the surround is the distant region that leads to depolarization).

Spatial antagonism is an important concept in visual processing. The response of a bipolar cell depends on the distribution of the light in its receptive field, not simply on the total amount of light. Bipolar cells start to take account of the relative amount of light, or *contrast*. The hyperpolarization of a bipolar cell depends on the amount of light falling on the center of its receptive field, relative to the amount falling on the surround. This kind of processing of spatial information will be discussed in much greater depth in Chapter 5.

The bipolar cell shown in Fig. 4.8 is typical of one type that is found in the retina. There is also another kind of bipolar cell that is a mirror image of this one. The second type depolarizes when light is shone directly on the receptors above the cell, and hyperpolarizes when the light

is in the surround part of its receptive field. To distinguish between them, this second type of bipolar cell is called 'center depolarizing', while the cell shown in the figure is called 'center hyperpolarizing'. The two types of bipolar cells generally correspond to the two anatomical types mentioned on page 62; most of the center-depolarizing cone bipolars are invaginating, while most center-hyperpolarizing cone bipolars are flat (Famiglietti & Kolb, 1976; Stell et al., 1977). While the division by anatomical types is not perfect (Saito et al., 1983; Sterling, 1983) it is a reasonable general rule (Boycott & Hopkins, 1993), and the 'violations' often involve bipolars that both invaginate and make some conventional synapses (Hopkins & Boycott, 1995). In any case, the division into mirror-image systems persists throughout the retina. **BOX 4.10**

The demonstration program shows both hyperpolarizing and depolarizing bipolar cells. The ones directly under the stimulus hyperpolarize or depolarize, respectively, when the light is present. Notice that those on the right do the opposite; the hyperpolarizing bipolars depolarize when light is flashed far from the receptors they contact directly, while the depolarizing bipolars hyperpolarize.

> **Box 4.10** Synaptic mechanisms of the bipolar cells
>
> The responses of depolarizing bipolar cells are opposite to those of the hyperpolarizing cells shown in Fig. 4.8. Since they both receive inputs from the same receptors, there must be a difference in the way transmission works at the synapses onto these two cell types. The transmission from receptors to hyperpolarizing bipolars is 'sign conserving' (the bipolars mimic the depolarization or hyperpolarization), while that from receptors to depolarizing bipolars is 'sign inverting' (these bipolars do just the opposite). If both types of bipolar cells receive the same transmitter from the receptors, they must use it to operate different channels.
>
> Horizontal cells and depolarizing bipolars require chlo-ride ions to function, but hyperpolarizing bipolars do not (Miller & Dacheux, 1976). Furthermore, the transmitter seems to close ionic channels in the depolarizing bipolars, but open channels in the hyperpolarizing type (Toyoda, 1973; Kaneko *et al.*, 1994; Maple & Wu, 1996). All of this implies that the channels in these two types of bipolars are different. Pharmacological investigations of the synaptic chemistry have shown that the appropriate systems are present in the retina (Miller & Slaughter, 1986). In fact, the transmitter is glutamate (see Appendix), and bipolars of different type have different types of glutamate receptors (Hirano & MacLeish, 1991; Pourcho, 1996)

Inner plexiform layer

Bipolar cells represent the output of the first stage of retinal processing, in the outer plexiform layer. The signals within bipolar cells are conducted radially inward (by electrotonic conduction) to the inner plexiform layer, where the next major processing steps occur. Here, bipolar cells communicate with amacrine cells and ganglion cells.

There is another specialized kind of synapse that is found in the inner plexiform layer: the *dyad*. At a dyad, a bipolar cell terminal with a synaptic ribbon is presynaptic to two amacrine cells. One of the amacrine cells, in turn, is presynaptic to the *same* bipolar cell terminal (Dowling & Boycott, 1966; Dowling, 1968). (At some dyads, the bipolar is presynaptic to an amacrine cell and a ganglion cell, as in Fig. 4.9.) The result of this arrangement is a *feedback* of the amacrine cell onto the bipolar cell.

Amacrine cells

Return to Fig. 4.8, and look at the responses of an amacrine cell. The response to a spot of light (fourth row, left) is a depolarization that appears rapidly at the onset of the light, but dwindles to nothing by the time the light is about to be extinguished. This is a different kind of response from those of receptors, horizontal cells, and bipolar cells. In those cells, presentation of light led to a depolarization that was at least partially maintained for as long as the light was present; this is called a *sustained* or *tonic* response. The amacrine cell shown here, on the other hand, produced its response when the light level *changed*, but gave little or no response when the light was steady (regardless of whether it was steadily on or steadily off); this kind of response is called *transient* or *phasic*. The sustained response is a signal that something is present, while the transient response is a signal that something has just changed. It is a general property of the visual system from this level onward that responses are at least somewhat transient. Some cells maintain a level of activity throughout the duration of a stimulus, but nearly all cells are considerably more active at the instant a stimulus appears (or disappears) than after it has been present or absent for a while (see Appendix). BOX 4.11

The response of the amacrine cell in the figure to an annulus is similar to its response to the spot. There is a transient depolarization at the onset of the light (called an ONSET response) and a second

Box 4.11 Other types of amacrine cells

Although amacrine cells recorded in *Necturus* seem to be transient cells like the one shown in Fig. 4.8, many of those in other animals give sustained responses (Kaneko & Hashimoto, 1969; Murakami & Shimoda, 1977; Chan & Naka, 1976; Kolb & Nelson, 1981; Weiler & Marchiafava, 1981; Nelson, 1982). Sustained amacrine cells can be further subdivided into depolarizing and hyperpolarizing types.

There is a tremendous diversity of anatomical types of amacrine cells in the retina (Kolb, Nelson, & Mariani, 1981;

Mariani, 1990; MacNeil & Masland, 1998). Some of the types are distinguished by their overall anatomy, some by their connections to other cells, some by their response type (Bloomfield, 1991), and some by the chemical transmitter they release (see Massey & Redburn, 1987). While a few of these cell types have been implicated in specific functions (Masland & Tauchi, 1986; Vaney, 1986), the roles of most of them are still not clear (Morgan, 1991). Only the 'traditional' transient amacrine cells are shown in the demonstration program.

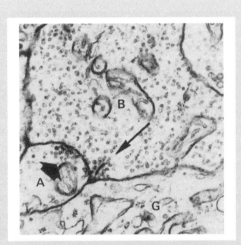

Fig. 4.9 A dyad in a human retina. The bipolar cell (**B**) is presynaptic to an amacrine cell (**A**) and a ganglion cell (**G**). Where the three join, a synaptic ribbon (*thin arrow*) may be seen in the bipolar cell. The collection of vesicles in the amacrine cell process (*fat arrow*) indicates where the amacrine cell is presynaptic to the bipolar cell. Electron micrograph from Dowling, J. E. and B. B. Boycott (1965) *Cold Spring Harbor Symp. Quant. Biol.* 30: 393–402. Reprinted by permission of the author and publisher.

depolarization at the offset of the light (called an OFFSET response). As the stimulating light is moved farther from the cell body, the relative sizes of the ONSET and OFFSET responses shift; the spot produces almost no OFFSET response, while the annulus produces a larger OFFSET than ONSET response. This cell apparently has a concentric receptive field, but the center and surround simply contribute different components of the response. The amacrine cells in the demonstration program all depolarize briefly when the light first comes on, and again when it first goes off, regardless of whether the amacrine cell you are watching is directly under the light or off to the right. Like horizontal cells, amacrine cells provide information about the general region of the retina, and are the lateral elements of the inner plexiform layer. The spatial processing begun in the outer plexiform layer continues in the inner plexiform layer.

You have already seen that the processing in the outer plexiform layer is concerned with spatial contrasts. The amacrine cells and their synapses in the inner plexiform layer also process another kind of contrast: temporal contrast. Transient responses are signals of change; transient cells respond only when there is an abrupt change in stimulation, and ignore steady stimuli. Killing a subset of amacrine cells by genetic manipulation greatly reduces the transient nature of ganglion cell responses (Nirenberg & Meister, 1997). **BOX 4.12**

Box 4.12 Amacrine cells as spiking neurons

There is another interesting aspect to the responses of the amacrine cell shown in Fig. 4.8. At the leading edge of the ONSET response to the spot and the OFFSET response to the annulus, there is a spike-like depolarization in excess of the bulk of the response. This spike is usually not considered an action potential, as it is *graded*—its amplitude is different when the stimulus is stronger or weaker. It is also much slower than the typical action potentials observed in true spiking neurons, and there are rarely more than one or two of these 'spikes' in a given response (Toyoda *et al.*, 1973).

However, some amacrine cells do apparently produce true action potentials (Bloomfield, 1996; Stafford & Dacey, 1997; but see Taylor & Wässle, 1995), as do in-

terplexiform cells (Feigenspan *et al.*, 1998). The spike is apparently caused by a regenerative amplification like the amplification that causes an action potential (Werblin, 1977; Eliasof *et al.*, 1987). Active amplification may be important for allowing signals to spread throughout the entire amacrine cell (Bloomfield, 1996), and probably accounts for the rapid rise of the amacrine cell response; notice that it reaches a peak considerably before the bipolar cells that provide its input. For example, Nelson (1982) has suggested that this function of one type of amacrine cell in the rod pathway (called the AII amacrine) may be responsible for the time course of the rod-driven responses.

Ganglion cells

Finally, the cells that receive the fruits of all this processing and communicate it to the brain are the ganglion cells, located at the inner edge of the inner plexiform layer. These cells are the subject of the next chapter, so not much will be said here. Suffice it to say that ganglion cells generally have spatially antagonistic (center versus surround) receptive fields, and may be transient in their responses (like the amacrine cell in Fig. 4.8) or relatively sustained (like a bipolar cell). Note that even the 'sustained' ganglion cells show a gradual loss of response in the absence of a changing stimulus, accounting for the Troxler fading that prevents us from seeing the blood vessels coursing over our retinas (see Chapter 3).

Like the hyperpolarizing and depolarizing bipolars that form a mirror-image pair, there are ganglion cells that are excited by the onset of light in their receptive field centers (*ON-center*) and ganglion cells inhibited by light in the center (*OFF-center*). The two systems continue in parallel through the retina, with a third system that combines features of both arising in the inner plexiform layer (the amacrine cell shown has what is called an *ON–OFF* response, and presumably receives excita-

tory inputs from both hyperpolarizing and depolarizing bipolars) (Marchiafava & Torre, 1978). Even the supposedly one-to-one cones of the fovea show this divergence, with each cone communicating with three ganglion cells (Sjöstrand *et al.*, 1994).

The ON-center ganglion cells have their dendrites in the part of the inner plexiform layer that is nearest the ganglion cell layer, which seems to be the level where mostly invaginating (center-depolarizing) cone bipolar cells make synapses. The OFF-center ganglion cells send dendrites through the inner plexiform layer to make synapses at its outer portion, where mostly flat (hyperpolarizing) bipolar cells terminate (Famiglietti & Kolb, 1976; Nelson & Kolb, 1983). The ON–OFF type may send a spray of dendrites through the entire plexiform layer, or have two distinct layers of branches. In any case, the ON-center ganglion cells receive direct excitation from depolarizing bipolar cells, and the OFF-center ganglion cells from hyperpolarizing bipolars (Miller & Dacheux, 1976; Naka, 1977).

However, it also seems likely that the ON-center ganglion cells receive inhibition from the hyperpolarizing bipolars, and the OFF-center ganglion cells receive inhibition from the depolarizing bipolars (Sterling, 1983; Müller *et al.*, 1988; Boycott & Hopkins, 1991). Thus, their responses

Box 4.13 The pathway for rod signals

The preceding discussion has concentrated on the pathway from cones to ganglion cells. What happened to the rods? In fact, the rods have a somewhat parallel system, with their own bipolar cells, although the two pathways converge onto the same ganglion cells (except, of course, in the fovea, where there are no rods).

There is a puzzling asymmetry in the rod pathway, however: there is only one type of rod bipolar cell. Each rod bipolar invaginates the spherules of many rods and (like the invaginating cone bipolars) produces a depolarizing response to light (Nelson & Kolb, 1983). Yet there are responses to both onset and offset of lights that are effective only for rods. This is because the rod bipolar does not synapse directly on the ganglion cells. Instead there is a special amacrine cell, called the AII amacrine, that merges the rod pathway to the cone pathway. The AII makes both electrical gap junctions and chemical synapses with the amacrine and bipolar cells of the cone pathway (Kolb & Nelson, 1983; DeVries & Baylor, 1995). In this way, it can excite the 'ON' pathway through electrical connections, while inhibiting the 'OFF' pathway through chemical synapses.

In addition, rods communicate directly with cones through electrical synapses. When rods are stimulated to the point at which each one absorbs about one photon, the rod signals pass through the cones and 'borrow' the cone pathway (Smith *et al.*, 1986; Vaney *et al.*, 1991; see Vaney, 1994).

---

are actively increased when the one kind of bipolar is depolarized, but actively decreased when the other is depolarized. This 'push–pull' action allows the cell to respond well to either direction of change, brightening or dimming (Levine & Shefner, 1975, 1977; Sterling, 1983; Derrington, 1990; Kremers *et al.*, 1993; Bilotta *et al.*, 1995; Chichilnisky & Wandell, 1996; see review by Schiller, 1995). BOX 4.13

Summary

For a summary of this processing, refer to the schematic shown in Fig. 4.10. In it, you see stylized pictures of receptors (at the top) and the other cell types leading to the ganglion cells (at the bottom). In the circle representing each cell's body is a graph showing the response of that cell to a light flashed on the receptor at the left. The cells in the column to the right are not directly illuminated by the flash; for them, the light is in the surround part of their receptive fields, as with the annular stimuli in Fig. 4.8. Synapses between cells are shown by Vs (presynaptic element) covering round spots (postsynaptic elements). The animation on the CD-ROM accompanying this book is just a more elaborate version of this figure.

Starting at the top, the receptors hyperpolarize when the light is flashed; in effect they say, 'there is light shining on me'. A receptor that is illuminated hyperpolarizes far more than one that is not. The horizontal cells say, 'there is light somewhere', as they integrate signals from a large number of receptors and hyperpolarize when light falls anywhere in their vicinity. As the receptor is releasing transmitter in the dark and stops releasing it in the light, the transmitter released by the receptors must be excitatory to the horizontal cells.

The two bipolar cells shown in the figure are both of the hyperpolarizing type. The one on the left hyperpolarizes in response to the slowed release of transmitter from the receptor on the left; the receptor transmitter must also be excitatory for the hyperpolarizing bipolar. The bipolar on the right depolarizes. As the receptor synapsing on it was not significantly affected by the light, this response must be caused by the slowing of transmitter release by the horizontal cell. If slowed transmitter leads to depolarization, the transmitter must be inhibitory; that is, the synapse is *sign-inverting*. It is possible, however,

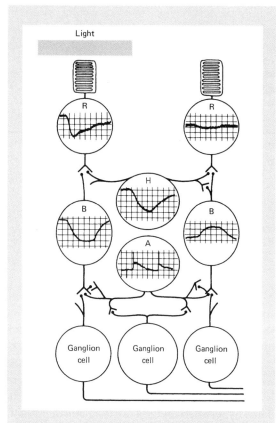

Fig. 4.10 Summary of the connections between cells in the vertebrate retina and the responses of each cell type. From Dowling, J. E. (1970) Organization of vertebrate retinas. *Invest. Ophthalmol.* 9: 655–680. Reprinted by permission of the publisher and the author.

the bipolar cells say, 'there is more (or less) light here than in nearby regions'.

The amacrine cell shown receives inputs from bipolar cells in a relatively large area of retina. It gives phasic responses to changes in bipolar cell outputs; it says, 'something just changed'. These synapses are apparently excitatory (Marchiafava & Torre, 1978). The transient nature of the amacrine cell responses is not well understood, but it is probably due to both the ionic amplification that gives the graded 'spike' (Werblin, 1977) and feedback at the dyad (Dowling, 1970). The feedback could be a negative regulation by which the response is 'shut down' after the initial surge because of its own activity (Tachibana & Kaneko, 1988; Maguire *et al.*, 1989; Neal & Cunningham, 1995), or a positive boosting by its own bootstraps (Freed *et al.*, 1987). Possibly, all three mechanisms contribute.

Finally, the ganglion cells receive signals from the bipolar and amacrine cells in the inner plexiform layer and relay information to the brain. Werblin & Dowling (1969) hypothesized that the transient ganglion cells receive their input from the amacrine cells, while sustained ganglion cells receive input from bipolar cells and sustained amacrine cells (Chan & Naka, 1976).

Notice the similarities between the two plexiform layers. In each, an array of elements presents information (receptors for the outer layer, bipolar cells for the inner layer). The 'output' is read by another array of cells—bipolar cells at the outer plexiform layer, and ganglion cells at the inner. There are lateral elements (horizontal cells and amacrine cells) in each layer that effectively cause an antagonism between signals going directly to the 'output' cells and signals coming from the sides. There are feedback loops (horizontal cells to receptors and amacrine cells to bipolar cells) that moderate the flow of information and tend to make the responses more transient. And, at each layer, there are more types of specialized 'output' cells than in the previous array (hyperpolarizing and depolarizing bipolar cells, ON-center and OFF-center, sustained and transient ganglion cells). Further specialization of the cell types is discussed in

that the 'inhibition' actually consists of horizontal cells depolarizing the receptors (Toyoda, 1973; Toyoda & Kujiraoka, 1982). In any case, the surround part of the bipolar receptive field seems to be caused by the activity of horizontal cells (Naka, 1977). The importance of the surround contribution relative to that of the center is modulated by feedback by way of the interplexiform cells (see Chapter 6).

There also would be center-depolarizing bipolars giving opposite responses to these (they are shown in the animation). Each in their own way,

Box 4.14 A simulation of the retina

To see all of these effects in action, run the retinal simulation program on the CD packaged with this book. In that simulation, you will see a schematic retina, much like that in Fig. 4.1(b). For information on any given cell type, click on the cell.

The polarization of all the cells is indicated by color. When you 'flash a light' on one group of receptors, you can see them hyperpolarize. The hyperpolarization is copied by all the horizontal cells and by those hyperpolarizing bipolars that contact the illuminated receptors; the depolarizing bipolar cells depolarize. Amacrine cells depolarize briefly both when the light first appears and when it is turned off.

The simulation only shows the sustained ON-center and OFF-center ganglion cells. Ganglion cells continuously show strong depolarizing pulses (action potentials) which change their rate of occurrence depending on the turning on or off of the 'light', the location of the particular ganglion cell relative to the light, and the type of the ganglion cell. Each time you flash the stimulus, the responses of one ganglion cell (you can select which by clicking the selection dot beneath the cell of your choice) are displayed as if on an oscilloscope in the window at the upper right of the screen. You will also hear the response as if it were fed to an amplifier and loudspeaker; each action potential produces a click. You can choose to watch the responses of the cells directly under the stimulus or those off to the right. In the next chapter you will learn more about the receptive fields of ganglion cells, and the different types of ganglion cells in the retina.

Chapters 5, 7, and 8. The transformation of the information at each layer is subtle, but the cumulative effects are considerable by the time the information is conveyed from the retina to the brain. **BOX 4.14**

Suggested readings

A good review of the chemistry of photopigments, including all the steps involved in bleaching pigment with light (which were not discussed here) is 'Molecular basis of visual excitation', by G. Wald in *Science* (162: 230–239; 1968). An excellent review of retinal anatomy is by Wässle & Boycott in *Physiological Reviews* (71: 447–480; 1991). For a classic review of the structure and function of the retina (though now slightly out of date), see: 'Organization of vertebrate retinas' by John E. Dowling in *Investigative Ophthalmology* (9: 655–680; 1970). Frank S. Werblin presents a more up-to-date view in his review in *Investigative Ophthalmology and Visual Science* (32: 459–489; 1991). Both of these reviews were transcripts of their respective talks upon winning the Friedenwald Award. Dowling has updated the material in his review for a chapter in *The encyclopedia of human biology* (Academic Press, 1991, pp. 615–631).

A number of readable reviews may be found in a special issue of *Trends in Neurosciences* published in May 1986. Articles in that issue review topics relevant to this chapter, such as the structure of rhodopsin, the cGMP cascade, synaptic relationships between receptors and bipolar cells, neurotransmitters in the retina, the role of interplexiform cells, and the structure and function of amacrine cells. Other articles are relevant to Chapter 5. You may also want to read the *Scientific American* article 'The functional architecture of the retina' by R. H. Masland (November 1986) for a review of the types and functions of amacrine cells. This article has been reprinted in *The biology of the brain: from neurons to networks* (R. R. Llinás, ed., W. H. Freeman, 1989).

If you wish to tackle a serious and advanced study of the vertebrate retina, you cannot do better than read portions of *The vertebrate retina* by R. W. Rodieck (W. H. Freeman, 1973). This work is a veritable encyclopedia of what was known of the retina as of 1973. Visual pigment chemistry is covered in

Chapters 2 and 3. The structure of the retina is discussed in Chapters 13 and 15; in addition, the book includes a translation of Ramón y Cajál's classic 1893 monograph *La rétine des vertébrés*.

A newer book on many of the same topics in John Dowling's *The retina* (Harvard University Press, Cambridge, MA, 1987). This book covers all the topics from light transduction in receptors to ganglion cell responses, with an emphasis on those areas in which Dowling has made major contributions.

Chapter 5
Retinal ganglion cells and lateral antagonism

In the last chapter, you learned about the anatomical structure of the retina and the response properties of retinal cells. This chapter focuses on the cells that provide the retina's output to the brain, the retinal ganglion cells. Ganglion cell axons exit the eye at the optic disc (blind spot) to form the optic nerve. All the processing functions subserved by the retina must therefore be observable in the responses of ganglion cells. It is for this reason that a separate chapter is devoted to ganglion cells; not only is this background necessary in order to analyze the responses of visual cells in the brain, but the same principles recur throughout all the sensory systems.

Ganglion cell responses

The ganglion cell is a neuron that codes information by firing action potentials; it was originally believed to be the only cell in the retina that does not employ decremental conduction as its sole means of information transmission. You saw in the previous chapter that some large amacrine cells and interplexiform cells may also produce impulses, possibly even trains of action potentials (Bloomfield, 1996; Feigenspan *et al.*, 1998). Some horizontal cells may also produce regenerative spikes (Blanco *et al.*, 1996). Nevertheless, the ganglion cells are the only ones that seem to encode information by complicated trains of action potentials, and, even if they are not alone in this property, you must understand this code to understand the ganglion cells. It is not surprising that the ganglion cell should be different from other retinal cells in this regard, as it is the only cell in the retina that has to transmit information over very long distances. Because it fires action potentials, its responses can be recorded extracellularly (see Appendix). A single cell's responses can therefore be observed with minimal damage to the cell or the network of neurons of which it is a part.

To appreciate what kind of signal this is, you should run the demonstrations for Chapters 4 and 5 on the CD packaged with this book. The window in the upper right of the simulation for Chapter 4 showed the trains of action potentials produced by an ON-center or an OFF-center ganglion cell. The simulation associated with this chapter allows you to select one of the subtypes of ganglion cell (discussed later in this chapter), and observe its 'responses' to various stimuli presented at various positions on the retina. You will not only see the responses evolve as voltage *versus* time while seeing the stimulus, but you will hear the 'click' of each action potential as the signal is fed to an audio amplifier. Electrophysiologists normally listen to the responses in this way; it is often easier to detect responses from the sound than from watching an oscilloscope.

Figure 5.1 shows the responses of actual ganglion cells to spots of white light centered on their receptive fields. These cells were in a goldfish, whose visual system is fairly representative of vertebrates. In Fig. 5.1(a), the response of one ganglion cell is displayed as a train of action potentials.

One property of ganglion cells evident from Fig. 5.1(a) is that they are not silent in the absence of stimulation. Before the onset of the stimulus, the cell fires action potentials; this is called the *maintained discharge* of the cell. If you have been running the demonstrations on the CD (as you should be!), you will already have seen that the ganglion cells in the 'Retina' demonstration (Chapter 4) were continually firing action potentials. Although the maintained discharge may be influenced by the level of steady background illumination, it is present even if the eye is placed in total darkness.

The origin of the maintained discharge is a matter of some contention; some investigators argue

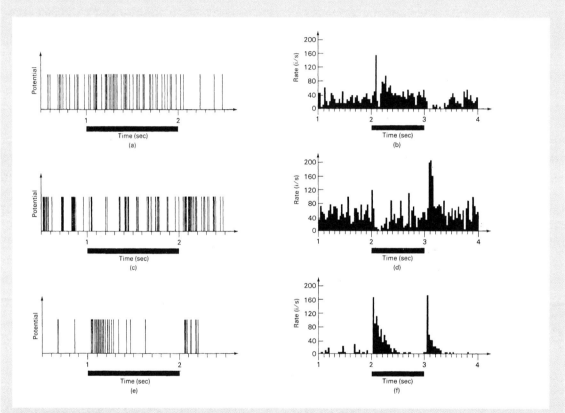

Fig. 5.1 Responses of ganglion cells to small spots of light. The duration of the stimulus is marked by the dark bar below each response. (a), (c), and (e) show the spike trains for an ON-cell, an OFF-cell, and an ON–OFF cell, respectively. (These are computer-generated plots of data from goldfish ganglion cells; see Appendix.) (b), (d), and (f) are peristimulus time histograms (PSTHs) of the same responses; each PSTH is an average of 30 stimulus presentations. Spikes have been cumulated in 25 ms bins.

that it is caused by spontaneous activity of receptors that occurs even in the dark (Rodieck, 1967; Barlow & Levick, 1969), while others believe that it is intrinsic to the ganglion cell itself (Hughes & Maffei, 1965; Schellart & Spekreijse, 1973; Brivanlou, *et al.*, 1998), and still others contend it arises from somewhere between the receptors and the ganglion cells (Frishman & Levine, 1983; Levine *et al.*, 1988). Whatever its origin, it serves a useful purpose that will be discussed shortly.

The cell in Fig. 5.1(a) responds to the ONSET of light by firing a burst of action potentials; this high rate of firing decays to a plateau after the stimulus has been present for short time, although the firing rate is still somewhat higher than it was in the dark. At stimulus offset, the firing rate is temporarily reduced below the level of the maintained discharge, and gradually returns to the firing rate that was observed before the stimulus. This cell therefore responds with excitation to light onset and inhibition to light offset (an ON response), and so is an ON-center cell (ON-cell for short). As you saw in Chapter 4, there are two responses to each stimulus: the response to stimulus initiation is called the ONSET response, while the response to stimulus termination is called the OFFSET response. ON-cells, therefore, respond to small spots with excitatory ONSET responses and inhibitory OFFSET responses. (In the demonstration program, this response could be obtained from an ON-center X-cell.)

Figure 5.1(b) shows the same response in a slightly different way. Instead of displaying the action potentials themselves, the response is shown as a *peristimulus time histogram* (PSTH). To obtain a PSTH, the time axis is divided into a sequence of uniform bins. For each bin, the action potentials occurring during that time are counted and plotted as a frequency histogram. This produces a representation of the rate of firing action potentials as a function of time, relative to the stimulus presentation. Often, the histograms from a series of identical stimulus presentations are averaged.

The PSTH histogram serves as a means of examining the shape of a given response that is simpler than looking at the times of occurrence of every single action potential. The demonstration program will accumulate a PSTH if you present the identical stimulus to a 'cell' more than once. Each time you repeat the same stimulus, the new response is averaged with the previous responses in the PSTH at the lower right of your screen; as you average more and more responses, the PSTH becomes smoother and 'cleaner'.

Figure 5.1(c) and (d) display the response of a second type of ganglion cell. This cell is inhibited at the onset of the spot, and excited by its termination (OFF response). Such a cell is called an OFF-cell; its response pattern is the opposite of that displayed by an ON-cell. A similar response could be obtained from an OFF-center X-cell in the stimulation.

After inspecting the responses of these cells, a possible function of the maintained discharge should become clear. A ganglion cell can respond to light with either excitation or inhibition, but the only way that the inhibitory component is revealed is by a reduction in the firing rate below the level of the maintained discharge. If the cell were perfectly silent in the absence of stimulation, an inhibitory response would go unnoticed, as the cell cannot fire fewer than zero spikes. Thus, inhibition at the ganglion cell level would be lost to the next synapse in the processing hierarchy. The presence of the maintained discharge therefore provides for a baseline from which an inhibitory response can deviate.

Figure 5.1(e) and (f) show how a third type of ganglion cell responds to the same stimulus. It has both an excitatory onset response and an excitatory offset response; that is, firing rate increases both at light onset and at light offset (ON–OFF response). This is an ON–OFF cell, and it signals a change in light level without regard to whether the change is toward more or less light. An ON–OFF cell is also available in the simulation.

A property common to all three types of cell is that both onset and offset of the light are signaled by the cells. The presence of both ONSET and OFFSET responses is a fundamental property of sensory systems. At the ganglion cell, the ONSET and OFFSET responses would be expected to be related to each other; if a stimulus produces a large ONSET response, it is likely to produce a large OFFSET response, and vice versa. Evidence has shown, however, that ONSET and OFFSET responses are, in fact, produced by separable pathways converging onto the ganglion cell (Levine & Shefner, 1975, 1977; Levine & Zimmerman, 1988). In this sense, the ONSET and OFFSET responses are manifestations of the push–pull operation of the retina mentioned in Chapter 4.

ON-center and OFF-center ganglion cells represent the start of a pair of parallel pathways in the visual system (often called the ON and OFF pathways). Even though each type signals both increments and decrements, each is clearly better at indicating the direction of change that produces increased firing. After all, rate can increase dramatically, but can never go below zero (you can't have fewer than zero spikes). The ON and OFF pathways are complementary in that the ON pathway is best suited to telling us about increments of light (how bright or white something is) while the OFF pathway indicates decrements (how dark or black). Even though the responses are roughly mirror images, the information carried by ON- and OFF-center cells is largely independent (Warland *et al.*, 1997).

Ganglion cell receptive fields

So far, you have seen the responses of retinal ganglion cells to spots of light falling directly on the place in the retina in which the cells are located. Like other cells of the retina, however, ganglion cells are more responsive to stimulation in certain parts of the visual world than in others; the area to which a ganglion cell is sensitive is its receptive field.

The first detailed investigation of the receptive fields of mammalian retinal ganglion cells was done by S. W. Kuffler (1953), who used small spots of light to map the responses of ganglion cells in the cat retina. He found two distinct parts to the receptive fields of most ganglion cells. For cells that gave ON responses to presentation of diffuse light flashes covering much of the retina, Kuffler found that there was a specific area of the retina that also

gave ON responses to stimulation by small spots; he noted where in the visual field ON responses were elicited by marking those locations with plus signs (Fig. 5.2). Surrounding this central region, however, was an area in which stimulation by small spots produced an OFF response. This was one of the first demonstrations of the spatial antagonism that has since been reported for various other retinal cells (see Chapter 4). Figure 5.2 illustrates the receptive field of this type of cell; the region in which small spot stimulation produced ON responses is the *center* of the ganglion cell receptive field, while the area marked with negative (–) signs that envelops the center is the *surround*. The center of the field seems to correspond to the spread of the dendritic field of the ganglion cell itself (Peichl & Wässle, 1983), so the surround must be due to the lateral signals carried by amacrine and horizontal cells.

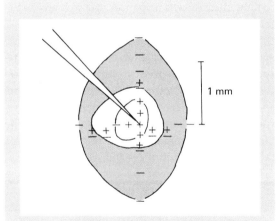

Fig. 5.2 Mapping the receptive field of a cat retinal ganglion cell. Center region marked '+' yields ON responses when stimulated with small spots; the region marked '–' responds with OFF responses; the intermediate region marked '±' gives ON–OFF responses. The microelectrode is drawn in for illustration. From Kuffler, S. W. (1953) Discharge patterns and functional organization of mammalian retina. *J. Neurophysiol.* 16: 37–68. Reprinted by permission.

Kuffler found that most ganglion cells possessed this antagonistic center/surround organization, but that the response to light onset of the center region was excitatory in some cells and inhibitory in others. In the case where center stimulation produced an OFF response, surround stimulation produced an ON response.

Perceptual effects accounted for by center/surround antagonism

The center/surround organization of retinal ganglion cells means that the response of the ganglion cell to stimulation of one portion of the receptive field can be modified by stimulation of a neighboring area. This relationship between neighboring areas of retina is called *lateral antagonism*,[1] it is a mechanism that allows a single ganglion cell to be selectively sensitive to contrast within its receptive field, rather than simply responding to the total amount of light directed onto the field. You read about a similar effect in bipolar cells in Chapter 4. In ganglion cells, the effect is stronger because it reflects the processing of both the outer and inner plexiform layers. BOX 5.1

Consider the ganglion cell whose receptive field is shown in Fig. 5.3. In part (a) of this figure, an edge is positioned so that light covers the entire receptive field when the stimulus is presented; it produces an ON response, as shown on the right. When the edge is moved so that all of the receptive field center is stimulated but only a portion of the surround receives illumination (Fig. 5.3b), the response evoked by stimulus onset is significantly greater than in (a). This cell is therefore more sensitive to an appropriately positioned edge than it is to a diffuse light stimulus of the same intensity covering the entire receptive field. When the edge is positioned so that only the surround of the cell is stimulated (Fig. 5.3c), the cell responds in a different way than it did to the stimuli in (a) and (b) of the figure; it produces an OFF response. You can observe this in the simulation program: select an X-cell (either ON-center or OFF-center), and stimulate it with a vertical edge in various positions.

[1] Lateral antagonism is commonly known by another name, lateral inhibition, which you may encounter in your other reading. The word 'inhibition' was applied when the process was first discovered in the eye of the horseshoe crab (see Box 5.4); in that animal, light directly on a receptor always caused an increase in firing that was decreased (inhibited) by light to the sides. In vertebrates, however, the response in the center of a field may be either an increase in firing (ON response) or a decrease in firing (OFF response). For an OFF-center cell, the light to the side increases the firing, so it is very odd to refer to this increase as 'inhibition'. Nevertheless, the increase in firing is antagonistic to the response in the center (a decrease). Many workers therefore prefer to say lateral antagonism, as a way of avoiding confusion when responses may be either ON or OFF.

Box 5.1 The many faces of lateral antagonism

'Center/surround antagonism', 'lateral antagonism' and 'contrast sensitivity' are all different ways of describing the same phenomenon—that the visual system *makes comparisons* between light levels. Later you will learn about still another way to look at this, in terms of spatial frequency or Fourier analysis (Chapter 9), and see the same phenomenon described as 'attenuation of low spatial frequencies'. Recently, it has been subsumed into a more general concept, a 'law of repulsion' (Barlow, 1997).

This is probably a good place to mention that lateral antagonism is not a fixed entity. The strength of lateral antagonism depends on the level of adaptation (see Chapter 6), which may be another way of achieving the effect of comparing lights despite overall shifts in their levels (Barlow, 1997). It is probably equivalent to say that antagonism depends on the history of contrast in the field. That is, there is *contrast gain control*, particularly at higher levels than the retina, that adjusts the sensitivity to contrast (Shapley & Victor, 1979).

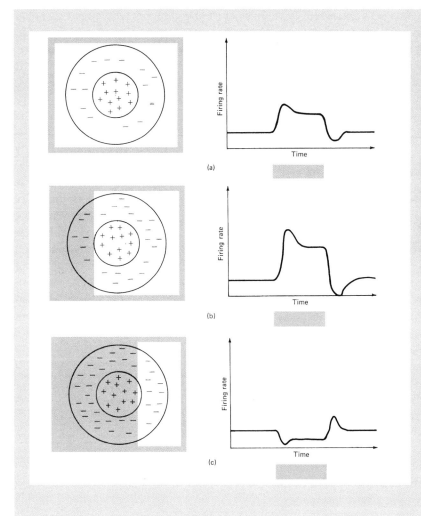

Fig. 5.3 Responses (PSTH) of a hypothetical ON-center retinal ganglion cell to an edge of light positioned at different places. (a) Light covers the entire receptive field; response shown to the right is an ON response. (b) Edge is positioned so the entire center region is stimulated, but much of the surround is still in darkness; ON response is enhanced relative to that in (a). (c) Only the surround is stimulated; an OFF response is produced.

Ganglion cells are sensitive to contrast within their receptive fields, rather than responding only as a function of total illumination within the field. There are numerous ways to demonstrate the visual system's preference for contrast, and a number of them are shown in Figs 5.4–5.8. In these demonstrations of lateral antagonism in the visual system, the phenomena are treated as if they were exclusively a property of retinal ganglion cells. It is important to note, however, that lateral antagonism occurs at many levels within the visual system, and that the perceptual effects described here

are enhanced by interactions other than those at the ganglion cell level.

The pattern in Fig. 5.4 produces an effect called a *Mach band*, after its discoverer, Ernst Mach. The light distribution is shown under the pattern; the light uniformly and smoothly increases from left to right. But you probably see a vertical dark band (marked D) that occurs just to the left of the luminance gradient, and a vertical light band (marked B) just to the right of the gradient. These light and dark bands are not present in the physical stimulus; they exist in your perception of the stimulus

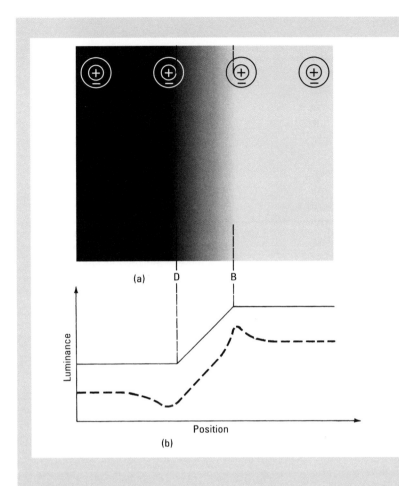

Fig. 5.4 Mach bands. (a) Mach band pattern, with the receptive fields of four ON-center ganglion cells projected onto it. (b) Luminance gradient (*solid line*), along with the perceptual brightness gradient it produces (*dotted line*).

To demonstrate that the bands are not physically present, cover the gradient part of the pattern. Take a sheet of paper and slowly move it across the figure from the left, while keeping your eye on the light Mach band. The band will vanish when the gradient is covered—just before the paper reaches it. Similarly, bringing the paper across from the right will make the dark band vanish just before the paper reaches it.

because of the way your visual system responds to the stimulus. (Prove this to yourself by covering part of the pattern with a sheet of blank paper, as described in the figure caption.)

To see how the responses of ganglion cells can account for your perception of Mach bands, suppose that the stimulus in Fig. 5.4(a) is projected onto the retina. An image of the stimulus therefore falls onto an array of ganglion cells, each with its own receptive field; a selection from this array of ganglion cell receptive fields is shown at the top of the Mach band pattern. For convenience, suppose that all of these are ON-center cells, and consider the response of each cell, starting from left to right on the figure. The leftmost ganglion cell, like other cells near it that are not shown, is uniformly illuminated at a low light level; it therefore fires at about its maintained discharge rate.

The second cell is not stimulated uniformly— although the center portion of its receptive field is illuminated at the same level as its neighbors to the left, the right half of its surround is on the edge of the intensity gradient, and is therefore receiving more light. Compared to cells on the left, this cell is receiving more light in its surround and the same amount of light in its center; as the surround is inhibitory, the response of this cell is less than the response of the first cell in the row. That is the reason you see a dark bar at this location on the pattern. The ganglion cells are signaling less light at this position than are the cells to the left.

The same reasoning can be applied to the perception of the light band at the right of the luminance gradient. Start with the right-hand side of the row of ganglion cells; the first cell receives the same high illumination over its entire receptive field. Its firing is therefore only slightly higher than its maintained discharge rate. Now consider the second cell from the right; its receptive field center is illuminated at the same level as the cells to the right of it, but the left part of its surround is illuminated less than the right part because of its proximity to the gradient. The surround of this cell, therefore, exerts less of an inhibitory effect on the response of the cell than do the surrounds of cells to the right. The result of this is a greater response from the cell. The greater responses of cells at this location along the pattern produce the perception of a light band.

Center/surround interactions produce a brightness gradient like that shown by the dotted line in Fig. 5.4(b). The perceptual effect is one that tends to enhance the brightness difference between the two steady-state levels. This is, in fact, the probable

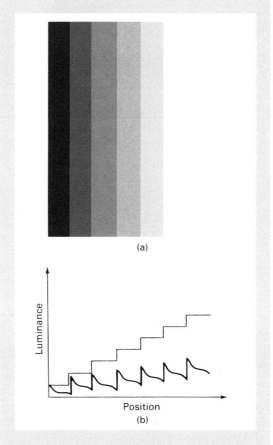

Fig. 5.5 Series of equal luminance steps. (a) The pattern; (b) luminance and perceptual brightness gradients.

Box 5.2 Why aren't there mach bands everywhere?

Why do you not see bands at all borders? Various hypotheses have been put forward. Some suggest that the effect of lateral antagonism is like taking spatial derivatives (looking for rates of change of light). When the change happens too abruptly, the changes at the one border cancel those at the other (Marr, 1982; Watt & Morgan, 1983). Another suggestion is that the sharp edge prevents the visual system from detecting the bands by a process called *masking* that you will encounter in Chapter 9 (Ratliff,

1984). Another way of thinking about it is that it is simply a matter of how the brain interprets the pattern of firing. When the bands are contiguous, they are interpreted as indicating a real edge (which it normally is); when they are separated, as in the Mach pattern, the bands can be separately seen. Assumptions about how the brain might interpret patterns of firing in the sensory pathway are called 'linking propositions' (Teller, 1984).

purpose of lateral antagonism—it acts to emphasize borders while neglecting to some extent uniform brightness levels. If you have a clear idea where the borders are, the brightness on either side of the border is known by implication and does not have to be coded specifically by the visual system. <u>BOX 5.2</u>

The staircase illusion shown in Fig. 5.5 is another example of your visual system's tendency to emphasize borders. Although the actual physical stimulus is a series of luminance steps, the perception is that each step is brighter at its left border and darker at its right border. This has the effect of producing a brightness distribution like that shown as a dotted line in Fig. 5.5(b). As with the Mach band in the previous figure, the borders between adjacent steps are perceptually more extreme than is the case for the physical stimulus. The mechanism for the enhancement of borders in the staircase illusion is just like that described for Fig. 5.4

An illusion that demonstrates even more strongly the fact that your visual system is selectively sensitive to borders is the Craik–O'Brien illusion shown in Fig. 5.6. In this figure, you should

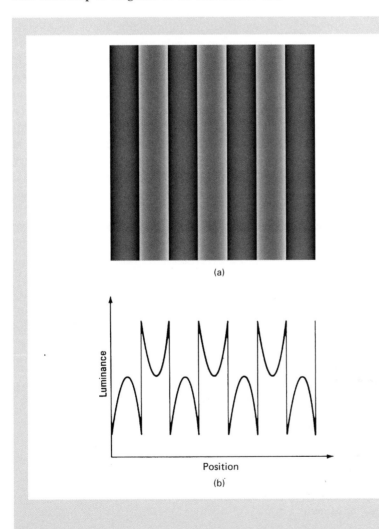

(a)

(b)

Fig.5.6 Craik–O'Brien illusion. (a) The luminance in the middle of all bars is the same, even though it looks as if there are light and dark bars. (b) The actual luminance gradient.

see a pattern consisting of light and dark bars. A look at the luminance distribution taken through the figure, however, reveals that the luminance in the middle of the 'light' bars is identical to the luminance in the middle of each 'dark' bar, (prove this by covering the borders with pencils). The abrupt luminance drop is enhanced by lateral antagonism and is perceived as a border. The gradual changes in luminance are not paid much attention, however. The result is a perception of a brightness change at the borders, but no concomitant perception of the gradual changes on either side of the borders. The ganglion cells provide only a signed contrast signal, regardless of the mean level of illumination (Troy & Enroth-Cugell, 1993). Note also that higher centers must 'fill in' the missing information between the borders; this happens from edge to center, even if the blind spot is enclosed in the filled-in area (Paradiso & Hahn, 1996). Lest you get too convinced that lateral antagonism at the ganglion cells explains all these phenomena, you should be aware that this illusion can also be created by 'second-order effects', in which there is no actual change in luminance at the 'border' (Lu & Sperling, 1996). In Chapter 9 you will read about other ways of thinking about this illusion.

The strength of the Craik–O'Brien illusion can be seen by comparing Figs 5.6 and 5.7. In Fig. 5.7, the bars are actually uniform in their luminances, as is shown by the luminance distribution in part (b) of the figure. The magnitude of the abrupt change at each border is identical to that in Fig. 5.6; when the two figures are compared with each other, it is hard to decide which figure reflects a real luminance difference between adjacent bars. The fact that the 'dark' bars in Fig. 5.7 are actually darker does not seem to add additional information to the visual percept; what the visual system seems to be concentrating on is the borders, to the exclusion of information about steady-state levels.

A final demonstration of the effects of lateral antagonism is shown in Fig. 5.8. This pattern is known as the Hermann grid; it is merely a series of horizontal and vertical white bars placed across a black background. By staring at the center of this grid you should get an impression of dark spots at the intersections of the white bars. These dark spots are not present in the intersection that you actively stare at, but occur in the periphery of your gaze.

The dark spots are a straightforward result of lateral antagonism. Consider the responses of the

---

Box 5.3 Why isn't there a dark spot in the center of the Hermann grid?

Disappearance of a dark spot at the center of the intersection of two white bars when you fix your gaze upon it is probably caused by the non-homogeneity of the retina. When you stare directly at an object, an image of the object is placed on the fovea. Acuity is maximized in the fovea; the highest density of cones in the retina is found in this region (see Chapter 4). In addition, along with the high concentration of receptors in the fovea, there is also a large number of ganglion cells receiving inputs from single foveal receptors. Ganglion cells in this region have much smaller receptive fields than they do elsewhere in the retina.

The fact that ganglion cell receptive fields are small in the fovea means that when you gaze at a particular intersection of white bars in the Hermann grid, the cells with the image of the intersection projected onto their receptive fields are so small that both the center and surround of each cell lie within that intersection. Therefore there is no effect of the surrounding black squares, and you do not have an impression of a dark spot. Images of intersections that are projected onto extrafoveal regions of the retina, however, stimulate cells whose receptive fields are much bigger than those in the fovea, so that the situation sketched in Fig. 5.8 is obtained. If you look at the figure from across the room, the image of the figure will be much smaller on your retina, and a gray spot may be apparent at the intersection on which you fixate.

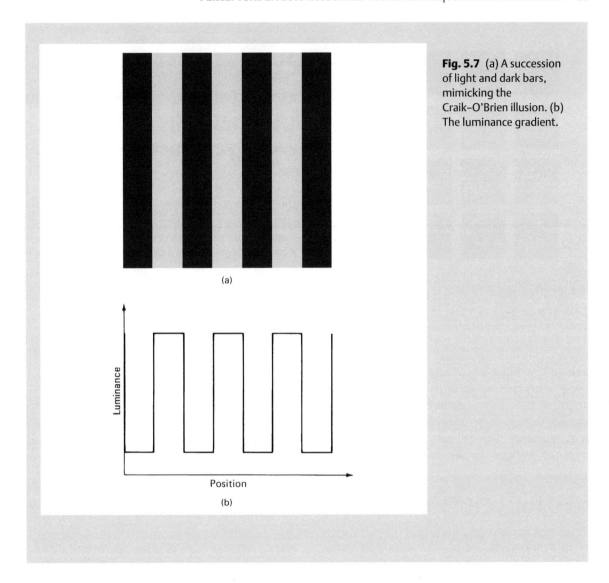

Fig. 5.7 (a) A succession of light and dark bars, mimicking the Craik–O'Brien illusion. (b) The luminance gradient.

(a)

(b)

two ON-center ganglion cells whose receptive fields are sketched on the figure. The cell on the right has one white bar projecting through the center of its receptive field, and through part of its surround. The cell on the left has the identical light distribution in its center, but an additional white bar is projected through its surround. This cell, therefore, receives more light in its surround than does its neighbor; it responds at a lower level because of greater antagonism by the surround. Hence the dark spots. <u>BOX 5.3</u>

Most of this chapter so far has been about just one particular aspect of ganglion cell function: lateral antagonism. This was done partly because it is an important function, but also because lateral antagonism provides a good example of a property general to all sensory systems; that is, sensory systems act to condense the information present in the physical world down to certain specific aspects that are essential to the organism. An animal dependent on its vision needs to know about borders; given that information, the

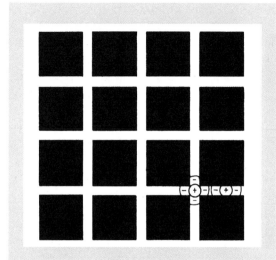

Fig. 5.8 The Hermann grid, with two ganglion cell receptive fields projected onto it.

nism reduces the *redundancy* of the visual scene (Laughlin, 1990). BOX 5.4

Ganglion cells with special coding characteristics

Antagonism between the center and surround of the receptive field serves to 'tune' the cells' response properties; instead of reporting light, they report contrasts. However, certain ganglion cells may selectively respond to much more specific features of the visual world. Just as the processing pathway split into 'ON' and 'OFF' at the outer plexiform layer, additional parallel systems may be found after the inner plexiform layer. The rest of this chapter considers some of the specialized kinds of ganglion cells that have been observed.

What the frog's eye tells the frog's brain

The frog retina seems to extract specific features from the visual world, while ignoring more global

animal can make unconscious inferences about the illumination within a given contour. Selective attention to borders reduces the amount of information that must be taken in by the visual system, allowing the animal to concentrate on essential features. In this sense, lateral antago-

---

Box 5.4 Lateral antagonism in a primitive invertebrate

You have seen the properties of lateral antagonism as it occurs in vertebrate visual systems; however, the earliest experiments on this subject were performed on the lateral eye of the horseshoe crab, *Limulus*, an animal whose visual system is vastly different from ours. As you saw when you met *Limulus* in Box 3.11 (p. 46), the lateral eye of the horseshoe crab is made up of about 800 tiny facets, or ommatidia, each of which has its own lens, receptors, and output fibers that form an optic nerve. The response recorded at these output fibers reflects, in general, the amount of light being projected onto the particular facet from which the fiber originated.

Hartline and his co-workers (Hartline, 1949; Hartline, *et al.*, 1956; Hartline & Ratliff, 1957) found that the response to light of fibers coming from one facet could be reduced by shining light on a nearby facet. The amount that the excitation in one facet was reduced by simultaneous stimulation of another facet depended on how close the two facets were to each other, with the inhibitory effect decreasing with distance. Thus there is a lateral inhibitory network in the *Limulus* eye by which excitation in one region affects the responses to light of a neighboring region. Functionally, this is similar to the lateral antagonism produced in the vertebrate visual system as a result of the interactions between the center and surround regions of the ganglion cell receptive field. Using somewhat different mechanisms, both types of visual systems employ lateral antagonism to enhance the response to borders in the visual world.

properties. Lettvin *et al.* (1959) studied the properties of frog retinal ganglion cells and found four types of cells with distinct processing characteristics. The properties of the four cell types provide an illustration of how a sensory system can be selectively sensitive to a small subset of inputs from the physical environment.

One type of ganglion cell was called a *sustained contrast detector* (Lettvin *et al.*, 1959). These cells did not respond at all to changes in overall illumination if the light was diffusely distributed throughout the receptive field of the cell. If an image of a lighted edge passed through the receptive field, however, the cell responded vigorously. This response could be *direction-dependent*; that is, a response might be generated when the stimulus moved through the receptive field in one direction, but be absent or reduced if the edge moved in the opposite direction. Sustained contrast detectors send information about specific aspects of the visual world. Not only is this type of cell selectively sensitive to light/dark borders, but it also prefers movement of the border at certain velocities and only in certain directions. When such a cell is firing, therefore, the information it sends is considerably more specific than a mere statement of how much light is falling on its receptive field.

A second type of ganglion cell was called a *net convexity detector*. These cells provided perhaps the most dramatic illustration of feature detectors yet discovered. Net convexity detectors respond poorly to changes in illumination within the receptive field, and to light/dark edges moving through the field at any speed or in any direction. What they respond best to is the movement of a small, dark object in their receptive field. The response of the cell to such an object persists as long as the object remains in the field; if it is moved into the field and just left there, the response will persist until it is finally moved out again. Although the response is maintained to a stationary spot, the cell prefers movement within the receptive field, with jerky movements producing larger responses than smooth ones. The size of the spot is not crucial, but it must be darker than the surrounding level of illu-

mination to evoke any response. If an array of spots (each of which is capable of producing a response if presented alone) is moved into the field of a cell, little or no response is produced. If one of the spots moves relative to the others in the array, however, the response evoked is similar to what would occur if that spot were alone in the field.

This type of cell is sensitive to a specific pattern of visual stimulation. In fact, a little reflection might lead to the conclusion that the patterns that best activate net convexity detectors are of crucial importance to frogs: they are similar to the movements of insects in the natural habitat! Net convexity detectors have been given the nickname 'bug detectors'. Their activation may indicate the location of a potential food source. With this type of information coming into the brain, the amount of central processing that must be performed before a response can be initiated is greatly reduced. For an animal such as the frog, with a fairly small number of different behaviors in its repertoire, this type of sophisticated peripheral processing is an efficient way of analyzing the visual world.

The other two types of ganglion cells in the frog retina have somewhat less specific feature-detecting properties. *Moving edge detectors* (also called ON–OFF units) (Hartline, 1938; Barlow, 1953) are insensitive to changes in diffuse illumination, but are quite responsive to light/dark edges moving in any direction through the receptive field. This type of cell increases its firing in response to movement of either a light or a dark edge; it is thus concerned only with movement, and not with the actual amount of illumination. *Net dimming detectors* give a prolonged response to the extinction of a diffuse light stimulus; they also respond to any moving stimulus regardless of its size, shape, or contrast, in direct proportion to the amount of dimming that the stimulus produces when passing across the receptive field of the cell.

The four types of cells just described comprise the great majority of all retinal ganglion cells found in the frog. The frog brain does not receive from the retina anything remotely similar to a photographic representation of the visual world.

Rather, it receives a catalog of features whose correct detection is crucial for the animal's survival. From the sustained contrast detectors and net dimming detectors, the frog receives information about objects moving about, perhaps indicating potential predators. From the net convexity detectors comes information about potential sources of food. This type of information is what is necessary for the animal to survive, but it in no way provides a general picture of the visual world.

The frog is noted for its specialized retinal feature detectors, but ganglion cells that seem to be tuned to special features in the visual world are found in all animals. Cells with concentric center/surround mechanisms seem to comprise the largest class of ganglion cells in most mammals, but significant numbers of cells are sensitive to either the orientation or direction of a moving stimulus.

Direction selectivity

Direction-selective ganglion cells give excitatory responses to both onset and offset of a flashing spot anywhere within their receptive fields, but give responses to a moving stimulus that depend on its direction of movement (Barlow & Hill, 1963). Figure 5.9 shows the receptive field organization of such a cell, along with its responses to a bar of light moving in various directions through its receptive field. This cell responds most strongly to a bar moving upward through the field; as the direction of movement varies from upward-going, the response decreases and is non-existent for stimuli moving vertically downward. The response of this cell does not depend on whether the bar is brighter or dimmer than the background. **BOX 5.5**

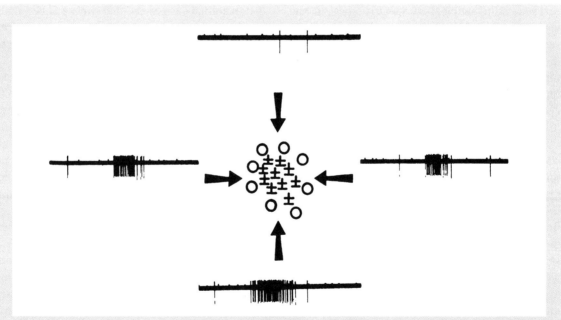

Fig. 5.9 Responses of a directionally sensitive ganglion cell from a rabbit. Center portion of the figure shows the receptive field of the cell, mapped with small spots. The response patterns were all generated by a moving stimulus traveling across the receptive field in the direction indicated by the arrow. The stimulus was a bar of light. From Barlow, H. B., R. M. Hill and W. R. Levick (1964) Retinal ganglion cells responding selectively to direction and speed of image motion in the rabbit. *J. Physiol.* 173: 377–407. Reprinted by permission.

Box 5.5 Direction selectivity—a result of inhibition

Direction selectivity provides another example of how antagonism (in this case, inhibition) 'tunes' cells to respond to specific aspects of the environment. The model of a direction-selective cell presented by Barlow & Hill (1963) suggests that there is a delayed inhibition signal that proceeds in one direction. That is, light at point A (say, on the right side of the receptive field) excites the ganglion cell through the bipolar cells directly under the receptors stimulated by the light, but also sends a slower inhibitory signal to the terminals of bipolar cells at point B to its left. When the moving light reaches point B, the signal that it is there arrives at the same time as the inhibition from A, so there is no excitation of the ganglion cell; nevertheless, an inhibitory signal is sent to C to preclude firing when the light gets there. For such a cell, there will be virtually no fir-

ing for a stimulus moving from right to left, which is called the 'null' direction. A stimulus moving left to right, on the other hand, always precedes the inhibition it leaves behind, and so the cell can fire continuously as the light moves through its field. This is then called the 'preferred' direction.

Updated versions of this simple model have withstood rigorous testing (Pennartz & van de Grind, 1990). Pharmacological studies of direction-selective cells have demonstrated the importance of an inhibitory signal, which is carried by the neurotransmitter gamma-amino butyric acid (GABA) (Pan & Slaughter, 1991). Motion detectors in higher centers of the cortex also depend on inhibition of the null direction rather than on increased excitation of the preferred direction (Mikami, 1992).

Orientation selectivity

Orientation-selective units are not so concerned with the direction of movement of a stimulus as much as they are selective to its orientation

(Levick, 1967). Figure 5.10 shows the receptive field of an orientation-selective unit, along with responses to rectangular stimuli that move through the receptive field at different angles. This cell has a horizontally elongated receptive

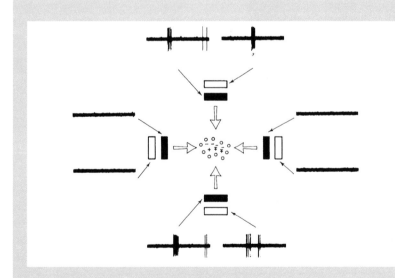

Fig. 5.10 Responses of an orientation-selective ganglion cell from a rabbit. Center of the figure shows the receptive field of the cell; responses to light and dark bars oriented either vertically or horizontally are shown surrounding the receptive field. From Levick, W. R. (1967) Receptive fields and trigger features of ganglion cells of the rabbit's retina. *J. Physiol.* 188: 285–307. Reprinted by permission.

field, making it more sensitive to stimuli that are wider than they are tall. White or black bars that are moved upward or downward through the field evoke a vigorous response that is independent of direction. If the bars are rotated by 90° and passed horizontally through the field of the cell, however, no response is seen. If this cell were stimulated with stationary flashing bars of the same size, it would respond strongly to bars oriented horizontally, and make little or no response to bars oriented vertically. Thus, this cell is selectively sensitive to the shape of the stimulus, as opposed to its direction.

X-cells and Y-cells

Most ganglion cells that have been recorded from the retinas of higher mammals (primarily cat and monkey) have concentric center/surround receptive field organizations. This does not mean, however, that they are all identical in their processing characteristics. In fact, ganglion cells with concentric receptive fields have been classified into several distinct groups on the basis of both anatomical and functional characteristics.

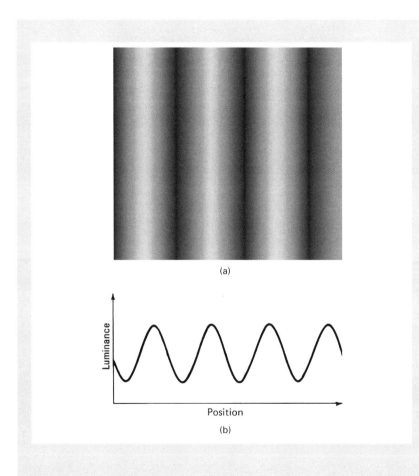

Fig. 5.11 (a) A sinusoidal grating. (b) Luminance distribution for the grating.

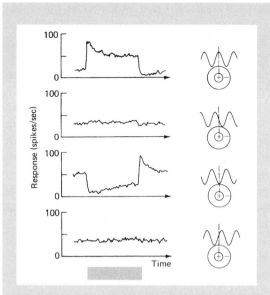

Fig. 5.12 Responses (PSTH) of an X-cell to stimulation by a grating positioned in different ways within the receptive field. The position of the grating is shown on the right of the figure. Grating was substituted for a uniform field of the same mean luminance during the time indicated by the dark bar under the bottom PSTH. From Enroth-Cugell, C. and J. G. Robson (1966) The contrast sensitivity of retinal ganglion cells of the cat. *J. Physiol.* 187: 517–552. Reprinted by permission.

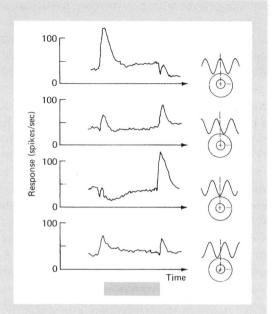

Fig. 5.13 Responses (PSTH) of a Y-cell to stimulation by a grating positioned in different ways within the receptive field. Same conventions as in Fig. 5.12. From Enroth-Cugell, C. and J. G. Robson (1966). Reprinted by permission.

Enroth-Cugell & Robson (1966), recording from ganglion cells in the retina of the cat, used stimuli called *sinusoidal gratings* to distinguish between what they named *X-cells* and *Y-cells*. Figure 5.11 shows an example of a sinusoidal grating (to be discussed in detail in Chapter 9); it is simply a succession of light and dark gradations. Enroth-Cugell & Robson presented a grating to the receptive field of a ganglion cell for a short time period, and then replaced it with a diffuse light stimulus that was of the same luminance as the average of the grating. They varied position of the grating with respect to the receptive field of the cell. Sometimes a dark bar covered the receptive field center, sometimes a

light bar covered it, and sometimes parts of both portions covered the center.

Enroth-Cugell & Robson found that they could distinguish between two types of ganglion cells on the basis of the responses to the grating stimuli—Fig. 5.12 shows the responses of an X-cell. When the light bar covered the center, the cell increased its firing; when the dark bar was over the center, the cell decreased its firing. By manipulating the exact placement of the grating, however, a position could be found where the presentation produced no response. At this position, the average illumination on the receptive field center and on the receptive field surround from the grating was equal to the illumination provided by the diffuse light. This type of cell, therefore, averages the amount of light falling on its receptive field, and responds accordingly.

Y-cells, on the other hand, respond quite differently when stimulated with gratings. As Fig. 5.13 shows, no matter how the grating is positioned on the receptive field, a response to the onset and/or the offset of the presentation is always obtained. Y-cells, therefore, care about more than just the total amount of light falling on their receptive fields; the spatial configuration of the light is also important. That is, while X-cells only respond to the grating presentation when it produces a change in the total effective amount of light falling on the receptive field, Y-cells respond whenever there is a change in the spatial arrangement of the light. This is a non-linearity. **BOX 5.6**

X-cells differ from Y-cells in a number of other ways. They are differentially sensitive to moving stimuli, with X-cells responding well to slow movements of a stimulus, and Y-cells preferring rapidly moving stimuli across a wide field. Y-cells have larger receptive fields than X-cells (Enroth-Cugell & Robson, 1966) and Y-cells have thicker axons that conduct action potentials significantly faster than those of X-cells (Stone & Freeman, 1971).

In general, Y-cells respond to stimuli in a fairly transient manner, showing strong response components primarily at stimulus onset and offset; X-cells, on the other hand, usually respond in a more sustained fashion (Saito *et al.*, 1970). While some researchers invoke this difference in response type as a way to classify cells, it should be noted that all cells become more transient in brighter lights. Larger receptive fields collect more of the background light, so it is possible that this difference may be partly due to the Y-cells being more light-adapted (see Jakiela *et al.*, 1976).

The retinal distributions of X- and Y-cells differ;

Box 5.6 A model for the non-linearity of Y-cells

The non-linearity of the Y-cells seems to be a fundamental property—actually, it is their *defining* property (but see Gaudiano, 1994). How can it be explained? A model presented by Shaul Hochstein and Robert Shapley in 1976 indicates how such a response property could arise, and makes it easier to predict what to expect of various stimuli. Similar models will be needed to understand the responses of cells in the cortex, so these concepts will serve you well.

Hochstein & Shapley (1976) accepted that the X-cell receptive field can be well described by the linear model confirmed by Enroth-Cugell & Robson (1966; see Box 5.7, p. 91). They suggested that Y-cells are like X-cells with an added feature: subunits that sample local regions within the receptive field. Each subunit is itself a smaller center/surround receptive field—in fact, subunits may be about the size of an X-cell field in the same area, since Y-cell fields are about three times as large. But the subunits have a non-linearity called a *rectifier*: they can signal increases in responses, but not decreases. In many ways, this is like a ganglion cell with no maintained discharge. Since

there cannot be fewer than zero spikes, there is no difference between nothing happening and inhibition.

Because the subunits each respond to a relatively small region at various locations within the field, a stimulus that is 'null' for the large, linear center and surround will be optimal for *some* subunit *somewhere* in the field (Hochstein & Shapley suggested that about 100 subunits cover a field). That subunit will send excitation to the ganglion cell, increasing its firing. Some other subunits will be optimally inhibited at the same time, but since they cannot signal the inhibition, they cannot cancel the excitation from the excited subunits. As a result, there is a response to any change in the pattern in the field, because any change will excite some subunits. This is added to the responses from the linear center and surround. Thus, in Fig. 5.13, the clear excitatory onset or offset response is visible when the pattern is not in the null position (although the inhibitory portion is largely canceled by the excitation from the subunits), and the excitation from subunits dominates at each change in what would be the 'null' position (in which the linear portion is silent).

the former are concentrated in the central retina, while the latter occur more or less uniformly throughout the retina (Fukuda, 1971).

At any particular location in the retina, Y-cells are larger, suggesting the cells may be differentiated by structural criteria (Cleland *et al.*, 1975). In a heroic series of experiments, Heinz Wässle and his coworkers have been able to show that X-cells and Y-cells are anatomically distinct (Peichl & Wässle, 1981; Wässle *et al.*, 1981 a,b). They did this by recording from many ganglion cells in a small area of cat retina, and noting the exact locations at which each X-cell or Y-cell was found. They then stained the retina to reveal certain anatomical types, and correlated the locations of these types with the positions of the X-cells or Y-cells. They found that the Y-cells corresponded to a rel-

atively rare, large cell called the *alpha cell*, while X-cells corresponded to a smaller cell called the *beta cell*. The relative rarity of Y-cells was a surprise, for physiologists had seen more Y-cells than any other type. This is probably because the large cell bodies and axons are more easily recorded by microelectrodes. BOX 5.7

Consideration of the properties of X- and Y-cells, summarized in Table 5.1, has led to the hypothesis that they have radically different functions (Rodieck, 1979; Sherman, 1979). Y-cells seem to be important for orienting to new, potentially important stimuli, while X-cells, because of their smaller receptive fields, may function to provide more detailed information from stimuli after they have been attended to and fixated on the fovea. The Y-cells each cover a larger area, perhaps allowing a

---

Box 5.7 The serendipitous discovery of X- and Y-cells

There is an interesting story behind Enroth-Cugell & Robson's discovery of X- and Y-cells. When they began their experiments, they did not realize there were two types of ganglion cell. Their purpose was to verify a model of the receptive field that they expected would apply to all ganglion cells.

The model, proposed by Rodieck & Stone (1965), provided a specific mathematical description of the way the center and the surround were sensitive to lights at different positions. The model suggested that the center and surround are each described as Gaussian functions (a mathematicians' term for what you probably know as the 'normal distribution'), and the resultant receptive field is thus the 'difference of Gaussians', or DOG. The DOG was sought in the cat retina!

Enroth-Cugell & Robson took an unusual approach to the problem: analysis by linear systems theory, for which sinusoidal gratings are the fundamental stimulus. Sinusoidal gratings had never been tried in a physiological experiment, although gratings were being used in visual psychophysics (see Chapter 9). In fact, John Robson was a pioneer in the use of sinusoidal gratings, and hoped to show (1) that they were useful for physiology, and (2) that the model could account for the quantitative details of the psychophysical findings.

The analysis technique for which gratings are suited depends on the cell combining influences from different parts of its receptive field in a linear manner. Before the analysis could be applied, therefore, this property had to be verified for the ganglion cells. The exchange of a grating for a uniform field, as described above, was Enroth-Cugell & Robson's test for this kind of linearity. A cell would 'pass' the test (be spatially linear) if gratings positioned such that a bright bar and a dark bar that shared the field center elicited no response. As you saw, X-cells passed that test (Fig. 5.12, second and fourth rows), and these were used to verify the model. Y-cells 'failed' the test (Fig. 5.13), and so were not suited for the study originally planned.

Enroth-Cugell & Robson realized that some cells being different could be important (in an early draft, Y-cells were called 'I-cells', for 'interesting'). Although a large part of the paper is devoted to the analysis of X-cells (which confirmed the DOG model as they had originally intended), there is also a discussion of the dichotomy they found. Their paper is one of the most widely cited in the vision literature, and most of the references are to the X-cell and Y-cell distinction.

Table 5.1   A comparison of X-, Y-, and W-cells and their anatomical correlates (based on cat retina)

	X-cells	Y-cells	W-cells
Response type	Brisk	Brisk	Sluggish
Spatial summation	Linear	Non-linear	Can be any
Response timing (tendency)	Sustained	Transient	Can be any
Receptive field	Center/surround	Center/surround	Various
Size of receptive field center	Small	Large	Huge
Anatomical type	Beta	Alpha	Gamma
Cell body/axon size	Medium	Large	Small
Axon conduction velocity	Medium	Fast	Slow
Main density	Central retina	Everywhere	Peripheral retina
Relative number (in cat)	55%	4%	41%
Main target in brain	Thalamus (only)	Thalamus 1 brainstem	Brainstem mainly

better analysis of direction of motion (Marr, 1982). The smaller receptive fields of X-cells allow for finer discrimination (and perhaps identification) of a stimulus. You will see in Chapters 7 and 8 that the X- and Y-cells are related to parallel systems that can be identified at higher levels of the visual system.

Although it is very difficult to record from ganglion cells in the human retina, a similar dichotomy of anatomy and function has been described in other primates (Peichl, 1991). In addition, psychophysical studies indicate that there is a similar separation of function in the human visual system. Investigators have been able to distinguish between what have been called *sustained* and *transient* mechanisms within the human visual system (Tolhurst, 1973; Breitmeyer & Ganz, 1976). The sustained system is slower in its response to stimuli, but has better acuity. The transient mechanism, on the other hand, is significantly faster in its response, but is much less sensitive to fine spatial patterns. Of course, that does not prove that the X- and Y-cell types form the basis of the sustained and transient mechanisms in human vision. Indeed, as you will see in Chapters 7 and 8, another distinction similar to that between X- and Y-cells seems to be even more important in the primate visual system (Williams *et al.*, 1991).

W-cells

There is also a significant third system in the retina. The W-cells are a heterogeneous group of cells with large receptive fields (but small cell bodies, making them very difficult to record) that are almost as numerous as the X-cells in cat (Stone & Hoffmann, 1972; Stone & Fukuda, 1974), although quite a bit rarer in primates (Wässle & Boycott, 1991). They may be either spatially linear and relatively tonic, like X-cells, or non-linear and phasic like Y-cells (Sur & Sherman, 1982), and include the motion-selective and other specialized cell types as well as ordinary center/surround cells (Rodieck, 1979; Rowe & Cox, 1993). Anatomically, they seem to correspond to *gamma cells*, a diverse group of cells that have in common small cell bodies, large but very sparse dendritic fields, and extremely thin axons (Boycott & Wässle, 1974; McGuire *et al.*, 1986; Stanford, 1987).

The responses of W-cells are different from those of X-cells and Y-cells in that they are 'sluggish', rather than 'brisk' (Cleland & Levick, 1974). To understand the difference between a brisk response (X- or Y-cell) and a sluggish response (W-cell), think of how you respond to a challenge in a lively debate. That is brisk. Now think of how you respond to someone trying to wake you from a deep sleep. That is sluggish.

Another difference between W-cells and other cells is their target in the brain. W-cell axons leave the eye with other axons in the optic nerve, but few of them go to the main target—the lateral geniculate nucleus of the thalamus (see Chapter 7). Instead, they terminate on groups of cells near (or buried inside) the main target or go to the brainstem. X-cells, on the other hand, seem to go almost exclusively to the main part of the lateral geniculate nucleus. Y-cells often split, sending branches to both the main target and the brainstem. Properties of the W-cells are also summarized in Table 5.1.

Perhaps the best way to appreciate the differences among the ganglion cell types is to play the simulations of each in the demonstration program on the accompanying CD. Note the differences between the 'sluggish' W-cell responses as compared with the 'brisk' X-cells and Y-cells. Note also the responses to each change by Y-cells, especially when the stimuli are balanced between ON and OFF responses (such as the centered edge or the grating in 'null' phase, which is when it is at either extreme position).

Test yourself: If you click 'Let the computer choose', it will select one of the seven possible cell types at random. You will not be able to see the representation of the receptive field, but you can select and present as many different stimuli as you like, and see the responses. When you think you know what type of cell it is, click the check box next to its name (check boxes will replace the round selection indicators).

Suggested readings

Books that discuss properties of the retina generally include the ganglion cells. The books recommended in Chapter 4 are therefore also relevant for this chapter (*The vertebrate retina* by R. W. Rodieck, 1973; *The retina* by J. E. Dowling, 1987). Topics relating to lateral interactions in the retina are nicely covered by T. N. Cornsweet (Academic Press, 1970) in his book, *Visual perception.*

A compendium text that has been suggested before is *Vision: coding and efficiency* (C. Blakemore, ed., Cambridge University Press, Cambridge, 1990), a volume in honor of Horace Barlow. 'Is there more than meets the eye?' by Vaney & Hughes (pp. 74–83) gives considerable information about the retinal coverage of the various types of ganglion cells. The chapter 'Neural interactions underlying direction-selectivity in the rabbit retina' by Clyde Oyster (pp. 92–102) discusses movement-selective cells.

There are two (at least) *Scientific American* articles that expand on the topics covered in this chapter. C. R. Michael's 'Retinal processing of visual images' (May 1969; offprint #1143) is a good treatment of ganglion cell physiology. For an authoritative treatment of Mach bands and lateral interactions, see F. Ratliff's 'Contour and contrast' (June 1972; offprint #543). Michael's article is reprinted in *Perception: mechanisms and models* (W. H. Freeman, 1972), while Ratliff's article may be found in *Recent progress in perception* (W. H. Freeman, 1976).

The May 1986 issue of *Trends in Neurosciences* also includes several articles on ganglion cells.

Chapter 6

Light adaptation and dark adaptation

You have seen how the visual system detects and processes patterns of light, and thereby learned about a number of important kinds of processing that are performed by the retina. This been a simplified story, however, for you have not yet seen one of its most remarkable feats: *adapting* to different levels of illumination.

You might not think that there is a problem here. For any given scene, some parts of the retina are stimulated by relatively intense lights, and other parts are stimulated by relatively weaker lights. What more do you need to know in order to identify objects in the visual world? In fact, that (plus information about color, movement, and so on) is all you want to be told by your retinas. The question addressed by this chapter is how they can perform this task over a wide range of luminances—the most intense lights are about 10^{13} (or 10 000 000 000 000) times more intense than the weakest lights you can detect. But the firing rate of a neuron can range only from 0 to maybe 500 action potentials per second. Because of the inherent noisiness in the firing, there are only a very limited number of discriminable levels a neuron can signal; if the entire 10^{13} range were divided into those levels, you would be unable to see subtle (and not so subtle) gradations.

If you are a photographer, you will have faced a similar problem. The difference in density be-tween clear (unexposed) film and solid black (exposed) film is only about 100 : 1. With indoor film, which is very sensitive to light, you can take pictures inside a dim room by opening the diaphragm of the lens wide to let in the maximum amount of light, and setting a long exposure. In the bright outdoors you must close the diaphragm to a small opening and use a fast shutter speed; otherwise the picture will be overexposed and come out solid white. If your camera does not have a wide enough range of diaphragm openings and shutter speeds, less sensitive film must be used in sunlight.

The eyes of the photographer fiddling with the camera are functioning in the same extremes of light. True, the iris (which is like the camera's diaphragm) can close in bright light and open in dim light, but the change in area is trivial compared with 10^{13}. Moreover, while you can change the exposure speed (the time the shutter is open) on the camera, you cannot do the same with your eyes: the retina is continuously exposed to light. For the retina to work effectively in any illumination, it must be capable somehow of changing its sensitivity to light. Like the photographer, you can 'change the film'; you have what amounts to a day retina and a night retina, but each one is adjustable in sensitivity over a wide latitude.

Sensitivity versus response measures

What is meant by 'sensitivity'? Although you probably have a pretty good feel for what it means to be 'sensitive' to light, there is a more technical meaning. You will need to understand the difference between sensitivity and response to understand adaptation. The following exercise should help explain these concepts.

The curve in Fig. 6.1(a) characterizes the rhodopsin of human rods; it therefore also characterizes the rods themselves. The hyperpolarization of a rod depends on the number of photons captured; the number of photons captured depends on the number delivered and their wavelengths (according to the percentage absorption curve). It would seem that this curve is all you need to characterize the responses of a rod to any given light. For example, a given number of photons at 550 nm will produce just about half as much effect as the same number of photons at 500 nm, and so forth. Alternatively, you might expect that given the responses of a receptor to lights of various wavelengths, you should be able to see if the pigment in the receptor was rhodopsin (with an absorption curve like that shown in Fig. 6.1a) or something else.

But there is a catch: the hyperpolarization of the receptor, although it is related to the number of photons absorbed, is not *linearly* related. That is, the hyperpolarization due to the capture of, say, 2000 photons is *not* necessarily twice the hyperpolarization due to the capture of 1000 photons. For this reason, you must be careful about how to measure the characteristics of a visual cell when you wish to determine what visual pigment is responsible for the cell responses.

There are two general methods available: response measures and sensitivity measures. Response measures are simpler (and quicker) to obtain. Sensitivity measures require more elaborate experiments, but reveal more about the intrinsic properties of the cell under study. To see why this is so, you need to understand how the non-linear relationship between the number of photons absorbed and the amount of hyperpolarization affects response measures, and why it does not contaminate sensitivity measures.

You can characterize the relationship between numbers of photons captured and amount of hyperpolarization for a particular receptor by presenting lights of various irradiances, all at the same wavelength, and recording the responses. When response (hyperpolarization) is plotted against the irradiance (which is proportional to the average number of photons captured), you obtain a curve called a *stimulus–response curve*, as shown in Fig. 6.2.

Suppose you have impaled a receptor with a microelectrode and wish to determine whether the pigment it contains is pure rhodopsin. You might choose some irradiance (number of photons to include in each stimulus flash) and record the hyperpolarization to flashes of various wavelengths. Because you are providing a constant number of photons in each flash, the percentage absorption curve tells you the number of photons absorbed at each wavelength (the number absorbed is the percentage times the number in each flash). This is shown in Fig. 6.1(a). Consider three wavelengths: 500, 450, and 400 nm. The number of photons absorbed at each wavelength may be read from the axis on the left: they are the three values labeled A, B, and C (corresponding to 500, 450, and 400 nm, respectively).

The receptor pigment does not absorb the same number of photons from each of the three lights; therefore the hyperpolarizations produced by the three lights should be different. The actual hyperpolarizations in response to the three wavelengths depend not only on the number of photons absorbed but also on the stimulus–response curve. As an extreme example, notice that the stimulus-response curve shown in Fig. 6.2 becomes nearly horizontal (or *saturates*) at high levels. Once the saturation has been attained, further increases in the

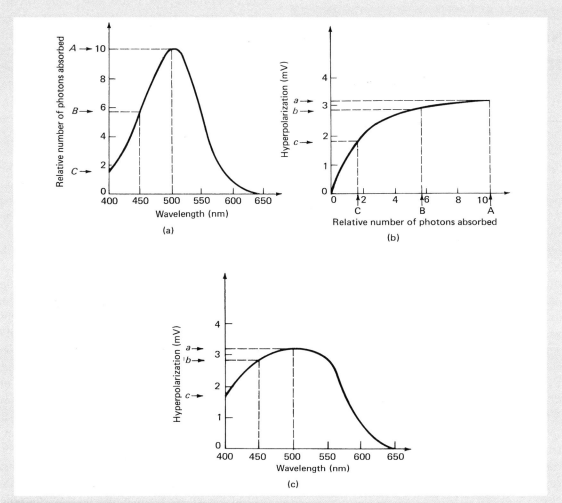

Fig. 6.1 Demonstration that a curve of responses as a function of wavelength does not reproduce the absorption curve of the pigment in a receptor. (a) The number of photons that would be absorbed at each wavelength; this curve was shown in Fig. 4.6. Three particular wavelengths are indicated, with absorptions marked A, B, and C. (b) The stimulus–response curve shown in Fig. 6.2; the responses (a, b, c) that would be expected from the three absorptions (A, B, C) are shown. (c) The responses that would he expected at each wavelength (with a, b, and c indicated).

number of photons absorbed have no further effect on the response. If the three test lights were presented at a sufficiently high irradiance (so that the number of photons absorbed from even the 400 nm light were sufficient to reach the saturation), they would all evoke the same response. More photons would be absorbed at 500 than at 400 nm, but each would evoke maximal hyperpolarization.

Of course, when you notice that all stimuli are producing the identical response, you would guess what the problem is, and use a more moderate ir-

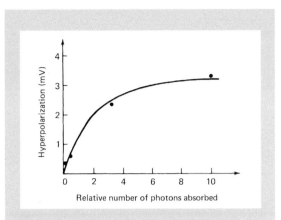

Fig. 6.2 Stimulus–response curve from a single rod in *Necturus*. Response is shown as a function of the relative number of photons absorbed (actual number of photons is about 3300 times larger). Based on Normann, R. A. and F. S. Werblin (1974) Control of retinal sensitivity. 1. Light and dark adaptation of vertebrate rods and cones. *J. Gen. Physiol.* 63: 37–61. By copyright permission of the Rockefeller University Press.

radiance. This improves matters, but does not solve the problem completely. Return to the three wavelengths in Fig. 6.1 with the three corresponding moderate photon absorptions *A*, *B*, and *C*. Figure 6.1(b) shows a stimulus–response curve, with the numbers of photons corresponding to *A*, *B*, and *C* indicated on the x-axis. From the y-axis, you can read the amount of hyperpolarization that each stimulus would evoke; they are labeled *a*, *b*, and *c*. You could now plot the hyperpolarization as a function of wavelength (Fig. 6.1c) for the three points and all other wavelengths. This curve is what you would have obtained in the experiment; it peaks at the right wavelength for rhodopsin, but has a distorted shape (compare with Fig. 6.1a). You would not be able to determine whether the pigment was pure rhodopsin, some other pigment, or a combination of pigments. The curve in Fig. 6.1(c) is a *response measure*: it is not a good way of looking at the spectral characteristics of the receptor.

A more satisfactory way to examine spectral characteristics is to use a *sensitivity measure*. Sensitivity means basically what you expect by intuition, although the exact definition is somewhat confusing. In sensitivity measures, you choose a specific magnitude of response; for each wavelength of light, the stimulus is adjusted until it produces exactly the requisite amount of response. Sensitivity is then defined as the inverse of the energy required to produce the criterion response, or $S = 1/I_{criterion}$. The inversion may seem like a strange thing to do, but it is the reason that sensitivity follows the intuitive definition. High sensitivity means a minimal stimulus is required to produce a response; low sensitivity means the light must be far stronger.

You encountered measures of this type in Chapter 2: *threshold* is simply one possible criterion that you could choose. If you measured threshold for detecting lights of different wavelengths, the *spectral sensitivity function* derived would depend only on the pigments in the receptors; it would not depend on the stimulus response curve of the subject or the cells conveying the responses. The response is always the same (just visible, 10 mV hyperpolarization, or whatever), so each point is at the same response level on the stimulus–response curve. The shape of the stimulus–response curve, therefore, can have no effect on the outcome; the function measured is the absorption curve.

To measure the sensitivity of a receptor, find the irradiance at each wavelength that gives a particular amount of hyperpolarization (say, 10 mV). As the amount of hyperpolarization is always the same, the same number of photons must have been captured from each of the stimuli. If a 400 nm light requires four times as many photons as a 460 nm light in order to give the same response (see Fig. 6.1a), the percentage capture at 400 nm must have been one-quarter of that at 460 nm. Then the sensitivity for 400 nm is one-quarter that for 460 nm (sensitivity is the inverse of the intensity). Table 6.1 presents a comparison of the sensitivities and percentages of absorption for five wavelengths. The percentages of absorption

Table 6.1   Sensitivities and percentages of absorption for five wavelengths

Wavelength (nm)	Percentage of absorption	Number of photons required	Sensitivity
400	1.75	57.1	0.0175
450	5.65	17.7	0.0565
500	10.00	10.0	0.1000
550	5.05	19.8	0.0505
600	0.52	192.3	0.0052

in the second column are read directly from Fig. 6.1(a). The third column gives the number of photons that would have to be delivered to result in the absorption of one photon at each wavelength (on average, that is—note that in a real experiment, the numbers of photons would be many times higher so you would not run into the absurdity of a fraction of a photon). Verify that the products of the numbers in columns 2 and 3 of Table 6.1 are 1.0 (remember to divide the numbers in column 2 by 100, because they are percentages). The last column is the sensitivity; it is 1 over the numbers in the third column. Notice that the numbers in the last column agree with those in the second (again allowing for a factor of 100 because the numbers in column 2 are percentages).

Dark adaptation

Consider the problem that you create for your eyes when you go to the movies in the afternoon. You step from the bright sunlight outside the theater into the gloomy rows of seats. At first, it is hard to see anything except the aisle marker lights and the relatively bright picture on the screen. It is hard to avoid stepping on people while groping your way to a seat. After a while, however, you can see quite well. People who were jostled on the way in can be seen so clearly that you could recognize them. It is as if there were much more light available in the theater.

This is an uncontrolled psychophysical experiment that most people have performed without thinking about it. Consider a controlled version of the same experiment: a subject is allowed a period of time to stare at a bright surface (a controlled amount of adaptation, rather than 'sunshine in the streets'), and then is placed in total darkness. Spots of light of low radiance are shown on a screen; the subject is asked to detect them. Threshold is determined as a function of the time in darkness, as described in Chapter 2.

This experiment was performed by Hecht *et al.* (1937) using a small red spot of light on which the subject fixated. The result is shown in Fig. 6.3. As the subject remained in the dark after the adapting field was extinguished, threshold dropped; the change was most rapid immediately after being placed in the dark and tapered off to a fairly stable threshold level by 5 or 10 min. This stable plateau represents a lowering of threshold of about 2 log units, or an improvement in the subject's ability to detect the red light by about a factor of 100. The improvement in sensitivity with time in the dark is called *dark adaptation*.

The increase in sensitivity represented by the curve in Fig. 6.3 was observed when a subject was tested with a small red light presented to the fovea. It shows an improvement to a new level of sensitivity. Hecht and coworkers found a more striking result when larger test spots of violet light were used (Fig. 6.4). As with the red test spot, there was a rapid improvement immediately after the adapting field was extinguished, apparently leveling off

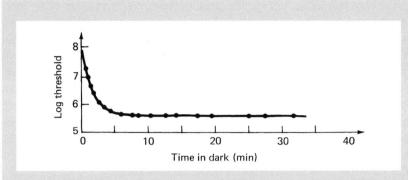

Fig. 6.3 Threshold intensity of a small, red flash of light as a function of time in the dark after exposure to an adapting light. From Hecht, S., C. Haig, and A. M. Chase (1937) The influence of light adaptation on subsequent dark adaptation of the eye. *J. Gen. Physiol.* 20: 831–850. By copyright permission of the Rockefeller University Press.

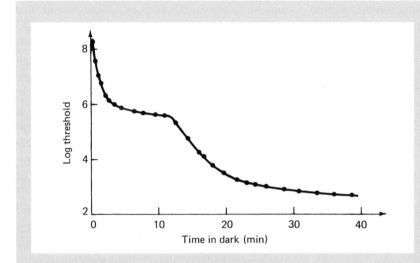

Fig. 6.4 Threshold intensity of a large, violet flash of light as a function of time in the dark after exposure to an adapting light. From Hecht *et al.* (1937). By copyright permission of the Rockefeller University Press.

to a new threshold about 1 log lower than the original. But about 10 min after the adapting field was extinguished, the threshold suddenly plunged again. Over the next 20 min it dropped another 3 log units (1000-fold), and finally settled at a value far lower than before.

What happened? There must be two distinct mechanisms; one of them acts rapidly, reaching a plateau in under 10 min, while the other is much slower but apparently more potent. The plateau represents the absolute threshold of the faster system; the break in the curve at about 10 min represents the transition from one system to the other, and the final plateau represents the absolute threshold of the slower system.

The system that reached its threshold first is called the *photopic* system. When it is operating, as it does in relatively bright illumination, we are said to be in the photopic state. The slower system, which accounted for the extremely high sensitivity after about 20 min, is the *scotopic* system; when we are dark-adapted and sensitive to dim lights, we are said to be in the scotopic state. You may recall these two systems from Chapter 3.

The spectral sensitivities of the two systems can be measured by performing the experiment of Fig. 6.4 (large test stimulus) with test lights of various wavelengths. The initial plateau (before the break) represents the threshold of the photopic system some time after the adapting field is extinguished. The inverse of the threshold is the sensitivity, so you can plot the sensitivity of the photopic system as a function of wavelength (dashed curve in Fig. 6.5). Similarly, the final plateau reached after a long time in the dark (absolute visual threshold) represents the threshold of the scotopic system. You can plot the sensitivity of the scotopic system on the same axes (solid curve in Fig. 6.5). When you do this, you may note several interesting things.

First, notice that the scotopic system is more sensitive than the photopic for all wavelengths ex-

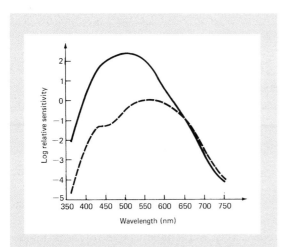

Fig. 6.5 Relative sensitivity of the photopic (*dashed*) and scotopic (*solid*) systems as a function of wavelength. From Wald, G. (1945) Human vision and the spectrum. *Science* 101: 653–658. Reprinted by permission. Copyright 1945 by the AAAS.

cept the very longest. When you are fully dark-adapted, the weakest lights you can detect (except reds) are detected by your scotopic system. Second, notice that the shapes of the photopic and scotopic spectral sensitivity curves are different. The photopic system is most sensitive at 555 nm (green light), although the scotopic system is still more sensitive even at that wavelength. The scotopic system is most sensitive at 505 nm (blue-green). In fact, 505 nm is the light to which you are the most sensitive when dark-adapted.

The change in spectral sensitivity going from the photopic to the scotopic state is called the *Purkinje shift*. It is basically a shift in the peak sensitivity of the eye as a function of adaptation. Two stimuli that are equally 'bright' to the photopic observer (have equal photopic luminosity) will not appear equally bright to the scotopic observer, and vice versa. An orange flower and a blue flower may seem about the same brightness (although obviously different in color) in sunlight, but in moonlight the blue flower will appear relatively light and the orange flower relatively dark. This effect was first described by J. E. Purkinje, who pointed out that in the dim light of early dawn reds look blackest of all the colors; as light increases, the blues emerge first, but their brightness is overtaken by the yellows and greens in the full light of day (Purkinje, 1825).

The scotopic peak at 505 nm may ring a bell. You saw in Chapter 4 that the peak of the rhodopsin (the rod pigment) absorption curve is 505 nm. This is not a coincidence. In fact, if the scotopic spectral sensitivity curve is plotted on the same coordinates as the spectral absorption curve of rhodopsin, the two curves are virtually identical (Hecht *et al.*, 1942). There is a strong implication here: rods are the receptors of the scotopic system.

If the rods serve the scotopic system, it seems reasonable to surmise that the other class of receptors, the cones, serve the photopic system. (Although no cone pigment matches the photopic spectral sensitivity curve, that curve can be closely approximated by a combination of the three cone types). Several other kinds of evidence also support the conclusion that rods serve the scotopic system and cones serve the photopic system:

1. Lights presented to the fovea stimulate only the photopic system, while lights presented outside the fovea affect the scotopic system at absolute threshold. That is why the demonstration of the adaptation of the photopic system in Fig. 6.3 was performed with a light in the fovea, and the scotopic system became evident when a larger stimulus light was used (Fig. 6.4). As you may recall from Chapter 4, cones are most concentrated in the fovea, while rods are absent from the fovea but are most numerous just outside it (see Fig. 4.3, p. 53). The spectral sensitivity (at absolute threshold) for stimuli presented to the fovea is that of the photopic system (dashed curve in Fig. 6.5); the drop in threshold when placed in the dark does not show a break to the scotopic system when the test flashes are presented to the fovea. Only test spots presented outside the fovea, where both rods and cones are present, yield dark adaptation curves with two branches (as in Fig. 6.4) having an absolute visual sensitivity after a long time in the dark that matches the sensitivity of the scotopic system (solid curve in Fig. 6.5). As only the photopic system can be demonstrated in the fovea, where there are only cones, cones must be the receptors that serve the photopic system.

Just as the best location for a photopic stimulus (one that is detected by the photopic system) is in the fovea, the best place to present a scotopic stimulus is outside the fovea. The sensitivities of the two systems as a function of placement on the retina match the measured distributions of the cones (photopic) and rods (scotopic) (see Fig. 4.3, p. 53). There is a consequence of the difference in retinal location of the peak sensitivities of the scotopic and photopic systems that may be familiar: the scotopic system, which is more sensitive than the photopic (Fig. 6.5), is most sensitive slightly off-axis. To detect a dim light when you are fully dark-adapted, it is best to look slightly above or below where it might be (you could look to the side, but then you might place the image on your blind spot,

which is totally insensitive). This is a trick used by amateur astronomers, and taught to soldiers who stand guard duty at night.

2. Rods and cones in the back of the eye are 'aimed' at the center of the pupil, from which the light should come (see Chapter 3). Cones, in particular, have inner segments that serve to channel the light to the outer segment when the light is coming directly down their axes (Enoch, 1963). This makes cones more sensitive to light coming from the center of the pupil than from the edges, wasting the light from the edges but giving a clearer image (the light from the edges is less well focused). Cones function in bright light and so can afford to waste light; rods need all the light they can get, and therefore do not waste the light from the edge of the pupil. An experimenter can arrange for all the light in the stimulus to pass through a small point in the pupil, and locate that point in the center or at the edge of the pupil. If the light is effective for cones, the stimulus entering through the edge of the pupil will be less effective than that entering through the center. This is the *Stiles–Crawford effect* (Stiles & Crawford, 1933); it is far more pronounced for photopic than for scotopic stimuli.

3. The scotopic system is served by a single type of receptor; a rod can only hyperpolarize in proportion to the number of photons absorbed. There is no way for a rod to signal whether it caught one of 10 available photons at 505 nm, or one of 20 available photons at 550 nm. There is thus no way for the rod to signal the color of the light—it is color-blind. The cone system, on the other hand, has three distinct members (cones with somewhat different spectral sensitivities). With relative absorptions of a light by the three different classes of cone, the nervous system can extract information about the color of the light (see Chapter 14 for a full discussion of this). You can see colors when in the photopic state but not in the scotopic state. In the dim of night, when you can see forms and shapes, you are color-blind except for some reds, to which the photopic system is more sensitive than the scotopic.

Now that you are persuaded (well, you should be) that rods subserve the scotopic system and cones subserve the photopic, look again at what happens when you are suddenly placed in the dark and asked to detect a green light. Follow the course of dark adaptation of rods and cones in Fig. 6.6. When you were in the light (adapting field) before the experiment began, both rods and cones were made less sensitive; that is, the retina was *light-adapted*. The rods, however, were far more affected by the adapting field than were the cones; that is, the sensitivity of the rods became less than that of the cones. Quite possibly, the rods were made so insensitive as to be unresponsive. When the adapting field is extinguished, both rods and cones start to dark-adapt, becoming more sensitive. The cones, being more sensitive to begin with and adapting faster than the rods, determine the threshold for the first test flashes. You are still in the photopic state and, as the cones are detecting the test, can see its color.

After a few minutes your cones have approached their ultimate sensitivity, and threshold levels off. Your rods, of course, are still changing dramatically, but since their threshold is still higher than the cone threshold, the light is detected by the cones. We know that the rod curve is doing what we say it is, as studies of people who have a genetic abnormality that causes them to lack cones show dark-adaptation curves like the 'rod' curve in Fig. 6.6 (Rushton, 1961a).

During this photopic period, you have color vision, relatively good acuity, relatively rapid responses to flickering light, and show the Stiles–Crawford effect. Your peak sensitivity is at about 555 nm, and maximum sensitivity is in your fovea.

At some time after 5 min in the dark, the increasing sensitivity of your rod system causes its threshold to fall below that of your cones. Because the rods become more sensitive, they are the receptors that determine threshold. You can see dimmer and dimmer lights, until the ultimate

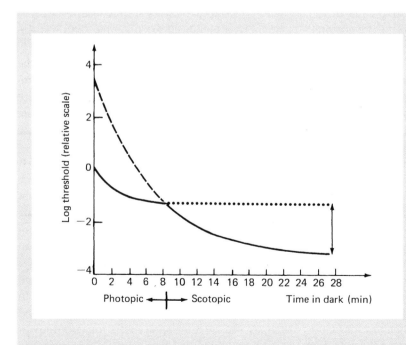

Fig. 6.6 Theoretical course of adaptation of the cones (*dotted*) and rods (*dashed*) as a function of time in the dark. *Solid curve* shows the drop in threshold, determined by the more sensitive system. Test light = 550 nm.

absolute scotopic threshold is approached some time after 30 min.

Scotopic vision is characterized by a lack of colors for threshold stimuli—the test flash looks colorless or pale blue (Trezona, 1970), there is poorer acuity, and responses to flickering light are slower (a light that could be seen to be alternating between bright and dim at a rapid rate in the photopic state may now look like a steady light). The Stiles–Crawford effect is minimal, peak sensitivity is at 505 nm, and the most sensitive part of your retina is slightly outside the fovea. There is a summary of the characteristics of the photopic and scotopic systems in Table 6.2. But note that some of these effects may be due to processes occurring in more central visual areas, not in the retina itself (Lee *et al.*, 1992; Carandini & Ferster, 1997).

In the scotopic state, lights at threshold are detected by the rods, and their color is not sensed. If a light is made stronger, however, it also stimulates cones, and color can be detected. The arrow in Fig. 6.6 shows the additional amount of light that must be added to a threshold light to make its color evident; this separation is called the *photochromatic interval*. Lights in this range of intensities (between absolute threshold and the photopic threshold) are visible, but uncolored. The photochromatic interval is different for different wavelengths; it depends on the relative sensitivities of the photopic and scotopic systems. Short-wavelength stimuli have large photochromatic intervals, as the difference in sensitivity between the systems is large in this region of the spectrum.

Lights longer than about 650 nm show no photochromatic interval; their color is seen as soon as they are detectable, as the photopic system is more sensitive than the scotopic at these long wavelengths. <u>BOX 6.1</u>

Light adaptation

The changeover from cones to rods as the eye dark-adapts is striking, but it is actually not as remarkable as the fact that each system, rod or cone, changes its sensitivity dramatically as it remains in the dark. Similarly, each system adjusts its sensitivity according to the lighting. If a system is most sensitive in complete darkness, adding a 'background' light quickly reduces sensitivity. This adjustment of sensitivity is known as light adaptation.

Light adaptation refers to the change in sensitivity to lights that are superimposed on a steady background light. While the stimuli could be either brighter or dimmer than the background, it is usual to refer to *increment sensitivity*; that is, how much light must be added to the background to be detected. You may recall this problem from Chapter 2, where you saw that Weber's law was the typical sensory system's solution to the problem. According to Weber's law, the size of the just noticeable increment is directly related to the luminance it is seen against; that is, the same *contrast* is

Table 6.2 A comparison of properties of the photopic and scotopic systems

Property	Photopic system	Scotopic system
Receptor type	Cones	Rods
Retinal location for highest sensitivity	Fovea	Outside fovea
Wavelength of peak sensitivity	555 nm	505 nm
Acuity	Good	Poor
Sensitivity	Moderate and bright lights	Dim lights
Type of vision	Color or black and white	Black and white only
Sensitivity to part of pupil light enters	Sensitive	Not sensitive

Box 6.1 | Interactions between rods and cones

Although the rods and cones may seem to be two independent systems, there is evidence that they interact. If there is an inhibitory interaction between them at the point at which one receptor type is more active than the other, it can inhibit the weaker type and so prevent it from having as much influence on the visual signal.

Psychophysical experiments provide evidence for an interaction between rods and cones. The scotopic threshold is different for background lights of the same scotopic effectiveness that have different *photopic* effectiveness (Makous & Boothe, 1974; Frumkes & Temme, 1977; Ingling, *et al.*, 1977); that is, activity in the cones affects the rod threshold. Other evidence for rod/cone interaction comes from recordings in single horizontal cells; the range of intensities over which input from both rods and cones can be demonstrated in a horizontal cell can be changed by using anesthetic drugs that apparently affect interactions (Whitten & Brown, 1973).

The ganglion cells of the retina have input from both rods and cones (Barlow *et al.*, 1957; Adams & Afanador, 1971), so the interaction of the systems must be complete by that level of processing. Shefner & Levine (1977, 1981) studied rod/cone interactions by recording the activity of ganglion cells in goldfish. We stimulated with lights effective only for rods or only for cones; there was greater interaction when the two stimuli overlapped than when they were somewhat separated (although still within the center of the ganglion cell receptive field). This difference implies an interaction that is distance-dependent: rods and cones that are close to each other interact more strongly than those that are somewhat separated. A similar interaction has been demonstrated in cats (Levine *et al.*, 1987), and can be demonstrated psychophysically in humans (Benimoff *et al.*, 1982; Drum, 1982; see Levine & Frishman, 1984).

just noticeable. At higher backgrounds, the system is somehow 'cranked down' so that a larger increment is needed to give the same (threshold) response (Shapley & Enroth-Cugell, 1984).

What kind of change could there be in the way the retina responds to light? The solid curve in Fig. 6.7(a) shows how a cell in the visual system might respond to various strengths of stimulation. For very low stimulus strengths, there is no response; as the strength increases, so does the response. But there is an upper limit to the responses a cell can generate, so the cell would eventually saturate. The curve shown in Fig. 6.7(a) is drawn from an equation commonly used to represent the responses of visual cells (Naka & Rushton, 1966).

A steady background light would appear along the curve at some new operating point, such as the solid circle at the middle of the curve. Increments (or decrements) of light superimposed on that background would then cause changes in response from that middle level. (Since this graph shows responses versus the log of stimulus strength, the size of the response would grow directly with the logarithm of *contrast* as long as the contrast was

low enough to stay on the approximately straight central portion of the curve.)

But an even stronger background would place the 'operating point' at the nearly horizontal saturated part of the curve (open circle). Even very large increments would not cause any change in response (and because of the log axis, the changes would be truly enormous). How could the system compensate for the bright background?

You have perhaps found one solution to being in too bright a light: you put on dark glasses. A dark filter would reduce every light (background and increment) by the same fraction. On a log axis, a constant factor is equivalent to a constant shift (see Appendix), so the same cell (wearing dark glasses) would operate on the dashed curve shown to the right of the original solid curve. The very strong background would be at the middle of the curve in Fig. 6.7(a) (cross), and the situation would be exactly as it was for the moderate background (solid circle). If you are looking at a picture and the illumination increases, you can get back to exactly where you had been by putting on the appropriate dark glasses. But you do not need the glasses,

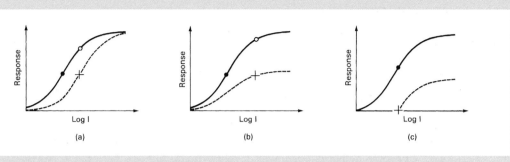

Fig. 6.7 Responses of a hypothetical visual cell *versus* the logarithm of stimulus strength. (a) The *solid curve* is like that in Fig. 6.2, except for the logarithmic axis. The *dashed curve* shows the relation in a steady strong background (*open circle on solid curve*) that effects a change in sensitivity. (b) The same relationship as in (a), but the *dashed curve* represents the relationship if the background effects a multiplicative change. (c) Responses to increments derived from the curves in (b).

because your visual system light-adapts, shifting your curves *as if* you were wearing the glasses. BOX 6.2.

Physiology of adaptation

The simplest way to explain adaptation would be to assume that the loss of sensitivity in brighter lights occurs because there is less pigment available to capture photons. You may recall from Chapter 4 that a visual signal is initiated by a pigment molecule capturing a photon, and that the probability of a capture depends on both the number of photons and the number of available pigment molecules (among other things). Each time a molecule captures a photon, it isomerizes—that is, bleaches—and is temporarily unavailable to catch more photons. A bright light bleaches a large number of molecules; that decreases the number

Box 6.2 The difference between gain and sensitivity

Notice that the dark glasses, representing a change in sensitivity, do not have the same effect as simply decreasing the *gain* of the cell. Gain refers to the multiplier between input and output. If you divided the responses represented by the solid curve in Fig. 6.7(a) by some factor, the curve would shrink, as shown by the dashed curve in Fig. 6.7(b). This picture illustrates the same situations for a gain-changing system. True, the sensitivity would be decreased by the background (a greater increment would be needed to give the same response), but the high background would still saturate the responses.

Suppose, instead of looking at the absolute response in Fig. 6.7(b), you looked at the increment responses—that is, the change in response due to the flashes against the background. You could ignore the steady response due to the background (as visual cells, which are somewhat transient, essentially do), and just see the changes. You would then see a set of curves like those in Fig. 6.7(c). This looks like adaptation because the curves shift to the right, but it is not the same as the change in sensitivity illustrated in Fig. 6.7(a). A pure change in sensitivity is represented by a shift of the curve horizontally, not a change in the vertical scale of the curves.

remaining, so that there are fewer photon captures for the incoming stream of light. Hecht (1937) proposed that bleaching of pigment molecules by light causes the loss of sensitivity associated with bright backgrounds, and that gradual recovery of bleached molecules (by regeneration) in the dark accounts for the increase in sensitivity observed in Figs 6.3, 6.4, and 6.6.

Life is not that simple. Enormous changes in sensitivity occur with virtually no pigment bleaching (Granit *et al.*, 1938). Of course, sensitivity is lower when pigment is bleached, but there is an important kind of adaptation that does not require significant bleaching. This has been termed 'neural' or *field adaptation*, by Rushton (1965). Recovery from field adaptation is relatively fast, compared with adaptation caused by the bleaching of pigment (which Rushton called *photochemical* or *bleaching adaptation*).

Where in the retina does adaptation occur? Obviously, the effect of reducing the amount of

pigment occurs in the receptors themselves, for that is where the pigment is. But if significant adaptation occurs with only minimal pigment bleaching, it might occur anywhere in the retina, or even higher in the visual system.

Do individual receptors adapt? Cones apparently show adaptation like that illustrated in Figure 6.7(a) (Malchow & Yazulla, 1986), but it is possible that rods (at least in retinas that also have cones to take over at higher illuminations) do not adapt very much (but see Perlman & Normann, 1998). Rods in our retinas, as judged by those in monkeys, may mainly shift to new operating points, like the circles on the solid curve in Fig. 6.7(a) (Baylor *et al.*, 1984). But rods in other animals do adapt. Grabowski & Pak (1975) showed that the sensitivity of individual salamander (axolotl) rods changed far more than could be predicted by the amount of pigment bleached. Similar results were obtained from the frog by Hemila (1977). A study of toad rods, exactly like the study of monkey rods that

Box 6.3 Adaptation pools

Adaptation that occurs in the proximal retina nonetheless has a restricted extent; the pools do not extend across the entire retina, as adaptation is at least somewhat local. It is reasonable to wonder whether the adaptation pools are somehow linked to the ganglion cell receptive fields.

One line of evidence indicates that the adaptation pools are indeed so related. Cleland & Enroth-Cugell (1968) and Enroth-Cugell & Shapley (1973) found that the change in sensitivity of a cat ganglion cell depended on the effective amount of light falling on the center of the field. That is, a small intense adapting field would have the same effect as a larger, less intense field if the two were equally effective in exciting the ganglion cell. It did not seem to matter how the light was distributed within the receptive field as long as it had the same effect on the center of the receptive field.

On the other hand, Easter (1968b) placed small adapting spots within the receptive fields of goldfish ganglion cells, and tested their effect on the sensitivities to test spots at various positions within the fields. He found that the effect on a test spot was determined by how near it was to the adapting spot; there were local adaptation pools within the receptive field center. Similar results have been obtained from frog by Burkhardt & Berntson (1972).

Some resolution to this apparent contradiction can be found in the work of Tong & Green (1977). They placed adapting lights within the receptive fields of rat retinal ganglion cells, and tested the effects on variously positioned test spots. As did Easter, they found a tendency for the effects to be greatest near the adapting spots; however, the greatest effect was often at a point between the adapting light and the middle of the receptive field (Cicerone & Green, 1980). In other words, there was also a component that was associated with the receptive field center, as noted by Enroth-Cugell & Shapley. There are likely to be at least two different components of adaptation, corresponding to two different levels in the retina. The pools of the outer retina are associated with the local area around the adapting light, but there is apparently pooling associated with the ganglion cell receptive field center. It should also be noted that these results were obtained with different animal models, and different animals may place heavier reliance on different pools.

Box 6.4   The stages of retinal adaptation

In an elegant series of studies, Laura Frishman and her colleagues used the ERG to examine the stages of adaptation of the scotopic systems of higher vertebrates (see Box A. 8, p. 493s). They isolated the components of the ERG that arise from receptors, from rod bipolar cells, and from spiking neurons deeper in the retina. To determine the pure receptor response, Robson & Frishman (1995) treated retinas with chemicals that blocked the transmission from rods to rod bipolar cells (remember, there is only one type of rod bipolar, unlike the richer system available to cones).

They also removed the portion of the response due to spiking cells by treating the retina with a compound that prevents action potentials (Viswanathan *et al.*, 1996). By subtracting the various other components from the complete ERG, they could reconstruct the pure responses of the rod bipolars.

Once the ERG was separable into a part due to receptors (a-wave), a part due to rod bipolars (b-wave), and a part due to spiking neurons (the scotopic threshold response, or STR; Sieving *et al.*, 1986), the responses of each part of

➡

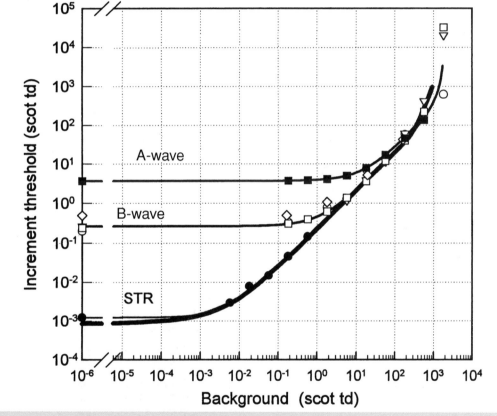

Fig. 6.1 Threshold *versus* intensity curves for components of the scotopic ERG compared to human psychophysical data. The a-wave (solid squares) represents the responses of receptors; the b-wave (open squares and diamonds) represents rod bipolar cells; the STR (solid circles) represents spiking neurons. The solid curve is the human scotopic threshold function measured psychophysically (after Aguilar & Stiles. 1954). Note that this is log-log paper (see Appendix), so a straight line with a slope of one means the increment is proportional to the background — that is, such a line represents Weber's Law (see Chapter 2). Scot td, scotopic trolands (a photometric measure). From Xu, L. (1998). Effects of Light Adaptation on the Activities of Rod-driven Bipolar Cells in the Cat Electroretinogram. (College of Optometry, University of Houston, Master's Thesis).

(BOX 6.4 CONTINUED)

the retina could be examined with light flashes of various intensities against various strengths of steady, adapting backgrounds. Various intensity flashes were used in order to achieve a valid establishment of a threshold sensitivity (see Fig. 6.7). The threshold for each component was then plotted as a function of background (Fig. 6.8). For comparison, the psychophysical function is shown as a solid curve (after Aguilar & Stiles, 1954). This function was obtained, like those in Figs 6.3 and 6.4, by asking people whether or not they could see a light flash.

The a-wave, due to the rods themselves, shows no change in threshold until the very highest backgrounds (where the rod signal is probably also 'borrowing' the cone pathway through gap junctions—see Box 4.13, p. 69).

Thus, very little adaptation occurs at the level of the rods themselves. The b-wave, on the other hand, begins to show a change in sensitivity at moderate backgrounds, possibly accounting for the psychophysical effects over the upper half of the scotopic range. The STR, although it can only be recorded at the lowest levels, begins to change its threshold at about the same background level as is observed for the psychophysical data. It therefore appears that adaptation is complete by the level of the ganglion cells (Frishman & Sieving, 1995; Frishman *et al.*, 1996). Notice, however, that adaptation occurs in stages within the retina, and not all at one level.

showed minimal adaptation, indicated a shift like the change to the dashed curve in Fig. 6.7(a) (Lamb *et al.*, 1981). And it appears that some adaptation occurs in human rods as well (Hood & Birch, 1993; Kraft *et al.*, 1993).

Receptors adapt, but there is further adaptation in the proximal retina. Like lateral antagonism, all adaptation does not occur in a single stage. One clue that there is adaptation after the receptors is that adaptation is not localized to individual receptors. Light in one spot also affects the sensitivity for lights in nearby regions; that is, receptors act as if they were affected by lights in a larger region, called an *adapting pool* (Rushton, 1965). These pools were first demonstrated by an ingenious psychophysical experiment in which it was found that the adaptation caused by a stroboscopic flash (too brief to allow for any eye movement) was independent of whether it was spread uniformly over an area or concentrated in fine bars alternating with dark areas (Rushton & Westheimer, 1962). Since the receptors in the dark areas were not spared, they must have been adapted by the light in the nearby bars, even though they did not receive any of that light directly. Pooling is not demonstrable for cones, however (Cicerone *et al.*, 1990). <u>BOX 6.3</u>

There is considerable further change in sensitivity proximal to the receptors. Later stages of adaptation have been found in recordings from single cells in the retina of the mud puppy *Necturus* (Werblin, 1971; 1974; Chaparro *et al.*, 1995). <u>BOX 6.4</u>

Afterimages

There is a set of visual phenomena that are apparently related to the process of adaptation. They are called *afterimages*—literally, images seen after the stimulus is no longer present. There are two major classes: *positive* and *negative*. Afterimages are illustrated in the demonstration program for Chapter 6 on the CD accompanying this book. There are three different images (the first is black and white, the other two are in color) that you can try. In each case, you should stare at the tiny blinking dot in the center of the image; try to move your eyes as little as possible. After about 30 s, the picture will disappear and be replaced by a uniform field. You should see an afterimage of the original picture.

Positive afterimages

A positive afterimage is one that looks like the fading ghost of the original stimulus. Stare at a bright light and then look at a black surface; there will be

Box 6.5 Mechanisms of adaptation

What mechanisms might lead to field adaptation? One intriguing possibility is that there is a 'parametric feedback', in which activation of receptors serves to change the properties of the retina by some mechanism such as exhausting neurotransmitter, inactivating synapses, or accumulating some extracellular 'dark adaptation substance' (Barlow, 1977b). You have already encountered an intracellular adapting substance that might play a role in receptors: calcium (Lamb, 1990; McNaughton, 1990; Chappell & Naka, 1991; Koutalos & Yau, 1996; see Box 4.6, p. 57).

A possible candidate for an adaptation substance in the inner retina that has received considerable attention is potassium. Potassium ions (K^+) are released into the extracellular environment whenever cells depolarize (see Appendix). Added to the extracellular fluid, K^+ has little or no effect on the sensitivity or responses of receptors, but has an effect on the b-wave of the electroretinogram that is analogous to the effect of background lights (Dowling &

Ripps, 1976; Dowling, 1977; see Frishman *et al.*, 1988 for a discussion of K^+ and the electroretinogram). It is therefore possible that K^+ accumulating in the extracellular environment causes a slight depolarization of retinal cells and leads to the loss of sensitivity we call light adaptation.

Finally, the neurotransmitter dopamine (DA) plays a role in adaptation. Dopamine is released by amacrine and interplexiform cells (Dowling, 1979; Dacey, 1990; Kolb *et al.*, 1990) and has the effect of reducing the coupling between cells that communicate by gap junctions (Hedden & Dowling, 1978; Djamgoz *et al.*, 1981; Dowling, 1989; Dong & McReynolds, 1991, 1992; Harsanyi & Mangel, 1992; Hampson *et al.*, 1992; Weiler & Akopian, 1992; McMahon & Brown, 1994; Perlman & Ammermüller, 1994; Wu, 1994). This has multiple effects upon the transmission of signals in both plexiform layers.

---

a bright image of the light. This is the positive afterimage. It sometimes does not appear immediately, but 'develops' after a brief delay. The afterimage gradually fades from view, although it is often possible to revive it by blinking hard, or looking briefly at a differently colored surface. To see a positive afterimage in the demonstration, you must clear the check-box near the lower right.

A positive afterimage is made of 'light' that is not there; this 'light' generated by retinal activity, has been called *dark light* (Barlow, 1964). In fact, the higher visual thresholds immediately following the offset of an adapting light can be considered as if they were caused by dark light against which the test flashes must be detected. The recovery of sensitivity with time in the dark can be equated with the gradual fading of the dark light (or afterimage), and the state of adaptation at any moment can be expressed in terms of the equivalent background light that, if present, would yield the same sensitivity.

Dark light is probably caused by continued hyperpolarization of the receptors following offset of

a strong light (Penn & Hagins, 1972; Baylor & Hodgkin, 1974; Kleinschmidt & Dowling, 1975). Even the delay in onset of the afterimage may be identified with a brief dead period observed in the receptors (Baylor & Hodgkin, 1974). The reason for the continued hyperpolarization is not completely known, although it is reasonable to assume that bleached pigment molecules that have not yet regenerated continue to signal the presence of light by the fact of their isomerized state.

Afterimages do not last for the 30 min or so that is required for complete recovery of sensitivity. The reason for this is that they cannot move on the surface of the retina; they are anchored by being produced in the receptor cells in a particular area. The stimulation associated with them is therefore wholly unchanging, and as you know from Chapters 4 and 5, the cells of the retina are not interested in unchanging stimuli. The afterimages move with the retina, and fade as 'adaptation' occurs. A similar phenomenon occurs with actual lights that stimulate the retina without being allowed to move across it as the eye moves. These are called *stabilized images*.

Negative afterimages

A negative afterimage is induced the same way as a positive one, except that following exposure to the original stimulus, the subject looks at a light gray or white surface. The afterimage on the surface has the same form as the original stimulus, but the contrast is reversed. Areas that were bright in the original appear dark, while areas that were dim in the original appear bright (like a photographic negative). If the original stimulus was colored, the colors are also reversed, with greens appearing where there had been reds, yellows for blues, and so forth. The significance of these color reversals is discussed in Chapter 14. To see negative afterimages in the demonstration, check the box (the way it is when you start the program).

To induce a negative afterimage, the luminance of the screen on which it is to be seen must be at least at the threshold for seeing a light at that level of adaptation (Gosline *et al.*, 1973); that is, the lightness of the screen must be such that it is visible. That is a clue to the nature of the negative afterimage: the adaptation pools in the areas exposed to bright light have been adapted, so the cells in those areas of retina are less sensitive. The screen on which the afterimage is seen provides uniform light, but when the light falls on less sensitive areas of the retina it has less effect. It could even be below threshold, if the adaptation is strong enough and the screen is relatively dim. The areas of screen being sensed by strongly adapted areas of retina appear dim, and the other areas appear relatively brighter. Hence, there is a negative afterimage.

Like a positive afterimage, a negative afterimage is stabilized on the retina. It therefore also fades more rapidly than would be expected from the time course of dark adaptation. It can be revitalized by blinking the eyes or changing the luminance of the screen on which it is seen, as these activities cause changes in the otherwise static af-

terimage. In fact, brightening the screen leads to a negative afterimage and dimming the screen leads to a positive afterimage. This is consistent with the idea that local areas adapted by light are less responsive; by brightening the screen, the areas adapted by light parts of the original pattern brighten less than other areas, giving a negative afterimage. Dimming the screen causes less OFF response in the adapted areas; they dim less than the surrounding regions, causing a positive afterimage (Williams & MacLeod, 1979). <u>BOX 6.5</u>

Suggested readings

One of the clearest descriptions of the process of dark adaptation and the properties of the photopic and scotopic systems that we have encountered is in the book *Visual perception*, by T. N. Cornsweet (Academic Press, New York, 1970). In particular, Chapter 7, 'Cones and cone pigment', describes the differences between rods and cones, and explains the significance of the photopic and scotopic spectral sensitivity curves.

The psychophysics of dark adaptation, and the identification of the pigments of the photopic and scotopic systems are presented by W. A. H. Rushton in 'Visual pigments in man' (*Scientific American*, November 1962; offprint #139). This article is reprinted in *Perception: mechanisms and models*, by R. Held and W. Richards (W. H. Freeman, San Francisco, 1972). A good treatment of the way individual neurons within the retina adapt to different background levels of light is presented by F. S. Werblin in 'The control of sensitivity in the retina' (*Scientific American*, January 1973; offprint #1264). This article is reprinted in *Recent progress in perception*, by R. Held and W. Richards (W. H. Freeman, San Francisco, 1976).

A more detailed discussion of adaptation may be found in *The retina*, by J. E. Dowling (Harvard University Press, 1987). You could also look at 'Visual adaptation and retinal gain controls' by R.

Shapley and C. Enroth-Cugell, in *Progress in Retinal Research*, 3:263–346. This is an excellent review of the mechanisms of adaptation in the retina, though it is quite technical and may prove difficult in places.

There are also several relevant chapters in *Vision: coding and efficiency*, edited by Colin Blakemore (Cambridge University Press, Cambridge, 1990), a book that is also mentioned in connection with other chapters. The chapter by T. D. Lamb ('The role of photoreceptors in light-adaptation and dark-adaptation of the visual system', pp. 161–168) is a good source for reading about adaptation by photoreceptors. H. B. Barlow ('A theory about the functional role and synaptic mechanism of visual after-effects', pp. 363–375) discusses afterimages. A somewhat related chapter on the invariances adaptation can cause, by T.E. Cohn ('Spatial and temporal summation in human vision', pp. 376–385), is also relevant to Chapter 12.

Chapter 7

The primary visual areas of the brain

So far, all you know about the visual system concerns processes that occur in the eye itself. Three chapters' worth! Even at the peripheral level, you saw the existence of a number of sophisticated coding mechanisms. In this chapter, you will trace the pathways of the visual system from the point at which ganglion cell axons leave the eyeball and follow them into the cerebral cortex of the brain. You will see how higher processing centers act on the incoming signals to detect specific features of the visual world. This chapter concentrates on the pathway to primary visual cortex and the responses of cells in these still lower-order areas. In the next chapter, you will see how cortical areas are organized into parallel, cooperative pathways.

The visual pathway

Figure 7.1 shows three sketches of a human brain seen from different angles: part (a) presents a side view, with the front of the brain toward the left; part (b) shows the middle (or *medial*) surface, as if the brain were sliced right down the middle. The surface visible on the outside (of both) is a thin sheet of tissue called the *cerebral cortex*. It is only about 2 mm thick, but its many folds and invaginations give it an extremely large surface area, about 2000 cm^2 in humans (Hubel & Wiesel, 1977). The cerebral cortex is phylogenetically the newest part of the brain; it is large and highly specialized in higher mammals, but is relatively small in lower mammals such as rodents, and is minimal in fish and amphibians.

The part of the cortex that first receives the visual signal is shaded in Figs 7.1(a) and (b); it is the back part of the cortex, and is given the name *occipital cortex*. Within this region of the brain, there are a number of differentiable visual areas (creatively named *visual area I*, *visual area II*, and so on). These areas are somewhat hierarchically organized; visual area I (also called *striate cortex* or V1) receives visual information from lower centers while providing input to a number of secondary cortical regions (Van Essen, 1979).

Photographs of human brains are presented in 'Brain anatomy' on the demonstration CD accompanying this book (the side view of Fig. 7.1(a) is on the left and the medial view of Fig. 7.1(b) on the right). When you first select 'Anatomy of the brain' from the drop-down menu for Chapter 7, you will see these views with V1, V2, and V3 labeled, along with a number of other visual areas.

As are many other parts of the body, the brain is a *bilaterally symmetric* organ; that is, it is composed of two half-brains (called cerebral hemi-

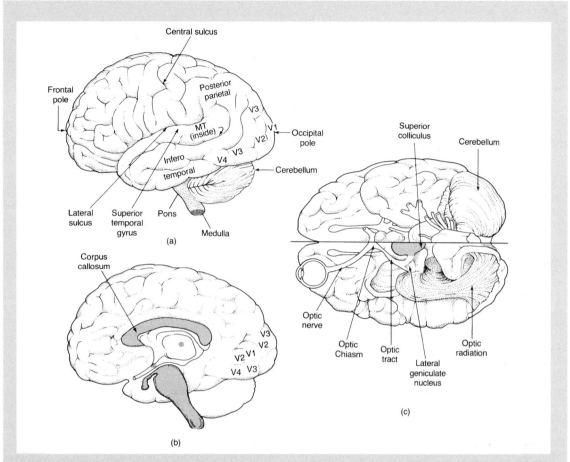

Fig. 7.1 The human brain. (a) Side view showing the major primary visual areas. (b) View of the middle surface of a brain that was cut down the middle. Cut structures are shown shaded. (c) View from underneath the brain, showing the optic pathway. The left half has been dissected to reveal the structures of the early visual pathway.

spheres) that are nearly mirror images of each other. The two halves are connected to each other by the *corpus callosum*, which is a thick band of nerve fibers (see Fig. 7.1b or the cut brain on the right in 'Brain anatomy'). The visual areas mentioned in the previous paragraph are found in each of the hemispheres.

The pathway of the visual system from the eye to the cortex is shown schematically in Fig. 7.2. The axons of retinal ganglion cells leave the eyeball at the optic disc, forming the optic nerve. The optic

nerves from both eyes run underneath the brain (see Fig. 7.2) and intersect at a junction called the *optic chiasm*. At the chiasm, the nerves branch, forming the two *optic tracts*. Some of the fibers continue through the intersection toward the half of the brain on the opposite side from the eye from which the fibers originated; the opposite side of the brain is called the *contralateral* hemisphere. The rest of the fibers do not cross to the opposite side of the brain, but change their direction of travel at the optic chiasm and stay in the same half of the brain as the eye

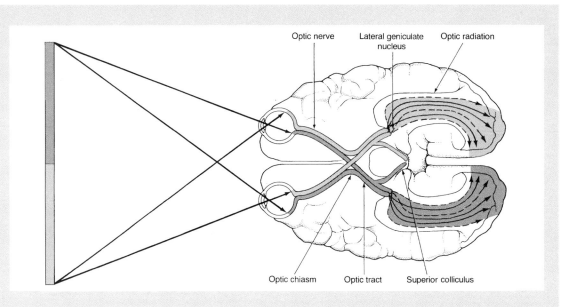

Fig. 7.2 View of the early visual pathway, showing the partial crossing of optic nerve fibers at the chiasm. A visual field, shaded to the right and light to the left, is shown. Pathways are shaded in agreement with the part of the field they serve.

from which they came; the half of the brain on the same side is said to be *ipsilateral* to that eye.

Which fibers cross from one side of the brain to the other at the optic chiasm is determined by where on the retina they originated. As shown in Fig. 7.2, fibers coming from the side of each retina closest to the nose (*nasal retina*) cross at the chiasm and go into the contralateral side of the brain. Fibers that originate in the area of each retina toward the temples (*temporal retina*) do not cross at the chiasm and stay on the ipsilateral side of the brain. Therefore optic nerve fibers from the temporal side of the left retina and the nasal side of the right retina both go to the left half of the brain, while fibers from the nasal side of the left retina and temporal side of the right retina go to the right half of the brain. Of course, the division is not perfect, with some cells very near the division projecting to the 'wrong' side (Levick *et al.*, 1981; Sugishita *et al.*, 1994). This 'slop' is presumably like the 'feathering' where new paint is blended to the old when a wall is patched.

This scheme of some fibers crossing to different parts of the brain may seem like a strange way to design a visual system, but a little reflection should affirm that the arrangement is indeed sensible. Your eyes are at the front of your head, so both eyes see almost the same region of the visual world. If you cover one of your eyes, there is very little change in how much of the world you see. Only about 30° at the extreme periphery is the sole province of one eye. (To get an idea of how much is seen by only one eye, stare at a point across the room and quickly cover your right eye with your right hand. Notice that only things to the extreme right disappear from view.)

This large overlap of the fields of view could be confusing for the visual system if it had no way of collating the corresponding information from the two eyes. The partial crossing of ganglion cell axons at the optic chiasm allows fibers from both eyes receiving information about the same point in visual space to project to the same part of the brain. In Fig. 7.2, you can see that a stimulus in the right half of the visual field projects an image onto the nasal half of the right retina, and an image onto the temporal side of the left retina; these are the two half-retinas that are combined by the redistribution of fibers at the optic chiasm. Similarly, an object on the left half of the visual field produces images on the nasal portion of the left retina and the temporal portion of the right retina. The right half of the brain receives information about the left half of the visual world, regardless of the eye from which the information comes, while the left half of the brain receives its input from the right half of the visual world. BOX 7.1

This description of which optic nerve fibers cross from one side of the brain to the other at the optic chiasm applies only to those animals that have their eyes in the front of their heads looking forward, including humans and many predators. This eye placement is such that there is extensive duplication of visual processing by both eyes; the right eye sees almost the identical stimulus array as the left, and vice versa. Although redundant, this arrangement has one great advantage that will become clear later: it aids the perception of visual depth or distance. Animals that are predators require a high degree of depth perception, as their survival depends on being able to judge correctly where their next potential meal is located. Hunted animals, on the other hand, are less concerned with judging the exact position of an object in space; it is much more important for them to have as wide a visual field as possible. Such animals, therefore, have their eyes placed on the sides of their heads, rather than at the front. This gives them a larger field of view, at the expense of a well-developed sense of visual depth. For these animals, virtually all optic nerve fibers cross to the contralateral side of the brain, so the left hemisphere sees the right half of the world and vice versa.

The lateral geniculate nucleus

After the optic nerve fibers have passed through the optic chiasm, they go into the brain proper. The ones discussed here terminate in the *lateral geniculate nucleus* (LGN; more properly the dorsal LGN, or LGN$_d$). The LGN is part of a larger section of the brain called the *thalamus*, which is tucked under the corpus callosum on both sides of the brain (it is labeled in the photograph on the CD). The ganglion cell axons bundled into the optic tract make synapses onto cells in the LGN.

A cross-section of the LGN of a monkey is shown in Fig. 7.3, where you can see it has six distinct

Box 7.1 Damage in the pathways from eye to brain

The division of visual fibers going to the brain is graphically demonstrated by the visual deficits produced when different parts of this pathway are damaged by strokes, tumors, or injuries. Tests of where in the visual field a patient cannot detect stimuli can be accurate indicators of where the damage (called a *lesion*) can be found.

Not surprisingly, if one of the optic nerves is destroyed, vision from that eye is completely lost. Loss of vision affecting only one of the eyes must be near (or in) that eye.

Pressure on the optic chiasm can lead to *bitemporal hemianopia*, in which each eye loses the vision on its own side while the main central portion remains unaffected.

This is a result of damage to the crossing (nasal) fibers of the chiasm. This may seem rather fanciful, but it is exactly the deficit that occurs when there is a tumor of the pituitary gland, which is located just beneath the chiasm. As the tumor expands, it compresses the center of the chiasm, damaging the crossing fibers.

Damage higher in the pathway (optic tract, lateral geniculate, or optic radiation) causes *homonymous hemianopia*, in which there are blanks (also called *scotomas*) in the visual field. The defects are essentially the same in both eyes, since by this time fibers serving the same visual area travel close together.

Fig. 7.3 Cross-section of the right LGN of an adult monkey. The preparation was stained with a chemical called cresyl violet to make cell bodies appear dark in the photograph. Arrows point to the six layers. The heavy gray arrow represents the sample electrode track discussed in the text. From Hubel, D. H. and T. N. Wiesel (1977) Functional architecture of macaque monkey visual cortex. *Proc. R. Soc. Lond. Ser. B.* 198: 1–59. Reprinted by permission.

layers. An odd feature of the LGN is that optic nerve fibers from the two eyes remain segregated at this level. Cells in layers 2,3, and 5 of the LGN receive their inputs from the ipsilateral eye—that is, from the eye on the same side as that LGN. Layers 1, 4, and 6 receive input from the contralateral eye. Even though the LGN receives inputs from both eyes, the information from the two eyes does not get combined.

Within any one layer of the LGN there is a topographic representation of the world; that is, the visual field is mapped onto the surface of the LGN, so that neighboring LGN cells have receptive fields that are nearby in the visual world. The central or foveal regions of the retina project onto a relatively large part of the LGN, so that the topographic representation is distorted to give the central part of the retina more space than the peripheral regions. The heavy representation of cen-

tral regions reflects the fact that this part of the retina has a higher concentration of both receptors and ganglion cells, and is specialized for high-acuity vision. Since the projection on the retina is relatively undistorted, there is a high density of cells in the central region, where the most information must be obtained. In the LGN, the cell density is approximately uniform, so the volume serving the central region must be larger to accommodate the larger number of cells.

The topographic representations of the visual field from the two eyes are in register, but as an electrode makes a vertical penetration through the LGN (as is indicated in Fig. 7.3 by the dark arrow), cells from one eye are encountered, followed by cells driven by the other eye as one passes to the next layer. Still, the receptive fields of the cells driven by different eyes are affected by stimuli in the same location in the visual field (Hubel &

Wiesel, 1961; Wiesel & Hubel, 1966). The fact that cells in different layers are in register with each other provides an opportunity for interactions between layers; in fact, such binocular interactions have been reported (Sanderson, *et al.*, 1971; Schroeder *et al.*, 1990).

There are two types of cells in the LGN: *principal* cells (also called *relay* cells) and *interneurons* (Burke & Sefton, 1966). The axons of interneurons remain within the LGN itself and provide a system for further processing at this level. Principal cell axons, however, leave the LGN and course outward to the cortex in a diffuse spray called the *optic radiation*

(see Fig. 7.2). The receptive field properties of principal cells and interneurons are similar (Dubin & Cleland, 1977).

Responses of LGN neurons

In general, the responses of LGN cells closely resemble the responses of retinal ganglion cells. The majority of cells recorded from LGN have concentric center/surround receptive field mechanisms; the major difference between these and retinal ganglion cells is that the surrounds of LGN neurons are somewhat stronger than those of ganglion

---

Box 7.2 Who needs an LGN?

The LGN is something of a puzzle. It sits in the visual pathway, taking up a chunk of valuable brain real estate, interposing an extra synapse, and adding noise to the visual signal (Levine & Troy, 1986; Levine *et al.*, 1996). Yet it seems to do relatively little. (Remind you of anyone you know?) True, there is added lateral antagonism, and some temporal sharpening. It also exaggerates the difference between the X- and Y-cells in their sensitivities to motion (Frishman *et al.*, 1983), but this effect is so slight that it can be entirely negated by choice of stimuli (Cleland & Lee, 1985).

The increased variability of LGN firing is somewhat curious. The cells of the LGN seem to have two distinct modes of firing: in the 'sustained' or 'transfer' mode, the LGN discharges are much like those of the retinal ganglion cells, although somewhat more variable (McCormick & Feeser, 1990). In this mode, visual information is relatively faithfully transmitted to the cortex. The other mode, which occurs when the LGN cells are hyperpolarized by inputs from the brainstem, is phasic and 'bursty' or oscillatory. This state, which occurs during sleep, is poor for relaying information but produces a burst of impulses to provide a 'wake-up' signal if something important happens (Lu *et al.*, 1992, 1993).

A possible clue as to why so much brain volume is devoted to this structure is that the LGN receives a large share of its input (more than half) from parts of the brain other than the retina (Singer, 1977). These inputs come from the brainstem (pons, medulla, and tectum), other parts of the thalamus, and from the cortex to which the LGN projects.

The brainstem inputs may 'turn off' the visual signal during eye movements, so you do not see the world jump when you move your eyes (Noda, 1975). You can demonstrate this effect, called *saccadic suppression*, by looking at yourself in a mirror. Look at your left eye; now look at your right eye. You know you moved your eyes, but did you *see* them move? Perhaps only some cells must be silenced; indeed, it appears that the suppression occurs only for those cells in the *magnocellular* division, which will be discussed in the next section (Burr *et al.*, 1994; Burr & Morrone, 1996).

A similar suppression occurs during eye blinks (Hari *et al.*, 1994). You can observe this effect with the demonstration 'Blink suppression' associated with this chapter on the CD. The computer screen will have an annoying flicker as it darkens briefly on a regular basis. If you time your eye blinks so they coincide with the screen darkening (the cue beep can help you), the darkening will be almost unnoticeable. There is also suppression of the inputs from one eye when the two have inconsistent images, as discussed in Box 11.6, p242 (Wang, *et al.*, 1994).

The inputs from the cortex represent a feedback, like that in the retina. This feedback may affect the properties of LGN cells themselves. For example, cooling the cortex (which temporarily disables it) weakens the surrounds of LGN cell receptive fields (McClurkin & Marrocco, 1984). This feedback loop may play a more important role in determining cortical cell properties (Martin, 1988a; Cudeiro & Sillito, 1996; Murphy & Sillito, 1996).

cells (Hubel & Wiesel, 1961). The result of this increased surround strength is to make the responses of LGN cells to diffuse illumination weaker than the responses of ganglion cells to similar stimuli. The increase in lateral antagonism over that shown by retinal ganglion cells is very slight, however (Kaplan *et al.*, 1979).

LGN cells also show a weak increase in the preference for stimuli changing in time (So & Shapley, 1981; Hamamoto *et al.*, 1994). There is also some weak orientation tuning (this is a major property in the visual cortex, as you will see in the sections that follow) in about one-third of the cells (Thompson *et al.*, 1994 a,b). Thus, the processes that you saw in retina acting to make cells more specific to particular stimuli seem to act again in the LGN. But the effect is slight, and LGN cells are barely discriminable in their responses from their retinal ganglion cell counterparts. In fact, it is most common for a cell in the LGN to receive its excitatory drive from a single retinal ganglion cell (Cleland & Lee, 1985). <u>BOX 7.2</u>

The distinction between X- and Y-cells is maintained at the level of the LGN; both have been found in the LGN of cats (Cleland *et al.*, 1971; Shapley & Hochstein, 1975) and monkeys (Dreher *et al.*, 1976; Sherman *et al.*, 1976). Not surprisingly, cells that have Y-like properties in the LGN receive their synaptic inputs from retinal Y-cells, with LGN X-cells receiving input from retinal X-cells (Stone &

Hoffmann, 1971; Fukada & Saito, 1972; Cleland & Lee, 1985).

The parvocellular and magnocellular divisions

The two eyes are segregated into separate layers in the LGN, but why are there *six* layers? There is an important further subdivision in the brains of primates (including monkeys, apes, and humans), which you may be able to discern in Fig. 7.3. Look closely at the two deep (ventral) layers (1 and 2), and you will see they are 'grainier' looking than layers 3–6. That is because the cells in layers 1 and 2 are larger; the cells in layers 3–6 are smaller and more numerous. Layers 1 and 2 are grouped under the label *magnocellular* (magno for 'large'), and layers 3–6 under *parvocellular* (parvo for 'small').

There are important differences between the properties of cells in the parvocellular and magnocellular layers (Table 7.1). Given the close link between ganglion cells and LGN cells, there must also be comparable differences between the ganglion cells projecting to those layers, and that is also true (Leventhal *et al.*, 1981).

Comparison of the properties of parvocellular and magnocellular cells (Table 7.1) with Table 5.1 (p. 92) suggests that these cells are homologous with the X- and Y-cells of the cat. But there is still controversy over whether this is really the case.

Table 7.1   Properties of parvocellular and magnocellular cells in the LGN

	Parvocellular	Magnocellular
Retinal input	Type B (or P)	Type A (or M)
Spatial summation	Linear	M_x linear, M_y non-linear
Field size	Small	M_x medium, M_y larger
Response timing	Sustained	More transient
Layers in LGN	3, 4, 5, 6	1, 2
Axon conduction velocity	Slow	Faster
Sensitivity to contrast	Poor	Good, but saturates
Sensitivity to colour	Many cells	None
Projection to V1 (layers)	4A, 4Cβ	4Cα

Kaplan & Shapley (1982) pointed out that magnocellular cells could be either X-like or Y-like in their spatial summation, but the (very X-like) parvocellular cells are different from the magnocellular X-like cells in several ways (Benardete *et al.*, 1992). One particularly notable difference is that the parvocellular cells are the only ones sensitive to differences in color (see Chapter 14). Moreover, parvocellular cells are fairly insensitive to low contrasts, so only magnocellular cells can detect ghostly images. Figure 7.4 compares the responses of cells in the magnocellular and parvocellular systems to gratings of various contrasts. The parvocellular cells respond poorly, giving almost no response until the contrast is at least 25%. The magnocellular cells respond well at very low contrasts (under 10%), but soon saturate; there is little increase in response beyond 30% contrast. However, this difference in gain may be secondary

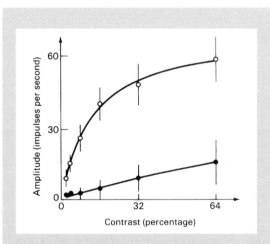

Fig. 7.4 Comparison of the responses of parvocellular and magnocellular cells to different contrast levels. The figure shows the mean of eight magnocellular cells (*open circles*) and 28 parvocellular cells (*solid circles*). From Kaplan, E. and R. M. Shapley (1986) The primate retina contains two types of ganglion cells, with high and low contrast sensitivity. *Proc. Nat. Acad. Sci.* 83: 2755–2757. Reprinted by permission.

to the differences in receptive field sizes, much as the sustained-transient differences between X- and Y-cells could be attributed to their receptive field sizes (Croner & Kaplan, 1995).

Kaplan & Shapley proposed that the magnocellular cells include the X- and Y-cells of the cat, and parvocellular cells represent an additional system. Certainly, one would expect fewer color-sensitive cells in the cat, which is nearly color-blind. In any case, it appears that the magnocellular system does a considerable share of the visual task: it detects low-contrast stimuli of various sizes, and is probably more sensitive to motion. The parvocellular system is more sensitive to the finest details and to color, is not sensitive to faint patterns, but may be better at discriminating between contrasts (Shapley & Perry, 1986). As you will see shortly, the parvocellular and magnocellular cells project to different systems in the visual cortex. These two systems remain somewhat distinct in their further projections to higher cortical areas, although they intercommunicate at many levels. Many workers consider them the roots of parallel visual processing systems. These parallel systems occupy a large part of the discussion in Chapter 8.

While Kaplan & Shapley argued that the parvocellular system is a 'new invention' of the primate, with the older X- and Y-cell systems constituting the magnocellular system, the anatomy seems to indicate that parvo and magno are refinements of X and Y (but see Silveira & Perry, 1991). There are large ganglion cells, comparable to the α cells of cat (but referred to as **A** cells in order to avoid confounding what may really be a different type that just seems similar). These are relatively rare—about 10% of the ganglion cell population (Wässle & Boycott, 1991). Small, bushy cells reminiscent of the β cells (called **B** cells) are much more numerous—about 80% of the population (Wässle & Boycott, 1991), and project exclusively to the thalamus (Peichl, 1991). These two types project to the magnocellular and parvocellular layers of the LGN, respectively, and are therefore sometimes labeled **M** and **P** types, respectively, to indicate their magno and parvo destinations. Unfortunately, an older classification of

Box 7.3 Layers of the LGN

A division of the LGN into at least four layers accommodates the parvocellular and magnocellular systems (with one layer per eye in each). Why, then, are there four parvocellular layers? The answer is not certain, but it is possible that they allow correct registration of the images from the two eyes despite different image disparities, as discussed in Chapter 11 (McIlwain, 1995). Alternatively, they may represent a further subdivision into the ON-center and OFF-center systems you saw in the retina in Chapter 5 (Wilson *et al.*, 1996). This division is clear in at least one mammal, the ferret (Zahs & Stryker, 1988; Roe *et al.*, 1989), and seems to occur in the macaque monkey as well

(Schiller & Malpeli, 1978; Michael, 1988). There are hints of a similar subdivision *within* each layer in the cat LGN (Bowling & Wieniawa-Narkiewicz, 1986; Thurlow *et al.*, 1993), which may correspond to the magnocellular layers of the monkey (Shapley & Perry, 1986). This could explain why there are not also four magnocellular layers.

But wait! There are some extra layers that are slipped between these six. These are called the *interlaminar* layers (literally, the 'between layers' layers) or *koniocellular* layers, and seem to be the destination of the W-cells that send axons to the LGN (Lachica & Casagrande, 1993).

ganglion cells used the same two letters to abbreviate a shape distinction between large 'parasol' cells and smaller 'midget' cells—thus naming 'p' the larger (M-cell) and 'm' the smaller (P-cell). With 26 letters to choose among, retinal anatomists and physiologists managed to choose the same pair for opposite meanings! BOX 7.3

Visual area 1 (V1)

The principal cells of the LGN send their axons to V1 (on the same side of the brain). Figure 7.5 shows a cross-section through the visual cortex of

Box 7.4 Layers of the primary visual cortex

The layering of V1 naturally represents a segregation of function, and we are beginning to understand some of the differences among layers. As noted, layer 4 is mainly an input layer, receiving information from the LGN. An exception, unique in sensory cortex, is that the middle sublayer of layer 4 (called layer 4B) apparently does not receive direct LGN input, and projects to other areas of cortex forward of V1 (Tootell *et al.*, 1988a). It is because of the striped appearance of this part of cortex that V1 is also called striate cortex; this area can be easily distinguished from the other two visual areas in occipital cortex, which lack some of the striations seen in Fig. 7.5.

Layers 2 and 3, above layer 4, project to the next higher visual area, V2. The deeper layers of V1 project to lower centers in the brain (Gilbert, 1983). Layer 5 projects to the superior colliculus (see Box 7.5), while layer 6 provides the projection back to the LGN.

There is also a stylized interconnection among the layers. The magnocellular input arrives near the middle of layer 4; actually, it is near the top of the lowest sublayer,

called layer 4Cα. This layer projects directly above itself, to layer 4B, which is the unusual part of layer 4 that projects out of V1. It also has a weak projection within V1 in layers 2 and 3, into special regions called 'blobs', which you will learn about shortly. The magnocellular input also projects strongly into layer 6 (Tootell *et al.*, 1988b).

The parvocellular inputs go to the lowest part of layer 4, called layer 4Cβ. Some also go to the uppermost part of layer 4, called layer 4A, although this may not be true in humans (DeBruyn *et al.*, 1993). These layers project strongly to layers 2 and 3, and from there to 5 and 6 (Gilbert, 1983).

There is considerable interchange of information among the layers, with most of the projections being radially oriented (that is, cells communicate mainly with those directly above or below them). There is also lateral intercommunication, with interconnections being made among specific groups of cells in nearby cortex (Gilbert & Wiesel, 1985; Eysel *et al.*, 1988; Komatsu *et al.*, 1988; Ts'o & Gilbert, 1988).

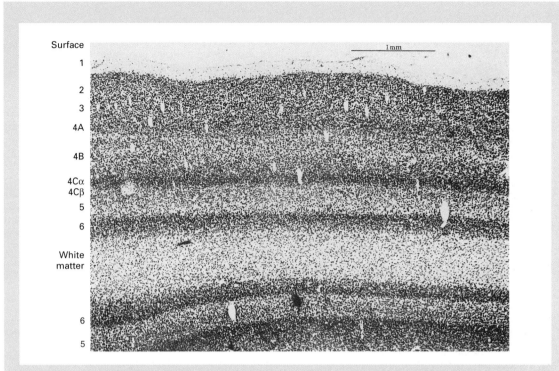

Fig. 7.5 Cross-section of a monkey striate cortex, stained with cresyl violet. The cortical layers are marked along the left of the figure. From Hubel and Wiesel (1977). Reprinted by permission. For the general orientation of this section, see Fig. 8.2(b)

a monkey brain that has been stained to show cell bodies (Hubel & Wiesel, 1977). The cells are arranged in layers that are somewhat less distinct than those found in the retina and LGN. Axons of lateral geniculate principal neurons terminate in layer 4 of the cortex. The magnocellular cell axons go near the middle of layer 4, while the parvocellular cell axons terminate above and below them, at the edges of layer 4. BOX 7.4

As in the LGN, the surface of the visual cortex is organized so that the receptive fields of cortical cells create a topographic map of the visual world. This is called a *retinotopic map*. Not surprisingly, much more cortical area is devoted to the central or foveal regions of the visual field; in fact, this magnification of foveal regions is even more extreme than that seen in the LGN (Daniel &

Whitteridge, 1961; Hubel & Wiesel, 1974b), although it is consistent with the densities of ganglion cells in the retina (Wässle *et al.*, 1990). Unlike the LGN, however, the map on the cortex is repeated several times; the different visual areas in occipital cortex all have separate representations of the visual world mapped onto them. This multiple topographic representation in the several areas probably reflects the fact that each area is performing different processing tasks, all of which require knowledge of the location of a stimulus within the visual field. BOX 7.5

Blindsight

Box 7.5 indicates that while the main pathway for vision is through V1, some function remains even

Box 7.5 Other visual pathways

The only visual pathway considered in this book is the *geniculostriate* pathway (from retina, to lateral geniculate, to striate cortex), but there are a number of other places in the brain that receive direct inputs from retinal ganglion cells. They include other parts of the thalamus, and parts of the hypothalamus and brainstem. The importance of these areas is shown by the fact that removal of the striate cortex in non-primates does not lead to complete blindness (Van Essen, 1979). In humans and monkeys, its removal does cause blindness, although, as you will learn in this section, some very limited visual function remains (Richards, 1973; Mohler & Wurtz, 1977; Van Essen, 1979; Solomon *et al.*, 1981; Cowey, 1996).

One area of the brainstem that has received considerable attention is the *superior colliculus* (or *visual tectum*), located on the rear part of the brainstem just under the cerebellum (see Fig 7.1 and 7.2; it is also labeled on the photographs on the CD). Cells in the outermost layers of the superior colliculus receive branches of ganglion cell axons, in particular from Y-cells and W-cells (Rodieck, 1979), but *not* from X-cells (Fukuda & Stone, 1974). In lower animals, cells in the superior colliculus are motion- and direction-selective (Berman & Cynader, 1972; Michael, 1972; Chalupa & Rhoades, 1977), although this does not appear to be the case in primates (Updyke, 1974; Marrocco & Li, 1977). Cells deeper in the superior colliculus also respond to inputs from other sense modalities (Bisti *et al.*, 1974; Stein *et al.*, 1975; Chalupa & Rhoades, 1977).

Given all of this, plus the fact that the superior colliculus is located near the part of the brainstem responsible for eye movements, it is generally believed that the superior colliculus plays an important role in orienting behavior and visual tracking of a target (Wallace *et al.*, 1993). In fact, cells in the monkey's tectum have been shown to be more responsive to a moving spot of light when the monkey is awake and actively following the spot with his eyes than when he is not (Wurtz & Mohler, 1976). Similarly, cells in the superior colliculus of monkeys have been found to discharge action potentials immediately before the monkey's eyes move (Wurtz & Goldberg, 1971). Its removal causes a behavioral deficit in visual tracking by the cat (Norton, 1974) and the hamster (Schneider, 1969). Superior colliculus activity seems directly related to the localization of the target of saccadic movements (Sparks & Porter, 1983). This area, therefore, seems to coordinate eye movements and visual information. It plays a role in the localization of objects in the visual world, but pattern analysis seems to be performed by the geniculostriate system (Van Essen, 1979).

when this pathway is destroyed. This surviving visual capability in the presence of seemingly total blindness is called *blindsight*. It has been a topic of considerable interest (and controversy) for some time.

One difficulty in studying blindsight is that it is present only in a small number of people who have suffered damage to their visual cortex. Thus, our knowledge is based on specific cases, and they are cases in which the damage is not neatly defined. There is always a chance that whatever caused the damage to V1 also affected other parts of the brain. There is also a possibility that the damage to V1 is not quite complete, and there may be spared 'islands' of functioning cortex within the 'blind' area (Fendrich *et al.*, 1992).

Vision without V1 seemingly must be due to direct projections to other parts of the cortex, or in-

direct projections from the brainstem. There are such projections. Higher cortical areas in monkey can respond (though not with the normal precision) in the complete absence of V1 (Girard *et al.*, 1992).

The ability to perform visual tasks in the absence of conscious perception leads to a notion that will be explored in the next chapter: that conscious vision is only a part of the visual system's task, and different parts of the visual system participate in different tasks. For example, subjects who show *neglect* ignore visual information from one side of the world, but may still be able to react to visual stimuli on that side; this is less severe than blindsight despite its similar appearance (Berti & Rizzolatti, 1992). Perhaps more like blindsight, Goodale *et al.* (1991) reported a woman who lost the ability to see the form and shape of objects due to damage from carbon monoxide poisoning. When they showed her a slit oriented at various angles, she was unable to say in which direction it was leaning (although she had normal speech), or choose a line parallel to it. She would even confuse vertical with horizontal. But when they asked her to pick up a card and put it into the slit (like putting a credit card into an ATM), she did so just about as quickly and smoothly as a normal person. Her conscious self was unaware of the orientation of the slit, but her brain still could guide her hand correctly.

This suggests that she has separate conscious perception and motor control systems. Is this true in normals? The answer seems to be 'yes'. Figure 7.6 shows an illusion of size (you will see other size illusions in Chapter 12). The central circles in each part of the figure are the same size, but the one surrounded by small circles appears larger than the one surrounded by large circles. To make them appear the same, you could make the circle surrounded by large circles physically larger. But if the center circles are real disks on a table, and you are asked to pick them up, as you reach toward them you spread your thumb and forefinger the correct amounts for their *actual* sizes, even though you are convinced of their illusory sizes (Aglioti *et al.*, 1995). The possible substrates for these separate pathways will be discussed in Chapter 8.

Properties of cells in visual cortex

While properties of LGN neurons remain similar to those exhibited by retinal ganglion cells, cells in the visual cortex have quite different response characteristics. As with the more peripheral cells, cortical cells respond to stimulation only within a restricted region of the visual field, although in general their receptive fields are larger than those of ganglion or LGN cells. These receptive fields are 'locked' to retinal locations, moving in the visual world as the eyes move (Gur & Snodderly, 1997). After all, there is a retinotopic map on the surface of the cortex.

Within their receptive fields, however, most cortical cells will not respond to presentations of diffuse-light stimuli, but require instead patterns of specific shapes and orientations. Responses were first recorded from single cells in the cat visual cortex by Hubel & Wiesel (1959, 1962, 1965a), who found that most cells could be placed in one of the categories that they named *simple* and *complex*. This classification scheme also applied to monkey cortical cells (Hubel & Wiesel, 1968). In the sections that follow, you will read about the different categories of cortical neuron that have been described. You will find it much easier to appreciate the response properties that differentiate among them if you 'follow along' with the Chapter 7

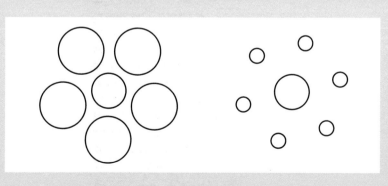

Fig. 7.6 The Titchener size illusion. The central circles in each half of the figure are the same size; the surrounding circles make them appear different.

'Cortical cell responses' demonstration on the CD accompanying this book.

Simple cells As their name implies, simple cells have receptive fields that are, well, simple. An example of a simple cell receptive field is shown in Fig. 7.7. While this cell has antagonistic receptive field mechanisms similar to those of the ganglion cell center and surround, the areas are not circularly symmetric or concentric with each other. There is a long thin area in the central portion of the field in which onset of a small spot of light evokes a modest excitatory response (marked by the '+' in Fig. 7.7c), while stimulation of either of the two antagonistic flanks that surround this central region produces an OFF response (marked '−' in Fig. 7.7c).

Although this simple cell may respond weakly to the presentation of small spots of light, it is far more sensitive to the presence of a bar-shaped stimulus appropriately oriented within its receptive field. Figure 7.8(b) shows responses to bars of light whose widths correspond to that of the central region of the receptive field. Horizontally placed bars evoke no response whatsoever from this cell, but presentation of a vertical bar, the extent of which corresponds to the central area of the receptive field, results in a vigorous response. This selectivity is exactly what would be expected given the shape of the receptive field of this cell, as the vertical bar covers the entire excitatory area but does not intrude on the antagonistic flanks. Thus, simple cells are selectively sensitive to stimuli of particular orientation and position. Note, however, that while the cell in Fig. 7.7 is sensitive to the orientation and width of the bar stimulus, it does not particularly care about the length; given a bar that is long enough to cover

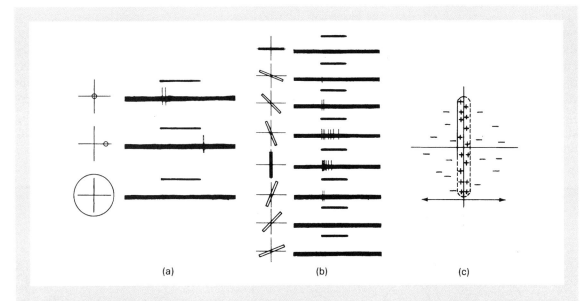

(a)   (b)   (c)

Fig. 7.7 Responses of a simple cell in the visual cortex of the cat, and the receptive field map derived from those responses. (a), (b) Responses to presentations of small spots and bar stimuli, respectively. The bar over each response trace denotes when the stimulus was present, and the stimulus position is shown at the left of each trace. (c) Map of the receptive field, with '+' denoting excitatory areas and '−' denoting inhibitory areas. From Hubel, D. H. and T. N. Wiesel (1959) Receptive fields of single neurones in the cat's striate cortex. *J. Physiol.* 148: 574–591. Reprinted by permission.

the excitatory portion of the receptive field, additional length is irrelevant.

Not all simple cells have receptive fields that look like the receptive field in Fig. 7.7. Figure 7.8 shows the receptive fields of five other simple cells; clearly there is quite a bit of variability. The central region of the receptive field may be either excitatory or inhibitory, and the preferred orientation can be at any angle (although in this figure all the cells have the same orientation preference). In addition, as is shown in Figs 7.8 (c) and (e), the antagonistic flanks may not be symmetric about the central region of the receptive field; in fact, the receptive field displayed in Fig. 7.8(e) has only one inhibitory area and one excitatory area that are adjacent to each other.

What all of these cells have in common is that their properties can be determined by mapping their receptive fields with stationary stimuli (at least in principle). For example, the cell in Fig. 7.8(a) fires in response to the onset of a small spot presented anywhere within the diagonal central region, and fires in response to the offset of a spot that is flashed in either of the antagonistic flanks. By moving such a spot throughout the receptive field of this cell, you could determine the extent of both the central region and the flanks; with this information, the orientation, placement, and width of a bar that will evoke the maximum response from this cell could be determined. As you will see, this is a property not shared by complex cells.

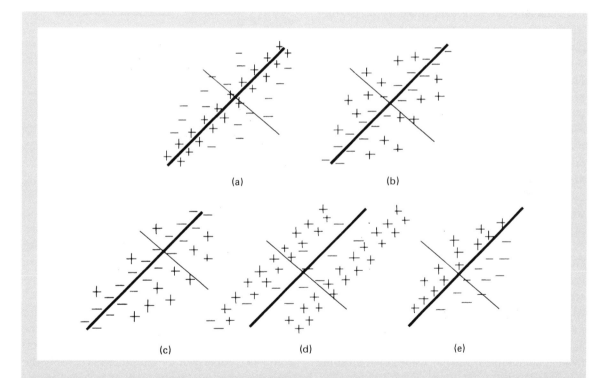

Fig. 7.8 Receptive field maps of five different simple cells in the visual cortex of the cat. A '+' denotes excitatory areas, and '–' indicates inhibitory areas. The solid lines are parallel to the preferred stimulus orientation of each cell. From Hubel, D. H. and T. N. Wiesel (1962) Receptive fields, binocular interaction and functional architecture in the cat's visual cortex. *J. Physiol.* 160: 106–114. Reprinted by permission.

Complex cells Simple cells give a vigorous response to onset of a bar of light only if the bar is of the correct size, orientation, and position within its receptive field (the responses are usually opposite for a bar darker than the rest of the field). Complex cells generally share the same type of requirements for orientation and size of the stimulus, but are less restrictive as to its position. Typically, they do not care whether the bar is light or dark. While simple cells have fairly distinct excitatory and inhibitory regions within their receptive fields, complex cells do not; in fact, complex cells usually give no responses at all when they are stimulated with small flashing spots.

Figure 7.9 shows the responses of a complex cell to bars of various sizes at various positions within its receptive field. Like a simple cell, this cell is selectively sensitive to a bar stimulus of a certain width and orientation; however, the bar can be placed anywhere within the receptive field of the cell without affecting the magnitude of response. Thus, the response of a complex cell signals the presence of a stimulus of a certain orientation, without reference to the specific position.

In addition, complex cells are often selectively sensitive to movement of the stimulus in a specific direction. Complex cells may be specifically tuned for different ocular disparities (differences between the images in the two eyes; see Chapter 11), which corresponds to different distances in front of the eyes (Ohzawa *et al.*, 1996). __BOX 7.6__

End-stopped cells Some cells also select for optimal length of a stimulus bar, in addition to being sensitive to its orientation and width. For example, while the optimal stimulus for a complex cell might be a bar of some particular width oriented at 45° from the vertical, the cell might only respond to such a stimulus if the bar were less than some particular length.

When Hubel & Wiesel (1965a) discovered cells with this property, they considered them a third class of cortical neurons, which they called *hypercomplex* cells. But there is some doubt as to whether they form a truly separable group. Dreher (1972)

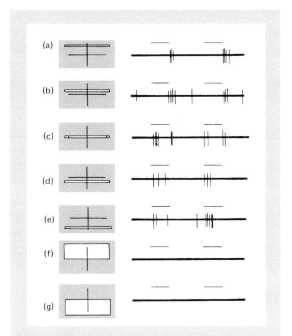

Fig. 7.9 Responses of a complex cell in the visual cortex of the cat. Stimulus position is shown to the left of each response; the stimulus is shown by an open rectangle, with the position of the receptive field referenced by the crossed lines. The bar over the response shows when the stimulus was present. From Hubel and Wiesel (1962). Reprinted by permission.

found that cat hypercomplex cells could be divided into subgroups according to whether the receptive field properties resembled simple or complex cells. For either subgroup, the feature that distinguished a cell as hypercomplex was its specificity for stimulus length. Workers now generally prefer to refer to cells as simple or complex, and add the label *end-stopped* for those that have the 'hypercomplex' property of length preference. (Only the complex type end-stopped cell is included in the demonstration on the CD.)

Figure 7.10 shows the responses of an end-stopped cell to its preferred stimulus, which is an edge moving through its receptive field in a particular direction. Unlike a complex cell, the extent of

Box 7.6 The variety of complex cells

The definition of complex cells is not as precise as could be hoped, and there are sometimes disagreements between groups of workers about whether the categorizations made by one group are correct. What makes a cell 'complex' is that its responses are in some way independent of a stimulus feature that logically should make a difference. Thus, it should matter where a bar is placed, given that the cell does not simply add all light indiscriminately (that is, it does not respond to a wider bar, or one of the 'wrong' orientation). It should matter whether it is a black bar on a gray field or a white bar on a gray field, but for many complex cells, the responses are the same for either contrast. On the other hand, it should not matter (in a symmetric field) whether the bar sweeps from left to right or from right to left, but many complex cells are direction-selective. Of course, not all complex cells display all of these anomalies. It is even possible for a cell to be considered complex that does not care about stimulus orientation (DeValois *et al.*, 1982). The original explorations of cortical cells emphasized orientation, but researchers now realize that complex cells encode much more complex kinds of information about what is in their visual fields (Kjaer *et al.*, 1997).

Perhaps the most accurate statement of what makes a cell complex is that it is spatially non-linear. Most simple cells sum influences within their receptive fields in a linear fashion, similar to the responses of X-cells (Movshon *et al.*, 1978a; DeAngelis *et al.*, 1993; Jagadeesh *et al.*, 1994; Jagadeesh *et al.*, 1997). Of course, simple cells are not completely linear—nothing in biology is completely linear. Simple cells have the usual non-linearities of converting light to firing rate (Albrecht & Geisler, 1991; Reid *et al.*, 1991; Jacobson *et al.*, 1993). But complex cells are strongly non-linear in the same sense as Y-cells (Movshon *et al.*, 1978b). Given this, one might consider the Y-cells as low-level complex cells.

That does not mean, however, that Y-cells must be the sole inputs to complex cells, although that suggestion has been proposed (Hoffmann & Stone, 1971; DeValois *et al.*, 1982). Alternatively, Heeger (1992) has noted that to model complex cells requires an interconnected network of cells, a model that cannot be simplified (Emerson *et al.*, 1992; Lehky *et al.*, 1992). As you will see (in Box 7.7) the question of how these cells are 'made' is further complicated by the variety of subtypes of complex cells.

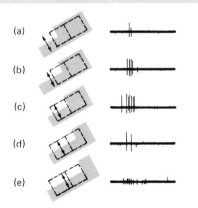

Fig. 7.10 Responses of an end-stopped (hypercomplex) cell in the visual cortex of the cat. Stimulus position is shown to the left of each response, with the receptive field sketched as a dashed rectangle. From Hubel, D. H. and T. N. Wiesel (1965a). Receptive fields and functional architecture in two non-striate visual areas (18 and 19) of the cat. *J. Neurophysiol.* 28: 229–289. Reprinted by permission.

Box 7.7 The wiring of cortical cells

How might the properties of the various cortical cells come about? Hubel & Wiesel (1962, 1965a) hypothesized that the three types of cells they identified (simple, complex, and hypercomplex) are hierarchically organized. In their view, simple cell properties can be explained by the convergence of a number of LGN fibers with their receptive fields aligned in a straight row. That is, the LGN cells that provide the direct input to a simple cell have receptive fields whose positions (on the retina) correspond to the central region of the simple cell field (see Fig. 7.11). Additional rows of LGN cells (of the opposite type) could be responsible for the antagonistic flanks. The flanks represent additional lateral antagonism, for they superimpose on the weak flanks that would be created by the aligned surrounds of the LGN fields. The lateral antagonism begun in the outer plexiform layer of the retina gets enhanced in the inner plexiform layer, enhanced again in the LGN, and enhanced further in the cortex.

Complex cells could be formed from ranks of simple cells of the same preferred orientation. The synaptic connections would have to be such that the simple cells could only excite the complex cell, not inhibit it. Thus, if any simple cell were active, the complex cell would fire, but a broader stimulus covering many of the simple cells would be ineffective because none of the simple cells would respond to a stimulus that extends into its antagonistic flanks (Hubel & Wiesel, 1962).

This is an attractive hypothesis, but it is apparently not quite right. There are extensive intracortical connections between layers, so many cortical cells do receive inputs from other cortical cells. But many cells receive only (or mainly) direct LGN input. Hoffmann & Stone (1971) showed that both simple and complex cells received direct input from the LGN, with simple cell input coming from X-

cells and complex cell input from Y-cells. Responses of cat cortical cells tend to reinforce the notion that simple and complex cells represent parallel processing systems and not a hierarchical one. Simple cells tend to prefer more slowly moving stimuli than do complex cells, so much so that stimuli moving at velocities preferred by complex cells may be virtually ineffective for most simple cells (Movshon, 1975; for a review, see Stone *et al.*, 1979).

Input from aligned rows of LGN cells can account for simple cell properties (Reid & Alonso, 1995, 1996), but how can complex cell properties be created if not by superposition of simple cells? Spitzer & Hochstein (1985) suggested a model in which a complex cell receives inputs directly from two rows of LGN cells. These are probably X-cells (for Y-cells are too rare to account for much of the input; see Lennie, 1980). The rows of LGN cells form *subunits*, which are combined non-linearly. The non-linearity is called rectification: it means the cells can only signal excitation, not inhibition. In effect, the rows of LGN cells are the simple cells of the Hubel & Wiesel hierarchical model. This is exactly the kind of model proposed for Y-cells (see Box 5.6, p. 90), which seem to have a large number of subunits that can only excite the cell (Cleland *et al.*, 1973; Hochstein & Shapley, 1976). A specific model for how this could occur has been presented by Mel *et al.* (1998). In their model, subunits are built of clusters of inputs on the complex cell dendrites. The synapses in a local cluster come from aligned LGN cells, much as simple cell fields are built by inputs from aligned LGN cells. Voltage-sensitive channels in the dendrites allow the subunits to behave as if they were separate neurons with rectifying thresholds and active propagation to the complex cell soma.

Different types of complex cells can be modeled by different combinations of two or more overlapping or non-overlapping subunits, with some also receiving inputs

→

Fig. 7.11 (Facing page) Hypothetical hierarchical scheme illustrating how receptive field properties of cells in the visual cortex could be built up from the receptive fields of more peripheral cells. In this conception, LGN cells feed into simple cells that are the inputs to complex cells. (a) LGN cells, with fields indicated to the left, combine to form the field of a simple cell (*right*). Three rows of LGN cells, with all cells in each row of the same type, provide the inputs. The profiles below the field maps show the relative amount of excitation or inhibition (as a function of position in the receptive field) for the cells above the profiles. Linear summation means both excitation and inhibitory influences are transmitted, and so can cancel. (b) Simple cells with a common orientation preference in the same general region combine to form a complex cell field. Some of the simple cells have an ON middle region, and some have an OFF middle region. Non-linear summation means each simple cell can only signal that it is excited but cannot provide an inhibitory signal to cancel the excitation from other simple cells.

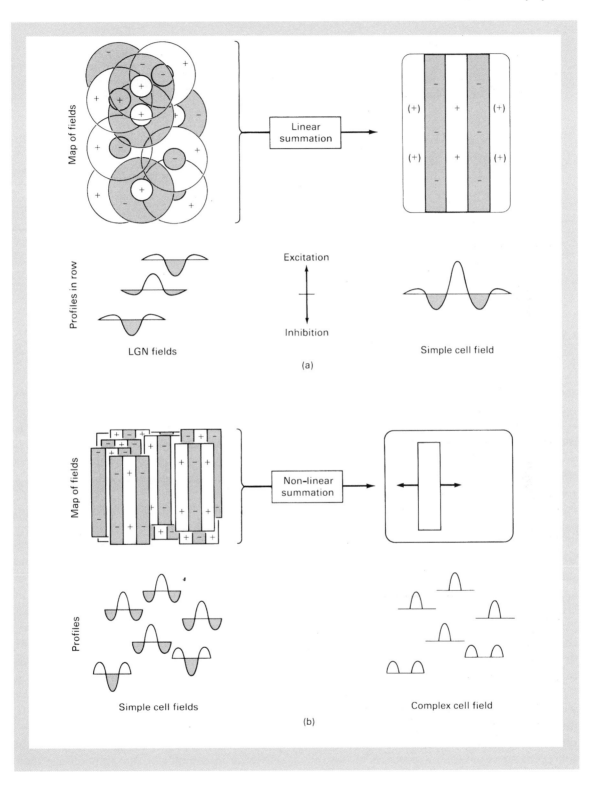

Map of fields

Profiles in row

Linear summation

Excitation

Inhibition

LGN fields

Simple cell field

(a)

Map of fields

Profiles

Non-linear summation

Simple cell fields

Complex cell field

(b)

(BOX 7.7 CONTINUED)

from other cortical cells, and some receiving all their inputs from other complex cells (Spitzer & Hochstein, 1985). The fact that some complex cells respond to both dark and light bars may be because they receive inputs from both ON and OFF cells (Heggelund, 1981; Tanaka, 1985).

Another mechanism that tunes the responses of cortical cells is antagonism, in this case inhibition between cortical cells. For example, the antagonistic flanks of the simple cell shown in Fig. 7.7 cause the cell to fire when a light in a flank is extinguished; this is presumably the OFF-SET response of the OFF-center LGN cells in that flank. But there is also inhibition during the presentation of the light in the flank, and this is probably due to inhibition from other simple cells in the same column (Ferster, 1988). Similarly, the orientation selectivity of cortical neurons is sharpened by inhibition from cells with similar preferred orientations (Hata et al., 1988; Bonds, 1989; Allison & Bonds, 1994; Crook et al., 1998). It is possible that orientation tuning is enhanced by cells with the same preferred orientation but slightly different optimum positions and by inhibition from cells with different preferred orientations (Ferster & Koch, 1987). Either of

these mechanisms can be disabled by drugs that affect inhibitory transmitters in the cortex (Sillito & Versiani, 1977; Sillito et al., 1985; Wörgötter & Eysel, 1991; Crook & Eysel, 1992; Sato et al., 1996; Crook et al., 1997).

Other models for complex cells depend upon the fact that the rich interconnections among layers of cortex can generate a complex network of cells. These models invoke both inhibition and excitation to generate the necessary properties (Lehky et al., 1992; Volgushev et al., 1993; Somers et al., 1995; Hammond & Kim, 1996; Sillito & Jones, 1996; Heeger et al., 1996; Stratford et al., 1996). It appears that orientation preference is fine-tuned by interactions among cells in various orientation columns, but the dependency is weak compared with the basic organization imposed by the inputs from the LGN (Toth et al., 1997).

---

the edge in the direction perpendicular to the direction of movement is a crucial variable; if the edge is made wider than the optimal size in this direction, or is moved only slightly from its optimal position, no response is produced.

It is attractive to consider cortical cells as either simple or complex, and either end-stopped or not end-stopped; however, more recent evidence indicates that this may not be valid. When properties of cortical cells in both cat and monkey were studied in detail, they were found to show a wide range of specificities to stimulus length, with no apparent break point that could be used to discriminate end-stopped from non end-stopped cells (Schiller et al., 1976a; Gilbert, 1977). It is possible, therefore, that length specificity is a receptive field property that is shared by most cortical cells to some degree. <u>BOX 7.7</u>

This discussion of receptive fields may have led you to think of the cortical wiring as fixed and immutable. In fact, there is now evidence that cortical receptive fields change according to the context of the visual stimuli, probably because of

feedback connections from 'higher' cortical areas (see Chapter 8). In addition, experience can change receptive field properties (Ohzawa et al., 1996; Frégnac et al., 1996a; Debanne et al., 1998). This is presumably a part of 'visual learning'—the process by which we learn to perceive (see Chapter 10).

Concentric cells   Orientation selectivity may seem to be the hallmark of cortical cells, a radical departure from the concentric, nearly circular, center/surround antagonism seen in the retina and LGN. When concentric cells were encountered in cortex, therefore, they were generally ignored in the belief that these were recordings from the ascending fibers of the LGN principal cells. However, as clusters of these cells were found in cortex (Michael, 1981), it was gradually conceded that this was still another class of cell in cortex (Hubel & Livingstone, 1983). Many of these cells seem to be specific for the color of a stimulus (Michael, 1981).

Binocular cells One property that many cortical cells have in common is that they receive their visual inputs from both eyes. This is in marked contrast to LGN cells, which only respond to visual stimuli presented to one eye or the other. Cells that receive input from both eyes are called *binocular* neurons; V1 is the first level in the visual system where the inputs from the two eyes combine. When the receptive field of a binocular cortical neuron is examined, it is found that the fields mapped from the two eyes almost always completely overlap. (A certain percentage of cells have non-identical receptive field locations; their function in the perception of depth will be discussed in Chapter 11.) This overlapping should not be surprising; if a single cell received inputs from two different areas in the visual field depending on which eye was being stimulated, it would be impossible to tell whether a response from that cell meant that a stimulus was in one location or the other.

Not only are the receptive field locations from the two eyes usually overlapped in a binocular cell, the particular response properties are also the same. Thus if a cortical simple cell responds best to a bar of light flashed at an angle of 30° from the horizontal when the right eye is stimulated, the optimal stimulus from the left eye is also a bar at 30°. If the same optimal stimulus is presented to both eyes simultaneously, the response of the cortical cell will be greater than if just one eye were stimulated. Binocular neurons are therefore most effectively activated by stimuli presented to both eyes.

Cortical cells and perception

Primary visual cortex contains a rich variety of cell types. How do these cell types relate to perception of the visual world? One approach has been to ask to what parts of a complex stimulus a particular cell might respond. For example, if you were presented with an equilateral triangle, most cells in the cortex would not respond. Only those cells whose receptive fields lie on the borders of the triangle would respond, and then only if their preferred orientation matched the orientation of that border. Simple cells require exact placement of the border; end-stopped cells would have to be appropriately near a corner.

Because the cells of the cortex respond best when specific patterns are present in their receptive fields, they have been described as *feature detectors*. The idea is that feature detectors are each abstracting the particular aspect of the pattern to which they are specific. In the triangle example, the features were the borders of the triangle (which had already been emphasized by the process of lateral antagonism in the retina), and the three corners. The simple and complex cells that detected the sides of the triangle were 'straight line at 60°' detectors; the base was detected by 'horizontal line' detectors. The corners would be detected by end-stopped cells. The significant features are abstracted by detectors; an appropriate constellation of active cells would then be the effective stimulus for a 'triangle detector' higher in the processing hierarchy. This idea is developed further in Chapter 10.

It makes intuitive sense for the perception of a triangle to depend on recognition of the three sides and angles, but there are problems when the feature detector model is extended. A triangle detector is a cell that fires when a correct pattern of cells fire; is there then an 'hourglass detector' that fires when the two appropriate triangle detectors are active? Is there a 'jack-o-lantern detector' sensitive to the output of three triangle detectors and a 'pumpkin detector'? Is there a cell somewhere that recognizes 'mother standing at the door'? These higher-order detectors would have to have 'learned' their stimuli through experience; that is not a problem for a cortical cell (Katz & Callaway, 1992; Frégnac *et al.*, 1996a, b), but how many cells are there available to become specific detectors? Each percept would have to be embodied by a constellation of cells, or the death of a single neuron (which happens all the time) would cause the loss of ability to recognize a particular thing.

There is a danger in describing cortical cells as feature detectors; it makes you forget that each cell responds to a variety of stimuli. A cortical cell could be defined as a '55° tilted line detector' because when you tested it with lines of various orientations, it responded best (or exclusively) if the line was oriented at 55°. Unless you also tested for it, you cannot know that the cell would not prefer a *double* line, or a checkerboard, or a wavy line, or ... The nature of the detector depends on the way it was identified experimentally. (A noted neurophysiologist illustrated this point in a lecture by suggesting that if he were to pour his glass of water over the head of a person in the first row, the person would probably let out a scream; he asked if that means we should define this wet individual as a 'water detector'.)

plexiform layer of the retina feeds to the outer layer via interplexiform cells; the cortex (layer 6) projects back to the LGN. Similarly, higher visual areas project to V1. Cooling V2 (which effectively disables it) has subtle but potentially important effects on V1 (Sandell & Schiller, 1982). It is not fair to consider responses of V1 as if they independently told the whole story.

If you think of the entire network of cells in all layers of the visual system as a whole, you can appreciate that one particular cell would not have a single, immutable function. It would participate in many visual tasks, in ways that might not be well related. Indeed, there are properties of even a simple network of cells that are not 'given' by the individual cells; these are called *emergent properties* (Sejnowski *et al.*, 1988). You will see how

---

Box 7.8 What is a neuron 'saying'?

There is another danger in identifying cells by their responses: there may be more to a response than the number of action potentials a cell fires. The particular temporal pattern with which the cell responds may carry more information than the firing rate itself (see Richmond & Optican, 1990; Gawne *et al.*, 1991). The relative timing of spikes among neurons is being recognized as an important parameter in determining their effectiveness (Liu *et al.*, 1992;

Alonso *et al.*, 1996; Usrey *et al.*, 1998). Cells 'reporting' different aspects of the same stimulus object seem to fire in synchrony (Eckhorn & Obermueller, 1993; Funke & Wörgötter, 1997) with systems of oscillations across areas of cortex (Krüger & Becker, 1991; Engel *et al.*, 1992). You will see these ideas about how different aspects of the same stimulus may be associated to create a unified percept in Chapter 10.

Lines, edges, and corners are effective stimuli for cortical cells and are the kinds of features you intuitively expect the brain to extract. An alternative interpretation of the function of cortical cells is that they are 'spatial frequency analyzers', a concept you will study in Chapter 9. The spatial frequency notion will require some development to make it clear; for now, just be aware that there are alternatives to the feature-detection model.

There is still another possible interpretation of these cells' responses. Cortical cells do not act alone. Not only do they have neighbors, but they also interact with the 'higher' cells to which they project. You have seen several places in which there is feedback in the visual system: the inner

perception might be an emergent property of the nervous system in Chapter 10. <u>BOX 7.8</u>

Suggested readings

For those who want to know more about responses of cells in the visual cortex, probably the best thing to do is to read some of the original work. Hubel and Wiesel have written an extensive (and very readable) review of their work on monkey (*Proc. R. Soc. Lond. Ser. B.*, 198: 1–59; 1977); an earlier classic paper of theirs that also makes good reading is the

1962 paper on visual cells in cat cortex (*J. Physiol.*, 160: 106–154; also reprinted in many collections including *Perceptual processing: stimulus equivalence and pattern recognition* (P. C. Dodwell, ed., Appleton-Century Crofts, 1971).

A readable and up-to-date version may be found in *Eye, brain, and vision*, by D. H. Hubel (Scientific American Library, 1988). Hubel's collaborations with Torsten Wiesel laid the groundwork for much of what was discussed in this chapter (and the next), and resulted in their sharing a Nobel Prize. His book is even more relevant to the next chapter.

Actually, the best means to appreciate the way article cells respond and how they differ is to spend some time with the demonstration program for Chapter 7. If one picture is worth a thousand words, an interactive experience must be worth 10 000.

Chapter 8
Architecture of vision in the cortex

Iɴ Chapter 7, you learned that the information from the two retinas passes to the LGN and then to the primary visual cortex, V1. Cells in V1 seem to be selective for attributes of the stimulus, such as color, orientation, and direction of motion. You also saw that in addition to the X-type and Y-type, and ON-center and OFF-center cells of the retina, there are simple and complex cells of various types, and a subdivision into the parvocellular and magnocellular pathways. This chapter discusses how some of these attributes are sorted out in the cortex. You will learn about the anatomical arrangement in V1, and the projections into 'higher' cortex. You will see that the parvocellular and magnocellular pathways form parallel, but interdependent, streams in the visual system.

Functional architecture of the visual cortex

The visual cortex is a thin sheet of tissue on which a map of the visual world is imposed. Cortical cells, however, possess many other properties besides their receptive field location, such as optimal angle of orientation and extent of binocularity. To understand how the cortex performs its function of analyzing the visual world, scientists naturally asked how it organizes the visual information that its cells are designed to detect. In order to approach this question, Hubel & Wiesel (1962, 1968, 1974a, b) systematically investigated the organization of the cortex by recording from cell after cell and seeing how the properties of cells varied with their locations within the cortex.

Orientation columns

One property Hubel & Wiesel investigated was the optimal orientation of a visual stimulus. They made multiple electrode penetrations through the cortices of monkeys and cats, and determined the orientation specificity of each cell they encountered. The cells encountered in two electrode penetrations into V1 of cat cortex are shown in Fig. 8.1. The solid lines show the paths of the electrode, with the short lines that intersect them representing the optimal stimulus orientation for each cell. For the electrode track on the left in the figure, all of the cells in the upper part of the penetration had horizontal optimal orientations, with orientation gradually shifting to an angle of about 45°. It is not a random distribution; instead, cells with similar optimal orientations seem to be stacked one upon another.

This is a general finding; when an electrode penetration is made perpendicular to the surface of the cortex, all of the cells in that penetration

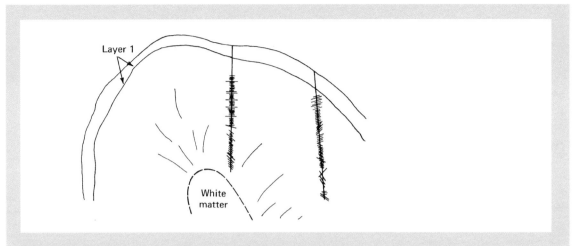

Fig. 8.1 Cross-section of cat visual cortex, showing the orientations of cells encountered during two electrode penetrations. Cells encountered during a given penetration tend to have similar preferred orientations. From Hubel, D. H. & T. N. Wiesel (1962) Receptive fields, binocular interaction and functional architecture in the cat's visual cortex. *J. Physiol.* 160: 106–154. Reprinted by permission.

show the same, or very similar, preferred stimulus orientation. The penetration shown in the right side of the figure illustrates what happens when the penetration is not perpendicular to the cortical surface; in this case, the electrode passes through regions of constant orientation, but there is a fairly systematic change in preferred orientation along the electrode track. The penetration shown in Fig. 8.2 is even more oblique; optimal orientation of the cells encountered is plotted versus electrode distance. Orientation changes smoothly for short distances, but there are also abrupt shifts in preferred orientation.

These data led Hubel & Wiesel to conclude that the cortex was organized into what they called *orientation columns*, within which all cells possessed the same optimal stimulus orientation. In a block of about 1 mm², all possible orientations are represented.

Ocular dominance columns

The preferred orientation of a visual stimulus is represented along the surface of the cortex; the re-sponses of cortical cells, however, vary along other dimensions as well. One dimension of interest is *ocular dominance*, the extent to which a cell responds to stimulation delivered to one eye or both. Some cortical cells in the cat are monocular; they respond only when one of the eyes is stimulated and are blind if that eye is closed. Most cells are binocular; they receive inputs from both eyes, so they respond (at least to some extent) if either eye is closed. However, even the binocular cells may favor one eye, so most cells can be assigned either a right- or a left-eye preference.

To examine ocular dominance, Hubel & Wiesel (1965b, 1968) went through the same procedure as when they found orientation columns; they made multiple electrode penetrations through the surface of the cortex, and the ocular dominance was determined for each cell encountered. They found that if the electrode track was perpendicular to the surface of the cortex, all of the cells recorded from a single penetration would be dominated by the same eye. Thus, the columns of cortex are specific for ocular dominance as well as orientation. **BOX 8.1**

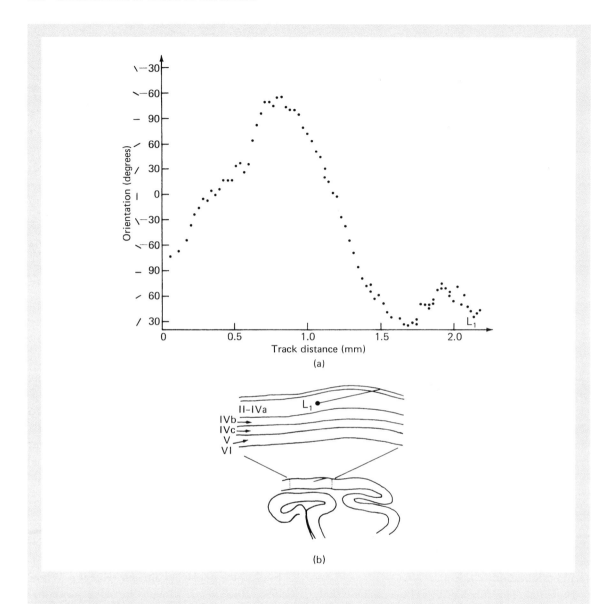

Fig. 8.2 (a) Graph of orientation versus electrode position for an electrode penetration that was nearly parallel to the surface of the cortex. (b) The actual track of the electrode during the penetration graphed in (a). From Hubel, D. H. and T. N. Wiesel (1974) Sequence regularity and geometry of orientation columns in the monkey striate cortex. *J. Comp. Neurol.* 158: 267–294. Reprinted by permission.

From Fig. 8.3(b), which shows the anatomical shapes of the ocular dominance columns, you can see that 'columns' is probably not the most appropriate term for the way ocular dominance is organized in the cortex. In fact, the cells seem to be arranged in slabs. There are clear strips of cells of similar ocular dominance that wend their way irregularly along the surface of the cortex. These

Box 8.1 Visualizing the columns in visual cortex

It is possible to show the existence of both orientation and ocular dominance columns by anatomical methods. A substance called 2-deoxyglucose (2-DG) accumulates selectively in regions where the cells are actively firing action potentials. Cell groups that have high concentrations of 2-DG can be treated so that they appear to be darker on a photographic plate than do regions where 2-DG has not accumulated (see Appendix). Hubel *et al.* (1978) injected a monkey with 2-DG, after which they stimulated both eyes with a field of unidirectional stripes. After 45 min of this stimulation, the brain was treated to show regions with high concentrations of 2-DG, so that cortical areas that were actively responding to the striped stimulus were darkly stained. Figure 8.3(a) shows a tangential section through the visual cortex from a monkey brain treated in the above manner. You can clearly see a pattern of darkly

stained patches that represent the orientation columns sensitive to the stimulus presented.

Hubel & Wiesel (1974a, 1977) used another anatomical technique to reveal the shapes of the ocular dominance columns. They injected into the vitreous humor of one eye a radioactive substance that is actively absorbed by the cell bodies of neurons. This substance gets absorbed by retinal ganglion cells and transported down their axons to the LGN, where it is taken up by LGN neurons and transported to the visual cortex. In the visual cortex of an animal treated in this manner, only those neurons that are functionally connected to the injected eye show the presence of radioactivity. Figure 8.3(b) shows a section of a monkey brain after this experiment; the pattern of ocular dominance columns is much clearer than that of the orientation columns shown in Fig. 8.3(a).

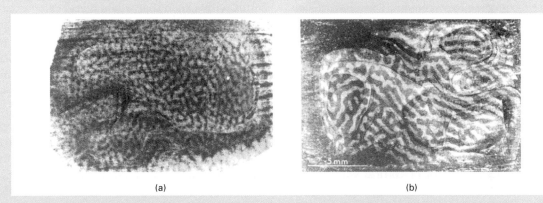

(a)   (b)

Fig. 8.3 (a) Pattern of orientation columns in monkey cortex, treated with 2-deoxyglucose. (b) Pattern of ocular dominance columns in the same region of cortex as in (a). Columns were made visible by radioactive proline injected into one eye and transported to the visual cortex. From Hubel, D. H., T. N. Wiesel and M. P. Stryker (1978) Anatomical demonstration of oriented columns in macaque monkey. *J. Comp. Neurol.* 177: 361–380. Reprinted by permission.

strips remain about equal in width throughout their extent. Although columns may not be the most accurate way to describe the organization of the cortex, it is convenient to continue to use that term here.

The surface of the cortex has at least three types of visual information represented on it. Not only is position in the visual world determined by cortical location, but the preferred orientation and level of

binocularity of a cell are also related to where it is in the cortex. At first, this may seem like a confusing way for the visual system to be set up, because as you move from one location of the cortex to another, you might be changing location of the visual field, preferred orientation, and binocularity all at the same time. If this is the case, you would think that all cortical cells having their receptive fields in a certain location would also only have one optimal stimulus orientation and one ocular dominance level. In fact, this problem does not arise, because of the arrangement of the cortex into what Hubel & Wiesel (1974a) called *hypercolumns*.

A hypercolumn is defined as a collection of either orientation or ocular dominance columns such that the collection includes one set of all possible orientations or ocular dominance levels. Therefore, an orientation hypercolumn is a region of cortex that includes orientation columns for all stimulus orientations, and an ocular dominance hypercolumn includes cells receiving principal input from one eye or the other. Hubel & Wiesel (1974a, 1977) found that the sizes of both types of hypercolumns were about the same throughout the cortex; a lateral movement of about 1 mm along the surface of the cortex is sufficient to traverse a complete hypercolumn. This distance corresponds well to the distance on the cortex an electrode must travel to change the receptive field locations of the cells encountered. Therefore, within a given 1 mm by 1 mm (by 2 mm thick) chunk of cortex, all the cells have approximately the same receptive field location, and a full range of preferred orientations and ocular dominance levels.

Notice that while all hypercolumns occupy about the same amount of cortical volume, the amount of visual space covered by each depends on the sizes of the receptive fields of the cells within the hypercolumn. In fact, the distance between the centers of the receptive fields represented by neighboring hypercolumns (that is, the difference in location of receptive fields of cells about 1 mm apart) is about half of the average receptive field size (Hubel & Wiesel, 1974b). You already know (Chapter 4) that acuity is best in the fovea, and becomes coarser toward more peripheral parts of the retina; in other words, the receptive fields of ganglion cells (and cortical cells) serving the fovea are smallest, and those for peripheral retina are largest. If the foveal receptive fields are small, the amount of visual space served by each foveal hypercolumn is small, and many hypercolumns are needed to cover the relatively

small visual area of the fovea. As all hypercolumns are the same size in cortex, this means a relatively large amount of cortex must be devoted to the small visual area of the fovea. This is the case; as you saw in Chapter 7, maps of the retinotopic projection on the cortex show a tremendous magnification of the fovea relative to the remainder of the visual field.

Blobs

The photographs in Fig. 8.3 reveal two remarkable systems of columns that correspond to those inferred from single-cell recordings. Still another kind of patterning was found accidentally in the visual cortex of monkey before its physiological correlate was recognized. Margaret Wong-Riley treated the cortex with a stain that would reveal cytochrome oxidase, an enzyme involved in the energy system of cells. She hoped to be able to show changes in activity of areas of cortex, like those shown by 2-DG, with a stain that did not diffuse as readily and thereby 'smear' the pattern. Her staining did show changes in energy use (De Yoe *et al.*, 1995). But, to her surprise, the overall levels of cytochrome oxidase, even in the absence of visual stimulation, showed a patchy distribution, with puffs of high activity spattered in the upper layers of the V1 cortex (Wong-Riley, 1979; Wong-Riley *et al.*, 1993). These puffs, generally known by the elegant name *blobs*, form chains that run down the middles of the ocular dominance columns (see Fig. 8.4).

It was soon found that the blobs are the lairs of the concentric cells of the cortex (Hubel & Livingstone, 1983). They contain the majority of the cells exclusively devoted to color (Martin, 1988b; Ts'o & Gilbert, 1988), in addition to a weak magnocellular input (Tootell *et al.*, 1988a). Note that 'color' means both color in the usual sense of the word—red, green, blue and so on—and shades of gray. The areas of cortex between the blobs (called the *interblob* regions) receive parvocellular input but seem more sensitive to the presence of boundaries than nuances of color (Tootell *et al.*, 1988b; Born & Tootell, 1991). Many of these cells

Fig. 8.4 Cytochrome oxidase activity in the visual cortex of a squirrel monkey. V1 is at the left, V2 to the right. Blobs can be seen in V1. Thick stripes and thin stripes, separated by pale stripes, can be seen in V2. From Livingstone, M. S. and D. H. Hubel (1988) Segregation of form, color, movement, and depth: anatomy, physiology, and perception. *Science* 240: 740–749. Copyright 1988 by the AAAS. Reprinted by permission.

are sensitive to colors, but only where the colors define edges or borders (Leventhal *et al.*, 1995). While the cytochrome oxidase blobs are found in the upper layers (2 and 3), the functional column apparently extends through the entire cortical sheet, interrupted by the magnocellular parts of layer 4 (Ts'o & Gilbert, 1988).

Hubel & Wiesel envisioned the cortex as mapping ocular dominance along one direction and orientation along the direction at right angles to ocular dominance—a Cartesian graph of ocular dominance *versus* orientation. Since then, special dyes have been found that allow visualization of the activity patterns in a patch of cortex in a live animal while a stimulus is present (Blasdel & Salama, 1986; Bonhoeffer & Grinvald, 1991, 1993; Blasdel, 1992a; Obermayer & Blasdel, 1993). Separate pictures are taken of a patch of cortex

with each of several differently oriented stimuli being presented. These pictures are then superimposed, with each printed in a different color so the areas responding to each orientation may be differentiated. An example of one of these 'false color' pictures forms the background of the demonstration 'Cortical columns' on the CD accompanying this book (image from Blasdel, 1992b; it was also used as the cover of that issue of the *Journal of Neuroscience*).

Baxter & Dow (1989) found that a concentric model provided a good fit to orientation data from long electrode tracks like those in Fig. 8.2, a finding supported by multiple electrode recordings (Maldonado & Gray, 1996). More recently, a technique for visualizing the activity of the cortex directly by imaging it under near-infrared light has allowed simultaneous mapping of orientation, ocular dominance, and spatial frequency in the cat cortex. These maps show distinct pinwheels of orientation preference, with their hubs centered within ocular dominance columns and tending to be in areas of low spatial frequency preference (Hübener *et al.*, 1997).

Figure 8.5 summarizes the current view of cortical layout. The block represents a cube of cortex about 2 mm in size; the cortical surface is at the top, the white matter underneath. The slabs parallel to the right front face (labeled 'L' and 'R' for the left and right eyes) are the ocular dominance columns. Their borders become blurry, particularly away from layer 4; cells driven exclusively by only one eye occur mainly in the middles of the columns. The blobs are shown centered in the ocular dominance columns. They are shown solidly in layers 2 and 3, where the cytochrome oxidase stain is most distinct, but are also indicated in the deeper layers where they are functionally present. Each blob forms the hub of an orientation pinwheel. For some pinwheels, clockwise rotation represents clockwise rotation of the stimulus; for others, the direction is reversed (Bonhoeffer & Grinvald, 1993). Each pinwheel encodes all possible orientations for a particular visual field, dominated by one eye or the other.

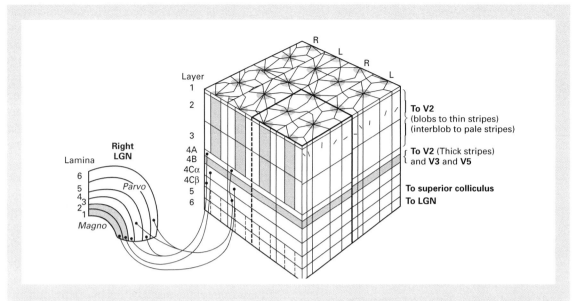

Fig. 8.5 Model of V1 cortex showing two hypercolumns for ocular dominance, two orientation hypercolumns, and the blobs. The sketch of a right LGN shows the projections from each lamina
to the appropriate ocular dominance column, with the parvocellular layers projecting to cortical layers 4A and 4Cβ and the magnocellular layers to cortical layer 4Cα. The major outputs of the layers are indicated to the right (although the fibers actually exit through the bottom of the cortex). Other inputs are not indicated. Be sure to run the demonstration 'Cortical columns' associated with this chapter on the CD accompanying this book.

The cortical layers are labeled at the left, and their outputs are indicated to the right. The sketch of an LGN to the left shows outputs of its six layers dividing among the lamina and ocular dominance columns of the leftmost hypercolumn. Magnocellular influences are shaded along the left face of the cube.

Notice that Fig. 8.5 represents two complete cycles of ocular dominance, with two blobs and orientation pinwheels in each. The receptive fields in one pinwheel are essentially in the same location. In each neighboring pinwheel, there is another complete representation of all orientations, with receptive field locations shifted by about half a field width (Hubel & Wiesel, 1974b).

The best way to visualize this is to watch the surface of the cortex 'light up' as stimuli of different orientations are presented. This is simulated in the demonstration of 'Cortical columns' on the CD.

When you start the demonstration, you will see the false color representation of a monkey's cortex, with white lines superimposed to indicate orientation. When you click 'Show model cortex', you will see ideal, clear pinwheels; click 'Fill in model' to see these pinwheels blurred into a reasonable approximation of the actual cortex pattern. When you show a stimulus, the cortex becomes gray, except for those columns that respond to the selected orientation in the idealized pattern. If one eye is covered (click the check-box above and to the right of the cartoon of the eyes watching the stimulus), the activity in the columns corresponding to that eye is extinguished. If the stimulus is moved to a slightly different location (check-box to the right of the stimulus), activity is extinguished in pinwheels in the retinotopic region no longer stimulated. If the stimulus rotates instead of maintaining a constant orientation, the pinwheels appear to rotate. **BOX 8.2**

Box 8.2 Interpretations of cortical organization into columns

Hubel & Wiesel's original model of cortical organization was a rectangular coordinate system plotting orientation *versus* ocular dominance. This model was accepted for many years. The model now preferred suggests that the orientation columns are not parallel slabs but segments that intersect at the blobs. Each hypercolumn represents a polar coordinate system; within each pinwheel (preferring one eye or the other), the *angle* represents orientation. The principle of the hypercolumn, however, is that a small cortical region can encode all ocular dominances and preferred orientations, plus information about color. This idea is valid. The exact geometrical configuration of the hypercolumn is not as important.

But why were there two such different interpretations of the original data? One possibility is that some regions are slab-like and some are pinwheel-like (Blasdel, 1992a,b).

Remember, the slabs are not perfectly rectangular, and orientation and ocular dominance columns actually seem independent. Also, many of the orientation columns in adjacent pinwheels would approximately link, giving an appearance of longer slabs. Either model is an attempt to organize rather disarrayed patterns; the grid emphasizes the slab-like columns, while the pinwheels emphasize the discontinuities and interruptions (like the non-oriented blobs). Neither model is entirely satisfactory (Erwin *et al.*, 1995). What we may be witnessing is a difference in the ways patterns can be organized and encoded by the perceptual systems of the *scientists*—the topic of Chapter 10.

Development of cortical properties and effects of deprivation

Now you should have a picture of primary visual cortex (V1) in which cells with quite specific properties are found near other cells with similar properties. Thus, a column of cells in a single vertical penetration through cortex will share a common receptive field location, preferred orientation, and ocular dominance. A nearby column will have a nearby visual location, but may differ in the other properties. How did this specificity come about? Is it innate, or modified as a result of visual experience?

In an attempt to answer this question, Hubel & Wiesel recorded from cortical cells in cats and monkeys that were either newly born or several weeks old, but deprived of any visual experience since birth (Hubel & Wiesel, 1963; Wiesel & Hubel, 1974). In both species, they found that the properties of cells from visually naive animals were similar to those encountered in adult animals. In the

monkey, which is much more mature at birth than the cat, simple, complex, and end-stopped cells were all found, with orientation and direction specificity that was about as sophisticated as that in the adult. Both binocular and monocular cells were seen in about the same proportions as in the adult animal. Many response features seen in recording of cortical cells of mature animals were observed in cells from naive animals, especially if the anesthesia was light (Rodman *et al.*, 1993). In the cat, there were more differences, with cells recorded from newborn animals being much less responsive, and often less specifically tuned to particular features (Wiesel & Hubel, 1965).

Although some initial properties of cortical cells may be innate, it is possible to alter these properties by changing the visual environment of a very young animal. Ocular dominance is one property that can be changed in this way. Hubel & Wiesel (1962) assessed the binocularity of a great many cells in cat cortex and found that most cells in the cat cortex are binocular, at least to some degree. Of the relatively few monocular cells, about the same number of cells could be stimulated by the ipsilateral eye as the contralateral eye.

Ocular dominance columns are apparently present at birth (Horton & Hocking, 1996), but can be disrupted by visual experience. Wiesel & Hubel (1963) were the first to observe that if one eye of a kitten was kept closed for several months immediately after birth, more extreme changes resulted than if both eyes were kept closed. Instead of most cells responding to some extent to input from both eyes, cells in cats with one deprived eye were almost completely unresponsive to visual stimulation from that eye after it was reopened. There seems to be a critical period during which abnormal visual experiences can affect cortical properties; if after 4 months of normal visual experience, cats are monocularly deprived for any length of time, no changes are seen in cortical ocular dominance (Wiesel & Hubel, 1965).

Depriving one eye of visual stimulation is not the only way to modify the binocularity of cortical neurons. If one extraocular muscle from one eye is surgically severed, that eye will not be able to participate in conjugate eye movements with the other eye. The cat becomes 'cross eyed' (or 'wall-eyed', depending on which muscle is severed), and the two eyes have different images of the visual field projected onto them. This should disrupt binocular cortical neurons. Hubel & Wiesel (1965b) performed this experiment and found that there were approximately equal number of cells in the cortex driven by either eye, but that there were few binocular cells.

The contention that the cortex needs appropriate binocular input in order to maintain a population of binocularly driven cells received more support from an experiment by Blake & Hirsch (1975), who subjected kittens to a period of alternating monocular deprivation. For the first 6 months of each kitten's life, one eye was covered with an opaque contact lens for 1 day; the other eye was covered the next day, and so on. At the end of the 6 months the properties of cortical neurons were investigated; it was found, as in the study discussed in the previous paragraph, that cortical cells could be driven by one eye or the other, but there were few or no binocularly activated cells. It seems, therefore, that although binocular cells exist in cortex of newborn animals, they lose their

ability to signal binocular information when the animal's visual experience is restricted to situations in which this information is either useless or harmful.

If ocular dominance is so easily modified by abnormal visual experience, perhaps other cortical properties are equally plastic. Hirsch & Spinelli (1970) raised cats in complete darkness, except for 1-h periods each day during which one eye was presented with a stimulus consisting of vertical lines and the other eye was stimulated with an array of horizontal lines. After 10 weeks, the response properties of cortical cells were investigated. Not surprisingly, as the cats had had no opportunity for binocular stimulation, few cortical cells could be driven by both eyes. In addition, it was found that cells driven by the eye that was presented with the horizontal lines had receptive fields that preferred horizontal stimuli, while cells that had inputs from the eye receiving vertical stimulation were differentially sensitive to vertically oriented stimuli. Cells with preferred orientations in between horizontal and vertical were not found.

In a similar experiment, Blakemore & Cooper (1970) found that after rearing kittens in a visual environment that was limited to either vertical or horizontal stripes, most of the cortical cells recorded had preferred orientations that matched the early environment. Thus the orientation specificity of the visual cortex can also be altered by abnormal visual experience. These changes in physiological properties are accompanied by changes in morphology; Coleman et al., (1981) report a change in cortical dendrite organization after rearing in a striped environment similar to that used by Blakemore & Cooper (1970).

Still other properties of the visual cortex can be modified by experience. If cats are reared under stroboscopic illumination, their visual experience consists of a succession of still images, with movement being totally absent. Cortical cells of cats reared under these conditions show an abnormally low number of cells sensitive to direction of stimulus movement (Cynader et al., 1973; Cynader &

Box 8.3 How the cortex changes its wiring

What might actually be happening when the cortex is changed by experience? Coleman *et al.* (1981) demonstrated changes in the dendrites of cells in the cortex, but what kinds of changes happen? Do the unused synapses wither?

It appears in many cases that what happens is a suppression of the unused inputs, rather than their outright destruction. Chino *et al.* (1994) found an initial suppression of inputs when kittens were deprived in one eye; only later did the cells become truly monocular. But when the now dominant eye is removed, responses from the deprived eye are restored, albeit weakly (Chino *et al.*, 1995).

An even more striking demonstration is that if chemicals that block transmission at synapses are placed on the cortex, the deprived eye may actually have an advantage over the non-deprived eye (Hata & Stryker, 1994). Apparently, the 'useless' input is actively suppressed by competition from the active inputs (Antonini & Stryker, 1998). This also seems to be the case when damage to small regions of the retina force a remapping in the cortex; inhibition is decreased, allowing the deprived neurons to be activated by signals from nearby regions that were previously too weak (Chino, 1997).

Chernenko, 1976). In another experiment, kittens were raised so that their sole visual experience consisted of a stimulus array of stripes moving in one direction. Under these conditions, an unusually large percentage of cortical cells were found to be differentially sensitive to that direction of movement (Daw & Wyatt, 1976).

The general conclusion is that response properties may be genetically determined, but experience is necessary for normal development. But there are some indications that the genetic predisposition may be quite general, and the resulting organization may reflect the ways in which neural networks naturally form. In a fascinating set of experiments, Sur *et al.* (1988) removed the LGN from a ferret's brain and rerouted the incoming optic fibers to the auditory part of the thalamus (having removed the auditory nerve). The visual fibers made connections in this 'alien' area, and in fact formed a functioning visual system so that orientation-selective cells like those in normal visual cortex could be found in what had been auditory cortex. Similar results were obtained when hamster optic nerve was rerouted to somatosensory thalamus (Metin & Frost, 1989). Non-visual cortex innervated by a transplanted optic nerve even develops simple and complex cells similar to those in normal visual cortex (Roe *et al.*, 1992).

Perhaps there is some predisposition for cortical cells to organize their inputs and their communications with their neighbors to analyze for 'features', but the features must be whatever is available in the input. In this regard, it is interesting that when computers model cell networks (see Chapters 10 and 11), and the properties of intermediate cells between the defined input layer and output layer are 'optimized' by the computer, these intermediate cells spontaneously develop properties reminiscent of cortical cells (Lehky & Sejnowski, 1988). Moreover, the apparent properties of these cells (bar or edge detectors) are not obviously related to the task performed by the neural network (recognizing shape from shading). BOX 8.3

Projections to 'higher' cortical areas

In Chapter 7, you were introduced to parallel pathways in the LGN: the major parvocellular and magnocellular divisions, and the *interlaminar* (koniocellular) cells that lie between layers of the

LGN (Hendry & Yoshioka, 1994; Ding & Casagrande, 1997; Martin *et al.*, 1997). As the information passes to V1 and 'higher' areas there is considerable cross-talk (Krubitzer & Kaas, 1989), but these systems remain somewhat distinct.

V1 also contains at least three systems: the magnocellular pathway, the parvocellular pathway, and the blobs. Blobs seem to be largely parvocellular, but also have some magnocellular input (Yoshioka *et al.*, 1994) and koniocellular input. These three pathways remain distinct in their projections to V2 and V3, which are the next cortical areas forward of V1 (see Fig. 7.1, p. 113).

The magnocellular system, except for its weak projection into the blobs, is confined to layer 4 in V1 (see Chapter 7). From layer 4Cα, it projects to layer 4B, and from there directly to V2, V3, and V5 (DeYoe & Van Essen, 1988). In V2, this projection is to what are called the *thick stripes* (Livingstone & Hubel, 1987a). Thick stripes are part of a second cytochrome oxidase pattern found in monkey cortex (more or less clearly, depending on species). These stripes may be seen in Fig. 8.4, to the right of the blobs in V1. Instead of blobs, the cytochrome oxidase stain produces a banded pattern in V2. There are two sets of dark staining stripes interleaved: thick stripes and *thin stripes*. They are separated by *pale stripes* of weaker cytochrome oxidase activity (Olavarria & Van Essen, 1997).

The projections from layers 2 and 3 of V1, which are mainly parvocellular in origin, seem to go only to V2. The dark-staining blobs project to the thin dark stripes, while the pale interblobs project to the pale stripes. V2, consistent with its name, seems to be secondary to V1, with its three-stripe systems (thick, thin, and pale) corresponding to the three divisions of V1 (magnocellular, blob, and interblob, respectively).

These projections are summarized in Fig. 8.6. The figure is organized into columns to emphasize the parvocellular / magnocellular distinction. Although the figure emphasizes the projections 'upward' to higher cortical areas, virtually all of these projections are reciprocal; that is, the 'higher' areas also project back to the 'lower', so the flow should be considered as two-way traffic (Zeki & Shipp, 1988). **BOX 8.4**

V3 is 'third' in that it receives a projection from the thick stripes of V2, but its main input is directly from the magnocellular system in layer 4B of V1. Since that is also the main input to the thick stripes, V3 is really a parallel part of the magnocellular pathway.

The next area forward of V3 is V4, or, more accurately, the V4 complex (Zeki, 1983a). Nearly everything seems to converge onto V4: both the thin and the pale stripes of V2 (representing the parvocellular pathways), and V3 (representing the magnocellular). V4 is 'fourth' in that it receives inputs from V3, but it also receives a direct input

---

Box 8.4 Communication in the cortex is *not* on a one-way street

People often overlook the fact that there are projections from 'higher' to 'lower' cortical areas, but these may be as important as the 'forward' projections usually discussed (Barlow, 1997). The projections 'downward' come from cells with receptive field positions similar to, but somewhat broader than, those of the cells they project to (Salin *et al.*, 1992).

The reciprocal, or 'top down' connections may be responsible for effects you will encounter in Chapter 10 (Mignard & Malpeli, 1991), including the ability of mental imagery to interfere with direct perception (Craver-Lemley & Reeves, 1992). Response properties of cells in V1

can be changed by inactivation of V2, indicating that their tuning is dependent on information from the 'higher' center (Alonso *et al.*, 1993).

It has also been shown electrophysiologically that the responses of lower cortical cells may be modulated by the context of the stimuli exciting them. The receptive fields remain the same, but responses depend on whether the cell is looking at a part of the main figure, or an irrelevant piece of background. Such differences in response depend on the animal being awake, and thus able to perceive objects (Lamme *et al.*, 1998).

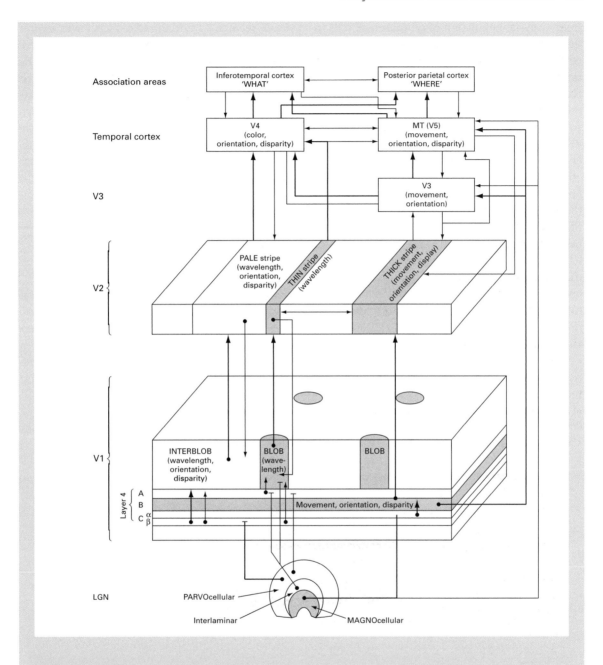

Fig. 8.6 Schematic diagram of the interconnections and possible roles of areas and subareas in primate cortex. The lateral geniculate nucleus is at the bottom, with progressively 'higher' cortical areas higher up the diagram. The parvocellular/ventral system is at the left, and the magnocellular/dorsal system is at the right. Based on a summary diagram by DeYoe, E. A. and D. C. Van Essen (1988) Concurrent processing streams in monkey visual cortex. *Trends Neurosci.* 11: 219–226. Reprinted by permission.

from a special population of interlaminar cells in the LGN (Lysakowski *et al.*, 1988). V4 is a large, heterogeneous collection of cells projecting into the inferotemporal cortex near the base of the brain (see Fig. 7.1, p.113 and 'Brain anatomy' on the CD).

The next visual area forward is sometimes called V5 because of its position (Zeki, 1983a), although it is at about the same logical level as V4. It is more often called the *middle temporal* region, or *MT*. It lies buried within a large infolding of the cortex called the *superior temporal sulcus*. For the most part, MT receives magnocellular inputs: from V3, from the thick stripes of V2, and directly from layer 4B of V1. However, there is also some input from the thin stripes of V2, and there is an interconnection between V4 and MT. In addition to its connection to V4, MT and its subdivisions project to the posterior parietal cortex near the top of the brain (see Fig. 7.1 and 'Brain anatomy' on the CD).

V4 and MT are shown next to each other in Fig. 8.6, but there is a striking physical separation of the pathways starting at that level. MT lies forward of V3, but many of its projections are to the parietal lobe *dorsal* to it (that is, toward the top of the

head; see Fig. 7.1 and the CD). V4 is lower, nearer the temples, and projects forward and downward (the *ventral* direction) toward the bottom of the brain (the temporal lobe; again, see Fig. 7.1 and the CD). Because of this split, these pathways are referred to as the *dorsal stream* and the *ventral stream* (Ungerleider & Mishkin, 1982). Both streams have at least some parvocellular and some magnocellular components, but they are separated into anatomically and functionally distinct streams projecting forward to rejoin in the prefrontal cortex (Young, 1992).

Functions of the 'higher' cortical areas

Some indication of possible functions of the cortical areas has been placed in each of the boxes of Fig. 8.6. These putative functions are based on the responses of cells in these areas and on deficits in function when these areas are damaged. Thus, Fig. 8.6 summarizes not only the streams and their interconnections, but also their possible roles in vision.

A word of caution is in order. It is easy to say that an area with many cells that respond to variations

---

Box 8.5 Sophisticated processing in the visual cortex

A fascinating glimpse of how processing in higher cortical areas may be more 'advanced' comes from a study by von der Heydt *et al.* (1984). They recorded from neurons in V1 and V2 of monkey, seeking cells that respond to edges. Such cells were easy to find in either area. However, the cells in V2 not only responded to edges of the correct orientation that were presented to their fields, but they also responded to edges of the correct orientation that were not really there (von der Heydt & Peterhans, 1989). Such non-edges, called *subjective contours*, will be discussed in Chapter 10 (see Box 10.6, p. 200). For now, just understand that these 'edges', which are not there but *appear* to be, can be created by the suggestion of an object overlaying a pattern. For example, in Fig. 8.7(a), you may 'see' a vertical white line connecting the slits in the two black rectangles. The line is not really there, but you may see it as if a thin white strip were lain across the picture.

A V2 cell receptive field is sketched between the black

rectangles (dashed oval). This cell responded best to vertical lines. When the black rectangles were moved left and right (together), the cell responded as if a line were being swept back and forth across its field. The response was not as strong as for a real line, but there was a response (although there was no change in the stimulus anywhere in its receptive field). And, after all, the perception of the subjective contour (the vertical white line in the area between the rectangles) is also weak.

A subjective contour depends on very subtle details of the stimulus. If you draw lines across the ends of the slits (so there is a thin white window in each of two complete black rectangles), the illusory white line vanishes (Fig. 8.7b). When the same cell was shown this very slightly modified stimulus, it also failed to 'see' the line, and gave no responses to sideways movement of the black rectangles (Peterhans & von der Heydt, 1989).

These properties are less easily found in the cells of V1

(Grosof *et al.*, 1993), and may be taken to indicate a closer agreement between the activity of the 'line detectors' of V2 and the actual perception of a line. But is this a function of V2? This property may depend on influences from other areas, including some 'higher' than V2. Responses to stimuli that are not really there but 'ought to be' may remind you of the 'filling in' that occurs in the blind spot (see Chapter 3). Projections from 'higher' areas with a broader view may reproduce the elements missing from the stimulus (Fiorani *et al.*, 1992)

Cells in V2 can respond to the orientation of areas de-fined by differences in texture or contrast, quite independently of changes in brightness. Imagine a pattern of vertical lines, with a horizontal band where the lines are smeared into a uniform gray. Even though this pattern has nearly no horizontal components, it excites a cell that is tuned to horizontal bars of about the same width as the blurry band. The smeared band has the exact same amount of light in it as the distinct pattern, so such a response cannot be explained by simple excitatory and inhibitory areas of input (Shapley, 1998).

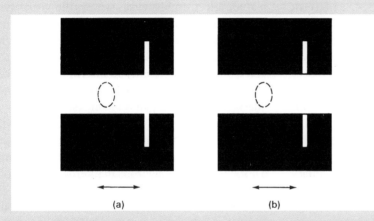

(a)   (b)

Fig. 8.7 Subjective contours and cells in V2. The black rectangles with slits were moved left and right, with the receptive field of the cortical cell as shown by the dashed ellipse. (a) Open slits create impression of a vertical white line through the gap between rectangles. A cell that responds to vertical lines responds to this stimulus. (b) Closing the slits negates the subjective contour (the white line); the cell does not respond to this stimulus. After von der Heydt, R., E. Peterhans and G. Baumgartner (1984) Illusory contours and cortical neuron responses. *Science* 224: 1260–1262. Copyright 1984 by the AAAS. Reprinted with permission.

in wavelength of the light is a 'color-sensitive' area and to forget that these cells may also have spatial, motion, or orientation preferences. As noted in Chapter 7, it is not fair to call a cell (or an area) a 'detector' of some feature simply because that is what it was tested for.

You will notice that most of the boxes indicate more than one function. In most cases, individual cells are sensitive along more than one dimension; in many cases, some cells in a particular area show one property, and other cells in that same area show

another. It is not uncommon to find clusters of cells in a higher visual area that seem to code for one property (like color) interspersed among clusters of other cells that are insensitive to that property (Zeki, 1983a). If the pattern of cytochrome oxidase stripes had not emerged in V2, we might consider it an area with all properties represented. Perhaps some finer organization will someday be recognized within the thick stripes, or in V3, V4, or MT (see Zeki & Shipp, 1988).

You have already seen specialization in V1. Cells

in the blobs are generally not selective for orientation or motion and are driven almost exclusively by one eye or the other. Many of them are interested in color; others are responsive to contrast. Cells outside the blobs are orientation-selective, and, when they are driven by either eye, may compare the positions of the stimuli in the two eyes, a difference referred to as *binocular disparity*. Cells in layers 2 and 3 (interblob) sometimes also care about wavelength. Cells in the magnocellular layer 4B often care about direction of motion.

Since these subdivisions of V1 project fairly directly to the thin stripe, pale stripe, and thick stripe divisions of V2, it is not surprising that those areas of V2 show similar preferences (Hubel & Livingstone, 1987). V3 receives its input from layer 4B and thick stripes and so shares the preferences of those areas. This does not mean that V2 and V3 are adding nothing to the processing begun in V1. For example, some cells in V2 respond specifically to motion of a stimulus across their receptive fields (with the eyes stationary), and do not respond when the eyes sweep across a stationary stimulus (Galletti *et al.*, 1988). The motion of the stimulus across the receptive field is the same in both cases; the difference is whether the *stimulus* moved. A preference for stimulus motion is even more prominent in V3 (Galletti *et al.*, 1990). This preference has not been reported in V1. Similarly, cells in V2 (in cat) have been reported to be sensitive to motion in depth (toward or away from the animal), not simply motion across the receptive field (Cynader & Regan, 1978). <u>**BOX 8.5**</u>

The ventral stream   Area V4 was originally thought to be a color processing area because of a large number of color-specific cells found in it, although these cells are found in clusters mingled with clusters of orientation-selective cells (Zeki, 1983a). There are at least two major systems: (1) a spatially broad, color-selective system that probably plays a major role in the perception of color; and (2) a spatially tuned, orientation-selective system that is probably important in pattern recognition. Of course, there must also be some depth

discrimination, since recognition of differences in distance are key to object recognition.

A role for V4 in pattern discrimination was demonstrated by Spitzer *et al.* (1988), who recorded from V4 of a monkey while it matched test bars against a sample (to be given a reward for correctly deciding if the test matched the sample). When the task was made more difficult ('false' test bars that were very similar to the sample in color or orientation), the cells became more selective, and gave larger responses to the 'correct' matching stimulus. In short, the task the monkey was engaged in had an effect on responses within the visual system. A broad feedback from 'higher' centers directs areas in 'lower' centers to search for specific patterns (Motter, 1994a,b). Damage in area V4 severely disrupts the ability to discriminate similar shapes in the affected region of the visual field (Merigan, 1996; Merigan & Pham, 1998).

The main target for V4 neurons is the inferotemporal cortex on the bottom of the brain. Like V4, inferotemporal cortex has multiple subdivisions (DeYoe *et al.*, 1994). Neurons in inferotemporal cortex may be selective for a particular shape, color, or texture anywhere within a relatively large area of visual field (Desimone *et al.*, 1985). That cells in higher cortex have more complex properties spanning a larger visual area than in primary cortex is consistent with their larger and more complex dendritic fields (Elston & Rosa, 1998). Cells may participate in many aspects of the processing, signaling which aspect they are dealing with by synchronizing their firing with other cells concerned with the same property (McClurkin & Optican, 1996).

Inferotemporal cortex seems essential for pattern perception (Iwai, 1985). Indeed, the columns in inferotemporal cortex seem to comprise cells specific to rather complex shapes in three dimensions (Tanaka, 1996). Neurons in this region, like the V4 neurons that supply their inputs, become selective for the particular stimulus parameters the animal is asked to discriminate (Fuster & Jervey, 1981).

Neurons in the inferotemporal cortex can be very selective for particular patterns. Neurons in

Box 8.6 Patients with damage to the ventral stream

Further evidence for the inferotemporal cortex as a 'what' system comes from observations of patients who have suffered damage in the ventral stream. If this area is damaged, usually because of multiple strokes (blood clots interfering with the blood supply to a part of the brain) or carbon monoxide poisoning, a number of interesting clinical pictures can appear.

One such deficit is called *prosopagnosia*, the inability to recognize faces. Patients with this problem can usually recognize objects, including faces, for what they are. But they cannot distinguish between objects in the same class. They cannot say if a particular face is familiar, or distinguish one person's face from another's. The deficit is not always limited to faces, but can extend to any set of similar objects among which distinctions must be made on the basis of relatively subtle differences. For example, a kennel owner who previously could identify each dog in the kennel may find all dogs indistinguishable. Patients with this disorder have normal *generic recognition*, but have suffered the loss of *specific recognition* within a given class (Damasio, 1985). Try to imagine what havoc such a problem could create in your life, even though your basic visual perception is completely normal.

Prosopagnosia is generally associated with damage on the right side of the brain (Carlesimo & Caltagirone, 1995), which is the side we think of as dealing with spatial relationships, rather than language. In addition, the type of prosopagnosia depends on the specific location of the damage. Recognition seems to be the task of more dorsal areas, while the more ventral parts connect to the limbic system deep within the brain to provide the emotional context; the medial surface seems to decide whether the face is familiar or unfamiliar (Szpir, 1992). Presentation of familiar faces generates activity in the amygdala, a limbic structure, while the task of deciding who the person is relies on memory structures like the nearby hippocampus (Seeck *et al.*, 1995). If the decision about whether the face

is familiar or not is wrong, it is possible to have the emotional affect without recognizing the person; there is a delusion that the person is an imposter. If the emotion is not triggered but recognition occurs, there is an impression that the person is a lifeless mask – think of the movie *Invasion of the Body Snatchers*; the person seems zombie-like, as if wearing one of those full-head rubber masks. The losses may be quite specific: for example, one case reported a person who cannot recognize objects but who *can* recognize faces—this person is superior to normals at 'find the hidden face' in a camouflage drawing (Holden, 1997).

Another deficit that can result from damage to visual temporal cortex, in this case on the left side (Rentschler *et al.*, 1994), is *alexia*, the inability to read. This is not to be confused with *dyslexia*, in which letter orders are reversed; you will read about that in Box 8.7 (p. 150) Alexia results when the visual association cortex is disconnected from the part of the left cortex that is responsible for language integration. Vision in the left field is completely normal—except for the inability to read. One irony is that these patients can write normally; however, they are apparently unable to read back what they have just written!

Other damage may specifically affect the color processing portions of this system. Patients with this condition often report that colors are 'washed out' or completely absent (Damasio, 1981). This rare color deficit is known as *achromatopsia*. It is not the same as color blindness (see Chapter 14), because while these patients report that everything is the same color, they still can see borders formed by differences in color only. They may also see grayed out blacks and whites, implicating the blob system in general (Livingstone & Hubel, 1987b).

---

monkey temporal cortex have even been reported to be selective for particular faces (Perrett *et al.* 1982; Tovee *et al.*, 1994). All of this suggested that the ventral stream is the system charged with identifying what we are seeing—in a word, the 'what' system. BOX 8.6

MT   MT, also called V5, is buried in the superior temporal sulcus. Zeki (1974) suggested this was a

movement area because it contains a high percentage of cells sensitive to movement, and because its columnar organization is based on direction of movement. The preponderance of motion-selective cells has been amply confirmed (Bruce *et al.*, 1981; Rodman & Albright, 1989). It has also been found that lesions in MT impair a monkey's ability to follow a moving target with its eyes (Dürsteller & Wurtz, 1988), or even to see that a pattern is moving (Newsome & Pare, 1988). In many ways, MT may be considered an 'island' of motion processing that serves both the dorsal and, to a lesser extent, the ventral streams. You will read more about the role of MT in motion detection in Chapter 13.

The dorsal stream   The other major stream is the magnocellular-dominated dorsal stream. Maunsell & Newsome (1987) referred to this as the 'motion pathway', although it clearly has a broader function than motion detection. One main station along the way is MT, whose major output goes to the posterior parietal cortex.

Posterior parietal cortex has been implicated in directing visual attention to a particular part of the visual field (Lynch *et al.*, 1977; Colby *et al.*, 1995). It has neurons that respond during eye movements, and others that are responsive only during fixation. The fixation neurons are often specific for location and distance of a target, suggesting they are concerned with the position of an object in space, taking account of eye position (Sakata *et al.*, 1980; Andersen *et al.*, 1985; Colby *et al.*, 1995) and even head position (Thier & Erickson, 1992). The neurons in this area also seem to integrate visual information with that from other senses, including *intended* hand posi-

---

Box 8.7 Patients suffering damage to the dorsal stream

Once again, the natural laboratory of clinical dysfunction can shed light on the normal role of a part of the brain. There is a considerable difference between the deficits caused by strokes affecting the inferotemporal cortex and those affecting posterior parietal cortex. A spectacular disorder called *Balint's syndrome* is due to damage in the posterior parietal cortex. Patients with this syndrome may have three distinct problems:

● The first prong of Balint's syndrome is a narrow visual attention field. This makes it difficult to perceive a whole structure from component parts (a condition called *simultagnosia*). If you show a patient with simultagnosia a photograph of a rural scene and ask him to describe what he sees, he may pick out a tree, or a pig, or a barn. However, he seems unable to integrate these components into a unified whole. He can apparently focus his attention on only a tiny part of the picture at any time. As a result, even if he initially saw the pig in the picture, he may be unable to find it again once he has turned his attention to something else. This has also been reported with mild generalized atrophy of the entire brain, implying that the ability to integrate may not be localized in the parietal cortex (Stark *et al.*, 1997).

● The second prong of Balint's syndrome is *optic ataxia*, a difficulty in reaching out for objects based on visual information. A patient with optic ataxia is unable to point accurately at an object, even though she sees it clearly. She can easily point to her nose, or the spot on her skin touched by a feather, or to any other object that pro-

duces somatosensory cues. The deficit is only apparent when visual cues are isolated. It is therefore neither a purely motor nor a purely sensory disorder. While this problem most usually occurs as part of Balint's syndrome, it is sometimes seen in isolation (Damasio & Benton, 1979).

● The third prong of Balint's syndrome is *ocular apraxia*, the inability to shift one's gaze to a new stimulus (apraxia in general refers to an impaired ability to perform complex motion programs, despite normal simple motor abilities). When the patient attempts to look toward a new or novel object, the eye movement is inaccurate. This problem occurs even though she has full eye movements and no visual-field defect evident in standard testing.

A familiar problem that seems to be associated with damage in the parietal cortex is dyslexia, a difficulty in reading. Dyslexics tend to jumble or reverse the orders of letters, reading 'dear' for 'read'. This may be a positional error, similar to Balint's syndrome (a mild simultagnosia), or a timing difficulty in scanning the letters as the eyes move across the line of print. It could also be an attentional problem, although it is harder to see why that would result in reversals. In any case, dyslexia has been associated with deficits of the magnocellular system (Lehmkuhle *et al.*, 1993; Kubová *et al.*, 1995; Cornelissen *et al.*, 1998).

tion (Robinson *et al.*, 1978) or eye movements (Duhamel *et al.*, 1992).

The posterior parietal cortex may also play a role in pattern vision (Iwai, 1985), but it seems its main role is in locating stimuli in space. For this reason, the dorsal stream is often referred to as the 'where' system, as opposed to the 'what' of the ventral stream (Ungerleider & Mishkin, 1982; Livingstone & Hubel, 1987b). 'Where' does not simply mean 'where is an object?', but also 'where are its parts?'; that is, 'where' is an essential component of integrating whole images. It may also be required by the 'what' system to allow it to identify the parts of objects being recognized, or the relationships of the parts of the object. **BOX 8.7**

Another view of the dorsal path is that it may play a role in directing attention to the salient parts of a stimulus, guiding the ventral stream's responses (Steinmetz & Constantinidis, 1995; Leonards & Singer, 1997; Steinman *et al.*, 1997). Neurons in temporal cortex respond differently depending on whether or not the item is the one sought, and this seems to be due to the attention paid to the item (Bushnell *et al.*, 1981; Chelazzi *et al.*, 1993).

A third possibility is suggested by the layout of the brain (see 'Anatomy of the brain' on the CD). Notice that the ventral stream diverts to the temporal lobe, where it has access to limbic structures—emotion areas like the amygdala, memory areas like the hippocampus, and the adjacent limbic cortex (Murray & Mishkin, 1998). This makes sense for its imputed memory-dependent, cognitive functions like identification and recognition. The dorsal stream, on the other hand (or lobe), aims toward premotor cortex, the part of the brain that plans and executes muscle movements (Tanné *et al.*, 1995; Lomber *et al.*, 1996).

Mel Goodale (1993, 1998) has suggested that while the ventral stream provides the visual input for the cognitive system, the dorsal stream evolved as the visual input part of the motor system. The dorsal stream provides accurate place information to guide your movements, although it cannot afford the time to check with memory to determine what the object is and what its properties are. The ventral stream communicates with memory to establish the identities and learned properties of objects; this is based on *relative* positions and would not be accurate for guiding specific motions. Box 8.7 indicates that the dorsal stream plays a major role in visually guided actions, including hand motions and eye movements. People with optic ataxia reach out the way you would with your eyes closed, making clumsy adjustments and corrections based on their errors. In contrast, if someone suddenly tosses something to you, you automatically stick out your hand and catch it (unless you are a klutz like me). You don't think about it, or recognize what it is, or plan the catch, you just do it. If you took the time to think about the trajectory, you would miss it.

In this view, the ventral stream helps you to choose a goal, while the dorsal stream guides you in accomplishing it. As noted in Chapter 7, the dorsal stream, being non-cognitive, could operate without your being aware of it (Milner, 1997; Goodale & Haffenden, 1998). Of course, the streams communicate with each other, so each system borrows information from the other. A dorsal stream devoid of 'what' information could direct you to pick up hot coals; a ventral stream devoid of position and motion information could decipher only the simplest images (Goodale, 1998). **BOX 8.8**

Vision and the parallel systems

You have seen that the dorsal and ventral systems serve somewhat different visual functions, mainly by studying cases of damage to the brain, or by noting what kinds of responses are found in various visual areas. It would be nice to understand how they interact in normal vision.

First, what divisions do we prefer? This discussion started with the parvocellular and magnocellular systems, but then you saw that they dominate the ventral and dorsal streams, respectively. You may also note that the parvocellular/ventral system has heavy representation of the central part of our visual field, while the magnocellular/dorsal

Box 8.8 What *does* the dorsal stream really do?

The last two putative functions suggested for parietal (and frontal) cortex are really closely related. One very important visually guided motor activity is aiming your eyes at what you want to see. Of course, you can direct your attention without aiming your eyes, but it is very difficult to do that, and you move your eyes much more slowly if you try to direct your attention to a place other than where you aim your eyes. Moreover, the same brain regions are involved in directing your eyes and directing your attention, so the motor act of aiming your eyes and the cognitive act of directing your attention may really be controlled by the same parietal system (Corbetta, 1998). Other visuomotor activity may be linked to this system as a generalization of the same process: direct the eyes, direct the hands, etc.

system has a greater input from the periphery (Sivak & MacKenzie, 1990). How shall we name the 'what' system and the 'where' system, assuming that is really the division of labor?

Livingstone & Hubel (1987b, 1988) chose to define the systems as parvocellular and magnocellular, and, through a series of demonstrations, tried to show what one system alone can do. Some of their demonstrations are reproduced on the CD accompanying this book. Livingstone & Hubel exploited the properties of the two systems, as indicated in Table 7.1 (p. 118), to devise stimuli that would selectively affect only one system or the other.

To isolate the parvocellular system, Livingstone & Hubel capitalized on the idea that magnocellular cells are 'color-blind'; that is, they are poor at discriminating between lights on the basis of wavelength alone. Livingstone & Hubel presented colored images that are *equiluminant*; meaning the luminances of the colors are matched (see Chapter 3). As you will read again in Chapter 14, a color-blind person cannot discriminate between two lights that are equal in luminance, even though to the rest of us they may appear different in color.

Imagine a green line on a red background. Vary the ratio of red to green light. At a high ratio, there is a bright red field with a dark line. Even a color-blind person would see that there is a dark line on a brighter field, without being able to tell the color of the field. At a low ratio, there is a bright green line on a dark field. Again, a color-blind person could easily see a light line.

Now consider what the color-blind person sees as the ratio is gradually leveled. The bright field becomes dimmer, while the dark line gets brighter. At equiluminance, they are the same brightness; the line and field blend perfectly into a smooth field. The exact ratio needed depends on the particular person and system, but it can be found. Of course, color-normals see a green line on a red field.

Be sure to look at the 'Equiluminant' demonstrations associated with this chapter to see these effects for yourself. In the demonstrations, you will be asked to find your own balance of the two colors you select, because people differ slightly in the exact balance of their color systems (so do computer monitors). Once you have adjusted your screen for your own color balance, you should get a much more convincing demonstration of these effects than if you were viewing the approximation to the average balance that would be printed in a color plate. (*Note*: in order for your computer to be able to produce the subtle variations in color necessary to balance the display for your visual system, it must be in at least 'high color' mode. The demonstration will give you an error message if it finds that your system does not allow a full-color display. If there is no message, you should be fine. If the message appears, see Box P2, p. vi).

The *assumption* is that, at equiluminance, the magnocellular system cannot discern the stimulus, but the parvocellular system can. Livingstone & Hubel noted that at equiluminance, pictures lose their apparent depth and structure. A picture that gives a strong impression of three-dimensionality in black and white (or at non-equiluminance) seems flat and two-dimensional at equiluminance. Complicated patterns are difficult or impossible to recognize at equiluminance. A pattern of moving dots that gives the distinct impression of spots on a rotating transparent sphere appears as spots dancing about at random when made equiluminant with the background (click 'Dot pattern'; view it at equiluminance and then in black and white).

Vision without the magnocellular system thus seems to lack depth and organization. In some ways, it is reminiscent of the effects of damage in the posterior parietal cortex (see Box 8.7, p. 150), which is a main recipient of the magnocellular pathway. Even the parvocellular function of recognizing a pattern is impaired, because the magnocellular system is needed to provide the information about depth and the relationship of the parts. You will learn more about the importance of the magnocellular system for the perception of depth in Chapter 11.

Perhaps it now seems like the parvocellular system is relatively unimportant. The magnocellular system is needed to see motion, depth, and spatial relationships; the poor parvocellular system seems to be left with only two 'minor' jobs: color (which is not essential), and filling in the details (these 'details' may include the texture of surfaces, which you will return to in Chapters 9 and 10). But this is like saying your left foot is responsible for your ability to walk, because if it is cut off, your right foot alone can only hop! Vision with the magnocellular system only (say, at low contrast) is not very good, other than for seeing that 'something moved'. It is a vision of indistinct, shadowy shapes. Just as the parvocellular system needs information from the magnocellular system to do its tasks, the magnocellular system requires information from the parvocellular pathways. They interact at many levels, so the capabilities of both working together are far better than would be expected from what each can do working alone. This kind of complicated intertwining of systems and processes will be evident many more times as you delve deeper into the process of perception.

At least two streams—but one perception

If the dorsal and ventral streams go their separate ways, why do we have only one percept? Perhaps we don't; as you learned, there may be visual information hidden from our conscious minds but available for guiding our hands. There are 'different ways of seeing' (Walsh & Butler, 1996).

Or perhaps the streams don't really go their separate ways—they interact at various levels (Merigan & Maunsell, 1993; Callaway & Wiser, 1996). They also maintain communication about which cells in each stream are related to the same stimulus. This seems to be accomplished by having those cells responding to a particular object fire in synchrony (Neven & Aertsen, 1992; Singer & Gray, 1995; Funke & Wörgötter, 1997). The 'binding' of parts of a complex stimulus will be examined again in Chapter 10.

The streams reconverge in the prefrontal cortex (Rao *et al.*, 1997). Frontal cortex is known to be important for producing voluntary eye movements, but probably plays other roles as well. It has been suggested that the frontal cortex is where 'meaning' is associated with the images, as this is where auditory information also becomes available (Watanabe, 1992). But even here, there is a dorsal–ventral distinction (Courtney *et al.*, 1996).

It is important to remember that the rich interconnections may allow perception to arise without there being a final, single terminus of the streams. Perhaps we should reconcile ourselves to the idea that each of the streams performs multiple functions, and many functions are shared (or replicated) in both streams. There are both special-purpose systems and multi-purpose systems (Schiller, 1996); we mislead ourselves if we try to force any given part of this complicated system into a predefined box.

Suggested readings

Chapters 2 and 3 of Kuffler & Nicholls' *From neuron to brain* (Sinauer Press, 1976) provide an excellent discussion of the functional architecture of the visual cortex. On the subject of plasticity of cells in the visual system, Chapter 15 of R. D. Lund's *Development and plasticity of the brain* (Oxford University Press, Oxford, 1978) provides a good review. Another review is Nigel Daw's presentation upon accepting the Friedenwald Award. 'Mechanisms of plasticity', in *Investigative Ophthalmology & Visual Science* (35: 4168–4179; 1994).

An excellent and readable account of how the cortex processes visual information is 'Brain mechanisms of vision', by Hubel & Wiesel (*Scientific American*, September, 1979). This article reviews the types of cells found in the cortex, but emphasizes their organization into orientation and ocular dominance columns. It further speculates about how particular visual patterns might be represented within the hypercolumns of the cortex. It may also be found in *The brain* (W. H. Freeman, 1979). It is also reprinted in *The mind's eye* (introduction by J. M. Wolfe, W. H. Freeman, 1986).

For a more up-to-date account of the parallel processing story and the roles of higher visual centers, read 'Concurrent processing streams in monkey visual cortex' by E. A. DeYoe and D. C. Van Essen in *Trends in Neurosciences* (11: 219–226; 1988). A brief account that is more concerned with the roles of these areas is 'Art, illusion and the visual system', by Margaret S. Livingstone (*Scientific American*, 258: 78–85; 1988). A more technical but readable version of this has been published by Livingstone & Hubel: 'Segregation of form, color, movement, and, depth: anatomy, physiology, and perception' (*Science*, 240: 740–749; 1988).

Another readable account may be found in David Hubel's *Eye, brain, and vision*, recommended for Chapter 7. Semir Zeki reviews the various visual areas and their interconnections in 'The visual image in mind and brain' (*Scientific American*, September, 1992, reprinted in *Mind and brain*; Freeman, 1993, pp. 27–39). A more technical article is his chapter 'The motion pathways in visual cortex' in *Vision: coding and efficiency*, edited by Colin Blakemore (Cambridge University Press, Cambridge, 1990, pp. 321–345). A somewhat different view may be found in *Spatial vision* by R. L. DeValois and K. K. DeValois (Oxford University Press, Oxford, 1988). Their book emphasizes the cortex as a processor of spatial frequencies, the topic of the next chapter.

Perception of faces has received considerable attention. *The artful eye*, edited by R. Gregory, J. Harris, P. Heard, & D. Rose (Oxford University Press, Oxford, 1995), recommended also for Chapters 10 and 12, includes considerable information on that topic. A book that concentrates mainly on face perception, including our emotional responses to faces, factors that help determine recognition, and some schemes for finding the fundamental features of face recognition, is *In the eye of the beholder*, by V. Bruce and A. Young (Oxford University Press, Oxford, 1998).

A relatively complete account of the parallel processing pathways is given by A. D. Milner and M. A. Goodale in *The visual brain in action* (Oxford University Press, Oxford, 1995). In addition to a good review of the parallel streams, they provide detailed descriptions of the deficits caused by brain damage, including both the clinical pictures in humans and models using animals.

Finally, Oliver Sacks writes entertaining anecdotal accounts of the effects of selective damage to parts of the brain. Of particular relevance for the discussion of the disruption of pattern perception is the tale of 'The man who mistook his wife for a hat' in his book *The man who mistook his wife for a hat and other clinical tales* (Simon & Schuster, 1985, pp. 8–21). Sacks also provides a fascinating account of a case of achromatopsia (where color blindness resulted from cortical damage later in life, rather than from a deficiency of one type of cone) in 'the case of the colorblind painter', which is in his book *An anthropologist on Mars* (Knopf, New York, 1995, pp. 3–41).

Chapter 9

Spatial frequency representation

IN specifying a visual scene, you naturally speak of areas of light and dark at particular locations in space. Those are the terms that describe visual stimuli presented to subjects (Chapter 2), or to the receptive fields of individual neurons (Chapters 4–8). In this chapter, you will learn about a different, but equally descriptive, way of specifying the visual scene: spatial frequency analysis. It is another way of describing visual stimuli, one that has attracted considerable attention in the past few decades. It is a description that you have probably never encountered before; because it is so different from other ways of discussing visual perception, it may seem rather confusing. Try to believe, however, that this material is not harder, it is just less familiar.

Some workers have considered it possible that at some level, spatial frequency analysis may be part of one way our nervous systems 'think about' the visual scene. In any case, it is a way that many researchers exploit to examine the workings of the visual system.

There are two major points to cover. First, you must learn what spatial frequency analysis is; only then can you think about the possibility that the visual system performs this function. The first part of this chapter is therefore devoted to developing the general concepts of spatial frequency analysis. Then you will read about evidence that the visual system includes channels that amount to spatial frequency detectors. Finally, you will be able to consider how the detectors could function in perception and demonstrate perceptual effects that may be explained by assuming this kind of analysis.

The concept of spatial frequencies

Spatial frequency representation is a *transformation* of the visual image into another, mathematically equivalent, representation. As such, it is just a mathematical trick that maps information into a different form. There is nothing controversial here; it is a mathematical truth that the two representations are of the same thing. If you look at a computer display in which there is a box with black letters on a gray background, you would describe it as a gray box with the words 'Warning! Program error at 11087'. But the monitor driver 'describes' it as 'color 128, color 128, color 128, color 0, color 128', etc. for all 20 000 pixels comprising the box. Which description is 'right'? Both convey the same information, although you might not know that by reading each of them. In this case, your description ('Warning! . . .') is much more efficient than that of the monitor driver.

The principle upon which the spatial frequency notion rests was stated by the French mathematician J. B. Fourier: any pattern that repeats itself over and over can be represented by the sum of a series of sinusoids. The mathematical procedure by which functions are approximated by sums of sinusoids is called a *Fourier transform*.

What is a sinusoid? A sinusoid, of which a sine wave is one example, is a continuous waveform that undulates in a smooth and regular fashion (see the Appendix). Figure A.8 shows a sine wave (repeated at the top of Fig. A.9). It is characterized by its amplitude (the maximum excursion of the clock hand, labeled *A* in Fig. A.9), and its *wavelength* (the time between corresponding points in successive *cycles*, labeled λ in Fig. A.9). The wavelength is

the length of a single cycle, or repetition. The *frequency* is the inverse of the wavelength. The equation of the curve in Fig. A.8 is

$$\theta = A \cdot sin(f \cdot t)$$
$$where f = 1/\lambda.$$

One other parameter is needed to characterize a sinusoid. The two waveforms shown in Fig. A.9 have identical wavelengths and amplitudes; however, they differ in *phase*. Phase refers to the difference in timing between the two waves; in Fig. A.9, the two waves are one-quarter of a cycle apart. This is, if the curve in Fig. A.9 (b) were shifted to the left by one-quarter of a cycle, it would superimpose exactly on the curve in Fig. A.9 (a). A single cycle of a sine wave is equal to a 360° change in angle, so a

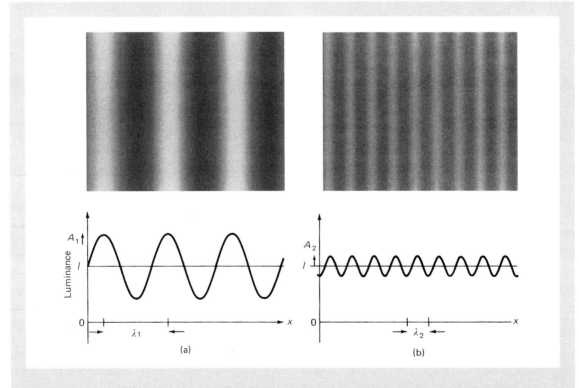

Fig. 9.1 Two sinusoidal gratings. The relation between luminance and distance across each grating is shown below it. The grating on the left is of low spatial frequency and high amplitude; that on the right is of higher frequency and lower amplitude. Both are at the same mean luminance.

one-quarter cycle change in phase is equal to a change of 90°. A 180° phase shift, or one-half-cycle change, would have the effect of completely inverting the wave; that is, where the original wave had its peaks, the phase-shifted wave would have its valleys, and vice versa (for more about sine waves, see the Appendix).

The sine waves in Figs A.8 and A.9 are functions of time, but sinusoids can also be functions of space. Ripples in a pond are waves in space. This chapter is about sinusoids in space, but the fluctuations of interest are not the elevations of ripples, they are increases and decreases in the luminance of a visual pattern. In general, the frequency of spatial sinusoids is expressed in the number of cycles per degree of visual angle. If it were in cycles per inch or per millimeter, you would also have to specify the viewing distance; by referring all measures to visual angle, the size of the retinal image is completely specified. You will learn more about visual angles in Chapter 12; for now, simply consider visual angle as a measure of distance along an image.

One point should be emphasized; the spatial frequency (f in the equation of a sine) is *inversely* related to the wavelength, or 'size' of the wave. A high spatial frequency (large f) is one with small wavelength; there are many cycles per degree. A low spatial frequency has a long wavelength, and there are few cycles per degree. A high-frequency pattern is therefore fine and detailed, with lots of waves in a small area. A low-frequency pattern represents long, smooth, drawn-out waves. As you will encounter high and low spatial frequencies throughout this chapter, it is essential to get this straight.

Fourier analysis

Now, if you are clear about what a sinusoid is, consider the Fourier transform. First, it is simpler to deal with stimuli that vary along only one dimension. Of course, real pictures vary in two dimensions. There are Fourier transforms of such images, but these are two-dimensional functions also, adding an extra complication to what may already

be a confusing story. By restricting the variations to one dimension, say horizontal, an entire stimulus is represented by a single function of luminance versus horizontal displacement. This function describes how the light varies across the field. In the vertical direction, the luminance is always the same as the points above or below. That is the description of a vertically oriented grating, as shown in Fig. 5.11 (p.88). For example, two sinusoidal gratings are shown in Fig. 9.1; below each is the sine function that represents the luminance at each horizontal point.

One of the demonstrations on the CD accompanying this book is called 'Fourier components of gratings' (it is one of the choices for Chapter 9). When you start this program, it will present a single sine wave, as in Fig. 9.1(a) or (b). You can use the slide adjustments to change the amplitude or phase of the sine wave. Each time you do so, the corresponding sine wave grating will be plotted in the top window; under it is its waveform, and under that a row with a shorter piece of grating, its waveform, and its equation. Each waveform in the lower window will superimpose on the previous ones, so you can see the effect of changing phase or amplitude (you can erase the old waveforms with the 'Reset' button).

There is one other thing to notice. Because there cannot be a negative amount of light at any point, the sine wave must be shifted up so that it never goes below zero. That is, the sine wave is a *modulation* about some mean amount of light, l, where l is greater than A, the amplitude of the sine wave. Rather than talk about the amplitude, A, we generally speak of the *contrast* of the grating. You have already encountered the concept of the Weber contrast (p. 15) as the relative increment of light superimposed on a mean background. For gratings, the luminance extends both above and below the mean level, and we define the *Rayleigh contrast* as the ratio of the amplitude to the mean, or

$$C = A/l$$

When $A = l$, the contrast is 1.0 (100%), and the dark troughs have zero light. As A becomes relatively smaller, the contrast becomes less, and the ripple a less and less significant part of the illumination.

The Fourier transform describes a pattern in space by the *component* sinusoids of which it is composed. Just as the wavelength spectrum of a light tells how much energy is present at different wavelengths, so the spatial frequency *spectrum* of a given pattern tells how much contrast there is in the pattern at different spatial frequencies. The spectrum of a visual pattern is presented as a graph of contrast versus spatial frequency. For example, the gratings in Fig. 9.1 or the demonstration consist of pure sine waves; each contains only the one frequency that is the frequency of that sine. Their spectra, shown in Fig. 9.2 and in the 'Spectrum' window near the upper right of your screen in the demonstration, indicate that there is contrast at only one frequency, and all others are absent.

The spectra and the sinusoidal curves are two different representations of the same thing. In Fig. 9.1 you see the actual patterns in space; in Fig. 9.2 you see their spectra. A spectrum looks very different from the actual light distribution, but it says unequivocally that the distribution of light is that shown in the corresponding part of Fig. 9.1.

Other simple sinusoids would also be represented by spectra in *frequency space* that are spike-like; the location of the spike depends on the frequency of the sinusoid. The height of the spike depends on the contrast of the sinusoid. A low-frequency sinusoid (coarse grating, as in Fig. 9.1a) is represented by a spike near the left end of the frequency axis (Fig. 9.2a); a higher-frequency sinusoid (fine grating, as in Fig. 9.1b) is represented by a spike to the right on the frequency axis (Fig. 9.2b). A high-contrast grating (Fig. 9.1a) is represented by a taller spike than that representing a lower contrast grating (Fig. 9.1b). When you change the amplitude of the sinusoid in the demonstration, you can see a corresponding change in the height of the spike representing it in the spectrum.

A single spike is the simplest spectrum one could imagine; only one spatial frequency is represented. For this reason, sinusoidal gratings are often the stimulus of choice for exploring the possibility that Fourier components play a role. Sinusoids are the most 'primitive' waveforms you can use, being the only waveform that is never distorted by any linear system (Shapley & Lennie, 1985).

Simple sinusoids are not what we generally see in the world about us. However, more interesting things can also be represented by spectra in frequency space. Fourier showed that it is possible to represent any pattern by its spectrum. As a demonstration, the next paragraphs show how one de-

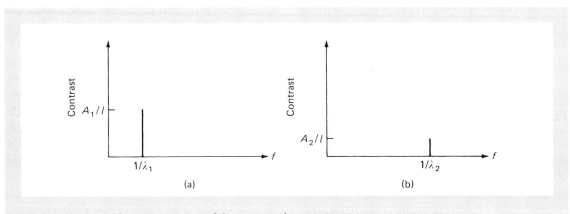

Fig. 9.2 The spatial frequency spectra of the gratings shown in Fig. 9.1.

composes one particular pattern into its component frequencies. The pattern is one that is commonly used as a stimulus: the square wave grating (Fig. 9.3). It consists of alternate light and dark bars. The pattern of light is thus described by a pattern of uniform areas—high intensity, then low, then high, then low.

You can play with adding components in the demonstration program. Click on 'Square wave' at the upper right. You will see the original sinusoidal grating at full contrast, just as it was when you started the demonstration. But now there will be additional rows available to add other sinusoids to this one. The three columns in the lower part of the demonstration are parallel representations of the building of a square wave from sines. The left column shows the actual patterns of light of each component (a sinusoidal grating); the middle column graphs luminance as a function of position for that component; and on the right are the corresponding equations. The resultant sum of these gratings is shown at the top, with its waveform traced in blue below it. To the upper right you can see the spectrum corresponding to the sum.

Begin with a sine wave whose wavelength is the same as the square wave you are composing. This is called the *fundamental* component; it is both the lowest frequency present and the largest component of the square wave. It is a sine in space, and therefore represented by a spectrum that is a single spike; its equation is given at the right. It is the only component present in the demonstration when you start it.

To the fundamental sine wave, add another sine at higher frequency but lower contrast. The particular wave needed is one-third the contrast and three times the frequency; it is called the 'third harmonic'. Click on its 'check box' to the right, and it will be drawn below the fundamental. The sum of these two components is shown at the top. Notice that the higher-frequency sine wave is negative where the fundamental reaches a peak; it therefore subtracts from the peak and flattens it. With just these two components, you can already see the form of the square wave emerging. The

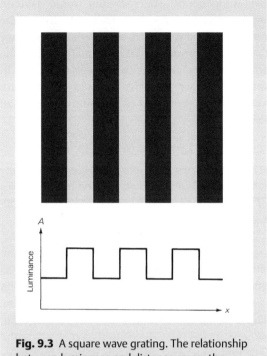

Fig. 9.3 A square wave grating. The relationship between luminance and distance across the grating is shown below.

spectrum of the sum of the two components is simply the sum of the spectra of the individual components; that is, two spikes. The equation of the curve is the sum of the two equations shown, namely:

$$1.00 \sin (fx) + 0.33 \sin (3 fx).$$

Now add another harmonic that is five times the fundamental in frequency and one-fifth of the contrast, the fifth harmonic (add it by clicking the next empty selection box on the right in the demonstration program). The pattern in space is an even better approximation to a square wave, and the spectrum now has three spikes.

If you continue in this manner, adding all the odd multiples (3, 5, 7, 9, etc.) of the fundamental frequency at contrasts proportional to the inverse of their frequencies, the sum approaches a square wave. (The program only allows the first five components.) The spectrum would have an infinite number of spikes (there are an infinite number of odd numbers), but the high-frequency components would be infinitesimally small. The equation corresponding to the spectrum has an infinite number of terms (one per component), and is best represented by the summation of an infinite series:

$$L(x) = \sum_{i=1}^{\infty} [1/(2i-1)] \sin [(2i-1)fx]$$

(This notation may be unfamiliar, but it just means what was said in words: add all the odd multiples of the fundamental frequency, each with an amplitude inversely proportional to its frequency.)

The spatial pattern, the equation, and the spectrum are all different representations of the same thing, but with one difference: the spectrum lacks one piece of information. As a result, a waveform cannot be uniquely determined from its spectrum. That missing information is the phase of each component, or the relative position of each along the left/right dimension. All that is implied by a spike on a spectrum is that there is a sinusoidal component of the given contrast at that frequency; it does not imply that this wave goes through zero at the same position as the fundamental. (The fact that all the components are sines and must pass through zero at the same points as the fundamental is unequivocal from the equations to the right.)

Suppose that alternate components were inverted—that is, peaked where these have valleys, and having valleys where these have peaks. This corresponds to a phase shift of 180°, as can be verified by considering the sine in Fig. A.9 shifted by one-half of a cycle or by changing the phase of the 'Simple sine wave' in the demonstration. If you take the same components but shift every other component 180°, the spectrum would be the same as before, but the waveform and equations are different. The resulting waveform can be seen in the CD demonstration by choosing 'Peaks add' from the top right. There is the same fundamental component with the same harmonics, but two harmonics have a phase shift of 180°. The result of the phase shift is that the peaks add, rather than sub-

tract; instead of leveling the peaks of the fundamental, the harmonics build them higher and narrower.

When the peaks add instead of cancel, the peaks and troughs could exceed 100% modulation, requiring negative light in the troughs! For this reason, all the components of the compound gratings were actually made smaller than indicated. The 'Peaks add' grating tends toward a pattern of alternating dark and light lines on a field of gray. Another adjustment can be made: invert the alternate components, but instead of dividing each amplitude by the frequency, as for the square wave, divide by the frequency squared. Then the harmonics are not as large as for the square wave. When this full complement of harmonics has been added, the waveform is a *triangle wave*; it clearly looks quite different from the square wave or 'Peaks add', although its spectrum is similar. You can try this combination by clicking 'Triangle wave' at the upper right.

Now stop and consider what you have learned so far. For every pattern in space, which can be represented by a function showing the luminance as a function of position, there corresponds a Fourier transform that can be graphed as a spectrum of contrast versus frequency. The function of luminance versus position is a direct map of the pattern; it is the way one would generally think about what the pattern 'is'. The spectrum is quite different looking; however, it is a convenient way of describing the pattern mathematically. In what follows, gratings will be described only by their spectra, for the corresponding equations tend not to make pleasant reading. Remember, however, that the actual Fourier transform of patterns also contains information about the phase that is simply not shown in the spectra.

The modulation transfer and contrast sensitivity functions

For every pattern in space there corresponds a Fourier transform; for every Fourier transform there is a corresponding pattern in space. Suppose you have an optical system (a camera or telescope) and wish to know how good an image of some pattern it can make. By looking at the quality of the images produced for input patterns that are pure sinusoidal gratings, you can predict how the optical system will perform for any arbitrary input. If the pure gratings are all of the same contrast, the performance of the optical system can be defined by the contrast of the image at each frequency. The plot of the relative image contrast versus frequency is called a *modulation transfer function* (MTF).

A hypothetical example is shown in Fig. 9.4(a). This is the MTF of a typical camera lens; all frequencies lower than f_0 are reproduced without a loss of contrast, but higher frequencies are progressively less well reproduced. A grating at a frequency less than f_0 would appear as strongly in the image as in the original pattern, but a high-frequency grating (closely spaced bars) would be reproduced with lower contrast; if it is of sufficiently high frequency, its image would be a uniform gray field. This is typical of optical systems: low frequencies (large things) are reproduced well, but high frequencies (tiny details) are lost.

Suppose this same optical system is knocked out of focus. Some high frequencies that had been reproduced well are lost; only the lowest frequencies survive. In general, when an image is out of focus, the highest frequencies are lost (the fine details are blurred out of existence).

The MTF of the optical system lets you predict the image that will be formed of any pattern it might reproduce. If the pattern contains only components less than f_0 (and is in focus), it is reproduced perfectly. If there are components greater than f_0, they are diminished according to a factor corresponding to their frequencies. Components near f_0 are made slightly smaller, while those well above f_0 become vanishingly small. If you take the spectrum of the pattern, and multiply each component by the factor implied by the MTF for its frequency, you obtain the spectrum of the image. By Fourier mathematics, the light distribution in the image may be reconstructed from that spectrum. (Again, remember that you need the phase information. In fact, components with frequencies such that their amplitudes are made smaller also have their phases changed. That is why an out-of-focus point looks like a blurry ring.) **BOX 9.1**

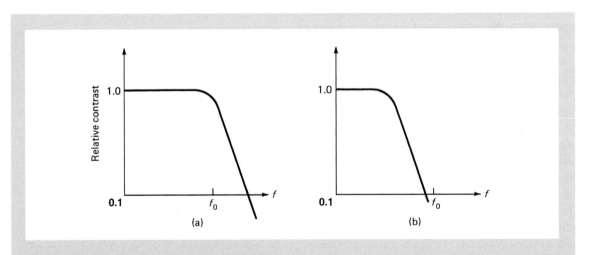

Fig. 9.4 Hypothetical transfer functions of a physical optical system, showing relative contrast in the image as a function of spatial frequency. (a) A reasonable optical system, well focused. (b) The same system with the image out of focus.

Box 9.1 Why Fourier transforms are really simpler

The spectrum of an image is simply the point-by-point product of the spectrum of the pattern and the MTF of the optical system. This simplicity is the principal mathematical advantage of transforms such as the Fourier transform. If you wished to know the output of an electronic circuit given a particular input, or the motion of a mechanical structure (bridge or tower) given a particular mechanical perturbation, or the path of a vehicle or ship with a particular steering system given a particular command, you would be faced with a difficult and complicated differential equation (differential equations are the subject following advanced calculus). On the other hand, you can take the transform of the input, simply multiply by the MTF, and have the transform of the system output without ever having to resort to calculus or differential equations. The only problem is performing the transformations to and from frequency space, and that problem is solved by published tables of functions and their corresponding transforms.

Up to this point, the MTF has referred to a physical optical system; but the human visual system is just a high-class optical system. In fact, it includes a physical optical system in the traditional sense: the cornea and lens of the eye, which form the image on the retina (see Chapter 3). The tests that an optometrist or ophthalmologist make to determine visual acuity are really just another way of characterizing the MTF of your eyes.

The visual system, however, includes more than the eye. There is no guarantee that all components imaged on the retina will be perceived (although any that are degraded by the cornea and lens certainly will *not* be seen). Psychophysics can determine the MTF of the entire system: cornea, lens, retina, visual cortex, and whatever interprets patterns of firing within the cortex. The way this is done is to measure the *contrast sensitivity* for sine wave gratings at all spatial frequencies.

Contrast sensitivity is defined (as are other sensitivities) as the inverse of the contrast required to attain threshold. Measuring contrast sensitivity is thus like making any other threshold measurement; the contrast is found at which the subject is just barely able to detect that the target is a grating rather than a uniform gray field (any of the methods discussed in Chapter 2 can be used). Obviously, it is easier for a subject to say whether there was a grating than to indicate the apparent amplitude of the modulation. When contrast threshold is measured at each frequency and the results plotted versus spatial frequency, a *contrast sensitivity function* (CSF) like the one shown in Fig. 9.5 is derived. The CSF represents the underlying function (see Chapter 6 for a discussion of sensitivity *versus* response measures). The MTF and CSF are identical if the system is linear.

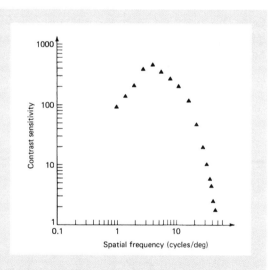

Fig. 9.5 The contrast sensitivity function (CSF) of a human observer; contrast sensitivity as a function of spatial frequency. From Campbell, F. W. and J. G. Robson (1968) Application of Fourier analysis to the visibility of gratings. *J. Physiol.* 197: 551–566. Reprinted by permission of the Cambridge University Press.

What does the CSF in Fig. 9.5 tell us? For one thing, like the MTFs in Fig. 9.4, there is drastic attenuation of very high frequencies. In fact, it is perfectly reasonable to expect this, as the cornea and lens comprise a physical optical system of limited capability that transmits very high frequencies poorly. It is probable, however, that the exact shape of the high-frequency end of the curve is also partially determined by the processing performed by the retina and cortex.

The other noteworthy feature of the CSF in Fig. 9.5 is that the very low spatial frequencies are also attenuated. This is not like the characteristics of physical optical systems and is thus likely to reflect a physiological property of the visual system. **BOX 9.2**

As a matter of fact, you already know of a physiological process that attenuates low spatial frequencies: lateral antagonism (see Chapter 5). Remember that lateral antagonism has the effect of reducing the responses of ganglion cells when they are situated in a broad area of uniform illumination (low spatial frequency). A ganglion cell with its receptive field centered on the broad plateau of a low spatial frequency grating, as shown in Fig. 9.6(a), receives considerable antagonism from the well-illuminated surround of its receptive field. This is inhibition that reduces the firing of the cell from the level that it might have attained because of the illumination of its excitatory center. If the grating were of a higher frequency, as shown in Fig. 9.6(b), the center could be about as well illuminated as in (a), but the major part of the surround would lie in the relatively darker troughs. The response in this case would be considerably greater, for there would be less antagonism.

Now suppose the grating were of an even higher frequency, so that several cycles could fit within the center of the receptive field (Fig 9.6c). The center and surround would each have light areas and dark areas in about equal proportion, and the response would be expected to be less than in Fig. 9.6(a). The excitation and inhibition are balanced, as in Fig. 9.6(a); high frequencies should therefore be attenuated as well.

If lateral antagonism can be equated with the low spatial frequency attenuation noted in the CSF, the CSF can be considered an 'explanation' for those visual effects attributed to lateral antagonism. You can 'explain' Mach bands and similar effects by applying the CSF to the spectra of these patterns. In general, these arguments are rather complicated, but there is one that is amenable to graphic demonstration. This is the Craik–O'Brien illusion (Fig. 5.6, p.81) The light distribution in the Craik–O'Brien illusion is one with 'glitches' in an otherwise uniform field, but the appearance is

Box 9.2 A pattern to see your own CSF

There is a particular pattern that enables you to see the shape of your own CSF. This pattern is reproduced as a demonstration on the CD accompanying this book. (Select 'See your CSF' from the Chapter 9 menu. The pattern will only be an approximation if you have not set your color resolution to 'True color'; see Box P2). The pattern is a grating in which the spatial frequency increases from left to right, and the contrast increases from top to bottom. Along any vertical strip of the figure the frequency is the same; along any horizontal strip the contrast is the same. You should see a pattern in which the medium-sized 'bars' in the middle are the tallest—they are tallest because they are visible at lower contrast (farther up on the figure). The higher-frequency stripes to the right and the lower-frequency stripes to the left are at just as high a contrast, but they cannot be seen because the human eye is less sensitive to those frequencies. Click on the bar that appears tallest, and then move to a different distance from the screen. (This changes the spatial frequencies in cycles/degree; move away from the screen, and all the frequencies become higher.) The peak should appear to move to a different position, indicating that it is a function of the visual system, not the way the figure was reproduced on your screen.

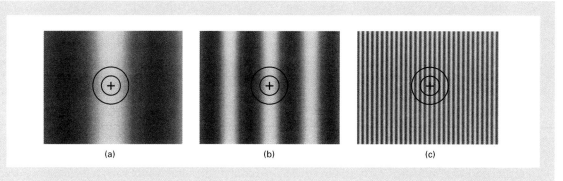

Fig. 9.6 How lateral antagonism can account for the lower sensitivity to low spatial frequencies. (a) A ganglion cell receptive field being stimulated by a very low-frequency grating; both center and surround are well lit, so inhibition cancels much of the excitation. (b) The same receptive field with a grating of optimal frequency. The center is well lit, but the surround is in the dark, so there is little inhibition. (c) The same field stimulated by a very high-frequency grating. Both the center and the surround are about as well lit as if the field were uniform (no grating).

of fairly uniform steps in brightness. The pattern shown at the top left of Fig. 9.7 should appear as alternate bright and dark bands, even though the actual illumination in the center of each band is the same.

The third column in Fig. 9.7 shows the spectra associated with the illusion and the two other patterns shown below it. You can better understand the spectrum for the illusion by seeing how the illusory pattern can be broken into two components: a sine wave and a square wave. If the sine wave in the middle row is added to the square wave at the bottom, the illusory pattern will result (you can convince yourself of this by doing some mental addition). The spectrum of the sine is a single spike; the spectrum of the square wave is a series of spikes (as in the 'Fourier components' demonstration). The sum of these spectra is thus the series of spikes shown at the top of the third column. Note that the sine in the middle row is 180° out of phase with the fundamental of the square wave; that is, it is actually *subtracted* from the square wave.

Consider what happens if each of the spectra is multiplied by the CSF in Fig. 9.5. The lowest frequencies are attenuated, so the pattern the brain receives that generally means square wave (bot-

tom) is as shown at the lower right. The sine wave, which is of low spatial frequency, is attenuated to near invisibility. The spectrum of the square-plus-sine (top) is similar to the spectrum of the square wave, so the two look alike, and the illusory pattern is seen as the more familiar square wave pattern. Put another way, the sinusoidal component (that is, the only physical difference between the illusory pattern and the square wave pattern) is nearly invisible, so the illusory pattern cannot be distinguished from a square wave. The Craik–O'Brien pattern and the square wave pattern are both members of the same 'equivalence class'—patterns that are physically different but give rise to the identical neural signals (Ratliff & Sirovich, 1978). They must therefore look alike; that they both appear as square waves might be because the visual system is set up to detect edges (and therefore also square waves) by a kind of Fourier analysis (Campbell et al., 1978). **BOX 9.3**

The Craik–O'Brien illusion works well near threshold, where the low-frequency fundamental may well be imperceptible. At higher contrasts, the difference between the illusory figure (Fig. 9.7a) and the square wave (Fig. 9.7c) is easily seen (although it may still appear that the centers of the light and dark bars are not the same luminance).

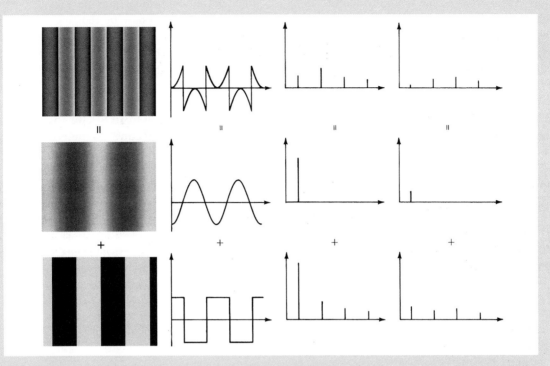

Fig. 9.7 The Craik–O'Brien illusion explained in terms of the CSF. The left graphs show the distribution of light in space, the middle graphs show the spectrum corresponding to each pattern, and the right graphs show the *effective* spectra (how effective each component should be if it is weighted according to the CSF in Fig. 9.5). *Top*: The Craik–O'Brien pattern. *Middle*: A low-frequency sinusoid. *Bottom*: A square wave. The sum of the bottom two rows is the Craik–O'Brien pattern in the top row.

Box 9.3 Another way to think about the Craik–O'Brien illusion

Because the Craik–O'Brien illusion is really a square wave with its fundamental component removed, it is sometimes also called the *missing fundamental* illusion. Actually, the pattern in Fig. 9.7(a) is not a missing fundamental illusion, for the sine subtracted had the same contrast as the square wave. If you look carefully at the 'Fourier components' demonstration, you may notice that the fundamental component actually has a greater contrast than the resultant square wave (there is a factor of $4/\pi$ that was not mentioned). Therefore, in Fig. 9.7, most, but not all, of the fundamental component of the square wave was subtracted. Notice that because of this mathematical quirk, a 100% contrast square wave actually contains a fundamental component that is greater than 100% contrast!

You can demonstrate that the Craik–O'Brien illusion is really a 'missing fundamental' by removing the fundamental component of the square wave (built from the first five components) in the demonstration program of Fourier components of gratings. First, include all the components to make a reasonable square wave. Then click the check-box to the right of the fundamental [$1.00\sin(fx)$], so that it is cleared. Without the fundamental, you have a missing-fundamental illusion. Note that it is a fair approximation to the Craik–O'Brien pattern.

Burr (1987) explored the way in which the apparent brightness of the bar centers changed at higher contrasts and concluded that there are really two systems: at low contrasts (below 10%) there is a contrast-dependent system; at higher contrasts, brightness is matched. This changeover may remind you of the dual magnocellular and parvocellular systems discussed in Chapters 7 and 8. The magnocellular system operates well at low contrasts, while the parvocellular system is nearly ineffective at contrasts less than about 10%. It thus appears that this illusion may 'fool' the magnocellular system but not the parvocellular.

The multiple-channel hypothesis

The foregoing discussion emphasized the fact that spatial frequency analysis is no more than an alternative, equivalent description of patterns you might otherwise describe in terms of light and dark. The explanations of Mach bands and the Craik–O'Brien illusions in terms of the CSF might be thought of as representing new and different explanations of these phenomena; in fact, if the shape of the CSF can be attributed to lateral antagonism, this is no more than the old explanation couched in terms of spatial frequencies. Just as spatial frequency is an equivalent description of the visual stimulus, the CSF provides an equivalent description of the process of lateral antagonism.

In short, this alternative way of describing things may not be more appropriate than the old familiar descriptions. But you may recall a promise to show that it is possible that the visual system pays attention to component spatial frequencies.

Evidence suggesting that the human visual system might perform some kind of Fourier analysis was introduced by Blakemore & Campbell (1969). They measured the CSF of a subject, as previously described. Then they had the subject inspect a high-contrast sinusoidal grating. The inspection grating changed in phase by 180° eight times per second, so that the subject would not simply form an afterimage of the grating (see Chapter 6). Still, for a minute or so the subject saw only a high-contrast pattern at a single spatial frequency. Following this exposure, the subject's CSF was again measured. The two CSFs for the same subject, one before inspecting the high-contrast grating and one after, are shown together in Fig. 9.8. The CSF before exposure to the grating is shown as a solid line; it is like the CSF shown in Fig. 9.5. (The only difference is that there is not as much attenuation of low frequencies as in that other figure; this is probably because Blakemore & Campbell used a lower overall light level.) The CSF measured after exposure to the high-contrast grating is shown by the data points; it is markedly depressed

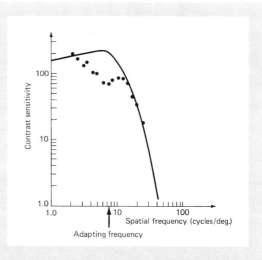

Fig. 9.8 A CSF before (*solid curve*) and after (*data points*) adaptation to a high-contrast grating at the spatial frequency indicated by the arrow. From Blakemore, C. and F. W. Campbell (1969) On the existence of neurones in the human visual system selectively sensitive to the orientation and size of retinal images. *J. Physiol.* 203: 237–260. Reprinted by permission of the Cambridge University Press.

for frequencies near the frequency of the inspection grating (indicated by an arrow).

A similar result was obtained when other spatial frequencies were used for the inspection grating. Whatever was used, the CSF was depressed for test gratings near that frequency, but unaffected for those much higher or much lower. Inspection of a high-contrast grating has the effect of making low-contrast gratings of similar frequency much harder to detect, but has little or no effect on gratings significantly different in frequency.

How might one explain such a result? Blakemore & Campbell invoked a hypothesis (first made by Campbell & Robson, 1968) that there are a number of separate *channels* in the visual system. Each of the hypothetical channels is

'tuned' to a relatively narrow range of spatial frequencies. Thus, some channels are specific for low spatial frequencies; these channels would be activated only when there are large smudges (low frequencies) in the visual field. Other channels are specific to high frequencies and are activated only when there are fine details (high frequencies) in the visual field. Others are specific for the frequencies in between. Detection of the presence of a grating depends on activating any channel; the one that will be activated first (and determine the threshold contrast) will be the one that is best tuned to the spatial frequency of the grating.

The overall CSF should therefore be determined by the peak sensitivities of each of the component channels, or the *envelope* of the separate channels.

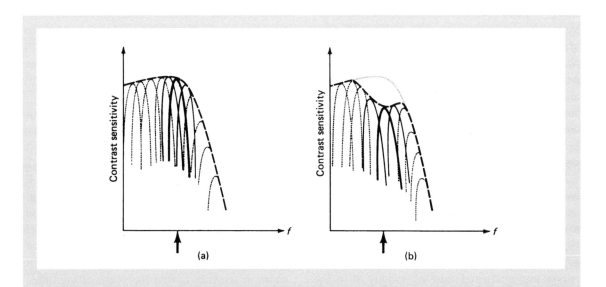

Fig. 9.9 How the CSF could be composed of frequency-selective channels. (a) The CSF (*dashed*) is the envelope of a number of separate channels, each sensitive to a narrow range of spatial frequencies. A stimulus at a particular frequency (*arrow*) would have its greatest effect on the channel shown as a dark solid curve; it would have less effect on the channels shown by light solid curves, and virtually no effect on those shown by dotted curves. (b) The result of adapting to a high-contrast grating at the frequency shown by the arrow. The channel shown by the dark solid curve is made much less sensitive; the channels shown by light solid curves are less affected, and those shown by dotted curves are unaffected. As a result, the CSF (*dashed*) shows a notch in sensitivity for spatial frequencies near the adapting frequency. Modified from Blakemore and Campbell (1969). Reprinted by permission.

How a CSF is made from the sum of separate channels is shown in Fig. 9.9(a). The CSF is shown as a dashed curve, with some of the channels of which it is composed shown as dotted and solid curves.

Blakemore & Campbell assumed that a channel adapts when it is strongly stimulated. When a channel adapts, it becomes less sensitive; that is, a higher-contrast grating is needed to stimulate it. This could be exactly like adaptation of retinal neurons; when they are vigorously stimulated, they become less sensitive. Adaptation depends on stimulation, so the most stimulated channel will be the most severely adapted one, while less stimulated channels will be less adapted.

Suppose that the subject inspects a high-contrast grating at the frequency shown by the arrow in Fig. 9.9(a). The channel most stimulated by the grating is the one that peaks at that frequency; it is shown as a heavy solid curve. As each channel covers a band of frequencies, other channels that peak at nearby frequencies will also be affected by the grating; they are shown by light solid curves. Channels that peak at frequencies well above or well below the grating frequency, however, will be virtually unaffected by the grating (dotted curves).

Adaptation means a loss of contrast sensitivity; this means an adapted channel has its sensitivity curve moved downward. Figure 9.9(b) shows the same channels after adaptation to a high-contrast grating at the frequency marked by the arrow. The channels shown by dotted curves are unaffected, and are exactly as in Fig. 9.9(a). The channels shown by solid lines have been adapted by the grating, and are shifted downward from their former positions; the most adapted curve is the one that peaks at the frequency of the inspection grating (dark solid curve). The envelope indicating the sensitivity of the most sensitive channel at each frequency (dashed curve) is the notched CSF as observed by Blakemore & Campbell.

Channels as Fourier analyzers

The Blakemore & Campbell experiment suggested that there are separate channels tuned to different spatial frequencies. Now let's leap to an assumption about the function of these channels: as each channel is preferentially tuned to a particular band of frequencies, activity in that channel signals how much contrast there is at that peak frequency in the visual stimulus. The visual system analyzes a scene by determining the contrast at each of the spatial frequencies; it does this by noting the activity in each of the spatial frequency channels (Graham & Nachmias, 1971).

If this is true, the visual system performs a crude Fourier analysis of the visual scene. If you arrayed all the channels along a line in the order of the spatial frequency to which each is most sensitive, the activity in each channel (firing rate of neurons) would represent the spectrum of the visual stimulus, as extracted by the visual system. Like the spectra in the 'Fourier components' demonstration, it is a representation of the contrast at every spatial frequency.

Might we recognize patterns by their spectra? Graham & Nachmias (1971) compared the detection of gratings made of two components. The two components they used were like the fundamental and first harmonic of a square wave; that is, a sinusoid plus another sinusoid at three times as high a frequency (see the 'Fourier components' demonstration). The harmonic could be combined with the fundamental in phase ('Square wave'), or 180° out of phase ('Peaks add'). When the harmonic is in phase, it tends to flatten the peaks of the fundamental; when the harmonic is 180° out of phase it enhances the peaks of the fundamental.

Subjects could just detect that there was a grating when the fundamental was of high enough contrast to be detected. The contrast required in the fundamental was the same whether it was presented alone (no harmonic at all), or with the harmonic in either the 'peaks add' or 'square wave' configuration. The harmonic, when it was below threshold, had no effect on the detection of the fundamental. This confirmed an earlier observation by Campbell & Robson (1968) that the threshold for seeing a square wave is determined by the threshold for its fundamental component. When only the fundamental component is above threshold, the square wave cannot be discriminated from a sine wave (see also Campbell *et al.*, 1978; Badcock, 1984b).

As the contrast of the harmonic component increases, it ultimately exceeds threshold. When it does, the pattern no longer looks the same as a simple sinusoidal grating. The contrast of the harmonic at which it is seen is the same regardless of whether the harmonic is presented alone (no fundamental), or in conjunction with the fundamental (also confirming Campbell & Robson). Threshold for detecting the combination is about the same when the harmonic is in phase as when it is out of phase (but see Akutsu & Legge, 1995). This demonstration of independence is actually surprising considering that the overall contrast of the pattern (difference between brightest bar and dimmest) is considerably greater in the 180° out-of-phase configuration ('Peaks add') than in the in-phase configuration ('Square wave'). **BOX 9.4**

But there are problems with the simple idea that information is encoded by the activities in a large number of independent channels, each tuned to a specific spatial frequency. First, the number of channels is not as large as the early experiments had suggested. Careful psychophysical measurements have indicated that there may be relatively few channels. Williams *et al.* (1982) report only four size-sensitive mechanisms at each retinal location. Wilson *et al.* (1983) suggest six channels. Watson & Robson (1981) vote for 10 channels in two distinct subsets: seven operate at low temporal frequencies, while three operate only at high temporal frequencies. Whatever the actual count, there are apparently too few to provide more than a very coarse Fourier analysis. (It should be noted, however, that a much finer Fourier analysis could be extracted from a few broad channels; see Chapter 14 for how the visual system performs an exquisite analysis of wavelength from the information in only three color channels.)

Another objection concerns the specificity of the channels. Clearly, if there are few channels and each is very narrow in bandwidth, they cannot effectively span the frequency range. In fact, the bandwidth is limited by the mathematics of the requirement that each channel also somehow specify the position of a stimulus. In order for a channel to be narrow in its spatial frequency selectivity, it must accept input from a large spatial domain. Conversely, to be selective for a particular location, a channel must be broad in its spatial frequency bandwidth. Thus, a perfect

---

Box 9.4 On the importance of phase

The equivalence of the 'square wave' and 'peaks add' combination gratings bears further comment. It is the result to expect if phase information has been lost, as the only difference between the two patterns is their phases. At high-contrast levels, well above threshold, the two patterns do not look alike: the 'square wave' pattern looks like pairs of bright bars and dark bars, while the 'peaks add' pattern looks like a bright bar, medium bar, dim bar, etc. Near threshold, however, the phase information seems lost, and the two are equivalent.

Given that the two patterns do not look alike at high contrast, the phase information must be carried some-where in the visual system. Where and how it is carried have been the object of considerable speculation (Stromeyer *et al.*, 1973; Atkinson & Campbell, 1974; DeValois, 1978). Perhaps the most straightforward suggestion is that phase is encoded by the retinotopic location of the channels stimulated (Ochs, 1979). Recent workers suggest that localization is independent of the spatial frequency channels (Burbeck, 1987; Polat & Sagi, 1993), with the difference between a 'square wave' and a 'peaks add' wave being coded specifically as the profile of the luminance pattern (Badcock, 1984a).

Box 9.5 A compromise between Fourier and point-by-point information

The argument in this paragraph has led to the suggestion that the visual system has arranged a compromise. Receptive fields must be small to allow localization, but if there is to be spatial frequency analysis, the bandwidths cannot be too broad. The compromise is to have moderate-sized receptive fields that provide moderate bandwidth channels. In fact, the visual system seems to have made the compromise rather well, having receptive field sizes that jointly optimize spatial localization and spatial frequency selectivity (Daugman, 1984). The resulting channels are a close approximation to the real part of a function called a *Gabor filter*. Some workers in recent years have embraced the notion that it is this compromise, rather than a real Fourier analysis, that the visual system uses (for example, Porat & Zeevi, 1989); others disagree (Stork & Wilson, 1990)

---

spatial frequency channel would have an infinite spatial receptive field. As the field narrows, the spatial frequency selectivity broadens, until a point receptor (perfect spatial localization) accepts all spatial frequencies equally. <u>BOX 9.5</u>

Masking

Additional evidence that the visual system might actually encode a visual scene according to its spatial frequency components comes from an experimental paradigm called *masking*. Masking refers to using one stimulus to hide another. It is not a new technique, having been used in visual experiments for at least 30 years before the spatial frequency notion was proposed (see Chapter 10). The particular kind of masking experiments that have been invoked to support the spatial frequency idea are analogous to experiments that have long been known in audition. As you will see in Chapter 16, the auditory system performs a Fourier analysis of the temporal frequencies of sound waves in analyzing pitch. The proponents of spatial frequency analysis by the visual system often draw the analogy of the temporal frequency analysis in the ear.

There are three basic kinds of masking experiments: *simultaneous, backward*, and *forward masking*. In each, there is a test stimulus the presence of which the subject is requested to detect, and a masking stimulus that makes detection more difficult than it would be if the test stimulus were presented in isolation. This is not the same as adaptation, in which viewing of a stimulus makes the mechanism responsible for its detection less effective; in masking, the mask typically affects other mechanisms than the one being tested (Ross & Speed, 1991).

In simultaneous masking, both the test and the mask are presented at once; if both are visual patterns, they may be printed one on top of the other on the same piece of paper. The masking pattern serves to distract the viewer from the stimulus; this is the principle of camouflage (see Chapter 10).

Backward masking occurs when the mask stimulus is presented immediately after the test stimulus; forward masking occurs when the mask precedes the test. As the timing is critical, a special piece of equipment, called a *tachistoscope* (often referred to as a t'scope), is used. The tachistoscope has the capability of presenting several different patterns, either superimposed or singly, with any timing the experimenter chooses. The timing circuitry is precise enough to allow presentations of less than a millisecond (1/1000 s). <u>BOX 9.6</u>

The point about masking that is relevant here is that effective masks (those that prevent detection of the test) may lie within a *critical band* of spatial frequencies near those of the test patterns they are masking. This is consistent with the multiple channel hypothesis, for if the stimulus pattern is detected by the relative excitation of the various channels, the perception of the stimulus will be disrupted only if the mask also affects those same channels. If the mask only affected channels that peaked at spatial frequencies much different from

Box 9.6 Metacontrast

A special name has been given to backward masking in which the test figure and the mask fall on different areas of retina: it is called *metacontrast*. Weisstein (1968) suggested that metacontrast may be explained as a form of lateral antagonism, by assuming that the antagonistic effect (from the mask) develops more slowly than the excitatory effect (from the test). It is likely, however, that metacontrast is more complex than simple retinal interac-

tion; for example, Bernstein *et al.* (1976) have suggested that the mechanism of metacontrast for short delays between mask and test may be different from the mechanism for long delays. They also suggest that information about the test and the mask are extracted separately before the two interact.

those of the test stimulus, the channels carrying the information about the pattern would be unaffected. A mask of spatial frequency much different from the stimulus would be as ineffective as if the mask were far away from the stimulus in space; an ink spill on the desk next to the book does not interfere with reading, but an ink spill on the page could create a problem.

A demonstration of the significance of the spatial frequency content in simultaneous masking was made by Harmon & Julesz (1973). Their stimulus, that is test and mask simultaneously, is shown in Fig. 9.10. If it looks like an abstraction of gray boxes, prop up the book and look at the figure from a distance (or take off your glasses if you wear them). The picture was made by a computer process that divided a portrait into boxes and printed each box with the average intensity in that box. This has the effect of removing high frequencies; any detail smaller than the width of a box must be averaged out. It also has the effect of adding some high frequencies, namely those that define the edges of the boxes.

Figure 9.11 illustrates graphically what the computer has done in creating Fig. 9–10 from a portrait. Figure 9.11(a) shows a hypothetical spectrum of the original picture, with components at all frequencies; Fig. 9.11(b) shows the result of the computer processing: all the picture frequencies higher than the repeat frequency of the boxes (indicated by an arrow) have been removed. In their places are the frequencies defining the boxes; essentially, the boxes are square

waves and so appear as a series of odd multiples of the box frequency (recall the 'square wave' demon-stration). The hypothetical spectrum of Fig. 9.10 is shown in Fig. 9.11(b).

What happens when you blur the figure by moving away from it or taking off your eyeglasses? Blurring an image removes the high-frequency components (see Fig. 9.4); the high-frequency components that are removed are the ones the computer introduced by making sharp boxes. The spectrum of the blurred picture is shown in Fig. 9.11(c); it is nearly the same as what the spectrum of the original would be if it were blurred. There is no way to recover the lost high frequencies of the original portrait, but you can remove the additional high frequencies that made the picture information hard to see. The blurred boxed picture is about as good as a blurred original—not great, but recognizable.

The portrait is masked by the high frequencies introduced by the computer; according to the channel hypothesis, only those additional frequencies similar to the frequencies surviving in the picture should be effective in masking it. If you blurred only slightly, removing the highest frequencies but leaving the first few components of the boxes, the masking should still be quite effective. This can be seen in Fig. 9.11(d). You cannot yet say that the slight blur that removes the very highest frequencies is less effective because those frequencies are dissimilar from the frequencies in the picture; it may simply be that you have not removed enough of the masking energy.

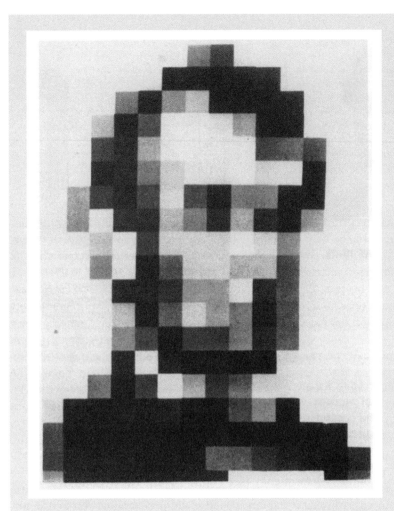

Fig. 9.10 Computer-processed portrait. Courtesy of International Business Machines Corporation.

To check for that possibility, Harmon & Julesz (1973) prepared a picture in which the masking frequencies of Fig. 9.11(d) were removed, and the higher frequencies missing there but present in Fig. 9.11(b) were restored. This cannot be done by defocusing, but requires computer processing. The result is shown in Fig. 9.11(e); the high frequencies are present, but the lowest frequencies due to the boxes are gone. The picture is about as recognizable as when all the high frequencies are removed (Fig. 9.11c); that is, the frequencies introduced by the boxing do not all mask the picture—only those within the critical band near the picture frequencies affect recognition of the photo, because only nearby frequency channels affect those carrying the picture information (Cannon & Fullenkamp, 1991). BOX 9.7

Perceptual effects

The preceding experiments provide evidence for separate channels tuned to different spatial frequencies, and further imply that the channels function as spatial frequency detectors. Now, what visual effects can be explained by assuming that each channel actually signals a particular spatial frequency when it is active?

Apparent size Because spatial frequency roughly correlates with the size or extent of patterns, it is natural to expect that any manipulation that distorts the pattern of which channels are most responsive would distort the apparent size of a figure. If the high-frequency channels were somehow disabled, only the low-frequency components would be sensed; low frequency corresponds to large patterns, so the pattern would appear larger than if all channels were functioning normally.

This is the premise of a demonstration prepared by Blakemore & Sutton (1969). They used adaptation to a high-contrast grating to reduce the sensitivity of channels at a particular spatial frequency; they then found that other gratings at frequencies slightly above or slightly below that of the adaptation grating appeared to be of higher or lower frequency than they actually were.

Their demonstration is shown in Fig. 9.12. First, look at the two square wave gratings on the right; notice that the one on the top and the one on the bottom are identical. Now adapt to the two gratings on the left; fixate on the horizontal line between the two, and move your gaze back and forth along this line to avoid creating an afterimage of the two gratings. Do this for about a half minute.

Now look at the dot between the identical gratings on the right. The grating on the top should appear to be of a higher frequency than the one below; that is, it should look like narrower bars spaced more closely together. Adapting to the low-frequency grating on the upper left caused the appearance of the medium-frequency grating on the upper right to shift toward higher frequencies; adapting to the high-frequency grating on the lower left caused the medium-frequency grating on the lower right to appear lower in frequency. As you see both at once, you make a direct comparison of the two appearances, and the difference is apparent. Changes in appearance as a result of looking at an inspection figure had

been known for some time under the name *figural aftereffects* (FAE).

To understand how the channel hypothesis explains this effect, consider Fig. 9.13. For simplicity, assume that there are only three channels concerned with the detection of the gratings shown in Fig. 9.12 (you can also neglect the harmonics in these gratings, which are, after all, square waves). The three channels labeled 1, 2, and 3, are shown in Fig. 9.13 as being equally sensitive. Suppose that the gratings on the right in Fig. 9.12 are at the peak frequency for channel 2 (t in the figure). When these gratings are presented (before any adaptation), they evoke a large response from channel 2, and smaller responses from channels 1 and 3. Gratings of slightly higher frequency evoke less response from channels 1 and 2, but more response from channel 3; for example, a high-frequency grating at h would evoke equal responses from channels 2 and 3 and a much smaller response from channel 1.

Now suppose this system is adapted by a low-frequency grating, as in the top part of Fig. 9.12. The adapting frequency is marked a in Fig. 9.13; the adapting grating has a large effect on channel 1, a moderate effect on channel 2, and virtually no effect on channel 3. Channel 1 therefore adapts the most, channel 2 somewhat less, and channel 3 practically not at all, as shown by the sensitivities in Fig. 9.13(b). The responses evoked by the test grating (at frequency t) in channels 2 and 3 are now approximately equal, with a much smaller response in channel 1. This is essentially the response pattern that would be evoked by a grating at the higher frequency h before adaptation. If the system has no way of compensating for the adaptation of the channels, it has to assume that the stimulus evoking these responses is of frequency h; that is, adaptation to the lower-frequency grating causes the test grating to be perceived as a higher frequency than it actually is. It is easy to see that if the adapting grating had been at a higher frequency than t, channels 2 and 3 would be most affected and the test would appear to be of lower frequency. This was the case for the bottom half of Fig. 9.12. **BOX 9.8**

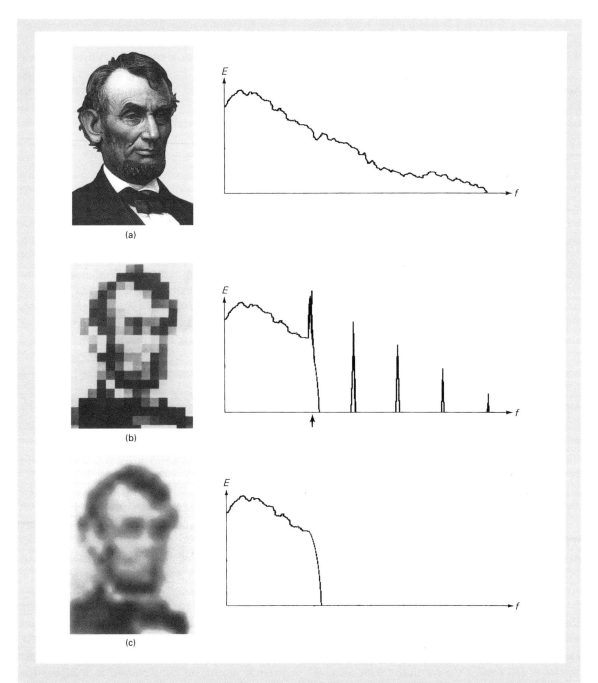

Fig. 9.11 Various manipulations on the computer-processed photograph of Fig. 9.10. Hypothetical spectra in the right-hand column correspond to each picture. Original (a) courtesy of Life Picture Service. Processed versions from Harmon, L. D. and B. Julesz (1973) Masking in visual recognition: effects of two-dimensional filtered noise. *Science* 180: 1194–1197. Copyright 1973 by the AAAS. Reprinted by permission of the publisher and authors.

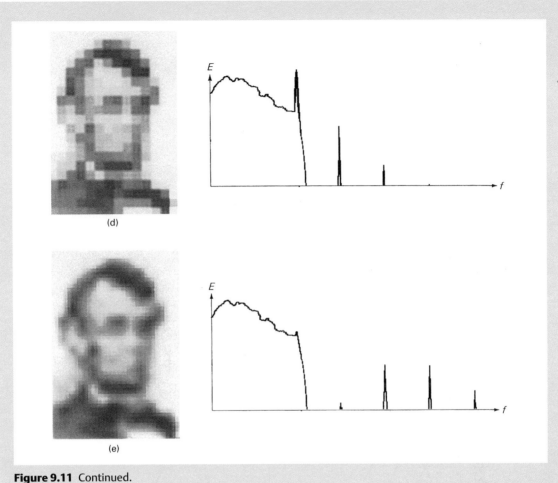

Figure 9.11 Continued.

Box 9.7 Another explanation for the Lincoln picture

There is another way of explaining the influence of the boxes in Fig. 9.10. Sufficient information that this is a picture of Lincoln is carried by low spatial frequencies, which are best seen by the magnocellular system. The parvocellular system 'sees' the high spatial frequencies, and, if the discussion at the end of Chapter 8 is correct, uses that high-frequency information along with information from the magnocellular system to identify the stimulus. In Fig. 9.10, the parvocellular and magnocellular systems con-

tradict each other, so the pattern cannot be found. When the high frequencies are removed, the parvocellular system has only the information from the magnocellular system to go on, but that is enough information to make the correct identification. In this regard, it is noteworthy that identification is enhanced if the picture is moved about (or the eyes move rapidly across it); remember, motion favors the magnocellular system.

Fig. 9.12
Demonstration of spatial frequency adaptation. Inspection pattern on the left; test pattern on the right (see text). From Blakemore, C. and P. Sutton (1969) Size adaptation: a new aftereffect. *Science* 166: 245–247 Copyright 1969 by the AAAS. Reprinted by permission of the publisher and authors.

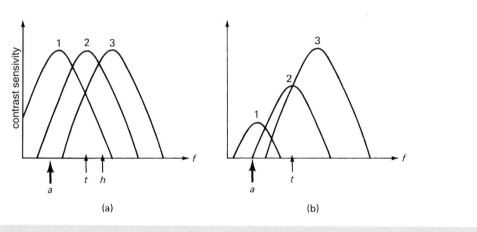

Fig. 9.13 Explanation of the effect in Fig. 9.12, showing only three channels. (a) Three equally sensitive channels, with frequency of adaptation grating (*large arrow*), frequency of test grating (*t*) and a slightly higher frequency (*h*) indicated. (b) The same three channels after exposure to the adaptation grating has depressed the sensitivity of channels 1 and 2. Test and adaptation grating frequencies are indicated by arrows.

Orientation The patterns you have seen so far varied along one dimension only; the gratings were always oriented the same way. A bit of thought should convince you that a two-dimensional pattern must have two dimensions of frequency components, and that there must be separate sets of spatial frequency analyzers corresponding to different orientations. In fact, this is the case. Adaptation to a vertical grating (bars that run up and down) has virtually no effect on the detection of a grating of the same frequency that is oriented horizontally (bars running across) (Blakemore & Campbell, 1969). Vertical and horizontal frequencies are detected by their own sets of channels.

Just like the selectivity of the channels for spatial frequency, selectivity for orientation is not perfect (Olzak & Thomas, 1991). Adaptation to a grating that is tilted slightly from vertical affects the detection of a vertical grating of the same frequency, although not quite as much as it would have done had the adaptation grating also been vertical. The greater the angle between a test grating and an adapting (or masking) grating, the less effective is the adaptation (or masking).

Figural aftereffects based on adaptation to specific orientations may easily be explained by the multiple channel hypothesis. If you adapt to a grating that is tilted slightly to the right of vertical, a subsequently viewed vertical line will appear to be tilted to the left (for example, Gibson, 1937). The explanation could be made using Fig. 9.13, only this time the abscissa would be labeled 'angle of inclination', and all three channels would be tuned to the same frequencies. In effect, then, there is a third dimension of the channel picture: preferred orientation of the channels. If channel 1 is most sensitive to an orientation to the right of vertical, channel 2 is most sensitive to vertical, and channel 3 is sensitive to the left of vertical, adaptation would affect channels 1 and 2, causing the vertical test (t) to appear to be tilted left of vertical. **BOX 9.9**

Motion and color Direction of motion is also selected by channels in the visual system. Among vertically oriented channels, there are some that

prefer leftward motion, and some that prefer rightward motion. ('Stationary' gratings, where there is equal motion in both directions because of eye movements, would affect both directions equally.) Adaptation to a rightward moving vertical grating of a particular frequency will affect detection of any vertical grating of the same frequency, but will have the greatest effect on another vertical grating of the same frequency that is moving to the right at a similar speed (Pantle & Sekuler, 1969; Pantle, 1970).

Another aspect of the channels is that they may be color-selective (Bradley *et al.*, 1988). Inspection of an orange and black vertical grating and a blue and black horizontal grating causes a black-and-white vertical grating to appear bluish green and a black-and-white horizontal grating to appear slightly orange (McCollough, 1965). If you adapt to a red vertical grating and a green horizontal grating by alternately viewing one and then the other, and then inspect a pattern made of black-and-white gratings of the same frequency (Fig. 9.16), the vertical black-and-white areas appear greenish, and the horizontal areas appear reddish. View Fig. 9.16 after running the 'McCollough Effect' demonstration associated with Chapter 9 on the CD. Rotate the book 90°, and the colors reverse. The reason that a red stimulus produces a green afterimage and vice versa is explained in Chapter 14. **BOX 9.10**

Physiological basis of the channels

It is now time to ask what these hypothetical channels might be. What would be the shape of a receptive field that is suited to detecting spatial frequencies? The expected receptive field profile is, as you might expect, a sine wave. A sinusoidal profile, with an infinite number of excitatory hills and inhibitory valleys, would be ideal for detecting an infinite sinusoidal grating—but it would be *too* good. The channels are not exquisitely selective;

Box 9.8 A classical figural aftereffect

The most famous FAE is the one studied by Köhler & Wallach (1944), reproduced in Fig. 9.14. First, notice that the four white squares in the lower part of the figure are equally spaced about the fixation cross in the center of (b). Next fixate on the cross in (a) of the figure for about a minute. Then stare at the fixation cross in (b); the two squares on the left side of the figure should appear further apart than the two on the right. (This is somewhat related to the Titchener size illusion in Fig. 7.6.)

Early attempts to explain aftereffects such as this one postulated electrical fields on the cortex (subsequently shown not to exist), or relied on eye movements (since shown to be irrelevant). Ganz (1966) proposed an explanation based on lateral antagonism, but his explanation is not wholly satisfactory. We can follow the lead given by the explanation of the Blakemore & Sutton effect, however, and explain other figural aftereffects in terms of the multiple channel theory. In this case, the black square in Fig. 9.14(a) is smaller than the space between the boxes; it therefore adapts higher-frequency channels and makes the space between the two boxes on the left appear to be of lower frequency (larger) than it is.

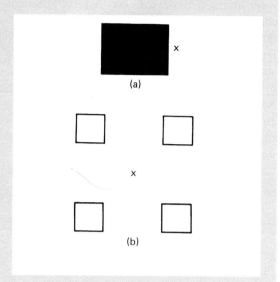

Fig. 9.14 A figural aftereffect of size. Adapting to the pattern at the top causes an apparent shift in size of the test pattern, below. From Köhler, W. and J. Wallach (1944) Figural aftereffect, an investigation of visual processes. *Proc. Am. Philos. Soc.* 88: 269–357. Reprinted by permission.

they accept a fairly wide band of frequencies. Mathematics tells us that a not-quite-so-selective channel would have a profile in pattern space that looks like the one shown in Fig. 9.17. There would be a large central area, flanked by an antagonistic surround, then a much less potent facilitatory region, and so on. Of course, the 'sign' (excitatory or inhibitory) is arbitrary, so the same picture upside down would serve just as well.

If you neglect the very weak areas outside the first inhibitory surround, this is a cross-section of an ON-center ganglion cell receptive field. It has an excitatory center and an inhibitory surround. In fact, this is very much like the profile predicted by the difference-of-Gaussians model (see Box 5.7, p. 91). Different ganglion cells with different sized receptive fields would be differentially selective for spatial frequencies.

The ganglion cell receptive fields lack some important attributes, however. For one thing, they are circularly symmetric, and not orientation-selective as the channels are. They also seem not to have any extra excitatory and inhibitory regions beyond the surround.

When you think of all the properties of the channels (tuning for frequency, orientation, direction of motion), you should naturally suspect the cortex of having the cells corresponding to the channels. Albrecht *et al.* (1980) reported that both the simple and complex cells of the monkey cortex are considerably more selective for spatial frequencies than they are for the widths of bars. Cortical cells also seem to be implicated by the fact (not previously mentioned) that adaptation by a grating presented to one eye affects detection of a grating presented to the other eye.

Box 9.9 Checkerboards and two-dimensional Fourier analysis

Fig. 9.15 A checkerboard pattern, and four gratings whose detection might be affected by adaptation to it. Top gratings are vertical; bottom are oriented at 45°. Gratings on the right have a wavelength corresponding to the size of the checkerboard pattern (two squares); those on the left have a wavelength $1/\sqrt{2}$ times as large.

The fact that the channels are tuned to spatial frequency and orientation suggests a further test of the Fourier analysis idea. Consider a checkerboard pattern, as shown in Fig. 9.15. Although it seems that the components of a checkerboard are vertical and horizontal, like the edges of the boxes it is made up of, the principal Fourier components are oriented *diagonally* (Kelly, 1976). You can verify this by defocusing the checkerboard; when only the lowest frequency components are seen, it appears as a sort of plaid at 45° to vertical. Moreover, the fundamental frequency is not determined by the edge-to-edge size of each pair of squares, as you might expect; it is determined by the length of the diagonals of the squares. This spacing is smaller than the edge-to-edge size of each pair of squares by a factor of $\sqrt{2}$.

➡

(Box 9.9 continued)

According to Fourier analysis, adapting to a checkerboard should have the greatest effect on a grating oriented at 45° to the edges of the board, at a spatial frequency whose wavelength is √2 smaller than the repeat size of two squares. This prediction was tested (Green *et al.*, 1976), and found to be correct. The grating most af-

fected by adapting to a checkerboard such as that in Fig. 9.15 would be the one on the lower left in the figure. A similar result was obtained by May & Matteson (1976).

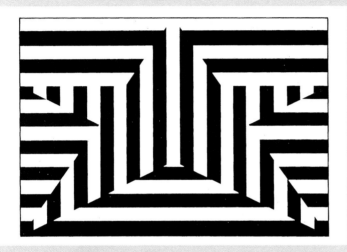

Fig. 9.16 The McCollough effect. First adapt to the red-and-black and green-and-black gratings of 'McCollough effect' among the demonstrations for Chapter 9 on the CD accompanying this book; then inspect this figure.

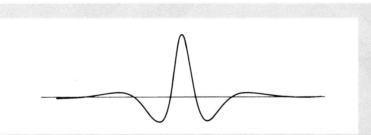

Fig. 9.17 Receptive field profile corresponding to a channel like those postulated. From Stromeyer, C. F. and S. Klein (1974) Spatial frequency channels in human vision as asymmetric (edge) mechanisms. *Vision Res.* 14: 1409–1420. Reprinted by permission of Pergamon Press, Ltd.

Simple cells of the cortex have most of the requisite properties; they are orientation-selective, can be motion-selective, and can have a profile such as the one in Fig. 9.17. (In the cortex, the central region is long and thin, and the antagonistic regions are the 'flanks'; see Figs 7.6 and 7.10.) In

Box 9.10 Is the McCollough effect really sensory?

An interesting and disturbing finding is that the McCollough effect is very long-lasting. If you looked at the colored gratings in the demonstration program for a long time (more than a minute or two, which you can do by recycling the program), you would see the colors in Fig. 9.16 for a long time. The effect lasts hours, days, and sometimes even weeks! This, of course, is very odd for a sensory effect. It suggests that these aspects are not part of the primary sensory process, but occur much higher in the brain. Murch (1976) has suggested that the McCollough effect is actually a form of classical conditioning. Consistent with this, the McCollough effect has been re-

ported to vary with the amount of sleep a person has had, just as other learning tasks do (Lund & MacKay, 1983).

It is also disturbing that the McCollough effect is 'global'; that is, the colored 'adapting' or 'conditioning' gratings do not have to be presented anywhere near where the test pattern will be (Dodwell & O'Shea, 1987). This is not consistent with the kinds of classical conditioning proposed (Karni & Sagi, 1991), but also is not consistent with relatively localized spatial frequency channels. For these reasons, it is possible that color is not an attribute of the spatial frequency channels after all.

fact, simple cortical cells also have the additional excitatory and inhibitory regions suggested in Fig. 9.17 (Maffei & Fiorentini, 1976; Schiller *et al.*, 1976a). Jones & Palmer (1987) presented a model of cortical simple cells as Gabor filters. Maffei & Fiorentini (1973) reported a progressive narrowing of the spatial frequency selectivity as one progresses from retina to lateral geniculate to cortical simple cells.

The complex cells of the cortex do not have receptive fields like the one in Fig. 9.17, as their fields cannot be mapped in the traditional way. They certainly do, however, have all the other properties such as orientation and motion selectivity. Selectivity of complex cells to gratings of various frequencies has been measured (Glezer *et al.*, 1976; Schiller *et al.*, 1976b), and found to be appropriate for a role as frequency channels, Spatially periodic areas of excitability have been reported (Pollen & Ronner, 1975; Pollen *et al.*, 1978).

A number of researchers have argued that cortical cells have the requisite properties to perform spatial frequency analysis. DeValois *et al.* (1982) found cells with narrow bandwidths, appropriate for a multiple channel system (see also Robson *et al.*, 1988). Moreover, there is a correlation between

spatial frequency tuning and orientation tuning such as would be expected for two-dimensional spatial filters. The spatial frequency tuning is apparently sharpened by a frequency-specific inhibition between cortical cells, as one would expect if spatial frequency were a feature that is being analyzed (DeValois & Tootell, 1983; Greenlee & Magnussen, 1988). Adaptation of single cortical cells to gratings caused the greatest decline in sensitivity for gratings that were identical in orientation and spatial frequency (Carandini *et al.*, 1998), just like the spatial frequency channels. Single cells were also found to be 'fooled' by the missing fundamental illusion (similar to Fig. 9.7) (Albrecht & DeValois, 1981).

The question of how phase (spatial position) might be encoded is also a concern. Simple cells can encode phase (Pollen & Ronner, 1981), but much of the cortical projection to higher areas is from complex cells. Complex cells apparently do not encode phase, for they do not care where in their field a stimulus may lie (Lee *et al.*, 1981; Pollen & Ronner, 1982). However, they do apparently encode the *relative* phase of components of a compound grating, and relative phase is what is needed to distinguish square waves from 'Peaks add' or triangle waves (Pollen *et al.*, 1988).

Box 9.11 Is spatial frequency analysis a part of perception

Does spatial frequency analysis play a role in the way we perceive the world? Fourier analysis provides a tool for the study of the visual system, but that does not mean that perception is based on that formulation. There are investigators who maintain that the only reason there is evidence for spatial frequency analysis is that the tests were done with stimuli intended to reveal these particular aspects. In their view, the visual system processes spatial frequency information concomitant to processing other, more relevant features.

For example, Ullman (1986) suggested that there are receptive fields of various sizes in order to provide for multiscale computations. In his view, receptive fields such as those in Fig. 9.17 serve to locate lines. In a complex scene, a mixture of different-sized line detectors is far more efficient at finding all the lines than is a collection of identical detectors. It would also be difficult to discriminate scenes based on spectrum alone, as most natural scenes have a spectrum in which amplitude is roughly inversely proportional to spatial frequency (Tadmor & Tolhurst, 1993), making phase the more important attribute.

There are a number of phenomena that fly in the face of spatial frequency predictions. Plaid patterns (the sum of two gratings with different orientations) can appear to move in directions in which there is no Fourier component (Alais et al., 1996). Other combinations of gratings give rise to the appearance of components that are not present in the stimulus (e.g. Chubb & Sperling, 1988; Solomon & Sperling, 1994; see the review by Derrington & Henning, 1993). These effects depend on non-linear processing, which certainly is a characteristic of the visual system, and also is a violation of the fundamental assumptions of Fourier analysis. These known non-Fourier outputs must somehow combine with the Fourier outputs to give a coherent perception (Wilson & Mast, 1993).

On the other hand, it is difficult to dismiss the apparently elaborate channel system that seems so suited for spatial frequency analysis. It has been suggested, by Graham (1979), that the channels are vital for the mechanism by which we perceive textures, the general roughness or graininess of objects. In her view, the actual identification of objects is based on features coarser than those detected by the spatial frequency channels (see Chapter 10); the channels are suited for abstracting secondary characteristics of the object, such as texture (Lamme et al., 1992). This may remind you of a suggestion in Chapter 8 that the coarse magnocellular system located parts of an object while the finer-grained parvocellular system 'filled in' the details that are often essential for identification of the object. Remember, too, that V2 cells were capable of detecting regions that were defined by texture (see Box 8.5, p. 147).

In this regard, it is noteworthy that there may be one or only a few transient (possibly magnocellular) channels, and several sustained (perhaps parvocellular) channels. The parvocellular system might perform a Fourier analysis to represent textures, which are recognized independently of the particular placement of details. For example, you recognize a lawn without any reference to the particular placement of the blades of grass; you may not even 'see' any of the individual blades. The cells apparently tuned for spatial frequency may be part of a texture system (von der Heydt et al., 1992).

The extreme view is that an approximation to Fourier analysis is an integral part of visual perception (Carl & Hall, 1972). According to this, the spatial frequency components extracted by the visual system form a 'pattern' in the frequency domain that is compared with the spatial frequency component patterns stored in memory in order to classify the stimuli presented. This view is currently not in favor.

Summary

This chapter was intended to do two things: to introduce the concept of spatial frequency (Fourier) analysis, which is a commonly used method for characterizing the visual system, and to explore the possibility that the visual stimulus might at some level be analyzed in terms of the spatial frequency components into which it may be decomposed. In this latter respect, the visual system might perform a Fourier analysis of the stimulus—rather than a representation of the luminance at each point in space, there would be a representation of the contrast at each spatial frequency. This would be realized by a series of frequency-selective channels, perhaps cortical neurons. The firing of a given cortical neuron would be interpreted to indicate the presence of contrast at a particular frequency, in the appropriate orientation, moving in the right direction at the appropriate speed, and possibly of the correct color. <u>BOX 9.11</u>

Fourier analysis is no more than another way of representing a pattern in space; it is mathematically equivalent to the more familiar point-by-point description. Perhaps it is surprising that the visual system could operate with a description that we find bizarre, but we do not normally have access to the inner workings of our brains. All we know of the processing is the output, the perception that is generated as the final step. How the nervous system gets from input to perception is hidden from our view; it is, in fact, the topic of this entire book.

Suggested readings

Few secondary or general sources have a treatment of the spatial frequency idea; this reflects in part the conceptual difficulty the material poses. One exception is the clear exposition in *Sight and mind*, by L. Kaufman (Oxford, 1974); Chapter 13 develops the concepts of the MTF and the channel hypothesis from a viewpoint somewhat different than the one taken here. A simpler treatment of the way components add to generate complex patterns and of the significance of the MTF may be found in *Visual perception*, by T. N. Cornsweet (Academic Press, 1970), Chapter 12 (this treatment does not include the channel hypothesis). For those interested in the mathematical basis of Fourier analysis, consider the rigorous but clear and well-illustrated book *The fast Fourier transform*, by F. O. Brigham (Prentice-Hall, 1974), Chapters 1–5.

Further illustrations of gratings and the CSF can be found in a *Scientific American* article entitled 'Contrast and spatial frequency,' by F. Campbell and L. Maffei (November 1974; offprint #1308). Another *Scientific American* article, 'The recognition of faces', by L. Harmon (November 1973; offprint #555) includes discussion of computer 'boxed' pictures such as the portrait in Fig. 9.10. Both of these articles have been reprinted in the collection *Recent progress in perception*, edited by R. Held and W. Richards (W. H. Freeman, 1976).

A more recent review of this field may be found in the chapter 'Mechanisms for coding luminance patterns: are they really linear?', by Andrew Derrington, in *Vision: coding and efficiency*, edited by Colin Blakemore (a volume mentioned in other 'Suggested readings' sections), pp. 175–184.

Chapter 10
Form perception

IN the past several chapters you saw physiological evidence that the visual system extracts useful information from the retinal image while it neglects less informative aspects. You saw that the cells of the retina are sensitive to *changes* (spatial and temporal). Whether you express the spatial tuning as spatial frequency filtering that emphasizes higher spatial frequencies, or as a lateral antagonistic network that emphasizes steep gradients, you are saying the same thing: the cells of the retina are more excited by the presence of a border than by a uniform light. You also saw that the cortex contains cells that seem to be specific for particular features in the array of information presented by the ganglion cells. You can express the relevant features as spatial frequencies or as lines of particular orientations; either way, cortical cells act to extract information of significance for analysis of the visual scene.

This chapter asks how the features detected by cortical neurons might be used to effect perception. The physiological data say only so much about the process; from this point onward it is a guess as to what physiological correlates there might be for the observed facts of perception. To help with this guess about how the visual system does its job, you will see how engineers have solved a similar problem.

But first, what is meant by perception? Perception is the development of an internal representation of the outside world based on the information presented by the senses. The representation is a functional description of the environment. It enables you to categorize the objects and images you see; the categories into which stimuli are placed by subjects are often the only data available to measure a subject's perceptions. Bear in mind, however, that categorization is not the same thing as perception: a sieve categorizes ore particles according to their sizes, but you would never accuse a sieve of perceiving (MacKay, 1967).

The information from which a percept is formed comprises the 'features' reported by lower-order processors in the sensory system. These features provide a way of summarizing the scene without requiring a point-by-point description. Sutherland (1973) pointed out that a description could be at a number of different levels. For example, consider the pattern in Fig. 10.1(a). When you look at the figure, there is a pattern of light and darkness projected onto your retinas; those receptors onto which the image of a black line is projected are in relative darkness compared with those receiving a projection of an image of white paper. You could describe the figure by listing which cones are in light and which are in darkness. This is essentially the form of the message a TV station sends to your television.

Your retinas do not pass a point-by-point representation of the image to your brain, however; you already know that only ganglion cells with their receptive fields near one of the lines fire at rates significantly different from their maintained discharges. Cortical cells are specifically tuned to lines of appropriate length and orientation; you

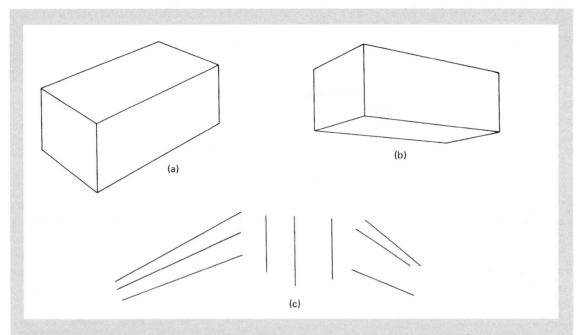

Fig. 10.1 Visual stimuli: (a) a visual pattern; (b) a pattern that can be seen to be another view of the object in (a); (c) the component lines of which the pattern in (a) is composed.

might therefore describe the figure as a collection of nine lines, each at a particular orientation, meeting at seven angles. This is one kind of description the cortex appears to be presenting.

You might now speculate that cells in some other part of the cortex, sensing particular patterns of excitation of the visual cortical cells, could signal certain plane figures that are formed from the lines. At this level, you could describe Fig. 10.1(a) as a collection of three quadrilaterals, each sharing two edges with the other two.

Rather than any of the above descriptions, you are most likely to describe Fig. 10.1(a) as a rectangular solid box with three sides visible. That is what you probably first saw when you looked at the figure. It is also the only level of description that would enable you to realize immediately that the objects in Fig. 10.1(a) and (b) are the same, viewed from different perspectives. This point was emphasized by a school of psychology that arose around 1900, called *gestalt*. In the gestalt view, the whole figure is imbued with a property as a unit that is not evident when it is analyzed as a collection of features. The solidity of the box is not simply an extension of the nine lines from which it is constructed. The same nine lines, rearranged as in Fig. 10.1(c), give an impression that is nothing at all like the object in Fig. 10.1(a); the properties of the latter depend on the picture in its entirety.

Pattern recognition

A perceptual system capable of determining the three-dimensional nature of Fig. 10.1 is obviously performing complex processing tasks. How might a perceptual system analyze the two-dimensional properties of a stimulus? In particular, how might it go about recognizing that Fig. 10.1(a) can be described as three quadrilaterals? Cells in the visual cortex can recognize lines, but how can you recognize three lines as a triangle, or another three lines as the letter *A*? This is the problem of pattern recognition.

The simplest form of recognition might be the task performed by a sieve; an object is 'recognized' only when it possesses certain size and shape characteristics that match the properties of the sieve. In a similar way, you might compare a stimulus to a set of possible alternative patterns and reply 'this one' when the stimulus matches one of the patterns. This scheme is called *template matching* (Selfridge & Neisser, 1960); it is the way the bank's computer 'reads' the stylized letters and numbers printed along the bottoms of checks.

The premise of template matching is that each stimulus pattern is matched to templates that are internal to the recognizer. The templates must be able to be shifted in orientation or position to be the same as the image, and changed in relative size to effect a match. This would allow an *H* to be recognized as an 'H', no matter whether the image looks like **H**, **н**, or *H*, and no matter where in the visual field it may be. There remain the questions of how the shifting of position or changing of size is accomplished, and how the mechanism decides it has done all it can and still failed to match a particular template.

There is evidence for template-matching activity in human perception. Subjects asked to recognize that two pictures are different views of the same object (like the two views in Figs 10.1a and b) take an amount of time to make their decision that depends on how much of a 'mental rotation' of the stimulus must be made for the two views to match (Shepard & Metzler, 1971). This mental rotation can even be shown to have a neural correlate in the motor cortex of monkeys (Georgopoulos *et al.*, 1989; Georgopoulos *et al.*, 1993; Pellizzer & Georgopoulos, 1993).

When a subject is shown a novel pattern (a shape the subject has never seen before), the tendency is to classify it as similar to some known shape except for some set of noted deviations. That is essentially how we see patterns in the clouds: a

cloud may look like a dog with two tails, or a face with no nose.

When a subject is shown a pattern that can be interpreted in either of two ways (an ambiguous figure, discussed later in this chapter) after being shown a pattern that is unambiguously one interpretation or the other, the interpretation of the ambiguous version depends on which unambiguous interpretation was shown. If each of the unambiguous versions is presented to separate areas on the retina, the interpretation given to the ambiguous pattern tends to agree with the unambiguous version that was shown to the same area of the retina as the ambiguous pattern (Wallach & Austin, 1954). This implies some kind of position preference for the template. There is also some dependence on position within the overall visual field (Dill & Fahle, 1997), although it is relatively minor (Braje *et al.*, 1995; Tjan *et al.*, 1995).

There is also physiological evidence for templates of sorts in the inferotemporal cortex. Inferotemporal cortex is in the ventral 'what' pathway apparently charged with identification of objects (see Chapter 8). Cells in this area maintain information about the features of objects, 'knowing' about the comparison object when the animal is asked to recognize a particular stimulus object (Eskandar *et al.*, 1992).

There are, however, a number of serious problems with the template theory. The main problem is that figures that are easily recognized as being of the same class may be quite different physically. A pattern can be drawn with clean black lines on white paper, or it can be done in smudgy pencil; it could be white chalk on a blackboard. Nevertheless, all three are immediately perceived as the same. Perhaps the feature detectors have somehow cleaned up the smudgy image and treated white on black as equivalent to black on white, but how does the template tolerate wide deviances in details of the figure?

Even more disturbing, a character may be recognized as one thing, even though it more closely matches the ideal template of another. For example, most people would identify the character on the left in Fig. 10.2 as a distorted 'A', but it is more similar to the template for an 'R'. Two people's handwritten Hs are probably quite different, but you can still read other people's handwriting (well, usually). You have no hesitancy in recognizing a drawing of a face as a representation of the same thing you immediately recognize on the heads of your friends, but think how different these patterns are. It is hard to imagine how templates could achieve these results.

The major alternative to a template matching scheme is a 'feature-extracting' model. You have already seen that cortical cells seem to be specific to certain features of the visual scene, such as lines, angles, and slopes. It is from such features that the visual system may first construct what David Marr (1976) termed a 'primal sketch'. These would be the 'primitives' from which the percept is constructed (although, as Ullman (1986) pointed out, the primitives could just as well be spatial frequencies or Gabor-like components; see Chapter 9).

Features such as edges, curves, and lines are the parts of a visual scene that convey the most information about the scene. Attneave (1954) pointed out that there is considerable *redundancy* in a visual image (that is why compression techniques like 'GIF' can reduce the size of a picture file). Attneave suggested that if you play a 'guessing game' in which you attempt to guess the color of each pixel successively, the only places you will make mistakes are where there is an as yet undiscovered contour, or where a contour suddenly changes direction. In short, the contours and their limits (corners) contain the information that must be guessed; filling in the solid areas is a foregone conclusion. In fact, it is the same foregone conclusion that the retina assumes the cortex will make when it sends messages only about boundaries. This incorrect assumption provides the basis for perceiving the Craik–O'Brien pattern as uniform stripes separated by sharp borders (see Fig. 5.6, p. 81).

Artificial intelligence

Assuming that features such as lines, edges, and corners are the raw materials from which the percept will be built, how might the higher centers proceed to recognize patterns? When the question is phrased in that way, it is natural to ask the related question: how might one build a machine to recognize patterns? Models of perception that start with the feature-extraction notion tend to look like pattern recognition schemes designed for

Fig. 10.2 Distorted 'A' (*left*) more nearly matches the template for 'R' (*center*) than for 'A' (*right*). From *Visual information processing* by Kathryn T. Spoehr and Stephen W. Lehmkuhle. Copyright © 1982 by W. H. Freeman and Company. Reprinted with permission.

computers (Uhr, 1973), and theories in this area of perception draw heavily from the field of artificial intelligence (for a further discussion, see Barlow *et al.*, 1972).

Artificial intelligence models share many features. Nearly all have a hierarchical structure; that is, the outputs of the computations made at one level go to a higher-level structure that performs the next level of processing. You have already seen the lowest levels of a hierarchical structure: ganglion cells extract information about changes in luminance from the array of cones; cortical cells extract information about lines of various orientation from the array of ganglion cells; and presumably the higher-level detectors extract information about specific patterns from the array of cortical neurons. At each level, the information about the visual scene is represented in progressively more abstract form.

A closer look at one particular artificial intelligence model may help to clarify the way models of this sort operate. The model is called 'pandemonium' (Selfridge, 1959), and is a classic that is sufficiently general that many other models are considered special cases of pandemonium.

Pandemonium assumes a hierarchical organization; at each level is a population of demons, imaginary creatures who scurry about performing their assigned tasks. The demons at each level are individuals, but they have in common a similar level of complexity. Demons at each level receive their information from the inferior demons below them, and in their turn serve the superior demons at the next level above. Communication is by shouting: each demon yells about how well the information it received fits the ideal of what it is programmed to seek, and the demons at the higher level extract their information by listening to what lower-level demons shout to them. Hence the name pandemonium, in reference to the general confusion generated by all the shouting demons. (It is no coincidence that the word 'demon' is embedded in 'pan**demon**ium'. The word is derived from the name of the principal city of Hell in *Paradise lost*.)

The demons at the lowest level are the *image demons*. Each reports whether there is light at a particular place in the visual field; they may correspond to cells in the retina or lateral geniculate nucleus. *Feature demons* listen to all the image demons, but each is hoping to find different groupings of image demons that are shouting loudest. There are 'vertical line' feature demons, 'left curve' feature demons, 'right angle' feature demons, and so forth (feature demons are reminiscent of cortical neurons).

The feature demons hope to be noticed by their supervisors, the *cognitive demons*, Each cognitive demon seeks evidence from the shouts of the feature demons that will support a claim that what it is programmed to recognize is present. The better the evidence, the louder it shouts in hopes of attracting the attention of the omnipotent *decision demon* that ultimately decides what pattern was present.

At each processing level there are demons (detectors) that recognize specific patterns of activity in the demons at the next lower level. The demons at any level are acting in *parallel*; they all look at the same input information at the same time. The concept of parallel processing is a key feature of the pandemonium model. In fact, Selfridge & Neisser (1960) use the term pandemonium to refer to *any* parallel processing model. Parallel processing stands in sharp distinction to the *serial* processing often supposed to underlie template matching.

The pandemonium model also is a serial model, because each level depends on the shouting of the demons at the next lower level. The levels are thus serially arranged, while the demons within each level act in parallel. Now consider how both the purely serial and purely parallel processors might work.

As an example of a serial processing template-match, take a computer that is programmed to recognize various encoded numbers. In its memory bank is a list of the codes, and a corresponding list of the numbers each represents. A code is given to the machine to identify; it is compared with each of the codes in the memorized list until it is found to match one of them. At this point the search ends, and the number corresponding to the match is reported. How long it takes to recognize the input code depends on how far down the list the search has to go before the match; the *average* search time depends on the length of the list that is searched.

Parallel processing allows for greater speed. A parallel processor would have a small special computer for each possible code. The input code goes to all the computers at the same time; the answer gets typed out by the one computer that found the code that matched the pattern in its memory. The search time would not vary from input code to input code. The search time would remain extremely short regardless of how many possible codes there were, but the cost of the system (one computer per code) would increase.

Perhaps of even greater importance for a perceptual system, parallel processors are less prone to make mistakes. A wrong decision at an early stage would lead a serial processor down the wrong path. For example, if one of the first tests of the character in Fig. 10.2 was for a vertical line on the left (which would be found), the later tests would be among 'B', 'D', 'F', and so on. 'A' would no longer be under consideration, and so could never be found. A parallel processor would simultaneously seek all the possible features, and so the vertical left line would sound only one false note in a chorus otherwise proclaiming an 'A'.

Now the distinction between template matching and feature extracting seems blurred. Templates can be compared in parallel (in fact, the bank machine that reads the numbers on checks does make its comparisons in parallel). What then are 'feature detectors' but parallel templates for particular patterns in the input array? The feature demons form an array (not in physical space, but in a 'feature' space), and cognitive demons are templates that match particular patterns in feature space. You can think of feature-extracting as a more elaborate kind of template matching, with the added sophistication of parallel processing and hierarchical structure.

The advantage of hierarchical structure is that the information presented to the templates is processed into a form that can be readily examined. Moreover, the processed information retains only those aspects of the stimulus array that are relevant for pattern recognition. There need not be a large number of 'equivalent formulation' templates, because the essence has been extracted for presentation to the template. The feature-extraction models, therefore, can overcome many of the objections to ordinary template-matching models, even though they are essentially a kind of template matching at each level. <u>BOX 10.1</u>

Top-down processing

Most of the models you have seen so far have been hierarchical; that is, information received at the lowest levels is processed by higher levels that pass it on to still higher levels. There was no provision for feedback from higher levels affecting the way the lower levels process information. You may recall, however, that the inner plexiform layer of the retina sent information back to the outer plexiform layer (Chapter 4), that the visual cortex projected back to the LGN (Chapter 7), and that higher cortical areas sent information to lower areas (Chapter 8). It should not be surprising, then, that processing is not a one-way street. In fact, once everything is interconnected, there really is no 'top' (Barlow, 1997). The signal goes around and around in an infinite loop, a process known to computer theorists as *recursion*.

One way in which a 'higher' level may be affecting 'lower' levels will be discussed later in this chapter, under the heading 'Perceptual set'. This refers to effects of context, in which what is perceived depends on what is expected. It is due to these higher influences on perception that you may clearly 'see' a threatening person lurking in the shadows of a dark alley; if you stay around to investigate, the 'person' turns out to be a smudge on the wall or a cat on a garbage can.

In a less exciting setting, 'higher' centers can assist the more primitive in finding the appropriate features. For example, our knowledge of the

Box 10.1 PDP networks

Artificial intelligence theory has embraced a formulation that is superficially similar to the pandemonium model. It is called *parallel distributed processing*, or PDP. In PDP, there is a neural network consisting of layers of cells. Cells in the lowest layer receive a pattern of input from the environment. They communicate with cells in the second layer, with each cell in the lowest layer sending its message to each cell in the second layer. Cells in the second layer communicate with the cells in the third layer, and so forth (a minimum of three layers is necessary for it to work; Minsky & Papert, 1969). A computer made of neurons has been dubbed 'squishy ware' (Gregory, 1995, p. 22).

So far, PDP sounds like pandemonium. However, all cells in a layer do not 'hear' all cells in the next lower layer equally well. The linkages from various cells have different strengths, or weightings, so that a particular cell may receive most of its information from a small subset of the lower level cells. Moreover, some linkages can be negative, so some lower-level cells can have an inhibitory influence on some of the cells in the next layer.

An important theoretical difference between PDP and pandemonium is that the cells in PDP do not have the personalities of demons. Cells in one layer are not identified as 'image demons', and those in another as 'cognitive demons'. No cell is dubbed a 'vertical line detector', or an 'H detector'. Activity in a cell is just that: activity. It is not a shout of 'I see a horizontal bar'. Thus, the same cell may participate in the perception of innumerable different stimuli.

What makes the PDP networks 'perceive' is that they are modifiable. A pattern of inputs leads to a pattern of outputs depending on the array of connections among the cells of the various levels. An algorithm that adjusts those connections molds the output toward a 'desired' pattern. The strengths are adjusted 'adaptively', until the pattern is learned. This adjustment requires 'training'—the network must somehow be told in what direction to adjust the connections. Training information may come from other networks serving other sense modalities; your facial vision network is told it correctly identified your friend when your auditory network recognizes the correct voice and your tactile network feels the hug or handshake.

Of particular relevance for a perceptual system, which must perceive myriad different patterns, is that learning a new pattern does not eradicate earlier learning. That is, there are enough connections, with so many possible ways to get from a particular input pattern to a particular output pattern, that many different codings can coexist in a PDP network.

There are PDP networks that recognize human faces, that process speech, or that read (Bien, 1988). Other PDP networks deduce the shape of objects from patterns of shading (Lehky & Sejnowski, 1988). PDP networks can make generalizations, and give reasonable 'responses' to poorly defined stimuli (Mel, 1997). The invariances you will encounter in Chapter 12 can also be found in models with interconnected networks (Neven & Aertsen, 1992). Even the apparent mental rotation effect that seemed to substantiate the template model can be simulated (Edelman & Weinshall, 1991).

Not all computer models are strictly hierarchical; some make use of feedback from 'higher' layers to 'lower'. This, of course, is just like the connections of cortex, in which messages pass in both directions (see the next section). A class of models that make use of feedback is called 'Hopfield nets', after John Hopfield, who popularized them (Hopfield, 1982). The idea has been further extended by Gerald Edelman (1987), who uses the term 'reentrant processing' to refer to the interconnection of neural networks. A sophisticated model for color perception is built on this principle (Wray & Edelman, 1996). Indeed, Edelman and his coworkers at the Salk Institute argue persuasively that reentrant processing is one of the keys to the understanding of consciousness (Tononi & Edelman, 1998). But the models can be so complicated that we can't really understand them; all we know is that the computer somehow solved the perceptual problem and got an answer similar to that which a human would arrive at.

general morphology of human faces can help to guide the cells that must detect the rather subtle variations in contrast that define cheekbones, nose, etc. The downward projections of the higher centers can influence cells in the supposedly more primitive centers by facilitating their responses to edges in places they 'should' be, but inhibiting responses where there ought not to be features, or by synchronizing activity across wide areas (Przybyszewski, 1998).

These less dramatic influences of higher centers in guiding the performance of lower levels are referred to as *top-down processing*. Since accurate perception is ultimately guided by the stimulus presented, it is sometimes hard to see evidence of top-down processing. One of the best examples (although it was not presented by its authors as top-down processing) is an experiment done by Johnston & McClelland (1974). They presented brief (tachistoscopic) arrays of four letters, and asked subjects to determine whether a particular target letter had been presented. In one condition, subjects were asked to fixate the center position and read the word; in the other condition, they were told which position the target would be in (if it was presented), and to watch only that position. Surprisingly, subjects did better reading the whole word than monitoring the critical position. That is, it was easier to read an entire four letter word and deduce whether it contained the target letter anywhere within it than to find the target letter in a forewarned position. One would think we recognized the letters in order to read the words, but in this experiment the words were read to identify the component letters. A similar result was obtained for finding lines embedded in coherent or incoherent figures (Weisstein & Harris, 1974; Wong & Weisstein, 1982).

Development of figure and ground

Given what you now know of physiology, you can probably imagine how the feature demons might work. What about the cognitive demons? Cognitive demons organize features into patterns, and it is these patterns we perceive.

Organization of features

The question of how features are organized into whole 'figures' was actively researched by the gestalt psychologists in the beginning of the 20th century. They observed that when features were organized into a figure, the figure existed as an entity that was greater than the sum of its individual features. You saw this earlier, when you noted that the objects in Figs 10.1(a) and (b) consist of more than three quadrilaterals, or the nine lines Fig 10.1(c). Figures 10.3–10.12 will further demonstrate this point.

Notice that the grouping of features into figures is spontaneous and automatic; you do not have to think about it to make it happen. For this reason, these processes are referred to as *preattentive processing*—they happen before you pay conscious attention. For example, finding the one red letter in a display of green letters is a quick process, and it doesn't matter how many green letters are strewn around to distract you. Preattentive processing works through a parallel search process. More complex searches, such as finding a particular word in a list, are carried out in serial, so the average time it takes to find the target word depends on the number of words in the list.

The Gestalt psychologists derived a compendium of the rules by which features (they did not generally use that term) are organized into a coherent whole. The principles of organization are relatively obvious once they have been stated, so they will be discussed only briefly. For a more elegant discussion, see Wertheimer (1923; abridged and translated into English by his son in 1958); see also Hochberg (1971a) and Kaufman (1974).

Two of the Gestalt principles are concerned simply with the grouping of features; that is, which features will be seen as being part of the same subpattern. The first of these is the *principle of proximity*; the other is the *principle of similarity*.

Proximity Proximity means nearness; things that are close to each other seem to go together. The

Fig. 10.3 Grouping by proximity.

dots in Fig. 10.3 are immediately perceived as four pairs and a single, rather than three triplets. You tend to group nearby items together; however, this is not a simple collation by proximity of the images upon your retina. When you view a person standing in front of a car, the images of the person and the car may be contiguous, yet you do not see person-and-car as a unit. BOX 10.2

Similarity The *principle of similarity* states that like things group together. Some examples are given in Fig. 10.5. In Fig. 10.5(a) you see diagonal groups (even though all the elements are equally spaced) because you tend to group solid circles together with other solid circles, and open circles with other open circles. In Fig. 10.5(b) you see that there is more involved than the amount of stimulation,

as the Xs group together and the Os group together even though neither is darker than the other. Some complex processing of the shapes must take place before the grouping. This is evident in Fig. 10.5(c), where there is an obvious boundary between the vertical/horizontal elements and the diagonally oriented ones, although the boundary between different vertical/horizontal elements is less clear (Beck, 1972).

The relative importance of proximity versus similarity may be gauged by putting them into conflict (Hochberg & Silverstein, 1956). For example, in Fig. 10.6(a), the principle of proximity would dictate that columns be visible, while the principle of similarity would predict the appearance of rows. The chances are you can see Fig. 10.6(a) either as rows of Xs between rows of Os

Box 10.2 Perceived proximity is more important than retinal proximity

Kaufman (1974) provided an elegant demonstration of the importance of perceived proximity rather than retinal proximity. It is shown in Fig. 10.4. In both halves of this figure, the dots are closer to their neighbors to the sides than to the ones above or below; as a result, each figure looks like horizontal rows of dots. If you view the figure as a stereogram, however (see Box P1, p. vi), you will see three *columns* of dots, each column at a different distance than the others. The differences in distance (depth) are greater than the distances in height, so you organize the figure into columns. The apparent spatial proximity dominates, rather than the retinal proximity (Rock & Brosgole, 1964).

Since the real location is more important than the retinal location, it is reasonable to suspect that the dorsal 'where' pathway may be involved. This is also consistent with the idea that the lower spatial frequencies are important in these groupings. Remember, the low spa-

tial frequency magnocellular system is dominant in the dorsal pathway.

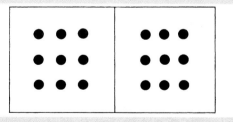

Fig. 10.4 From *Sight and mind: an introduction to visual perception* by Lloyd Kaufman. Copyright © 1974 by Oxford University Press, Inc. Reprinted by permission.

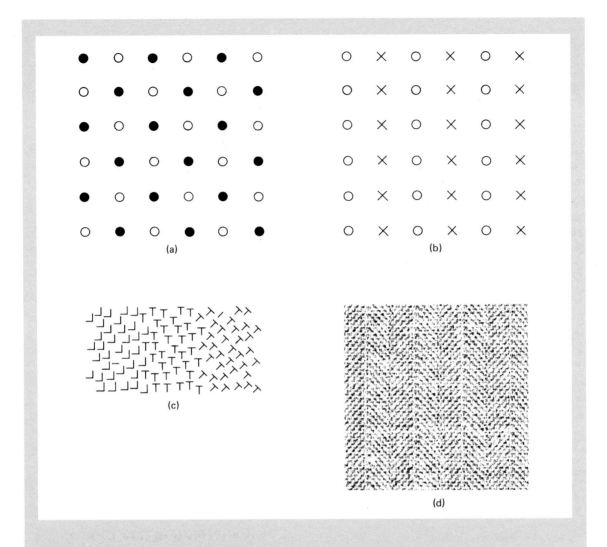

Fig. 10.5 Grouping by similarity. (a) Dots of similar darkness are grouped. (b) Columns are seen because circles group with circles and Xs with Xs. (c) The pattern divides into two segments distinguished by orientation (even though the Ts in the middle segment are really the same figure as in the right segment but for a rotation of 45° (d) A herringbone pattern. All the elements (and spatial frequency components) are diagonal but vertical stripes are seen. Part (c) from Beck, J. (1966) Effect of orientation and of shape similarity' on perceptual grouping. *Percept Psychophysics* 1: 300–302. Reprinted by permission of Psychonomic Society Inc. and the author. Part (d) from Marr, D. (1982) *Vision* (Freeman, New York).

or as columns of 'things'. You probably cannot see both at once. We seem to be capable of choosing whether to see the individual elements in the array, and thus group by similarity, or to ignore their identities and group by proximity.

Adjusting the spacing between columns can favor one principle over the other so that subjects almost never group the 'wrong' way; this gives a metric relating proximity and similarity. <u>BOX 10.3</u>

Box 10.3 Texture

Recognition of the boundaries in Fig. 10.5(c) is often cited as an example of texture discrimination. Julesz (1981) refers to a texture discrimination system that is preattentive, recognizing units of the pattern called textons. Textons are discriminated by statistical properties, not simply orientation (Bergen & Adelson, 1988) or spatial frequency (Julesz & Krose, 1988). These discriminations depend on non-linearities, presumably at higher levels (Victor & Conti, 1991). Nevertheless, textures may be identified as early as the LGN (Nothdurft, 1990).

A preattentive process would presumably be performed by parallel, rather than by serial search. In fact, Sagi & Julesz (1985) report that recognizing *where* aberrant textons are embedded in a pattern is indeed a parallel process. On the other hand, recognizing *what* the aberrant

elements actually are is a serial process in which attention is focused on each element in turn. This is an example of how different aspects of the same visual image can be processed in different ways, presumably by separate systems. Notice that '*where*' and '*what*' have also been attributed to the dorsal and ventral pathways, respectively (see Chapter 8).

If textures are handled by a separate system from that which identifies patterns, you might expect a separate physiological correlate of that system. A class of complex cells in visual cortex, localized in two bands in layers 3 and 5, seem to be the texture-sensitive cells (Edelstyn & Hammond, 1988). These cells respond well to patterns of random dots, and are not particularly sensitive to direction of motion of the patterns.

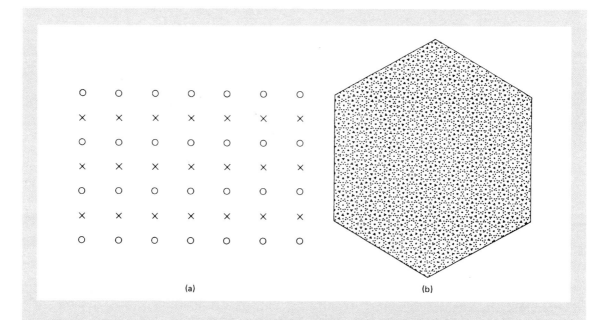

(a) (b)

Fig. 10.6 (a) Competition between grouping by proximity (columns) and grouping by similarity (rows). (b) Demonstration of active grouping when multiple possibilities are available. (b) from Marr, D. (1982).

As you look at Fig. 10.6(a), you may notice the grouping switching between the possibilities. That is because there is ambiguity, and you can control which version you wish to perceive. This

phenomenon will come up later in this chapter. An even more striking example of the active grouping process may be seen in Fig. 10.6(b). Marr (1982) describes this figure as one that 'seethes

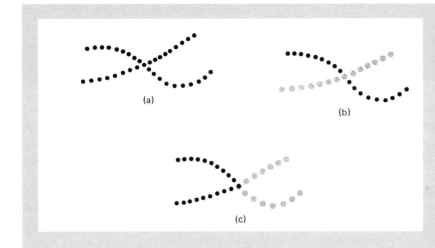

Fig. 10.7 An example of continuity. (a) A pattern seen as two curves. (b) The two curves into which most people divide the pattern in (a). (c) Alternative pairs of curves that are generally not seen in (a).

with activity as the rival organizations seem to compete with one another. All of these principles, which are concerned with the question of which things 'go together', are aspects of the binding problem (see Box 10.5, p.198).

Pragnanz The remaining Gestalt principles are slightly more abstract; they suggest that features are grouped according to *pragnanz*, which is generally translated as 'good form'. You see things as belonging together if they will combine to form a 'good' figure; the better the figure, the more strongly they tend to group.

What makes a figure 'good'? One aspect is *continuity*, the appearance of a single entity. For example, the dots in Fig. 10.7(a) are seen as two curves that cross at the center, as indicated by the dots of different darkness in Fig. 10.7(b) (where grouping by similarity ensures the groups to be demonstrated are the ones that are seen). These two continuous curves have more pragnanz than simple grouping by proximity (as indicated in Fig. 10.7c).

Another aspect closely related to continuity is *common fate*, which applies to patterns that are changing in time. Common fate means that items that are moving in the same direction at the same speed are grouped together. Slowly moving high clouds are seen as distinct from more rapidly moving low clouds. You can see how dots moving to-

gether segregate from dots moving in a different direction by running the demonstrations of depth from motion (for Chapter 11) on the CD accompanying this book; note particularly 'transparency' and 'motion parallax'. You can also see this effect in the motion demonstration (for Chapter 13) called 'Macro and Micro Fields'.

Still another principle of pragnanz related to continuity is *closure*, the tendency to see figures as unitary, enclosed wholes. You not only prefer figures that are enclosed, you may even perform the enclosing yourself in your mind's eye. Figure 10.8 is an example of this; you have no difficulty in

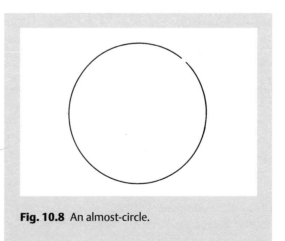

Fig. 10.8 An almost-circle.

seeing the figure as a circle, even though it fails to meet the simplest definition of a circle as a 'plane, closed figure'. In fact, at a quick enough glance you might not even notice the small gap in the circumference. Bear this figure in mind when you read about subjective contours in a few pages.

Another contributor to pragnanz is *symmetry*, which is when the right half of a figure is a mirror image of the left half. In geometry, symmetry could be about any axis, not just the vertical midline, but people seem to be considerably better at detecting this form of symmetry than any other (Barlow & Reeves, 1979). Preferences for left–right symmetry are probably related to the fact that small children seem nearly unaware of left–right inversions (for example, in writing the alphabet) although they rarely confuse top and bottom (Rock, 1974). A symmetric form may be more readily perceived than an asymmetric one; for example, the symmetric array of open circles embedded in a background of dots (Fig. 10.9a) is more readily perceived as a form than the asymmetric array (Fig. 10.9b) (the form is only visible in any case because of grouping by similarity).

Good forms are easier to see (as is the form in Fig. 10.9a) than less good forms (Fig. 10.9b); they are also harder to decompose into other shapes. As an example, it is harder to see a circle as a forward C butted against a backward C than it is to see the figure in Fig. 10.10(a) as the combination of the two patterns in Fig. 10.10(b). <u>**BOX 10.4**</u>

The foregoing should give an intuitive sense of what is meant by pragnanz, but it would be better to be able to define it in a more precise way. Two lines of investigation into the quantification of pragnanz are particularly worthy of mention. The first is to equate it with simplicity: a good figure is less complex than a poor figure. Complexity can be defined as a weighted sum of a number of attributes such as curvature, angularity, number of sides, and the ratio of the perimeter squared to the area (P^2/A) (Attneave, 1957; Stenson, 1966). Alternatively, complexity may be related to the number of features (lines, angles, areas) that need be sampled in order to apprehend the entire figure (Vitz & Todd, 1971).

The other way to look at pragnanz also equates it with simplicity, but of a different kind. In this view, simplicity means low information content, with information defined in the strict mathematical sense used in communication theory. Information is measured by how many 'bits' are needed to specify a figure. If a figure is a member of a class that could only contain two figures, a single bit is needed (one two-choice question must be answered); if there are four members of the set, then two bits are needed (two questions: one to divide the four into two groups, and one to decide which of the two remaining is 'it'). Eight figures in a class requires three bits and so on. Using this reasoning, the more predictable the figure, the less information the figure contains. Very predictable

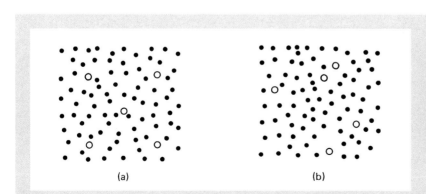

Fig. 10.9
Demonstration of the goodness of symmetry. (a) A symmetric pattern of five circles in a field of dots. (b) An asymmetric pattern of five circles in a field of dots.

(a)   (b)

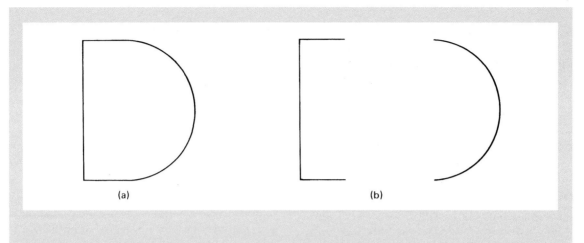

Figure 10.10 Decomposition of a figure into two good forms: (a) the figure; (b) the two components.

Box 10.4 Reconciling spatial frequency and the gestalt principles

It is possible to consider the gestalt principles from the standpoint of the spatial frequency concepts presented in Chapter 9 (see Ginsburg, 1975). At least some of the principles may be restated in terms of the spatial frequency spectra of the patterns.

Perhaps the most direct example is closure. The near circle in Fig. 10.8 has a spatial frequency spectrum that differs from the spectrum of a whole circle only in the very highest spatial frequencies. If both the circle and the near circle were filtered to remove the highest spatial frequencies (that is, slightly defocused), they would look the same. Closure may be interpreted as a tendency to pay the most attention to the medium spatial frequency components (which are also the largest components). In fact, this particular figure has been used for some time as a test of high-frequency capabilities, or *acuity*. It is called a *landolt C*. A person whose eyes are being tested is shown small landolt Cs with their gaps oriented differently, and must say where the gap is (12 o'clock, 6 o'clock, 9 o'clock, and so forth — see Box 3.7, p. 42). Acuity, or ability to see fine details (high spatial frequencies), is defined by how narrow a gap can be located accurately.

Proponents of the spatial frequency hypothesis have pointed out that the grouping demonstrations may be 'explained' by their spatial frequency components (Ginsburg, 1975). Clearly, there is a strong diagonally oriented component in Fig. 10.5(a) and a vertical component in Fig. 10.6(a). These low-frequency components might easily be used to group elements.

The patterns in Fig. 10.5(b) and (c) depend on high spatial frequencies, for it is the details of the elements that are important. Nevertheless, it is notable that there are strong diagonal components in only one of the regions in Fig. 10.5(c).

Others argue that spatial frequency is not an essential ingredient. Marr (1982) points out that a herringbone pattern (Fig. 10.5d) has absolutely no energy in any vertical Fourier component, yet is seen as vertical stripes. Similarly, if the dots in Fig. 10.3 are replaced with dark and light 'ripples' on a medium-gray background, the grouping persists even though there are no low-frequency components (Janez, 1984).

figures are, in general, said to have good form. This way of looking at figural goodness was suggested independently by Hochberg & McAlister (1953) and Attneave (1954). Attneave found that the visibility of figures partially obscured by extraneous details was inversely related to their information content. He also found that figures that seemed complicated but were symmetric, and which therefore

Box 10.5 The binding problem

How does the nervous system actually group features and decide which 'belong' to which figures? The problem of associating features into a cohesive unit is known as the *binding problem*. Recently, a considerable body of work has been devoted to the hypothesis that binding is accomplished by synchronized oscillations of the neurons encoding the various parts of a single object (Eckhorn *et al.*, 1988; Gray & Singer, 1989; Engel *et al.*, 1992; Eckhorn & Obermueller, 1993; Singer & Gray, 1995; Funke & Wörgötter, 1997). In this view, cells responding to features that are part of the same object in a complicated scene are linked by the fact that they are firing in synchrony; cells concerned with other objects are in synchrony with each other, but in a different temporal pattern than those responding to the first object. Synchrony is usually believed to be expressed by oscillations at a particular frequency, but may instead be due to different latencies (delays) in response timing (Hopfield, 1995; Gawne *et al.*, 1996).

Not everyone agrees that synchronous firing is the key

to binding. It has been suggested that the synchrony is an epiphenomenon of the fact that there are oscillations, or an accident of the fact that there are maintained discharges in so many cells (Ghose & Freeman, 1992; Ghose *et al.*, 1994). Kiper *et al.* (1996) attempted to disrupt or assist the coherent oscillations by flickering the various parts of a stimulus object; there was no apparent effect upon binding.

Nevertheless, there does seem to be synchronization of cells responding to the same stimulus. If it is not involved in binding, what might it actually be doing? One possibility is that the synchronous firing calls attention to the cells that are all firing in unison; in this sense, it is how attention is focused upon an object (Carvalho & Roitman, 1995). In this regard, it is interesting that when attention shifts in binocular rivalry (when two different stimuli are presented to the two eyes, only one can be seen at a time; see Box 11.6, p. 242), only the cells responding to the stimulus being perceived continue to oscillate (Fries *et al.*, 1997).

contained no more information than apparently simpler figures, were as visible as the seemingly simpler ones. (In fact, they were slightly more visible, indicating that information content is not the whole story). <u>BOX 10.5</u>

Figure and ground

Assume then that features are organized into figures. What next? Do their properties somehow change? The answer is yes; the figure becomes a distinct entity with properties that set it apart from the remainder of the scene. The figure becomes real and apparently solid (the gestaltists said it had 'dingstoff'—'thingness'). The rest of the scene, referred to as the *ground*, seems less substantial, and appears to recede behind the figure.

The distinction between figure and ground is illustrated by Fig. 10.11. This is an ambiguous pattern; it can be seen in either of two ways. On the one hand, it can be seen as two silhouetted faces staring at each other, nearly nose-to-nose, and on

the other hand, it can be seen as a white vase or goblet, in front of a black wall. Once you have seen it each way, you can easily switch from the one to the other. The thing to notice, however, is that when you see the two faces they appear to be sub-

Fig. 10.11 A pattern in which figure and ground may exchange roles. The pattern may be seen either as two silhouetted faces or as a white vase.

stantial; they stand in front of the white background (of no particular depth or substance), and the borders between the black and white areas 'belong' to the black faces. When the vase is the figure, the reverse is true: the white vase seems to be in front of a non-descript black background, and the contour seems to belong to the white vase.

Notice that you can see only one interpretation (faces or vase) at a time. Switching occurs spontaneously, or you can control which you see. The implication is that attention is important for perception. The control of attention has been attributed to the parietal cortex (see Chapter 8), which is in the dorsal stream and may not be part of the conscious perception pathway. In this sense, note that it is easier to attend to objects in the lower part of the visual field, which has stronger connections to parietal cortex (He *et al.*, 1996). This idea will make a reappearance shortly.

Once a figure has become evident, it seems to be imbued with a strength and reality that resists dissolution into its elements. For example, run the 'Motion from form' demonstration on the CD. It may seem that the pattern on the screen (initially Image #1) is just a random grouping of meaningless shapes. The same would be true for 'Image #2'. When you click 'Alternate images', the rapid alternation of the pictures should look jumpy and disorganized. In fact, the two images are photographs, at extremely high contrast, of faces (after Mooney, 1951). To see the faces, click 'Reveal actual picture' for each. Once you see the faces, the pictures no longer look like a smattering of meaningless blobs; they acquire a three-dimensional depth that was not evident before you saw what they were. When you now click 'Alternate images', you see coherent motion.

The faces demonstrate another point: despite the apparent emphasis the retina places on contours, a perceived figure need not be neatly bounded by a complete outline. Closure may play a part, but in these cases, there is less contour present than absent. In fact, contour information alone did not allow recognition of the faces in the demonstration (Cavanaugh, 1991b).

Similarly, four appropriately placed dots are immediately seen as forming the corners of a square, even though none of the contours of the square is present. It is sometimes possible to suggest contours where there are none, and still form a figure. The suggested contours are generally called *subjective contours* (Schumann, 1904). An example of a triangle formed by subjective contours is shown in Fig. 10.12; the three vertices are suggested as superimposed on the three black circles, but the sides themselves are not drawn. Despite the lack of actual sides, the triangle appears as a quite distinct figure. It has the properties you have already learned to expect figures to have: it appears to have substance, it appears to be in front of the ground, and the subjective contour 'belongs' to the triangle rather than to the eclipsed circles. The triangle also has one other feature commonly associated with the figure: it appears lighter than the ground. This is an anomalous brightness, as the triangle consists of the same white paper as the rest of the page; it somehow seems that there is a change in lightness at the subjective contour, even though the contour is not actually present. **BOX 10.6**

Fig. 10.12 A triangle generated by subjective contours. After Coren (1972) Subjective contours and apparent depth. *Psych. Rev.* 79: 359–367. Copyright © 1972 by the American Psychological Association. Adapted by permission.

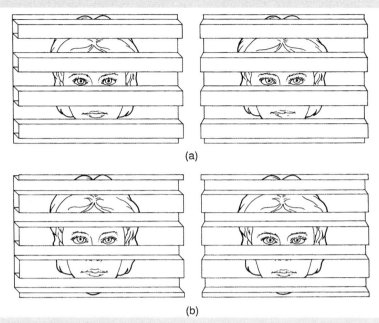

(a)

(b)

Fig. 10.13 The same strips of a picture give different results when made to appear behind occluding strips (a) or when pasted on the strips (b). View these stereograms as indicated in Box P1 (p. vi) From Braddick, 0. (1988) Contours revealed by concealment. *Nature* 333: 803–804. Based on work by Nakayama, later published in *Perception* 18: 55–68 (1989). Reprinted by permission of the author.

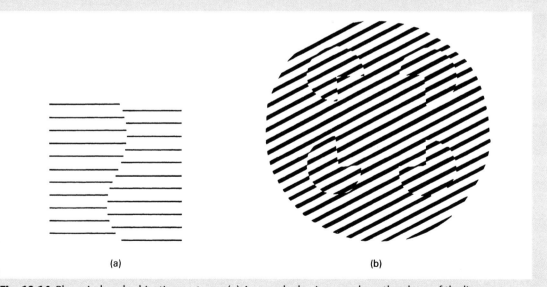

(a)   (b)

Fig. 10.14 Phase-induced subjective contours. (a) A curved edge is seen where the phase of the lines changes. (b) The corners of a subjective square are generated by 'pac-men' that are themselves generated by a phase change (from Petry & MeShane, 1988). Part (a) from Gaetano Kanizsa, *Organization in vision: essays on gestalt perception* (Praeger, New York, 1979, p. 204). Copyright © 1979 by Gaetano Kanizsa. Reprinted with permission.

Subjective contours, like the triangle in Fig. 10.12, are sometimes interpreted as the visual system's means of 'explaining' an apparent occlusion of one set of objects (the black circles) by an overlying object (the white triangle). That being determined, the triangle appears lighter (compared to the circles), and so appears whiter than the surrounding paper. Notice the top-down flow of information: the occlusion generates the boundary (an edge, which should have been a primitive) and the edge generates the lightness gradient (which should be how you find edges).

A confirmation of the occlusion hypothesis can be found by deliberately making the occluder lie in front of or behind the occluded pattern (Braddick, 1988). The stereogram in Fig. 10.13(a) is set up so that the horizontal strips appear in front of the face; that in Fig. 10.13(b) is set up as if the face were 'painted' on the strips. Notice that the same strips of face appear quite different in the two stereograms. This is consistent with recordings from area V4 (in the ventral pathway) in which occluded patterns are detected by neurons (Kovács et al., 1995).

Subjective contours do not require luminance gradients. Figure 10.14(a) shows a curved edge created by a change of the spatial phase in the striped pattern. This can even give rise to a second-order effect, as shown in Fig. 10.14(b): four 'pac-men' are generated by phase changes (the shift in position of the stripes) like the curve in part (a). The pac-men in turn generate a square that stands in front of the striped background.

While subjective contours are not as compelling as real contours, they can be as potent. They give rise to the tilt aftereffect (look at a set of slightly leaning lines for a few minutes, and vertical lines seem to lean in the opposite direction) just about as well as real lines (Greene & Verloop, 1994). Subjective contours can also generate optical illusions, as you will see in Fig. 10.17. Subjective contours are apparently low-level phenomena, in that attention is not needed for them to appear (Davis & Driver, 1994). They

Fig. 10.15 Demonstration that humor is subjective (and illusory). By Meyer, G. E. (drawn by S. Petry) (1987) *Perception* 16: 412.

'jump out' in parallel, indicating preattentive processing (see page 191).

Are both the dorsal and ventral pathways involved? Recognizing the occluded pattern seems to be a 'what' function, but recognizing the depth is a 'where' function. There are at least two aspects to subjective contours: the sharpness of the edge and the brightness of the surface. These aspects can be dissociated. Sharpness of the contour is enhanced under conditions that favor the parvocellular system; on the other hand, the brightness of the illusory shape is enhanced when the magnocellular system should be most active (Petry & Siegel, 1989). Moreover, the completion of subjective contours occurs in two temporally distinct phases, implying contributions by at least two systems (Ringach & Shapley, 1996).

One last demonstration relates subjective contours to figure-ground processing. Figure 10.16 is a stereogram of a subjective contour—maybe. When the frames are fused, the two black bars are seen in front of the vertical lines. But it is possible to see either a subjective contour (a white banner stretched between the bars and occluding two lines below) or not see one (the bars just happen to float above the four vertical lines. Rubin *et al.* (1996) found that when the upper cross is fixated, so the possible occluding banner is in the lower visual field, the subjective contour is seen. When the lower cross is fixated, so the bars are in the upper visual field, no subjective contour is seen. They note that this makes sense in that intricate, crowded patterns are generally below our gaze, not in the sky. But they also note that the lower visual field has stronger connections to parietal cortex, which you have already seen is implicated in figure/ground segregation (page 199).

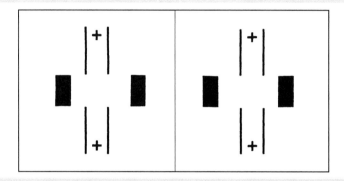

Fig. 10.16 Stereogram demonstrating a subjective contour that is not always there. When viewed as instructed in Box P1 (p. vi), the two black bars should appear to be in front of the vertical lines. This can be interpreted either as the two bars framing an occluding banner that blocks two vertical lines, or as two bars floating in front of a pattern of four vertical lines. Fixation on the upper cross generally yields the former percept, while fixation on the lower cross yields the latter. After Rubin, N., Nakayama, K. and Shapley, R. (1996) Enhanced perception of illusory contours in the lower versus upper visual hemifields. *Science* 271: 651–653.

The solidity of figures formed of subjective contours may be demonstrated by showing that they are nearly as effective as real contours in generating illusions. Look at Fig. 10.17. In part (a) of the figure is a familiar illusion, the *Poggendorf* figure. This is the usual way presenting this illusion; the interposition of the rectangle makes the two visible segments of the line appear to be misaligned. Confirm their alignment by placing a straight edge along the lines, or by sighting along them from the edge of the page. (There are nearly as many theories about why this occurs as there are psychologists who have devoted attention to it; many postulate either an interaction of the interrupted line with the contour of the rectangle, or an overestimation of the acute angles formed between the line segments and the contour.) You can test yourself on this illusion with

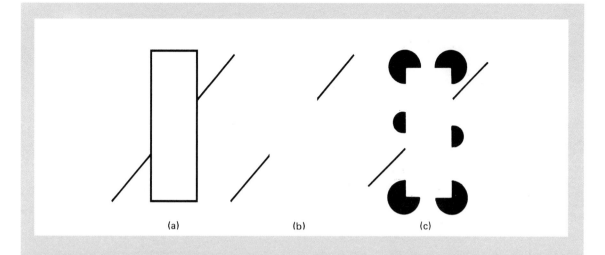

Fig. 10.17 The Poggendorf illusion. (a) The standard pattern: the presence of the rectangle makes it difficult to see that the diagonal line on the right aligns with the diagonal line on the left. (b) The same diagonal lines as in (a) without the rectangle. Alignment is easy to determine. (c) The illusion with a rectangle generated by subjective contours. Most people find alignment hard to determine.

the 'Optical Illusions' demonstration for Chapter 12 on the CD.

Figure 10.17(b) shows the same line segments as in (a), without the rectangle. In this case there should be no difficulty seeing that the line segment to the right aligns with the one on the left. Figure 10.17(c) repeats the same line segments, eclipsed by a rectangle formed by subjective contours. Most people find that there is an illusory effect caused by the subjective rectangle; most likely, the continuation of the line to the left appears to fall below the segment to the right.

Another indication of the importance of the figure as a whole is the demonstration that it can have properties independent of its parts. This is demonstrated when the same shape takes on a new identity because of a change in orientation. The two shapes in Fig. 10.18 are identical but for a rotation by 45°. On the left it is a square; on the right a diamond. Turn the book 45° and cover the frame around the figure; the diamond is really a square turned on end. Until this intellectual discovery is made, however, the diamond and the square are perceived as different figures. For example, an obvious attribute of the square is that the four corners are right angles, but this is not as obvious for the diamond. Even the apparent sizes of the figures are affected; most people judge the diamond as slightly larger than the square. BOX 10.7

Simultaneous masking

You have already encountered visual masking in Chapter 9, as a method of demonstrating that test patterns of a particular spatial frequency are most affected by other patterns of similar frequency. Visual masking is a far older idea than the spatial frequency channel hypothesis; the original masking experiments were performed in the hope of elucidating the way in which figures are perceived. Both simultaneous masking and backward masking have been exploited toward this end.

Simultaneous masking, in which the test pattern and the mask are present at the same time, is camouflage. If the test is enough like the mask,

Fig. 10.18 A square and a diamond. The diamond is the same as the square except that it has been rotated 45°. All the corners are right angles, but this is not as obvious in the diamond as it is in the square. Even the apparent sizes of the figures are affected, the diamond seeming larger than the square.

Box 10.7 Frames of reference

Whether an equilateral quadrilateral will be seen as a diamond or a square depends on its orientation; this implies a frame of reference against which orientation is measured. In Fig. 10.18, the shape to the left appears to be a square because it is oriented the same way as the book (which you are presumably holding right side up). Your perception of vertical being toward the top of the page was further enhanced by the rectangular frame around the entire figure. In this case, there is no conflict between actual vertical (the pull of gravity), retinal vertical (the direction on your retinas from forehead to cheeks), and apparent vertical (the frame around the picture).

Now disrupt any one of these cues to vertical and see whether the percept goes with it or with the others. For example, tilting the book and your head 45° to the side while looking at Fig. 10.18 should have no effect on your perception of the square and the diamond; gravity is not a very important cue to the vertical. The visual frame is the most important cue in this case: turning the book 45° but leaving your head erect is not likely to change the square into a diamond. (It might have some effect on the diamond in that you *can* see it as a square; remember, however, that you have rotated only a part of the visual frame: the room around the book remains vertical.) Changing the visual frame, on the other hand, has a potent effect. Figure 10.19 shows a pattern of diamonds. The diamonds in the line along the top of the figure are seen as diamonds, but the cluster in the lower right create a 45° frame of reference, so the figures can easily be seen as squares (Attneave, 1971). Notice that the same figures in the

upper right can be seen either as diamonds or as squares, depending on which other figures they are grouped with.

Rock (1974) pointed out that the visual frame of reference is dominant only in the case of simple figures such as squares and diamonds. More complex figures, such as letters or faces, depend more strongly on retinal orientation than on the visual frame of reference. This is why when you read lying on your side in bed, you must also turn the book sideways. Rock demonstrated his point

Fig. 10.19 A pattern of diamonds that can be seen as either diamonds or squares. From Attneave, F. (1971) Multistability in perception. In *Recent progress in perception*, by R. Held and W. Richards. Copyright © 1976 by Scientific American, Inc. Reprinted with permission by W. H. Freeman and Company.

(a) (b)

Fig. 10.20 Invertible figures: (a) when the book is turned upside down, a different face is seen; (b) the word 'saturn' becomes 'uranus' when turned upside down. (a) from 'The perception of disoriented figures', by Irvin Rock. Copyright © 1974 by Scientific American, Inc. All rights reserved. (b) Copyright Chicago Sun Times.

with a series of 'invertible' faces, faces that look like one person when viewed right side up but appear to be a different character when viewed upside down (180° rotation). Look at the face in Fig. 10.20(a); now turn the book upside down and look at it again to see the alternative face. Turning the book over changes both the retinal and the visual frame of reference for vertical. You could change the visual frame by turning the book over, but maintain the retinal orientation by also turning yourself over. The easiest way to do this is to hold the book upside down behind your legs and bend over to view it from between your knees (don't try this demonstration in a public place). You will see only the face that you saw in the normal right side up orientation of the book. This applies not only to faces, but also to other complex stimuli like writing. The invertible logo in Fig. 10.20(b) was designed by space scientists working on an interplanetary probe that would fly past Saturn, then go to Uranus.

Why does retinal orientation seem the most important for complicated stimuli? Ahissar & Hochstein (1997) suggest that for simple figures, learning is easily generalized, but for more complicated figures it is bound to the specific orientation and position. This implies a template-like linkage to the retinotopic map. It is noteworthy that retinal orientation is more important than gravity, even though you are better at judging true vertical than judging parallel to the axis of your head (Darling & Hondzinski, 1997).

The visual influence upon the sense of vertical was explored in a series of experiments by Leonard Matin and his colleagues. They had subjects look into a large box that was tipped toward or away from them, and locate the point that they judged to be at eye level. They found the influences of gravity and visual field structure added to produce the net apparent eye level and apparent tilt (Matin & Fox, 1989). These effects could be produced by a single tilted line, as long as there were no other visual indicators of vertical (Matin & Li, 1994). Interestingly, the apparent tilt could be independent of the influence on apparent eye level (Li & Matin, 1998). Matin further suggested that this dissociation might be because the judged angle is a property of the ventral stream while the apparent eye level is determined by the dorsal stream. To test this idea, he and Mel Goodale used the tilt-box apparatus to test the subject with extensive ventral stream damage (see 'Blindsight' in Chapter 7). As expected, her apparent eye level was diverted as normal, even though she could not judge the tilt (Servos *et al.*, 1995).

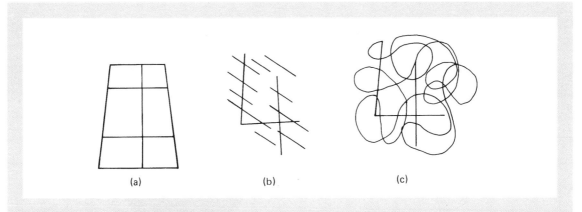

(a)   (b)   (c)

Fig. 10.21 Camouflage (simultaneous masking) of the numeral 4. (a) The 4 is well masked. (b) and (c) The 4 is poorly masked.

it will be effectively hidden. One way in which the test and mask must be similar is in terms of their spatial frequency spectra; this was demonstrated in Fig. 9.11 (p.174-5), in which Lincoln's portrait is hidden best when the mask (boxes) has energy in spatial frequencies near those of the portrait. Other aspects of the mask also play a role, and these are often predicted by the principles of organization. If the mask is as likely to be grouped with the features as the features are with each other, incorrect groupings will be made and the figure will be obscured. For example, in Fig. 10.21 the same figure, a printed numeral 4, is hidden in all three parts of the figure. The camouflage is best in part (a), where the masking elements are just like the figure elements, and approach them in ways that promote closure, continuation, and general pragnanz. In Fig. 10.21(b) the camouflage is not as good, despite the similarity of the mask elements to the figure, because closure and continuation are not implied. In Fig. 10.21(c), the mask elements are somewhat different, and continuation works against confusing the figure with the mask. Similar principles may be invoked to explain the camouflage in Fig. 10.22; the person is hard to see because he fits the 'S' of the writing by continuation. **BOX 10.8**

For simultaneous masking to be effective, the mask and target must share certain properties, including location. If the mask and target appear to be at different distances from the observer, there is less masking (Lehmkuhle & Fox, 1980; Schneider *et al.*, 1989). This can be arranged with stereoscopic images. For example, the letter hidden in the stere-

Box 10.8 Masking and binding

Masking is a way of defeating the binding of appropriate features to the same object. As suggested in Box 10.5 (p.198), binding may be accomplished by the synchronous oscillation of cells responding to different parts of the same object. In this respect, it is interesting that a particular cortical EEG rhythm becomes evident in the brains of subjects who are searching for hidden objects in a complex field (Tallon-Baudrey *et al.*, 1997). When the stimulus and camouflage are not different in some way, there is nothing to make the oscillations settle on a particular subgroup of cells while excluding others.

Fig. 10.22 Camouflage on a mountainside. A person is seated cross-legged before the first S in 'SAVES'.

ogram of Fig. 10.23 is difficult to find in either frame alone. But when the frames are fused, the letter stands out clearly from the masking lines.

Perceptual hypotheses

Up to this point, it may have seemed that the categorization of stimuli is the principal goal of a perceptual system. Except for an occasional reference to your ability to influence perception by conscious effort, you may well have wondered whether the human visual system is anything more than a fancy version of the machine that reads the code numbers on bank checks. It is now time to try to deal with those properties that set it apart from a sieve that sorts ore by size.

Synthesizer models

An alternative to a model in which a stimulus is channeled to the appropriate cognitive demon is one in which an internal representation consonant with the stimulus is constructed by an active synthetic process (Neisser, 1967). In this kind of model, perception is viewed as an active process in which you, the perceiver, make and test hypotheses about what physical things in the outside world could give rise to the pattern of stimulation

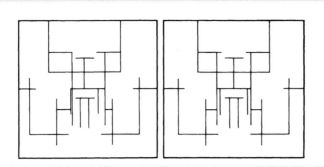

Fig. 10.23
Stereogram in which depth information 'unmasks' the hidden letter. View according to instructions in Box P1 (p.vi).

reported by your retinas. There is a distinction between two kinds of stimuli: the *distal stimulus*, which is the real set of objects 'out there' in the world, and the *proximal stimulus*, which is the pattern of stimulation on your retinas (see Fig. 10.24). This same distinction will prove important in understanding distance perception and constancies, which comprise the next two chapters.

The act of perception, then, is to make a best guess about what distal stimulus is likely to correspond to the proximal stimulus being sensed. This subconscious guess is termed a *perceptual hypothesis*. Active synthesis theories postulate that an internal model is built, and predictions of how the model should appear are compared with the proximal stimulus. If the comparison proves valid, the hypothesis is accepted and you 'see' the model you have constructed; if it is at variance with the facts

(the proximal stimulus), you reject or modify the hypothesis. Probably the best example of an analysis-by-synthesis perception model is the motor theory of speech perception (Liberman, 1957), which you will encounter in Chapter 18. The construction of models of the three-dimensional world (Marr, 1982) will be considered in Chapter 11. In each case, the hypotheses about what is being seen guide the way the sensory information is used to make the models. In this sense, these schemes include top-down processing. BOX 10.9

Although the synthesis of an internal model is quite different from the operation of a decision demon, it is not necessary to assume that perception is either synthetic or feature extracting (or template matching). MacKay (1967) pointed out that both a parallel set of feature extractors (he refers to these as 'filters') and a synthesizer

---

Box 10.9 Is it *really* a perceptual hypothesis?

The term 'perceptual hypothesis' has fallen into some disfavor, partly because it has been around for so long that it just seems 'old fashioned'. A more serious objection is the implication that perception involves some kind of reasoning process, although even complex perception is quite rapid and automatic (Thorpe *et al.*, 1996). Nevertheless, there seems to be no escaping the idea that the system must somehow infer what reality led to the stimulation received. This has been rephrased as a 'most likely interpre-

tation' (Stoner & Albright, 1992). The network theorists think in terms of a neural network that searches a 'possible solution' space for the optimum (read 'most likely') solution (read 'hypothesis'). While this approach begins to address *how* the hypothesis is synthesized, the fact remains that, functionally, the perceptual system makes a guess about what distal stimulus is likely to correspond to the proximal stimulus being sensed.

have their own distinct advantages. The parallel filters have the advantage of speed (see p. 189-90), while the synthesizer has the advantage of generality. The synthesizer would take a long time to build a model from 'scratch', but it could presumably eventually construct one for nearly any input. The parallel filters are fast, but an inordinate number of them would be needed to cover all possible inputs (and in designing a system, it would be impossible to be sure all possible future contingencies have been covered). MacKay suggested that the perceptual system is designed to capitalize on the advantages of each: a set of parallel filters extracts features from the proximal stimulus, and it is this highly digested representation of the stimulus that is presented to the synthesizer.

Cognitive learning

There is another aspect of perceptual systems that is undoubtedly essential. Suppose there are cognitive demons; how could there be a demon that recognizes the letter H? It is absurd to believe that English speaking people are born with the alpha-

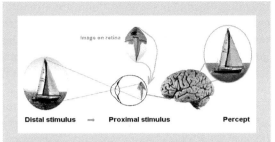

Fig. 10.24 Proximal and distal stimuli. The perceptual hypothesis is the link that allows the percept to represent the distal stimulus.

bet built into their cognitive systems. When we speak of a perceptual hypothesis, whether it is a guess about the real world or an active synthesis of a model of the world, we must ask how the rules for making these guesses were derived. At some point, at least some of perception is learned.

A theory of form recognition based entirely on learning was proposed by Hebb (1949). It is called the 'cell-assembly theory', and postulates that for each proximal stimulus some particular group of cells is excited. When these groupings recur, the

Box 10.10 Learning to see

Some evidence for the importance of early experience in 'teaching' perceptual systems how to perform their tasks comes from a few cases in which humans who were blind from birth have had their sight restored later in life.

Cataract operations were performed successfully in the 1770s. When sight was restored, the patients went through a period of 'learning to see'. One patient was 'far from making any judgment about distances' and 'could form no judgment about . . . shape'. This young gentleman often forgot which was the cat and which the dog, and was ashamed to ask; but catching the cat (which he knew by feeling) he was observed to look at her steadfastly, and then setting her down said, 'So Puss, I shall know you another time' (Priestly, 1772, p. 722).

Modern accounts of restored sight bear out this early account. Gregory (1978) and Gregory & Wallace (1963)

reported on the restored sight of a man who had undergone a corneal transplant. Although the patient did not 'suddenly see' when the bandages were removed, he was capable of considerable visual perception after a few days. He was not really required to learn to perceive, however, for he had already learned to map the world using his other senses. What he was required to do was to learn how the visual stimuli he was receiving corresponded to the familiar tactile and auditory stimuli accompanying them. He performed best at perceiving things he knew from his other senses, but had considerable difficulty with purely visual phenomena (such as judging height from a window). He did show evidence of visual learning, in that his drawings of the world gradually came to include features he did not know by touch, such as writing.

synaptic attachments among them are strengthened; cell assemblies in the association cortex would link assemblies corresponding to particular interpretation of the world (derived from various senses). This is essentially the basis of the neural network idea (see Box 10.1, p.189).

Our current understanding of how learning (of any kind) occurs in the brain is still too incomplete to justify a much more specific description. Synapses might be strengthened, new ones may form, or chemical changes might occur in neurons; all of these effects have been shown (for a review, see Fiorentini & Berardi, 1997). The important point is that some kind of learning must be required to 'teach' the brain how to perceive. This does not mean that all of perception is learned; you have already seen in Chapter 8 that cells of the visual cortex have many of their adult properties in the neonate. Aberrant visual experience seems only to modify or negate these 'inborn' properties (a kind of 'learning' in the cortex). However, even these properties can be modified by recent experience (Gilbert & Wiesel, 1992; Weinberger, 1995; Frégnac *et al.*, 1996; Eysel *et al.*, 1998). **BOX 10.10**

Perceptual set

If there is cognitive learning, perception is to some extent a function of what has been learned. There are two factors at work here: one is the overall question of what demons have been developed, what pattern of network connections strengthened, and what perceptual hypotheses encouraged; the other is the question of which of the many available sets of demons or connections or hypotheses to test first in the current situation.

The first factor supposes a difference in perception among people of differing perceptual backgrounds, more generally a *cultural* difference. Anyone accustomed to the English alphabet will immediately perceive two poles with a crossbar at midheight as an H, but that description would probably not occur to a Japanese person. We immediately recognize a distant airplane as a large, distant object, but a transplanted prehistoric person might see it as an odd, slow-flying bird—very likely 'seeing' the wings flapping.

These cultural differences have been invoked to explain differences in the susceptibility of certain groups of people to illusions that seem to depend on misinterpretation of line figures (these illusions will be discussed in Chapter 12). Segall *et al.* (1963) reported differences between European and African people, and attributed them to the Europeans' familiarity with a 'carpentered environment'. That is, Europeans are accustomed to straight walls, roads, and so on, and easily form impressions of depth from the implications of linear perspective (see Chapter 12). People not familiar with linear perspective are not fooled by the illusions; they simply do not make the same perceptual hypotheses when shown a pattern of non-parallel straight lines. This interpretation has come under some criticism; for example, Jahoda (1966) verified the findings for Europeans and people from undeveloped countries, but found no difference between the people from undeveloped countries who lived in carpentered environments and those who lived in uncarpentered environments. This does not mean that perceptual experience plays no role, only that this particular cultural difference may not account for the differential results with these illusions.

The second factor, *set*, depends on the more immediate experience of the perceiver. This may best be demonstrated by perception of what have been called *ambiguous figures*. Ambiguous figures are patterns that can be perceived in either of two ways; often, the perception switches back and forth between the interpretations once each has been seen. Such a pattern is shown in Fig. 10.25, called the 'my wife and my mother-in-law' drawing (Boring, 1930). This pattern can be seen as either an old woman with her chin down, or a young woman with her head turned nearly away looking over her shoulder. With slight modifications, the figure can be made much less ambiguous, much more likely to be seen as the 'wife' (Fig. 10.26a or as the 'mother-in-law' (Fig. 10.26b). Leeper (1935) used similar unambiguous drawings to define the set for subjects who were shown the ambiguous version. Subjects shown the 'wife' first saw the young woman when shown the ambiguous version, while those shown the 'mother-in-law' saw the old woman.

This might be considered a demonstration of the persistence of a figure, however, rather than of the influence of set. Quite possibly when you first saw Fig. 10.25 you saw only the younger or only the older woman and could not find the other until you used Fig. 10.26 as a guide. Once you saw it both ways, however, you probably had little trouble in seeing either configuration. Similarly, once you see the faces in the images in the 'Motion from form' demonstration on the CD, they appear spontaneously whenever you look at them. The person in Fig. 10.22 may have gone unnoticed when you first looked at the picture, but once you saw him he stood out vividly.

Perhaps a better demonstration of set is the way you interpret particular patterns according to context. For example, you have no difficulty in seeing that Fig. 10.27 shows the word 'title' written twice: once in capital letters, once in lower case. You also have no difficulty in recognizing that the straight vertical line that is the second letter in the upper-case version is an 'I', while the identical straight vertical line that is the fourth letter in the lower-case version is an 'L'. You perceive the same single stroke differently depending on whether you are in capital or lower-case mode.

Context effects can be even more complex than a change of mode. You have no difficulty with Is and Ls in mixed upper- and lower-case writing. You also can immediately perceive an ambiguous letter in one form or another depending on context. For example, the second letters in each of the two 'words' in Fig. 10.28 are physically identical, but you read the figure as 'THE CAT'.

Another example of the way context guides your hypothesis making is shown in Fig. 10.29. When you first glanced at this picture, you probably saw a gesticulating Japanese character. Closer inspection reveals that the head and hand are made up of

Fig. 10.25 'My wife and my mother-in-law'. An ambiguous figure from Boring, E. G. (1930) A new ambiguous figure. *Am. J. Psychol.* 42: 444–445. Reprinted by permission.

miniature figures. Once you notice them, they are hard to avoid seeing—but when you first looked at the picture, the lines seemed only to represent the larger face and hand. Interpreting the lines as part of the larger figure rather than the unexpected component figures is another indication of top-down processing affecting the way you handle sensory information.

Illusions dependent on perceptual hypotheses

There are numerous visual illusions and effects that help demonstrate the role of perceptual hypothesis-making. This section will deal only with those concerning formation of figures. In Chapter 12 you will encounter a larger group of illusions explicable by faulty perceptual hypotheses about depth and distance.

Fig. 10.26 Unambiguous versions of Fig. 10.25: (a) the young woman; (b) the old woman.

Impoverished cues You have already seen an example in which you needed guidance to make *any* perceptual hypothesis: the high-contrast faces in the 'Motion from form' demonstration on the CD. When you first saw these images they made no sense, and alternating between the two meaningless images failed to give an impression of coherent motion. When you clicked 'Reveal actual picture' for each of them, you saw what they really were. After that, you should have had no difficulty seeing the faces.

Ambiguous and reversible figures Ambiguous figures, such as the wife/mother-in-law in Fig. 10.25, can be interpreted in either of two ways because either of two perceptual hypotheses can be accepted. You may begin with the hypothesis that the loop to the left is a face; which means the triangular projection on the far left is a nose, the black band below is a necklace, and so on. As each part falls into place, no hypothesis need be rejected, and the young lady is seen. Alternatively, if the first hypothesis was that the

Fig. 10.27 Effect of context on perception. A straight vertical line can be seen as either an I (in TITLE, a) or as an l (in title, b).

THE CAT

Fig. 10.28 Effect of context on perception.

loop to the left is a nose, then the triangle is a wart upon it and the band is a mouth. No hypothesis need be rejected, and the old lady is seen. There are no details drawn completely enough to cause the rejection of any particular hypothesis. In the unambiguous versions shown Fig. 10.26, certain details are drawn too well to satisfy the 'wrong' hypothesis: the necklace/mouth is too distinctly a necklace in Fig. 10.26(a) to satisfy the 'mouth' hypothesis, and too clearly a mouth in Fig. 10.26(b) to satisfy the 'necklace' hypothesis.

You have also seen another ambiguous figure, in which the figure and ground could exchange roles (these are generally referred to as *reversible* figures). This was Fig. 10.11 (p.198), which could be seen either as a white vase or two silhouetted faces. Either hypothesis can be taken as 'true', so

Fig. 10.29 Japanese woodcut of a man by Hiroshige (early 1800s). Notice that the head and hand are made of tiny figures.

either figure may appear. Since both hypotheses cannot be true at the same time, it is nearly impossible to see both the vase and the faces simultaneously. Whichever you see as the figure at a given time takes on the attributes of a figure. There is also a demonstration of the active nature of our perceptual processes in both the wife/mother-in-law figure and the vase/faces: you can see either pattern in whichever configuration you wish by an act of willing it to be so.

One of the most famous reversible figures is shown in Fig. 10.30(a); it is the Necker cube. As all the edges of the cube are shown (like a cube made of wires), it is possible to see the Necker cube in either of the configurations shown in Figs 10.30(b) and (c). Once both have been seen, the cube seems to oscillate between them.

If you build a cube out of toothpicks or wires, and view it (with one eye) from an angle that makes it look like a Necker cube, you may be able to see the same apparent reversals as in the drawing. There will however, be, a striking effect. The real cube is not symmetrical like the drawing; the nearest edges project a larger image on your

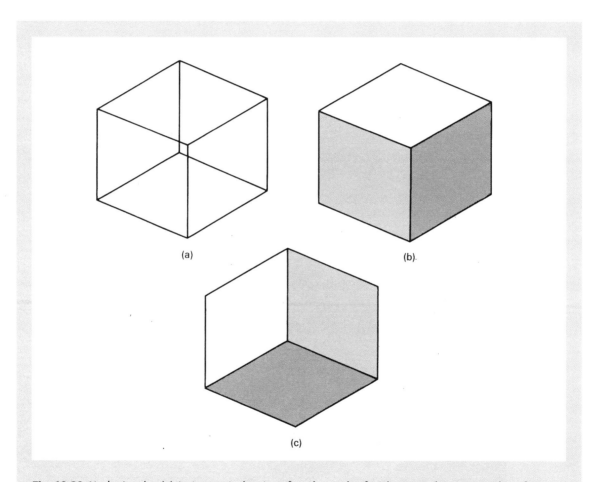

(a)

(b)

(c)

Fig. 10.30 Necker's cube. (a) An isometric drawing of a cube made of sticks; it may be seen in either of two configurations. (b), (c) Unambiguous cubes illustrating the two possible configurations of the Necker cube in (a).

retina than the edges farther away. This is a natural result of linear perspective (see next chapter), and causes no concern. When the figure reverses, however, those edges that appear closest are actually farther away, and therefore project smaller images. Distant edges projecting larger retinal images are not consonant with your experience and tend to invalidate the perceptual hypothesis that they are farther away (making the real cube harder to reverse than the drawing in Fig. 10.30a). To restore consistency, a second hypothesis, that the farther edges are also physically larger, must be made. This is what happens: when the cube reverses, it also appears to distort into a non-cubic hexahedron. This distortion can be seen in the drawing in Fig. 10.31(a), which is an accurate perspective view of a Necker cube. When it appears to be in the position of the cube in Fig. 10.30(c), for which the perspective is correct, it is a cube; when it reverses, it distorts. Similarly, the perspective drawing of a fanfold paper in Fig. 10.31(b) distorts when it is reversed so that the corner marked with a dot seems closest (which requires

considerable effort). This demonstration can also be done with a real folded sheet of paper viewed with one eye.

This raises a point about perceptual hypotheses: you tend to make the simplest hypothesis consistent with the proximal stimulus. You can consciously invoke a less simple hypothesis that requires further hypotheses to maintain internal consistency, but you generally choose the simpler solution. This is demonstrated by the patterns in Fig. 10.32. Both of these patterns are views of Necker cubes: part (a) is a familiar view, and part (b) is from a perspective that makes the forward corner and rearward corner superimpose. It is possible to see the former as a plane figure consisting of 12 lines (which it is), but the tendency to organize it into a cube is nearly overpowering. A cube is a simple hypothesis that explains the location of the 12 lines. The illustration in Fig. 10.32(b), however, is easily seen as either a plane figure or a cube. It is slightly easier to see it as the former; that is, as a hexagon with the three diagonals drawn in. The simpler hypothesis prevails.

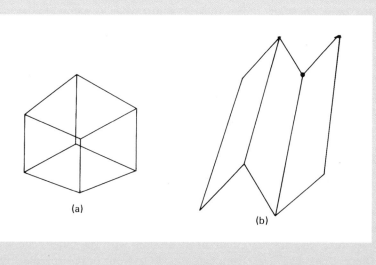

(a)

(b)

Fig. 10.31 (a) Necker cube drawn in correct perspective for the configuration of Fig. 10.30(c). When it is perceived in the configuration of Fig. 10.30(b), the cube appears distorted. (b) Another reversible figure drawn in correct perspective. It appears distorted when the corner
marked with a dot is seen as closer to the observer than the adjacent corners.

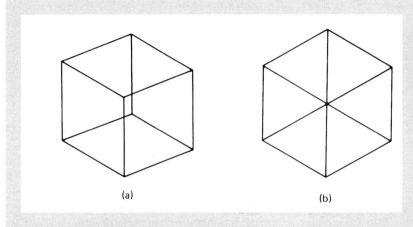

(a)

(b)

Fig. 10.32
Demonstration of the efficacy of the simplest perceptual hypothesis. (a) A Necker cube; this is generally seen as a three-dimensional cube. (b) A Necker cube viewed along a major diagonal; this figure is more often
perceived as a plane hexagon with the diagonals drawn.

Artists exploit the tendency to view the simplest alternative. Perceptual hypotheses about depth, coupled with the learned facts about perspective, allow two-dimensional canvases to appear to have depth, and theatrical stage flats to simulate a real scene. Other demonstrations are even more deliberately misleading. Figure 10.33(a) shows what appears to be a chair of sticks; in Fig. 10.33(b) you see the same 'chair' viewed from a slightly different perspective. Sticks that appeared to be adjoining other sticks because of their apparent proximity prove to be a considerable distance away. The simplest hypothesis is that these sticks really do touch (Gogel, 1970), and there really is a chair; no cues are given to dispel this idea. Even after seeing the real situation, it is nearly impossible not to see the chair when viewing from the correct position.

There is an excellent natural example similar to this phenomenon: the stars all appear as if they were affixed to a dome forming the sky. The stars that form the Big Dipper look like a single unit (grouped by proximity, forming a good figure) even though they are all at incredibly different distances from us. Even with the intellectual knowledge that the stars are not equidistant, it is difficult not to see them as a group, for there are no cues to disrupt that simplest of hypotheses.

Another kind of misleading object was devised by Adelbert Ames, the designer of the 'chair' in Fig. 10.33. Ames' trapezoidal window is shown in Fig. 10.34. It is just what its name implies: a window of trapezoidal (rather than rectangular) shape. As you are accustomed to rectangular windows, you make the hypothesis that this is a rectangular window that casts a trapezoidal image because it is being viewed from an angle: the large side seems closer. If a trapezoidal window cut from cardboard is mounted on a spindle, as shown in the figure, it can be made to rotate uniformly in one direction. When the taller edge passes closer to the observer there is no difficulty; but when the taller edge, which appears closer, passes *behind* the spindle, the observer thinks it is again passing in front. The window seems to oscillate in its motion, with the taller edge waving from side to side in front of the spindle. The hypothesis of a waving window is apparently easier to accept than the actual situation of a trapezoidal window rotating in a complete circle.

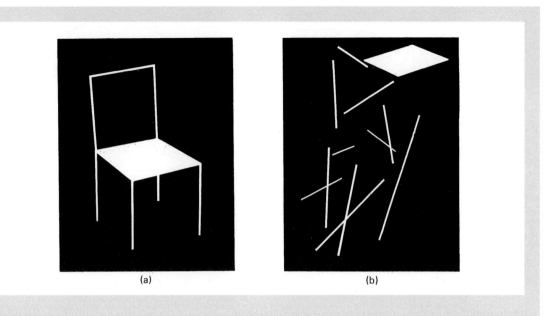

Fig. 10.33 Ames' chair: (a) when viewed from the correct point, the chair is seen; (b) when viewed from another position, the chair becomes a collection of sticks in space. From W. H. Ittelson (1968) *The Ames demonstrations in perception* (Macmillan, New York). Reprinted by permission of the author.

Now, if some other object, such as a pencil, is affixed to the window so that it projects through the frame, a bizarre effect occurs. There is no difficulty in seeing that the pencil is normal and following a circular orbit, which is both the actual case and the simplest hypothesis. It is inconsistent, however, for the pencil to travel in a circular path while the window oscillates, without the pencil somehow moving independently of, and passing through, the window frame. Additional hypotheses must be made to rectify the conflict between the circling pencil and oscillating window. Different observers make somewhat different hypotheses; most report the window oscillating and the pencil bending around as if made of rubber, then cutting through the frame at the extreme of each cycle. (Of course, any cues that the tall edge of the window is actually not nearer than the short edge tend to destroy the illusion.

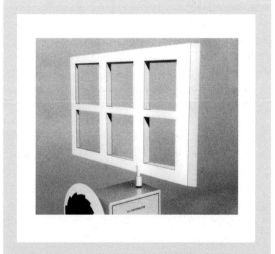

Fig. 10.34 The Ames trapezoidal window.

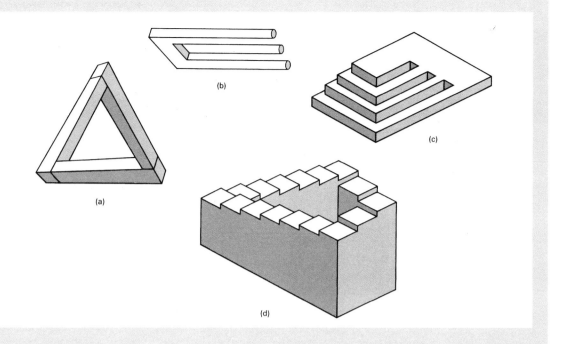

Fig. 10.35 Some impossible figures: (a) impossible triangle; (b) structure in which two arms become three prongs; (c) 'Ziggurat', a more subtle violation of structure; (d) perpetual staircase (also used in the demonstration program for this chapter). Parts (a) and (d) from Penrose, L. S. and R. Penrose (1958) Impossible objects: a special type of visual illusion. *Br. J. Psychol.* 49: 31–33. Reprinted by permission of the British Psychological Society. Part (c) from Draper, S. W. (1978) The Penrose triangle and a family of related figures. *Perception* 7: 283–296. Reprinted by permission of Pion, Ltd., London.

Box 10.11 Demonstration of impossible figures and sounds

Figures like this can be very entertaining, and often show up on children's placemats. Bell Laboratories took the perpetual staircase and combined it with a perpetual tone in a 2-minute film entitled 'A pair of paradoxes'. In it, a ball is seen bouncing down the stairs; each bounce is accented by a tone that seems one step lower than the previous one, although in the end it does not get any lower either.

The tone is the invention of R. N. Shepard (1964). It consists of a number of sine waves (an octave apart) in a bell-shaped envelope. That is, the lowest frequency is very low amplitude, and the amplitudes grow with frequency until the middle frequency; successively higher frequencies are lower amplitude. At each step, every tone moves down in frequency (by one note), growing or shrinking in ampli-

tude according to its new position in the envelope. The lowest tone eventually shrinks to nothing and disappears, while a new (but very weak) highest tone takes its place at the top. The shrinkage at the bottom is unnoticed, as is the growth at the top because of all the other tones. All that is noticed is the shift as every tone steps down one note.

Want to hear it? That is the background that plays when you start the demonstration program on the CD accompanying this book. (In this case, the steps are up instead of down, but the principle is the same.) The Chapter 10 demonstration 'Impossible figures', replicates the Bell Labs movie with downward steps.

For this reason, the window is best viewed with only one eye, preferably from some distance. A movie of the rotating window is generally more effective than the actual apparatus.)

Impossible figures Finally, there are patterns that are not exactly illusory, but which can be disturbing because there is no way to make a complete set of perceptual hypotheses that will be internally consistent. These are the *impossible figures*, drawings that cannot be physically realized. Four examples (of many) are shown in Fig. 10.35. The triangle on the left looks as though it might be built of three wooden slats (like a pool ball rack), except that the perspective is different for different corners. Any given corner is a perfectly valid joint, but as one follows from corner to corner the third simply will not mate. There is no reasonable hypothesis that is consistent with the proximal image, because the total pattern violates spatial closure (Draper, 1978).

The drawing in Fig. 10.35(b) is an even more extreme example. The left half of the figure is a perspective drawing of a U-shaped rectangular block; the right half is a drawing of three round rods. A reasonable hypothesis can be made about either half of the figure, but the two are inconsistent. The significance of the six horizontal lines changes halfway across: the third line down, for example, is the rear underside of a square beam on the left, but becomes the *top* edge of the second rod to the right. (Obvious as the impossibility may seem, I spent more than 10 minutes painstakingly pointing out these inconsistencies to my 6-year-old son, and in the end he was still not convinced that we couldn't build one of these if we tried hard enough! At that age, he had not yet learned all the rules for making consistent hypotheses across his visual field.)

The examples in Figs 10.35(c) and (d) are more subtle. In part (c), the perspectives on the left and the right sides disagree. In part (d), there are no changes in the meanings of particular lines, and no apparent inconsistencies—until you realize that if you start climbing steps at any place you will go completely around the structure, always climbing, and be back at the starting point. The trick here is that the perspective is wrong; the whole structure is designed on a spiral in the opposite direction (Gombrich, 1961). <u>BOX 10.11</u>

All the pictures in Fig. 10.35 share the property that the visual system has no difficulty 'understanding' each part of the picture, but that the parts are inconsistent with each other. Apparently, local processing can invoke perceptual hypotheses that apply to local regions. Minsky & Papert (1969), pioneers of the artificial intelligence approach to vision, referred to this ability to isolate portions as the 'context problem'. However, it is clear that some larger process must integrate these local hypotheses into a unified percept. This larger process is missing in Balint's syndrome (see Box 8.7, p. 150).

Impossible figures have been used in works of art, most notably in the drawings of M. C. Escher. An elaborate version of the perpetual staircase (Fig. 10.35d) forms the basis of his 'Ascending and descending', in which the details and buttresses of the building camouflage the distortions of the stairs. Failures of spatial closure like those in Fig. 10.35(a) are featured in 'Belvedere'. 'Waterfall', shown in Fig. 10.36(a), is another use of the impossible triangle. This perfectly reasonable waterfall turns a wheel, then flows downhill along its course to arrive again at the top of the falls. The sketch of the watercourse in Fig. 10.36(b) shows how the picture is actually a double impossible triangle. Notice how the craft and elaboration hide the source of the deception.

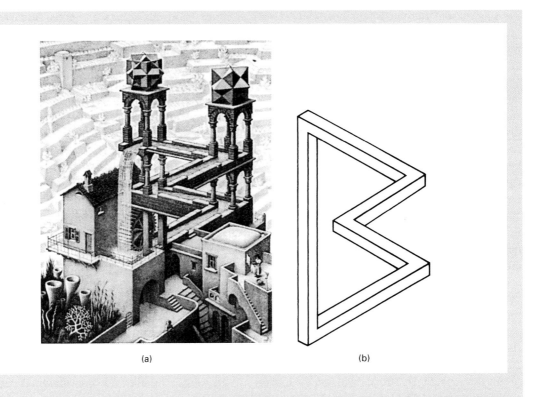

(a)   (b)

Fig. 10.36 (a) An impossible scene: M. C. Escher's 'Waterfall' © 2000 Cordon Art B.V. -Baarn- Holland. All rights reserved. (b) The shape of the watercourse in (a), revealing how it is essentially like Fig. 10.41(a). After Draper, S. W. (1978). Reprinted by permission of Pion, Ltd., London.

Suggested readings

Several books have treatments of form perception that are readable and comprehensive; they differ considerably, however, in their points of view. A modern view of the more traditional topics may be found in *Sight and mind*, by Lloyd Kaufman (Oxford University Press, Oxford, 1974). A comprehensive view of the traditional topics is given in Julian Hochberg's 'Perception. I. Color and shape', which is Chapter 12 of *Experimental psychology*, by J.

W. Kling and L. A. Riggs (Holt, Rinehart, and Winston, 1971). A cognitively oriented presentation that includes some of the work in artificial intelligence is given by Ulrich Neisser in his book *Cognitive psychology* (Appleton-Century Crofts, 1967). A more philosophical view is given by Paul Churchland in *The engine of reason, the seat of the soul* (MIT Press, 1995). The first few chapters are particularly relevant to this discussion. (Churchland is a philosopher who is married to Patricia Churchland, one of the leading neural network modelers.)

A number of *Scientific American* articles bear on specific topics covered in this chapter; in most cases, the titles reveal the contents. O. G. Selfridge and U. Neisser present 'Pattern recognition by machine' (August 1960; offprint #510). 'Visual illusions', by R. L. Gregory (November 1968; offprint #517) also includes illusions covered in Chapter 12. 'Texture and visual perception', by B. Julesz (February 1965; offprint #318) has some material pertinent to the next two chapters, but also includes a modern view of organization by similarity, and of the concept of symmetry. How an infant first begins to perceive shape and form is the subject of 'The origin of form perception', by R. L. Fantz (May 1961; offprint #459). All of these articles are reprinted in the collection *Perception. mechanisms and models*, edited by R. Held and W. Richards (W. H. Freeman, 1972). An article that deals with ambiguous figures and the figure ground/relationship is called 'Multistability in perception', by F. Attneave (December 1971; offprint #540); a similar theme is explored by M. L. Teuber in 'Sources of ambiguity in the prints of Maurits C. Escher' (July 1974; offprint #560). 'The perception of disoriented figures', by I. Rock (January 1974; offprint #557) stresses the importance of the frame of reference in perception. These three articles, plus the Julesz article mentioned above, are reprinted in *Recent progress in perception*, edited by R. Held and W. Richards (W. H. Freeman, 1976). The articles by Attneave, Gregory, Julesz, and Rock also appear in *Image, object, and illusion*, by R. Held (W. H. Freeman, 1974). A classic discussion of 'Subjective contours' was presented by G. Kanizsa (April 1976). A newer treatment of ambiguous figures may be found in 'The interpretation of visual illusions', by D. D. Hoffman (December, 1983). Both of these are reprinted in *The mind's eye* (introduction by J. M. Wolfe; W. H. Freeman, 1986).

Accounts of restored vision in adults who had been blind from birth can be fascinating. You already read briefly about the case described by Gregory (1978); you may wish to read it in more detail in *Eye and brain*, 3rd edn McGraw-Hill, New York, 1978, pp. 194–200). A more detailed case history is called 'To see and not see', by Oliver Sacks. It can be found in his book *An anthropologist on Mars* (Knopf, New York, 1995, pp. 108–152). Sacks' essay was the basis for the movie 'At first sight'.

A beautifully illustrated book that covers many of the topics in this and the next four chapters is *Perception*, by Irvin Rock (Scientific American Books, 1984). In addition to explaining the principles of perception, Rock provides examples of how these principles are used in art and apply to everyday scenes. A book that uses extensive examples from art, but also includes a considerable discussion of illusions and the basic visual principles, is *The artful eye*, edited by R. Gregory *et al.* (Oxford University Press, Oxford, 1995). A similar treatment that also concentrates on analyzing particular artists' works is *The eye of the artist*, by Michael Marmor & James Ravin (Mosby, St Louis, 1997). A study of how visual science principles apply to art is presented by Semir Zeki, a noted vision researcher, in *Inner Vision: an exploration of art and the brain* (Oxford University Press, 2000). Another book of interest is *Art and illusion*, by E. H. Gombrich (Princeton University Press, 1961). Basically an art book, there is an emphasis on the use of illusory, impossible, and ambiguous figures in works of art. The latter four books are also relevant to Chapter 12.

The application of artificial intelligence to cognitive processing is a new and exciting area, but it is hard to find appropriate readings. Two articles appearing in *Science* in 1988 merit attention for giving specific examples of how neural networks might perform cognitive functions. The first is by P. S. Churchland and T. J. Sejnowski: 'Perspectives on cognitive neuroscience' (242: 741–745). The second is by T. J. Sejnowski, C. Koch and P. S. Churchland: 'Computational neuroscience' (241: 1299–1306). *Science* is written at a technical level, but these articles are generally accessible. For those who are serious about understanding how cognition could be based on neural interactions, there is *Neural Darwinism: the theory of neuronal group selection*, by G. M. Edelman

(Basic Books, 1987). Edelman discusses ways in which synapses might change as a network 'learns' to recognize objects, and he proposes a way in which neurons might coalesce into functional groups. He presents a model for a cognitive system in which functional groups interact at various levels—strikingly like the various brain regions discussed in Chapter 9. However, this book is recommended only for the most serious students, as it is conceptually difficult and written in a way that seems almost deliberately opaque.

Chapter 11
Depth perception

Aʟʟ the information you have regarding the visual world comes from stimulation of your two retinas. Your retinas, although curved into hemispheres in the back of your eyeballs, are two-dimensional layers of tissue. How does stimulation of two-dimensional retinal surfaces get translated by your brain into perceptions of depth or distance? Such perceptions are an integral part of your world; when reaching for a glass of water on a table, you must know exactly what position in space that glass is occupying. The activities of hitting tennis balls, shooting baskets, and just walking around on a city street all require vast amounts of information about spatial relationships between you and the physical world, as well as among various objects within the physical world.

You can divide the cues available for depth perception into several fairly distinct classes. *Monocular cues* are those that require the use of only one eye. Some monocular cues may be available from a stationary inspection of the visual scene; these are the types that are employed by artists and are therefore called *pictorial cues*. Others are only present when either the observer or the objects in the visual scene are in motion; these are called *kinetic cues*. A final source of monocular information regarding depth can be obtained from the state of accommodation of the lens as it focuses on a given object.

Another class of depth cue is available because your brain receives two views of the visual world, one from each eye. These are *binocular cues*, derived from the fact that the two retinal images are

slightly different from each other. In addition, information regarding the state of contraction of the extraocular muscles of your two eyes may be used by your brain to determine the point in space at which your eyes are pointing.

In this chapter, you will learn about these cues, and about attempts to determine which ones are the most important for your perception of depth. In addition, you will read about the physiological mechanisms that underlie the processing of some of these depth cues.

Monocular depth cues

Pictorial cues

Size If an object is placed at different distances from you, the size of the retinal images produced by that object varies in inverse proportion to its distance. For example, an object placed 5 m away casts an image on the retina that is double what the image size would be if the same object were moved so that it were 10 m away. Thus, the size of the retinal image can act as a cue for determining how far away the object actually is. (As you will see in Chapter 12, perception of distance can also affect apparent size.)

There are two different ways in which this cue might be applied to the perception of depth. If you are looking at two similar or identical objects whose distances from you are different, they cast images whose sizes are also different. When making judgments regarding the relative positions of the two objects, the *relative sizes* of the images may be considered. To make this judgment, you do not have to know anything about the actual sizes of the objects; it is necessary only to assume that they are really similar.

Many investigators have shown that under these conditions relative size can be an effective cue. Ittelson & Kilpatrick (1951) presented subjects with two balloons at the same distance from the subjects; the sizes of the balloons could be controlled by bellows. When the balloons were viewed monocularly under dim illumination (to eliminate other depth cues), the relative distances assigned to them by the subjects depended on the relative sizes. When the two balloons were of equal size, they were viewed as being the same distance away, but when they were different in size, the larger one was always thought to be closer to the subject.

A demonstration of the effectiveness of relative retinal image size as a cue for distance is given in Fig. 11.1. (If this figure is not compelling, it is because the cue of relative size is acting in opposition to the other depth cues that are present; for example, under the conditions you are viewing the figure, it is clear that all the triangles are actually lying in the plane of the book. For this figure to give a convincing feeling of distance, you would have to view it under conditions in which it was not so clear that the stimuli were on the same piece of paper.)

Although relative size can clearly play a role in the perception of depth, there are other size cues that are also effective. *Familiar size* applies when the actual size of an object is known to the viewer. For example, everyone knows the approximate size of an automobile, but the size of its retinal image varies with distance from the viewer. If familiar size is an effective cue for distance, the absolute retinal image size of the car tells the viewer approximately how far away the car actually is. For example, Epstein & Baratz (1964) found that when extremely familiar objects such as coins were used as stimuli, their sizes affected how far away subjects judged them to be. For objects that subjects were less familiar with, changing the size had no effect on distance judgments.

The importance of familiar size as a cue for depth seems to depend also on what other cues are available. Under rich stimulus conditions, familiar size is not used in distance judgments (Fillenbaum *et al.*, 1965); subjects generally use the size cue in experimental situations in which other cues were not available (Schiffman, 1967).

Interposition If two opaque objects are in the same line of sight, one occludes the other. This is *interposition*, and its effectiveness can be seen in Fig. 11.2. Although all of the geometric forms in the figure lie in the plane of the paper, the circle is seen as lying behind the rectangle, which seems to be

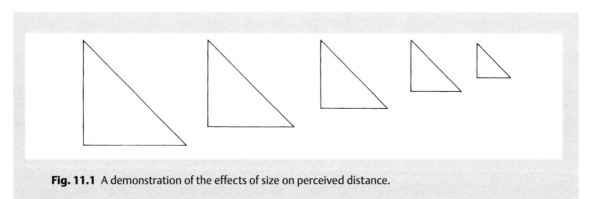

Fig. 11.1 A demonstration of the effects of size on perceived distance.

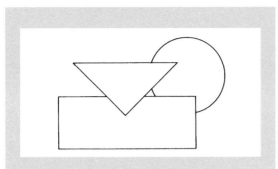

Fig. 11.2 Interposition as a cue for distance.

behind the triangle. The relative depths of the three objects can be deduced from the facts that the circle is blocked by both the rectangle and the triangle, while the rectangle blocks the circle but is blocked by the triangle.

The above interpretation is not the only one that could be given to this figure; the forms in Fig. 11.2 could conceivably be the ones shown in Fig. 11.3, in which case their relative distances could be anything. One reason that you get the illusion of depth from Fig. 11.2 instead of seeing the forms as shown in Fig. 11.3 was discussed in Chapter 10. If there is a choice between perceiving something as a complicated form or as a simpler form, you generally perceive the simplest shape possible—that is, you tend to maximize figural goodness (pragnanz). Perceiving the forms in Fig. 11.2 as a triangle, rectangle, and circle is simpler than having to conceptualize the rather complex shapes in Fig. 11.3. In this case the perception of depth allows you to code the ensemble of lines and curves in Fig. 11.2 more easily than if they were all thought of as being coplanar (see Fig. 10.32, p. 216).

Lighting and shadow Objects that have depth associated with them usually cast shadows; these shadows can be used to give the impression of a three-dimensional form even on a two-dimensional surface. Consider the photograph of a crater shown in Fig. 11.4. There is a clear impression of the depth of the crater, at least partially because of the shadow. To see the importance of the shadow gradients on perception, turn the book upside down and look at the photo again. The shadow gradients are now reversed; because of this, you should get the strong impression of a hill. A more abstract demonstration of this same phenomenon is shown in Fig. 11.5.

Since greater depth is indicated by deeper shadows, less depth is perceived when the lighting is directed straight onto a surface. This is why the full moon looks like a flat disk, while the half-moon, with sunlight grazing the night–day delimiter, clearly has a ball-like shape (Nayar & Oren, 1995). BOX 11.1

Clarity and elevation Look at the scene in Fig. 11.6. The person is obviously closer than the river and valley. Of course, interposition plays a role here, but a large part of the appearance of depth is due to the relative *clarity* of the person. Particles of dust and moisture in the atmosphere interrupt and scatter the light; the longer the light path from object to

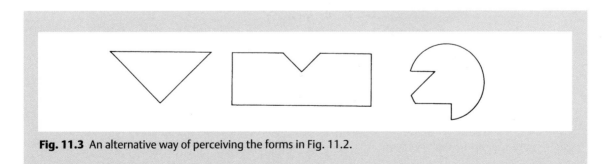

Fig. 11.3 An alternative way of perceiving the forms in Fig. 11.2.

Box 11.1 Neural network models of depth perception

Workers in artificial intelligence have found that the apparently simple relationship between depth and shadow can be quite difficult to implement in machine vision. A considerable amount of effort has been devoted to the problem of deducing the shapes of objects from the shades of gray in a two-dimensional photograph. It is *relatively* easy to determine the appearance of objects to be expected given their surface properties and the lighting conditions; extraordinarily life-like representations can be generated as computer graphics requiring only a few *hours* of computation (Greenberg, 1989; those times have been dramatically reduced in the decade since then). The reverse problem, determining the object given the image, does not even have a unique solution. It is what is called an 'ill-posed problem'—soluble only when the observer moves around and thereby obtains multiple images to compare (Aloimonos & Rosenfeld, 1991). Quite complicated algorithms have been devised, but these require assumptions about the nature of surfaces and the lighting conditions in order to reach their solutions (Brown, 1984). Our visual systems solve the same problems instantly. Newer approaches in which neural networks 'learn' to recognize the shapes seem to be more successful than strictly mathematical approaches (Lehky & Sejnowski, 1988; Sejnowski *et al.*, 1988).

observer, the less crisp the image. (In this sense, clarity is not loss of focus, but loss of *contrast*.) Clarity can thus serve as a cue for distance.

Figure 11.6 also illustrates the cue of *elevation*, the location within the picture frame. As you look from nearer objects to farther, the farther objects are generally higher in the visual field. Except for the person, this is especially true in Fig. 11.6. The closest objects (the rock and plants) are at the bottom of the picture; midrange objects (the river and roads) are higher; the farthest objects (the valley at the left side of the picture) are at the very top of the frame. Objects represented higher in a scene tend to be perceived as being further away.

Fig. 11.4 Lighting and shadow as a cue for depth. Turn the book upside down and the crater turns into a hill. Photo courtesy of the US Dept of Energy.

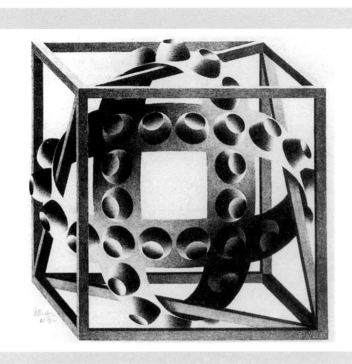

Fig. 11.5 Drawing by M. C. Escher using light and shadow as a depth cue. M. C. Escher's 'Cube with ribbons' © 2000 Cordon Art -Baarn– Holland.

Perspective   Imagine standing in the middle of a long boardwalk, gazing down the walk as it recedes toward the horizon, as shown in Fig. 11.7. The railings along the walkway are parallel as they extend away from you, and you perceive them as such; however, the retinal image of the railings is far from parallel. The images of the portions of the near railings are quite far apart on the retina, just as they are well separated from each other in the figure. Look farther down the walkway, and their images on the retinas become closer together, tending toward a single point at the horizon. This is exactly what happens in Fig. 11.7. This phenomenon is termed *linear perspective*; it is a ubiquitous component of retinal images, and imparts a strong depth component to line drawings and photographs. (You can see this picture at equiluminance as 'Photo #4' in the demonstrations for Chapter 8 on the CD; notice how little depth is conveyed at equiluminance.)

Linear perspective is a necessary consequence of projecting a three-dimensional world onto a two-dimensional surface (a retina, photographic film, or drawing paper). For any object that extends in depth away from the observer, the near portions of the object cast larger images on the retina than the more distant portions. Another example of linear perspective is shown in Fig. 11.8; in this photograph of the inside of a winery, the casks near the camera take up much more of the picture than the areas farther away. Just as the railings in Fig. 11.7 seemed to converge at the horizon, the line of casks converges with distance down the length of the cellar, as do the ceiling details and lights at the top of the figure.

Texture   Another depth cue is derived from the depth-dependent change in size of details in a two-dimensional representation of a three-dimensional world. This is called *detail perspective*, or *texture*

Fig. 11.6 Scene demonstrating depth due to clarity and elevation.

gradients (Gibson, 1950). Imagine again standing on the boardwalk depicted in Fig. 11.7; besides the fact that the railings appear to converge as they recede from the observer, the spacing between adjacent posts decreases with distance from the observer. The reason for this is the same as for the railings converging; although the distance between the posts is the same in the physical world, the posts more distant from you project closer together on your retina than those that are near you. In the case of the photograph in Fig. 11.7, the camera's film takes the place of your retina, and you get the same impression of depth by looking at the photograph. In this example, a texture gradient combines with linear perspective to produce an impression of depth.

A graphic demonstration of texture in the absence of any linear perspective cues is given in Fig. 11.9. The halves of the figure differ only in the placement of the horizontal lines, but there is a strong depth impression in (b) and not in (a). This impression comes from the fact that the lines in (b) form a texture gradient, while in (a) they are equally spaced. In this example, the only cue providing depth information is the texture change; it is strong enough to produce a depth impression in the absence of other cues.

If you prop the book up and step back from it, you may notice that the apparent depth in Fig. 11.9(b) seems less compelling. This is true even though you can still see the lines plainly. What is different when you step back is that the image is smaller; that is, everything is shifted to higher spatial frequencies. Perhaps appearance of depth depends on a system that is most sensitive to lower spatial frequencies — such as the magnocellular system (see Chapter 8). If that is so, depth should not be evident when the pattern is made effective only for the parvocellular sys-

Fig. 11.7 An example of linear perspective.

Fig. 11.8 A second example of linear perspective.

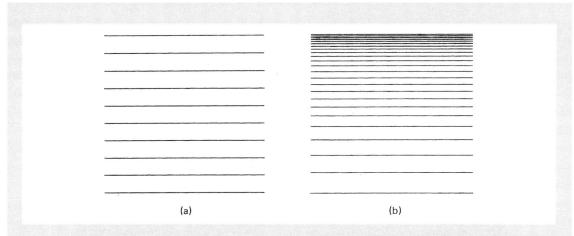

    (a)   (b)

Fig. 11.9 An example of pure texture as a depth cue. (a) and (b) are similar except for the texture gradient in (b), which gives it a strong depth component.

tem. Another way to achieve this is to produce the picture in Fig. 11.9(b) at equiluminance, so the color-blind magnocellular system cannot see the lines even though the parvocellular system allows the viewer to see that they are present. When this is done, viewers report seeing lines, but with no apparent depth (Livingstone & Hubel, 1987b). You can see this for yourself in the equiluminant demonstration 'Line drawing' on the CD, for Chapter 8. This is an indication that the magnocellular system is required for the appearance of depth from pictorial cues. **BOX 11.2**

Box 11.2 A great painter's comment on pictorial representation

Pictorial cues were employed to make a statement about the nature of artistic representation in the painting *Les Promenades d'Euclide* by René Magritte (Fig. 11.10). A view of the world extending in depth is seen through a window, as if it were a pictorial projection on the window. In front of the window is an artist's canvas with the same pictorial representation painted on it, so that it appears you are actually seeing the world through the canvas. (Of course, this entire scene is itself painted on a canvas, seen through the eye of the camera that photographed the painting.) All the pictorial cues you have read about can be seen in this painting: distant buildings are smaller than nearby buildings; the nearby objects (such as the pointed tower just left of center) are interposed between the viewer and more distant objects; there are shadows cast by buildings and the tower; the distant horizon is higher than the buildings and is less distinct; the sides of the street (right of center) converge as the street recedes toward the horizon (linear perspective); and the textures in the street become finer the farther down the road you look.

Notice in particular that the pointed tower and the street are formed by identical triangles having their apices coincident with the horizon. Whether you take the converging lines to imply linear perspective (as in the street), or an erect conical object (the tower), depends on context, texture, and shadowing. Thus, the convergent point of the tower is perceived as much closer than the point at which the road disappears over the horizon, and the triangle forming the street seems larger than the one forming the tower. Chapter 12 will discuss how the perceived distance of objects affects their perceived sizes.

Fig. 11.10 *Les Promenades d'Euclide* by René Magritte. Notice the pictorial cues are all used to generate a feeling of depth in the picture-within-the-picture. Notice also that the tower and road are formed by identical triangles but are perceived differently because of context, shading, and texture gradients. The Minneapolis Institute of Arts. Reprinted by permission.

Accommodation

When you shift your visual attention from a nearby object to one that is far away, your lens adjusts its shape to maintain a sharp image of the particular object to which you are attending. This is accommodation, as discussed in Chapter 3. The fact that the level of activity of the ciliary muscles is correlated with the distance of the object to be viewed means that your brain could use this information to make decisions about the distance of the object.

There is considerable doubt as to whether information regarding the state of accommodation of the lens provides a usable distance cue. Hochberg (1971b) reviewed the literature on this question and concluded that there is little reason to believe that the state of accommodation is an important cue for the perception of distance. Other species, such as owls, may make more use of this cue than we do (Wagner & Schaeffel, 1991).

Kinetic cues

All the cues discussed so far involve a stationary subject looking with one eye at a stationary visual scene. In this section the subject might remain one-eyed, but additional depth cues become available when either the subject or the stimulus is moving in space.

When you move within the physical world, objects that are stationary in space nevertheless have images that continuously change position on your retina. The relative movement of objects at different distances from the observer is called *motion parallax*. Motion parallax occurs in many situations—for example, while looking out the window of a moving car or train. If your eyes are fixated on the horizon in

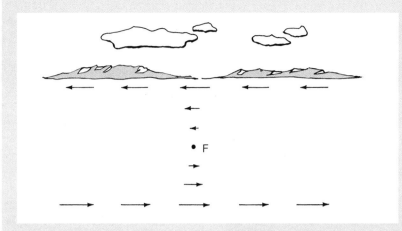

Fig. 11.11 Motion parallax as a cue for depth. If a subject fixates on point *F* and is moving to the left, all objects more distant than *F* will move with the subject, while objects in front of *F* will move in the opposite direction. This is shown as a demonstration of 'Depth from motion of random dots' (click 'Motion parallax') on the CD accompanying this book. From Gibson, J. J. *The perception of the visual world*. Copyright © 1950 by Houghton Mifflin Company. Used with permission.

such a situation, then all objects closer than the horizon move in the opposite direction from the vehicle. If you attend to an object a moderate distance away, however, all components of the visual world situated behind that object appear to move with you, while everything in front of that object moves in the opposite direction (Fig. 11.11).

This effect is demonstrated in 'Depth from motion', associated with this chapter on the CD. The topmost choice button, 'Motion parallax', causes the random dots in the display to move according to the pattern indicated in Fig. 11.11. This should give a clear impression of depth, even though the dots are all the same size and no other cues are pre-

---

Box 11.3 Motion parallax from a simple gesture

You need not move about in the world to cause motion parallax. Your eyes are farther forward in your head than the axis about which your head pivots on your neck. When you turn your head from side to side (as you normally do to look around yourself), you also move your eyes from side to side. To see the motion parallax induced by turning your head, 'just say no'. Close one eye and hold the index finger of each hand out in front of you, so that one finger is quite near your eye, and the other is about 18 inches away. Keep your fingers steady, and turn your head from side to side while fixating on the far finger. Under these conditions, as you turn your

head in one direction, the image of the near finger should move in the opposite direction. Now perform the same experiment while fixating on your nearer finger; the image of your far finger should move in the same direction as your head. Finally, if you fixate on something behind your far finger (for example, the wall), the images of both fingers move in the direction opposite to your head movement, but the image of the closer finger appears to move much faster than the other. In fact, just rotating your eyes with your head stationary provides a small motion parallax (Enright, 1991).

sent. You can confirm that there are no other depth cues by clicking 'Stop motion'. <u>BOX 11.3</u>

Motion parallax clearly is a potential source of information about the relative distances of objects in space. Many studies have been performed to try to isolate this cue from other sources of distance information, to see just how effective it really is. As far as your retina is concerned, moving objects in space can exactly mimic movement of the observer, and thus many of these studies held the subject still and manipulated the external environment.

In one such study, Gibson *et al.* (1959) used a point-source shadow projector to simulate motion parallax cues in the absence of other depth information. The shadow projector simply consisted of a light source that lit a projection screen viewed by the subject on the other side of the screen from the light. One or more transparent plastic sheets erratically covered with splattered paint or talcum powder could be placed between the light and the screen; the shadows of these irregular patterns were then projected onto the screen and seen by the observer. Fig. 11.12 shows a schematic of the shadow projector.

Gibson *et al.* (1959) placed two splattered plastic sheets parallel to the projection screen. The sheets were moved across the field such that the projected image from one sheet moved faster than that from the other. Thus the observer saw a moving textured field with some elements moving faster than others, just as if sheets at different distances were being viewed directly while the observer was moving and the sheets remained stationary. Under these conditions, subjects reported an impression of depth; however, they could not always determine which sheet was beyond the other. Notice that they could recognize the two sheets because of common fate (see Chapter 10). You can see this effect for yourself by selecting 'Transparency' from the 'Depth from motion' demonstrations associated with this chapter on the CD accompanying this book.

Motion parallax is a cue that is derived from the observer's movements. In the shadow projector experiments and on the CD, stimulus motion simply mimicked effects that in the real world would have been produced by movements of the subject. There is, however, a related class of motion cues that depends on movement in the physical world. Wallach and his colleagues (Wallach & O'Connell, 1953; Wallach *et al.*, 1953) used the

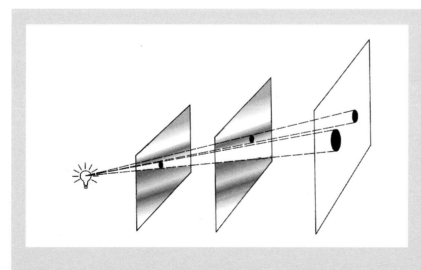

Fig. 11.12 A schematic of the kind of shadow projector used by Gibson *et al.* (1959).

shadow projector technique described above, except that between the light source and the projection screen they placed a rotating object oriented in different directions. For example, a straight rod could be positioned so that the top of the rod was tilted toward the projection screen and the bottom was toward the light source (Fig. 11.13). It was then rotated in the horizontal dimension about a point at the center of the rod. When the rod was positioned so that it cast a vertical shadow on the viewing screen, the length of its shadow was smaller than when it was rotated one-quarter of a cycle in either direction. The different shadows produced by the different positions of the rod are shown in Fig. 11.13; as the rod rotated, the shadow changed both in orientation and in length.

When a rod was rotated in the manner described above, subjects viewing the continuously changing shadow received the clear impression of a rod rotating in three dimensions; that is, they perceived the shadow as three-dimensional much in the way that they would have perceived the rod itself. Thus, even though the shadow was in two dimensions, it produced an impression of depth.

Wallach and his coworkers called this the *kinetic depth effect* (KDE).

A related effect may be obtained from a field of about 50 dots that each move in ellipses at the same frequency. This is the pattern that would arise if opaque dots were placed at random on a transparent, rotating sphere, and you were looking at the shadow of the dotted sphere. If the sphere were stationary, you would see a circular field of random dots. When the dots move, the sphere 'jumps out' as a three-dimensional shape. However, if the dots are made equiluminant with the background (such that the two colors are equally effective for the magnocellular system), there is no apparent depth. Instead of a rotating field, you see a circular field of dots that are apparently moving about at random (Livingstone & Hubel, 1987b). As noted for depth from texture, it appears that the magnocellular system is needed to perceive depth. This rotating sphere is among the 'Equiluminant demonstrations' associated with Chapter 8 on the CD (it is the 'Dot pattern', which is only available after the colors are balanced). Be sure to view it both at equiluminance and in black and white.

Fig. 11.13 Demonstration of the kinetic depth effect (KDE). A rotating bar casts a shadow that changes in both orientation and length, producing a three-dimensional impression.

Binocular depth cues

The monocular cues for depth that have been discussed so far in this chapter allow for a fairly accurate perception of the three-dimensional world. If you have ever had to wear a patch over one eye for any length of time, you know that these cues are adequate for most perceptual needs. People with only one eye can drive cars, catch baseballs, and perform many other tasks requiring an exact impression of the depth associated with the physical world. By comparing your perceptual experiences under monocular and binocular conditions, however, you know that depth perception is enhanced by the use of two eyes. In this section, you will see some of the depth cues that depend on binocular vision.

Convergence

As mentioned earlier in this chapter, there are accommodative changes in the lens that accompany changes in stimulus position for objects quite close to the eye. Associated with accommodation are eye movements called disjunctive eye movements (see Chapter 3). Disjunctive eye movements occur as a stimulus moves either toward or away from a subject.

In the example shown in Fig. 11.14, a subject is staring at an object located at point A in space. The eyes are therefore positioned so that an image of the object is projected to both foveae; as point A is located directly in front of the two eyes, the eyes have been rotated so that their gazes are not parallel, but converge at point A. If the stimulus is moved from point A to point B as shown in Fig. 11.14(b), two physiological changes occur. First, accommodation takes place, with the lens assuming a more rounded shape to provide the extra refractive power to maintain focus of the stimulus on the retina. In addition, a disjunctive eye movement occurs, with both eyes turning inward to maintain the stimulus' projection onto both foveae. This is an example of *convergence*: the two eyes turn inward to prevent double vision. If you now reverse the sequence and move the stimulus from point B back to point A, the two eyes rotate away from each other; that is, they *diverge*.

The amount of convergence between the two

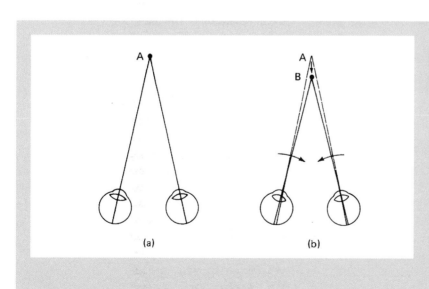

(a)   (b)

Fig. 11.14 An example of convergence.

eyes is a potential source of depth information. In fact, unlike most other cues for depth, the angle at which the eyes converge to produce an image of the stimulus at corresponding points on the retinas provides a measure of the absolute distance between the observer and the stimulus. The absolute distance between the observer's head and the point at which the lines of sight of the two eyes intersect can be calculated with simple trigonometry, given the distance between the two eyes and the angle of convergence (Fig. 11.15). Of course, our visual systems do not perform a trigonometric calculation, but it is reasonable to expect to learn the distance significance of the convergence signal.

Although accommodation and convergence are closely related phenomena, evidence supporting the contention that people use convergence cues to make decisions about depth is much stronger than the evidence regarding accommodation. Heinemann *et al.* (1959) presented luminous discs to subjects *dichoptically*; that is, separate discs were presented to the two eyes so that each eye only saw one disc. By simply changing the lateral position of the discs, they could manipulate the amount of ocular convergence that was necessary to maintain the image of the discs on corresponding points of the retinas. When the stimuli were arranged so

that convergence was increased, the subjects reported the discs as being smaller than when the eyes were caused to diverge, even though the physical size of the retinal images was the same in both cases. Large amounts of convergence accompany the viewing of a nearby object; as the retinal image size was constant in both cases, it makes sense that the stimuli were perceived as being smaller when the convergence cues indicated the object was nearby. Thus, apparent size changes of the stimuli provide support for the idea that convergence is used as a depth cue (see Chapter 12). Other experiments on this subject have yielded similar results (Leibowitz, 1971; Komoda & Ono, 1974).

In these studies, there were no changes in accommodative state as the stimuli to the two eyes were moved. Other experiments investigating the importance of convergence as a cue for depth have employed conditions in which accommodative and convergence information were in conflict; that is, the amount of lens accommodation necessary to place the stimulus in sharp focus was inconsistent with the convergence necessary to keep images of the stimulus located on the corresponding areas of the retina. Under these conditions, depth judgments were made solely on the basis of the convergence information, ignoring the state of accommodation of the lens (Gogel & Sturm, 1972;

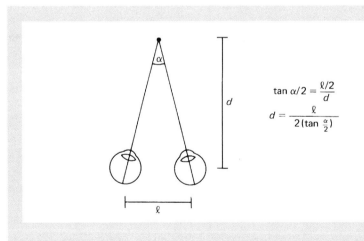

$$\tan \alpha/2 = \frac{\ell/2}{d}$$

$$d = \frac{\ell}{2\left(\tan \frac{\alpha}{2}\right)}$$

Fig. 11.15
Demonstration of how ocular convergence can provide information about the absolute distance between observer and point of fixation.

Ritter, 1977). These experiments confirm that ocular convergence information is far more important for depth perception than information arising from state of accommodation.

Binocular disparity

The two eyes converge or diverge in order to place images of the stimulus being attended to on corresponding locations of the retinas. In general, however, the two eyes receive slightly different views of the world by virtue of their different locations on the head. Because of this difference, corresponding areas of the two retinas do not always receive exactly the same visual image. This phenomenon is known as *binocular disparity*, or *binocular parallax*; it provides an important cue for binocular depth perception.

Binocular disparity is illustrated in Fig. 11.16. In this figure, two eyes are shown fixated on a nearby square stimulus. Because this is the stimulus being attended to, images of the square are projected to corresponding locations on the foveae of the two retinas. The images of the closer stimulus in the figure, the circle, cannot be projected onto the retinas without some disparity. From the perspective of the right eye, the two stimuli are quite close together, while from the left eye, they look as though they are considerably farther apart. The fact that the views from the two eyes look different is a cue that the stimuli are at different distances from the observer.

Notice that what is important is that the two views look different, not which object appears 'displaced'. If the gaze were directed at the circular stimulus, then the square would have been projected on two different locations in the two retinas. Whatever object you fixate on, other objects at the same distance appear at corresponding points on your two retinas, while objects at different distances do not.

The direction and magnitude of binocular disparity provide information about which of the two objects is closer to the observer, as well as relatively how far apart the objects might be. To

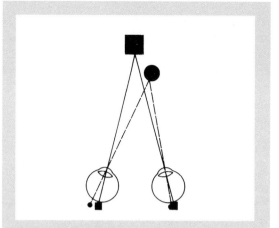

Fig. 11.16 Binocular disparity. The square and circle are imaged quite close together on the right retina, but are imaged considerably farther apart on the left retina. If the observer fixates on the square, there must be a disparity in the retinal locations of the image of the circle.

see how the direction of the disparity gives information about relative distance, consider the stimulus configuration portrayed in Fig. 11.17. In this case, two stimuli are arranged so that one is directly behind the other. If you fixate on the close-up stimulus (the disc), the more distant square appears as if it is to the left of the disc when viewed by your left eye, but seems to be located to the right of the disc when viewed monocularly by your right eye. This is an example of *uncrossed disparity*; it occurs for objects further than the fixated point.

To demonstrate uncrossed disparity, hold your finger out in front of you so that it is directly in line with a light switch on the far wall. If you fixate on your finger, and alternatively close one eye and then the other, the light switch should appear to be to the left of your finger when viewed through your left eye, and should seem to be to the right of your finger when looked at by your right eye.

Alternatively, if you hold your finger in front of you but fixate on the switch, the position of

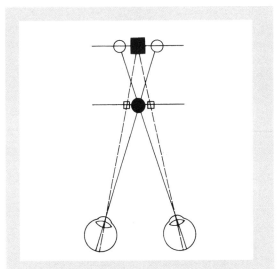

Fig. 11.17 Crossed versus uncrossed disparity. If the observer fixates on the circle, the disparity of the position of the square on the retinas is of the uncrossed variety. If the observer fixates on the square, there is crossed disparity of the images of the circle.

your finger should change as a function of which eye you use. When viewed with your left eye, your finger appears to be to the right of the wall switch, while it moves to the left of the switch when you open your right eye and close your left. This is a case of *crossed disparity*; it occurs when an object is closer than the fixated point. In Fig. 11.17, crossed disparity occurs when the observer fixates on the square and looks at the relative position of the disc under monocular conditions.

From this, it should be clear that stimuli either in front of or behind an object to which an observer is attending have some amount of binocular disparity. What about objects that are the same distance from the observer as the object being fixated? Figure 11.18 shows two eyes that are converged so that point F in the figure is imaged on the foveae of both eyes. In such a situation, there are many other points in the visual field that are also imaged on corresponding points of the two retinas. These points define a concave surface in front of the viewer.

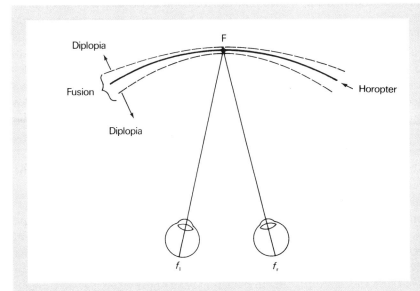

Fig. 11.18 The horopter. If you fixate on the point *F*, the middle solid curve represents the surface of points whose images are projected at corresponding locations on your retinas. This is the horopter. For locations off the horopter but within the bounds of the two dashed curves, there is retinal disparity, and you will see the object in depth. Outside of these bounds, double images result.

The middle curve in the figure shows a horizontal slice through this surface, which is called the *horopter*. For a given fixation distance, all points on the horopter have images that fall on corresponding points of the two retinas, in the same way that the single point being fixated on falls on the identical retinal area of the two eyes (specifically, the fovea). All of the points on the horopter are perceived as being at the same distance from the observer as the fixation point *F*. All points not on the horopter for this particular fixation distance stimulate disparate retinal points.

If a stimulus is placed outside the region bounded by the two dashed curves, the visual system will not be able to combine the two images of the stimulus into one single percept, and a double image of that stimulus will result. This is *diplopia*, or double vision. The dashed curves delimit the region in which the visual system can combine images; this region is called *Panum's fusion area*. A stimulus that is in Panum's area is seen as a single object at a different depth from the fixation distance. As it is seen as a single object even though it stimulates disparate regions of the two retinas, the visual system is said to *fuse* the two images.

Within the limit of Panum's area, objects that stimulate disparate retinal regions in the two eyes produce an impression of depth. This fact was realized many years ago; in 1838, the English physicist Charles Wheatstone invented a device called a *stereoscope* that took advantage of binocular disparity cues to produce pictures with striking depth. The stereoscope took two pictures of the same visual scene that were slightly different in perspective (that is, one picture was taken from the position of the right eye, and a second picture was taken from the position of the left eye), and projected one picture to each eye. When the pictures (called *stereograms*) were appropriately positioned in space, the viewer had the impression of a single scene with a distinct depth component. The modern version of Wheatstone's stereoscope is the stereo slide viewer that allows the observer to view dichoptically (one picture to each eye) photographic slides of the same scene that have been taken by a stereo camera (you have probably seen a Vue-Master, with its wheels of tiny images). A stereo camera is just a camera that has two lenses and two film compartments, separated by about the same distance that separates our two eyes. The shutter opens simultaneously for the two parts of the camera, so that the same scene is photographed from the different perspectives. Viewing the photographic stereograms in the viewer results in a striking impression that the scene is three-dimensional, rather than a flat picture (see Fig. P2, p.vii). **BOX 11.4**

The pictures viewed with Wheatstone's stereoscope or with modern stereo viewers are usually of familiar scenes having strong contours associated with them. That is, the stimulus presented to each eye is well defined in shape and readily identifiable. In a series of studies on binocular perception, Julesz (1964, 1971, 1974) asked whether these factors were necessary for binocular disparity to produce a sensation of depth. He had subjects dichoptically view a pair of stimuli that he called

---

Box 11.4 Stereoblindness

A small percentage of people do not get an impression of depth when they look through a stereo viewer. These people are called *stereoblind* (see Box P1, p. vi). There are a number of causes of stereoblindness; the most common one seems to be a disruption of normal binocular experience in childhood. For example, if a person grows up through early childhood with a cataract in one eye, or if one eye is very nearsighted and the other is normal, stereoblindness may result. Such monocular deprivation in childhood is quite similar to the deprivation experiments Wiesel & Hubel (1963) performed on kittens. When one eye was deprived in these experiments, the kittens grew up with a lack of binocular cells in their visual cortex (see Chapter 8 and later in this chapter).

random dot stereograms, an example of which is shown in Fig. 11.19.

The patterns in Fig. 11.19 were generated by computer to be a random array of black and white dots. The computer began at the upper left corner of the right-hand frame; for each position in the top row, it selected a random number to decide whether to make that point (pixel) black or white. It then moved to the next position to the right, and did the same, until it reached the middle of the row. From the middle onward, it read the preceding sequence backwards to fill in to the right edge. This made the row mirror-symmetric, which allows the stereogram to be viewed by either the direct or the mirror method (see Box P1, p. vi) (most random dot stereograms do not have this mirror symmetry). It then filled in the second row from the top, then the third, until the entire right panel was filled. Each half of the panel is completely random. You can see the mirror symmetry about the vertical midline because symmetric figures are 'good' (see Chapter 10), and therefore stand out.

The left panel is a duplicate of the right panel, except that a square region in the center has been displaced to the right. If you follow the line of mirror symmetry in the left panel, you can see that it jogs 2 mm to the right about one-third of the way down; it returns to the central position about two-thirds of the way down. To create this panel, the computer simply reproduced the outer portion of the panel on the right. It moved each dot in the central portion 2 mm to the right. The rightmost 2 mm of the central portion, which would have overlapped the unchanged right side of the panel, was omitted. Similarly, the gap that was created when the leftmost part of the middle portion was moved to the right (away from the unchanged left portion) was filled with a new sequence of random dots.

The end result is that each panel is an array of random dots. Were it not for the mirror symmetry imposed in the right panel (and copied into the left), they would each be completely random and formless. However, the outer parts of the two are identical, and the central portions are also the same except for the rightward shift. When the patterns are viewed dichoptically, the shifted area is not imaged on the exact corresponding locations of the two retinas; that is, there is binocular disparity. If this disparity produces an impression of depth in the absence of any pictorial or kinetic depth cues, it would be a demonstration of the strength and importance of binocular cues in the perception of depth.

View the stereogram in Fig. 11.19 using the method described in Box P1. After a few seconds, there should be the sensation of a distinct square floating in front of the rest of the pattern. (If you cannot see this, you will just have to take the word of the rest of us.) It takes a noticeable time before

Fig. 11.19 Random dot stereograms. View this figure using the method described in Box P1 (p.vi). You should see a square floating in space.

Box 11.5 'Magic eye' stereograms

Earlier editions of this book proclaimed this emergence of depth 'a surprising thing'. Until the early 1990s, few people had ever seen a random dot stereogram. But then a psychologist devised a clever way to make large random dot stereograms that could be viewed without glasses. Instead of two separate frames to fuse, as in Fig. 11.19, a random pattern was repeated in columns about as wide as the average distance between human eyes (with appropriate slight shifts to produce the disparity needed for depth). Fusing adjacent columns was equivalent to fusing the adjacent frames in Fig. 11.19. But because the frames continued to replicate (with further relative shifts between adjacent columns), a large scene could be rendered and viewed as the eyes wandered across it. (To maintain

divergence, people were told to concentrate on the reflections in the glass covering the picture, or to start close and slowly back away.)

If you were awake in America in the early 1990s, you saw these images on posters, calendars, and books. Images from dinosaurs to landscapes were depicted (generally under the rubric 'magic eye'), and games magazines published mazes in which the paths were 'raised' by this method. Shareware computer programs let people create their own images on their home computers.

And is the psychologist a multimillionaire? Sadly, his university foresaw no practical use for the idea, and so it was never patented in his name.

the image appears, and the effect continues to grow stronger as you continue to view it. Obviously, this is not a preattentive process, and must depend on considerable interaction among brain areas. In fact, imaging studies show that finding form in random dot stereograms involves at least 20 different brain areas, almost none of which are involved in detecting form from luminance differences (Gulyas *et al.*, 1994). **BOX 11.5**

The appearance of the random dot stereogram is not surprising if there are disparity detectors that interpret disparity as depth. But it is surprising

that disparity can be determined when there is no overall structure in the images in the two eyes. The implication is that the binocular comparison can precede the determination of form (Pettigrew, 1990). How do the detectors determine which dots go with which? Clearly, in this case they cannot base it on corresponding points in independently recognized figures (Julesz, 1974). Similarly, it cannot simply be an alignment of contrasts, for images of opposite contrast can also fuse to form a three-dimensional image (see Fig. 11.20).

Another feature that does not seem to aid in the

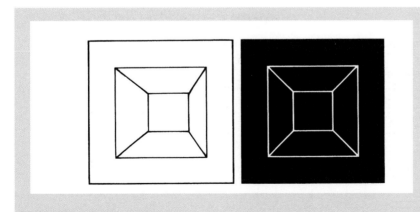

Fig. 11.20 Stereo pair that gives an impression of depth despite having opposite contrasts in the two frames. View according to the instructions in Box P1 (p. vi). After Helmholtz (1924).

Box 11.6 Binocular rivalry

When your two eyes are presented with similar views of the same scene with a small amount of binocular disparity, you see a single unified scene that includes a strong depth component. What happens when the disparity between the scenes presented to your eyes is too great, say if your eyes are presented with totally different stimuli? Under these conditions, a condition called *binocular rivalry* results.

For example, view the two patterns of lines oriented in different directions in Fig. 11.21 as a stereogram. There is no way that these two patterns can be integrated to produce a unified percept; you should see a horizontal pattern for a period of a few seconds, and then spontaneously change to seeing the vertical pattern. It is likely that part of the field will be seen as vertical lines and part as horizontal, giving a 'patchy' appearance that shifts with time. In other words, you see each region monocularly with the one eye, and then with the other, but the information from your two eyes does not fuse to form a single binocular percept. (If you are stereoblind and have one eye that is very dominant, you will not experience this alternation.) When you see the stimulus presented to the right eye, that eye is *dominant*, while the left eye is being *suppressed*.

Under the conditions of binocular rivalry, where the two eyes are presented with equally compelling stimuli, subjects report frequent fluctuations of which eye is dominant and which is suppressed. If one eye is presented with a well-defined stimulus and the other with a blank field, however, the eye that is seeing the stimulus will almost always be dominant (see Fahle, 1982). You can verify this for yourself by covering one eye with your hand; instead of alternating between seeing the world with one eye and seeing darkness with the other, you only see the world.

Therefore, your uncovered eye has become your dominant eye in this situation.

Binocular rivalry results in the suppression of information coming from one eye under conditions in which the two eyes receive very disparate inputs. But there is almost always some disparity between the images of the world projected onto the retinas. How does the visual system unite the two slightly different pictures of the visual world? One possibility is that you somehow fuse images that are slightly disparate into one percept that has a depth component associated with it. If this is the case, then you should not have a dominant and suppressed eye when looking binocularly at a visual scene; instead, information from both eyes should be processed simultaneously. Blake & Camisa (1978) were able to demonstrate that, in fact, when a subject dichoptically viewed patterns that were either identical or only slightly different from each other, both eyes were equally sensitive in detecting the presence of a small flash that could be presented to either eye. When the subject viewed a patterned scene with one eye and a blank field with the other, the eye with the blank field presented to it was always less sensitive to the test flash than the eye receiving patterned stimulation. From this study, Blake & Camisa concluded that when the two eyes viewed the same or similar scenes, the visual system used information from both eyes equally to create a single fused percept. Under conditions of binocular rivalry, however, information from the suppressed eye was actively ignored. For the test probe to attract attention, it must be presented to the dominant eye (Schall *et al.*, 1993); motion, however, can still be detected by the suppressed eye (Wiesenfelder & Blake, 1991).

The alternation of the dominance of the two eyes is reminiscent of the spontaneous alternation of two inter-

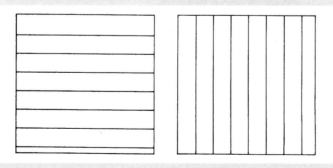

Fig. 11.21 Two competing patterns that cause binocular rivalry when viewed dichoptically. View this figure using the method described in Box P1 (p. vi).

pretations of an ambiguous or reversible figure like those in Figs 10.6, 10.11, 10.25, and 10.30 (Leopold & Logothetis, 1996; Sengpiel, 1997). You may recall from Box 10.5 (p.198) that oscillations might account for the binding of features into objects, and that the oscillation only persisted for those objects seen by the dominant eye during binocular rivalry (Fries *et al.*, 1997).

matching process is color (Livingstone & Hubel, 1987b). In addition, equiluminant random dot stereograms do not produce a perception of depth (Lu & Fender, 1972). As was the case for depth from texture and depth from motion, it appears that depth from stereopsis depends on the magnocellular system. **BOX 11.6**

Of course, the monocular and binocular cues are ultimately combined into a single percept. A good example of this integration may be seen in Fig. 11.22. In this stereo pair, the two vertical bars appear to be in front of the horizontal bar both because of the monocular cue of interposition, and because of their relative disparity. But there is no stereoscopic cue to the depth of the middle segment of the horizontal bar; its image is identical in both frames. It appears at the same depth as the end segments because of the monocular information that it is to be interpreted as a continuation of the two end segments (Marr, 1982). **BOX 11.7**

The combined information from monocular and binocular cues tells you the relative distances of objects from yourself. However, this is not how you perceive the world. If it were, all the distances would change every time you moved, and relative positions of objects would be difficult to comprehend. David Marr, in an influential monograph (1982) published shortly after his death, referred to this viewer-centered representation as the '2½-D sketch'. It is not the flat, two-dimensional representation of edges captured by the 'primal sketch', but neither is it a real three-dimensional model of the world. That representation must be derived from the 2½-D sketch.

Physiological studies on binocular depth perception

The visual cortex is the logical physiological substrate that might mediate binocular depth perception, as that is the first place in the visual system that has binocular cells. Most of the binocular cortical cells discussed in Chapter 7 have receptive fields from the two eyes that correspond quite

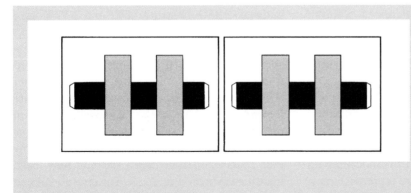

Fig. 11.22 A stereo pair in which the depth of the middle segment is given entirely by monocular cues. View according to the instructions in Box P1 (p. vi). From *Vision* by David Marr. Copyright © 1982 by W. H. Freeman and Company. Reprinted with permission.

Box 11.7 What if I put my stereoscope slides in backwards?

What happens when the binocular and monocular cues disagree? Very often, the monocular cues override the binocular cues, because they provide the only sensible interpretation. For example, imagine a stereogram of a face in which the frames are reversed. Binocular disparity tells you the tip of the nose is further than the eyes or ears. This is not an impossible situation—you could be looking at the inside of a mask—but it is so unusual that the top-down information 'this is a face' overrides the binocular information and you see it as a normal, uneverted face—a fact Wheatstone himself noticed. But if you walk past this stereogram, the motion parallax also conflicts with the perception of a normal face—the consistent interpretation (which is what you perceive) is that the face is turning

twice as fast as you are walking past it (Barlow, 1997). (It should be noted that Barlow's interpretation is *not* that this is evidence of top-down processing affecting the perception, but of repulsion by the 'usual' associations.)

While strong pictorial cues dominate over binocular cues, binocular cues can sometimes dominate over pictorial cues (Buckley *et al.*, 1989; Buckley & Frisby, 1993). You saw examples of this phenomenon in Chapter 10. The grouping by proximity of depth in Fig. 10.4 is one example. An even more 'interpretive' example was given in Fig. 10.13, in which the slices of a picture of a face were interpreted either as a face behind a set of slats, or a poster cut into strips.

---

closely with each other. That is, there is little or no disparity in the positions of the receptive fields of the eyes. Such cells are effectively stimulated by objects at the fixation distance, but to perceive objects either in front of or behind the fixation point, there should be binocular cells that have receptive fields with disparate retinal receptive field positions.

Binocular cortical cells with disparate receptive field locations have been found in the brains of a variety of animals, including cats (Barlow *et al.*, 1967; Nelson *et al.*, 1977), monkeys (Hubel & Wiesel, 1970), and owls (Pettigrew & Konishi, 1976). In the monkey, Hubel & Wiesel found that the binocular cells encountered from V1 all had receptive fields that showed no binocular disparity, but that cells in V2 often responded best to dichoptically presented stimuli that were slightly displaced in some way. These cells often did not respond at all to monocular stimulation, and responded best to a very small range of disparities. Some cells respond to zero disparities (locations on the horopter), some to disparities representing positions in front of the horopter, and others to positions behind it (Clarke *et al.*, 1976; Poggio & Talbot, 1981). Ohzawa *et al.*, (1997) reported complex cells

with disparity sensitivities twice as good as their position sensitivities.

To what systems do these cells belong? You have seen several instances in this chapter in which equiluminant stimuli failed to produce a depth effect, implicating the magnocellular system. As you learned in Chapter 8, the magnocellular system responds well to depth, and leads ultimately to a system that accurately locates 'where' a stimulus is. Indeed, the cells tuned to specific disparities near the horopter, or to detecting crossings of the horopter, seem to be found in the magnocellular pathways: the thick stripes of V2, and in V3 (Poggio *et al.*, 1988).

Of course, the parvocellular system also responds well to depth, as it must if it is to determine 'what' the objects are. It is not clear whether the parvocellular system's depth capabilities are dependent on those of the magnocellular system or whether they represent a parallel determination of distance. In this regard, it is noteworthy that coarse and fine depth systems have been identified (Norcia *et al.*, 1985). The question of parallel versus shared information will arise again at the end of Chapter 12. **BOX 11.8**

The experiments previously discussed indicate that there are binocular cells in the cortex that

Box 11.8 Depth perception throughout the visual system

Depth is important for locating objects, locating oneself, guiding movements, and for identification of objects, so it is not surprising that some kind of depth perception can be found in all the visual pathways (Tyler, 1990). Some areas are essential for specific aspects of depth perception; for example, lesions in V2 disrupt stereoscopic vision (Cowey & Wilkinson, 1991). Other areas seem to be influenced by the interpreted depth, probably through connections with areas that analyze depth. For example, neurons in V1 can respond to 'nearness' or 'farness' of a stimulus, nearly independently of the size of the *retinal* image (Dobbins *et al.*, 1998).

Other areas have cells that seem to fit the bill for real depth perception. In Chapter 13, you will encounter cells that are concerned with motion in depth, or motion relative to the observer (rather than relative to the retina or relative to the rest of the world). Obviously, the interpretation of motion is closely tied to the interpretation of space. The nervous system must convert from the retinal coordinates to the coordinates of the real world, which are independent of the observer. Does it employ Marr's 2½-D sketch? Battaglini *et al.* (1996) report cells in the premotor area (where the dorsal stream is aiming) that seem to respond according to the 'real' position of the stimulus relative to the animal. Such a system could be the neural representation of the 2½-D sketch.

have the capability of participating in the perception of visual depth. The question still remains, however, of whether the presence of these binocular cells is necessary for binocular depth perception to occur. To investigate this problem, Blake & Hirsch (1975) took advantage of the fact that if kittens are raised with alternating monocular visual stimulation (so that each eye receives stimulation, but never both simultaneously), their cortex contains abnormally few binocularly responsive cells (see Chapter 8). Blake & Hirsch tested such cats for their depth perception abilities, and found that they were inferior to normally raised cats in this regard. On other behavioral tests of visual performance, such as visual acuity, the monocularly reared cats performed normally, suggesting that the deficit was specifically in their abilities to perceive depth.

Psychophysical experiments performed on human subjects also support the contention that binocular cortical cells are necessary for binocular depth perception to exist. Blake & Cormack (1979) attacked the problem in the reverse way from Blake & Hirsch's experiment. They found a human population that was stereoblind, and tried to determine whether these people had binocular cells in their visual cortices. The experimenters reasoned that if stereoblind observers had only monocularly responsive cells, they should be superior to normal subjects in tasks that required deciding to which of the two eyes a given visual stimulus was presented. They found that this was indeed the case; normal observers often had great difficulty in determining which eye a given stimulus was presented to, but stereoblind observers performed this sort of task with facility. It therefore seems quite likely that the binocular disparity cells discovered by Hubel & Wiesel and others do mediate the binocular perception of depth.

Suggested readings

The chapter on visual space perception in C. H. Graham's *Vision and visual perception* (Wiley, 1965) provides a detailed and fairly complete treatment of the topic of depth perception. Even more complete are the two chapters on depth and binocular stereopsis in Lloyd Kaufman's *Sight and mind* (Oxford University Press, Oxford, 1974). Many of these topics are also considered by Maurice Hershenson in *Visual space perception* (MIT Press,

1998). Finally, J. J. Gibson presents the topics of depth and distance perceptions quite elegantly in *The perception of the visual world* (Houghton Mifflin, 1950); the book is somewhat dated, but still quite useful.

Bela Julesz has written an excellent review of his work on binocular depth perception that appeared in *American Scientist* (62: 32–43; 1974). In addition, Julesz has written two articles for *Scientific American* on this topic: 'Texture and visual perception' (February 1965), and 'Experiments in the visual perception of texture' (April 1975; offprint #563). The former article has been reprinted in *Perception: mechanisms and models*, edited by R. Held and W. Richards (W. H. Freeman, 1972), while the latter article can be found in *Recent progress in perception*, edited by R. Held and W. Richards (W. H. Freeman, 1976). Also in the 1976 collection is 'The neurophysiology of binocular vision', by J. Pettigrew (*Scientific American*, August 1972; offprint #1255); another relevant *Scientific American* article that has

not been reprinted elsewhere is 'The resources of binocular perception', by J. Ross (234: 80–87; 1976; offprint #569).

The process of determining depth from shadows and grays, such as in Figs 11.4 and 11.5, is considered in 'Perceiving shape from shading', by V. S. Ramachandran (August, 1988); this article is reprinted in *The perceptual world*, edited by Irvin Rock (W. H. Freeman, 1990).

Two more recent (although somewhat more technical) articles are concerned with modeling the process of extracting depth information from the two eyes. A brief review of competitive models is given by Blake and Wilson in 'Neural models of stereoscopic vision' in *Trends in Neurosciences* (14: 445–452; 1991). A thought-provoking but quite readable account by one of the most eminent visual system theorists alive today is 'The knowledge used in vision' by Horace Barlow in *Philosophical Transactions of the Royal Society of London (series B)* (352: 1141–1147; 1997).

Chapter 12
Perceptual constancies
. . . and illusions

Now you have some ideas about how you can see and recognize an object (Chapter 10) and how you can locate it (Chapter 11). Next, you can consider how you perceive certain attributes of the object—its size, shape, and color. Despite the fact that a given object can be viewed from different angles or distances in a variety of different lighting conditions, you will usually be able to correctly identify the physical characteristics of the object. The physical sizes, shapes, and colors do not change in these different viewing conditions. Similarly, the apparent sizes, shapes, and colors tend not to change; they remain constant. That is what is meant by the *constancy* of these properties.

This is really *the* fundamental problem for a perceptual system: how to create a logical and stable internal representation of the world (which is, of course, logical and stable) from the distorted and changing representations delivered to the sensory receptors. It is the heart of the problem identified by Ragnar Granit, a Nobel laureate for his early work in visual physiology, in his inquiries into the functioning of the brain (Granit, 1977):

> [W]e must not underestimate what the interpreting brain itself adds to make the seen world more intelligible than does a pure peripheral input, dependent though the cortex is on information from feature detectors. The purposive brain requires a considerable degree of invariance, size constancy, a fixed verticality, approximately invariant surface colors, some constancy

of velocity and direction of movement and, above all, a steady world; in short, a large number of what one is fully entitled to call 'reliable illusions.' They are all constant errors with respect to the informational content of the primary sensory message. A world in which, for instance, my hands all the time varied in size with the retinal image would be intolerable! And so the brain does what no computer can imitate: in growing and developing, it creates the world it needs.   (page 128)

Constancies: the world doesn't seem to change because of your angle of view, changes in lighting, or your distance from objects. *Illusions*: things aren't always as they seem; two equal lines appear to be of different lengths because of the picture they are embedded in; two patches of the same gray appear to be different because they are surrounded by different colors. As Granit put it, constancy is a necessary illusion. Perhaps illusions are unwarranted constancies.

As an example, consider an all-too-familiar object: this book. It has certain physical properties, such as size ($7\frac{3}{8} \times 9\frac{1}{4}$ inches or 246×189 mm), shape (rectangular solid), and color (red cover). As it is carried about, it can be seen from various angles (straight on, tilted, edge on, and so forth) but it always appears as a rectangular solid. You see it from various distances (right next to you on the table, over there on the desk where you 'forgot' it) but it does not appear to grow and shrink in size when viewed from different positions. You see it in bright sunlight on your way home (with lots of light reflecting from its cover to your eye) and in the dim light of the hallways (with little light reflected even from the pages), yet the cover always appears red and the pages white. In this chapter, in addition to examining the way in which you perceive the size, shape, and color of objects, you will also see a number of visual illusions that result from inappropriate judgments of these attributes.

Lightness constancy

The first constancy to consider is *lightness constancy*. The more general term for this is *color constancy*, for it concerns the ability of the observer to assign a judgment of color to an object despite changes in the illumination. However, this discussion is of the whiteness or blackness of uncolored ('gray') objects, and 'color' brings to mind changes of hue; hence the narrower term 'lightness'.

Actually, it is not lightness at all that we are dealing with, for objects generally do not radiate their own light. They reflect light from some source such as the sun or an electrical fixture. This is really about the *reflectance* of an object, which is the percentage of the light incident on it that is reflected from it. That light that is not reflected is absorbed by the object; what percentage of light is absorbed and what percentage reflected depends on the pigmentation and texture of the surface. A rough object that is highly pigmented will be an excellent absorber and will appear black. A rough reflective object, on the other hand, will absorb very little light and reflect nearly all the light incident upon it; such an object will appear white. The blackness or whiteness of an object depends on its reflectance (another term for this is *albedo*); black objects have reflectances of only a few percent and white objects have reflectances around 90%. It is really a property of the object that is being judged, so it is better to use the term lightness rather than *brightness*, a term that is commonly used to mean the same thing (another term that is occasionally used is *whiteness*). Regardless of the name it is given, it should be borne in mind that the subjects are asked to rate target objects as white, black, or shades of gray, and not to say how much light appears to emanate from them. The term *brightness* will be used when subjects are asked to judge the total amount of light emanating from (or reflected by) a scene or object (see Arend & Goldstein, 1987).

Optical measuring devices (including your eyes) cannot measure reflectances directly; all that photodetectors (including rods and cones) can do is respond to the light they are receiving. To measure reflectance, a physicist would measure the light incident upon an object as well as measuring the light coming from it; the ratio of these two measurements is reflectance. Your eyes only receive information regarding the reflected light and not the incident light. You respond to the light reflected from an object, which is the product of the incident illumination times the reflectance.

Consider a sheet of white paper. It has a high reflectance, perhaps 90%. Imagine looking at the sheet of paper in a room lit by a single light bulb; the paper reflects 90% of the light incident upon it, but 90% of a small number is still a small number. Now consider a black cat, whose furry coat absorbs most of the light incident upon it; the reflectance may be as low as 5%. When the cat walks in the sunlight, only 5% of the incident light reflects off the fur—but 5% of a very large number is still a lot of light. There may be thousands of times more light reaching your eye from the cat fur in sun than from the paper indoors, yet the cat looks black and the paper white. How do you make these determinations?

Suppose the same black cat steps in front of your car headlights some dark night on a clear open road. If the light bathes the cat but there are no other objects also in light, the cat will look ghostly white. You cannot detect that a small percentage of the light is being reflected because it is hard to estimate how much light is incident upon the cat.

Box 12.1 The shadow

Shadows present an interesting situation. If two identical objects are seen against the same surface but a shadow falls across only one of them, they still appear the same color and lightness. Nonetheless, it is clear that the one in shadow has less light coming from it; the judgment of lightness seems to be one of reflectance rather than of light reflected.

When a shadow falls across a relatively uniform surface, you can generally recognize it for what it is: a shadow. You can clearly see that the shadowed area is 'darker', yet you do not think of the surface as being different in the area of the shadow. (Sometimes you can be fooled by an odd fold in the surface and mistake a shadow for a stain; in that case the shadowed area does appear to be different from the rest of the surface.

Conversely, you may sometimes mistake a stain for a shadow.)

As an example, take a sheet of white paper and cast a shadow on it. The shadow should be relatively crisp and distinct; a reasonable arrangement is shown in Fig. 12.1. Here, a wooden ruler casts a clear shadow if the only light in the room is a single bulb at some distance; it is best if the bulb has no lampshade. (You could use the sun as a source, but then the shadow would move slowly as the earth rotates on its axis.)

The shadow cast by the ruler is relatively distinct, but there should be no trouble recognizing it as a shadow. This recognition is due in part to the fact that the shadow's edge is slightly blurred. The shadow cast by an object lit by a finite light source has two parts: the

➡

Fig. 12.1 A shadow cast on paper

(Box 12.1 CONTINUED)

umbra, or darkest part, is where the surface on which the shadow falls is fully shielded from the light source; the *penumbra*, or outer shadow, is the part near the edge where the source is only partially eclipsed, so the light is partly diminished. This slight blurring of the shadow's edge helps to indicate the fact that the dark area is a shadow and not a different surface.

If you now remove the blurred edge and replace it with a firm outline, the shadow changes its nature (Wallach, 1963). To do this, take a dark pencil or black felt-tipped pen and carefully outline the shadow, as shown in the figure. (This is why the sun makes a poor light source: you do not want the shadow to move away from its outline.) The outline into which the shadow exactly fits makes it look like a different surface from the rest of the paper; when it is outlined, it also appears darker than it did as a simple shadow. Perceptions of lightness depend on the apparent illumination of the surface being judged.

That is also why the moon appears self-luminous in the sky. It is reflecting sunlight, but observers on the night-time earth cannot see that source of illumination.

This was the basis of an experiment performed by Gelb (1929). He had observers look into a dimly lit room in which there was a black disc. A projector, hidden from the observers' view, cast a bright beam of light on the disc so that it was well lit, but no other visible object in the room received any of the extra light. The disc appeared white; in fact, with a bright enough light from the projector, it appeared self-luminous (see Henneman, 1935). When Gelb placed a small rectangle of white paper in the beam just in front of the disc, however, the disc immediately appeared black and the paper white. It was as if the white paper, revealing the true nature of the illumination, dispelled the question of how much light was incident, and lightness could be correctly judged. When the paper was removed, the black disc again appeared white, indicating that the observers' conscious (or intellectual) knowledge of the situation did not contribute to the perception.

The converse demonstration can also be performed. Kardos (1934) set up a field of objects lit by a single source, with a white disc for the observer to judge. A solid object (out of the observer's view) cast a shadow only on the white disc, which then appeared black. Removing the screens that hid the true situation so that the observer was intellectually aware of the shadow did not reverse the illusion. The cues for lightness constancy must reside in the scene being observed, not in the intellectual knowledge of the observer. <u>BOX 12.1</u>

Simultaneous contrast

That judgments of lightness depend on the perceived illumination of objects raised the question of how the incident illumination can be estimated. Wallach (1948) suggested that we simply compare the amount of light reflected by the object in question with the amount of light reflected from adjacent regions in the visual field. Thus an object of moderate reflectance should look lighter in front of a black background than it would in front of a white background. This is called *simultaneous contrast*.

The idea of simultaneous contrast was an alternative to the theory of *adaptation level* (Helson, 1948, 1964). Adaptation level refers to the mean luminance of a field; the visual system is presumed to respond to changes above and below the average level of luminance (and average hue as well). In the experiments you will read about here, the only things in the visual field other than the test objects being judged are uniform surrounding fields; the average luminance of the scene is therefore really just the luminance of these surrounding fields. In the real world, objects are surrounded by complicated arrays of other objects of various shades and sizes. These would determine the adaptation level; from the point of view of simultaneous contrast, some average of those objects nearest (or bordering) the test object would be taken as the surrounding luminance. The difference between the simultaneous contrast and the adaptation level theories would therefore reside in how large an area surrounding the test object would determine the surrounding (or adaptation level) luminance. It would also depend on whether the surround was taken to be that area adjacent to the test object in the proximal stimulus, or those things perceived to be near the test object (in distance as well as position). It should also be noted that the adaptation level depends in part on the recent history of illumination, as well as on the current scene.

Simultaneous contrast is demonstrated among the 'Illusions and constancies' on the CD accompanying this book. When you adjust the shade of gray of the right circle (against a white background) to match the gray of the left circle (against a black background), you will probably make it too light. You are trying in some measure to make it relatively lighter than its background, just like the one on the left. When you think you have a match, click 'Accept the match' to learn how close you came (in addition to being told how your setting compared, you will see both circles against the same black background). Click 'Try it again' to see if you can compensate for the illusion.

Another demonstration can be found in Fig. 12.2. Careful inspection should show that the shaded ring is uniform; if you now create a border between the part of the ring against the black background and the part against the white background, the two half-rings will appear to be different in lightness. (To create a border, draw a line along the division between black and white.) The border is necessary because the ring is perceived as a single 'good' figure (see Chapter 10), and tends to appear homogenous in color; the border breaks it into figures that can each take on a different lightness (Koffka, 1935; see also Berman & Leibowitz, 1965).

Wallach (1948) measured simultaneous contrast by projecting a disc of light on a screen in an otherwise dark room. When the disc was shown in isolation, it appeared self-luminous; when it was

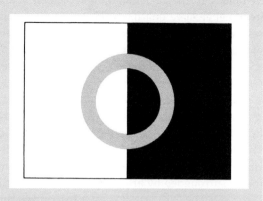

Fig. 12.2 Simultaneous contrast; when a line is drawn along the border between black and white, the halves of the ring appear different.

surrounded by an annulus of light (of either lesser or greater intensity) the disc seemed to be white or gray. How light or dark it appeared was influenced by the annulus surrounding it; an annulus of higher luminance made the disc appear dark, and an annulus of lower luminance made it appear light. A second disc (of different luminance) surrounded by an annulus was shown on the other side of the display; the subject's task was to adjust the luminance of the annulus surrounding the second disc so that the second disc appeared the same color (lightness) as the first. Wallach found that the two discs appeared equally light when the ratios of their luminances to the luminances of their respective annuli were the same. For example, a 200-unit disc could exactly match a 100-unit disc if the former were surrounded by a 400-unit annulus, and the 100-unit disc by a 200-unit annulus. Similar findings had been reported in 1894 by Hess and Pretori.

The rule that the lightness of an object is given by the ratio of its luminance to that of its surround is quite attractive for its simplicity, and for the relatively direct way it can be related to the physiology of the visual system. Another way to express the ratio rule is to say that we are responsive to the *contrast* of an image. Remember concentric receptive fields of retinal ganglion cells (Chapter 5) and lateral geniculate neurons (Chapter 7); these cells respond to contrast. Increasing light in the center of a ganglion cell receptive field increases its response (increased inhibition is also an increased response), but light falling in the surround decreases the center-driven response. The net response is therefore given by the balance of the light in the center and the light in the surround. This is the premise of lateral antagonism, as discussed in Chapter 5; a moderate light appears dimmer if surrounded by bright light, and brighter if surrounded by darkness. It is safer to describe this phenomenon as lateral antagonism than by the specific receptive field structure by which lateral antagonism is achieved, for one would not expect the test discs in a psychophysical experiment to coincide exactly with the centers of receptive fields of ganglion cells. The principle that nearby light diminishes the responses in a particular area does, however, apply. **BOX 12.2**

The ratio rule is simple but, not surprisingly, it does not work over large ranges. Heinemann (1955) studied the apparent brightness of discs surrounded by annuli over a wide range of luminances and ratios of luminances. When a test disc was surrounded by a much dimmer annulus, the brightness of the test disc was only slightly affected by the luminance of the annulus. Only when the luminance of the annulus was nearly the same as that of the test disc did the annulus make the test seem dimmer. When the annulus luminance surpassed that of the test disc, the test disc abruptly looked very dark.

Jameson & Hurvich (1961) tested the ratio principle more directly. They presented a display of five neighboring patches of known reflectances. The incident lighting illuminating the entire display was varied by a factor of about 10; at each illuminance level the ratios of the luminances of the patches remained constant (being given by the ratio of the reflectances). Like Heinemann, Jameson & Hurvich had their subjects estimate the brightness of each patch by setting the luminance of an isolated matching patch, but this experiment shows the effects of changed luminance when the ratio of test to surround is constant.

If the brightness of the test patch were determined by the ratio of its luminance to the luminances of its neighbors, the brightness would be unaffected by changing the illumination; this is what happened when the ratio of test patch luminance to surround luminance was not too extreme. For that situation, the ratio rule worked perfectly (as it had for Wallach).

When the luminance of the test patch was either much greater or much less than that of the surround, however, the ratio rule failed. When the test patch was much lighter than its surround, its apparent brightness increased with increased illumination. In that case, it is possible that the patch was so much lighter than the surround that the

---

Box 12.2 The ratio 'rule' and ganglion cell responses

You learned that the center and surround of a ganglion cell receptive field seem to interact subtractively (Rodieck & Stone, 1965; Enroth-Cugell & Pinto, 1970), so you might wonder why a ratio rule should be expected. The answer lies in the fact that the firing rate of a ganglion cell in response to light is approximately proportional to the logarithm of the light intensity (Easter, 1968a; Naka & Rushton, 1966; Levine & Abramov, 1975). The logarithmic rule would apply in both the center and the surround of the receptive field; taking the difference between the responses in those two areas therefore represents subtracting the logarithms of the incident luminances. Subtracting logarithms is mathematically equivalent to taking a ratio, so the response of the ganglion cell is proportional to the logarithm of the ratio of the luminances in the center and surround of the receptive field. Of course, this is an approximation and it does not hold for extreme ratios.

Box 12.3 'Mondrians', retinex theory, and contrast

The failure of the ratio rule may be an artifact of the relatively simple displays used in the experiments previously discussed. The ratio rule works quite well when the stimuli are more complicated (Arend & Goldstein, 1987).

More complicated stimuli are made of various sized and shaped patches of shades of gray (or, in some cases, color). These stimuli are known as 'Mondrians', after Piet Mondrian, the Dutch painter whose paintings these stimuli resemble. Mondrians are just abstract versions of the complicated images in the real world. The accuracy of judgment of lightness of patches in Mondrians under various conditions of illumination led Land & McCann (1971) to postulate a theory of lightness perception that they call the *retinex* theory. In this theory, lightness is built up from the ratios of luminances at the various borders. The lightness of each patch buried within the pattern is computed by cumulating the differences at each border crossed as one goes from some reference point to the patch in question.

There is an added feature built into retinex theory to allow for the fact that luminance may change gradually across parts of an image; these gradients are what we encounter in a picture illuminated from one side. If they are gentle enough, the gradients may be imperceptible, for they represent extremely low spatial frequencies. The retinex theory deliberately excludes gradients by postulating a threshold below which a change in luminance is imperceptible. You have already seen how gradients may be ignored compared to the edges of an image in the Craik–O'Brien illusion (Figs 5.6 and 9.7). Thus, the background gradient in the lower part of Fig. 12.3(a) is ignored for the computation, and the retinex is 'fooled' into seeing the circles as having different lightnesses. In fact, you are also fooled by gradients, as you can see in Fig. 12.3(a). All the small gray circles are actually identical, but some are placed against a dark ground (so they appear light) and others against a light ground (so they appear dark). You can demonstrate that the circles are really identical

➡

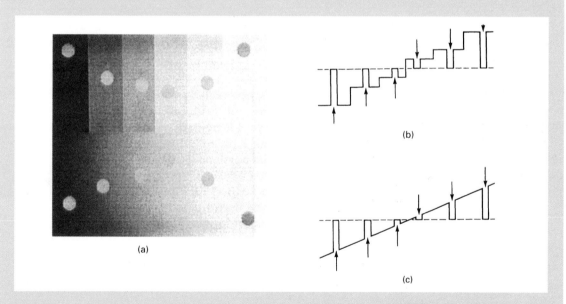

(a)

(b)

(c)

Fig. 12.3 (a) Patterns in which identical circles appear to have different lightnesses because of the background against which they are viewed. (b) Sketch of luminance versus position (through the centers of the circles) in the upper half of (a). Arrows indicate the circles, with luminances matched to the horizontal dashed line. (c) Luminance profile for the lower half of (a). From Shapley R. (1986) The importance of contrast for the activity of single neurons, the VEP and perception. *Vision Research* 26: 45–61. Reprinted by permission of Pergamon Press, Ltd. and the author.

(Box 12.3 CONTINUED)

by covering the picture with a sheet of paper with holes punched over each gray circle. The grays seen through the holes will be the same.

The retinex theory is satisfactory for the circles placed against a gradient, as in the lower part of Fig. 12.3(a), but the borders of the step-like background in the upper part of the figure should be well above the threshold. We should be aware of the steps against which the circles are seen. As a result, the retinex theory predicts that all the circles in the upper part should be seen veridically; that is, they should appear to be equal in lightness. This is clearly not the case. Anomalies such as in Fig. 12.3 have led some to question the retinex theory's reliance on the global changes in luminance. Shapley (1986) criticized retinex on these grounds, and proposed that the perception of lightness is based on the average contrast at the borders of each area being judged. As a result, the only contrasts of importance in Fig. 12.3(a) are at the borders of the small circles. This way, their relative lightnesses are correctly predicted to be judged as different in both the upper and lower parts of the figure. A similar demonstration on a Mondrian pattern is shown in Fig. 12.4. Here, the square in the upper left is of the same luminance as the circle at the

lower right, but appears lighter because of the darker surrounding boxes.

Notice that both the retinex theory and Shapley's contrast theory measure contrast at the borders. The difference is that retinex simultaneously includes *all* borders, while Shapley considers only the borders of the patch being judged. This closely parallels the older controversy of adaptation level versus simultaneous contrast. Both of those theories compared luminance in the patch being judged to an 'average' background luminance; adaptation level considered *all* of the background, while simultaneous contrast considered only those parts near the patch being judged.

Other theorists have considered the importance of 'object-oriented' brightness (Blommaert & Martens, 1990); that is, brightness is associated with the object, not just the contrast of a patch against neighboring patches. Such processing has been built into computer models for brightness (Pessoa *et al.*, 1995). In the next section, you will see how higher 'cognitive' factors may influence the perception of brightness.

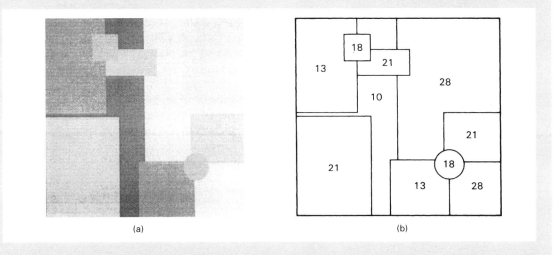

(a)   (b)

Fig. 12.4 Mondrian pattern in which two patches of identical luminance appear different in lightness because of the surrounding patches. (a) The small square in the upper left is the same gray as the circle in the lower right. (b) Sketch of the pattern, with relative luminances of each patch indicated. From Shapley R. (1986) The importance of contrast for the activity of single neurons, the VEP and perception. *Vision Research* 26: 45–61. Reprinted by permission of Pergamon Press, Ltd. and the author.

surround was nearly irrelevant, and the patch was like a luminous source similar to the matching patch. In the limit, if the surround were perfectly black, the test patch and matching patch should be set to be physically identical.

The case in which the test patch is of considerably lower reflectance than the surround is rather interesting. Increasing the incident illumination seemed to cause a decrease in the apparent brightness of the test patch; more light on the patch made it darker! This is not as paradoxical as it seems, however, when you consider that the brightness is determined by the luminance of both the object and its surround. Increasing incident illumination increases the luminance of the test patch, but it also increases luminance of the surround. The brighter surround causes the dimmer test patch to appear even blacker. When incident illumination is very low, everything appears a general gray; increased illumination brings out the surround and makes the patch appear relatively blacker (Hochberg, 1971a). **BOX 12.3**

Cognitive factors in lightness and brightness

It would be nice to be able to say that the perception of lightness and brightness can be explained by the physiology of the retina. Can we predict the apparent lightness of a surface by knowing the pattern of light on the retina? Lateral antagonism from areas surrounding the surface in question obviously plays a part in determining the lightness of the surface, but other perceptual aspects of a display affect apparent lightness or brightness.

You have already seen an example of how higher processing of the image plays a role in perception of lightness. A shadow appears darker when it is outlined (see Box 12.1, p. 249), even though the outline is a minor part of the pattern on the retina. Similarly, the division of the ring in Fig. 12.2 into two parts (by drawing a line across the border) was necessary to show the effect of simultaneous contrast on the apparent grayness of each half.

A graphic demonstration of this point can be seen in Fig. 12.5. This is a reversible figure similar to the ones you saw in Chapter 10; it may be seen as a tube with the opening to the right (so that the shaded crescent on the right is the inside of the tube), or with the opening to the left (so the crescent on the left is the inside). With a bit of concentration, you should be able to see the tube in either configuration, just as Necker cubes could be seen in either of two configurations. The thing to notice here, however, is that whichever shaded crescent is seen as the inside of the tube appears slightly lighter than the other (mirror image, but otherwise identical) crescent. Coren & Komoda (1973), who devised this figure, suggested that the reason for this is that the inside of a real tube receives less illumination than the outside; when the inside of a tube is seen as reflecting the same amount of light as the outside, the perceptual hypothesis is that it must be of higher reflectance (lighter in color) than the outside. Here, the pattern on the retina is absolutely unchanged as the figure reverses; the change in perceived brightness is a result of the interpretation of the pattern.

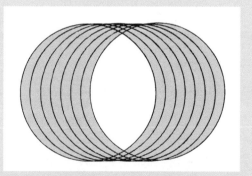

Fig. 12.5 Ambiguous 'tube' which may be seen opening to either the left or the right. The brightness of each shaded crescent depends on the configuration seen. Figure 7.9 from *Sensation and perception*, by Stanley Coren, Clare Porac, and Lawrence M. Ward, copyright © 1979 by Harcourt Brace, Jovanovich, Inc. Reprinted by permission of the publisher.

Perceived depth can also affect the perception of lightness (Hochberg & Beck, 1954; Mershon & Gogel, 1970). Again remember the Craik–O'Brien illusion (Figs 5.6 and 9.7), in which two equally luminous areas looked different because the one gradually faded to light while the other faded to dark, meeting at a strong border. If this identical luminance pattern is shaped to look like a book lying open, the fading looks like the natural shadows in the gutter of the book, and the two areas appear equally bright (Knill & Kersten, 1991). In this case, the simple perceptual hypothesis is that the curved pages lead to shading of identical surfaces.

Gilchrist (1977) provided a good demonstration of the effect of perceived lighting on brightness. His observers looked through a peephole (to limit depth cues) into a room with a doorway that opened into a second room. The subject was asked to judge the lightness of a test piece of paper fastened inside the door frame. The test stimulus could be a square, overlapping the corner of a paper in the far room so that it clearly was within the first room, or it could have been notched it so that it appeared to be behind the paper in the second room. The apparent color of the paper depended on which room it appeared to be in—that is, how well it was lit. The difference between the patterns reaching the observer's retina is slight; the lightness must have been determined in part by the interpretation given to the patterns. You can see this effect for yourself in 'Apparent lightness', the second choice among the 'Illusions and constancies' demonstrations on the CD accompanying this book. A gray rectangle is made to appear behind a picture on the wall of the far, dimly lit room in the left photograph. A rectangle of the same area appears to be fastened to the door frame in the right photo. You can adjust the luminance of the right rectangle so it seems to be the same shade of gray as the left one; you should find you make it too light because you think it is receiving

---

Box 12.4 Brightness of a flickering light

In addition to the spatial factors that contribute to the perception of brightness, there is a temporal factor. Under certain circumstances, a flickering light can appear brighter than a steady light of the same mean luminance; this phenomenon is known as *brightness enhancement*.

A light can be flickered (turned on and off regularly, as if viewed through the blades of a slowly turning fan) at any rate. If the rate is slow enough, the flicker is obvious, and it is easy to judge the brightness during the time the light is on. As the rate of flicker increases, it becomes harder to see that the light is actually flickering and not steadily on. For example, fluorescent lights flicker at a rate of 120 cycles/s (a fluorescent tube becomes almost completely dark 120 times each second), yet the light appears steady. Flicker at such a rapid rate is too fast to be detected; it exceeds the *critical fusion frequency* (CFF), the rate at which a flickering light appears steady. The effective light coming from such a flickering light is the average amount of light in a cycle, or the average of the light half-cycle and the dark half-cycle.

When a light flickering at about 10 cycles/s is compared with steady light of the same average luminance, the flickering light appears brighter (Bartley, 1938). The subject can easily detect the fact that the flickering light is not steady, but cannot correctly compensate and judge its brightness.

This phenomenon may be explained by recalling some characteristics of the responses of ganglion cells in the retina. The responses of ganglion cells are minimal in steady light; there is a peak of response when the light first comes on, and a much lower plateau of response while it is steady (see Chapter 5). A flickering light is continually re-exciting the peak response. On the average there is more activity in ganglion cells stimulated by a flickering light than in those stimulated by a steady light of the same average luminance, so the flickering light appears brighter (Walters & Harwerth, 1978). This enhancement has been demonstrated in single cell recordings in animals such as the cat (Enroth, 1952; Grüsser & Creutzfeldt, 1957; Hughes & Maffei, 1966) and the horseshoe crab, *Limulus* (Ratliff *et al.*, 1969).

the brighter lighting of the foreground. (Note also that the relatively bright rectangle 'behind' the picture on the left makes the mat in its frame appear darker than in the same picture in the right room.) A similar effect of apparent lighting has been reported by Adelson (1993). <u>BOX 12.4</u>

Size constancy

Size constancy refers to the ability to judge correctly the sizes of objects despite the differences in the retinal images cast by them as they are viewed from different distances. The woman standing next to you projects a larger image on your retina than does the man across the room, but she does not seem larger than him. The size of the proximal stimulus (retinal image) is intimately related to your distance from an object, so it is clear that your ability to judge size is intimately related to your judgments of distance.

The relationship between size and distance is at the heart of the concept of *visual angle*. You have already encountered visual angles in speaking of eye movements and spatial frequencies, but here it must be defined it more carefully. The visual angle, θ, subtended by an object is the angle between the lines drawn from the opposite edges of the object through the center of the pupil of the eye. The geometry is shown in Fig. 12.6. Notice also that the projection onto the retina is defined by the same angle as the visual angle, for the rays from each edge of the object continue straight through the center of the optical system of the eye. The angle inside the eye is also θ, and the size of the image on the retina, a, is related to θ and y, the size of the eyeball. As the size of the eyeball (y) does not change for objects at various distances, the size of the retinal image depends only on the visual angle. Visual angle and the size of the retinal image (proximal stimulus) are interchangeable, because there is always a one-to-one relationship between them.

There is not a unique relationship between object size (distal stimulus) and visual angle, as the distance from object to eye can easily change. Consider Fig. 12.7(a); two people are viewed from two different distances. The closer person (at position 1) subtends a larger visual angle (θ_1) than the equally tall person at position 2 (θ_2). Their heights are the same, but the distances are different; as a result, the visual angles subtended by them are different and the retinal images are not the same size. The retinal image of person 1 will be about three times as large as the image of person 2, but the observer will correctly judge them to be equally tall if he or she can correctly infer their relative distances.

Figure 12.7(b) illustrates the opposite situation.

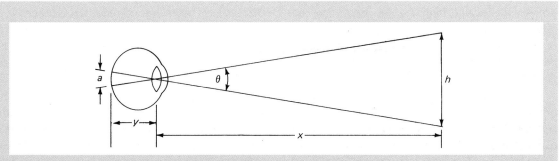

Fig. 12.6 Definition of visual angle. An object of height *h* at a distance *x* subtends a visual angle *θ*; this angle uniquely determines the size of the retinal image, *a*.

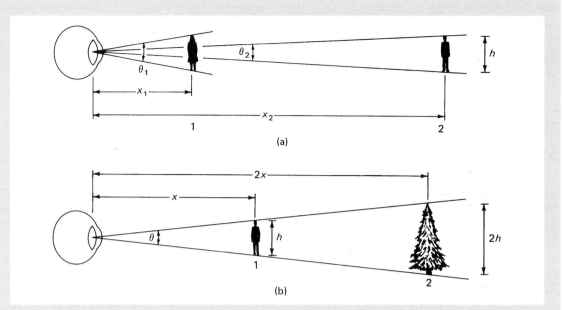

Fig. 12.7 Relationship of visual angle to size and distance. (a) Two objects of the same height at different distances subtend different visual angles. (b) Two objects of different heights at different distances may subtend the same visual angle.

Here, the person standing in position 1 is only half the distance from the observer as the tree in position 2. He is also half the height of the tree, so the ratios of height to distance for each are the same: if the person is at distance x and is of height h, the tree is at twice the distance ($2x$) and stands twice as tall ($2h$). They subtend the same visual angle, and project identically high images upon the observer's retina. Nevertheless, the observer can correctly judge the tree to be twice the height of the person if he or she can correctly infer their relative distances.

The key to size constancy lies in the last phrase of the two preceding paragraphs: 'if he or she can correctly infer their relative distances'. The cues to distance were the subject of the previous chapter; by making use of these cues, a distance is inferred, and perceived size follows directly from that inference. Of course, there is a certain amount of interaction, as the size of the proximal stimulus is also

an important cue for determining the distance between an object and the observer. If the object has a readily known familiar size (see Chapter 11), the distance can be known from the ratio of the actual size to the size of the proximal stimulus. This is possible if recognition is generally independent of size; cells in inferotemporal cortex seem to 'recognize' objects regardless of image size (Lueschow, *et al.*, 1994). In general, what the observer must do is make a perceptual hypothesis (see Chapter 10) about the size *and* distance of the object, using all the available distance cues and size cues (such as known size of the object), to build a model of the visual scene somewhere within the mind. Built into this process, of course, is the hypothesis-making that went into the determination of what was figure and what was ground, as well as actual identification of the figure. The end result is a simultaneous encoding of size and distance. Evidence of this interdependence may be seen in the responses of certain cells in area V4 (and even in V1 and V2), which respond to 'nearness' or 'farness' of objects independently of the image sizes (Dobbins *et al.*, 1998).

It is important to remember again that the making and testing of perceptual hypotheses is an unconscious process. You do not look at a scene and think: 'What could that be? Can I separate that set of lines into a closed figure? What figure is it? How far is it? Given that it is 500 m away and subtends a 21.8° angle, it must be, um, 500 times 0.4, or, ah, 200 m.' OK, it is a 200 m building 500 m away. Even when the inferences are wrong (as in optical illusions) and you are made *intellectually* aware of the actual situation, the misperception persists.

The classic experiment demonstrating the link between size estimates and perception of distance was performed in the corridors of Harvard University by Holway & Boring (1941). The subject was placed at the intersection of two corridors. Down one corridor was a disc whose size the subject was asked to judge. The disc could be at a number of different distances but whatever its distance, its size was selected so that it subtended exactly 1° of visual angle (Fig. 12.8). Down the other corridor was a second (comparison) disc at a constant distance, whose size could be adjusted. The subject's task was to set the size of the comparison disc in the second hallway so that it appeared to be the same size as the 1° test disc in the first corridor.

There are two distinct ways a subject could do this. As the test disc subtended exactly 1° no matter what its distance from the subject, the size of the retinal images could be matched by always setting the comparison disc to subtend 1°. The comparison disc was always at the same distance, so its size would not change as function of the distance of the test disc. On the other hand, the subject could set the comparison disc to be the same physical size as the test disc, making the comparison disc larger as the test disc was moved farther away

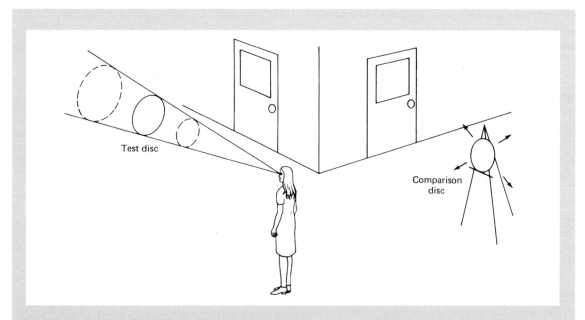

Fig. 12.8 Experimental arrangement for study of size constancy used by Holway, A. H. and E. G. Boring (1941) Determinants of apparent visual size with distance variant. *Am. J. Psychol.* 54: 21–37. Reprinted by permission.

(as the test disc was in fact made larger at farther distances in order to maintain the constant 1° angle).

The results of the Holway & Boring experiment for a number of different viewing conditions are shown in Fig. 12.9. The predictions based on the two possible strategies outlined above are shown by dashed lines. If the subject matched visual angle, which was constant, the horizontal dashed line marked 'constant visual angle' would result; if the size was correctly matched, the comparison disc would be made larger at larger distances, and the sloped line marked 'size constancy' would result.

Consider first the circles, resulting from the relatively natural condition of viewing with both eyes. In this condition, the subject presumably had as much distance information as possible. Size constancy seemed to be the rule, although there was a tendency to overcompensate (When the test disc was distant, it was seen as somewhat larger than it actually was.) As cues to depth were removed, size constancy worked less well. Thus, viewing with only one eye (removing all binocular cues) gave results in which the size was very slightly underestimated (triangles). A more drastic effect was

obtained by having the subject view the discs through a peephole (squares). The peephole removed the depth cues of motion parallax (if the subject's head moved, the subject simply did not see through the hole—see Chapter 11). With so few cues to depth, the subjects were nearly unable to determine the distance of the test disc, and tended to a compromise between size constancy and adjustment according to the size of the retinal image.

Finally, with the corridor darkened, curtains placed in front of doors to prevent any reflections, and viewing monocularly through the peephole, the discs must have appeared as luminous circles at indeterminate distances. In that case, the subjects very nearly obeyed the law of constant visual angle, for there was nothing else on which to base size judgments. This is what is referred to as an *unstructured field*, meaning there is no structure or form to give cues to size or distance. Holway & Boring's subjects set the size of the comparison disc approximately according to the visual angle of the test disc (Xs), although there was still a hint of size constancy in their settings. Presumably, some depth cues still remained, and were potent enough

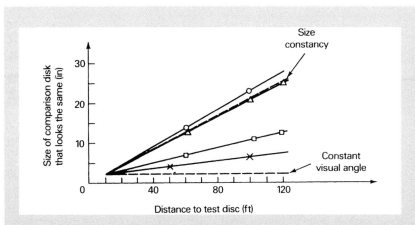

Fig. 12.9 Results of size constancy experiment—*slanted dashed line*: perfect size constancy; *horizontal dashed line*: judgments based on visual angle; *circles*: binocular viewing; *triangles*: monocular viewing; *squares*: viewing through a peephole; *crosses*: viewing through a peephole with curtains blocking stray reflections.

Box 12.5 Apparent size of afterimages

That the perceived size of an object is related to its perceived distance may be conveniently demonstrated by noting the apparent sizes of afterimages. An afterimage can be generated by staring fixedly at a high-contrast pattern. Gaze away from the high-contrast pattern after fixating for about 30 s to 1 min and stare at a blank (preferably gray) surface. After a moment or two, a reversed version of the original pattern should appear; this is because of local adaptation of the area of the retina that has been stimulated by the original pattern (see Chapter 6).

You can use the 'Afterimages' demonstration associated with Chapter 6 on the CD to see this effect. Instead of viewing the afterimage on your screen when the original image disappears and the screen goes blank, look at a blank wall across the room. Try it again, but move closer to the screen as soon as the afterimage forms.

The afterimage has a constant retinal size, as it is created by the specific cells within the retina that have been adapted. It therefore subtends a constant visual angle, regardless of the distance to the surface against which it is seen. The afterimage appears as if it were floating on the surface it is viewed against; the farther away the surface is, the farther away the afterimage appears. An afterimage of a particular pattern viewed against a surface that is as far from the observer as was the original pattern will appear to be the same size as the original pattern. If the afterimage is viewed against a surface farther away (for example, the far wall of the room), it will appear considerably larger than the original pattern used to generate it. Conversely, if it is viewed against a near surface (a sheet of paper held close to the eye), it will appear smaller. The apparent size of the afterimage, which subtends a constant angle, depends on its apparent distance. This relationship between size and apparent distance of an afterimage is called *Emmert's law*.

to allow the subject to realize the more distant test discs were somewhat further. (In a 1950 experiment, Lichten & Lurie used screens that hid the shadowy structure of the corridor. Their subjects were allowed to see only the stimuli, and based their settings of the comparison disc entirely on the visual angle of the test disc.)

There are two important lessons from these experiments. The first is that when a subject is allowed cues to the distance to an object, it is possible to compensate for the change of visual angle with distance and correctly judge the size; that is, within a reasonable range of distances, people maintain size constancy. The second lesson is that when the cues to distance are removed, the subject cannot correctly judge size, and must base estimates mainly on the visual angle subtended by them (see also Hastorf & Way, 1952; Zeigler & Leibowitz, 1957; Rock & McDermott, 1964). Although perceived size is clearly related to perceived distance, the relationship is not perfect. When an object is moved to a new distance, the size may be correctly judged as the same but the new distance may be incorrectly estimated. **BOX 12.5**

Illusions of size

You have already seen some optical illusions in Chapter 10: optical illusions are those delightful gimmicks that fool and amuse us while teaching us something about how the visual system works. The largest class of optical illusions, the ones most often found on breakfast cereal boxes, are the ones that give an erroneous impression of depth and therefore fool us about relative sizes. In these illusions, the apparent depth is not the same as the real depth, so the 'constancy' of size is an error.

The most straightforward way to produce such an illusion is to create an impression of depth by using the cues of linear perspective. For example, the picture in Fig. 12.10 shows an icy breakwater receding into the distance. All the cues (elevation, converging lines, fewer details) and past experience with beaches say that the end nearest the top of the picture is much farther away than the end at the bottom. The two ovals drawn on the picture are, in fact, identical in size and shape; they were drawn with the same template. They were drawn as if they were markings on the snow; the upper one appears farther away than the lower one. As a result, the upper one appears larger. Even after measuring the two ovals and understanding intellectually that they are the same size, the upper one appears larger.

The illusion that the two ovals in Fig. 12.10 are not the same size is a variant of an illusion called the *corridor illusion*, because it is usually represented as a long interior hallway. Any picture that gives the impression of receding into the distance can be used: a long hallway, a street, railroad tracks (an extremely popular one), a boardwalk (as in Fig. 11.7). The more distance cues provided, the more compelling the illusion will be.

The illusion can also be achieved with only minimal cues. For example, take Fig. 12.10, strip away all the cues but the converging lines, and replace the ovals with circles; this leaves another illusion, called the *Ponzo illusion* (Fig. 12.11; you can test how much the illusion fools you by trying to match the circles in the Ponzo illusion demonstration, which

is one of the illusions associated with this chapter on the CD). The Ponzo illusion is more often shown with the lines converging to the side, rather than above the circles, as if the book were turned through 90°; the argument about converging lines works in either case. In the Ponzo illusion, the two lines converging toward a 'vanishing point' may give the impression that the circle nearer this vanishing point is farther from the observer: it therefore appears larger. Demonstrate that the illusion is related to apparent depth by turning the Ponzo illustration (Fig. 12.11) upside down. When the lines converge at the bottom of the picture, there is little sense to the perspective. The apparent depth is diminished, and the two circles appear essentially the same size.

A famous depth illusion designed by Adelbert Ames is called the *Ames trapezoidal room*. As the name implies, this is a room of trapezoidal shape as shown in Fig. 12.12. An observer looks into the room through a peephole in the front wall (re-

Fig. 12.10
Demonstration of the corridor illusion. The two ovals drawn on the breakwater are physically identical.

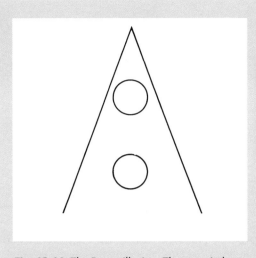

Fig. 12.11 The Ponzo illusion. The two circles are identical.

member, this prevents motion parallax, as well as enforcing viewing from a particular perspective and precluding binocular depth cues). The floor is

trapezoidal, and slopes downward toward the corner at *A*; the rear wall is a trapezoid with trapezoidal windows. It is much larger at *A* (which is in fact quite far from the observer) than at *B* (which is fairly close). The trapezoids are arranged so that the view through the peephole gives the same proximal stimulus as a normal view of an everyday. rectangular room. Figure 12.13 shows the view from the peephole.

Now, suppose two people are in the corners *A* and *B* (Fig. 12.13). They are essentially the same size, but the one in corner *A* is considerably farther from the observer at the pinhole than the one in corner *B*; he therefore subtends a considerably smaller angle. As the other cues indicate that the two are at the same distance, the perception is a difference in size (different visual angles at the same distance). This illusion is thus the converse of the corridor illusion, in which objects subtending the same visual angle appear different in size because the cues indicate a difference in distance. The Ames room demonstration is extremely

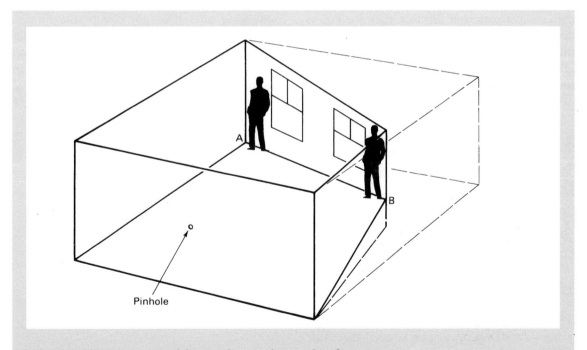

Fig. 12.12 The Ames trapezoidal room, showing the actual configuration.

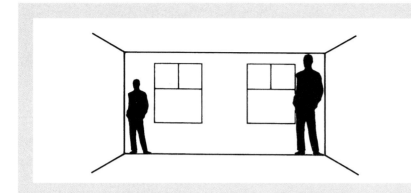

Fig. 12.13 View through the peephole into the Ames room of Fig. 12.12.

compelling—it is most disturbing to see two people in the actual room such that one is a hulking giant and the other a midget, and watch each shrink or grow as they exchange places in the room. Note that in this case the familiar sizes of the people, and the expectation of constancy of size of each, is overridden by the illusion due to apparent distance. BOX 12.6

There are other illusions that may well depend on a misperception of distance that are not as directly perspective-related. One of these is called the *Hering illusion*; it consists of a starburst pattern of lines superimposed on two straight parallel lines (Fig. 12.14). The straight lines appear bowed (you may have to convince yourself they are really straight by placing a ruler or the edge of a sheet of paper along each). One possible explanation for this illusion is that the lines converging to a point suggest greater depth in the center of the figure; the parallel lines do not become closer (in visual angle) when they are 'farther' and hence their separation appears greater. On the other hand, presenting the illusion as a stereogram so that the parallel lines appear to be clearly in front of the converging lines does not disrupt the illusion (Kaufman, 1974), indicating a mechanism other than apparent depth. Perhaps there is a distortion of the apparent angles made with the lines, as in the Poggendorf illusion (Fig. 10.17).

Similar to the Hering illusion is the *Wundt*

Box 12.6 Other explanations for these illusions

The illusions so far presented as illusions of distance can be explained in other ways. For example, the person on the right in Fig. 12.13 may look larger simply by comparison to nearby features of the room. The 'giant' is scrunched into a corner with the ceiling pressing his head, while the 'midget' just reaches the window. You would naturally judge a person to be huge who cannot fit into an apparently normal room, or car, or chair, without necessarily misperceiving distance. This is the trick used in movies to give the illusion of a miniature or giant person; a normal actor is placed among mis-scaled props (for example, in *Honey, I shrunk the kids*). Similarly, the upper circle in the Ponzo illusion (Fig. 12.11) is 'measured' by the closer lines near their vertex, and the ovals in Fig. 12.10 are 'measured' by the width of the breakwater.

At this point, size and distance are confused. The ovals in Fig. 12.10 are placed where the breakwater has different widths, but this is an inevitable result of linear perspective. If the breakwater did not change width, it would not appear to recede into the sea. Is the illusion due directly to the cues that also induce the impression of depth (as discussed in Chapter 11) or to the depth induced by those cues?

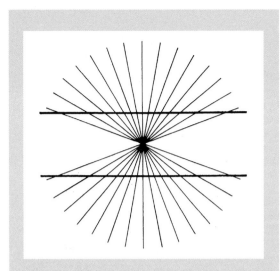

Fig. 12.14 The Hering illusion. The two lines are straight and parallel.

illusion; in fact it is like an inside-out Hering illusion (see Fig. 12.15). Here, the radiating lines give the appearance of a flattened spheroid, like a flying saucer. The horizontal parallel lines appear to converge either because they appear closer to the observer at their midpoints, or because of the distortion of the angles made with the radiating lines. <u>BOX 12.7</u>

An illusion that appears more distinctly depth-related is the *Jastrow illusion*, shown in Fig. 12.17. The two arcs appear to be parts of rings lying before you; the one higher in the frame appears farther away and therefore larger. In fact, the two shapes are identical. (This illusion, like the corridor and Ponzo illusions, works less well if turned upside down.)

Now for the most famous and perhaps the most controversial illusion, the *Müller–Lyer illusion* shown in Fig. 12.18. As everybody almost certainly has already been told, the two vertical line segments are equal in length (go on, measure them). Nevertheless, the one with the outward splayed tails appears longer than the one with the inward-facing arrowheads. You can measure your own ability to outguess the illusion by trying the Müller–Lyer illusion on the CD.

Why this illusion works has been the subject of considerable theorizing. Boring (1942) listed 12 different theories of the Müller–Lyer illusion presented in the first 12 years after it was devised! These include the possibility that the tails are somehow included in the estimate of the lines, that the angles are misjudged (as with the Poggendorf illusion) and seem to point at a 'false' line ending, that eye movements are greater when

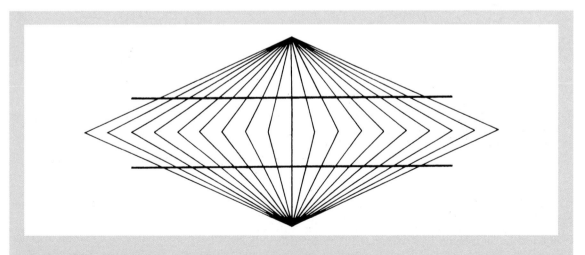

Fig. 12.15 The Wundt illusion. The two lines are straight and parallel.

Box 12.7 Shape illusions

The Hering and Wundt illusions are grouped with others in a class called 'shape illusions', as opposed to the size illusions that seem to depend on apparent distance. Other shape illusions are shown in Fig. 12.16. In the figure on the left, the radiating lines cause an apparent distortion of the regular shapes drawn on them. The square is actually a perfect square with straight edges (this is called the *Ehrenstein illusion*), and the circle is perfectly round (the *Orbison illusion*). The figure to the right is called the *Zollner illusion*; the long diagonal lines are actually straight and parallel. Like the Hering and Wundt illusions, these could be explained by effects of apparent depth or perspective, or could be more closely related to distortions of angle such as seem to dominate for the Poggendorf illusion in Fig. 10.17 and the 'Illusions and constancies' demonstration (Brigell & Uhlarik, 1980).

Perhaps a hint as to whether these are really illusions of distance (depth), rather than relative size or angle, can be found by asking whether the illusions are present when depth is not salient. In Chapter 11, you saw several indications that the magnocellular system is essential for the perception of depth. The magnocellular system seems to be color-blind; it cannot 'see' a stimulus that is equiluminant (see Chapter 8 and the 'Equiluminance' demonstrations on the CD). It was because equiluminant stimuli failed to produce a perception of depth that Livingstone & Hubel (1987b) concluded that the magnocellular system mediates depth. They also examined equiluminant versions of many of the illusions shown here, including the Poggendorf (Fig. 10.17), the Ponzo (Fig. 12.11), the Hering (Fig. 12.14), the Zollner (Fig. 12.16b), and the Müller–Lyer illusions (Fig. 12.18). They found no illusory effect at equiluminance in any of these. It thus seems that these illusions also require the participation of the magnocellular system. Of course, it is not clear whether they depend on the magnocellular processing of depth or on other functions of the magnocellular system.

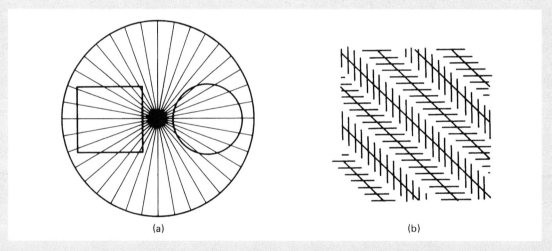

(a)   (b)

Fig. 12.16 Shape illusions: (a) the Ehrenstein and Orbison illusions; (b) the Zollner illusion.

the tails face out than in, that lateral interactions at the intersections of the tails and lines affect the positions of the maximum excitations, or that the Müller–Lyer figure gives a false impression of depth that accounts for the apparent size difference. This last possibility bears further examination.

The principal proponent of an apparent distance explanation for the Müller–Lyer illusion is R. L. Gregory, who likens the two figures to an exterior

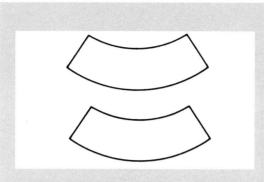

Fig. 12.17 The Jastrow illusion. The two shapes are identical.

corner of a building and the interior corner of a room (see Fig. 12.19). The exterior corner, which contains the arrows-in figure, should appear to approach the observer from the page, while the interior corner, containing the tails-out figure, should appear to be behind the page. The arrows-in figure should appear closer; because the visual angles are the same, the 'closer' figure should appear smaller.

This explanation depends on the notion that the apparent depths of the straight lines in the

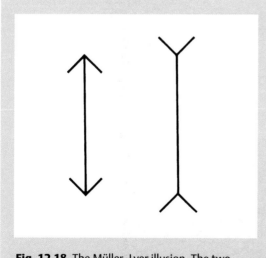

Fig. 12.18 The Müller–Lyer illusion. The two vertical lines are equal.

Müller–Lyer figures are different. Gregory (1970, 1978) had subjects report the apparent depth of the figures by setting the apparent distance of a comparison spot, and found a depth difference commensurate with the illusion. An even more potent test was to use stereograms of the Müller–Lyer figures and see if disrupting the apparent depth by an overriding binocular cue could disrupt the illusion. This was reported by Gregory & Harris (1975), who found a normal amount of distortion when the stereograms were appropriate to the differences in depth expected from geometric considerations, but a much diminished illusion when the stereograms were reversed so that the arrows-in figure appeared farther away than the tails-out figure (Fig. 12.20a). In other words, a binocular cue that opposed the apparent geometric cue seemed to cancel the illusion. BOX 12.8

The moon illusion

Finally, here is one of the most compelling illusions, one 'devised' by nature rather than human beings. It is the *moon illusion*, in which the zenith moon (directly overhead) appears smaller than the horizon moon. (The same effect applies to the sun, but staring directly at the sun can permanently damage your eyes.) It may actually surprise you to learn that the moon does *not* in fact change size as it 'travels' across the sky; it always subtends the same visual angle (about 1/2°) whether it is high overhead or the huge harvest moon just over the treetops. It is *not* magnified by some strange effect of the more dense atmosphere near the horizon (it is actually slightly compressed in the vertical direction), nor is it closer to you at the horizon (it is very slightly farther away at that point). Nevertheless, the horizon moon appears larger than the zenith moon.

As with any good illusion, there are several theories to explain this one (Ross & Plug, 1998). Holway & Boring (1940) suggested that the zenith moon appears smaller because you must tilt your head back to see the moon overhead; this was shown not to be so by Kaufman & Rock (1962), who used mirrors

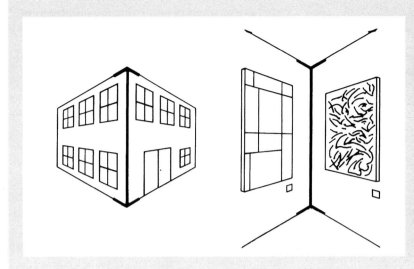

Fig. 12.19 Drawing indicating how the Müller–Lyer figures could be perceived as indicating depth.

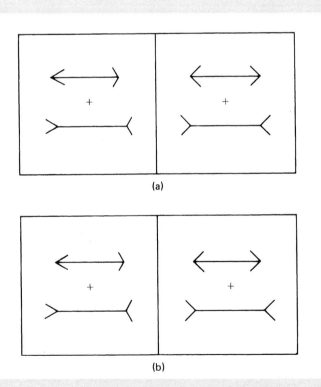

(a)

(b)

Fig. 12.20 Stereograms that attempt to abolish the depth effects of the Müller–Lyer illusion. Note there is an illusion in each panel. Stereograms should be viewed according to the instructions in Box P1 (p. vi). (a) The horizontal lines are displaced in depth; this should cancel the illusion. (b) The arrowheads are made to appear in the wrong depth for the interpretation in Fig. 12.19; this should not affect the illusion.

Box 12.8 Well, how do *you* explain these illusions?

The idea that there is a depth-related explanation for the Müller–Lyer illusion is accepted by many psychologists, but certainly not all (for arguments against a size constancy explanation see Day, 1965; Massaro & Anderson, 1970; Waite & Massaro, 1970). Even the demonstration that a stereogram depth reversal cancels the illusion does not settle the issue, for a depth reversal of the kind described by Gregory & Harris would be expected to give a size illusion that would cancel the illusion regardless of its actual origin. A more appropriate test would seem to be one in which the stereogram causes the arrowheads to face the 'wrong' way without affecting the apparent distances of the lines. Pitblado & Kaufman (1967) set up a stereogram in which the lines to be judged were unchanged in apparent depth but the arrows-in lines appeared to come toward the observer, and the tails-out lines appeared to recede. They found no disruption of the illusion in these circumstances, and concluded that the Müller–Lyer illusion is not dependent on apparent distance.

A stereogram reproducing the effect that Pitblado & Kaufman found non-disruptive is shown in Fig. 12.20 (b); it should be compared with the apparently disrupting stereogram of the type used by Gregory & Harris, shown in Fig. 12.20(a). The difference between the two is that in Fig. 12.20 (a) the ends of the wings are in the same plane as the fixation cross, while the horizontal lines lie in front of or behind that plane. In Fig. 12.20(b) it is the horizontal lines that are in the same plane as the fixation cross, while the wings extend in front of or behind the plane. (Both parts are set up so that the direction of the wings from the horizontal lines is the opposite of that postulated by Gregory in explaining the illusion). Note, however, that neither stereogram is so effective that you cannot convince yourself the illusion is either present or absent as desired.

There is another lesson here, which can be applied to a number of other experiments that claim to have 'ruled out' one or another explanation of this (or other) illusion. The lesson is that perceptual hypotheses are based on all kinds of cues—there is no one cue that leads inevitably to a particular hypothesis. It is thus possible that under different circumstances illusions could arise from different sources. It is probable that there is no single explanation for any given illusion (Fisher, 1970; Coren & Girgus, 1973; Morgan & Casco, 1990).

to view horizon moons overhead and zenith moons straight ahead. They found that nearness to the perceived horizon was the essential cue to achieve the effect. Others (Restle, 1970) have argued that the illusion is explicable by the relative expanse of sky surrounding the moon. The size of a horizon moon is measured relative to the small stretch of sky separating it from the horizon, while the zenith moon is measured against the vast expanse of sky between it and the rest of the world. Similar size comparison effects can be invoked to explain the Ponzo illusion (Fig. 12.11), in which the apparently larger circle is also 'squeezed' by the converging lines. Similarly, in Chapter 9 you saw that adapting to low spatial frequencies made subsequently viewed patterns appear to be of higher spatial frequency (that is, smaller). A direct example of this effect is the Titchener illusion, shown in Fig. 7.6 (p. 123) in connection with the experiment demonstrating that illusions that fool you do not

fool your visually guided hand motions (Aglioti, *et al.*, 1995).

An interesting explanation for the moon illusion, and the one most commonly accepted, is that it is an illusion of apparent depth (Kaufman & Rock, 1962; Rock & Kaufman, 1962). The idea is that the moon is seen as if it were on the 'surface' of the sky. If the sky were perceived as a hemispheric bowl, there would be no illusion; however, the sky is perceived as a flattened bowl that is closer at the zenith than at the horizon (as if it has gradually settled over the millennia). Clouds, when they are present, seem to heighten this flattened bowl effect, for clouds overhead are, in fact, closer than those at the horizon, and they appear closer in the sense that there is more visible detail in overhead clouds than horizon clouds. When thunderstorms roll in we seem to be sandwiched between two parallel planes, for the curvature of the earth is too slight to detect.

Figure 12.21 shows a section of our clouded-over plane, indicating how the overhead clouds are actually closer than the distant clouds. We do not see the two planes extending to infinity with a gap between sky and earth, however; the two seem to converge, and we conceive this as a flattened dome. Figure 12.22 shows the flattened dome of the sky with a truly hemispheric dome indicated by dashes.

The moon maintains a constant visual angle in its travels across the sky; it is equivalent to moving a 'moon-disc' along the true hemisphere (dashed). But you perceive it as if it were traveling on the flattened bowl. (The projections of the moon in two positions are shown in Fig. 12.22.) The moon appears larger at the horizon because it seems farther away, and it appears smaller overhead be-

cause it seems nearer, yet subtends the same visual angle. This idea is corroborated by the fact that afterimages also display the moon illusion when viewed against the sky (see Box 12.5, p. 261).

There is a catch to this explanation, however. The horizon sky appears more distant than the zenith sky, but the horizon moon appears *closer* than the zenith moon. The low harvest moon seems to float above the treetops, practically within reach. If it appears closer, why does it not appear smaller? Kaufman & Rock recognized this problem, and proposed that the judged distance to the horizon moon is influenced by its perceived size. That is, the horizon moon appears larger than the zenith moon because it appears to be on the more distant horizon sky; it is then judged to be closer than the zenith moon because it is appar-

Fig. 12.21 Indication of why the sky at the horizon should appear more distant than the zenith sky.

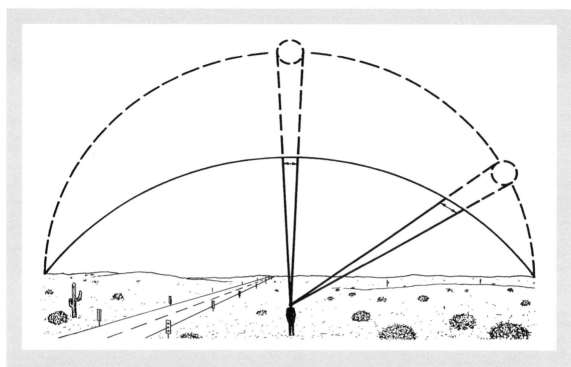

Fig. 12.22 The moon illusion. The sky is perceived as a flattened dome (*solid*) against which the equal visual angle moon is projected After Kaufman, L. and I. Rock (1962).

ently larger. In effect there are two distances: a 'registered' distance that the perceptual system uses in gauging size, and a 'judged' distance that is the overt estimate the observer would give of distance. (Rereading this last paragraph will probably not help you at all.) <u>BOX 12.9</u>

Shape constancy

The third kind of constancy is called *shape constancy* (or *object constancy*). It refers to the ability to perceive the shape of the distal object rather than the shape of the proximal stimulus. This is also known as 'perspective invariants theory', which is reviewed by Pizlo (1994).

Shape constancy is really a special case of size constancy. Distortions of the shapes of plane figures are caused by the fact that different parts of the figures are at different distances from the observer; those parts farthest away subtend smaller visual angles than corresponding parts of the same size that are nearer. Shape constancy is really nothing more than the reconstruction of the correct relative sizes of the parts of a figure given their relative distances from the observer. To do this accurately, the observer must correctly infer the slant at which the figure is viewed.

To comprehend the kinds of distortions undergone by the proximal stimulus, you need to understand the concept of the *frontal plane projection*. A frontal plane is like a window between the world and your eyes. If you traced the scene on that window, you would have a pretty good representation of the retinal image (like Magritte's painting in Fig. 11.10). In fact, the photograph taken by a camera

Box 12.9 Two kinds of distance perception — two pathways?

The two kinds of distance proposed by Kaufman & Rock are a form of parallel processing. Judged distance is the one you tap when you ask a subject how far away something is. Since it is available to the conscious mind, it seems likely that this resides in the ventral pathway. Among its determinants are size; for example, your judgment of how high an airplane is when you are watching from the ground may be largely determined by your judgment of the familiar size of a plane of that type. Registered distance, on the other hand, is not available to your estimation apparatus; it is an internal datum used by the size-estimating system. It is tempting to think of it as residing in the dorsal pathway, but there is no evidence for an actual anatomical separation of these constructs.

You have seen how the parallel pathways in the cortex may duplicate similar functions. For example, orientation selectivity is a property of both the magnocellular and parvocellular pathways at all levels above the lateral geniculate. Presumably, each requires this information for the tasks it performs, even though the two systems perform somewhat different tasks. Livingstone & Hubel (1987b) have argued that the movement-sensitive system displays orientation selectivity that is independent of the orientation selectivity evident in the texture or pattern system. Judged and registered distance may be evidence of duplication in parallel pathways at another level of processing. Similar interactions may occur in the judgment of size (McKee & Smallman, 1998).

held at your eye is a frontal plane projection of the scene. The advantage of referring to the frontal plane is that it demonstrates the geometry of objects viewed at different angles.

Figure 12.23 illustrates the frontal plane, and the frontal plane projections of a slanted circle and square. The circle is foreshortened into an ellipse, and the square becomes a trapezoid. These are the shapes of the proximal stimuli that are projected by those distal stimuli; note that there would be no difference in the shape of the pattern on the retina between a square seen from an angle and a trapezoid seen straight on. Shape constancy refers to the fact that a subject can perceive a square when the proximal stimulus is a trapezoid (and the distal stimulus is a square at a slant).

You can thus expect a relationship between the perceived slant of an object and the apparent foreshortening, just as there was a relationship between the size and the apparent distance (Koffka, 1935). This is, in fact, at least partially true, as shown by Beck & Gibson (1955). They showed subjects a display in which a triangle was mounted at 45° to a vertical background. On the background were two triangles, one of which was physically identical to the slanted one, and the other of which

was identical to the frontal plane projection of the tilted triangle. When the subjects viewed the display through a peephole so that they could not detect the slant of the test triangle, they chose the triangle with the same frontal plane projection as being the same as the tilted one. When the subjects viewed the display with both eyes, they chose the physically identical triangle as the same. The apparent shape was determined by the perceived slant. These results should remind you of the perception of eye level in a slanted environment (see Box 10.7, p. 205).

Similar findings have been obtained in experiments in which the shapes of tilted objects were to be judged (Thouless, 1931; Langdon, 1951; Miller & Bartley, 1954; Nelson & Bartley, 1956). As a general rule, the matched shape lies between the frontal plane projection and the real shape. The more cues to the slant, the more like the real shape an object appears.

With more complicated shapes, you can recognize an object despite rotations of about 40°. But we must encode a more three-dimensional view (see Chapter 10), and if we are once offered three views about 120° apart we can recognize an object from any other view. Cells in area V4 seem to

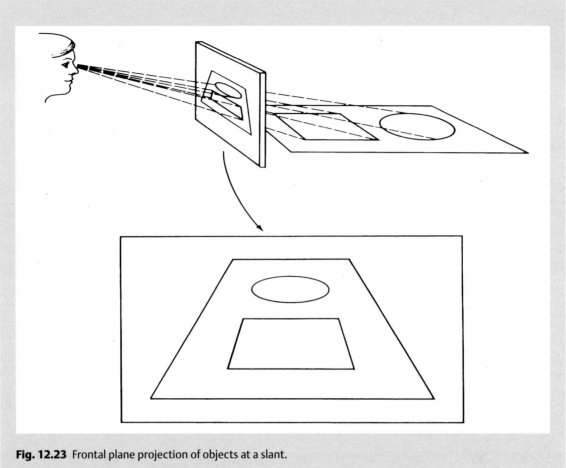

Fig. 12.23 Frontal plane projection of objects at a slant.

have similar capabilities (Logothetis & Pauls, 1995).

Regression to the real

When an observer (not a trained artist) is asked to indicate the shape of a tilted object *as it appears in the frontal plane*, there is a tendency to draw a shape somewhat biased toward the actual physical shape. Thouless (1931) has called this 'phenomenal regression to the real object'. What that means is that you automatically correct for the registered tilt, just as perception of size includes an automatic correction for registered distance. This is also known as 'view invariance'.

This may explain the way children draw before they learn the rules of perspective. For example, Fig. 12.24(a) is a 'clear glass of water' drawn by a 6-year-old. Notice the overly round top and bottom of the glass; the child knew they were circular, and so drew them as nearly round. (Isn't this what Picasso did when he showed both a profile and frontal view of a face in the same picture?) Figure 12.24 (b) provides an interesting comparison. It is a drawing of a glass made by a congenitally blind woman. Notice the same tendency to show the top and bottom as circular. The line down the middle represents the front of the glass, a 'feature' not normally drawn by the sighted.

Distortion of shape is not confined to our talents

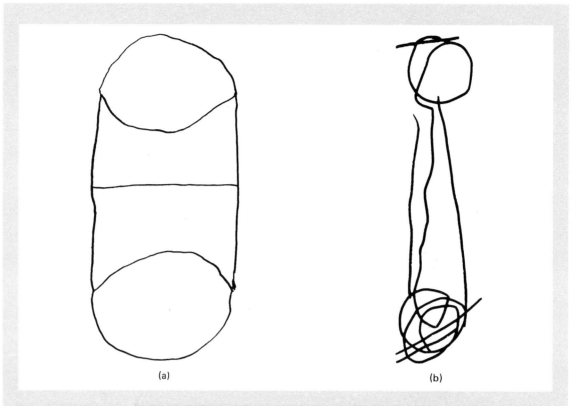

Fig. 12.24 (a) A 'clear glass of water' showing exaggeration of the circles at top and bottom (drawing by Matt Levine, age 6). (b) Drawing by a congenitally blind woman. From Kennedy, J. M. (1980) Blind people recognizing and making haptic pictures. In *The perception of pictures*, ed. M. Hagen, Academic Press, New York, pp. 263–303. Reprinted by permission.

in drawing pictures. Coren *et al.*, (1979) present an interesting demonstration, shown in Fig. 12.25. The figure shows a drawing of a box; the question is, could you lay a dime on the blank top of the box so that it would not overlap any of the lines of the drawing? Most people think they can. If you try, you will find that you were fooled into believing the top of the box was a square, and therefore had more area than it really does.

Another demonstration is on the CD. The last of the 'Illusions and constancies' is 'Shape constancy', which shows a few CDs scattered on a table. One is outlined in green; can you make the ellipse in the white area below the photo the same shape as the green ellipse? You will probably be surprised by

how much 'fatter' you set this ellipse. Your judgment of the green ellipse was affected by your perception of it as a circle at an angle. <u>BOX 12.10</u>

At this stage, you should note that just because there is a relationship between the perceived tilt and the estimated shape does not necessarily mean that there is a lawful compensation for tilt. In the physical domain, there is a trigonometric relationship: the height in the frontal plane is proportional to the cosine of the angle of tilt. The same is not necessarily true in the psychological domain. Nelson *et al.* (1961) had subjects look at luminous circles and ellipses in an otherwise dark field; the subjects had to draw the shapes they saw and indicate tilt by setting a 'tilt board'—a board

Box 12.10 Does familiarity breed regression?

When you think of regression to the real, you probably think that this carries an implication of some knowledge of the real object, based on past experience. Thus ellipses should look like circles, and trapezoids like squares; these are shapes that we are familiar with. But it does *not* appear that familiarity is the main influence on shape constancy (Thouless, 1931; Nelson & Bartley, 1956). The only hint

that familiarity might contribute to shape constancy comes from an experiment by Borresen & Lichte (1962). They used meaningless shapes and found the amount of regression to the real. There was always some tendency to correct for the viewing angle, but the tendency could be increased somewhat if the subjects were first familiarized with the shapes that would be used.

on which their hands rested that could be moved to any angle (in the manner of an automobile gas pedal). The subjects thus reported both the perceived shape and the perceived tilt. The relationship found was *not* exactly the cosine law relating physical tilt and the frontal plane projection; in fact, the exact law depended on the amount of texture in the pattern. On the other hand, when subjects set visual comparisons to both shape and tilt, shape and tilt are found to trade off as a true invariance (Kaiser, 1967). The point, however, is that the perceived tilt and perceived shape are not necessarily brought into a perfect trade-off. This is comparable to the fact that the perceived size and judged distance are not in an exact inverse relationship either, as are real size and distance.

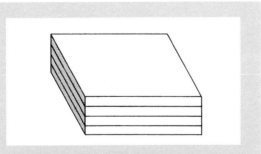

Fig. 12.25 Demonstration of shape constancy. Will a dime fit on top of the box? Figure 14.2 from *Sensation and perception*, by Stanley Coren, Clare Porac, and Lawrence M. Ward, copyright 1979 by Harcourt Brace Jovanovich, Inc. Reprinted by permission of the publisher.

Illusions of shape

Examples of illusions that depend on shape constancy are hard to single out, as shape constancy and size constancy are intimately related. After all, the former is a way of allowing for the shrinkage of the far edge of a figure that is viewed at an angle. The following examples, therefore, can also be taken as examples of size constancy.

One example is the Ames trapezoidal window, discussed in Chapter 10 (Fig. 10.34, p.217). In that example, a window shaped like a trapezoid was rotated; because the larger edge always appeared closer, the window seemed to be rocking rather than rotating. The shape constancy mechanism was fooled into taking the trapezoidal shape as the frontal plane projection of a tilted rectangle. Alternatively, according to size constancy, we simply take the larger edge to be closer. In fact, both statements amount to the same thing.

Shape constancy can be summarized by saying that it is the principle by which objects are seen as their correct shapes despite their being viewed at an angle. You judge the shape of an object by taking into account its tilt and not simply by the shape of its frontal plane projection. For this reason, photographs and paintings can convey correctly the shapes they portray despite the distortions of these shapes. You treat these representations as frontal plane projections, and perceive them as you would your own naturally occurring frontal plane projections. You also automatically compensate for the projected sizes of the

Box 12.11 Pictures of pictures

Pictures represent a remarkable second level of transformation that you can accept with no difficulty. A photograph is a frontal plane projection from the position of the camera. There is little problem in understanding how, when you view a photo straight on, you can interpret ellipses as circles in the real scene (as, for example, the paper plates in Fig. 12.26, which are ellipses in the photo but are obviously circular plates on the table). What is remarkable is that you can view the photograph from the side (not too extremely) and still correctly perceive the scene portrayed.

The next level of abstraction is generally beyond our capabilities. Take a photograph of a photograph from one side, and the picture within the picture looks distorted. This is true even if the photograph of the photograph includes ample information about the way it was taken, as in Fig. 12.27. Here is obviously a scene in which the photo of Fig. 12.26 is a part. You are unable to compensate for the distortion of the frontal plane represented by a photograph of it, and the scene in the photo-in-the-photo looks distorted. Now the images of the plates are in fact approximately circular, but look like strange ellipses.

Fig. 12.26 Child setting a picnic table. Shapes are correctly perceived despite distortion into the frontal plane of the camera.

Actually, you do not compensate perfectly. You may have seen a portrait in which the subject is staring straight out of the frame. As you walk past such a painting, the eyes in the portrait seem to follow you as you move about the room. Objects such as eyes and pointing fingers in pictures fail to rotate because the point of view cannot change; Wallach (1987) invokes a compensatory mechanism that normally would prevent apparent rotation of real objects as we walk by them (a problem considered in the next chapter). Surprisingly, while the amounts by which objects rotate in a painting may differ, the spatial relationships among them do not seem to change (Goldstein, 1979).

You saw that the distortion caused by looking at a picture from an angle was automatically compensated for, up to a point. If the angle is really extreme, the process breaks down. This breakdown is the reason traffic instructions painted on the roadway must be made in such tall, stretched-out letters; they would not be legible in normal proportions. The distortions of extreme angles are also exploited in a form of painting called anamorphic art; some of these pictures were painted so that the subject could only be seen correctly when viewed at an extreme angle. An example is shown in Fig. 12.28. To see the subject of this painting, you must look at it from the right side, with your eye practically touching the book.

Fig. 12.27 Photograph of a photograph. Notice the distortion of the objects in the embedded photo (which is Fig. 12.26).

Fig. 12.28 Anamorphic art. Viewed straight on, the picture is quite distorted, but viewed from the right at an extreme angle (close one eye and let the other practically touch the page) it is a clear portrait of Edward VI. By courtesy of The National Portrait Gallery, London.

images, and see objects in the picture in their appropriate relative sizes. <u>BOX 12.11</u>

Suggested readings

There are several popular paperbacks available that concentrate on the illusions and constancies of vision. Two that are readable (although the reader is cautioned that they are not without bias toward their author's positions) are by R. L. Gregory. One, *The intelligent eye* (McGraw-Hill, 1970) is noteworthy for its treatment of illusions and impossible or ambiguous figures, and for the inclusion of a large number of stereograms that can be viewed with the red/green goggles included in the book. The other is *Eye and brain*, 3rd edn (McGraw-Hill, 1978), which includes somewhat more reference to the research literature.

Another book of interest is *Visual illusions*, by M.

Luckiesh (Dover, 1965; reprinted from a 1922 edition). Despite the fact that the book was written more than 75 years ago, the discussions of illusions and contrast are surprisingly up to date. The chapters of particular interest are Chapter 4 (geometric illusions), Chapter 6 (angles), Chapter 7 (illusions of distance), and Chapter 8 (brightness contrast).

Surface color perception, by Jacob Beck (Cornell University Press, 1972) is devoted almost entirely to lightness and brightness perception. Much of the discussion is concerned with general theories of lightness constancy, with experimental evidence presented as it bears on theoretical positions. Of particular note is Chapter 7, which deals with anomalous illumination and shadows.

Chapter 8 of E. H. Gombrich's book *Art and illusion*, 2nd edn (Princeton University Press, 1961) deals with portrayal of depth and shape, and some illusions due to perceived depth. Note also *The artful eye*, edited by R. Gregory, J. Harris, P. Heard and D. Rose (Oxford University Press, Oxford, 1995) and *The eye of the artist*, by Michael Marmor and James Ravin (Mosby, St Lovis, 1997). (These books were also recommended in Chapter 10 for their treatments of the principles of perception as applied to fine art.)

There are three pertinent *Scientific American* articles, all of which have been reprinted in the collection *Perception: mechanisms and models*, edited by R. Held and W. Richards (W. H. Freeman, 1972). They are 'Visual illusions', by R. L. Gregory (November 1968; offprint #517), which discusses illusions of depth (including the Müller–Lyer illusion) and impossible figures; 'The moon illusion', by L. Kaufman and I. Rock (July 1962; offprint #462), which presents their account of the moon illusion; and 'The perception of neutral colors', by H. Wallach (January 1965; offprint #474), a discussion of simultaneous contrast and lightness perception. A more recent article is 'Geometric illusions', by B. Gillam (January 1980); this article is reprinted in *The mind's eye* (introduction by J. M. Wolfe, W. H. Freeman, 1986), and in *The perceptual World*, edited by Irvin Rock (W. H. Freeman, 1990). This latter collection of *Scientific American* articles also contains Alan Gilchrist's account of how spatial relationships help to determine the apparent lightness of a surface: 'The perception of surface blacks and whites' (March 1979).

Finally, for a discussion on the survival value of illusions and their (mis)interpretation, see David Miller's 'Brain processing of optical input: the perception of visual reality' in *M.D. Computing* (11: 34–42; 1994). A very complete book with chapters by leaders in this field is *Perceptual constancy*, edited by V. Walsh and J. Kulikowski (Cambridge University Press, Cambridge, 1998).

Chapter 13
The perception of movement

THIS chapter is about an important topic in visual perception: how you perceive the movement of objects through space. At first glance, this might seem to require only a straightforward extension of ideas that have been presented earlier; if you know something about form perception, object constancies, and the identification of objects that have depth associated with them, what more do you have to know to understand how the same phenomena are perceived when moving? As usual, however, nothing is as simple as it seems. The perception of movement is a complex topic, at least partially because observers (and their eyes) do not remain stationary while viewing the world. How does the visual system differentiate movement that is caused by the external environment from movement caused by the organism itself? Even when a subject is relatively stationary, eye movements are occurring during which the position of the entire visual world is shifted on the retina. How do you avoid perceiving these shifts as large-scale movements in the world?

People perceive motion either by detecting position shifts of the image of a stimulus on the retina, or by using eye movements to follow a moving object so that the object's image is maintained in approximately the same retinal location. R. L. Gregory (1978) named the perceptual system that responds to movement of an image across the retina the *image–retina system*, while the system responsible for following the position of a stimulus with eye and head movements is called the *eye–head movement system*. This chapter discusses

both of these ways of detecting movement. In addition, you will learn about the phenomenon of apparent movement, a class of events in which there are strong impressions of movement under conditions in which the stimuli are actually stationary. This is in contrast to real movement, where the stimuli are actually moving in space.

The motion-sensing systems

Image–retina system

The most straightforward type of movement perception occurs when a subject is relatively stationary and movement of the stimulus image across the retina is the critical event (Fig. 13.1). In the studies you will encounter in this section, the subject's eye movements were rarely if ever controlled; however, most of the effects revealed by these studies would still be seen in the absence of eye movements. These experiments, therefore, investigate the properties of the image–retina movement system.

Motion thresholds One of the first steps in characterizing a sensory system is to determine its thresholds, or limits of operation, as well as investigating factors that affect those thresholds. In

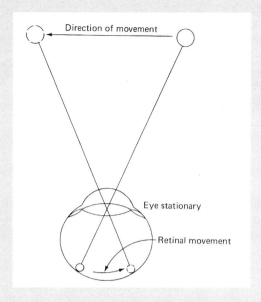

Fig. 13.1 The image–retina system. As the stimulus moves, the image also moves across the retina. Adapted from Gregory (1978).

most experiments investigating motion thresholds, the duration of the stimulus is held constant while the velocity of the stimulus is varied. Threshold velocities determined in this way have been named *isochronal* thresholds (Leibowitz, 1955).

One of the most important determinants of motion thresholds is the location on the retina of the moving image. Objects whose images pass through the center of the retina have much lower movement thresholds than stimuli presented to the retinal periphery (Aubert, 1886); that is, much slower movements can be detected. This may seem somewhat surprising in view of the fact that the periphery is often thought of as being selectively sensitive to novel or sudden movements, with a higher proportion of movement-sensitive ganglion cells than in the fovea (recall the 'Peripheral vision' demonstration on the CD in Chapter 3). The absolute number of retinal cells in the periphery is much smaller than in the center, however; in addition, the size of retinal ganglion cell receptive

fields grow with eccentricity, so a greater extent of motion may be necessary for it to be resolved.

Leibowitz *et al.* (1972) have shown that much of the deficit in peripheral movement perception is caused by optical factors that degrade images in this region of the retina. They compared movement thresholds in the presence and absence of lenses that were designed to minimize peripheral refractive error. The results are shown in Fig. 13.2; although movement thresholds rise as a function of eccentricity for both conditions, the effect is much greater in the condition in which refractive errors were not corrected. When stimuli move at relatively fast speeds, the peripheral retina is superior to the fovea in detecting movement (Bhatia, 1975). This reversal in what portion of the retina is most sensitive to movement probably occurs at a stimulus velocity such that sustained ganglion cells (perhaps the X-cells that project to the parvocellular system) are not effectively stimulated, but more transient ganglion cells are still quite responsive.

Other factors besides retinal position affect thresholds for detecting the motion of stimuli. One factor that has a large effect is the presence of reference points in the visual field; many studies have shown that thresholds obtained using a single stimulus in a homogeneous field may be much higher than when the field includes stationary reference points. It seems that this improvement only occurs under conditions when the stimulus duration is fairly long; for durations shorter than 4 s, it does not matter whether reference points are present or not (Harvey & Michon, 1974). These data suggest that there might be different mechanisms responsible for the perception of motion of stimuli presented quickly and for those stimuli that remain for longer periods of time. Note, however, that this difference could also be partly due to drifts in eye position that would only be significant with the longer exposure times.

Motion aftereffects   When you read about retinal ganglion cells in Chapter 5, you learned that cells

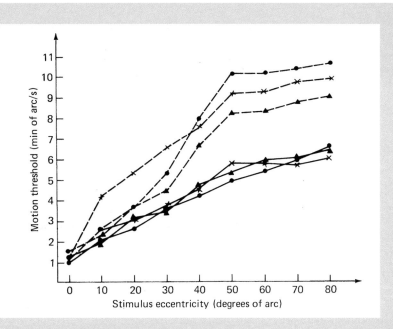

Fig. 13.2 Motion thresholds for three observers as a function of stimulus eccentricity: *dashed* functions are derived from experiments with no correcting lenses; *solid* functions come from experiments using lenses that best focus images in the retinal periphery. From Leibowitz, H. W., C. A. Johnson and E. Isabelle (1972) Peripheral motion detection and refractive error. *Science* 177: 1207–1208. Copyright 1972 by the AAAS. Reprinted by permission of the publisher and author.

found in frog and rabbit retinas were selectively sensitive to movement. Some cells responded to movement of a stimulus in one direction but were completely unresponsive to movement in the opposite direction. In higher animals (cats and monkeys), ganglion cells are not generally sensitive to movement in a specific direction; however, many cells in the visual cortex are (see Chapter 7).

Directionally selective cells in the human visual system could form the basis of the image–retina movement system. In fact, there is evidence for the presence of direction-specific movement detectors in the human visual system. The supportive evidence comes mostly in the form of investigations of a phenomenon called the movement aftereffect (MAE). Most people who stare at a waterfall for a couple of minutes and then look away get an illusion of the objects they are looking at (trees, rocks,

etc.) floating upwards. This effect is called the waterfall illusion, and is an example of an MAE. Examples of MAEs abound in the natural world; for instance, a passenger sitting in a train that has come to a stop often has the feeling that the stopped train is moving backwards. Or if you watch all the closing credits on a video, and they scroll up the screen at a steady rate, the entire TV may seem to be moving downward after the credits have ended. <u>BOX 13.1</u>

The most common explanation for MAEs is that they are caused by adaptation of the motion-specific detectors that are tuned to the direction of movement of the stimuli in the scene being viewed. For example, in the waterfall illusion, all the detectors sensitive to downward movement are continuously stimulated while viewing the waterfall. If these detectors adapt and become less

Box 13.1 Demonstration of an MAE

One of the most striking motion aftereffects is the plateau spiral illusion. This illusion is usually demonstrated using a spiral placed on the turntable of a record player (remember those?). You stare at the spindle in the center of the spiral while the turntable is rotating for about 1 min and then stare at a neighbor's face. There should be a striking impression of continual contraction of the person's face. What is most disconcerting is that the impression is one of continual contraction, even though the face does not change size.

It's hard to find a phonograph these days, but you can get the effect viewing the 'Motion aftereffect' of the 'Motion demonstrations' listed for Chapter 13 on the CD accompanying this book. Instead of a rotating spiral making a continuously expanding field, you will see a field of blobs moving away from the center of the display. When the display is replaced with a photo, you see continual contraction.

sensitive, when the viewer shifts gaze and looks at other objects, all the movement detectors in the other directions will be activated more than the downward motion detectors, resulting in an impression of the scene moving upward. Consistent with this interpretation, cells in V1 that have a preferred direction of motion show adaptation mainly to motion in that preferred direction (Giaschi *et al.*, 1993). Both the phenomena and this explanation of them are reminiscent of the figural aftereffects discussed in Chapter 9. BOX 13.2

If MAEs are caused by adaptation of direction-specific motion detectors, perhaps a clue to where

in the visual system these detectors are located can be obtained by varying the conditions under which the aftereffect occurs. If the detectors are retinal in origin, there should be no interocular transfer of the effect; that is, if one eye is presented with an adapting stimulus that moved continuously in one direction, no aftereffect should be present in a test field viewed by the other eye. When Mitchell *et al.* (1975) performed this experiment, however, they found that MAEs were present under such conditions. This is strong evidence that the motion detectors being adapted by the adapting stimulus are not retinal in origin, but must be located at or after

Box 13.2 Letting an MAE determine perceived motion

Motion aftereffects also apply to moving stimuli. In the 'Moving dots' demonstration (viewed in black and white) of the Chapter 8 'Equiluminant demonstrations' on the CD, you saw a kinetic depth effect in which a field of moving dots presents a three-dimensional appearance of a rotating sphere. It is impossible to tell from this pattern which dots are on the 'near' side of the sphere and which are on the 'far' side. The result is that the direction of rotation is ambiguous; you cannot say whether the sphere is rotating clockwise or counterclockwise. As with other ambiguous stimuli (see Chapter 10), the direction of rotation seems to reverse spontaneously. You should see a rotating sphere when you set the black-and-white dots in motion,

and should be able to 'choose' whether it is rotating clockwise or counterclockwise.

Nawrot & Blake (1989) added an MAE to this ambiguity. They had their subjects adapt to an unambiguous rotating globe before showing them the pattern of dots. As a result of the pre-exposure, the ambiguous pattern was always seen rotating in the opposite direction from that of the globe. This is what one would expect if adapting to a globe rotating, for example, in a clockwise direction adapted all the 'clockwise' detectors, so the 'counterclockwise' detectors prevail to determine the apparent rotation of the field of dots. Notice, however, that this is quite different from adaptation of left-moving or right-moving detectors: it is adaptation to a rotation in depth.

the point in the visual system at which inputs from the two eyes have combined—that is, the visual cortex. This conclusion was further strengthened by Mitchell *et al.*'s observation that subjects who were stereoblind (that is, had poor binocular vision and depth perception presumably because of lack of binocular cells) failed to show interocular transfer of the aftereffect.

Other evidence that MAEs are central in origin depend on the fact that they are disrupted when there is binocular rivalry; when the two eyes see different directions of motion, neither displays the aftereffect (van der Zwan & Wenderoth, 1994). On the other hand, stimuli that induce motion within one eye's blind spot produce an MAE in the corresponding position of the other eye (Murakami, 1995), indicating involvement of cortex beyond V1. (You can see a 'filling-in' effect in the CD demonstration for Chapter 3 [Foveal and peripheral vision] by running the 'Blind spot' demonstration with a 'large stimulus'.) **BOX 13.3**

Other evidence for direction-specific motion detectors There have been several experiments designed to yield more information regarding the properties of the motion detectors. Levinson & Sekuler (1975) presented a grating moving in one direction at a constant speed, and manipulated the contrast of the grating to find a threshold level for which the grating could just be seen. They found that this contrast level did not change when a slightly subthreshold grating moving in the opposite direction was added to the visual display. This is evidence that, like the spatial frequency channels discussed in Chapter 9, the direction-specific motion detectors are independent of each other. For a stimulus to be above threshold, therefore, it must activate a particular detector or set of detectors above a certain level, and activation of a different detector (for example, with a grating moving in the opposite direction) will not affect the threshold of the first detector.

Other studies have further extended our knowledge about the direction-specific motion detectors. Tynan & Sekuler (1975) were interested in whether a moving stimulus had to be continuous through a field to activate the motion detectors in that field; they presented subjects with a stimulus array similar to that shown in Fig. 13.3, in which two sections of a moving grating were separated by a piece of black construction paper that covered the center of the grating. When subjects viewed this stimulus configuration, they reported seeing the grating continue through the construction paper, even though that portion of the array was completely blank. The 'phantom grating' seen on the blank part of the field looked considerably dimmer than the actual grating on either side, but it was of the same spatial frequency and traveled at the same speed. When the grating stopped moving and was held stationary, the phantom grating disappeared, and subjects saw the middle portion of

---

Box 13.3 Do MAEs demonstrate the existence of motion detectors?

Not everyone interprets the MAE as adaptation of motion detectors. For example, Chaudhuri (1990) showed that an MAE can be generated by *preventing* normal eye movements, so there is no retinal motion when the brain 'thinks' there should have been. This implies that outflow of information to the eye muscles is of importance for the perception of motion, an idea you will read more about shortly. Other higher processes are also involved. For example, running on a treadmill (where there is no visual motion because only your feet are moving) makes you move more slowly afterwards (Pelah & Barlow, 1996). Other explanations of the MAE include the 'law of repulsion', a kind of inhibition that develops as a result of association with the stimulus (Barlow, 1997), and 'recalibration' of the visual/vestibular system as a result of a lack of vestibular (body motion) input when the visual field is moving (Harris *et al.*, 1981).

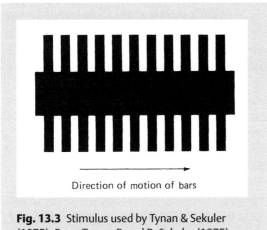

Direction of motion of bars

Fig. 13.3 Stimulus used by Tynan & Sekuler (1975). From Tynan, P. and R. Sekuler (1975) Moving visual phantoms: a new contour completion effect. *Science* 188: 951–952. Copyright 1975 by the AAAS. Reprinted by permission of the publisher and author.

the field as being blank. The illusion of a phantom grating seen when the grating was moving was therefore a product of a movement detection mechanism, rather than reflecting more general processes. When either the top or bottom portion of the grating was covered, the phantom grating was not seen; however, if the top portion of the grating was seen by one eye and the bottom portion by the other eye, the phantom grating was seen. This indicates that, like MAEs, the illusory moving grating is produced after the point at which the information from the two eyes has combined; that is, the visual cortex. Cells in the movement-sensitive posterior parietal cortex (dorsal stream) have been found that are sensitive to occluded (hidden) stimuli only if they are perceived as moving (Assad & Maunsell, 1995).

The movement detectors responsible for producing the phantom moving gratings in this experiment are fairly global in nature; they cover a large area of the visual field and tend to fill in blank areas surrounded by movement all in the same direction. Weisstein *et al.* (1977) performed an experiment that suggests that these are the

same motion detectors that provide the basis for motion aftereffects. They presented the same type of stimulus as Tynan & Sekuler, a moving grating with an obstruction covering the center portion. After inducing the phantom grating pattern, they tested for a MAE in the area of the field in which the phantom grating had been seen. Their results showed that under all conditions that produced a phantom grating, a strong movement aftereffect was also seen. This is evidence that the detectors responsible for the movement aftereffects are actually the same ones that produced the phantom gratings described by Tynan & Sekuler.

Directionality of motion detectors   In the preceding discussions, you were led to believe that motion detectors are stimulated by real motion in some direction, and probably inhibited by motion in the opposite direction. This is the model you read about in Chapter 5, and it seems to apply to many cortical cells as well (for example, Mikami, 1992). But motion can be perceived in a direction other than the directions in which things are really moving.

One kind of visual stimulus that shows this kind of motion is called a plaid. It consists of two gratings (usually sinusoids to avoid the complications of higher spatial frequencies—see Chapter 9) at right angles, each moving in the direction across its stripes. Thus, a horizontal grating moving upward would be superimposed on a vertical grating moving to the right. The appearance is of a plaid moving on a diagonal from lower left to upper right (Derrington & Suero, 1991). <u>BOX 13.4</u>

An example of perceived motion in a direction where there is no real motion may be seen in the demonstration 'Macro and micro fields' on the CD. When there is no motion, there is no indication of any kind of border in the field of dots. When you start the motion, the dots moving upward form a vertical stripe in the midst of those moving downward. This is an illustration of the Gestalt principle of 'common fate' you encountered in Chapter 10, but it is more generally known as 'contour from motion' in this form (Lamme *et al.*, 1993). But the

Box 13.4 The aperture problem

A plaid may not actually be devoid of motion in the diagonal direction. Consider a real plaid of black, white, and gray squares, which is what you would get by superimposing two square-wave gratings. The pattern you get by moving the gratings upward and rightward is exactly the same as if you printed a plaid on a sheet of paper and moved it diagonally—there just is no Fourier component moving in that direction. Nevertheless, diagonal motion is the 'most likely' explanation for what you see (Stoner & Albright, 1992), an idea that should remind you of the perceptual hypotheses you read about in Chapter 12.

On the other hand, if you considered a detector with a very small, local, receptive field focusing on a 'corner' of the plaid, it would detect diagonal motion. This is known as the *aperture problem*, and is of concern when a field of fi-

nite size is stimulated with a large grating or long line. Even if the line is actually slewing with motion partly along its length, it appears to move at right angles to its length. This is illustrated in the demonstration 'Motion past an aperture' which is among those associated with this chapter on the CD accompanying this book. When you start the demonstration, the lines moving behind the two circular 'cutouts' seem to move at right angles. When you choose 'Full view', the mask is taken away and you see that the pattern is really a chevron moving to the left. In 'Transparency', the mask is back in place but the lines show faintly through it; you can see them moving either at right angles or to the left.

---

downward-moving dots just to the right of the stripe reverse direction and move upward, while the upward-moving dots in the left of the stripe reverse and move downward; as a result, the stripe itself moves slowly to the right. Notice that the motion is to the right even though the only motion on the screen is up or down. There are at least two phases to this perception: local motion detectors recognize the upward and downward motion, and segregate the scene into vertical bands. A subjec-

tive contour is created, much like those you read about in Chapter 10. The rightward motion is then of the subjective contour. The perception of this more global motion is apparently by a long-range motion detector. BOX 13.5

Cortical motion detectors Retinal ganglion cells that seem to act as motion detectors were discussed in Chapter 5. Similarly, you saw in Chapter 7 that many cortical cells respond to specific

---

Box 13.5 Short-range and long-range motion systems

The idea of short-range and long-range motion detectors has come under considerable discussion (see Braddick, 1993). In general, the short-range process is associated with local contrast and segmentation of features, while the long-range process is more integrative and 'follows the features' (Chubb & Sperling, 1989; Georgeson & Hanis 1990; Snowden & Braddick 1990; Mingolla *et al.*, 1992). Ohtani *et al.* (1991) suggested that the two systems may be related to the sustained and transient systems (perhaps the sustained relates to the parvocellular system, or perhaps ventral stream, and the transient relates to the magnocellular, or perhaps dorsal, system). This could imply the

dorsal stream responds to global motion, while the ventral uses local motion to help determine 'what' objects are.

Not everyone agrees that the local–global distinction is valid. Grossberg (1992) argues that there are two systems, but one is 'static'—it determines form regardless of motion—while the other is specifically for determining shape from motion. Another suggestion is that the two systems differ in timing, not distance (Boulton & Baker, 1993a,b). And a number of workers find only a single system (Bischoff & DiLollo, 1990) or suggest the distinction is an artifact of the experiments (Cavanaugh, 1991a) or just an unnecessary complication (van de Grind *et al.*, 1992).

velocities of motion or directions of motion. An MAE similar to that found psychophysically may be observed in cortical cells (Hammond *et al.*, 1988; Hammond & Mouat, 1988). Thus, at least the simpler MAEs reflect the properties of cortical neurons.

As you saw, the areas of cortex involved with motion seem to be responsible for the MAE. Cells in the dorsal stream signal the perceived direction of motion, even when it is an aftereffect. This has been shown in area MT (Britten *et al.*, 1996) and in a nearby area called MST (Celebrini & Newsome, 1994). Neurons in these cortical areas have more complicated properties that are suited for detecting motion relative to a background. Cells in the lateral suprasylvian area in cat (probably homologous to MT in primates) respond best when a stimulus in the center of their receptive field moves in the opposite direction from a pattern of dots in the surround (von Grunau & Frost, 1983). Similar properties have been reported in MT of monkey (Komatsu & Wurtz, 1988b), and in tectum of pigeon (Frost & Nakayama, 1983). Such cells would recognize that the target is moving, rather than the eye sweeping across the target, because they respond to relative motion. They are therefore useful for recognizing the edges of an object moving among other objects or against a background and might help in deriving depth or shape from motion.

Eye–head system

When you attend to an object moving through your visual field, your eyes generally do not remain stationary; instead, they follow the path of the object. This can either occur through the use of head and body movements, or be caused by movements of the eyes themselves. As you follow the movements of the object, its images on your retinas will remain in approximately the same positions on your foveae (Fig. 13.4). Obviously, you are able to detect that a stimulus is moving under these conditions; just as obviously, the image–retina movement system cannot be respon-

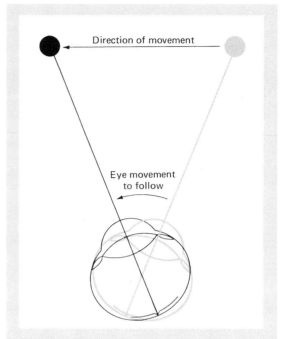

Fig. 13.4 The eye–head system. When a stimulus moves, the eyes follow so that the image of the stimulus remains fixed on the retina. Adapted from Gregory (1978).

sible for this perception of movement. When you follow the movement of a stimulus using eye movements, the background tends to stream past in the direction opposite to the direction of movement of the stimulus, providing a potential cue for the image–retina system to analyze. If you follow the movement of an illuminated stimulus against a dark background, however, movement is still perceived even though there is no moving background. This indicates that some other system must be operating under these conditions; it is what Gregory (1978) has termed the eye–head movement system.

There are two major classes of mechanisms that might account for the operation of the eye–head system. One possibility is the *inflow theory*, first suggested by Sir Charles Sherrington (1918); according to his theory, receptors in the eye muscles monitor the position of the eyes, and send this information to a hypothetical brain center that corrects the information coming in from the two eyes according to eye position (the eye–head center). The alternative way that eye position could feed into the eye–head center is known as the *outflow theory* of Helmholtz (1866). This theory suggests that it is not the receptors in the eye muscles that provide the necessary information about eye position, but that the neural signals sent by the brain to control the state of contraction of the extraocular muscles themselves serve as input to the eye–head center. Whichever way the system works, somehow the brain must be able to compare the signals coming in through the optic nerve with information about the speed and direction of movements of the eyes. These movements are often caused by changes in the state of contraction of the eye muscles, but they do not have to be. For example, the world moves around us as we walk from place to place, with or without eye movements. The information from the skeletal muscles about where and how fast the body is moving must be integrated with the visual images that are moving across our retinas, or else we would see the visual scene moving past us, instead of us moving past the visual scene.

Experimental evidence seems to favor the outflow theory. Consider what happens when you change the position of your eye by shoving it with your finger (gently, please!). If signals from your eye muscles were responsible for monitoring position, the world should remain stable, as they will accurately record position whether the movement was caused by an external push from your finger or the muscles themselves. If you perform this experiment on yourself, you should note that the world does in fact seem to move when you move your eye with a finger. Sherrington's inflow theory cannot account for this movement; however, the outflow theory does predict that movement will seem to occur in this situation. If the neural signal to eye muscles carries the critical information, this information will not be affected by an external (that is, by way of a finger) movement of the eyes; therefore the eye–head system will treat the shift

of images on the retina as being caused by movement of the world rather than the eyes.

Another way to demonstrate the validity of the outflow theory is to paralyze the eye muscles of a subject and have the subject attempt to move his or her eyes. The neural signals to the eye muscles are unaffected by paralyzing the muscles, but the eyes do not move so the image of the world on the retina remains stationary. Therefore, according to the outflow theory, it should seem that the eyes actually moved but that the world moved with them; in other words, the entire visual world should appear to jump from place to place. When the experiment was performed, this is exactly the result that was obtained (Howard & Templeton, 1966; Stevens *et al.*, 1976). If the system operated as suggested by inflow theory, the visual scene should seem to remain stationary. When the eye muscles were partially paralyzed, apparent position of objects could be explained by the errors in eye position (except in a complex field where other cues indicated position) (Matin *et al.*, 1982). Nevertheless, the question of inflow *versus* outflow is not settled. The situation is more complex than it seems, and other mechanisms may also be involved (Bridgeman *et al.*, 1994; Owens & Reed, 1994).

The eye–head movement system has two related functions: it must be able to monitor eye movements to keep your impression of the visual world stable as your eyes move from one position to another, and it must provide information about the speed and direction of a moving stimulus that is being followed using eye and head movements. When your eyes follow the movements of a stimulus, they do so with smooth pursuit movements (see Chapter 3). This type of eye movement only occurs when following a moving object; you cannot voluntarily make your eyes move in this manner. Saccadic eye movements, on the other hand, are under voluntary control and usually are not used to follow the movements of a stimulus; instead, they allow you to shift your attention from one aspect of the visual scene to another. When a saccadic eye movement occurs, therefore, the eye–head system can conclude that the images moving across the retina are a result of the eye movement and are not caused by the movement of a stimulus. Conversely, when a smooth pursuit movement occurs, it is because of a moving stimulus in the visual field, or because the subject is moving through the field. Cells have been found (in an area that responds both to vision and to limb movements) that respond to the motion of a stimulus *unless* the motion is caused by the animal's own motion (Hietanen & Perrett, 1996); that is, these cells must compute motion relative to the observer. <u>BOX 13.6</u>

Although experimenters have determined that the Helmholtz outflow theory provides a good explanation for the operation of the eye–head system, the actual parts of the brain that integrate neural signals that go to the eye muscles with those that come from the retina have not been well determined. Studies have identified some areas that are involved in this system, however. Miles & Fuller (1975), recording in a part of the monkey cerebellum called the flocculus, found

cells that responded only when the eyes were tracking a moving visual target. The firing rates of these cells were determined by the speed of the target; the faster the target moved, the faster the cells fired. Even when the monkey's head was mechanically moved by the experimenters while the animal was tracking a visual stimulus, the cells in this area of the brain were able to compensate for the head movements and respond in a way that accurately reflected the speed of the target. This area of the brain, therefore, is likely to be a part of the system that integrates visual and kinesthetic information to decide how objects in the physical world are moving.

Some of the integration of visual and extraretinal input can be seen in cells of the movement-sensitive area MT. A class of cells called pursuit cells respond when the eye is following (tracking) an object in an otherwise dark room (Komatsu & Wurtz, 1988a). Since the retinal image is stable during slow pursuit of the target, these cells must be responding to the movement of the eyes. Some

---

Box 13.6 Suppression of perceived motion during a saccade

The movements of a retinal image during a saccadic eye movement do not correspond to movement of objects in the visual world, so it is an advantage that the visual system has a way of ignoring them. One way that the visual system acts to disregard such moving images is to actively suppress the visual signals during a saccade. When visual sensitivity is tested during saccadic eye movements, it is found to be reduced by about a factor of 3 for a period of time shortly before, during, and after the movement (Chase & Kalil, 1972); such an inhibition even occurs in complete darkness (Riggs *et al.*, 1974). In general, thresholds for actual motion are higher when the motion occurs during a saccade, and the motion seems to have occurred after the saccade ended (Ilg & Hoffmann, 1993).

Suppression of sensitivity during saccades probably occurs at several levels in the visual system; however, Adey & Noda (1973) have found that, as early in the visual system as the lateral geniculate nucleus, the responses of cells can be suppressed during occurrence of a saccade. You may recall that suppression of the dimming due to eye blinks

seems to be a property of the lateral geniculate (see Box 7.2, p. 117).

An alternative mechanism for suppressing visual information present during a saccade is visual masking (see Chapter 9). Matin *et al.* (1972) showed that subjects perceived a vertical slit of light as a horizontal smear when the stimulus was present only during a saccade. When the stimulus remained after the saccade was over, however, the perception of the smear disappeared. Matin *et al.* hypothesized that this was an example of backward masking, whereby the stationary visual scene in the period after the saccade masked the stimulus that was present during the saccade. Campbell & Wurtz (1978) have found that forward masking also acts to suppress visual responses during saccades.

You can demonstrate the power of saccadic suppression by trying the following. Look at yourself in a mirror, and concentrate on your left eye. Now look at your right eye. Did you see your eyes move?

pursuit cells continue to respond even during eye blinks (Newsome *et al.*, 1988). These pursuit cells respond over a wide field, and prefer motion of a small stimulus in the direction opposite to that of the pursuit (Komatsu & Wurtz, 1988b). Unlike the smaller field cells that probably direct the pursuit motion, these larger cells are probably concerned with the perception of motion of the target. Note that although cells in the nearby motion area MST respond vigorously to motion, they do not respond to the movement of the background when the eyes are following a small, moving target in pursuit motion (Erickson & Thier, 1991).

Illusions of the eye-head system Information about the position of a moving target often comes from the efferent signals sent to control the eye muscles. Under certain conditions, however, this system provides insufficient or incorrect information, resulting either in an illusion of movement when in fact no movement has occurred, or in an inaccurate perception of the path of a moving object.

One illusion resulting in a faulty perception of movement is called the *autokinetic effect*; it occurs when a subject fixates on a small stationary object against a dark or undefined background. Under such conditions, the subject usually reports that the stimulus moves somewhat randomly within the field.

There are two types of mechanisms that might account for the autokinetic effect, and both seem to operate to some extent (Hochberg, 1971a). One possibility is that involuntary eye movements change the position of the stimulus image on the retina. As the movements are involuntary, there is no outflow of signals going to the eye muscles that the eye-head system can compare with image position, so that a perception of movement results. Matin & MacKinnon (1964) tested for autokinetic motion with a stabilized image, so that the retinal image could not move. They found that under these conditions the magnitude of the perceived movements was reduced, indicating that involuntary eye movements contribute to the autokinetic effect.

A second mechanism that may be partially responsible for the autokinetic phenomenon involves changes in muscle tension that normally occur during fixation on a stationary stimulus. While fixating for a relatively long period of time, the eye muscles fatigue, causing a change in the position of the eyes. The proponents of this mechanism suggest that because of this change in eye position, a voluntary signal to correct the drift will be emitted. This signal will be interpreted by the eye-head system as resulting from the movement of the stimulus in space, as the system had no information regarding the change in eye position that preceded it (Bruell & Albee, 1955). The validity of this mechanism rests on the assumption that the visual system is unaware of movements of the eyes that are not the result of neural directives from the brain; as you saw in comparing the inflow and outflow theories, this assumption seems to be valid.

Even when motion is actually present in the visual scene, the eye-head system does not always accurately reflect this motion. Smooth pursuit eye movements are limited in velocity, and sometimes the positions of the eyes lag significantly behind the target (Puckett & Steinman, 1969). This lag can produce inaccuracies in judging the path that a moving object follows. Festinger & Easton (1974) presented subjects with a target that moved along a square path at a velocity that could be varied by the experimenters. At stimulus speeds so rapid that smooth pursuit movements could not occur, the subjects accurately described the shape of the path that the target was following. At slower speeds, however, subjects reported a distortion of the path that changed with stimulus velocity. Figure 13.5 shows two perceived paths of the target. Both of the perceived paths are quite different from the actual path, which is a perfect square. This is a demonstration that the efferent information going to the eye muscles and feeding into the eye-head system does not always reflect the true position of a target in space. You can see this effect for yourself by running the demonstration 'Path of motion' associated with this chapter. The spot follows a perfectly square path.

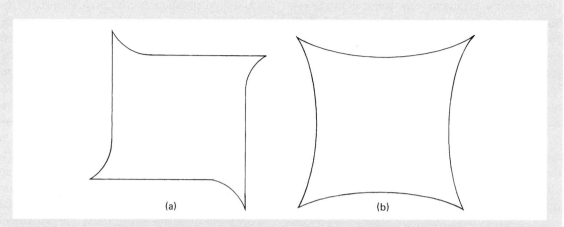

Fig. 13.5 Perceived stimulus paths for a stimulus moving in a square path. (a) Slow stimulus movement. (b) Faster stimulus movement. From Festinger, L. and A. M. Easton (1974) Inferences about the efferent system based on a perceptual illusion produced by eye movements. *Psych. Rev.* 81: 44–58. Copyright © by the American Psychological Association. Reprinted by permission. You can see this effect in the 'Path of motion' demonstration on the CD.

When visual information is sparse, as in the previous experiments, eye movements can be an important determinant of apparent motion. When the visual field is rich with information, however, these movements seem to be accounted for by the visual shifts they induce. For example, you are not fooled by your own body movements, which can have even more dramatic effects on the aim of your eyes than your eye and head movements. Perhaps an even more compelling argument is that you can watch and comprehend a movie in which the camera is moving. You clearly do not control the way the camera pans or moves, nor do you receive any kinesthetic or vestibular feedback about the motions the cameraman underwent, but you have no difficulty seeing which things in the scene are moving and which movements are due to the change in camera angle.

Perceived motion

This is leading to the question of how you perceive that something moved in the world, rather than that you moved relative to the world. That is, you want to know about things changing their spatial relationships with each other, or relative to you, as when something is flying toward your head. You are less interested in knowing that an image moved across your retina. But first, consider a case in which things seem to move, and there really was no motion.

Stroboscopic movement

When you watch a movie or a television show, there is absolutely no doubt in your mind that the images to which you are attending are physically moving. In reality, however, what you are seeing is a sequence of still pictures; movement is perceived because each picture is slightly different from the preceding one. Perceived movement caused by two or more stationary stimuli presented in sequence is called stroboscopic movement, and has a long history in perceptual psychology.

The classic experiment on this subject was published in 1912 by the German Gestalt psychologist Max Wertheimer; his method involved presenting in sequence two vertical lines placed close together. One line was exposed for a short time followed by a blank interval, then the second line was presented. By varying the length of the blank interval Wertheimer was able to produce a large number of different perceptual effects. If the blank interval was longer than 200 ms, the reported perception closely paralleled reality: subjects reported simply seeing two stationary lines with one being presented after the other. For intervals that lasted less than 30 ms, there was also no illusion — the two lines seemed to be presented simultaneously. With blank intervals lasting between 30 and 200 ms, a variety of movement illusions was obtained. The kind of movement reported depended on the exact interval length.

When the interval was relatively short (about 60 ms), the line seemed to move from one location to the other. Wertheimer called this optimal movement, while others have termed it beta movement (Kenkel, 1913). It is also referred to as *stroboscopic movement*. At longer intervals, the lines did not appear to move from place to place, but an illusion of movement persisted. This type of movement has been termed pure movement or phi movement. These illusions are collectively known as the *phi phenomenon*.

The world abounds with examples of the phi phenomenon. The signs that usher you into parking lots or movie theaters are often designed to produce stroboscopic movements. As noted, all of the motion on television and in the movies provides examples of this illusion. It is perhaps not surprising, given the massive use by the entertainment and advertising industries, that much research has been devoted to determining the exact stimulus parameters that affect the illusion of stroboscopic movement. Korte (1915) found a number of specific relationships between stimulus parame-

ters. He discovered that if the spatial distance between the two stimuli was increased, the blank interval also had to be lengthened in order to maintain the illusion at its optimal level. If the distance between the stimuli was kept constant, but stimulus strength was varied, it was found that the length of the blank interval had to vary inversely with strength to maintain the movement illusion. In other words, as the stimuli became dimmer, the blank interval had to get longer. Finally, when the blank interval length was held constant and the interstimulus distance was varied, the strength of the stimuli had to be increased as the distance was increased. These stimulus relationships have been named Korte's laws, and have subsequently been confirmed and extended by a number of investigators. While it may seem that most of the parameters of Korte's laws imply processing of motion early in the visual system (perhaps even in the retina), the 'interstimulus distance' includes distance in depth, not simply separation on the retina (Green & Odom, 1986). This implies processing at a higher level.

Is stroboscopic movement a special case of real movement, or are they independent phenomena? Most models of motion detection are set up to respond to either type of motion, for the delays between stimulation at separate points would be the same whether or not the stimulus traversed the intervening space (see Sejnowski *et al.*, 1988). Nevertheless, the question of whether they are really aspects of the same process remains. One indication that they may tap the same mechanisms is the finding that real motion in one direction can cancel apparent motion in the other (Gregory & Harris, 1984). BOX 13.7

Effects of context on the perception of motion

In many cases, the perceived velocity of a moving stimulus or even its direction of movement depends on the context in which the stimulus is seen. Workers who wish to measure the

Box 13.7 Presto! Change-O! (during stroboscopic motion)

One interesting aspect of the illusion of stroboscopic movement is what happens when the two stimuli in different positions are not identical, but differ either in color or in shape. It is easier to see stroboscopic movement between stimuli that are identical than between those that differ in shape, but motion is seen when the two stimuli are different (Shechter *et al.*, 1988). For example, in Fig. 13.6 (a), the stimulus in the first position is a square, while the stimulus that is presented after the blank interval is a triangle. When these stimuli are presented under conditions that evoke movement, subjects report not only that they perceive seeing the stimulus move, but that it seems to change shape smoothly from one type of stimulus to the other (Kolers & Pomerantz, 1971). If the subjects are asked what the shape of the stimulus was at some point in between the two positions, they report it looking more like the first stimulus if the point is nearer the position of that stimulus, and more like the second if the point is nearer that one.

However, if the two stimuli differ in color instead of shape, no such smooth transformation takes place. Kolers & von Grünau (1975, 1976) presented pairs of stimuli, the first of which was green and the second red (Fig. 13.6 b). They reasoned that if the visual system smoothly transformed shapes in the experiment previously discussed, perhaps it could transform colors in the same way. If so, as the stimulus appeared to move from one position to the other, it might continuously change color as it moved. When the experiment was performed, however, it was found that the stimulus stayed the same color as that in the first position until it passed the midway position between the two stimuli, where it abruptly changed to the color of the second stimulus. The fact that color changes abruptly while shape changes in a smooth manner suggests a major difference in the way that these two qualities are coded by the visual system.

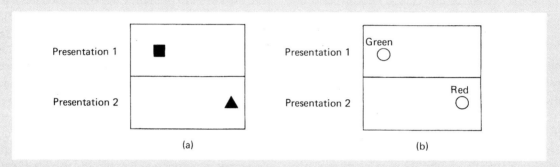

(a)   (b)

Fig. 13.6 Transformations of movement and color. (a) Sequential stimulus presentations where the stimuli are different in position and shape. The perception is of a moving stimulus that smoothly changes shape from a square to a triangle. (b) Sequential stimulus presentations of two colored discs, one red and one green, each in a different location. The perception is of a moving disc that abruptly changes color in the middle of the path.

movement sensitivity of single cells encounter a special kind of problem, because the receptive field of a cell is effectively an aperture or window (see Rubin *et al.*, 1995). When you look at a pattern like a line or set of stripes as it moves past an aperture, it appears to be moving at right angles to its orientation. A vertical line moving to the right and downward is indistinguishable from a vertical line

moving to the right (or moving to the right and upwards) when it is seen through a window (see Box 13.4 and try the 'motion past an aperture' demonstration on the CD).

The framework can also affect the apparent speed of movement. Consider the two situations shown in Fig. 13.7; in both cases, a continuous series of dark spots moves downward within a

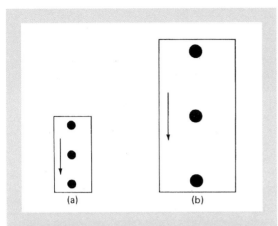

Fig. 13.7 Stimuli similar to those used by Brown (1931). The spots in the larger frame must travel twice as fast to be perceived as equal in velocity to the stimuli in the smaller frame.

rectangular framework. The only difference is that the framework on the right of the figure is twice as large as the framework on the left, as are the sizes of the spots and the physical distance between neighboring spots. If subjects are allowed to manipulate the speed at which the spots in the larger framework move, and are told to make the speeds in the two frameworks the same, they make the speed in the larger framework about twice the speed of the spots in the smaller framework (Brown, 1931). Thus, in order to make the velocities in the two situations seem identical, the velocity of the larger stimuli must be increased in direct proportion to the size of the framework.

This result makes sense if considered in light of what you know about depth perception. If two stimuli of similar form but different size are presented together, the larger one often seems as if it is positioned closer to the observer than the smaller one. If, in fact, the larger framework is regarded as being twice as close to the observer as the smaller framework, the actual velocity of the stimuli in units of visual angle per unit time would have to be twice that of the spots in the smaller framework in order for them to seem equal. This

effect explains why an airplane moving at several hundred miles per hour seems to move so slowly in the sky (where its distance is too great to estimate accurately).

Not only can the perceived speed of a moving object be affected by objects around it, but the perceived direction of motion can be changed as well. There are many situations in the physical world in which such effects occur; for example, consider a cloudy night sky with the moon ducking in and out of the drifting clouds. The moon is actually stationary relative to the clouds, but because clouds take up so much more room in the visual field than the moon, they appear to be stationary while the moon seems to move in the opposite direction from them. This is a phenomenon known as induced movement, where the apparent motion of the stimulus in question is 'induced' by movement of surrounding objects (Wallach, 1959). An artificial example of induced movement is shown in the 'Relative movement 1' demonstration for this chapter on the CD accompanying this book. The light blue rectangle is actually stationary on the screen, but seems to move leftward as the larger background moves to the right. Intuitively, it seems that the illusion of induced movement has a strong experiential base; usually in the real world, smaller objects move relative to the larger surrounding field. The importance of experience in this illusion is illustrated by the fact that objects that are known from experience to be mobile (people, airplanes, and so forth), are often more susceptible to induced movement than are objects that are usually stationary (Brosgole & Whalen, 1967). This is probably why the blue rectangle (which looks a bit like a window) shows a weak effect. Notice, by the way, that what happens is a small object seems to 'sail' in a large moving field (like the moon sailing through the clouds). This is neither inflow nor outflow, as the eyes do not move to track the apparently moving object (Owens & Reed, 1994). **BOX 13.8**

The importance of background in the perception of movement has also been emphasized in the work of James Gibson (1966, 1968; see the review

Box 13.8 Relative motion of a pigeon's head

Another 'natural' illustration of relative motion is shown in the demonstration 'Relative movement 2'. This is a cartoon (pardon my artwork!) drawing of a pigeon walking. As the bird walks, its head moves back and forth on its neck. It appears that the head moves back and forth in space. In fact, the head moves forward then stops while the body 'catches up'. You can see this by making the body invisible (a check-box to hide the body will appear after the first traverse of the screen) and watching the isolated head.

by Verri *et al.*, 1992). As an object moves through space, it successively covers different parts of the background and uncovers the portions through which it has just passed. Gibson called this process kinetic optical occlusion, and saw it as an important way for the subject to distinguish between objects moving through space and movement on the part of the subject through a stationary world. When a single object moves through space, the change in the texture of the background is limited to the region directly in front of and behind the object, while, if the observer is moving, there is a transformation of the entire visual world according to the principles of motion parallax (see p. 231-3). **BOX 13.9**

Where is the movement system in the brain? You encountered the specialized motion cells in MT, which receives most of its input from the magnocellular system. In Chapter 8, you learned that the dorsal stream might be largely responsible for analysis of motion. If this is so, a stimulus that the magnocellular system cannot discriminate from the background should not appear to move (even though the parvocellular system can see the stimulus). Such a stimulus is one that is equiluminant with the background.

Livingstone & Hubel (1987b) tested this hypothesis for a number of movement demonstrations. They cited evidence that equiluminant stimuli appeared to move more slowly than those with luminance contrast (Cavanagh *et al.*, 1984), and observations suggesting that stroboscopic motion disappears at equiluminance. From their demonstrations, they conclude that the magnocellular system is responsible for motion effects.

Nevertheless, some motion perception does depend on color.

On the other hand, a number of workers have found that MAEs can be obtained with equiluminant stimuli (Derrington & Badcock, 1985; Mullen & Baker, 1985; Papathomas *et al.*, 1991; Tyler & Cavanaugh, 1991), implicating a parvocellular motion system. Livingstone & Hubel counter that these effects may be the result of convergence of the parvocellular and magnocellular systems at higher levels, and do not imply that the parvocellular system itself encodes motion. Of course, you know that the two systems interact at a number of levels (see Fig. 8.6, p. 145), so some parvocellular influence should not be surprising.

Nevertheless, MT, at the gateway to the dorsal pathway, seems to be largely responsible for motion detection. You have already read about motion detectors in area MT and its nearby ally, MST. Even within MT, there seem to be subdivisions that are sensitive to different kinds of motion (Howard *et al.*, 1996). MT cells have responses that match well with the psychophysical responses to motion (Britten *et al.*, 1992), and a patient with damage to MT shows deficits that fit this picture of MT as a key area for motion perception (Vaina *et al.*, 1990).

MST cells seem more specific to the type of motion, including the flow fields Gibson suggested. Like MT, MST cells are clustered according to whether they are sensitive to rotation, expansion, contraction, or translation (Lagae *et al.*, 1994). MST cells respond to the motion, regardless of the stimulus that is moving (Geesaman & Andersen, 1996). Models for motion detection show that these responses are appropriate for the task of discrimi-

Box 13.9 The Pulfrich effect

One of the classic movement illusions is called the Pulfrich effect, as illustrated in Fig. 13.8. A subject viewing a pendulum swinging sees the pendulum bob moving from side to side along the same path. However, when one eye is covered with a filter that attenuates the amount of light reaching that eye (a lens from an old pair of sunglasses will do), the pendulum bob seems to move in depth in an elliptical path that goes forward and away from the observer.

Most investigators consider this illusion to be caused by the fact that receptors in the eye respond more slowly to

dim light than to bright light (Brauner & Lit, 1976; Gregory, 1978). The fact that the filtered eye receives less light from the stimulus causes it to respond more slowly, resulting in a delay in the transmission of signals from that eye. Therefore, at a given time, the position of the bob as seen from the filtered eye lags behind the position as seen from the other eye. This causes a binocular disparity that is consistent with a stimulus moving in an elliptical path such as that shown in the figure.

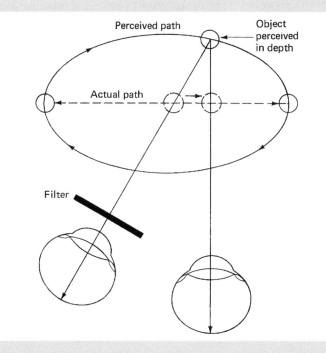

Fig. 13.8 The Pulfrich phenomenon. The eye with a dimmer image perceives the pendulum ball as lagging behind the position as seen by the eye without a filter. This is consistent with the ball actually traveling in an elliptical path, as shown.

nating between self motion and motion of objects around us (Zemel & Sejnowski, 1998). This processing apparently continues into other areas of parietal cortex (Siegel & Read, 1997). But don't become too comfortable with the idea of each cortical area performing its own circumscribed task; remember, these areas all interact. For example, even cells in 'simple' area MT show modification of their responses according to the interpretation of the stimulus (Stone & Albright, 1992).

Suggested readings

A number of books have detailed and well-written chapters on movement perception. The chapter on movement in Irvin Rock's book *An introduction to perception* (Macmillan, 1975) is interesting and easy to read. For more detail on apparent movement and movement illusions, see Julian Hochberg's chapter on space and movement in *Woodworth and Schlossberg's experimental psychology*, edited by J. W. Kling and L. A. Riggs (Holt, Rinehart, and Winston, 1971); for a more historical perspective, the place to go is C. H. Graham's movement chapter in *Vision and visual perception* (Wiley, 1965). The chapter on movement in L. Kaufman's *Sight and mind* (Oxford University Press, Oxford, 1974) provides the serious student with an excellent in-depth discussion of the topics of real and apparent movement. Interesting treatments may also be found in *The motion aftereffect*, edited by G. Mather, F. Verstraten and S. Anstis (MIT Press, 1998). Finally, a nice review is presented in 'Interactions between motion, depth, color and form: the utilitarian theory of perception', by V.S. Ramachandran in *Vision: coding and efficiency*, edited by Colin Blakemore (a book recommended in association with several other chapters), pp. 346–360.

Hans Wallach's *Scientific American* article, 'The perception of motion' (July 1959; offprint #409) gives good coverage of the topic of induced movement as well as other subjects, while Kolers' arti-cle, 'The illusion of movement' (October 1964; off-print #487), is a very interesting article covering just what the title says. Also worth reading is Johansson's article, 'Visual motion perception' (June 1975; offprint #564), which covers a number of topics not discussed in this chapter, such as the phenomenon of biological motion. The perception of motion in the phi phenomenon, especially in cases in which the direction of motion may be ambiguous, is the topic of 'The perception of apparent motion', by V. S. Ramachandran and S. M. Anstis (June 1986). Finally, Sekuler and Levinson discussed their research on direction-specific motion detectors in an article entitled 'The perception of moving targets' (January 1977; offprint #575). The Wallach and Kolers articles are reprinted in *Perception: mechanisms and models*, edited by R. Held and W. Richards (W. H. Freeman, 1972), while the Johansson article is reprinted in *Recent progress in perception*, edited by Held and Richards (W. H. Freeman, 1976). The Ramachandran and Anstis article may be found in *The perceptual world*, edited by Irvin Rock (W. H. Freeman, 1990).

Chapter 14
Color vision

The physical stimulus

So far it may seem as if there is no more to the visual world than a quantification of light: more light, less light, light here, light moving there. But we also live in a world of colors. Color attracts attention, enhances contrast between objects of similar lightness, and even appeals to your aesthetic sense. It helps recognize objects; it is of particular value for finding and identifying food, for finding fruits among the leaves (Osorio & Vorobyev, 1996). It is especially useful when recognition depends on memory (Sachtler & Zaidi, 1992). Unlike your ability to comprehend objects, which is learned, color seems to be inborn. Blind people with their sight restored first recognize colors, long before they can identify objects and scenes (Sacks, 1995).

On the other hand, you know that color is not essential for visual perception. For years, TV and movies were in black and white, and no one had any trouble recognizing the images. In fact, nuances are sometimes better conveyed *without* color, which is why photographers and cinematographers still use black and white for some projects. Color may not be essential, but it adds another dimension to visual perception. Actually, as you will see, it adds two additional dimensions.

As real as color seems, it is, in fact, a purely psychological phenomenon. Light rays are not colored; they are radiations of electromagnetic energy of differing wavelengths. The attribute called 'color' is entirely a fabrication of your visual system.

The physical stimulus for color vision, as for any vision, is light. Different wavelengths of light distinguish different colors, just as different energies correspond to different luminances. As you recall from the beginning of Chapter 3, light may be described as either a wave phenomenon or a particle phenomenon. In speaking of colors, it is generally best to refer to the wavelength of light. Wavelength is measured in nanometers (nm): $1 \text{ nm} = 10^{-9} \text{ m}$, or 1/1000th of 1/1000th of a millimeter, which is itself 1/1000th of a meter.

When light is absorbed by a photopigment, however, it is more convenient to count the number of quanta (photons) captured, and to characterize each photon by its energy. Here, the energy of each quantum corresponds to the inverse of the wavelength of the light (Chapter 3). Rather than measure the total energy of the light (number of photons times their individual energies), one can count the number of photons.

The simplest kind of light to talk about would be one that is totally homogeneous—all the quanta having the same energy. Such a light would consist of a single wavelength only, and it would be completely characterized by its wavelength and total energy. A light of only one wavelength is as *pure* a light as possible, and is called *monochromatic* (*mono* = one, *chroma* = color).

It is difficult to produce a truly monochromatic light; lights called 'monochromatic' generally contain all wavelengths within a restricted spectral range. Natural lights, on the other hand, are *broad band*, the opposite of monochromatic. They contain significant amounts of a large portion of the electromagnetic spectrum. The light emitted by the sun contains nearly equal amounts of all wavelengths, and appears white to human observers. White is the least pure color there is.

Isaac Newton is credited with the first demonstration that sunlight is not qualitatively different from colored lights, but is merely the sum of all the colored lights. In his demonstration, white light from the sun passed through a slit that restricted the light to a fine line. The line of light impinged on a prism, where the rays were bent by refraction. The amount of bending of light depends on its wavelength; short wavelengths are refracted (bent) the most, and long wavelengths the least. As a result, the light was spread out and arrayed by wavelength on a white screen. This display, the 'spectrum', is a rainbow of color, ranging from the longest wavelengths (red light of about 700 nm) to the shortest (violet light of approximately 400 nm). The major spectral colors, in order, are: **r**ed, **o**range, **y**ellow, **g**reen, **b**lue, and **v**iolet.

Newton's prism decomposed white light into its spectral components; presumably, they could be recombined back into white light. Newton did this by using a lens to refocus the colors that had been dispersed by his prism, projecting a white patch in spite of the presence of the prism. In effect, the lens took the different wavelengths of light that had been spread out by the prism and

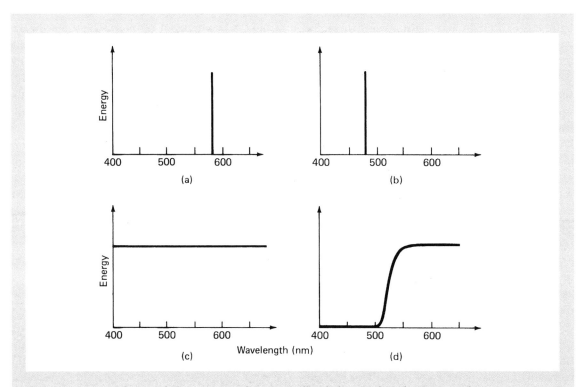

Fig. 14.1 Spectra of various lights. (a) Monochromatic yellow light, wavelength = 580 nm. (b) Monochromatic blue light, wavelength = 480 nm. (c) Equal energy white light. (d) Yellow light such as you might obtain by passing sunlight through yellow cellophane.

projected them onto the same area of screen. It thus *added* the colors back together to produce a white light.

How can you represent white light? Each of the colors of the spectrum may be characterized by its respective peak wavelength, but white sunlight contains all wavelengths. Everyday lights contain a range of wavelengths, but in differing amounts. The usual way to represent the physical nature of any light is by graphing its *spectrum* (a slightly different usage of the word than the 'rainbow' Newton's prism created). A spectrum is simply a catalog of how much energy there is at each wavelength in a given light—just as a spectrum represented contrast at each spatial frequency in Chapter 9. Graphically, it is a plot of energy versus wavelength, as shown in Fig. 14.1 Monochromatic lights have spectra that are single spikes at the wavelength of the light. Fig. 14.1 (a) shows the spectrum of a yellow monochromatic light, wavelength = 580 nm; part (b) shows a blue monochromatic light, wavelength = 480 nm; part (c) shows an equal energy white light, with all wavelengths equally represented; part (d) is the spectrum of a light that would appear yellow, although it clearly also contains wavelengths that by themselves would appear orange or red.

Newton wondered whether white light necessarily contained the entire spectrum or whether parts of it could be omitted. He tried selectively blocking bands of the spectrum before re-adding the components. He found that it was possible to block large amounts of the spectrum and still obtain white; if only four basic colors were present, white light resulted. Newton apparently never bothered to see whether even fewer primary colors would be sufficient, because the situation already seemed too artificial to be of interest to a physicist. As you will see, exactly three primary colors are necessary in general, and the implications of this fact are quite noteworthy.

Color mixture

Newton devised a system by which he could describe lights according to the spectral colors they looked like, with enough white added to make them less pure. The color itself is called the *hue*; the relative amount of color is the *saturation*. When two spectral colors are mixed, a new hue results. If the proportions of the two spectral lights are unequal, the mixture will be closer in hue to the wavelength that is represented in higher proportion.

Newton's system depends on the way the lights appear; that is, it is based on the psychological attributes of lights. The attributes of lights introduced at the beginning of this chapter (wavelength, energy, and purity) are physical attributes. There is a rough correspondence between these: wavelength is a major determinant of hue, energy has a great effect on the luminance (brightness), and purity influences saturation. But the terms cannot be used interchangeably. As you learned in Chapter 2, the hue of a given wavelength light depends somewhat on its energy (Bezold–Brücke hue shift), and the relative luminance of lights of the same energy depends on their wavelengths. Monochromatic lights (all of perfect purity, but different wavelengths) differ in saturation.

Additive mixture

At this point, it is best to clarify what happens when colors are mixed. In visual science, most color mixtures are *additive*, like Newton's recombination of the spectrum into white. Additive color mixture is exactly what it sounds like: two (or more) lights are added to each other to make a new light.

There are several ways to add lights. Newton's was the most direct: projections of each color are superimposed on a screen. This is also how lights are usually added in the laboratory. There are three or four projectors (each like a slide projector), all aimed at the same screen. Each projector has a filter or some other means of selecting a narrow band of wavelengths from the white light emitted by its bulb. Each also has a control that allows the total amount of light it emits to be changed. The light on the screen is the sum of the lights from each projector; for instance, if there are two projectors and each is fitted with so sharp a filter that it emits only a single wavelength, both wavelengths would be reflected from the screen. The spectrum of the light coming to the observer would be the *sum* of the spectra of the lights from each projector. **BOX 14.1**

Another way to add lights is to place the colored lights side by side in close proximity. If colored patches are small enough, you cannot resolve them separately. If several patches fit into each ganglion cell receptive field, the ganglion cells are unable to distinguish between patches and diffuse overlapped lights, and so respond as if the lights were superimposed. In fact, this is how a color television works. Examine the TV screen closely; it is made up of minute patches of red, green, and blue. Step back from the screen; the individual color patches merge, and what you see is the additive mixtures of the three colors. (It is also the principle explored by the pointilist school of painting.) **BOX 14.2**

The three primary colors of additive color mix-

ture are generally taken to be red, green, and blue. For reasons that should become clear later in this chapter, those three are the colors most capable of being added to make any other color. They are the only three colors on a color television screen, and are the three on a color mixing wheel.

Yellow seems intuitively to be a primary color, but in fact an excellent yellow can be made by the additive mixture of red and green (see the 'Color mixing' demonstration on the CD accompanying this book). White is also readily obtained from red, green, and blue. The additive mixture of all three, shown in the central fat triangle of the color mixing demonstration, is a white that cannot be distinguished from sunlight (a fact Newton stopped just short of discovering). If white is the sum of red, green, and blue, however, it must also be the sum of yellow and blue, as red and green mixed make yellow. In fact, if you take the pure spectral yellow that is exactly matched by the mixture of red and green and add it to blue, white results. Alternatively, you could split the lights a different way, and note that blue + green gives blue-green, and blue-green + red gives white (this also works with a spectral blue-green + red). Similarly, red + blue makes purple, and purple + green yields white (although there is no spectral light that appears purple). All these sums may be seen in the 'Color mixing' demonstration. **BOX 14.3**

The sums in additive mixtures do not depend on the actual spectra of the component lights. The yel-

---

Box 14.1 Laboratory color apparatus

The laboratory apparatus actually used to present color mixtures is more complex than described above. The 'projectors' are more precisely made than the slide projector you may have at home, with optics that are specifically designed to avoid any color distortion in the images. Each projector has neutral density (gray) filters that cut the light down to an appropriate level. Often, the control of wavelength is by *monochromators*, instruments that select a narrow band of light to transmit, and block the rest.

The projectors do not aim at a screen, but combine optically through partially reflecting mirrors and project directly through the pupil of the observer's eye onto the retina. This kind of projection system is called a *Maxwellian* view system; it is the same principle as the eyepiece of a microscope or telescope that projects an image into the eye.

Box 14.2 Temporal summation of colors

Still another way to add colors is to present them in sufficiently rapid succession that they cannot be resolved as separate flashes. When a light flickers at a rapid enough rate, it is perceived as steady—for example, fluorescent lights shut off completely 120 times every second yet they give what appears to be steady light (see Box 12.4, p. 254). If two colors were alternated (instead of alternating light and dark), their additive mixture would be seen. The mixture is additive because both colors would be in the mix-

ture—as a time average. The result is the same as physical superposition. This is the principle used in a color wheel, one of which may be lying around in your psychology department storage closet from pre-computer days. The color wheel consists of a motor that rotates a disc at high speed. Sectors of colored paper are attached so that when it rotates, the sectors fuse and the additive mixture is seen. At any point, the colors succeed each other at a rapid rate, and add.

Box 14.3 Demonstration of additive color mixtures

The facts of color mixture will be clearer (and more believable) if you demonstrate them to yourself. You should run the 'Color mixing' demonstration program and try each of the mixtures as you read about them.

The color mixing demonstration simulates what you would see if you had three spotlights (one producing red light, one producing green light, and one producing blue light) each shining a circular patch on a colorless screen. The spotlights are represented at the lower left. Where two circular patches overlap, the additive mixture color appears. These are in fact the real additive mixtures because the three color guns that paint your screen make pixels so small you cannot distinguish them (look with a strong magnifier). The red, green, and blue patches are obtained by turning on only that color gun and turning off the other two; where patches overlap, both (or all three) guns are active. The green gun paints the upper right patch; where it overlaps the red patch (to the left), yellow is produced; where it overlaps the blue patch (lower right), aqua is produced. Where all three overlap, the area is white (all three guns at the same strength). The gray background is produced by all three guns at equal strength, but a lower strength than in the pattern areas.

The color mixing demonstration requires high color resolution (see Box P2, p. ix). If your monitor is set for 256 colors (or less), the 'Color mixing' demonstration displays a yellow warning. You can quit the program and set your monitor for higher color resolution, or you can ignore the message and continue. If you continue, you will see the red, green, and blue pattern described above, but you will not be able to adjust the colors.

If, however, you have high enough color resolution, you will see the red, green, and blue pattern, with three slider adjustments to the right. The three sliders are labeled red, green, and blue, and allow you to adjust the strength of each of the colors (a box above each tells you what fraction of the maximum possible light you have selected). For example, if you set the blue to 0.00, only the red and green circles will remain, with a yellow lens-shaped intersection where they overlap. Increase red and decrease green, and the yellow becomes orange. Decrease red but decrease green even more and it looks brown. Increase the green, and the yellow becomes pea-green. Play with various two-way and three-way combinations and observe how the colors mix.

low that mixes with blue to make white light could be a mixture of red and green, or it could be any yellow, including a monochromatic yellow. If you add monochromatic yellow (580 nm) with monochromatic blue (480 nm), the resulting spectrum

would consist of two points (the yellow and blue spectra are given in Fig. 14.1; the result is shown in Fig. 14.2). This mixture, although obviously quite different *physically* from the white shown in Fig. 14.1(c), would appear white; in fact, the two whites

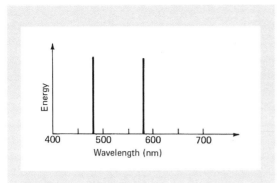

Fig. 14.2 Spectrum of the white light made by an additive mixture of monochromatic blue light (480 nm) with monochromatic yellow light (580 nm).

would be indistinguishable. Shown a white, you could not state whether it was equal energy, a mixture of 480 + 580, or any of the infinitely many other mixtures that make white.

Subtractive mixture

Although additive color mixing is typically used in visual science, you should know that there is another more familiar kind: *subtractive* color mixing. Subtractive mixing is the exact opposite of additive mixing, in which lights are superimposed so there is more light in the mixture than in either component; in subtractive mixing light is successively removed, so there is less light in the mixture than in either component.

The simplest way to conceive subtractive mixing is by considering stacking colored filters. A colored filter is a piece of material (for example, cellophane) that selectively removes some wavelengths of light while transmitting the others. A red filter makes white light red by removing all the short- and medium-wavelength light, leaving only the long-wavelength light. A common type of yellow filter passes medium- and long-wavelength light but attenuates short-wavelength light. It therefore makes equal energy white light look yellow (with a spectrum like that in Fig. 14.1d), but has virtually

no effect on long-wavelength light, and appears opaque in deep blue light.

A simple way to make subtractive color mixtures is by stacking filters so the light passes successively through two or more of them. Each filter blocks certain wavelengths while transmitting others; the characteristics of a filter are represented by a plot called the *transmission curve*, which shows the percentage of incident light that gets through the filter (is transmitted) as a function of its wavelength. Transmission curves for yellow and blue filters are shown on the left in Fig. 14.3 (b) and (d), which demonstrates the subtractive mixture of yellow and blue.

The mixture starts with white light containing all wavelengths (Fig. 14.3a). It passes into the yellow filter, which has a transmission curve (Fig. 14.3b) indicating that it allows most of the long- and medium-wavelength light to pass through it, but it subtracts (removes by absorbing) short-wavelength light. The result is yellow light containing long- and medium- but not short-wavelength light (Fig. 14.3c). The yellow light impinges on a blue filter (Fig. 14.3d) that blocks long- but transmits short- and medium-wavelength light. The result, shown in Fig. 14.3(e), is light of medium wavelength only; the long wavelengths were removed by the blue filter and the short wavelengths by the yellow filter. The medium-wavelength light remaining appears green, which is the subtractive mixture of yellow and blue (just like you learned in kindergarten). **BOX 14.4**

The resulting color in subtractive mixing is what is 'left over' when each filter has removed certain wavelengths. The physical stimulus is what indicates the color—there are no surprises like the sum of monochromatic blue and yellow. In fact, the mixture that results depends on the inefficiency of the filters. If you stacked ideal yellow and blue filters (that passed monochromatic yellow light and blue light, respectively), the mixture would not be green; it would be black, as *no* light could get through (Fig. 14.4).

The mixture of colored paints is also subtractive, for paint is essentially a suspension of microscopic

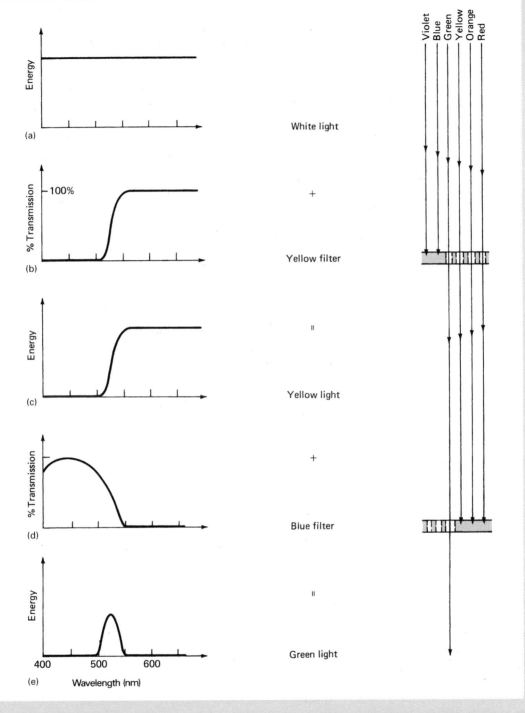

Fig. 14.3 Subtractive mixture of yellow and blue to give green. *Left*: Spectra or filter characteristics. *Right*: A schematic of the process.

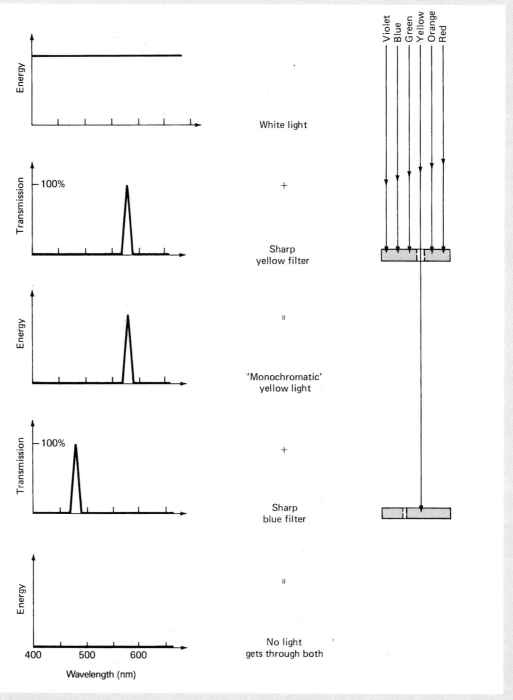

Fig. 14.4 Subtractive mixture with an extremely selective yellow filter and an extremely selective blue filter to give no light (black).

Box 14.4 Demonstrate subtractive mixing

Demonstrate subtractive color mixing by using some scraps of colored acetate. You can use candy wrappers, or the clear colored report covers sold in your bookstore. Get a piece of red, a piece of green, a piece of yellow, and a piece of blue. Hold any two scraps together, and the subtractive mixture results. Notice that holding red, green, and blue together results in a nearly opaque

combination: each filter removes some light, and if the filters are good enough, nothing gets through. This is in contrast to the generation of white by adding the three additive primary colors. Now stack yellow and blue, to get green. Remember, the additive mixture of yellow (the sum of red and green) plus blue gave white.

filters. When you paint a sheet of white paper green, you are covering it with a filter that prevents the reflection of long- and short-wavelength light, leaving only the medium wavelengths. When you mix paints, you are stacking the filters, and the rules of subtractive mixture apply. With each additional filter in the mixture, less light is transmitted; mixing all the colors in the paint box gives a muddy brown because very little gets through.

Psychophysics of color

A large body of experimental data has been collected to define the laws of additive mixture. The fundamental law is that any colored light can be matched by a combination of three primary lights. Any light, regardless of its actual spectrum, can be matched using only three primary colors; this includes white, spectral colors, or any other light there is. The primary colors themselves can, in fact, be almost anything—spectral (monochromatic) lights, or lights of some complex spectrum. The only restriction is that none of them can be matched by a mixture of the other two—if that were possible, there would actually be only two primaries.

Color matching is done by having the subject look at a 'split field', a display with two halves (Fig. 14.5). In one half of the field is the light to be

matched, in the other is the sum of the three primary colors to be used to make the match. The subject adjusts the amounts of each primary until satisfied that the two halves look identical. When the subject can detect no difference between the halves, a match has been made, and the amounts of each of the primary colors required can be recorded. The match is purely psychological, for the spectra of the halves can be quite different— they only *look* alike. Such a match is called a *metameric* match.

Remember, any three lights could serve as the primary colors (with that one restriction). Suppose you chose a system of primary colors in which the usual red was replaced with yellow. How could a subject match red light using only yellow, green,

Fig. 14.5 Stimulus display for metameric matching.

and blue? Suppose the light to be matched (the red) is on the left side of the split field; no matter how much yellow, green, or blue is added to the right side it can never become red. In particular, the more green that is added, the less red the field appears; what is needed is to put in less green. In fact, what is needed is less than none, a negative amount!

The physical correlate of negative light in a color match is light in the 'wrong' half of the field. That is, the match is made by putting some green primary in the left field, added to the color to be matched (the red). The red and green add to make yellow, which is matched by the yellow primary on the right—*voilà!* the two half-fields appear identical. You cannot create (*mix*) any color, but you can make a metameric *match* to any color with three primary colors if you are allowed to use negative amounts of one or more of the primary colors. In other words, the two half-fields can be made to look identical when three primary colors are available to be added to either one. Notice the distinction between mixing and matching colors: to mix is to create a specific color of some description; to match is to make two lights look identical (but not necessarily like the original light that is matched). **BOX 14.5**

Color space

The remarkable fact that three primary colors are sufficient for any and all metameric matches means that there is a simple way to represent any colored light. Think of the three primary colors in a matching experiment as the axes of a three-dimensional space (such as the one in Fig. 14.6); every light is represented by a point in that space, for it can be matched by a certain amount of primary color 1, an amount of primary color 2, and some amount of primary color 3. You need three dimensions because you need three primaries. Any light's appearance (*not* its physical make-up) can be completely specified by its location in the space; that is, by its *coordinates.*

The particular set of primary colors chosen was arbitrary. The only restriction was that no primary could be matched by a mixture of the other two. If a different set of primaries were chosen, the color space would look different; however, you can get back and forth between the two representations

---

Box 14.5 Negative light—an algebraic analogy

Negative light sounds like cheating, but in fact it is a way of saying that metameric matching is like an algebraic manipulation. The split field is an equation in need of solution: on the left is some value, the light to be matched, which you can call *x*. On the right is the sum of the three primaries (1, 2, and 3), the amounts of which the subject must choose to satisfy the match. There are thus three values, a_1, a_2, and a_3, which are the amounts of each primary selected to make the metameric match. The equation balances when values of the three have been chosen to make the two half-fields look identical: that is to say

$$x = a_1 + a_2 + a_3.$$

This 'equation' should be interpreted to say: 'light *x* looks like the additive mixture of a_1 of primary color 1, plus a_2 of primary color 2, plus a_3 of primary color 3'.

Suppose the solution required a negative second primary color; that is, a_2 is negative:

$$x = a_1 - a_2 + a_3.$$

In algebra, there would be no objection to rearranging this equation to read

$$x + a_2 = a_1 + a_3,$$

and the same is true in metameric matches. (The interpretation of the last equation is that there is a match when the light to be matched is added to a_2 of primary color 2 in the left field, and a_1 of primary color 1 is added to a_3 of primary color 3 in the right half-field.)

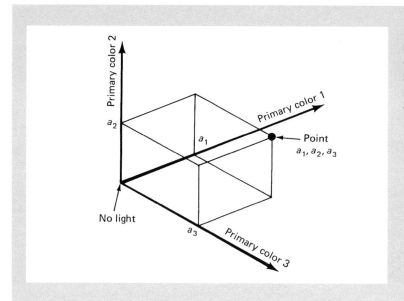

Fig. 14.6 Location of a point in color space. The color is specified by the amount of each primary color required to make a metameric match to it.

by noting that each primary in one space is a point in the other, and vice versa. The computations are tedious, but it is possible to get from any system to any other just by knowing the three primary colors used for each.

Three dimensions are a lot easier to deal with than the infinite number of color matches you might wish to describe, but making graphs in three dimensions is difficult. Wouldn't it be nice if you could represent color space on a two-dimensional plane, like a sheet of graph paper? Happily, you can do this with one simplification: consider each of the primary colors as a proportion of the total energy. Then the sum of the three primary colors used in any match must be 1.0 (unity—note, however, that the proportion devoted to any one primary could be greater than 1.0 because another might be negative). Since the sum is always unity, the system is reduced to two dimensions; the amount of the third primary color is completely determined by the amounts of the other two and the requirement that the three sum to unity. There are only two free variables (two degrees of freedom), so you need only two axes. Another way to look at this is to note

that the requirement of summing to unity means all colors are confined to a plane in the color space. This plane is shown in Fig. 14.7.

The CIE color diagram

Now you have reduced the three-dimensional color space to a plane by considering each primary color as a proportion of the total energy. It is important to remember that this two-dimensional plane still represents a three-color system. Each of the three primary colors is represented by a point in the plane, and the lines connecting these points (an equilateral triangle) are the axes of a color coordinate system (Fig. 14.7b). Three axes collapse into two dimensions because they have been given the special relationship that their sum is 1.

You could use the color plane in Fig. 14.7(b), but it is easier to work with axes that are perpendicular to each other, not at 60°. If you imagine stretching the triangle in Fig. 14.7(b) as if it were made of rubber, the angle at a_3 would straighten out into a right angle (this is a linear transformation that is mathematically straightforward). Now you have the normal-looking graph shown in Fig. 14.8. The

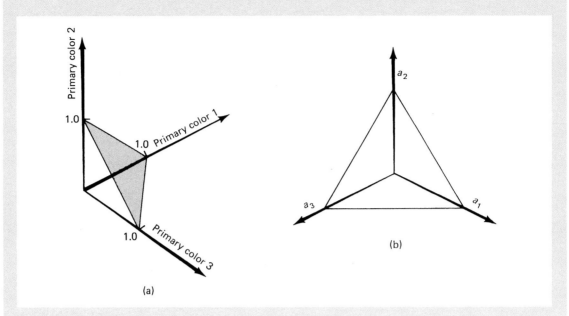

Fig. 14.7 The unit plane in color space. (a) Location of the unit plane in the color space of Fig. 14.6. (b) Direct view of the unit plane.

vertical axis is a_2 (the amount of the second primary color), the horizontal axis is a_1 (the amount of the first primary color), and the third primary color is at the origin.

You can put landmarks on this graph as soon as the three primary colors are specified. There is a standard set of primary colors that is almost invariably used, defined in 1931 by an international body called the *Commission Internationale de l'Éclairage* (International Commission on Illumination), or *CIE*. Although the primaries they chose may not be those we would pick today, all color data have been displayed on a color map derived from their primary colors (called the *CIE diagram*).

The first thing to show on the diagram are those lights it is easiest to define, the monochromatic lights. On Fig. 14.8 there is a curve, called the *spectrum locus*, that traces the location of all the monochromatic lights from 400 to 700 nm (some salient ones are indicated). The other interesting point is

equal energy white, which lies near the middle of the picture (marked 'W').

The CIE diagram summarizes all the facts of color mixture. To predict the color of an additive mixture of any two colors, find the coordinates of each, and draw the straight line that connects them. The mixture color lies on this line, at a distance from each of them inversely proportional to the amount of it in the mixture. (If lights were weights, and each weight sat on an end of the straight line, the appearance of the color mixture would be where the fulcrum must be placed for the seesaw to balance.)

As an example, suppose you mixed monochromatic green at 555 nm with monochromatic red at 620 nm. The line connecting those two colors is shown in bold on Fig. 14.9; in nearly equal mixture, the two exactly match monochromatic yellow (580 nm). That is, you cannot distinguish between monochromatic yellow and a mixture of monochromatic red with monochromatic green.

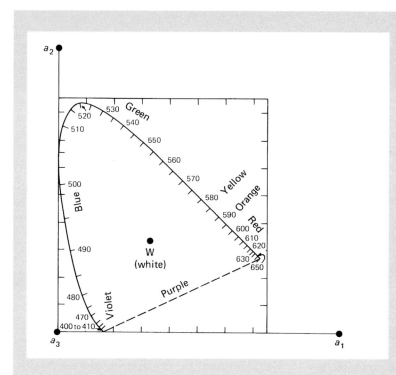

Fig. 14.8 The CIE color diagram (unit plane), showing the spectrum locus and white. Color appearances are indicated.

Now consider a mixture of monochromatic yellow at 580 nm with monochromatic blue at 480 nm. In nearly equal amounts they are indistinguishable from equal energy white (see Fig. 14.9). But you just saw that the monochromatic yellow is identical to a mixture of red and green; if the mixture yellow had been used instead, the same white would result from a sum of red, green, and blue. You can see that there are an infinite number of ways in which the identical white could be produced.

Now consider an equal mixture of 505 nm monochromatic blue-green with a monochromatic yellow-green of 550 nm, again shown in Fig. 14.9. The mixture lies inside the spectrum locus, but is clearly not white. In fact, it is equivalent to (it matches) a mixture of 520 nm green and white (with about twice as much of the green as the white). It is therefore fair to say that the 505 + 550 mixture is like a mixture of 520 and white. It is the same color (hue) but less saturated than monochromatic 520.

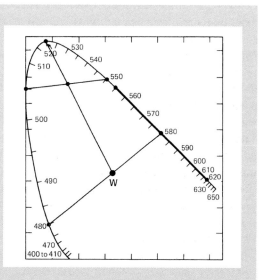

Fig. 14.9 Color mixtures on the CIE diagram. Each line represents a color mixture discussed in the text.

The spectrum locus is the purest and most saturated of real lights of any particular hue; lights inside it are less saturated than the corresponding spectral hues. As you can quickly convince yourself, mixtures of spectral lights are never more saturated than the spectral light of the matching hue. In general, the spectrum locus is a convex curve, so any mixture of two spectral lights is represented by a secant that lies within the locus (and is therefore closer to white than the locus itself). Except in the range from about 550 to 700 nm (where the spectrum locus is essentially a straight line), the mixtures of spectral lights are less saturated than the matching hue; as more and more spectral lights are added, the saturation declines, until all lights together yield the least saturated light, white.

As the purity of mixtures of spectral lights is never greater than 1, you may wonder if it is possible to achieve lights that are outside the spectrum locus—that is, more saturated than the spectral light of the same hue. The answer is yes, but not with real lights. The colors outside the spectrum locus may be matched by using negative amounts of some of the spectral colors. Such colors cannot actually be achieved as real lights, and are therefore called imaginary.

Now suppose that real colors are to be mixed with only three primary colors. Each primary color, if it is a real light, is represented by a point somewhere on or inside the spectrum locus. The three may be joined by a triangle; just as mixtures of spectral lights cannot extend outside the spectrum locus, mixtures of these three primary colors cannot extend outside the triangle connecting them. (Remember, you are using these primary colors to create colors and therefore cannot make use of negative amounts of them.) This explains why the three colors chosen as primaries for color television are red, green, and blue. They span the spectrum locus, which is the area of all real lights, as well as any three real colors possibly can. With any other choice, the triangle would be smaller, and some colors would be unobtainable.

Finally, consider the primary colors of the CIE diagram. All three are outside the spectrum locus; thus they are all imaginary. Primary color 1 is the 'red'; it consists of red light, strengthened in its redness by negative green. Primary color 2 is the 'green'; it has negative red and blue. Primary color 3 (at the origin) is 'blue'; it also has negative red in it.

The CIE diagram is only one possible diagram, but any other would be remappable into the CIE. The diagram is simply a convenient, standard way to summarize the rules of color mixture. That it works for all the color mixing experiments that have been performed demonstrates that it is sufficient for the specification of colors.

Implications for color theory

The color-matching experiments discussed in the last section showed that any arbitrary color could be exactly matched by an appropriate combination of three primary colors. This three-dimensionality of the human visual system is expressed formally by the CIE color space. It is reasonable to suppose that the three-dimensional nature of our color vision is related to the fact that we have three different cone types in our retina. To demonstrate this, start with a color vision system consisting of only one receptor type, and work up to a three-cone system.

Monochromacy

Consider a visual system with only one type of receptor. Suppose that the absorption spectrum of the visual pigment in this receptor is as shown in Fig. 14.10. From the figure, you can see that this receptor is most efficient at catching quanta (photons) when the stimulus is monochromatic light of 505 nm, with absorbance decreasing as the wavelength gets longer or shorter than 505 nm.

How does a visual system with only one type of

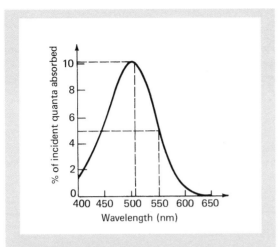

Fig. 14.10 Percentage absorption function for the visual pigment rhodopsin. From the nomogram of Ebrey, T. G. and B. Honig (1977). New wavelength-dependent visual pigment nomograms. *Vision Res.* 17: 147–141. Reprinted by permission of Pergamon Press, Ltd.

receptor respond to lights of different wavelengths? Take as an example an equal number of quanta of 505 and 550 nm light. From Fig. 14.10, you can see that the receptor absorbs about two times more 505 nm quanta than 550 nm quanta. If you increase the number of available 550 nm quanta by a factor of 2, the receptor will then absorb equal numbers of quanta from the two lights. The receptor's responses to the two stimuli under these conditions and identical; it has no way of distinguishing between the 505 nm stimulus and the (physically) much stronger 550 nm stimulus.

The above example is a manifestation of the *principle of univariance*. The principle may be stated in the following way: 'Each visual pigment can only signal the rate at which it is effectively catching quanta; it cannot also signal the wavelength associated with the quanta caught' (Naka & Rushton, 1966, p. 538). Saying that this receptor is more sensitive to 505 nm light than to 550 nm light means that it is better at catching 505 nm quanta than

550 nm quanta, and so will catch more of the 505 nm quanta given equal amounts of each. Once a quantum is caught, however, its effect on the receptor is completely independent of its wavelength. A receptor responds only on the basis of how many quanta it catches, with total disregard for their wavelengths. Each photon absorbed—of whatever wavelength—results in a single isomerization, as discussed in Chapter 4.

It should be clear by now that a visual system based on one receptor type has no capacity to distinguish color *per se*. In fact, with such a system, any one primary color can be made to match any colored light, simply by manipulating the energy of the primary light to match the luminance of the other color. Organisms that have this kind of visual system are called *monochromats*; such organisms have no ability to make discriminations on the basis of wavelength. Some rare types of genetic disorder result in people having monochromatic vision. This is the most severe form of color blindness, and will be described in a later section.

A final point should be made regarding the visual capacities of monochromats. They will confuse any two colors, including white. This is a direct consequence of the principle of univariance: the receptor response depends only on the number of quanta absorbed; it does not matter whether these quanta are all of the same wavelength (as is the case for monochromatic light), or if the quanta are from a continuum of wavelengths (as may be the case for white light). The only effect that wavelength has is on the probability of any given photon being absorbed by the receptor. **BOX 14.6**

Dichromacy

Now consider a hypothetical *dichromatic* visual system, one with two different receptor types. Suppose that the two receptors have absorbance spectra as shown in Fig. 14.11; receptor *A* has its maximum sensitivity at 500 nm, while receptor *B* has its sensitivity maximum at 600 nm.

Box 14.6 The world of the monochromat

What is the world like to a monochromat? You already know what it is like to see only gradations of luminance. When you watch a black-and-white movie, or look at a black-and-white photograph, your only clues to 'color' are lightness and darkness. If three people in such a picture are wearing the same style shirt, but one is red, one is navy blue, and one is dark gray, you would be unable to say the shirts are not identical, because all three come out the same shade of gray on the film.

Notice that becoming a monochromat (by looking at a black-and-white picture) did not mean you no longer had a normal visual system. As long as there is a reduction to one channel at any point in the pathway from stimulus to percept, the color information is lost. You would do no

better at judging the colors in a color TV transmission than in a black-and-white transmission if you only had a black-and-white TV set. It is thus possible for cells in the visual pathway to be monochromats, even though they receive information from more than one receptor type.

In several previous chapters, you read arguments that depend on magnocellular cells being monochromats. In particular, you saw demonstrations in which the magno-cellular pathway was inactivated by using equiluminant stimuli. You were told that whatever is lost in these condi-tions is a function of the magnocellular pathway (however, as you will soon see, some parvocellular cells are also monochromats).

Individually, each receptor obeys the principle of univariance; its response depends only on the number of quanta caught. In combination, how-ever, the system is more discriminating. As long as the signals from each receptor system can be compared, you can no longer make one spectral light match any other simply by manipulating their energies.

For example, look at the responses of each receptor to lights of 500 and 600 nm. Suppose each

light is presented for a duration of 1 s at an energy such that 1000 quanta impinge on each receptor. From Fig. 14.11, you can see that at 500 nm, receptor A absorbs 9% of the incident quanta, while receptor B absorbs 2%. At 600 nm, however, receptor A absorbs only 1.5% of the incident quanta, while receptor B absorbs 9%. If each stimulus contains 1000 quanta, the number of quanta actually absorbed by each receptor of the two wavelengths would be as shown in Table 14.1.

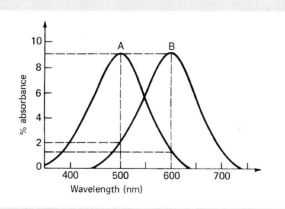

Fig. 14.11
Percentage absorption functions for two hypothetical visual pigments.

Table 14.1 The number of quanta of two wavelengths absorbed by each receptor

	Receptor A	Receptor B
500 nm	90	20
600 nm	14	90

A brief inspection of this table should make it clear that 500 and 600 nm lights cause different relative absorptions by the two receptors, no matter how the energy of either light may be varied. Equating the lights for one receptor inevitably causes a large discrepancy for the other. On the basis of these two receptors, it would always be possible to distinguish 500 nm light from 600 nm light. Therefore a visual system based on two re-

ceptors is capable of making discriminations based on wavelength in a way that a monochromatic system cannot.

A dichromat needs only two primaries to match all spectral colors (see Box 14.7), while color matching studies performed on normal human subjects require the use of three primary colors. Dichromatic systems are thus two-dimensional. There are a number of genetic disorders (to be discussed later) that result in a dichromatic visual system.

Another feature that distinguishes a dichromatic visual system from visual systems containing three types of receptors is that there is a wavelength of light that the dichromat confuses with white light. This is called the *neutral point*. The explanation is straightforward: white light excites both types of

---

Box 14.7 Why three primaries implies trichromacy

In general, any colored light can be matched by a sum of the same number of primary colors as there are color systems in the eye of the subject doing the matching. To see why this is so, imagine doing a color-matching experiment in which three primaries are offered to the subject. The arbitrary light to be matched is called x. The amounts of each primary color used to make the match (the variables over which the subject has control) are a_1, a_2, and a_3.

First consider monochromats; they have only one receptor system. The fraction of any light that receptor system will absorb is dependent on the spectrum of that light and the characteristics of the receptor; for any particular light, the absorbed fraction is simply a number. For this receptor system, called α, the fraction of primary color y it will absorb is denoted $R_\alpha(y)$; for x it is $R_\alpha(x)$, and so forth. The excitation of the receptor by any one light is the product of the amount of light and the fraction absorbed: for primary color 1 it is $a_1R_\alpha(1)$, and so on. The total excitation is the sum of the excitations due to all lights in the field, either x or the sum of the primary colors. For a match, the excitation from x equals that from the sum of the primary colors:

$$a_xR_\alpha(x) = a_1R_\alpha(1) + a_2R_\alpha(2) + a_3R_\alpha(3).$$

This is a single equation, so it has a unique solution only if

there is a single unknown variable. It may be satisfied using only a_1 (all other a values are 0) no matter what x is, because

$$a_xR_\alpha(x) = a_1R_\alpha(1)$$

has a unique solution. It could equally well be satisfied using just a_2 or a_3. If there are two or more unknowns on the right, there are an infinite number of solutions.

If the subject is not a monochromat, there is more than one receptor system, and *each* must be satisfied by the match. Each of these systems (β and γ) has an equation analogous to the equation for system α:

$$a_xR_\beta(x) = a_1R_\beta(1) + a_2R_\beta(2) + a_3R_\beta(3)$$

$$a_xR_\gamma(x) = a_1R_\gamma(1) + a_2R_\gamma(2) + a_3R_\gamma(3).$$

However many receptor systems there are, there is that same number of equations. Because in general a set of simultaneous equations has a unique solution when the number of unknowns is the same as the number of equations, there should be the same number of primaries (unknowns) as receptor systems (equations).

receptors with some ratio of excitation. Therefore, a monochromatic light that excites both receptors in that same ratio is indistinguishable from white.

In most dichromatic systems, the wavelength that is confused with white is fairly near the point at which the two receptor absorption spectra intersect; at that wavelength, the two receptors are excited in equal proportions. For receptors A and B, the intersection point is at about 550 nm; therefore, a stimulus in this spectral region is confused with the white light. Note that this is the *only* monochromatic light that would be confused with the white light. This property distinguishes dichromats from monochromats, who confuse all monochromatic lights with white light, as well as from trichromats, who do not confuse any monochromatic light with white.

Trichromacy

The color matching experiments discussed in the first part of this chapter were performed on trichromatic subjects—those whose color vision system is based on three receptors. Figure 14.12 shows absorbance spectra for three hypothetical receptors comprising a trichromatic system. Several features of this figure should be noticed. First, no single wavelength of light excites all three receptors in similar proportions to white light. Therefore no wavelength of light is confused with white light. Second, the presence of three receptors that all absorb some light throughout most of the visual range implies that the system is three-dimensional; that is, it takes three primaries to match a given light. This is, of course, the result obtained from the color-matching experiments. <u>BOX 14.7</u>

Trichromatic vision seems to be a pretty sophisticated kind of color vision. It would be perfectly possible, however, to construct a visual system based on four or more receptor types that would provide more information about the visual world than what is available to us. As Cornsweet (1970) has noted, an individual with a visual system based

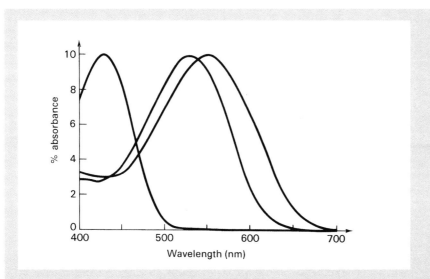

Fig. 14.12 Percentage absorption functions for three hypothetical visual receptors. These are the functions used by Smith, Pokorny, and Starr to model color mixing data. Assumes 10% absorption at the peak of each. From Smith *et al.* (1976) Variability of color mixture data–I. Inter-observer variability in the unit coordinates. *Vision Res.* 16: 1087–1094. Reprinted by permission of Pergamon Press Ltd.

on four receptor types would be able to see through color camouflaging that would fool a trichromatic observer.

Trichromatic theory

The preceding sections presented evidence that normal people have trichromatic color vision. The development of this conclusion required only the analysis of some fairly simple psychophysical experiments and the use of logic; no detailed knowledge of the structure or physiology of the human visual system was necessary. This conclusion was reached in 1807 by Thomas Young, who proposed that there must be three fiber types in the human eye. He made this suggestion based on his observation that all colors could be matched by a suitable mixture of three primary colors, without any knowledge of the nature or number of human photoreceptor types.

Young's trichromatic theory was formalized later in the 19th century by Hermann von Helmholtz (reprinted 1924), who proposed hypothetical excitation curves for each of the three types of fiber. Helmholtz used these curves to predict quantitatively the ability to make discriminations on the basis of wavelength.

The results of psychophysical experiments provided enough information for the general idea of trichromacy to become accepted doctrine. It was left to physiology, however, to provide the actual shapes of the absorbance spectra for the three receptor types. These measurements were made with a *microspectrophotometer* an instrument that directs a finely focused beam of light onto a single isolated cone. For each of a large number of wavelengths, the intensity of light transmitted through the single receptor was compared with the intensity of the light prior to passing through the receptor. If the values were similar, not much light at that wavelength was absorbed by the receptor. If the values were very different, the receptor must have absorbed a significant proportion of the incident light. By measuring the exact amount of light absorbed for a large number of wavelengths of light, a curve was derived showing the relative absorbance of the receptor versus wavelength.

This measurement was performed on the eyes of humans and other primates (Brown & Wald, 1964; Marks *et al.*, 1964). The investigators found that primate cones fall into three major groups, with absorbance maxima near 450, 525, and 555 nm. The shapes of the absorbance functions of human cones are shown in Fig. 14.13. These three curves provide a firm physiological basis for the trichromacy of human vision, although more recent work has indicated that there are two similar variants of the long-wavelength pigment and two variants of the middle-wavelength pigment (Neitz *et al.*, 1995).

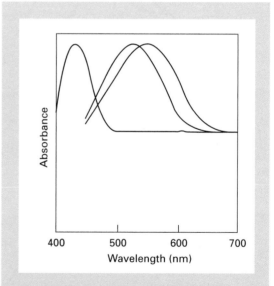

Fig. 14.13 Absorption spectra for pigments in human cones. From Merbs, S. L. and J. Nathans, (1992) Absorption spectra of the hybrid pigments responsible for anomalous color vision. *Science* 258: 464–466.

Notice that the three cone types represented by the absorption curves in Fig. 14.13 do not correspond to the primary colors. The long-wavelength-sensitive cone is *not* a 'red' cone in any way. It is sensitive to longer wavelengths than the other two cone types, but its peak sensitivity is at 555 nm—a light that appears yellowish-green. It is no more sensitive to lights that appear red (around 630 nm) than to lights that appear blue (around 450 nm).

Figure 14.13 shows the absorbance characteristics of the pigments in single human cones. In order to demonstrate that the absorbance characteristics of receptors are directly related to their response properties, the next logical step would

be to record directly the electrical responses of single cones to lights of different wavelengths. Experimenters have been successful in recording the responses of single cones from a number of different animals. For the carp, both spectrophotometric (Marks, 1965) and electrical response data (Tomita *et al.*, 1967) have been obtained. Figure 14.14 shows that the agreement between these two experiments is quite good, with both revealing the existence of three types of cones. (A fourth ultraviolet-sensitive cone found in fish would respond at shorter wavelengths than explored here.) Each individual cone contains only one of the three cone pigments. These results

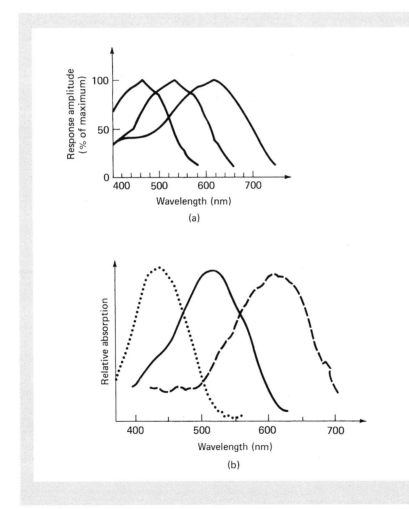

Fig. 14.14
Absorption spectra and electrophysiological receptor response versus frequency curves for fish retina. (a) Responses from single cones. From Tomita, T., A. Kaneko, M. Murakami and E. C. Pautler (1967) Spectral response curves of single cones in the carp. *Vision Res.* 7: 519–531. Reprinted by permission of Pergamon Press, Ltd. (b) Absorption spectra. From Marks, W. B. (1965) *J. Physiol. Lond.* 178: 14–32. Reprinted by permission.

have been confirmed in single cones of the macaque retina (Schnapf *et al.*, 1988).

Color defects

There are some people who either do not have trichromatic vision or have trichromatic vision with a weakened ability to make certain color discriminations. These people are sometimes called *color-blind*, although most of them do see colors and should more properly be called *color-defective* (but see Neitz, 1998).

There are many different kinds of color defect. An individual may possess trichromatic vision, but have one (or more) cone type that contains a visual pigment with abnormal spectral absorbance characteristics. Such a person is called an *anomalous trichromat*; he or she will require the usual three primary colors to make a color match, but the relative amounts of each will be different from what is required by a normal subject. In general, anomalous trichromats are usually poorer than normals at making wavelength discriminations in the red or green regions of the spectrum.

Dichromats

The most extensively studied color defects are those in which one of the three cone pigments is completely missing. There are three classes of dichromat, depending on which of the three pigments is absent: *protanopes* (lacking the long-wavelength-sensitive pigment), *deuteranopes* (lacking the medium-wavelength-sensitive pigment), and *tritanopes* (lacking the short wavelength-sensitive pigment). Protanopia was originally called 'Daltonism' because John Dalton, the English physicist, could not discriminate among reds, yellows, and greens. Ironically, there is now evidence that Dalton was actually a deuteranope (Hunt *et al.* 1995).

Most dichromats are either protanopes or deuteranopes, two categories often grouped as 'red–green defects'. These are sex-linked hereditary defects, with genes for the long- and medium wavelength-sensitive pigments located on one arm of the X-chromosome (Nathans *et al.* 1986b). When one normal gene is present, the person has normal color capability. Men have only one X-chromosome and women have two, so red–green color defects are rare in women (Nathans *et al.*, 1986a). About 8% of all US males have red–green defects (Piantanida, 1988). There are various forms of deuteranopia, depending on the nature and severity of the disruption of the gene for the middle-wavelength pigment (Neitz *et al.*, 1996). Tritanopia is much rarer, and is due to a defect on chromosome 7 (Nathans *et al.*, 1986b). <u>BOX 14.8</u>

Box 14.8 Animal color vision

The variations in color vision are interesting because of what they reveal about the human color vision system. Apparently, however, color vision evolved independently among various animals, so the color vision of other species can be somewhat different from ours. (What is more striking, however, is how similar to ours most of these other systems turn out to be.)

An interesting case is found among Old World monkeys, which are not so distant relatives of ours. Like us, they have an X-chromosome-linked visual pigment, but to have the pigment requires two different genes on two X-chromosomes. Thus, all the males are dichromats, since they can have only one X-chromosome. Females may have the two different genes and be trichromats, or have two identical genes and be dichromats like the males. Each has its advantages: trichromats have better color vision, and so may do better at picking out food by its color. Dichromats, on the other hand, do not make as good color discriminations, and so pay better attention to luminance; they are better at seeing through certain kinds of camouflage. These monkeys hunt in herds of both trichromats and dichromats, and so gain the advantage of each (Shyue *et al.*, 1995).

You already know the general properties of dichromatic vision; these include the ability to make color matches based on only two primaries and the existence of a wavelength that is indistinguishable from white light (neutral point). All dichromats share these properties; they differ only in the actual values of the color matching and the placement of the neutral point.

The CIE chromaticity diagram provides a useful way to summarize the properties of the different types of dichromacy. Imagine that the short-wavelength-sensitive cones are missing (a tritanope), so any discrimination that depends on the relative amount of stimulation of that cone type cannot be made. Since those cones are sensitive only to relatively short-wavelength lights, you can visualize their contribution as detecting the blue primary (lower left corner of the diagram). Of course, the other cones are also capable of detecting blue lights, so what is missing is not really a

spectral color or a primary. Nevertheless, for simplicity, you can imagine that what is missing is the ability to detect blueness. Notice that all the points on any line passing through the origin have the same ratio of green to red (the ratio is the slope of the line), and differ only in the amount of blueness.

Two such idealized lines, called *confusion loci*, are shown on the CIE diagram in Fig. 14.15. The actual point at which all such lines converge for a tritanope is not the origin; they are shown passing through the origin in Fig. 14.15 for the purposes of illustration. All the points a_1, a_2, ... on one line have the same green/red ratio, and so would look alike to a person with only the long-wavelength- and medium-wavelength-sensitive pigments. Similarly, the points b_1, b_2, ... (and W) on the other line would look like each other to such a person, although they would look different from the a points.

Figure 14.16 shows a chromaticity diagram with the confusion loci for a protanope drawn on it. All of the confusion loci are lines that emanate from

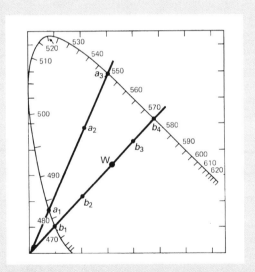

Fig. 14.15 CIE chromaticity diagram. Stimuli marked with as and stimuli marked with bs would be indiscriminable from each other if the blue fundamental were missing (makes the simplifying assumption that the blue fundamental is at the origin).

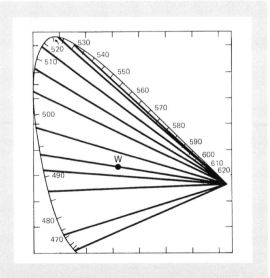

Fig. 14.16 Confusion loci for a protanope. From Le Grand (1957) *Light, color, and vision*. Chapman & Hall, London. Reprinted by permission.

Box 14.9 Why red–green dichromats confuse red with green

The fact that the spectrum locus is almost a straight line for wavelengths above about 550 nm also has important implications for normal human vision. Remember that the CIE diagram is a two-dimensional representation of a three-primary-color system, with the added assumption that the total amount of all primary colors is constant. In this representation, all colors that lie on a straight line can be matched with two primary colors; all you have to do is choose as primary colors the lights at each end of the line segment. All colors on the straight line between the two primary colors can be matched by varying the relative amounts of the primary colors. In this spectral range,

therefore, the human visual system is only two-dimensional; in other words, we are all dichromats for wavelengths above 550 nm. Dichromacy results because the short-wavelength-sensitive cones are almost totally unresponsive for wavelengths longer than 550 nm. If, as is the case for protanopes and deuteranopes, one of the other cone types is missing, the visual system will actually be monochromatic at longer wavelengths. The fact that a red–green confusion line runs along the spectrum locus for wavelengths above 550 nm (for both deuteranopes and protanopes) reflects this monochromacy.

the spectrum locus at 700 nm; the line that passes through the point W (representing white) intersects the CIE curve near 495 nm; near 495 nm is a wavelength that a protanope will confuse with white light. Notice also that the CIE curve itself is almost straight from 700 to about 550 nm. This also constitutes a confusion line, and means that a protanope confuses all spectral lights from about 550 to 700 nm. The pattern for a deuteranope is similar, although the lines are nearly parallel. **BOX 14.9**

Monochromats

A very small proportion of people have monochromatic visual systems. Most of these people lack all three cone types, leaving only the rod photoreceptors to mediate the visual process. The characteristics of rod monochromats include those discussed earlier for monochromats; they can make *no* distinctions solely on the basis of wavelength. In addition, rod monochromats have characteristics associated with scotopic vision: poor visual acuity and a strong tendency to be dazzled by bright lights. Another group of monochromats have only the short-wavelength-sensitive cones; interestingly, they can be dichromats at twilight when their rods contribute to vision (Reitner *et al.*, 1991).

A reminder: color blindness (monochromacy) is not the same as achromatopsia (see Chapter 8). A

monochromat confuses colors; once luminance is matched, the monochromat cannot tell that the two lights are different, or even detect a border between two matched areas. The achromatopsic has a cognitive failure to recognize colors, but still detects the border between matched areas. The colors are somehow 'different'—the achromatopsic just doesn't know in what way they differ.

Opponency

You saw in previous sections that trichromatic theory accounts for many characteristics of human color vision. Both the results of color-matching studies and the lack of a single wavelength that is confused with white light are consistent with the hypothesis that color information is encoded by the relative responses of the three cone types. There is a whole class of other visual phenomena, however, that are not easily explained by this model. In this section, you will first learn about the psychophysical results that are hard to explain on the basis of trichromatic theory, and then see another type of model that incorporates the trichromacy of human receptors and these additional data.

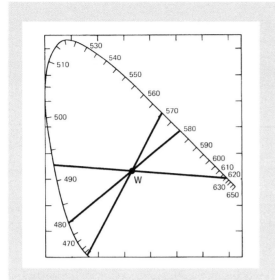

Fig. 14.17 Three pairs of complementary colors, plotted on the CIE chromaticity diagram.

Go back to the demonstrations of 'Afterimages' associated with Chapter 6 on the CD. Look at either 'After the holidays' or 'After the storm' with the box checked for 'Negative afterimage'. After staring at the inducing figure for 30 s, you should see the image in reversed colors when the white screen replaces it (allow a few seconds for the afterimage to appear). A green area in the inducing figure produces red in the afterimage (in conditions that favor the formation of negative afterimages—see Chapter 6); blue and yellow are paired in the same fashion. There is nothing in trichromatic theory that suggests a mechanism for this result.

Evidence that certain colors are paired with each other is present in, but not explained by, the CIE chromaticity diagram. Figure 14.17 shows a CIE curve with a family of lines that pass through the point W, corresponding to white light. Any one of these lines intersects the spectrum locus at two wavelengths. From the previous discussion of the properties of color mixtures, remember that the coordinates corresponding to a mixture of two

spectral lights fall somewhere on the straight line connecting them. Therefore an appropriate combination of the two lights connected by any one of the lines in Fig. 14.17 would result in a white light. White light can be produced by a combination of only two wavelengths; any pair that can be connected by a straight line drawn through W can be used for this purpose.

Pairs of colors that can be combined to produce white are called *complementary colors*. Blue and yellow are complementary, as are red and bluish-green, and reddish-yellow and greenish-blue. In fact, the same colors found to produce image–afterimage pairs also turn out to be complementary pairs. The fact that there is this kind of consistency across different experimental situations suggests that this pairing of colors is revealing something basic about human color processing.

The experimental technique of color naming reveals another class of phenomena that is difficult to explain on the basis of trichromatic theory. In this experiment, various monochromatic lights are presented to a subject, and the subject is asked to assign a color name to each light. The experimenter provides the names that can be used, for example, restricting the subject to three colors such as red, green, and blue. In that case, the subject would have to name all spectral lights using the three colors in any combination: greenish-blue, bluish-red, reddish-greenish-blue, and so forth.

One interesting result to come out of this type of experiment is that subjects have a hard time naming the whole range of spectral lights using only three color names (Judd, 1951). No matter what three names are used, subjects cannot satisfactorily name stimuli from all regions of the spectrum. When the list is expanded to four names, however, subjects are able to name any spectral light. The most satisfactory set of names is 'red, yellow, green, and blue', which are also the 'unique' colors. (You will encounter this set of four colors again in the description of the properties of color-opponent cells later in this chapter.) When subjects use these names to identify colors, the names fall into pairs that seem to be mutually exclusive: a subject never describes a light as 'reddish-green' or 'bluish-yellow' (Boynton & Gordon, 1965). Studies of the evolution of color names in various cultures indicate that there is apparently a genetic predilection for dividing the spectrum in this way (Berlin & Kay, 1969; Uchikawa & Boynton, 1987).

The requirement of four color names is rather difficult for trichromatic theory to explain, as the theory postulates the existence of only three chromatic systems. The fact that four names is the minimum set for naming the entire visual spectrum suggests the possibility that, at some point in the human color vision system, four channels are present (for a discussion of the biological significance of the color names, see Ratliff, 1976 and Abramov & Gordon, 1994).

To summarize, data accumulated from experiments on color afterimages, complementary colors, and color naming raise questions about the trichromatic model's ability to explain all color phenomena. Some of these problems were recognized in 1878 by Ewald Hering, who proposed an alternative model for the perception of color, called *opponent process theory*. The next section describes some of the basic characteristics of this theory (as modified by current investigators), and shows how it can account for the visual phenomena just discussed.

Opponent-process theory

Hering proposed that color vision is mediated by three complex 'substances', such that one supposed 'substance' accounts for distinctions between red and green, a second 'substance' would be responsible for blue versus yellow, and a third would be responsible for the white/black distinctions. These substances were postulated to be 'opponent', in the sense that the red/green substance might respond positively to red light but negatively to green light.

Contemporary supporters of opponent theory refer to opponent processes rather than substances, and believe that the red/green and yellow/blue processes are built by subtractive combinations of the three cone types. In this conception, opponent processes are results of the way the different receptor types are 'wired into' the retinal processing system. In later sections, you will learn about the physiological support for this model and how receptor systems might interact to form opponent processes.

In modern opponent theory, the white/black process is built from a combination of different cone types. Its purpose is to signal the brightness of a given light. The white/black process plays an important role in quantitative attempts to make the model account for various types of data; however, consider only the properties of the two chromatic processes for now.

The red/green opponent process is organized so that it responds in opposite directions to red and green lights. Therefore if you were to present a red stimulus, you should be able to null the response of the red/green process by adding some amount of green light. Hurvich & Jameson (1957) followed this line of reasoning to measure the strength of each opponent process as a function of wavelength. For example, to map out the red/green process, they presented subjects with a monochromatic stimulus, and asked them to add either green or red light to the stimulus until it looked 'neither red nor green'. If green light had to be added, the amount was recorded and assigned a positive sign; if red light was added, its amount was recorded and given a negative sign. If red light had to be added to the stimulus, Hurvich & Jameson reasoned that the original stimulus had evoked a green response from the red/green system, and that the amount of green excitation was opposite to the amount of red light that had to be added to cancel it. Similarly, if green light had to be added to produce a light that was neither red nor green, that meant that the stimulus before addition had evoked a red response from the red/green process.

Hurvich & Jameson plotted the relative amounts of green or red light that had to be added to the stimulus as a function of the wavelength of the

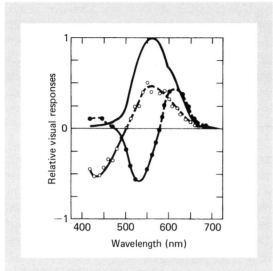

Fig. 14.18 Psychophysically obtained chromatic response functions for one observer. From Hurvich, L. M. and D. Jameson (1957) An opponent process theory of color vision. *Psychol Rev.* 64: 384–404.

stimulus; they called this the chromatic response function for the red/green process. They obtained the chromatic response function for the blue/yellow process in a similar way; that is, they measured the amount of blue or yellow light that had to be added to a stimulus to produce a light that looked neither blue nor yellow. These chromatic response functions are shown in Fig. 14.18. The open circles represent the yellow/blue process, with positive numbers implying the process is signaling yellow, and negative numbers implying the process is signaling blue. The red/green process is represented by the closed circles, with positive numbers implying red, and negative numbers implying green.

The chromatic response functions in Fig. 14.18 explain many of the phenomena that were troubling for trichromatic theory. For example, Fig. 14.18 shows why we need four words to name all the colors in the spectrum: the opponent processes model produces four different color responses. Even if these processes result from the activity of three cone types, there are four separable perceptual events (see Abramov & Gordon, 1994).

Colored afterimages can also be explained by the opponent processes shown in Fig. 14.18. As an example, suppose you stare continuously at an area of 490 nm light (which appears bluish-green). The red/green opponent process will give a vigorous green response to this stimulus. As you stare at this stimulus, the middle-wavelength-sensitive system (which is responsible for the vigorous response of the red/green system) will adapt, much in the way one adapts to a bright light. The adaptation of this system causes it to become less sensitive. When you transfer your gaze from the green to a white screen, the white light causes the red/green opponent process to respond. The fact that the middle-wavelength-sensitive system has been adapted shifts the balance of the red/green process to favor the long-wavelength-sensitive system. White light thus elicits the response normally associated with red light, resulting in a red afterimage. Other colored afterimages can be explained in a similar way. (Note that this explanation is virtually identical to the one given in Chapter 9 for aftereffects in which apparent size is affected. With a change in labeling of the axes, and the assumption that there is a subtractive comparison of the 'channel' responses, Fig. 9.18 could be used as an illustration for this paragraph.)

Physiological evidence for opponency

Although opponent process theory is an elegant explanation for a large variety of visual phenomena, it was criticized for many years because it required complex interactions for which there was no physiological evidence. The basis of this criticism disappeared with the discovery of cells in the visual system that behave in ways that are remarkably similar to Hurvich & Jameson's opponent processes.

The first physiological evidence for opponent processes came from the experiments of DeValois *et al.* (1966). These investigators used microelectrodes to record from single cells in the LGN of the macaque monkey, an animal whose color vision capabilities are similar to those of humans (DeValois *et al.*, 1974). The LGN cells were driven by illumination of the retina with diffuse monochromatic lights at a number of wavelengths. DeValois and his co-workers found four types of color-coded cell. One type of cell responded with excitation to the presentation of red light and inhibition to the presentation of green light; it was designated as +R–G. The converse of +R–G cells was also found; that is, cells that were inhibited by red light and would be excited by green light (+G–R). The other two types were selectively sensitive to yellow and blue lights; one was excited by blue and inhibited by yellow (+B–Y), while the other was of the reverse sign (+Y–B). Similar results were obtained by Wiesel & Hubel (1966).

The average spectral response curves for the +R–G cells and for the +Y–B cells are shown in Fig. 14.19. Notice that the responses of these cells closely resemble the red/green and yellow/blue opponent processes obtained psychophysically by Hurvich & Jameson (1957) and shown in Fig. 14.18. Hurvich & Jameson used their opponent process functions successfully to predict color-naming data, spectral saturation, and wavelength discrimination functions; therefore the responses of LGN cells should also be able to predict responses in the same experimental situations (DeValois *et al.*, 1966).

These spectrally opponent cells were found in the LGN; in more recent experiments, other investigators have found evidence for opponency while recording from more peripheral cells. In the central part of the monkey retina, more than half of all ganglion cells may be spectrally opponent (Gouras, 1968; DeMonasterio *et al.*, 1975). (Oddly, only three color opponent types have been reported in retina; the +Y–B cells seem to be absent—Dacey, 1996; Calkins *et al.*, 1998). **BOX 14.10**

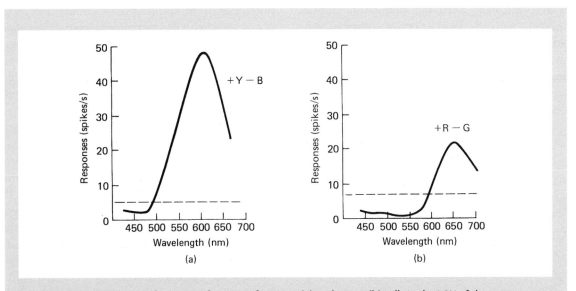

Fig. 14.19 Average spectral response functions for +Y –B (a) and +R –G (b) cells in the LGN of the macaque monkey. From DeValois, R. L., I. Abramov and G. H. Jacobs (1966) Analysis of response patterns of LGN cells. *J. Optical Soc. Am.* 56: 966–977. Reprinted by permission of the Optical Society of America.

Box 14.10 Simulation of color-opponent cells

It should not surprise you at this point that there is a demonstration of opponent cells on the CD accompanying this book. The demonstration is set up like the demonstrations of ganglion cells (Chapter 5) and cortical cells (Chapter 7). You are offered the three retinal opponent cell types, and the double-opponent cortical cell (see Box 14.11), as well as non-opponent cells (Box 14.12). As in the similar demonstrations, you can let the computer select a cell type, and you try to guess what it is from the responses.

You can see the responses to a small (center only) spot, an annulus (surround only), or full field; the light can be white, red, yellow, green, or blue.

One special feature of this demonstration is that you can bathe the field in a steady adapting light before flashing a test stimulus. The adaptation can be any of the colors available for testing. By adapting with colored lights, you can see the effects suggested for the color mechanisms under chromatic adaptation.

Retinal cells are organized in the typical center/surround manner that you encountered in Chapter 5; however, the center portion of the ganglion cell receptive field and the surround receive inputs from different types of cone. Figure 14.20 shows an example of a color-opponent monkey ganglion cell. Stimulation of the center region of the receptive field results in excitation of this cell, with this region being more sensitive to long-wavelength light. Surround stimulation inhibits the cell, with the most effective stimulus being green light. Note, however, that since both chromatic mechanisms are broad band, *any* color light in the surround will inhibit the cell. If this cell were stimulated with diffuse light of any color, the responses would be similar to those seen for LGN

cells. When the cell is illuminated with red light, the center region is stimulated more than the surround, as it is selectively sensitive to long-wavelength lights. Therefore the response of the cell is excitatory. Diffuse green light, on the other hand, stimulates the surround more than the center, resulting in net inhibition of the cell. Thus, when diffuse light is used, this cell closely resembles a +R–G LGN cell. When there is a luminance difference in the stimulus (for example, a grating of any color), this cell resembles a spatially antagonistic cell such as we discussed in Chapter 5. This cell would *not* respond well to an equiluminant grating (of the optimum spatial frequency for a luminance grating), for the center and the surround would be nearly matched. <u>BOX 14.11</u>

Color opponent cells provide an explanation for many visual phenomena. For example, afterimages are a direct consequence of organization into opponent cells. Consider the monkey's ganglion cell whose receptive field is shown in Fig. 14.20. If this cell is illuminated with bright, diffuse green light for a fairly long period of time, the receptors most responsive to such light are the ones providing input to the surround. Therefore these receptors are also the ones adapted by the green light; that is, they become less sensitive. Now suppose you turn off the green light and turn on a diffuse white light. This light excites all receptors, but the receptors feeding into the surround are desensitized and respond at a lower level. The response of

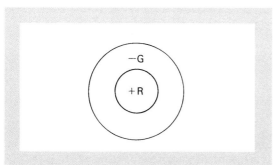

Fig. 14.20 Schematic of a receptive field of a color-opponent monkey ganglion cell.

Box 14.11 Color cells of the cortex

In the visual cortex, more complicated color opponent cells have been described (Ts'o & Gilbert, 1988). Some cells, called type I, are like those just described for the retina and LGN. Others, called type II, are spectrally opponent but not spatially opponent; that is, they are like the cell in Fig. 14.20, but with center and surround of identical size. A 'modified type II' cell is very similar, but has a larger additional surround that suppresses firing when light of any color falls on it. Finally, some cells are *double-opponent* (Daw, 1968; Michael, 1973). Such a cell is shown in Fig. 14.21. Both the center and the surround are color opponent; for any given color, the cell is spatially opponent. Notice that an equiluminant grating of the appropriate spatial frequency will have a strong effect on such a cell, unlike the type I cell in Fig. 14.20. There is some question about whether such cells are common (Michael, 1985) or rare (Ts'o & Gilbert, 1988) in V1 or even V2 (Kiper *et al.*, 1997).

The concentric color cells are found mainly in layers IVa and IVc (Michael, 1985), the layers to which the parvocellular cells of the LGN project. In the upper layers of the cortex, the color-sensitive cells are found in the cytochrome oxidase blobs (see Chapter 8), with each blob dedicated to a particular type of opponency (+R–G, +G–R, +B –Y, or

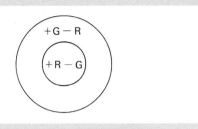

Fig. 14.21 Schematic of a receptive field of a double opponent cell.

+Y–B) (Ts'o & Gilbert, 1988). From the blobs, there is a strong projection to the thin cytochrome oxidase stripes in V2, where similar types of color-coded cells are found (Hubel & Livingstone, 1987)

In addition to these color cells, there are color-selective cells of the simple and complex types (Michael, 1979, 1981, 1985). Orientation-selective color cells are found in the interblob regions, with connections to the appropriately color-coded blobs (Ts'o & Gilbert, 1988). They probably account for the color selectivity of the pale stripes in V2.

---

this cell is therefore dominated by the center mechanism yielding an excitatory response, which signals to higher centers the presence of red light. This is the same explanation for afterimages that was given in the discussion of Hurvich & Jameson's (1957) opponent-color model; the difference is that, here, specific functions are assigned to physiological substrates.

Another phenomenon that may be related to the opponent cells is called Benham's top. Perhaps you have seen it: it is a half white/half black top with black circumferential bands going partway through the white half (see Fig. 14.22). When it is spun, weak colors appear in bands corresponding to the circumferential black bands. This can be explained by the OFF responses of the color opponent cells (Grunfeld & Spitzer, 1995), probably combined with the lateral effects of the differently colored surrounds of these cells (Tritsch, 1992).

There may also be a difference in the timing of the chromatic channels (Courtney & Buchsbaum, 1991). This may remind you of the explanations for brightness enhancement (Box 12.4, p. 256).

From trichromacy to opponency

The trichromatic and opponent-process theories were originally considered as two alternative explanations for the phenomenological appearance of colors. Color matching is trichromatic in that three primary colors are required to match any color, and both theories account for this fact. The major difference is that in trichromatic theory the three fundamental processes of color vision are all

Fig. 14.22 Benham's top. When rotated slowly, weakly colored bands appear.

sensitive to a broad range of wavelengths: one is most sensitive to the long wavelengths, one to middle wavelengths, and one to short wavelengths. In the opponent-process theory, the three fundamental processes include one broad-band system (the black/white) and two opponent systems (red/green and yellow/blue).

Opponent theory does not contradict trichromatic theory; it extends it. Hurvich & Jameson (1957) based their model on the existence of three types of cones, each with differing spectral sensitivities. The two opponent processes are formed by subtractive interactions among the three cone types. At the level of the cones there is trichromacy in exactly the form Young and Helmholtz suggested, as verified by spectrophotometry. By the level of the ganglion cells, there are opponent processes in the form of spectrally opponent cells; they represent the way the nervous system 'reads out' the information presented by the three sets of cones. It is what theorists refer to as a 'remapping' (Hurlbert, 1991).

Given the spectral absorbance curves of the three cone types, what are the interactions that produce opponent processes? The actual details become quite involved, and there is disagreement on a number of significant points. The fundamental idea that there is a subtraction (inhibitory interaction) of the responses of cone types is, however, generally accepted.

To illustrate, consider the red/green process. Abramov (1968) demonstrated that the +R – G and +G–R cells in the monkey lateral geniculate nucleus receive inputs from only the long-wavelength-sensitive and middle-wavelength-sensitive cones. (Ingling (1977) and Wooten & Werner (1979), however, argue that a short-wavelength-sensitive cone input is present under certain conditions, or is a very weak contributor — Sankeralli & Mullen, 1996.) The responses of these cells, which presumably comprise the monkey's red/green process, should therefore be derivable from the spectral sensitivities of the two cone types.

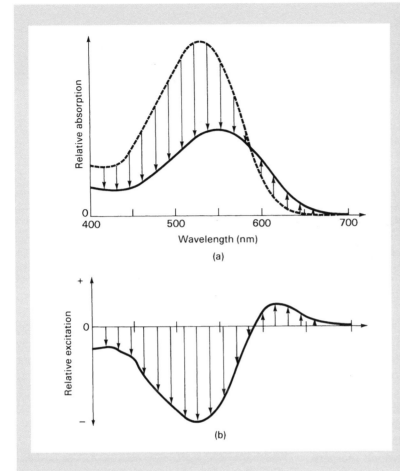

Fig 14.23 Demonstration of how chromatic response processes may be generated. (a) Relative absorption spectra for long- and middle-wavelength-sensitive visual pigments taken from long- and middle-wavelength-sensitive curves in Fig. 14.13. The relative heights of the two functions have been scaled so that they cross at 590 nm. (b) Chromatic response function obtained simply by subtracting the absorbance of the middle-wavelength pigment from that of the long-wavelength pigment, at each wavelength.

Figure 14.23(a) shows percentage absorption as a function of wavelength for the long-wavelength-sensitive and middle-wavelength-sensitive cones. Assume that a +R–G cell is excited by the long-wavelength-sensitive cones and inhibited by the middle-wavelength-sensitive cones. The response of a +R–G cell, relative to its maintained firing in the absence of light, is thus related to the difference between the number of photons absorbed by each of these cones. These differences are shown in Fig. 14.23(a) as arrows between the two absorption curves; upward arrows mean the long-wavelength-sensitive pigment absorbs more; downward arrows mean the middle-wavelength-sensitive pigment absorbs more. The differences

are plotted in Fig. 14.23(b). A +G–R cell would be made by subtracting in the other order and would thus be represented by the same curve inverted.

If you compare the curve in Fig. 14.23(b) with the red/green opponent process in Fig. 14.18, you can see that this simple model provides a reasonable approximation for the way the red/green process may be generated. Compare it with the +R–G cells shown in Fig. 14.19; the curves in general correspond quite well. (The main difference is that the cells compress the negative portions—after all, they cannot fire at a rate less than zero.)

The yellow/blue process is also made from a difference between the responses of cones, but in a somewhat more complicated manner. There is

Box 14.12 The non-opponent cells

The chromatically opponent cells are part of the parvo-cellular system in the cortex. What are the non-opponent cells that account for the black/white system?

DeValois *et al.* (1966), who described the four types of color opponent cells in the LGN, also found two classes of cells whose responses were of the same type regardless of the wavelength of light. One type always increased its firing when a light came on; the other always decreased its firing. They called these cells L-type, for they assumed these were the cells that signaled luminance. Since L-type cells were found among the color opponent cells of the LGN, it is likely that these cells were also in the parvocellular layers. (These cells are simulated for comparison in the 'Opponent cells' demonstration.)

Of course, you know of a type of cell that is not color-coded: the magnocellular cells. For a number of reasons, Lennie & D'Zmura (1988) reject the idea that magnocellular cells provide the achromatic signal. They argue that the opponent cells (which are the majority of parvocellular cells) carry both the chromatic and the luminance information (Creutzfeld *et al.*, 1991a). You have already seen that a type I cell (Fig. 14.20) responds to either color or luminance contrast. Lennie & D'Zmura suggest how different combinations of type I cells could form both a luminance and a chromatic pathway at higher levels. Nevertheless, magnocellular cells do seem to be responsible for the border between non-equiluminant fields (Valberg *et al.*, 1992) and for the flicker seen when the colors are not matched (Smith *et al.*, 1992)

unanimous agreement that all three cone types are needed to make a +Y–B cell or a +B–Y cell. The consensus is that the short-wavelength cones oppose the sum of the other two (Sankeralli & Mullen, 1996; Kolb *et al.*, 1997).

The antagonism between responses of different cone types has the effect of sharpening the wavelength selectivity of the retina. In this way it is analogous to lateral antagonism, which sharpens borders. In lateral antagonism, responses of receptors from one area subtract from those in another area—the result is that ganglion cells are more selective for the position of a stimulus. Antagonism (differencing) between cone types results in a sharpening of the spectral responses of the ganglion cell—cones 'from' one region of the spectrum subtract from those 'from' another region. The sharpening can be seen in the curves in Fig. 14.23. A +R–G cell is excited only by wavelengths between 600 and 700 nm, as compared with the long-wavelength-sensitive cones, which are excited to some extent by any visible light.

The initial analysis of color is at least a two-step operation (Hurlbert, 1997). The three cone types are the first stage of processing. They provide the initial basis for the essential trichromacy of color

mixing. The opponent cells are the second stage. Here, the selectivity of the system is sharpened by an antagonistic mechanism. The opponent processes explain the need for four color names, as well as the presence of complementary pairs and afterimages. **BOX 14.12**

Surface colors and color constancy

So far, this has been about the colors of isolated lights, or the two halves of a self-luminous display. But colors in the real world occur in complicated scenes. How do you perceive the colors of surfaces that are reflecting light from some source of illumination? You want those colors to be independent of the illumination. This is called *color constancy*, the tendency for a surface to appear a particular color despite the illumination conditions. It is exactly analogous to lightness constancy (see Chapter 12), except that, as you now know, there are three reflectance parameters needed to satisfy trichromacy.

Boynton (1988) discusses a list of 11 basic colors. There are the four colors you know about from opponency (red, yellow, green, and blue); there are three more 'achromatic' colors that you know from Chapter 12 (white, gray, and black); and there are four additional surface colors (orange, purple, pink, and brown). These 11 are 'basic' in that they are consistently recognized with minimal response times. The surface colors differ in their lightnesses; for example, brown is a darker version of orange. The 11 colors form clusters in a three-dimensional color space (Boynton & Montag, 1988; Boynton & Olson, 1990).

In a complicated display, the color of a particular patch is strongly dependent on what surrounds it. Put another way, the color of a surface is poorly related to the spectrum of the light emanating from it. A red shirt appears red in sunlight, electric light, and even in colored party lights (although there may be subtle differences, as you well know if you have ever matched colors in a store with fluorescent lighting and were surprised when you got home and saw them in daylight!).

Some of the most compelling demonstrations of color constancy have been devised by Edwin H. Land in support of his retinex theory (see Box 12.3, p. 253). In one, a colored scene (a still life with fruits, vegetables, and a wine bottle) was photographed three times in black and white through three different colored filters that roughly allowed only the long, the middle, or the short wavelengths to pass through. The three resulting uncolored slides were then projected through appropriately colored sharp filters and superimposed on a screen. This is a non-standard way to achieve a three-color separation, and the final product was a good full-color reproduction of the scene.

Now, by using only one projector at a time, Land was able to measure the amount of light in each of the three wave bands in any particular part of the picture (such as a red pepper). Not surprisingly, the image of the pepper was dominated by the long-wavelength light. Land then put a neutral filter in front of the red projector, so that there were equal energies in all three wave bands at the pepper when all three projectors were on. Nevertheless, the pepper appeared red! Of course, the relative amount of red in all other objects in the picture was also greatly diminished. The lights from the three projectors could be adjusted so that there were equal energies in the three wave bands in any one of the objects, but all the objects always appeared to be of the correct color. These demonstrations provide evidence that color perception is not well tied to the spectral composition of the light emanating from each point in a complicated image. <u>**BOX 14.13**</u>

How can we explain color constancy? One appealing idea is that adaptation 'readjusts' the color sensitivities of the system for an appropriate balance. If you view a scene lit by reddish light, the light reflected to your eyes from all the objects in the scene will be dominated by the long wavelengths. This will cause adaptation of the long-wavelength-sensitive mechanisms (long-wavelength-sensitive cones, $+R - G$ cells, and so forth), making your visual system less sensitive to longer wavelengths of light. The relatively weaker medium- and short-wavelength lights will thus be as effective as the powerful long-wavelength lights, restoring a balance similar to what would be achieved unadapted in white light. This is essentially an expanded (trichromatic) version of Helson's adaptation level theory for lightness constancy (Chapter 12).

Unfortunately for this idea, detailed analysis of how adaptation should affect simple and complex scenes does not agree with the data on color constancy (Brill & West, 1986). It cannot be based on assuming an average 'gray' background, for a few sparsely placed color dots can have a huge effect on the perceived colors (Jenness & Shevell, 1995). Moreover, colors are perceived correctly with very brief exposures to an image, and adaptation would be expected to take considerably more time (Land, 1986; Brill & West, 1986).

Another suggestion is that the observer 'knows' the illuminant of a scene, and therefore 'discounts' it in evaluating the colors of objects in the scene

---

Box 14.13 Land's two-color color mixing

Land is better known for an earlier color demonstration that may have inspired his development of retinex theory. In that demonstration, shown widely in the early 1960s, a still life was photographed twice in black and white: once through a green filter and once through a red filter. The two images were projected in register, the 'red' image through a red filter, the other with no filter. There was a surprising range of colors in the resulting image, even though it was dichromatic in that only two channels were used to encode it. (This two-color method is named for Land, but was actually in commercial use much earlier. From 1909 to the end of the silent movie era, color movies were produced by a process called 'Kinemacolor'. In Kinemacolor, alternate frames were projected with or without a red-orange filter, giving an additive mixture by their rapid superposition — Klein, 1936).

Land's two-color demonstrations were intended to show that there is more to color perception than simple trichromatic matching, and that they did. However, the colors in these demonstrations are not perfect, and modern retinex theory invokes three-color systems. As you would expect, the colors available with the two-color system are confined to a plane in the three-dimensional color space (Land, 1986).

(Boynton, 1988). The illuminant might be known by the direct reflections from shiny surfaces (Lennie & D'Zmura, 1988), or from the appearances of objects of known color. These mechanisms can be bypassed by presenting images of abstract, matt-finish surfaces. The stimuli so devised are called Mondrians, colored versions of the stimuli discussed in Box 12.3. (p.253). Mondrians are made as a collage of rectangular papers of various colors. When colored Mondrians are used, the apparent color of any given swatch is independent of the illuminant, just as for the still life images (Land, 1986). Even a goldfish judges the true colors of Mondrian patches when the illuminant is colored (Ingle, 1985). In these cases, the observer clearly cannot be evaluating the illuminant by its effect on familiar objects.

In order to achieve color constancy, there must be some computation across the entire image (Boynton, 1988; Churchland & Sejnowski, 1988; Foster *et al.*, 1997). In the retinex theory, ratios of energies at each border are computed in each of three broad energy bands (Land, 1986). Another possibility is a computation of the contrasts at the borders (see Box 12.3). There would be three contrasts to

compute, presumably in one non-opponent and two color-opponent systems.

There is physiological evidence for these computations. Second-order color cells in LGN (Nothdurft & Lee, 1982) and V1 (Zeki, 1983b) respond to the spectral composition of the lights with no apparent regard for the surrounding regions (but see Creutzfeld *et al.*, 1996). But cells in V4 respond to the apparent color rather than the spectral composition of patches in Mondrians (Zeki, 1983b). V4 is an area that has been implicated in color processing (Zeki, 1973), being the main receiving area for the V2 thin stripes (which receive their inputs from the V1 blobs; see Fig. 8.6, p.145). It thus seems reasonable that some cells in V4 engage in a third level process in which colors are represented by their appearance, and color constancy is maintained.

Of course, V4 is not the end of the process. You may recall that surface colors require 11 names, and V4 falls short of that categorization (Abramov & Gordon, 1994). Posterior inferotemporal cortex has cells with even more 'color perception' -like properties (this area is called V8 in humans, and TEO in monkeys — see 'Brain anatomy' associated with Chapter 7 on the CD). For example, Komatsu *et al.* (1992) report inferotemporal cells with responses corresponding to areas of the CIE color space; other cells seem to respond only to the saturation of stimuli. Experiments on color perception under different illuminants indicate that while some adaptation like that described earlier (and illustrated for 'opponent cells' on the CD) must occur at early stages, there must also be a cortical level of adaptation that represents position in the color space (Walsh, 1995).

The lessons of color vision are just like those of pattern vision: processing occurs at various levels, and the net effect is a cumulation of all the processing. Given the extensive feedback and interconnections of the cortex, it should not be surprising that no one area can be identified as 'the seat' of color vision.

Suggested readings

A careful and painstaking account of color perception is given by T. N. Cornsweet in *Visual perception* (Academic Press, 1970). Chapters 8, 9, and 10 are devoted to color, including color spaces, retinal physiology of color, and the psychological aspects of color. A somewhat briefer but slightly more technical account of the same topics may be found in Chapter 9 of *The psychobiology of sensory coding*, by W. R. Uttal (Harper and Row, 1973).

E. F. MacNichol, Jr, discussed physiological aspects of color vision, including details of cone pigment spectral sensitivities, in a *Scientific American* article called 'Three-pigment color vision' (December 1964; offprint #197). A somewhat unorthodox view of color vision is presented by E. H. Land in 'Experiments in color vision' (May 1959; offprint #223). The Land article is reprinted in the collection *Perception: mechanisms and models*, edited by R. Held and W. Richards (W. H. Freeman, 1972), pp. 286–298. Land's theory is further elaborated in his article 'The retinex theory of color vision' (December 1977; offprint #392). This article is reprinted in the collection *The perceptual world*,

edited by I. Rock (W. H. Freeman, 1990). An account of the genetics of color pigments and color defects is given in an article by Jeremy Nathans in *Scientific American* (260: 42; 1989)

Chapter 5 of *Surface color perception* by Jacob Beck (Cornell University Press, 1972) includes a discussion of the appearance of colored surfaces illuminated by colored lights. The approach taken is to consider the perception of the hue of these surfaces as an extension of the ways we perceive lightness of a surface (this book was recommended among the readings for Chapter 12). Land's color theory is discussed within this framework.

There are two comprehensive books by leading researchers in color vision that cover most of what was discussed in this chapter (plus several other aspects of color vision). These books are somewhat technical, but readable. They provide useful references on the CIE space and its fundamentals, and on specific forms of color defects, as well as presenting color-matching data and the physiology of color vision. *Human color vision*, by Robert M. Boynton (Holt, Rinehart, and Winston, NY, 1979) has a number of interesting demonstrations, and an appendix on the CIE space. *Color vision*, by Leo M. Hurvich (Sinauer Associates, Sunderland, MA, 1981) is illustrated with a large number of color plates; this book has a more complete coverage of opponent process theory. A somewhat shorter treatment that is technical but very readable is the review chapter by I. Abramov and J. Gordon, 'Color appearance: on seeing red—or yellow, or green, or blue' in the *Annual Review of Psychology* (45: 451–485; 1994).

An interesting book about color blindness (complete color blindness, in the form of rod monochromacy) is *The island of the colorblind* by Oliver Sacks (Alfred A. Knopf, New York, 1997, pp. 3–93). Sacks tells of an inbred island people who congenitally lack cone photoreceptors. Oddly, he refers to the condition as 'achromatopsia'; you may recall his account of cortical achromatopsia in 'The case of the colorblind painter', which was recommended in Chapter 8.

Chapter 15

The structure of the auditory system

So far in this book, you have read (in some detail) about only one sensory system, the visual system. This chapter begins your exploration of audition, the second most extensively studied sense. The treatment of audition follows lines somewhat similar to those followed for the visual system: first you will learn about the nature of the physical stimulus, and then about the physiological machinery that receives and processes the stimulus. You will study how the auditory system functions to produce the psychological impressions of loudness, pitch, and timbre, and for localization of specific sounds in space. Finally, you will learn about an auditory analog of form perception: speech perception.

Differences between light and sound Some of the differences between the sense of sight and the sense of hearing may be attributed to differences between the stimuli, light and sound. Both are forms of energy that travel as waves through space and allow you to sense what is happening at a distance. But light waves travel in nearly straight lines, while sound waves more easily bend around corners. This is because sound waves have a much longer wavelength than light waves, a difference that also limits the ability of sound waves to produce sharp images. That is both an advantage and a disadvantage; you cannot locate a predator precisely, but neither can a noisy quarry hide behind a rock.

An important difference between light and sound is that you see most objects by reflected light, but you hear them by sounds they themselves produce. You see a cat by light from the sun or a lamp bouncing off her fur, but you hear her by the meows she makes. Distinctive sounds are not dependent on the nature of some outside energy source in the way that the appearance of surfaces depends on the nature and amount of illuminant. Therefore, sounds do not present the constancy problem encountered for vision (see Chapters 12 and 14).

On the other hand, sound does bounce off other objects in the environment and is therefore 'colored' by the environment. Your voice sounds different in a small room, a large lecture hall, or outdoors. The ways in which sound reflects and is distorted is another cue to the space around you. Just as you might shine a flashlight around a dark room, some animals (such as bats) emit squeals that allow them to explore the dark. Congenitally blind people are quite good at comprehending their surroundings from the sounds that reach them.

An important difference between the senses of vision and audition is that vision is the sense that best creates a spatial world. Audition generally sequences events in time. Blind people may be said to live in a world structured by time; if they later regain their vision, they have difficulty comprehending the simultaneous unity of parts of an object (Sacks, 1995).

The physical nature of sound

In contrast to light, which is a type of electromagnetic radiation, sound is a purely mechanical phenomenon. It is produced by the vibration of an object, which results in the alternate compression and rarefaction of matter surrounding the object. The perturbations in position of the molecules are propagated as a wave that emanates in all directions from the object, even though the average positions of individual molecules may not change appreciably. In air, the presence of a sound wave is manifested by slight changes in local air pressure or concentration of air molecules in a particular location. Fig. 15.1 illustrates how the air molecules might be distributed about a regularly vibrating object (a loudspeaker). At any instant in time, there is an orderly and cyclical pattern of locations with high and low concentrations of air molecules.

The speed with which the waves move from a source depends on the medium through which they are traveling. In air, sound waves travel at a velocity of approximately 340 m/s; the velocity is considerably greater when sound waves travel through water, and even faster when traveling through metals.

One way of representing the sound produced by a given source is to graph the pressure changes that occur at a single point in space as a function of time. For example, if you measured the pressure changes at point A in Fig. 15.1 caused by the vibrating loudspeaker in the left center of the figure, you might obtain a function such as that shown in Fig. A.8 or A.9 (pp. 482 and 483). The function shown in the figures is a sine wave; sounds that can be represented by sine waves are called pure *tones*. From both the physiological and the mathe-

Fig. 15.1 Schematic representing the cyclic rarefaction and compression of air molecules caused by a uniformly vibrating object (a loudspeaker driven by a sine wave). Notice the decline in amplitude with distance from the source, and the 'shadow' behind the speaker.

matical points of view, pure sines are the simplest types of waveform to deal with (you should recall this from Chapter 9).

The period (P) of the wave is simply the amount of time between two successive maxima (or minima); that is, the length of time for one complete cycle to be carried out at a particular point in space. The *frequency* of the wave (f) is the reciprocal of the period; it is the number of cycles that occur in a 1 s interval. The frequency is measured in units of cycles per second, or *hertz* (Hz, after the physicist Heinrich Hertz).

The psychological attribute of sound that is most closely related to frequency is the pitch of the sound. You can hear how pitch changes with frequency by playing the demonstration 'Pitch and loudness' associated with Chapter 17 on the CD. When you click the various circles in the horizontal row, you will hear pure sinusoidal tones of the same amplitude but different frequencies (the frequency and amplitude are listed at the upper right of the graph, the waveform is shown below it). On the other hand, if you follow the vertical dots you will hear a tone of 400 or 6400 Hz at different amplitudes; even though these are all the same frequency, you may notice a slight variation in their pitches. The relationship between pitch and frequency and other factors that influence the perceived pitch of a tone will be discussed in Chapter 17.

Besides the frequency of a pure tone, two other characteristics of the stimulus that are of importance to the auditory system are the *amplitude* and the *phase* of the signal. The amplitude (*A*) of the sound wave may be defined in units of pressure or energy, and is related to the perceived loudness of the tone; the greater the amplitude, the louder the sound. As you will see later, however, loudness also depends on other factors, such as the frequency of the tone. The phase of the sound wave refers to the part of the cycle that is occurring relative to some fixed time. The two waveforms shown in Fig. A.9 have identical wavelengths and amplitudes; however, they differ in *phase*. You

should have already played with shifts in phase in the CD demonstration 'Fourier components' associated with Chapter 9. Phase becomes important to consider when a sound wave is being detected at two different points in space; for example, at your two ears. Properties of sine waves are more fully discussed at the beginning of Chapter 9 and in the Appendix.

Drawing the shape of a particular sound wave as a function of time is not always the most convenient way of representing the important characteristics of that sound. For pure tones, all you need to know to have a complete description of the sound are the frequency and amplitude of the signal. More complex sounds cannot be so easily described, however; the sound waves graphed on the left in Fig. 15.2 cannot be represented by a single frequency and amplitude pair. Fourier analysis separates these types of sound waves into their component sine waves of varying frequency and amplitude, just as it did for complex spatial stimuli in Chapter 9. Complex sound waves can be ex-

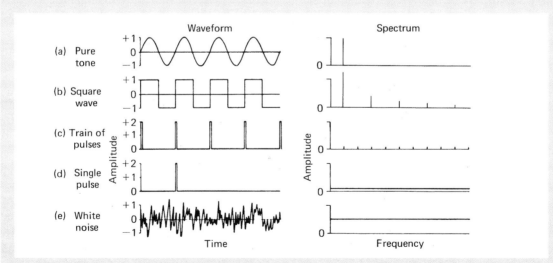

Fig. 15.2 Fourier spectra of a number of different sound waves. From Moore, B. C. J. (1977) *The psychology of hearing*. Macmillan Press, London. Copyright © Brian C. J. Moore. Reprinted by permission.

pressed by their spectra, where the amplitudes of sine wave components are plotted versus the frequency of the components.

You can see from the right side of Fig. 15.2 that sound spectra can be broken into two general classes. Complex sound waves that are periodic in structure (waveforms that continuously repeat) will yield spectra that consist of a discrete number of specific frequencies; for example, see the spectra associated with the sound waves in Figs 15.2 (a)–(c), and 15.4 (p. 339). Sounds that do not regularly repeat themselves are represented by spectra that are themselves continuous; that is, sine waves at all frequencies are represented in the signal to some extent. As examples, Figs 15.2 (d) and (e) show the waveforms and Fourier spectra for a single pulse and a white noise stimulus, two non-periodic signals. The spectra are continuous functions showing a range of frequencies for which there are non-zero amplitudes, in contrast to the spectra in Figs 15.2 (a)–(c). Both periodic and non-periodic complex sounds can be thought of as sums of pure tones with the frequencies and amplitudes expressed by their respective spectra. These are exactly like the spectra that you saw in Chapter 9.

Measurement of sound intensity

It is a general characteristic of sensory systems that discriminations on the basis of stimulus magnitude can be made over very large ranges of energy. You can make brightness discriminations over a range of approximately 11 log units, which corresponds to an energy ratio of 100 000 000 000 : 1. Similarly, your auditory system can respond differentially to stimuli the intensities of which vary over a 14-log unit range.

Because of the immense range of auditory intensities that must be considered, a modified logarithmic scale called the *decibel scale* (dB) was developed.[1] In a logarithmic scale, one particular energy level is chosen as a reference intensity, and

---

[1] The basic unit is actually the Bel, named after Alexander Graham Bell: 1 Bel corresponds to a change in intensity of a factor of 10, which is rather large. The Bel is therefore divided into tenths, and the new scale is called decibels.

Box 15.1 Scales for sound intensity

The SPL scale is referenced to a particular power (intensity) level, and so indicates the intensity in a sound regardless of its frequency. This is like the radiometric units of light (see Chapter 3) that measure the radiant power in a light without reference to how well such a light might be seen.

Environmental engineers concerned with the amount of noise workers are exposed to, or the amount of noise made by some machinery, use a sound-level meter. Sound-level meters usually have a switch that allows selection between two kinds of decibel scales, labeled 'A' and 'C'. The C weighting (also called dBC) is nearly independent of frequency (as the SPL scale actually is), so it indicates how much power there is, almost regardless of frequency.

The A scale (also called dBA) weights each frequency approximately according to the ability of the average human to hear that frequency. (When the reference for each reading is actually the threshold level for that frequency, as given in Fig. 17.1 (p. 373), it is called dB SL for 'sensation level'). This is comparable to the photometric measures of light. The weighting means that even if there is a lot of energy at a very high or very low frequency, it does not add much to the overall sound-level reading because we cannot hear it very well. Thus, these scales provide a reasonable estimate of how loud the sound should be perceived to be, regardless of its frequency spectrum (just as a photometric measure tells us how bright a light appears despite its color). This, of course, is the information an engineer needs to evaluate whether sound reduction efforts have paid off.

all other intensities are expressed as multiples of that reference level. The usual reference level is 10^{-16} watts per square centimeter (w/cm²; equivalent to a pressure of 0.0002 dynes/cm²), which is just barely audible for most people when the sound is a pure tone at 1000 Hz. (When a sound is specified using 10^{-16} W/cm² as a reference, the sound level is referred to as a sound pressure level, or SPL.) **BOX 15.1**

In the decibel scale, a difference of 10 dB corresponds to a 1-log unit (or factor of 10) change in sound intensity. Therefore an increase in intensity of a sound from 10 to 20 dB corresponds to a 10-fold intensity difference, while an increase from 10 to 30 dB represents a change in intensity by a factor of 100. The formula relating decibels to the intensity of a sound is

$$dB = 10 \log \left(\frac{I}{I_{ref}} \right)$$

$$= 10 \log (I/10^{-16} \text{ W/cm}^2)$$

$$= 10 \log (I) - 10 \log (10^{-16} \text{ W/cm}^2)$$

If, instead of measuring the intensity of a sound, you measured the pressure changes associated with that sound, the formula for calculating decibels would be different, because intensity is proportional to the square of the pressure:

$$I = P^2.$$

Therefore, the formula relating decibels to pressure (which is our ordinary measure of amplitude) is simply

$$dB = 10 \log \left(\frac{P^2}{P_{ref}^2} \right)$$

$$= 10 \log \left(\frac{P}{P_{ref}} \right)^2$$

$$= 20 \log \left(\frac{P}{R_{ref}} \right).$$

From the above formula, you can see that a 20 dB change in sound pressure level corresponds to a 100-fold change in the intensity of the sound, but only a 10-fold change in the pressure.

Similarly, a 6 dB change in pressure corresponds to a four-fold change in intensity but only a doubling in pressure (6 is twice 3, which is 10 times 0.3, the log of 2; see the Appendix). The sound levels in decibels of some familiar everyday noises are presented in Table 15.1.

The demonstration 'Pitch and loudness' (Chapter 17) on the CD allows you to alter the intensity of a 400 Hz or a 6400 Hz tone (vertical rows of dots). The obvious change is in loudness, although, as pointed out earlier, pitch does change a little. Notice on the graph of pressure versus time at the bottom of the display that the horizontal spacing stays the same (same frequency) while the amplitude changes. The steps are spaced 3 dB apart (intensity is given in the upper right of the graph), so you will see the amplitude change by a factor of 2 between adjacent steps. On the other hand, when you select the dots in the horizontal row, the amplitude (and intensity) stays the same while frequency changes. You can see that the wave on the graph at the bottom stays the same height while stretching or contracting horizontally. Notice that while pitch changes, the loudness also changes. The extremely high and extremely low frequencies are nearly inaudible, even though the middle frequencies at the same intensity are loud (assuming you have your sound system turned to a reasonable level).

Pure tones are produced by sources that vibrate in a sinusoidal fashion. Most vibrating bodies, however, do not move in such a simple way. For example, when a guitar string is plucked, it vibrates in a manner dependent on the nature of the string, the amount of tension applied to it, and the distance between the two rigidly held ends of the string. Figure 15.3 shows some of the ways that a string can vibrate if it is being held at two points (1 and 2 in the figure). In part (a), the entire string moves up and down in unison; the entire length of the string in this case corresponds to one-half of a complete wavelength. A second cycle length that will also be stationary at points 1 and 2 is shown in Fig. 15.3(b); in this case, the wave corresponds to one complete wavelength between the two points,

Table 15.1 Sound levels in decibels (dB) for a number of common sounds

Sound	Intensity level (dB)
Rocket launch (from 150 ft)	180
Jet plane take off (from 80 ft)	140
Pain threshold	130
Loud thunder	120
Inside subway train	100
Inside noisy car	80
Normal conversation	60
Normal office level	50
Quiet room	30
Soft whisper	20
Absolute hearing threshold (for 1000 Hz tone)	0

Note: levels are only rough guesses and may vary tremendously

so that the wavelength is half as long as the wave in (a). In other words, the frequency of the sound produced by the vibrations in (b) of the figure will be double the frequency of the vibrations illustrated in (a). The wave in (b) has an additional location besides the two endpoints at which the position of the string is constant; point 3 in the exact middle of the string is also immobile.

The frequency of the vibration in Fig. 15.3(b) could just as easily have come from a string whose

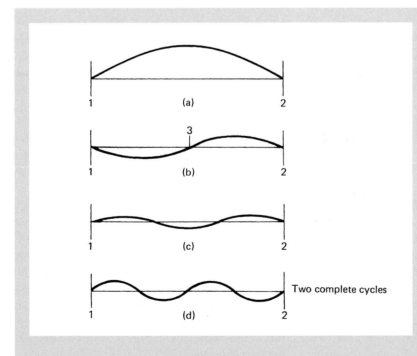

Fig. 15.3 Four ways in which a string fixed at two points can vibrate. The wavelengths of the vibrations of the string in (b), (c), and (d) are one-half, one-third, and one-quarter of the wavelength of the vibration of the string in (a), respectively, giving vibrations with frequencies two, three, and four times that in (a).

length was half the distance between points 1 and 2. If you decrease the length of the string by one-half, therefore, the lowest possible frequency will be exactly double the previous lowest frequency. This is easy to demonstrate on any stringed musical instrument that is handy. Take any string and pluck it; touch the string at a point exactly in between the two endpoints, and the observed pitch becomes higher. This change in pitch corresponds to a change in the primary frequency of the vibrating string by a factor of 2, in music, this change corresponds to one octave. You may have noticed that each tone in the 'Pitch and loudness' demonstration was double the frequency of the next lower tone. If you are musically savvy, you may also have noticed that they are all the same note, transposed by an octave. If you have perfect pitch you may also notice that the note is not well tuned—it is a slightly sharp G (about halfway between G and G#).

There are infinite numbers of other waves whose cycle lengths would conform to two stationary points at the end positions in Fig. 15.3. Parts (c) and (d) of the figure show two more examples of such waves; their wavelengths are one-third and one-quarter the wavelength of the wave in (a), respectively. Therefore the sound produced by these movements of the string will be three and four times that of the frequency of the sound produced in (a). The set of frequencies that can occur with stationary positions at points 1 and 2 will have frequencies that are integer multiples of the lowest possible frequency; that is, the frequency of vibration of the string in (a). This lowest possible frequency is the fundamental frequency; all the higher vibrations that are multiples of this are harmonics of that frequency.

You encountered harmonics before, in the discussion of spatial frequency in Chapter 9. In that chapter, you saw how a square wave grating could be generated by a sum of sine wave gratings (see also Fig 15.2b). Those sine waves included one that had the same frequency as the resulting square wave; this is the fundamental frequency for that square wave. All the other sine waves in the series were harmonics of that fundamental; they all had frequencies that were integer multiples of the fundamental frequency. Harmonics are also important in the generation of musical chords; pairs of notes that sound consonant (or harmonious) when played simultaneously almost always have fundamental frequencies that are related to each other as a ratio of small numbers.

Although musical notes often sound 'pure', they rarely are. Instead, they are composed of a fundamental frequency and a large number of harmonic frequencies that are present in varying amounts. The fundamental is what determines the pitch of the note, whereas the harmonics are important in producing a quality that is called the *timbre* of the sound. Figure 15.4 shows the waveform of an 'open' violin G string bowed with medium intensity, along with the spectrum of the waveform. The lowest frequency is the fundamental frequency, but there are also many harmonic frequencies present in the signal. In fact, the harmonics account for nearly all of the sound energy. These harmonics are generated by the vibrating string, but which of them are large and which are small depends on characteristics of the entire instrument. That is why a piano playing a G sounds different from a violin playing the same note. (Other differences are due to the rate of increase of the sound's amplitude, its duration, and its rate of decrease.)

Structure of the ear

The ear can be divided into three fairly distinct components, according to both anatomical position and function. The *outer ear* is responsible for gathering sound energy and funneling it to the eardrum. Just past the eardrum, the *middle ear* acts as a mechanical transformer, and transmits the sound to the *inner ear*, where the auditory receptors are located. This section will start by describing the properties of the outer ear and then follow

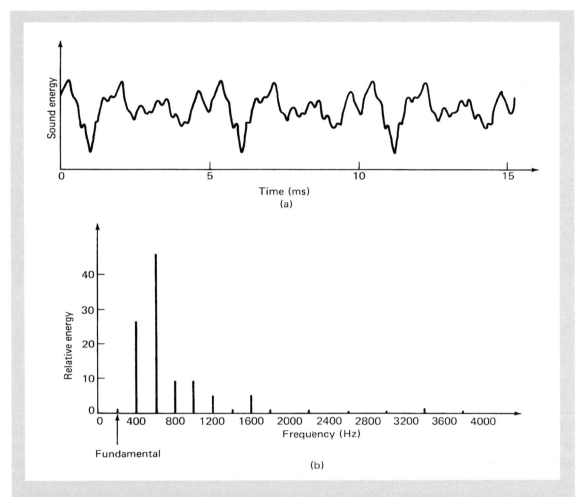

Fig. 15.4 Sound wave (a) and Fourier spectrum (b) of a violin G string. After Seashore, C. F. (1938) *The psychology of music*. McGraw-Hill, New York. Reprinted by permission.

the passage of the auditory information through the middle ear and inner ear.

The outer ear

Figure 15.5 shows a sketch of a human ear. The *pinna* is the most peripheral and noticeable portion of the ear; it is composed mostly of cartilage attached to the head by ligaments and muscles. In many animals, the pinna is an effective sound gathering device, with the ability to change position as a function of the location of the sound source. This is comparable to the way you redirect the aim of your eyes within your head to look directly at something. The human pinna, however, is immobile, so you must reposition your head to aim an ear at a sound source (although there are some people who can slightly wiggle their ears).

Our pinna is relatively smaller than the pinnae of many other animals with well developed auditory systems. Although its function as a sound-gathering device may be minor in humans, its

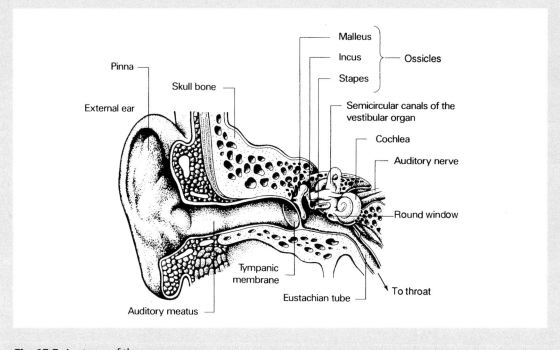

Fig. 15.5 Anatomy of the ear.

effectiveness can be increased by cupping a hand behind the ear. In addition, many studies have indicated that the shape of the pinna is important in the localization of sounds in space (Batteau, 1967; Freedman & Fisher, 1968). More will be said regarding auditory space localization in Chapter 17.

The largest depression in the pinna leads into the *external auditory meatus*, the tunnel that leads to the eardrum, or *tympanic membrane*. The meatus is about 2.5 cm long, and its length can have some influence on the sounds that reach the eardrum. Because of its physical shape, the meatus improves the selectivity of the auditory system for sounds that have frequencies in the range of about 3500 Hz, close to the midpoint of the human auditory range (Gulick, 1971).

Box 15.2 Vibrations of the eardrum

The eardrum is stretched tightly across the inner end of the auditory meatus, and is pulled slightly inward by structures in the middle ear. Because the tympanic membrane is not a uniformly stiff tissue, its vibration patterns in response to incoming sound waves are often quite complex. At fairly low frequencies (below about 2400 Hz), the membrane vibrates pretty much as a whole, although there are distinct areas of maximum and minimum excursion of the eardrum. As the frequency of the input sound is raised, however, the vibration pattern changes so that different parts of the eardrum are vibrating somewhat independently of each other (Tonndorf & Khanna, 1970).

The outer ear ends at the tympanic membrane, a three-layered tissue that vibrates in response to pressure changes in the external meatus. It is this vibration that ultimately leads to the perception of sound. <u>BOX 15.2</u>

The middle ear

On the other side of the tympanic membrane is the middle ear, which is an air-filled chamber containing three interlocking bones called the *ossicles* (literally, 'little bones'; these are the three smallest bones in your body). You can see in Fig. 15.5 that the tympanic membrane is attached to a bone called the *malleus* (Latin for hammer). The malleus is connected to the *incus* (anvil), which is a slightly larger bone that articulates with the *stapes* (stirrup). Movement of the final bone in this chain, the stapes, is the output signal of the middle ear. The stapes moves in and out of an opening in the cochlea called the *oval window*.

The function of the middle ear is to provide a mechanical transformer system that acts as an interface between the outer and inner ears. The reason for this interface is that the inner ear is a fluid-filled chamber, and so passage of sound information from the outer to the inner ear involves a boundary between air and fluid. You may have observed from personal experience that sound does not travel well across such an interface (try chatting with your pet goldfish, or talking to someone who is underwater); in fact, approximately 99.9% of the sound energy incident on an air/fluid boundary is reflected back within the air medium, so that only 0.1% of the energy is transmitted to the fluid (Wever & Lawrence, 1954). This is a decrease in energy of a factor of 1000, or a 30 dB difference. Such a reduction in energy between the inside and outside of the ear would make you very insensitive to sounds, unless an additional mechanism were present to counteract this reduction.

The middle ear provides two ways of doing so. The first has to do with the relative sizes of the tympanic membrane and the oval window into which the stapes moves. The effective area of the tympanic membrane is about 55 mm^2, while the oval window is on the order of 3.2 mm^2 (Békésy, 1960). Remember that intensity changes have been expressed in units of W/cm^2; if the total intensity remains constant, but the area in which it is expressed decreases, the intensity per unit area is proportionally increased. Put slightly differently, if the same force is applied to a large area and to a small area, the force applied to the small area will result in a bigger pressure change. This should not be too surprising; you can hit a wall with a hammer and only make a dent, but if you hit a nail with a hammer swung with the same force, all the force is concentrated at the small point of the nail, and it is driven into the wall. The tympanic membrane and oval window differ in area by about a factor of 17, so just by the difference in size of the two partitions, pressure (force per unit area) can be increased by this factor.

The other mechanism by which the middle ear transforms the auditory signal is the lever action of the three connecting bones: the malleus, incus, and stapes. Figure 15.6 shows how a lever system can increase the force of an incoming signal. In this figure, the lever is pivoting around a fulcrum at point C. The distance D_1 between the fulcrum and the point of the applied force is larger than the distance D_2 between the fulcrum and the position of the resultant force. The increase in force due to lever action is given by the following equation:

$$F_{resultant} = F_{applied} (D_1/D_2)$$

Therefore the closer the fulcrum is to the point at which the output force is applied, the larger the resultant force will be.

The ossicles of the middle ear are arranged so that they act as a lever in a way analogous to a simple lever. The length of the malleus corresponds to D_1, the distance between the applied signal and the fulcrum, while the incus acts as the lever portion between the resultant signal and the fulcrum. Measures of the lengths of these two bones indicate that the force of the incoming auditory signal is increased by the ossicles by a factor of about 1.3 (Wever & Lawrence, 1954; Fischler *et al.*, 1967).

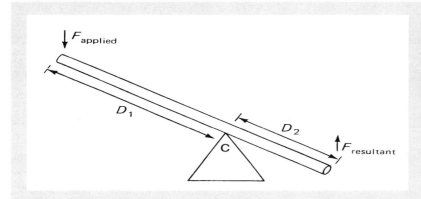

Fig. 15.6
Amplification with a lever. If D_2 is less than D_1, then the resultant force will be greater than the applied force.

The motion of the ossicles is hard to visualize in a static drawing, but you can get an idea of their action from the animation in the 'Mechanics of the auditory system' associated with this chapter on the CD. Choose 'Ossicles in the middle ear' and you will see an enlarged view of the middle ear with the ossicles in slow motion.

The combined effects of the difference in areas between the tympanic membrane and the oval window and the lever action of the ossicles produce an increase in the force of the auditory signal that can be measured experimentally. Békésy (1960) investigated the mechanical properties of the middle ear in human cadavers and found that it increased the sound pressure level by about 20–24 dB. The reduction in sound level caused by the fluid/air interface at the junction of the middle and inner ears is estimated to be about 30 dB;

therefore the action of the middle ear nearly counteracts this reduction.

The middle ear has another function in addition to the mechanical transformation of the auditory signal. When the auditory system is subjected to very loud sounds that may be potentially harmful to the inner ear, two sets of muscles in the middle ear contract and reduce the magnitude of the vibration transmitted through the middle ear. One of these muscles, the tensor tympani, is attached to the malleus; when activated, it pulls the tympanic membrane so that its stiffness is increased, and the magnitude of vibrations from incoming sounds is reduced. Similarly, the stapedius muscle connects to the stapes, causing it to retract from its normal position when the muscle is activated. This has the effect of reducing the amount of movement of the stapes in response to an auditory input. Both of

Box 15.3 The acoustic reflex

The acoustic reflex has many parallels to the pupillary reflex of the eye. Each acts to reduce the sensitivity of a sensory system when stimulus magnitude exceeds a certain level, although neither can protect the system from the damaging effects of very sudden and intense stimuli. In addition, the pupillary and acoustic reflexes are similar in that one cannot evoke either in just one eye or one ear.

A stimulus presented to one ear that is loud enough to evoke the acoustic reflex in that ear will necessarily evoke the reflex in the other ear, just as causing pupil contraction in one eye causes an equal contraction in the other eye. Of course, the eye also has a more effective protecting reflex, the blink.

these muscles contract reflexively in response to very loud noises and can cause reductions in sensitivity of the auditory system by as much as 30 dB (Reger, 1960). The combined synergistic response of the tensor tympani and stapedius muscles is called the *acoustic reflex*. <u>BOX 15.3</u>

The inner ear

The inner ear is a complicated structure encased in a *bony labyrinth*. Within the labyrinth are the *semicircular canals*, a series of fluid-filled tubes that are the primary receptor organs for the sense of balance. Continuous with the semicircular canals is the *cochlea*, a spiral-shaped structure that contains the cells that act as the auditory receptors. Figure 15.5 shows the relationship between the cochlea and the middle ear; the final bone of the ossicular chain, the stapes, transmits vibrations into the cochlea. The cochlea is filled with fluid, which is essentially incompressible, so movement of the stapes causes pressure changes in the cochlear fluid. It is these pressure changes that produce the movements that stimulate the primary auditory receptors.

Although it appears from the outside that the cochlea is a single coiled tube, there are actually three separate compartments within it. You could see this more clearly if you could unravel the cochlea, a process that is impossible in practice but easy on paper. (Bear in mind that the cochlea is a fluid-filled hollow in the skull, and not a structure unto itself.) As you will see, the properties of the cochlea do not depend on its being coiled into a spiral; this particular configuration seems to be more a matter of economy of space than of function. Figure 15.7 shows what the cochlea might look like if it were unraveled.

Of the three cochlear compartments, two are continuous with each other at the very tip, or *apex*, of the cochlea at an opening called the *helicotrema*. The oval window separates the middle ear from one compartment, the *scala vestibuli*. The scala vestibuli connects to the *scala tympani*, the chamber at the bottom of the unraveled cochlea; as the two compartments are continuous, both contain the same fluid. This fluid, the perilymph, is essentially the same in its composition as the extracellular fluid bathing most of the nervous system. At the part of the cochlea near the stapes, the scala tympani shares a wall with the middle ear through a flexible membrane called the *round window* (Fig. 15.5). When the stapes moves into the oval window, increasing the pressure within the cochlea, the round window acts to release the pressure by moving outward toward the middle ear.

The third compartment within the cochlea is the

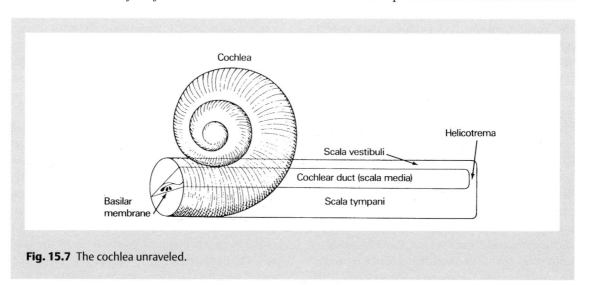

Fig. 15.7 The cochlea unraveled.

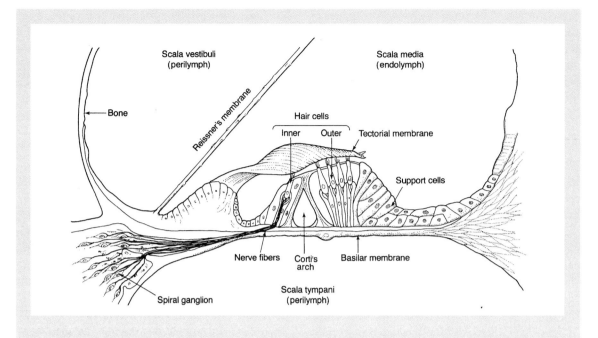

Fig. 15.8 Cross-section of the organ of Corti within a single turn of the cochlea. From *Hearing: physiological acoustics, neural coding, and psychoacoustics* by W. Lawrence Gulick, George A. Gescheider, and Robert D. Frisina. Copyright © 1989 by Oxford University Press, Oxford. Reprinted by permission.

cochlear duct or *scala media* (see Fig. 15.8). It is separated from the topmost chamber, the scala vestibuli, by *Reissner's membrane*. The structure separating the cochlear duct from the scala tympani is the *basilar membrane*. The cochlear duct is segregated from the two other cochlear compartments, and contains a fluid (*endolymph*) that differs from the fluid in those channels. Endolymph is very high in potassium, and low in sodium. The sensory organ responsible for transducing pressure changes into neural impulses lies within this duct.

On top of the basilar membrane is a structure called the *organ of Corti*, which is the primary auditory receptor structure. Figure 15.8 shows in some detail a cross-section of the unraveled cochlea with the organ of Corti. Just above the basilar membrane is a shelf of tissue called the *tectorial membrane*. On the basilar membrane sits a rigid inverted 'V' known as *Corti's arch*. On either side of the arch are the receptor cells themselves, the *hair cells*. These

cells are so named because of their ciliary projections, which are imbedded in the tectorial membrane. You have seen that visual receptors, rods and cones, also have modified cilia (see Box 4.4, p.54).

When the basilar membrane deforms in response to pressure changes in the cochlea, it produces lateral movements of the hair cell cilia. This lateral motion is visualized in the animation 'Basilar membrane', the middle button of 'Mechanics of the auditory system' on the CD. When you select this, you will see an enlargement of Fig. 15.8, with the basilar membrane slowly moving up and down as if in response to a very slow sound wave. Notice how the cilia on the tops of the hair cells (blue) get pulled left and right as the membrane moves. Through a transduction process, discussed in Box 15.4, this pulling of the hair cell cilia results in synchronous depolarization of the hair cells. The depolarization of the hair cells is the first neural signal in the auditory pathway. <u>**BOX 15.4**</u>

Box 15.4 How the cilia transduce sound

The transduction of sound energy into neural energy is rather different from the way light is transduced in the rods and cones of the eye. The cilia of each hair cell form a fairly dense bundle. The tips of the cilia are where there is a change induced by bending (Hudspeth, 1982). An extraordinarily fine filament links the tip of each cilium to the flank of its neighbor (Pickles *et al.*, 1984). The link is not quite as direct as a tiny string, and may even adjust its effective position to account for the bending (Baraniga, 1992; Meyer *et al.*, 1998). Nevertheless, it is as if the filament directly opened channels on the cilium tip when the cilia are bent in the preferred direction (Hudspeth, 1985). Actually, the result is a change in the probability of the channels being open, and the channels each rapidly oscillate between open and closed. The mechanical process is illustrated in the animation 'Hair cell cilia' in the CD demonstrations associated with this chapter.

The channels that open in the tips of the cilia are relatively non-selective about what ions they allow to pass through them (Corey & Hudspeth, 1979). However, potassium is very plentiful in the endolymph that bathes the cilia, so potassium is practically the only ion that actually flows through the channels. Usually, a flow of potassium hyperpolarizes a cell, because potassium is in relatively high supply inside cells and flows out. In the case of the hair cells, endolymph has even higher potassium levels than the cell, and the flow is reversed. Positive potassium ions *enter* through the channels and depolarize the hair cell (see Gulick, *et al.*, 1989). This depolarization leads to the release of chemical transmitter to the cells of the auditory nerve.

As in other synapses, the depolarization that leads to transmitter release acts through an intermediary: calcium. Depolarization opens channels in the base of the hair cell that allow calcium to enter the cell from the surrounding fluid (which is perilymph at the base of the cell). Calcium is instrumental for the release of transmitter. In the hair cell, it has still another function: it opens special potassium channels, called the calcium-gated potassium channels. But if you think that means there will be even more depolarization, there is still another surprise for you. Potassium *leaves* the cell through these channels, because the perilymph on the other side is low in potassium. Think of the hair cell as a lock in a potassium canal. The channels in the cilia are bathed in high-potassium endolymph, so that when they open, the potassium flows in. The channels at the base of the cell are bathed in low-potassium perilymph, so that when these channels open, the potassium flows out. Overall, potassium flows from endolymph to perilymph.

In any case, the potassium *leaving* the hair cell through the calcium-activated channels in the base results in repolarization of the cell, just as potassium channels throughout the nervous system normally lead to hyperpolarizing currents. This acts to 'quench' the depolarization caused by bending of the cilia. Bending lets potassium in, causing depolarization; depolarization opens calcium channels, letting calcium in to release transmitter and open the potassium channels in the base; these potassium channels let potassium out, ending the depolarization (Hudspeth, 1985).

Calcium may play still another role in the hair cell. The channels at the tips of the cilia are not very selective, and calcium can enter through them. Since calcium enters less readily than potassium, it may 'clog' the channel, so there is less depolarization when calcium is abundant than when it is rare (Corey & Hudspeth, 1983). This is similar to an effect calcium has in the rod outer segments (see Box 4.6, p. 58). In addition, calcium apparently affects the abilities of the channels to open, allowing it to make hair cells less sensitive (Corey & Hudspeth, 1983). In these ways, calcium may play a role in sensory adaptation, as it does in visual receptors.

Hair cells can be found on both sides of Corti's arch. Receptors on the side of the arch where the tectorial membrane arises are called *inner* hair cells, while the *outer* hair cells are located on the other side of the arch. Inner hair cells are arranged in a single row down the entire extent of the cochlea; all told, there are about 3500 inner hair cells in the human cochlea. The outer hair cells are arranged in rows on the other side of Corti's arch; the total number of outer hair cells has been estimated at about 20 000 (Goldstein, 1974).

There are structural differences between the inner and outer hair cells. Inner hair cells have about 40 cilia protruding from each cell, while outer cells have about 140 cilia (Moore, 1977). This may or may not account for the fact that outer hair cells are considerably more sensitive to weak auditory stimuli than are the inner hair cells, and are also more susceptible to damage on exposure to very loud sounds. There have also been suggestions that the two groups of receptors differ in how they respond to stimuli of a particular frequency (Billone & Raynor, 1973; but see Dallos *et al.*, 1982); how the auditory system as a whole codes the frequency of sounds is the subject of the next chapter.

The auditory pathway

The hair cells themselves do not have axons, but synapse within the organ of Corti onto the dendrites of auditory nerve fibers. Like rods and cones in the retina, hair cells do not fire action potentials, but release transmitter substance when they are depolarized (see Box 15.4). The innervation pat-

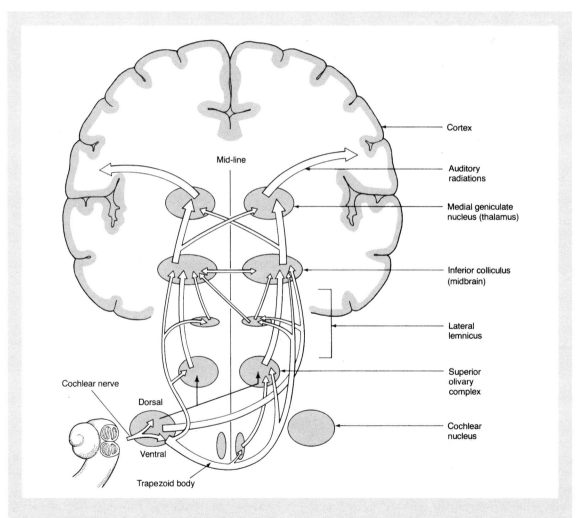

Fig. 15.9 Central pathways of the auditory system. From *Hearing: physiological acoustics, neural coding, and psychoacoustics* by W. Lawrence Gulick, George A. Gescheider, and Robert D. Frisina. Copyright © 1989 by Oxford University Press, Oxford. Reprinted by permission.

terns of the inner and outer hair cells have been shown to be completely independent (Kiang *et al.,* 1982). There is no convergence of the signal from inner hair cells; each fiber that contacts an inner hair cell contacts only the one. Instead, there is considerable divergence; each inner hair cell may contact up to 20 auditory nerve fibers. In contrast, the outer hair cells show considerable convergence, with a given fiber contacted by up to 10 outer hair cells. There is less divergence, with each outer hair cell synapsing onto only about four auditory nerve fibers (Goldstein, 1974). As a result, only about 10% of the auditory nerve fibers contact the outer hair cells, with 90% receiving exclusively from the inner hair cells (Spoendlin, 1970).

The auditory nerve fibers leaving the organ of Corti have their cell bodies in the *spiral ganglion.* (A ganglion is a group of nerve cell bodies outside the central nervous system.) The spiral ganglion is so named because it is situated right next to the cochlea and winds around in a spiral fashion just as the cochlea does. Approximately 30 000 auditory nerve fibers have their cell bodies in the spiral ganglion; this number is slightly greater than the total number of inner and outer hair cells in the cochlea. This is unlike the visual system, in which there are far fewer retinal ganglion cells than receptors.

The axons of cells in the spiral ganglion form the auditory nerve (vestibulocochlear nerve, part of the eighth cranial nerve), which enters the brainstem just under the cerebellum. Within the brainstem, almost all fibers of the auditory nerve synapse on cells in the *cochlear nucleus.* The relationships of the cochlear nucleus and higher auditory centers in the auditory processing system are shown in Fig. 15.9.

Most of the axons of cochlear nucleus cells cross to the contralateral side of the brain. As a result, much of the auditory information processed by each half of the brain comes from the ear on the other side of the head. This is in contrast to the visual system, where ganglion cell fibers cross from one side of the brain to the other or stay on the same side of the brain in nearly equal proportions. (Of course, this is also because our eyes look for-

ward and our ears aim to the sides; animals whose eyes aim to the sides show a crossing for both optic and auditory fibers.) Both crossed and uncrossed fibers from the cochlear nucleus synapse in an area of the brainstem called the *superior olivary complex.* This is the first location in the ascending auditory system to receive inputs from both ears, although most of the presynaptic fibers come from the contralateral ear.

From the superior olivary complex, axons travel one of two routes. Some fibers synapse in the *nucleus of the lateral lemniscus,* but the majority pass directly through this nucleus and synapse in the *inferior colliculus.* The inferior colliculus is a neighbor in place and function of the visual superior colliculus; together they form the tectum of the midbrain. At this level, there is another major pathway allowing information to pass from one side of the brain to the other, so that by this nucleus and higher up in the auditory system, information from the two ears is more nearly equally represented on both sides of the brain.

In addition to the pathway from one hemisphere to the other, fibers leaving the inferior colliculus project to the *medial geniculate nucleus* of the thalamus. This nucleus is a close neighbor of the LGN, the location of first synapse that the visual system makes within the brain. The structure of the auditory system is therefore not closely analogous to the visual system; while the visual system has a high level of neural processing carried out at the external sense organ, the auditory system has only one synapse before going into the brain. Before the auditory system reaches the equivalent level within the brain as the visual system, however, it passes through a sequence of up to five synaptic levels. Thus the auditory system performs many functions centrally that the visual system carries out in its periphery.

Just as lateral geniculate fibers project to the visual cortex, so do medial geniculate fibers project to the auditory cortex, whose location on the surface of the brain is shown in Figs 15.10 and 18.15 (p. 422). Auditory cortex bears some resemblances to the visual cortex. Most cortical cells within auditory

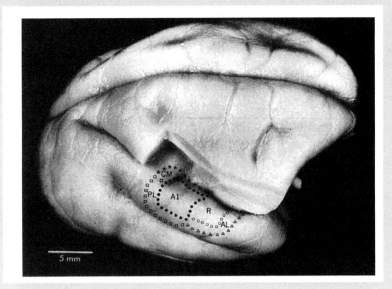

Fig. 15.10 Monkey brain partially dissected to show the areas of auditory cortex. From Imig, T. J. *et al.* (1977) Organization of auditory cortex in the owl monkey. *J. Comp. Neurol.* 171: 111–128. Reprinted by permission.

cortex receive input from both ears, just as most cells in visual cortex are binocular. In addition, a map of sorts is represented on the surface of the auditory cortex; there is a systematic relationship be-tween the spatial positions of cells within the cortex and the frequencies of sounds to which those cells are sensitive (Neff, 1961). This relationship is known as a *tonotopic map* and will be discussed in

---

Box 15.5 The top-down auditory system

The auditory system transmits information from the cochlea through a complicated processing system to the auditory cortex. There is another system, however, that follows a similar path through the brain, only in reverse. This is the descending auditory system, whose function is presumably to allow such phenomena as selective attention to favor input from one ear over the other. The final cell in this descending system has its cell body in the spiral ganglion of the cochlea and sends axons that synapse directly on the hair cells. The contacts that descending cells make with the hair cells are more diffuse than those of the auditory nerve fibers; one descending fiber will synapse on a relatively large number of hair cells. Thus this system provides a way of affecting a large portion of the receptor population, rather than affecting small numbers of cells separately from the rest of the cells in the cochlea.

Investigators have studied this system by electrically stimulating different nuclei from which the descending fibers arise, and looking to see what effect this stimulation has on activity of the auditory nerve. They found that stimulation of the descending pathway could reduce responses in the auditory nerve by an amount equivalent to a reduction in sound level of 18–25 dB (Desmedt, 1960).

The existence of a descending auditory system is not a difference from the visual system. It was mentioned in Chapters 7 and 8 that there are descending pathways from cortex to LGN, and from 'higher' cortex to primary cortex in the visual system. There may even be an analog of the fibers that go to the cochlea: fibers that descend from brain to retina. Such fibers are well known in lower vertebrates (Dowling & Cowan, 1966; Witkovsky, 1971), and may be present in mammals as well (Brooke *et al.*, 1965), although their existence is still not clear (Rodieck, 1973).

more detail in the next chapter. Some cortical cells require more specific stimulus parameters than just a particular frequency; many cells respond only to sounds coming from a particular location in space, while others respond only to onset or offset of a stimulus (Brugge & Merzenich, 1973).

In the tonotopic map, there is a systematic change in preferred frequency in the forward–backward direction along the cortex (see Fig. 16.9, p. 363). In the orthogonal direction, the position on the cortex is related to the amplitude of the sound (Suga & Manabe, 1982; Roe *et al.*, 1990). Within any vertical penetration through the cortex, the columns of cells have similar response preferences in frequency and amplitude. This arrangement is similar to the arrangement described for visual cortex (see Chapter 8), in which the column systems code for location, ocular dominance, and preferred orientation, rather than for amplitude and frequency. <u>BOX 15.5</u>

Suggested readings

Suggested readings for this chapter are included with those for Chapter 16.

Chapter 16
Frequency coding in the auditory system

IN the preceding chapter, you learned about the properties of the auditory stimulus and the structure of the auditory pathway. With this material as background, you are now ready to examine how the auditory system extracts features from the incoming stimulus to provide information regarding the pitch, loudness, and location in space of a stimulus. As you know from the demonstration 'Pitch and loudness' (which you should have run for the previous chapter, although it is associated with Chapter 17), the physical characteristic of the input stimulus that is most closely related to perceived pitch is frequency. In this chapter you will read about how the auditory system gets its information about the frequency of a sound, and how this information is transmitted through the auditory pathway.

The basilar membrane as a frequency analyzer

In Chapter 15, you saw how the basilar membrane wound through the cochlea, but you learned nothing about its physical characteristics. These characteristics, however, form a basis for our sophisticated ability to discriminate between sounds on the basis of pitch. Since the auditory hair cells respond to physical movement, and these cells are located on the surface of the basilar membrane, early auditory theorists had long been concerned with the role of this structure in the response to sound.

One early theory was that the entire basilar membrane vibrated in unison with the incoming sound wave, acting in a way similar to the diaphragm in a telephone. According to this theory (now called the *telephone theory*), hair cells located in all positions along the basilar membrane would be stimulated in synchrony, and the incoming sound wave would be replicated by the pattern of hair cell responses.

Other theorists, one of whom was the great German physiologist Helmholtz (whom you have already encountered as a pioneer of color theory), hypothesized that each location on the basilar membrane was independent of other locations, with each separate segment differentially sensitive to a very limited range of frequencies. According to his view (known as the *place theory*), information about the particular frequency of an incoming sound wave was coded by which segment of the basilar membrane vibrated in response to that sound, and therefore which subpopulation of hair cells was activated. As you will see in this chapter, both of these theories are still invoked to explain auditory pitch perception, although both theories have been significantly modified over the years.

Place theory

Start with the place theory. Helmholtz's idea was that neighboring regions of the basilar membrane are not connected to each other; he assumed that each section is under varying amounts of tension so that it resonates at a specific characteristic frequency when stimulated (in the same way that tuning forks or guitar strings vibrate at specific resonant frequencies). When a sound is presented with a frequency near the characteristic frequency of a particular section, that section would be set vibrating, and thus stimulate those hair cells attached to it.

The mechanical properties of the basilar membrane vary considerably from the *base* of the membrane (near the stapes) to the *apex* (near the helicotrema). At its base, the basilar membrane is fairly stiff, but at areas of the membrane farther away from the base, the membrane gradually becomes floppier. This transition from a stiff structure at the base to a floppy structure at the apex has great implications for the processing of sounds of different frequencies; a vibrating system that is stiff will tend to vibrate at higher frequencies than one that is floppy. The basilar membrane can therefore be expected to vibrate more strongly at its basal end when the input sound is of high frequency, and vibrate relatively more at its apex when the sound is of a lower frequency. As you know if you play guitar or other string instrument, the higher notes are played on thin, tightly stretched wires, while the deep bass notes are played on fatter and looser strings.

Georg von Békésy, the first scientist actually to observe the movements of the basilar membranes of humans, confirmed that different portions vibrated more or less according to the frequency of the input stimulus. Békésy (1947) exposed the basilar membranes of human cadavers and measured

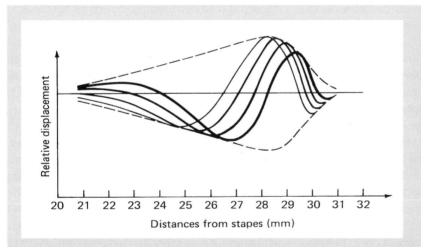

Fig. 16.1 Displacements of the cochlear membrane in response to a 200 Hz tone. The *solid curves* represent the patterns of displacement at four successive instants; the darker the line is drawn, the later in time that configuration occurred. The *dashed curve* is the envelope of maximum displacements. Note that the vertical displacements have been greatly exaggerated in this figure in order to make them visible; on the same scale as the horizontal axis, the vertical displacements would be less than 1/1000th as large as they appear here. (Be sure also to view the animation on the CD accompanying this book.) After Békésy, G. (1947) The variation of phase along the basilar membrane with sinusoidal vibrations. *J. Acoust. Soc. Am.* 19: 452–460. Reprinted by permission.

the displacement of the membrane at many locations along its length. But the basilar membrane is a continuous structure, and its response to incoming sound of a given frequency is due in part to its continuity. Békésy found that an auditory stimulus produced a *traveling wave* on the basilar membrane that traveled from the base end to the apex.

Although the waves originate near the stapes, their direction of travel does not depend on the origin of the stimulus for the wave. The movement of the stapes into the oval window causes a virtually instantaneous pressure change in the entire scala vestibuli. Increased pressure in the scala vestibuli causes the entire membrane to be pushed downward toward the scala tympani, the partition below the cochlear partition. It is this downward force exerted over the entire membrane that is the stimulus that causes the traveling waves to be generated. This was demonstrated by Békésy's observation that even when pressure changes were artificially initiated at the apex, traveling waves still traveled from the stapes to the apex on the basilar membrane.

Figure 16.1 shows the response of the basilar membrane to a steady pure tone, measured at four instants in time. The continuous curves show the displacement of the basilar membrane as a function of distance from the stapes (only the last one-third of the basilar membrane is shown; the entire membrane participates in the traveling wave). That this wave actually travels down the membrane can be appreciated by comparing the continuous curves; the displacement patterns displayed by the lighter curves represent sequential states of the membrane at very short times before the instants during which the patterns displayed as the heavier continuous curves were recorded. You can see that the entire pattern moves to the right, causing a change in displacement of all points along the basilar membrane.

The traveling waves in response to this same steady tone measured at many instants in time generate a function of all the maximum displacements of the membrane as a function of distance along the membrane (a time exposure photo-graph). Such a function is shown by the dashed curves. For this particular steady-tone input, the magnitude of the maximum membrane displacement increases gradually the farther one goes from the stapes. At a region of the membrane about 28 mm away from the stapes, the displacement reaches its maximum and then decreases rather abruptly at distances greater than 28 mm. The function relating maximum amplitude of displacement to position along the basilar membrane is called the *envelope* of the waves evoked by the stimulus.

Although the waves are traveling along the basilar membrane, the motion of the membrane itself is up and down. If you were sitting in a small boat at anchor in a sea with long, slow swells, you would see waves moving past you but your boat would just move up and down. If your boat were sitting on a giant's basilar membrane, each wave would grow as it approached some region, and then shrink as it passed away. How much your boat moved up and down would depend on how near to that maximum point you had 'anchored'; the envelope is nothing more than a map of the vertical excursion at each point. As the envelope is symmetric (that is, you go as far down in the troughs as you went up on the peaks), only the top half of it need be shown. **BOX 16.1**

The envelope of the wave displayed in Fig. 16.1 shows an area of maximum displacement at a certain position along the basilar membrane; the particular location of the maximum of a given envelope will depend on the frequency of the input sound wave. As the membrane is stiff and narrow near the stapes, high-frequency sounds will produce envelopes that have maxima closer to the stapes, while the responses to low-frequency sounds will be maximized closer to the apex. This is the physiological basis of the place theory.

Figure 16.2 shows the envelopes of patterns of vibration on the basilar membrane in response to a number of pure tones of different frequencies. The top curve shows the envelope for a very low-frequency tone; at this frequency, the entire membrane moves nearly as a unit, although the

---

Box 16.1 Traveling waves on the basilar membrane

You can see an animation of the traveling waves in the demonstration CD accompanying this book. Click on Chapter 16 and you will see a black screen like an oscilloscope. When you choose a frequency (click one of the circles inside the red oval), you will see a display of the displacement of the basilar membrane. Like Fig. 16.1, it is grossly exaggerated in the vertical direction, because if the scales were the same, the motion would be too small to see. Unlike the figure, the full length of the basilar membrane is represented; more significantly, the 'membrane' is in motion. The motion is slow compared with the actual frequencies (it would just be a blur, even if your computer could animate that quickly). For the first couple of seconds after you choose a frequency, a tone of that frequency will be played—click 'Silence' *before* clicking the choice of tone if you don't want to disturb others around you.

Although the animation is slow, you will be best able to appreciate the traveling waves at low frequencies. Start with 200 Hz (the frequency in Fig. 16.1). You will see the waves traveling from left to right (base to apex), with peaks and troughs growing to a maximum at about 28 mm and then shrinking toward the apex. The envelope is shown in green, with a vertical blue line marking the peak. As the waves pass the peak, the membrane moves up and down in a sinusoid, as you can see by watching the red circle marking the intersection of the blue line and the membrane.

At higher frequencies, the motion is hard to see because the changes are too great between frames. You will nevertheless be able to see the change in wavelength and in the position of the peak of the envelope.

---

greatest vibration is at the apex of the cochlea. The rest of the figure shows the responses to a series of stimuli of increasing frequency. As the frequency of the sound wave gets higher, the location of the displacement maximum moves closer to the stapes. The shape of the envelope also changes, becoming narrower as frequency increases. For fairly high-frequency tones, therefore, only a small portion of the basilar membrane moves to any significant degree, while the entire

membrane responds to low tones. If you choose different frequencies in the demonstration on the CD (see Box 16.1), you will see the envelope shift its position (although the motion is less realistic at the higher frequencies). **BOX 16.2**

Instead of measuring the maximum displacement of the entire basilar membrane in response to a particular sound wave, it is possible to measure the maximum displacement of a single point on the membrane in response to a large number of

---

Box 16.2 Measuring the motion of the basilar membrane

The techniques that have been used to measure the vibration of the basilar membrane deserve some mention. When Békésy (1928, 1942) first performed his experiments on cadavers, he obtained recordings of the position of the basilar membrane by viewing the entire cochlea using a light microscope under stroboscopic illumination. Thus, he could photographically record the position of the entire membrane at a given instant. The major problems with this method were that it could only be used with dead preparations, and the light microscope

did not give a high enough resolution to see the vibrations produced by anything but very loud sounds.

These problems were resolved with a technique that involved placing a small amount of radioactive material directly on the basilar membrane, and measuring the changes in the radiation emitted by the material when a sound wave caused vibration of the membrane (Johnstone *et al.*, 1970). This technique involves measuring the Doppler shift for emitted radioactivity; it allows much finer resolution of movement of the basilar membrane than is possible using a light microscope.

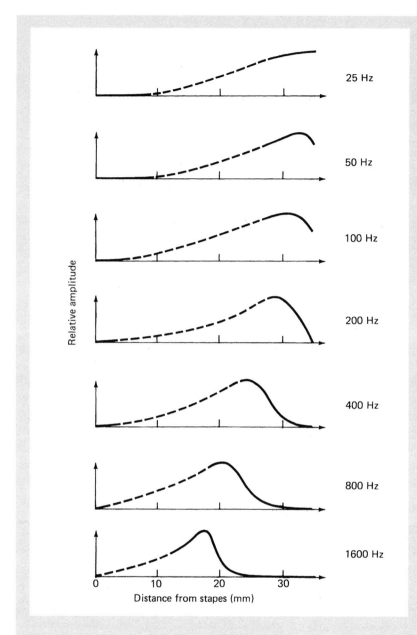

Fig. 16.2 Envelopes of vibration patterns on the basilar membrane for pure tones of different frequencies. Note the envelope for 200 Hz, the rightmost third of which was shown as the dashed curve in Fig. 16.1. From Békésy, G. (1960) *Experiments in hearing*. McGraw Hill, New York. Reprinted by permission.

sounds of different frequencies. Figure 16.3 shows a series of such functions, with each curve derived from responses of one particular location along the membrane. These functions are called *resonance curves*; they are a useful way of looking at the

response of the basilar membrane to sound, because they show how a single hair cell located at one position along the membrane would be stimulated by tones of different frequencies.

The resonance curves in Fig. 16.3 contain the

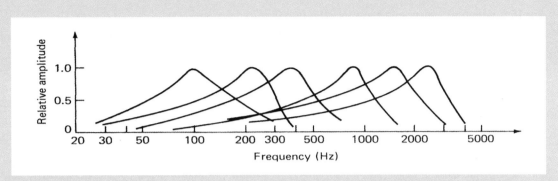

Fig. 16.3 Resonance curves at six different positions along the basilar membrane. From Békésy (1960). Reprinted by permission.

same information as the envelopes of basilar membrane vibrations shown in Fig. 16.2. In the first case, responses are measured for single frequencies at all points along the membrane, while in the latter case, responses at a single point on the membrane are measured at different frequencies. The two types of curves are simply alternate ways of displaying the same thing. For example, the second curve from the left in Fig. 16.3 peaks at about 200 Hz. From Figs 16.1 and 16.2, you can see that the part of the basilar membrane most sensitive to vibrations at 200 Hz is about 28 mm from the base (or about 6 mm from the apex); this curve must therefore correspond to that position on the basilar membrane. Similarly, the second curve from the right in Fig. 16.3 peaks at about 1600 Hz; from Fig. 16.2 you can estimate that it corresponds to a position about 17 or 18 mm from the base (just about halfway from base to apex).

The resonance curves in Fig. 16.3 have a number of important features. For example, at any particular point on the basilar membrane, one frequency maximally excites that point. This fact is of crucial importance; it means that the mechanical properties of the membrane allow the auditory system to distinguish one frequency from another by the location on the membrane that is maximally excited by a particular frequency. Thus if the response of the auditory hair cells at a particular location

along the basilar membrane is related to the amplitude of vibration at that location, the auditory system can get information about the frequency of a pure tone by attending to which hair cells are responding more than their neighbors on either side.

Another feature of the basilar membrane resonance curves that deserves mention is the fact that the curves are asymmetrical. For any given location on the membrane, the curve decays more gradually on the low-frequency side of the preferred frequency for that location than on the high-frequency side. Thus a tone that is lower than the preferred frequency will produce a larger displacement than a tone that is an equivalent amount higher. This is consistent with the shapes of the envelopes of maximum basilar membrane vibration shown in Fig. 16.2; lower frequencies cause the entire membrane to vibrate, so that any given location will tend to respond to a wide range of tones that are lower than the preferred frequency for that location. <u>BOX 16.3</u>

You have now seen strong evidence that the basilar membrane is involved in a frequency-to-place conversion for pure tone stimuli. How does this system respond to more complicated stimuli—for example, a combination of two pure tones? If the two tones are very different in frequency, the response of the membrane to the combination is two

Box 16.3 Why low frequencies are less selective than high frequencies

The asymmetry in which all parts of the cochlea respond better to frequencies lower than their best frequency than to higher frequencies is a common property of oscillators. Imagine a simple oscillator in which a weight is hung by a spring, as shown in Fig. 16.4 (you can try this yourself with a weight such as a pair of scissors hung by a rubber band). When the system is 'driven' slowly (the hand moving up and down in a slow sinusoid, as shown at the top), the spring stays the same length, and the weight also moves up and down. As the rate of motion increases, the spring starts stretching on the upward pulls, and contracting as the weight is still rising when the arm starts down. At the frequency that gives the maximum motion of the weight (middle of the figure), the weight and hand are completely out of phase. At even higher frequencies, the spring just stretches and contracts, and the weight stays practically stationary (bottom). The maximum motion of the weight is at the resonant frequency (middle). Notice that there is motion at lower frequencies (top), but not at higher frequencies (bottom).

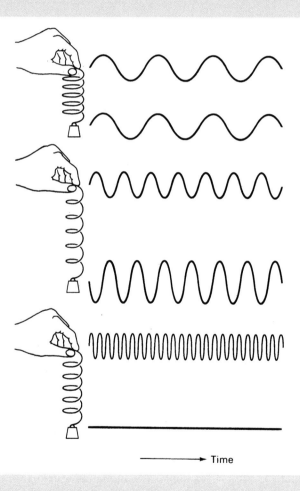

Fig. 16.4 Action of a simple oscillator: a weight hung from a spring, driven by sinusoidal up-and-down motion of the hand.

Time

essentially separate patterns of displacement. There are two local vibration maxima along the basilar membrane, with the locations of the maxima identical to where they would be if the tones were presented singly. In this way, the basilar membrane takes a complex tone combination and breaks it down into its component frequencies. For combinations of tones fairly far apart in frequency, then, the auditory system acts as a Fourier analyzer in the same way that the visual system may analyze the frequency components in a grating stimulus (see Chapter 9).

For tones that are close together in frequency, however, the response of the basilar membrane is more complex. If the two frequencies are quite close together, there will no longer be two discrete maxima; instead there is one fairly broad maximum that encompasses the locations at which each tone presented singly would produce its maximum response. This occurs even though the auditory system as a whole may be perfectly capable of discriminating between the two sounds when each is presented separately. Possible mechanisms by which the auditory system can resolve such stimuli will be discussed later.

Neural correlates of a place theory

In the preceding section, you saw evidence supporting the hypothesis that the basilar membrane is involved in a frequency-to-place conversion for any incoming sound wave. As most auditory nerve fibers receive from only one (inner) hair cell, the response of a given fiber should reflect the frequency selectivity of the location on the basilar membrane from which it comes. In fact, when microelectrodes are used to record the responses of single axons within the auditory nerve, such frequency selectivity is usually found.

There are several ways in which the frequency selectivity of single fibers can be demonstrated. One is to present to a single fiber a wide range of stimuli at different frequencies but identical intensity; the function generated when the responses to the stimuli are plotted against the frequency of each stimulus is called an *iso-intensity contour* (Rose *et al.*, 1971). Figure 16.5 shows a family of such contours for a single fiber in a monkey auditory nerve; each curve was generated using a different intensity level of the stimuli. Although at high intensities the contours are quite broad, for moderate intensities they reveal a single well-

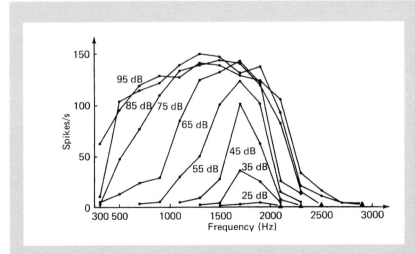

Fig. 16.5 Iso-intensity contours for a single auditory nerve fiber in the monkey. From Rose, J. E., J. E. Hind, D. J. Anderson and J. F. Brugge (1971) Some effects of stimulus intensity on response of auditory nerve fibers in the squirrel monkey. *J. Neurophysiol.* 34: 685–699. Reprinted by permission.

defined frequency maximum that corresponds to the location on the basilar membrane from which the fiber originated.

Another way to display the tuning characteristics of individual auditory nerve fibers is to employ a sensitivity measure rather than the response measure of the iso-intensity contour. (The usefulness of sensitivity measures over response measures was discussed in Chapter 6.) Figure 16.6 shows a set of functions called tuning curves, showing how the threshold intensity for a given fiber varies as a function of stimulus frequency. Each curve was generated by determining, for a single fiber, the lowest intensity of a pure tone that will produce a detectable response, across an entire series of pure tones. The frequency of the tone for which the threshold of a given fiber is lowest is called the *characteristic frequency* of that fiber.

Neural interactions in the auditory system Single locations on the basilar membrane and single auditory nerve fibers each respond selectively to a limited range of stimulus frequencies. Are the responses quantitatively similar to each other, or do neural interactions in the auditory periphery act to modify the signal? One way to investigate this question would be to generate tuning curves for both basilar membrane responses and auditory nerve fibers and to present them on the same coordinate system. Weiss (1964) combined the data from experiments by Békésy (1942) on the mechanical responses of the basilar membrane, and

by Kiang, *et al.* (1965), who recorded from single auditory fibers. The mechanical and neural tuning curves were qualitatively similar, but there seemed to be substantial quantitative differences. In particular, the neural tuning curves were narrower than the curves generated from the mechanical responses of the basilar membrane. In other words, the auditory nerve fibers seemed more finely tuned with respect to frequency than are specific locations of the basilar membrane. This suggested that some sort of neural interactive network acts to sharpen the frequency response before the level of the auditory nerve fiber.

One mechanism that would act to sharpen the neural response to pure tones would be a lateral inhibitory system analogous to that in the visual system. The antagonistic interactions between the center and surround of a retinal ganglion cell allow the visual system to enhance spatial borders; investigators interested in the auditory system reasoned that the same type of interaction between cells located at different positions along the basilar membrane could enhance the selectivity to certain frequencies.

More recently, however, measurements have shown that the difference between mechanical tuning and neural tuning is not very impressive after all (Khanna & Leonard, 1982; Dallos *et al.*, 1982). In fact, a careful comparison of mechanical and neural tuning at the same point in the same cochlea showed no significant difference at all (Narayan *et al.*, 1998). Much as one might expect a

---

Box 16.4 Why neural sharpening *seemed* to be present

The early work really seemed to indicate that there was neural tuning between mechanical vibrations of hair cells and the signal in the auditory nerve. It was even given a name: 'funneling'. Why were we fooled?

One problem is that measurements were made in different preparations. In order to observe a mechanical vibration, a window must be opened into the cochlea, and this can affect mechanical properties (Narayan *et al.*,

1998). The main problem, however, is that the mechanical recordings were done on cadavers. There is a reason why cadavers are colloquially known as 'stiffs'. Among other things, their basilar membranes may be less compliant than in living tissue (Dallos & Evans, 1995). In addition, the living cells may actually 'work' to improve mechanical tuning (see the next section).

mechanism like lateral antagonism, it seems not to be present, at least not at the most peripheral level. BOX 16.5

Mechanisms of frequency tuning Still another factor has been found at the level of the cochlea: the hair cells change their mechanical properties in response to commands from the descending auditory pathways (see Chapter 15) and in response to sound. The cilia can actually exert force against the tectorial membrane, and thereby affect their own vibration (Hubbard & Mountain, 1983; Brownell *et al.*, 1985; Dallos, 1996). Unhealthy (or dead) hair cells would not produce this response, and so the mechanical properties of the basilar membrane in such preparations might not be tuned in the same way as in a healthy preparation. Since the mechanical response depends on the electrical responses, this kind of mechanism could allow for tuning by coupling the mechanical and electrical properties of the hair cells (Weiss, 1982). BOX 16.5

If lateral antagonism is not present at the very first synapse of the auditory system, it certainly does exist at the next stage. Recording from cells in the cochlear nucleus, onto which auditory nerve fibers synapse, Rose *et al.* (1959) showed that the response of a cell to a stimulus at its characteristic frequency could be inhibited by the presentation of another stimulus at another frequency. This is illustrated in Fig. 16.7, where the response of a cochlear nucleus cell is plotted as a function of time. A steady tone at this cell's preferred frequency (5300 Hz) was presented continuously, while a second tone (at 4500 Hz) was presented for short time periods at regular intervals. The effect of the second tone presentation was to abolish completely the response of the cell, even though the preferred tone was still present.

Other experiments involving recording from neurons in the cochlear nucleus have provided more details regarding the extent of this lateral interaction. Greenwood & Maruyama (1965) recorded from cells in the cochlear nucleus that possessed an ongoing maintained discharge in the absence of stimulation. They found cells that responded with increased firing to stimuli within a restricted frequency range, but which actually reduced their firing below the maintained level when they were presented with stimuli just outside that range. Figure 16.8 shows an example of a

---

Box 16.5 Functions of the inner hair cells

A method has been developed by which the functioning of inner hair cells could be studied in the absence of outer hair cells. Kiang *et al.* (1970) found that when cats were treated with the antibiotic kanamycin, both inner and outer hair cells completely degenerated over large areas of the basilar membrane. While these investigators did not note a differential effect of the drug on inner and outer hair cells, Dallos & Harris (1978) found that it attacked outer hair cells preferentially over inner hair cells in the chinchilla. In animals treated with kanamycin, large sections of the basilar membrane could be found having inner hair cells that appeared to function normally with no outer hair cells present.

Dallos & Harris found that they could record from auditory nerve fibers coming from areas on the basilar membrane where no outer hair cells were present. They found that such fibers did respond to sound in a frequency-

selective way, but that the shapes of their tuning curves were markedly affected. The sensitivity of individual cells was much reduced, and the shape of the tuning curve was broadened, particularly on the low-frequency tail of the curve. Their conclusion was that the outer hair cells acted on the inner hair cells in some way to enhance the sensitivity of the cells in a frequency-dependent way.

We know that there is minimal neural sharpening by lateral antagonism in the cochlea itself. Moreover, more recent work indicates that the tuning of inner and outer hair cells is quite similar (Dallos, Santos-Sacchi, & Flock, 1982). For the outer hair cells to affect the tuning of the inner hair cells by a neural mechanism, their tuning might be expected to differ. Most likely, the outer hair cells affect the responses of the inner hair cells (and themselves) through their mechanical responses.

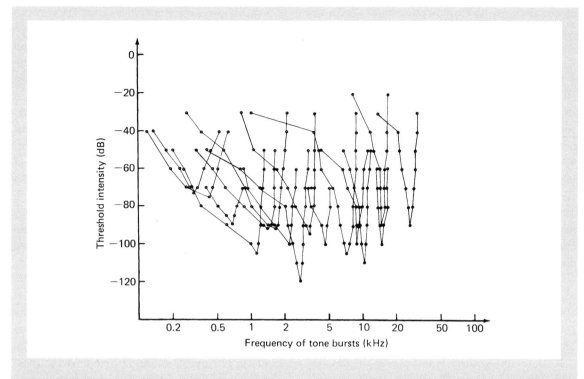

Fig. 16.6 Tuning curves for 16 auditory nerve fibers in the cat. From Kiang, N. Y-S., T. Watanabe, F. C. Thomas and L. F. Clark. (1962) Stimulus coding in the cat's auditory nerve. *Ann. Otol. Rhinol. Laryngol.* 71: 1009–1025. Reprinted by permission of the publisher and author.

cell with these inhibitory side regions. The dashed line in the center of the figure represents the tuning curve using a threshold criterion response; the extent of this curve shows the frequency and intensity ranges within which stimuli caused the cell to increase its firing. The shaded areas show the frequencies for which stimuli reduced the firing of the cell. The analogy of this type of cell to a retinal ganglion cell is striking; there is a center region on the basilar membrane within which stimulation will cause excitation of the cell, but there are areas just bordering on the excitatory center, activation of which will cause the cell to decrease its firing.

This type of interaction within the visual system resulted in the sharpening of spatial borders; enhancement of border responses along the length of the basilar membrane should result in increasing frequency selectivity of the system. (The analogy breaks down on close inspection, as the same frequency stimulus can cause either excitation or inhibition, depending on the intensity of the stimulus.)

Frequency coding in higher centers

Since auditory nerve fibers coming from particular locations on the basilar membrane project in an orderly fashion onto the cochlear nucleus, cells within this nucleus have preferred frequencies that vary as a function of their position in the nucleus. This orderly representation of preferred frequencies along the surface of the nucleus is a *tonotopic mapping*.

As you read in Chapter 15, tonotopic organization is also found in higher auditory centers. Just as there is a retinotopic representation of the vi-

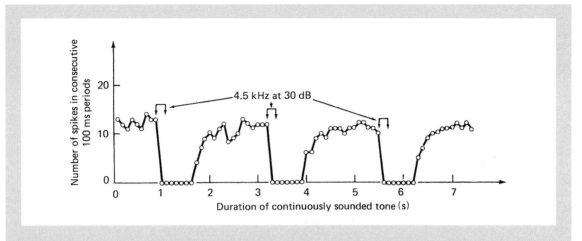

Fig. 16.7 Demonstration of lateral inhibition (funneling) in the cochlear nucleus. A 5300 Hz tone is presented continuously, with bursts of a 4500 Hz tone superimposed on the continuous tone. Firing is markedly reduced when the 4500 Hz tone burst is presented. From Rose, J. F., R. Galambos and J. R. Hughes (1959) Microelectrode studies of the cochlear nuclei of the cat. *Johns Hopkins Hosp. Bull.* 104: 211. Reprinted by permission.

sual world on the surface of the visual cortex, different positions along the basilar membrane are found to project systematically to specific locations along the surface of the auditory cortex (Merzenich *et al.*, 1975; Roe *et al.*, 1990). Figure 16.9 shows a map of the surface of the primary auditory cortex. The numbers shown are the characteristic frequencies of the cells encountered at each particular location. Going from left to right on the figure, the characteristic frequencies of the cells encountered progressively decrease. The dashed lines that run almost vertically within the figure are iso-frequency contours; along those lines, the preferred frequencies of the cells remain approximately constant. Left-to-right movement in the figure corresponds to forward-to-backward movement on the surface of the brain. Thus, within the auditory cortex, the preferred frequency of the cells decreases from the front to the back of the head.

A tonotopic map on the surface of the auditory cortex could simply be a consequence of the tonotopic mapping in the cochlea. In accordance with place theory, different positions along the basilar

membrane correspond to different frequencies. Thus, a map of the cochlea on the cortex would retain the tonotopic characteristics of the cochlea itself. You might then refer to this as a *cochleotopic* map, just as the retinotopic map in visual cortex also represents visual space. <u>**BOX 16.6**</u>

In summary, you have seen strong evidence that the auditory system processes information about the frequency of an incoming sound wave according to which location along the basilar membrane is maximally activated. The neural signals coming from the basilar membrane reflect mechanisms that act to make the tuning curves of individual neurons sharper than would be expected solely on the basis of the properties of the membrane. After the level of this interaction, however, auditory neurons do not undergo a noticeable neural sharpening process; tuning curves in the medial geniculate nucleus look quite similar to the tuning curves for auditory nerve fibers. In addition, the conversion from frequency to position that originates at the basilar membrane is maintained all the way up to the auditory cortex (but see Box 16.6).

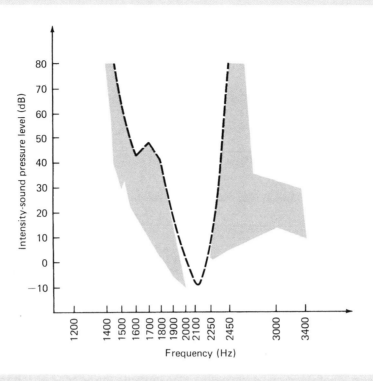

Fig. 16.8 Representation of excitatory and inhibitory response areas for a neuron in the cochlear nucleus of the cat. The *dashed line* in the middle of the figure is the excitatory tuning curve for the cell. *Shaded regions* show the inhibitory regions for this cell. Adapted from Greenwood, D. D. and N. Maruyama (1965). Excitatory and inhibitory response areas of auditory neurons in the cochlear nucleus. *J. Neurophysiol.* 28: 863–892. Reprinted by permission.

Box 16.6 A map of pitch on the cortex

In fact, the tonotopic map encodes the pitch of the stimulus. If complex stimuli are used, the location of the maximum response on the auditory cortex corresponds to the pitch, not the frequency components, of the stimulus (Pantev *et al.*, 1989). Since the mechanical vibration of the cochlea is purely dependent on frequency, there must be a transformation to what we recognize as pitch between cochlea and cortex.

Another way to demonstrate that pitch depends on more than the location on the cochlea is by directly stimulating the cochlea at locations that are inappropriate for the frequency of the stimulation. When Tong *et al.* (1983) did this on humans, they found two components, both interpreted as 'pitch'. One component corresponded to the location of the stimulation in the cochlea; this is the 'place' pitch. The second component corresponded to the *frequency* of the stimulus, independent of where it was applied within the cochlea. If it is correct that cortical cells do not show phase-locked firing (Brugge & Merzenich, 1973; Merzenich *et al.*, 1975), these signals must be somehow 'finding' the appropriate tonotopic locations in the cortex, despite their original cochleotopic locations. The important point is that the temporal frequency of the stimulus is not lost when it is inappropriately 'placed' on the basilar membrane. Some mechanism other than position on the basilar membrane must encode the temporal frequency. The next section discusses such a mechanism.

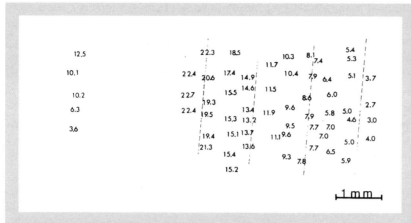

Fig. 16.9 Tonotopic map on the surface of the auditory cortex. Numbers reflect the peak frequencies (in KHz) of cells encountered at that location. From Merzenich, M. M., P. L. Knight and G. L. Roth (1975) Representation of cochlea within primary auditory cortex in the cat. *J. Neurophysiol.* 38: 231–249. Reprinted by permission.

Evidence for temporal frequency coding in the auditory system

Although the evidence for the place theory is compelling, there is some question about whether the tuning curves obtained for neurons in the auditory system provide a mechanism for frequency discrimination that is fine enough to account for the behavioral data. People can detect remarkably small differences in frequency; for a 1000 Hz frequency at a moderate intensity, you can detect a difference that is as small as 3 Hz (Moore, 1977). The narrowest tuning curves that were presented in the preceding section still seem to be too broad to account for such resolution.

An alternative to the place theory that might account for our well-developed abilities to discriminate between nearby frequencies was suggested many years ago by Wever & Bray (1930). They proposed that the entire basilar membrane vibrates in unison in response to a pure tone, with the vibration of the membrane matching the input frequency. They further suggested that the auditory receptors respond in such a way that the *temporal pattern* of the basilar membrane vibration is reproduced in the firing of the auditory nerve. You may recall that this alternative has been named the 'telephone theory', because the basilar membrane is hypothesized to act in a way analogous to a vibrating diaphragm in a telephone.

From the early work of Békésy, we know that the basilar membrane does not act precisely in the way proposed by Wever & Bray; however, it is still possible that some frequency information could be present in the pattern of particular auditory nerve firings (see Box 16.6). Wever & Bray proposed that if the frequency of the pure tone stimulus were low enough, auditory nerve fibers could respond by firing one or more action potentials at the same time in every cycle of the pure tone. Thus the response pattern of an individual nerve fiber would accurately reflect the frequency of the sound wave.

As neurons cannot fire much faster than, say, 1000 action potentials per second, however, this mechanism would seem to be limited to transmitting information about low-frequency tones only. Criticisms that a telephone theory would only be able to account for perception of low-frequency tones led Wever & Bray (1937) to modify their theory, and suggest that for higher-frequency sounds, every *individual* auditory nerve fiber did not have to give an exact reproduction of the pattern of the sound.

For frequencies of the input signal high enough that an individual nerve fiber could not fire fast enough to follow the signal, Wever & Bray proposed the operation of the *volley principle* illustrated in Fig. 16.10. In this figure, the sound wave illustrated at the top is at too high a frequency for a single auditory fiber to follow. According to the volley principle, however, each fiber fires only at a certain point in a cycle of the sound wave, although the fiber does not respond to every cycle.

In the figure, the eight fibers displayed are responding somewhat irregularly to the incoming signal. Even though every cell does not fire during every cycle of the sound wave, they are all responding in phase; that is, if on any cycle a given auditory nerve fiber does fire, it does so in the same relative position within the cycle. If auditory nerve fibers do respond in such a fashion, and the important signal for higher auditory centers is the ensemble or combination of the responses of many fibers, then the information is conveyed by the combined response of all the fibers that are responding to a given sound wave. The bottom trace in Fig. 16.10 shows the combined responses of the eight auditory fibers displayed in the rest of the figure; while none of the individual fibers reproduces the pattern of the wave, the combined response of all cells is sufficient to reproduce accurately the frequency of the incoming signal. Thus, according to the volley principle, frequency of the sound is coded by the response pattern of an ensemble of auditory nerve fibers.

This discussion of how response pattern could act to code the frequency of a sound wave has so far been entirely hypothetical, but there is physiological evidence for such a mechanism. Evidence has been found in the responses of sin-

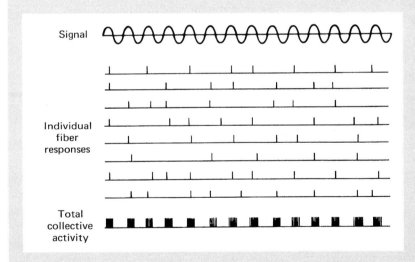

Fig. 16.10 The volley principle. The ensemble of fiber responses shown at the bottom has a pattern of responses that corresponds to the input sound wave, even though individual fibers are not firing fast enough to follow the pattern of the stimulus. Adapted from Wever, E. G., *Theory of hearing*. Copyright © 1949 John Wiley & Sons, Inc. Reprinted by permission.

gle auditory nerve fibers in the monkey. Rose *et al.* (1968) stimulated the monkey auditory system with pure tones of different frequencies, and constructed *inter-spike interval* histograms for each stimulus presentation. An inter-spike interval histogram is generated by taking all the times between successive action potentials produced by a single cell during a long period of firing, and collecting them into bins according to their durations. Thus all the intervals that were between 2 and 3 ms in duration would be counted in one bin; all the intervals between 3, and 4 ms long would be in the next bin, and so on. After this binning procedure is finished, the number of intervals that are in each bin is plotted as a function of the average duration of the intervals that went into that bin.

Figure 16.11 shows six inter-spike interval histograms obtained from one neuron, generated using stimuli of different frequencies. The horizontal axis plots the length of the interval, while the number of intervals of that duration is plotted on the vertical axis. In plot (a), the stimulus was a tone of 408 Hz; if the neuron fired one action potential at the same phase of each of two successive cycles of the stimulus, the interval between action potentials would be 1/408 = 2.45 ms. If the neuron missed a cycle, the interval between successive spikes would be twice that interval length (that is, 4.9 ms). The interval where two cycles were missed would be 7.35 ms, and so on. The histogram shown in plot (a) has a concentration of intervals that would be expected if the cell were firing at every cycle, as well as many intervals of lengths that are

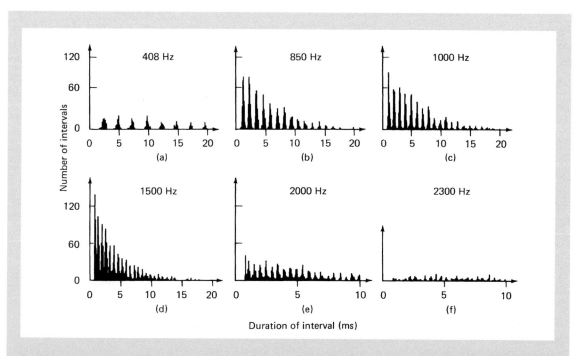

Fig. 16.11 Inter-spike interval histograms for a single auditory neuron in the monkey, for tones of different frequencies. From Rose, J. E., J. F. Brugge, D. J. Anderson and J. E. Hind (1968) Patterns of activity in single auditory nerve fibers of the squirrel monkey. In *Hearing mechanisms in vertebrates*, eds. A. V. S. de Reuck and J. Knight. Churchill, London. Reprinted by permission.

multiples of the interval expected if the cell were firing at every cycle. This cell, therefore, sometimes fires at consecutive cycles, sometimes fires every other cycle, sometimes every third cycle, and so on. Its firing pattern is an accurate reflection of the frequency of the incoming sound wave, just as the telephone theory would predict.

The other parts of Fig. 16.11 show inter-spike interval histograms of the same cell in response to different frequency sound waves. In plot (c), the stimulus is a tone of 1000 Hz; the volley theory would predict that most of the inter-spike intervals would be of length 1/1000 s (= 1 ms), or integer multiples of 1 ms. This prediction is borne out in the histogram; there are large numbers of intervals at 1 ms, but there also are concentrations at 2, 3 and 4 ms, and so on. The firing pattern of this cell reproduces the frequency of the sound wave for all of the stimuli in this figure except the 2300 Hz stimulus whose histogram is shown in plot (f). This is because the auditory fiber from which the recording is being made has its origin fairly close to the apex of the basilar membrane, and is therefore insensitive to high frequencies. Remember that, although this is evidence for temporal pat-terning as a way of transmitting frequency information, the place theory is also valid.

Auditory nerve fibers have been found that code frequency by the pattern of their response for frequencies up to 4000 or 5000 Hz (Rose *et al.*, 1968). Above that level, the variability inherent in neuronal firing becomes too great for such fine patterns to be resolved. Above the 5000 Hz level, therefore, frequency is probably coded solely by the place theory; remember that it is at these high frequencies that auditory nerve fiber tuning curves are at their narrowest, to give the finest discrimination on the basis of place. Below this frequency level, the preceding discussion raises the possibility that frequency may be coded using temporal pattern—as well as place—information, as proposed by Wever in 1949. Note that there is no direct evidence that the auditory system actually uses the temporal pattern information present in the auditory nerve fibers. In fact, it is unclear how the 'higher' centers would extract this information. But this encoding by firing patterns may remind you of the patterns and oscillations suggested for the 'binding' of features in visual cortex (see Box 10.5, p. 198). It is also possible to build

---

Box 16.7 The trade-off between sampling time and number of cells

The histograms in Fig. 16.11 were each generated from a long record of the firing of a single neuron during the presentation of a sustained pure tone. Gathering enough intervals for the pattern to emerge may require many seconds of firing. Your auditory system can detect the pitch of a tone from a much shorter sample, a fraction of a second. In that time, one cell might produce only about a dozen intervals, so the histogram from that one neuron would have only a few scattered bins with intervals in them.

The reason that the nervous system can determine pitch from a much shorter sample is that it has available to it the firing of a larger number of fibers. If you made a histogram from the intervals produced by 1000 neurons, you could obtain a picture like those in Fig. 16.11 in 1/1000th of the time. You could record the activity of the whole auditory nerve, but notice that if you could not keep track of which cell was producing which action potential it would do you no good. The phases would be different for different neurons (remember, this is a traveling wave, so it stimulates different cells at different times), and the volley would be smeared out. The nervous system must have a way of taking account of these phase shifts.

The higher centers in the auditory system can make use of the information from a large number of single cells. This is a point that is sometimes overlooked when we seek to understand a whole system from the activity of single cells. When you perform an operation like generating the histograms in Fig. 16.11, you are averaging over time; we implicitly assume that the statistics of any individual over a long time are the same as those of the ensemble at any moment.

a workable artificial cochlea based purely on temporal patterning (Wasserman, 1990). Later you will learn about some perceptual phenomena, such as auditory localization of sounds in space, that suggest that different mechanisms may be responsible for the perception of frequency above and below 5000 Hz. <u>BOX 16.7</u>

The perception of frequency

So far in this chapter, you have learned about various possible mechanisms by which the auditory system might abstract frequency information from a sound stimulus. It is now time to consider what kinds of discrimination people can actually make on the basis of frequency, as well as the effect that variations in frequency can have on the auditory percept. There are two psychological qualities that are affected primarily by the frequency content of a given auditory stimulus: the *pitch* and the *timbre* associated with the sound.

Pitch is a sound quality that is closely related to the frequency of a pure tone or the fundamental frequency of a complex tone containing many harmonics. Pitch is not identical to the frequency of a tone, however, just as the color of a light is not identical to its wavelength. You should have heard the pitch change when you changed the intensity of a 6400 Hz tone in the 'Pitch and loudness' demonstration of Chapter 17.

Timbre is a sensation that is related to the quality of the sound. Two sounds can be judged equal in pitch but may sound quite distinct because of differences in the timbre. This sensed quality is what accounts for the difference in the sound of, for example, a woodwind instrument and a violin playing the same musical note. Differences in timbre between two sounds of identical pitch are usually ascribed to differences in the harmonic content of the two sounds, while pitch is a function of the fundamental frequency.

The perception of pure tones

Pitch versus frequency   Pitch is the sound quality most closely related to the frequency of a pure tone. High-frequency tones are perceived as being of high pitch, while low-frequency tones are said to be low in pitch. The relationship between pitch and frequency is not a simple linear one, however. In order to make more precise statements about how the two are related, an arbitrary unit called the *mel* has been defined as the unit of pitch. The pitch of a 1000 Hz tone at 40 dB SPL has been given a fixed value of 1000 mel, and psychophysical scaling techniques have been used to determine the number of mels that are associated with different frequency tones. This is done using the method of magnitude production discussed in Chapter 2. A subject is presented with a 1000 Hz tone and is told that its pitch is 1000 mels; the subject is then asked to manipulate the frequency of a variable frequency tone until that tone has a pitch that is one-half as high as the 1000 mel tone. That tone is assigned a value of 500 mel. The subject can then find a frequency that is half the pitch of the 500 mel tone; that tone is assigned a value of 250 mel. In this way, an entire function relating frequency to mels can be generated.

Figure 16.12 shows an example of such a function. Frequency of the tone is shown using a logarithmic scale for the abscissa, while mels are displayed as the ordinate. This curve shows that pitch is not related to frequency in either a linear or a logarithmic fashion. Rather, the relationship is more complex.

Differential sensitivity   People can hear and assign pitch values to pure tones having frequencies that range from about 20 to 20 000 Hz. The range is largest in young children and decreases systematically as age increases. Below 20 Hz, a stimulus at high enough sound levels will still be perceived as present, but a subject will not be able to assign it a pitch. Rather, the perception a person has of an extremely low-frequency tone may be a 'chugging' sound (Geldard, 1972), with discrete sounds being

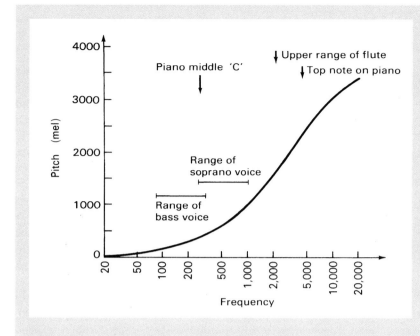

Fig. 16.12 Pitch (in mels) plotted *versus* frequency of an auditory stimulus. Fundamental frequencies of some musical reference points are indicated. One octave is represented by a doubling of the frequency. From Stevens, S. S. and J. Volkmann (1940) The relation of pitch to frequency: a revised scale. *Am. J. Psychol.* 53: 329–353. Reprinted by permission.

heard at every cycle. The very high-frequency sounds above about 18 000 Hz may not even be audible to many people, especially older people (see Box 17.1, p.376).

Although sounds have specific pitches within the frequency range of 20–20 000 Hz, you are not equally good at making discriminations between different frequencies throughout all portions of this range. By measuring the difference threshold (limen), or smallest frequency difference for which two pure tones can be discriminated, and repeating this measurement for a large number of reference tones, a function relating this difference threshold to the frequency of the reference tone can be obtained. Figure 16.13 shows a set of these functions, with each curve generated by using stimuli of a different loudness level. For a considerable portion of the auditory range, the difference threshold is about 1–3 Hz for moderate loudness levels; that is, humans can discriminate between two tones that differ in frequency by 3 Hz or less.

It is this very well-developed ability to make discriminations on the basis of frequency that caused

some auditory theorists to conclude that the auditory system must be making use of information present in the pattern of auditory nerve firings, in addition to place information. The fact that the size of the difference threshold starts increasing rapidly for frequencies above 4000–5000 Hz further strengthened this contention, as this is the frequency range in which auditory nerve fibers stop being capable of patterning their responses as a function of input frequency. If both pattern and place information were present in the auditory nerve signal for frequencies below 5000 Hz, but only place information was available for higher frequencies, such a decrease in differential frequency sensitivity could be easily explained.

Pitch versus intensity In Chapter 2, you learned about static invariances; for example, in the Bezold–Brücke hue shift, two lights of somewhat different wavelengths could be made to have the same hue by manipulating the intensities of one of the lights. There is an analogous auditory phenomenon: pure tones change in perceived pitch as their

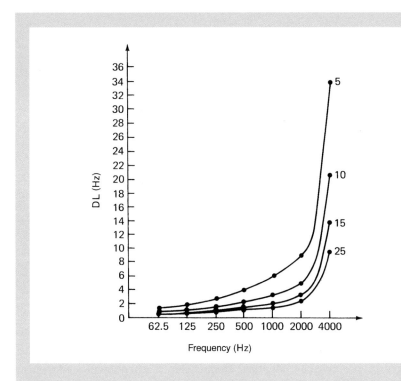

Fig. 16.13 The difference limen (DL) for pitch as a function of frequency, for four different loudness levels. From Harris, J. D. (1952) Pitch discrimination. *J. Acoust. Soc. Am.* 24: 750–755. Reprinted by permission.

amplitude is increased or decreased. Gulick (1971) showed this effect by presenting subjects with a standard tone of fixed frequency and intensity and asking them to match the pitch of the standard by manipulating the frequency of a comparison tone of a fixed intensity. He found that when the standard tone was above about 2500 Hz, very loud comparison tones had to be of a lower frequency than the standard in order to match the standard. In other words, as loudness increases, the perceived pitch increases. For standard tones lower than 2500 Hz, perceived pitch decreased with increasing intensity; that is, when the standard tone was of low frequency, loud comparison tones had to be of higher frequency than the standard in order for their pitches to match.

Box 16.8 The limited domain of pitch shifts

You might think that the fact that perceived pitch of a pure tone changes with intensity might cause severe problems for musicians. As different frequency tones are shifted in different directions, it would seem that the entire melody of a musical piece would be affected by the loudness at which the piece was played. Fortunately for those of us who appreciate music, however, the pitch shift only seems to occur for intensity changes of pure tones.

The sounds produced by musical instruments all have extensive harmonic structures; it is these structures that account for the different sounds among different instruments playing the same note. The presence of these harmonics is the reason that a musical note has the same pitch whether it is played loudly or softly. The reason that the auditory hue shift does not occur with complex sounds may be related to the phenomenon of periodicity pitch (see p. 371).

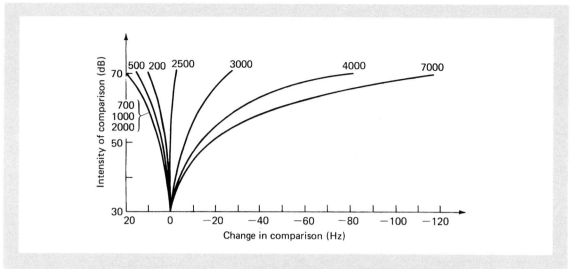

Fig. 16.14 Change of pitch with intensity. From *Hearing: physiological acoustics, neural coding, and psychoacoustics* by W. Lawrence Gulick, George A. Geseheider, and Robert D. Frisina. Copyright © 1989 by Oxford University Press, Inc. Reprinted by permission.

Figure 16.14 shows the changes in perceived pitch as a function of intensity for nine different frequencies. The abscissa is the change in frequency required for the comparison stimulus to match the pitch of the standard, at the intensity given by the ordinate. For a very high-frequency tone (7000 Hz), the pitch shift can be quite substantial; when the comparison stimulus is much louder than the standard, its frequency may have to be more than 100 Hz lower than the standard in order for a match to be made. You should have observed this effect in the 'Pitch and loudness' demonstration for Chapter 17. BOX 16.8

The perception of complex tones

Beats

If you are presented with a combination stimulus consisting of two pure tones of similar but not identical frequencies, a phenomenon known as *beating* occurs. To the listener, the stimulus does not remain at a constant loudness but seems to vary at a rate that depends on the frequency difference between the two tones. The reason that beats occur is illustrated in Fig. 16.15. When two tones are close in frequency, the relative phase difference between them varies slowly in time. In the left side of the figure, the two tones (shown by the top two sinusoids) are exactly in phase; when combined, the stimuli add together to produce a wave that is the sum of the amplitudes of the individual tones (bottom). At some points, however, the stimuli become out of phase with each other, so that when one wave is at a maximum, the other is at a minimum. When the tones are combined under these conditions, they cancel each other, as is shown in the middle of the bottom trace in Fig. 16.15. The amplitude of the total sound wave is very small at this time, so that the combined stimulus seems quite soft.

The rate at which the perceived loudness of a combination of two tones waxes and wanes depends on the frequency difference between them.

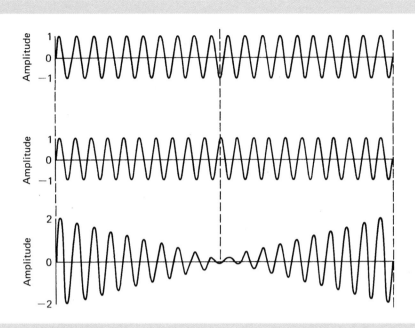

Fig. 16.15 Two pure tones of similar frequency adding together to produce beats. The top two traces show the individual waves, and the bottom trace is their arithmetic sum. Dashed vertical lines facilitate comparisons of phase.

For example, if a 500 Hz and a 501 Hz tone are presented together, the beat frequency is exactly 1 Hz; that is, the combination stimulus has one loud period and one soft period every second. For these types of combination stimuli, the perceived pitch is somewhere in between the pitches of the two components when presented separately.

Periodicity pitch

Combination stimuli that produce beats produce pitches that are similar to the pitches of the components (which must be similar). For other complex combinations, however, the pitch of the complex tone may not be at all close to the pitches of *any* of the components. Moore (1977) presented the example of a stimulus consisting of a sequence of very short clicks, occurring at a rate of 200 clicks/s. The pitch of such a stimulus will be very close to that of a 200 Hz pure tone, even though

the click stimulus contains significant amounts of energy at the harmonics of 200 Hz; that is, 400, 600, 800 Hz, and so on. Using electronic filtering techniques, it is possible to remove from this signal all of the 200 Hz component; in this case, the pitch of the remaining signal will still be that of a pure 200 Hz tone. In fact, it is possible to remove all but a small number of high-frequency harmonics, for example 2200, 2400, and 2600 Hz, without changing the perceived pitch of the stimulus. The timbre of the stimulus will change greatly as extra harmonics are added or subtracted, but the pitch remains remarkably constant. This phenomenon is known as *periodicity pitch*, or the perception of the *missing fundamental* (see also Chapter 9; 'missing fundamental' was an alternative name for the Craik–O'Brien illusion). This is a useful way to produce low-frequency tones in an organ. The fundamental frequency of an organ pipe depends on its length—longer pipes have a longer standing wave

Box 16.9 Pitch and the 'missing fundamental'

Many experimenters have attempted to determine the critical features that determine the pitch of a complex of high-frequency tones. A question that has received considerable attention is whether the observed pitch is due to the difference in frequency between the tones in the complex waveform, or whether other factors are also important.

Schouten *et al.* (1962) investigated the changes in perceived tone that occurred when the frequency differences between the component tones were kept constant while the absolute frequencies were varied; they found that the relative frequency differences were not the only important factors in determining the perceived pitch. If a complex tone with frequency components at 1800, 2000, and 2200 Hz is presented, the difference in frequency between the tones is 200 Hz, and the subjective pitch is similar to the

pitch of a pure tone at the fundamental frequency of the series, 200 Hz. Now consider what happens if a constant frequency is added to each tone, so that the individual components are, say, 1840, 2040, and 2240 Hz. The frequency differences have not changed, but the tones are no longer the consecutive harmonics of a pure tone at 200 Hz. In this case, a low-pitch sound is still heard, but the perceived pitch is not that of a 200Hz tone. Instead, the pitch is slightly higher, and it can be matched by a tone of approximately 204 Hz. Thus, neither the difference in frequency between the successive tones nor the presence of a fundamental frequency can completely account for the effect of periodicity pitch.

and a lower frequency. To get very low tones would require unrealistically long pipes. But the same pitch can be achieved by simultaneously sounding two shorter pipes that differ in frequency by the desired amount.

Several explanations for periodicity pitch have been proposed. According to one theory, non-linear properties of the basilar membrane cause vibrations to be set up at the place on the membrane corresponding to the fundamental frequency of the sound, whether or not that fundamental was actually present. This hypothesis can be fairly conclusively rejected, however, as experiments have shown that the missing fundamental will still be perceived even when the portion of the membrane most sensitive to the fundamental has been inactivated. Licklider (1956) presented the high harmonics of a low-frequency tone simultaneously with a wideband low-frequency stimulus that completely saturated the locations on the basilar membrane sensitive to low frequencies. Even under these conditions, the low-frequency pitch corresponding to the fundamental was heard. BOX 16.9

Suggested readings

For a more detailed look at auditory physiology, T. Glattke's chapter in *Normal aspects of speech, hearing and language*, edited by F. Minifie, T. Hixon, and F. Williams (Prentice-Hall, 1973) is a good place to start. For an even more complete treatment, turn to the chapters by M. H. Goldstein and V. B. Mountcastle in Mountcastle's *Medical physiology*, 13th edn (C. V. Mosby, 1974). The auditory periphery is also extensively and rigorously examined in P. Dallos' book *The auditory periphery* (Academic Press, 1973). Those interested in the particulars of frequency coding in the auditory system might try reading Békésy's *Experiments in hearing* (McGraw-Hill, 1960). Another good (and quite readable) discussion of this topic may be found in Chapters 3 and 4 of B. Moore's *Introduction to the psychology of hearing* (University Park Press, 1977).

A somewhat more advanced treatment of all the topics in Chapters 15 through 17 may be found in *Hearing: physiological acoustics, neural coding, and psy-*

choacoustics by W. L. Gulick, G. A. Gescheider, and R. D. Frisina (Oxford University Press, Oxford, 1989).

Scientific American articles relevant to the topics discussed in this and the previous chapter are numerous. They include Békésy's 'The ear' (August 1957; offprint #44), Warren & Warren's 'Auditory illusions and confusions' (December 1970; off-print #531), and Oster's 'Auditory beats in the brain' (October 1973; offprint #1282). The articles by Oster and by Warren & Warren are reprinted in *Recent progress in perception* (W. H. Freeman, 1976), while Békésy's article is reprinted in *Perception: mechanisms and models* (W. H. Freeman, 1972).

Chapter 17

Perception of loudness and space

THE last chapter told in some detail how the auditory system makes discriminations on the basis of the frequencies of the incoming waves. In addition to pitch and loudness, there are numerous other aspects of sound that you are capable of perceiving. This chapter is devoted to two of these properties: loudness and stimulus location in space.

Although the perception of loudness may seem like a simple task, it is complicated by interactions between the perceived loudness and the frequency of a given tone, as well as by the fact that the components of complex tones sometimes act as if their loudnesses add to each other, and sometimes act as if they are inhibited by each other. The perception of the location of a given sound is also a complex phenomenon, with the final percept resulting from a combination of monaural and binaural cues.

The perception of loudness

The loudness of an auditory stimulus is a psychological, not a physical, attribute of the stimulus. As such, it depends on the characteristics of the observer, as well as on those of the stimulus. The physical attribute of sound that is most closely correlated with loudness is intensity; however, because you are not equally sensitive to sounds of all frequencies, the perceived loudness of a tone depends on its frequency as well as its intensity. You should have heard the difference in the loudness of sounds of the same intensity but different frequencies in the 'Pitch and loudness' demonstration associated with this chapter but which was also suggested for the preceding two chapters. In this section, you will read about the loudness of pure tones, and then move on to the loudness of more complicated stimuli.

Pure tones

Absolute thresholds The minimum sound intensity that can be heard varies greatly as a function of stimulus frequency. People are most sensitive to tones of frequencies around 3000 Hz, with sensitivities decreasing for tones that are either higher or lower in frequency. Many investigators have obtained functions relating absolute auditory threshold to stimulus frequency, using a number of different experimental techniques.

One method involves delivering the stimuli using loudspeakers and measuring the sound pressure at the entrance to the auditory meatus. A threshold measured in this way is known as a *minimum audible field* (MAF). In contrast, when sounds are delivered through headphones, and sound levels calibrated using artificial ears, the threshold measure is called the *minimum audible pressure* (MAP). MAF thresholds are plotted as a function of frequency in Fig. 17.1. From this figure, you can see that threshold is minimized in the region from 2000–5000 Hz and rises steeply for frequencies above and below these levels. Many other animals (for example, dogs and bats) can detect frequencies far higher than those detectable by people. That is why dogs respond to whistles that humans cannot hear at all.

The threshold sound levels displayed in Fig. 17.1 produce extremely small physical displacements at both the tympanic and basilar membranes. Wilska (1940; as reported by Geldard, 1972) found that for sounds of frequencies to which the human auditory system is maximally sensitive, threshold sound levels caused movements at the eardrum that were on the order of 0.01 nm in total excursion. When you consider that the wavelengths of visible lights range from 400 to 700 nm, you can more fully appreciate what small movements the eardrum is making. Stevens & Davis (1938) have extrapolated from data on tympanic membrane movements to suggest that the physical response of the basilar membrane to near threshold sounds is even smaller, on the order of 0.001 nm. Such move-

ments are significantly smaller than the diameter of a single hydrogen atom!

The sensitivity function shown in Fig. 17.1 is a valid representation of the sensitivity of the human auditory system for only one particular group: young people. As we grow older, we become less sensitive to stimuli of all frequencies, but the maximum hearing losses occur for high-frequency tones. The progressive loss of hearing sensitivity with age is known as *presbycusis* (or *presbyacusia*); the details of this effect are shown in Fig. 17.2. In this figure, hearing loss (measured from a standard scale) is plotted as a function of frequency for each of two groups of people. The dashed line shows the auditory capabilities of a group of young men ranging in age from 18 to 30 years (0 dB means no difference from 'normal', which includes women); the solid black curve was derived from a group of men, all of whom were more than 65 years old. This group is at least 7 dB less sensitive than the younger group throughout the entire frequency range, with the maximum difference in sensitivity for frequencies greater than 1000 Hz. Remember, decibels are a log scale, and a 6 dB loss means twice as much intensity is needed to hear the tone. For frequencies above 5000 Hz, the older group is as much as 50 dB less sensitive than the younger

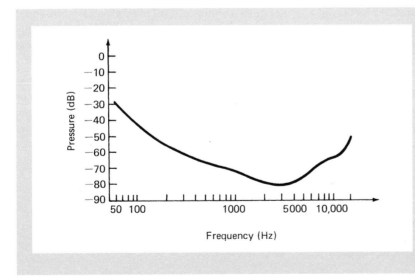

Fig. 17.1 Human auditory thresholds as a function of frequency. After Sivian, L. J. and S. D. White (1933) On minimum audible sound fields. *J. Acoust. Soc. Am.* 4: 288–321. Reprinted by permission.

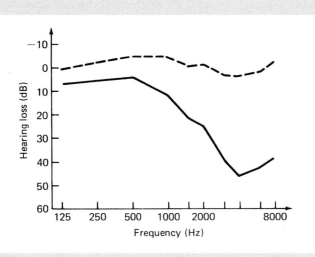

Fig. 17.2 Hearing loss as a function of frequency— *dashed curve*: losses for men ranging in age from 18 to 30; *solid curve*: losses for men over the age of 65. From Weiss (1963).

group (a factor of more than 300). Whether this age-related hearing loss is directly caused by some aging process or is the result of cumulative exposures to very loud sounds and illnesses is a question that has not yet been resolved. BOX 17.1

Equal loudness contours One of the most common problems in psychophysics is relating a subjective quality such as loudness to a physical quantity such as sound pressure level. Equal loudness contours provide a way of studying the details of this relationship: they are generated by taking a 1000 Hz tone at a specific intensity, and determining the sound levels at other frequencies that are subjectively equal in loudness to the 1000 Hz tone. For example, a subject might be presented with a 1000 Hz standard tone at 60 dB and then asked to manipulate the intensity of a 2000 Hz comparison tone until it matched the loudness of the 1000 Hz tone. The same 1000 Hz tone would then be compared with a 3000 Hz tone, the intensity of which would be manipulated until this tone was equal in loudness to the standard tone. In this way, intensities of tones at a variety of frequencies could be obtained so that all the tones matched the loudness of the 60 dB, 1000 Hz tone. These intensities could then be plotted as a function of frequency, yielding an equal loudness contour. All the tones with intensities and frequencies on the contour are subjectively equal in loudness; these sounds are assigned a loudness level of 60 *phons*. For any equal loudness contour, the loudness level in phons is defined as the decibel level of the subjectively equally loud 1000 Hz tone.

A series of equal loudness contours is presented in Fig. 17.3. For low loudness levels, the shapes of these curves closely resemble the sensitivity function shown in Fig. 17.1, as would be expected by

Box 17.1 Why hearing losses are in the high frequencies

It should not come as a surprise that most hearing losses are in the high frequencies. The frequencies lost are the ones for which the vibrations are essentially restricted to the base end of the basilar membrane (see Chapter 16).

These are therefore detected by a small subset of hair cells. Moreover, that subset of hair cells responds to all frequencies (see Chapter 16), and they are therefore the ones most likely to be 'worn out' with age.

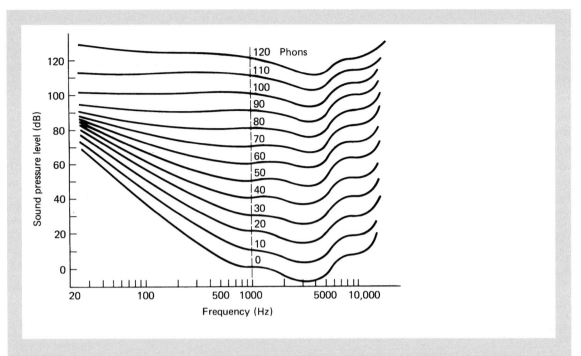

Fig. 17.3 Equal loudness contours. The curve marked '0' reflects the absolute sensitivity of the human auditory system. From Berrien, F. K. (1946) The effects of noise. *Psych. Bull.* 43: 141–161.

the fact that a threshold intensity versus frequency curve is really just an equal loudness contour. As loudness level increases, however, the contours change in shape, becoming much flatter than at lower levels. This means that the rate at which loudness grows with increasing SPL varies as a function of frequency. For example, the difference in sound level between two 1000 Hz tones at 60 and 70 phons is 10 dB (by definition). For a 30 Hz tone, however, two stimuli of 60 and 70 phons will only differ in sound level by about 3 dB. Clearly, we must know frequency as well as amplitude to determine loudness, just as we must know intensity as well as frequency to determine pitch. The 'Pitch and loudness' demonstration associated with this chapter is set up to look like this figure. By clicking dots in the horizontal row, you are cutting across the loudness contours.

The family of equal loudness contours displayed in Fig. 17.3 shows that you are more sensitive to low-frequency tones relative to high-frequency tones at high loudness levels than at low loudness levels. The equal loudness contours are more nearly flat above about 50 phons; below that level, the low-frequency sounds require more intensity to achieve comparable loudness with higher-frequency tones. Because of this, complex sounds that are identical in their frequency and phase components may sound different simply because of variations in loudness. For example, voices appear to have much greater low-frequency components when heard from a loudspeaker at full volume, giving them a quite 'boomy' sound (Moore, 1977). In addition, musical recordings that are made at a relatively high volume and then played softly often seem as if they are lacking in the bass range. This is because at low volumes we are relatively less sensitive to those low tones. Many stereos compensate for this effect by having a 'loudness' switch that adds extra bass at low volume levels.

Loudness scaling   Equal loudness contours define the phon scale, which relates subjective loudness level of an arbitrary tone to the intensity of a pure 1000 Hz tone that matches the arbitrary tone in loudness. A more direct way to create a scale for subjective loudness is to use the direct magnitude production techniques developed by S. S. Stevens and discussed in detail in Chapter 2. Stevens & Davis (1938) defined the *sone* as the

unit in such a loudness scale; 1 sone is arbitrarily assigned to be the loudness of a 1000 Hz tone at 40 dB intensity. To obtain a tone with a loudness of 2 sones, a subject is asked to manipulate the intensity of the stimulus so that the loudness is exactly twice that of the 1 sone sound. Similarly, 0.5 sone stimulus is one that is perceived to be exactly one-half the loudness of the original tone. Loudnesses that are not even multiples of the original 1 sone sound are obtained by bisection; that is, a 3 sone tone is one that is perceived as

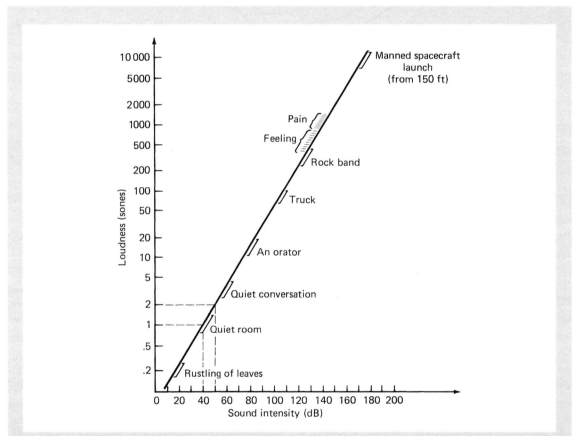

Fig. 17.4 Graph relating loudness in sones to the intensity level of a stimulus. Notice that many of the 'benchmark' sound levels indicated in Table 15.1 are marked on this figure. Figure 5.10 from *Human Information Processing*, 2nd edn, by Peter H. Lindsay and Donald A. Norman, copyright © 1977 by Harcourt Brace Jovanovich, Inc., reprinted by permission of the publisher.

Box 17.2 The power law in decibels

Stevens' power law, represented in Fig. 17.4, can be re-stated in a slightly different way: *loudness* doubles for every 10 dB increase in stimulus *intensity*. This statement sometimes misleads students into believing that 10 dB represents multiplication by 2. You recall, of course, that 10 dB actually represents a 10-fold change (see Chapter 15).

To understand why the power relationship implies a doubling of loudness for each 10 dB change in intensity, take the logarithm of the power relationship:

$$\log (loudness) = \log (k) + 0.3 \log (intensity)$$

Then, for every log unit change in intensity (which is 10 dB), there is a 0.3 log unit change in loudness. The antilog of 0.3 is 2 (log [2] = 0.3), so 10 dB represents a doubling of loudness. You can also read that result from Fig. 17.4: if you mark off a doubling of loudness on the *y*-axis (say from 1 to 2 sones), you will see a 10 dB change in intensity (in this case, from 40 to 50 dB).

midway between the loudness of a 2 sone and a 4 sone stimulus.

Stevens (1957) obtained loudness estimation data from a large sample of subjects and determined that loudness (in sones) was related to the sound intensity of a sound by a power law of the form.

$$loudness = k \, (intensity)^{0.3}$$

The relationship between decibels and sones is shown in Fig. 17.4; the straight line is obtained because sones are on a logarithmic scale and decibels are already in log units. (See the Appendix for an explanation as to why a straight line is expected when plotting this equation on log–log coordinates). BOX 17.2

You might wonder where the power law arises. In part, it is because you make a comparison of logarithmic functions (see Box 2.5, p. 18). In addition, at low frequencies, where the basilar membrane vibration is fairly linear, the cochlear nucleus produces a compression that approximates an exponential function. At high frequencies, the cochlear vibrations themselves produce the non-linear function (Zeng & Shannon, 1994)

The foregoing applies exclusively to pure tones. Stevens (1972) and others have proposed models that allow more complex sounds to be scaled according to their perceived loudness. These models all involve dividing the stimulus into a number of narrow frequency bands, and obtaining values for the SPLs within each band. The sone level of the total stimulus is then determined by summing the loudness of the individual bands. The complex tones whose scaled loudnesses are displayed in Fig. 17.4 were obtained in this way. According to the data presented in this figure, the loudness of a rock band is approximately three times greater than the noise of a nearby truck, which in turn is about 30 times louder than the sound of a quiet conversation. BOX 17.3

The coding of loudness changes The first parts of this chapter considered the psychophysical relationships between the intensity of a given auditory stimulus and its perceived loudness. From the data displayed in Figs 17.3 and 17.4, it is clear that the intensity range over which the human auditory system is capable of making loudness discriminations is about 130 dB (an energy range of more than $1:10^{13}$). This section considers how the auditory system might act to allow you to detect loudness changes over this extremely large range.

One possible way that the auditory system could code loudness changes is for individual auditory nerve fibers to respond differentially to sound levels throughout the entire intensive range. When Kiang (1968) recorded from single cat auditory nerve fibers, however, he found that they showed responses that ranged only over about 40 dB. In other words, the difference in intensity between a threshold stimulus and a stimulus that produces a maximal response from the nerve fiber is about 40 dB. Figure 17.5 shows the responses of an auditory nerve fiber as a function of sound level of the stimulus. For this cell, threshold is at about 25 dB, and the cell responds maximally for all sounds greater than about 65 dB.

If single nerve fibers do not respond across the entire range of auditory intensities, then perhaps different fibers have quite different auditory thresholds, so that loudness could be coded by simply noting which subpopulation of fibers is active. When a large sample of auditory fibers was examined from the cat auditory system, however, the variation in thresholds among the fibers in the sample was no greater than 20 dB for fibers with the same characteristic frequency (Kiang, 1968). Thus, if loudness of a pure tone stimulus were coded only by fibers with characteristic frequencies

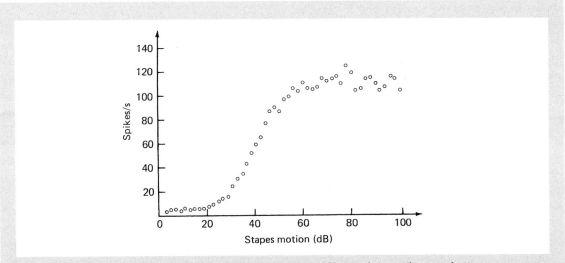

Fig. 17.5 Intensity response function for a single auditory nerve fiber in the cat. The stimulus is a pure tone at the characteristic frequency of the neuron. From Kiang, N. Y.-S. (1968) A survey of recent developments in the study of auditory physiology. *Ann. Otol. Rhinol. Laryngol.* 77: 656–675. Reprinted by permission.

equal to the frequency of the stimulus, the range of intensities over which loudness discriminations could be made would only be about 60 dB (20 dB threshold variability and 40 dB dynamic range). The fact that the human range is over 100 dB implies that fibers for which the stimulus frequency is not equal to their preferred frequency are also involved in the perception of loudness for that stimulus.

You know from Chapter 16 that basilar membrane vibrations for pure tone stimuli cover a large area of the membrane, and that these vibrations are reflected in the responses of the hair cells. Thus a pattern of excitation is produced in the auditory nerve such that fibers with characteristic frequencies close to the input frequency are firing more strongly than those fibers whose characteristic frequencies are very different from the stimulus. A way in which the auditory system might code loudness differences that would be consistent with the preceding data is that the shape of this excitation pattern might change as a function of the intensity of a stimulus.

Figure 17.6 gives an example of how such a mechanism might work. A pure tone with an intensity of 80 dB might produce a pattern of neural excitation along the basilar membrane that resembles the solid function in Fig. 17.6. Assume that the neurons most excited by this stimulus are firing at

their maximum level; therefore increasing the intensity of the stimulus causes no increase in firing by these cells. The cells with characteristic frequencies either higher or lower than the stimulus frequency are not firing at their maximum level, however, so increasing the stimulus intensity does cause these neurons to increase their response levels. The effect of increasing the stimulus intensity should therefore be to broaden the excitation pattern, as is shown by the dashed curve in Fig. 17.6; the firing in cells whose characteristic frequencies are near the input frequency is not changed, but cells with characteristic frequencies that are farther away from the input frequency will increase their responses. Thus, loudness would be coded by how broad the excitation pattern might be to a given stimulus. Recall from Chapter 15 that loudness may be encoded along the auditory cortex in the direction orthogonal to pitch (Roe *et al.*, 1990). This hypothesis seems the best to fit the available physiological and psychophysical data on the perception of loudness. However, functional neuroimaging now indicates that at least two different auditory cortical networks may be involved in the discrimination of loudness (Belin *et al.*, 1998).

Auditory fatigue and auditory adaptation In the course of our everyday experiences, we are exposed to sounds of many different loudness levels.

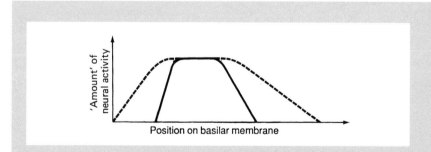

Fig. 17.6 Proposed mechanism for the coding of loudness. For high stimulus levels, further increases in stimulus intensity result in a change in the excitation pattern within the entire auditory nerve (*dashed line*), without changing the firing rates of the neurons most sensitive to the stimulus. After Moore (1977). Reprinted by permission.

Given this situation, a question that immediately arises is whether the auditory system—like the visual system—is capable of changing its sensitivity as a function of the level of ambient stimulation. The answer is an unequivocal 'yes', however, while all changes in visual sensitivity as a function of lighting conditions fall under the general category of adaptation, scientists interested in the auditory system have distinguished between two types of sensitivity changes. *Auditory fatigue* occurs in response to quite intense stimulation, and is usually measured after the fatiguing stimulus has been removed (Hood, 1972). *Auditory adaptation* is the reduction in sensitivity that occurs during the presentation of more moderate sounds.

To measure auditory fatigue, a fatiguing stimulus is presented for a period of time, and auditory thresholds are measured at various times after the original stimulus has been turned off. In the experiment for which data are shown in Fig. 17.7 (Postman & Egan, 1949), a 115 dB white (broad band) noise[1] was presented for several minutes, and the thresholds for different frequencies were measured at various times after the extinction of

the fatiguing stimulus. The reduction in threshold at various times after exposure to the noise is plotted against the frequency of the test stimulus in Fig. 17.7; hearing loss is greatest shortly after the fatiguing stimulus is turned off, with thresholds returning to near normal within 24 h. Even though the original stimulus included components at all frequencies, the hearing loss is much greater for high frequencies than for low ones; 30 s after the stimulus was turned off, thresholds were less than 10 dB higher than normal at 500 Hz, but were 50 dB higher than normal at 3000 Hz.

The fact that fatigue is greatest for high frequencies may be related to the phenomenon of presbycusis, wherein we become progressively less

[1] 'Noise' does not mean the sound is noxious. The term is used to mean any stimulus with a broad spectrum—that is, one that has all possible frequencies represented at approximately equal levels. Typically, this means the pressure (or radiance, for light) at any moment is chosen randomly and independently of what it was the moment before. 'White noise', analogous to white light with all wavelengths represented, contains all frequencies. It sounds like the hiss and static of a radio tuned between stations. If only a range of frequencies is included, it is called 'band-limited' noise. Sometimes, band-limited noise with a large bandwidth (range of frequencies) is called 'pink'.

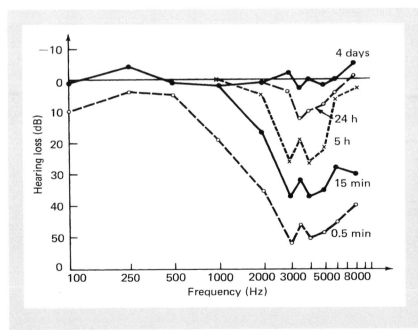

Fig. 17.7
Audiograms showing the changes in auditory sensitivity following exposure to intense stimuli. From *Experimental Psychology* by L. Postman and J. P. Egan. Copyright 1949 by Harper and Row, Publishers, Inc. Reprinted by permission of the publisher.

sensitive to high-frequency tones as a function of age. Compare the curves in Fig. 17.7 with the hearing loss of older men shown in Fig. 17.2 (dashed curve). Perhaps this permanent hearing loss is caused by cumulative effects of auditory fatigue.

Auditory adaptation effects are usually measured while the adapting tone is still physically present. The technique most commonly employed is called the *simultaneous dichotic loudness balance* (SDLB); it involves presenting the adapting stimulus to one ear, and asking the subject to manipulate the intensity of a tone presented to the other ear until it matches the loudness of the adapting tone. The intensity of the comparison tone thus serves as a measure of the loudness of the adapting tone.

Using the SDLB technique, investigators have found that if an adapting tone is turned on and left on for a long period of time, its perceived loudness decreases rapidly during the first 2 min of exposure, and reaches an asymptote by 3–7 min (Moore, 1977). The more intense the adapting tone, the greater the decrease in perceived loudness. In contrast to the phenomenon of fatigue, adaptation occurs approximately equally to both low and high frequencies (Jerger, 1957); in addition, adaptation is maximized when the adapting and comparison tones are of the same frequency.

Complex tones

This discussion has thus far centered around how the auditory system codes information regarding the loudness of pure tones. The auditory world is full of more complicated stimuli, however, and it is important to know whether such complex sounds are treated differently from pure tones. In general, the answer to this question is 'yes'; the auditory system responds quite differently to combinations of tones from the way it does to the individual components. In this section, you will read about some of these differences.

The loudness of complex tones and the concept of the critical band   Imagine an experiment in which a subject is presented with a complex stimulus consisting of equal intensities of stimulation for all frequencies between two limits. This type of stimulus is called band-limited; it is narrow-band if the two limits are close together, and wide-band if they are far apart. The *bandwidth* of such a stimulus is defined as the range of frequencies between the two frequency limits. When a subject is presented with a series of band-limited stimuli, with the bandwidth varying but the total energy of each stimulus remaining constant (Fig. 17.8), the subject's perception of the loudness of the stimulus

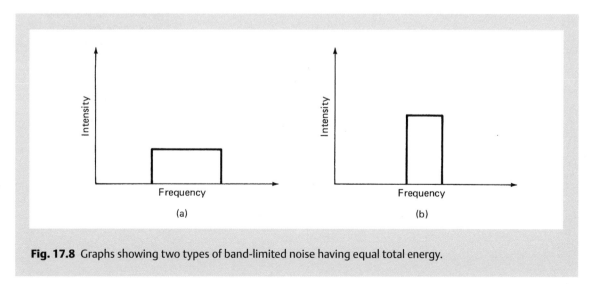

Fig. 17.8 Graphs showing two types of band-limited noise having equal total energy.

depends on the bandwidth. For narrow-band stimuli at moderate intensities, the subject judges the loudness of the stimulus to be the same as a pure tone of the same energy, the frequency of which is at the center of the frequency range of the stimulus. As the bandwidth is gradually increased—with energy held constant—the perceived loudness also remains constant; however, beyond a particular width, loudness starts to increase with further increases in bandwidth.

This phenomenon is shown graphically in Fig. 17.9, where the loudness of a series of band-limited stimuli with frequencies centered around 1000 Hz is displayed as a function of the bandwidth of the stimuli (Zwicker & Feldtkeller, 1956). Look for the moment at the 60 dB function; the loudness stays constant as stimulus bandwidth varies from 50 to 160 Hz, but it begins to rise steadily as bandwidth is further increased. The other functions show how the loudness of sounds of different intensity varies as a function of bandwidth; they show the same general properties, with loudness remaining constant for bandwidths below 160 Hz, and increasing as the bandwidth becomes greater. The exception to this rule is the function for the 20 dB stimulus,

for which loudness is completely independent of bandwidth.

This experiment suggests that if a complex tone consists of a fairly small range of frequencies, it will not be perceived as being as loud as a stimulus of the same total energy but with frequency components that are spread over a greater range. Experiments using combinations of pure tones instead of band-limited stimuli also lead to the same conclusion. If two pure tones of similar frequency are presented together, the loudness of the combination stimulus is less than if the two tones were quite different in frequency (Scharf 1961, 1970). The only exception to this rule occurs when the two tones are very weak, so that either tone presented alone might be below auditory threshold. In this case, the two tones are perceived as louder if they are similar in frequency than if they are very different (Gässler, 1954).

Complex tones of moderate or high intensity are perceived as louder when their components are not similar in frequency. In contrast, very soft complex tones seem to be louder when their frequency components are similar than when they are not. From these and other types of data, it is clear that

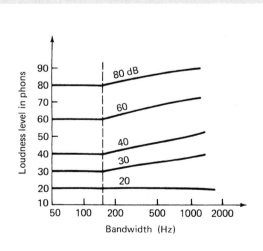

Fig. 17.9 Graph showing the loudness levels for bands of noise centered at 1000 Hz, as a function of bandwidth. The five different curves show the loudnesses for five different total energies. From Zwicker, E. and R. Feldtkeller (1956) *Das Ohr als Nachrichtenempfänger*. S. Hirzel, Stuttgart: Reprinted by permission.

complex stimuli are treated differently by the auditory system when they are restricted to a narrow range of frequencies from the way they are treated when the components are spread over a wider area. These considerations led to the development of what is called a *critical band theory*, which suggests that the auditory frequency range is divided into a number of bands. Combinations of tones that fall within a critical band are treated differently from combinations whose components fall into separate bands. The critical bands in audition are analogous to the visual spatial frequency channels discussed in Chapter 9.

According to critical band theory, two tones that fall in the same band will interact with each other, while tones in separate critical bands are treated essentially independently by the auditory system. When two fairly intense tones that excite the same critical band are presented together, they tend to inhibit each other, so that the total loudness of the combination is less than one would otherwise expect. If the two tones were different enough in frequency so that different critical bands were excited, then the interactions that reduced the perceived loudness in the first case would not be present, and the loudness of the combination stimulus would be greater.

The situation is somewhat different when the two tones in the combination stimulus are weak enough so that they are either near or below threshold when presented alone. In this case, tones close enough in frequency to excite the same critical band will sum their effects, so that the stimulus can be perceived even if the two components were each subthreshold when presented alone. If the tones are far apart in frequency so that they excite different critical bands, however, neither band is excited enough to signal the presence of a stimulus, and the combination cannot be heard at all. This reasoning accounts for the fact that the 20 dB function shown in Fig. 17.9 does not show the increase in loudness as a function of increasing bandwidth that is reflected in the functions derived from the more intense stimuli. At this level of intensity, the components within the same critical band do not inhibit each other, so that increasing the bandwidth to excite other critical bands does not reduce the amount of inhibition. BOX 17.4

In Fig. 17.9, the loudness of a band-limited stimulus centered at 1000 Hz is independent of bandwidth as long as the bandwidth is smaller than 160 Hz. Above this level, the perceived loudness increases as a function of increasing bandwidth. This implies that the size of the critical band centered around 1000 Hz is about 160 Hz; performing the same experiment with band-limited stimuli centered at different frequencies yields estimates of the sizes of the critical bands at different frequencies. Zwicker *et al.* (1957) performed this

---

Box 17.4 Critical bands and loudness

Critical bands complement the explanation of the coding of loudness represented in Fig. 17.6. If the frequencies of both tones are well within the range represented by the solid curve, the added energy of the second tone cannot raise the solid curve further; any tendency to broaden the curve (as a more intense single tone would) is offset by inhibitory interactions between the two tones. On the other hand, if the second tone is of sufficiently different frequency, it widens the area of stimulation, mimicking the dashed curve. For disparate frequencies, there is thus an increase in width of the curve, and therefore an increase in loudness.

When the tones are weak, on the other hand, the excitation is low. That is, the individual fibers are still within the range in which they can encode increases in stimulus by increases in firing (the sloped portion of the curve in Fig. 17.5). Adding energy in a nearby frequency to which the fiber is receptive increases the firing of the fiber. As a result, weak tones sum their effects within the critical band.

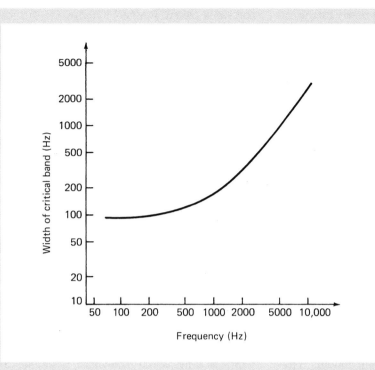

Fig. 17.10 Width of the critical bands as a function of center frequency. From Zwicker, E., G. Flottorp and S. S. Stevens (1957) Critical bandwidth in loudness summation. *J. Acoust. Soc. Am.* 29: 548–577. Reprinted by permission.

experiment, and obtained the results shown in Fig. 17.10. From this figure, you can see that the size of a critical band increases with frequency, going from about 100 Hz wide at low frequencies to more than 2000 Hz wide for frequencies greater than 10 000 Hz. Thus, at low frequencies, stimuli that are fairly close together in frequency excite different critical bands and are therefore treated somewhat independently by the auditory system, while high-frequency tones the same distance apart in frequency excite the same critical band and mutually inhibit each other.

Notice that above about 1000 Hz the curve in Fig. 17.10 can be approximated by a straight line with a slope of unity. Since this plot is on log–log coordinates, a slope near 1 implies that the width of the critical band is simply proportional to the mean frequency (see Appendix). For those frequencies for which there is a relatively narrow place of excitation on the basilar membrane, width of the critical band is proportional to frequency; at lower frequencies (for which the basilar membrane vibrates as a whole), the width of the critical band is essentially constant.

The preceding discussion may have led you to the conclusion that two tones that stimulate different critical bands are always treated separately by the auditory system. If so, this is a misconception. As you will see in more detail in the next section, two tones of very different frequencies can interact with each other, which raises the possibility that critical bands may extend over greater ranges than were indicated by the previously described experiments (Yost, 1992). In addition, critical bands are almost certainly not discrete, but rather are a series of extensively overlapping regions, like the overlapping receptive fields of retinal ganglion cells.

Auditory masking For suprathreshold stimuli, two tones presented simultaneously that excite the same critical band should interact with each other to reduce the perceived loudness of the combination tone, much in the way that visual stimuli with similar spatial frequency components mask each other (see Chapter 9). Another group of experiments that provides support for the concept of the critical band makes use of auditory masking. In these, the minimum intensity necessary just to hear a pure tone is determined both in the presence and in the absence of a continuous masking stimulus, which may or may not be similar in frequency to the pure tone. If the threshold intensity of the pure tone is increased by the presence of the masking stimulus, the stimulus has masked the pure tone by an amount equal to the difference in thresholds between the masked and unmasked situation. Usually, the louder the masking stimulus is, the more it will increase the threshold for the pure tone.

Figure 17.11 shows the results of a typical masking experiment (Egan & Hake, 1950). Here the masking stimulus was a narrow band of noise centered at 410 Hz. (Band-limited noise is often used as the masking stimulus to avoid the presence of beats, which would occur if the masking stimulus and the test stimulus were similar in frequency.) For a given intensity of the masking stimulus, the threshold intensities for pure tones of various frequencies are determined (test stimuli), and the difference between the masked and unmasked thresholds is plotted as a function of frequency. For all intensities of the masking stimulus, the amount of masking is greatest when the frequency of the test stimulus is equal to the center frequency of the masking stimulus, and the amount of masking increases as the intensity of the masking stimulus increases. In fact, when the center frequency of the masking stimulus and the frequency of the test stimulus are the same, a 10 dB increase in the intensity of the masking stimulus produces a 10 dB increase in its masking effectiveness.

As the test stimulus becomes more and more separated from the masking stimulus in frequency, the effectiveness of the mask decreases. For example, from Fig. 17.11, an 80 dB masking stimulus centered at 410 Hz will increase the threshold of a 410 Hz pure tone by more than 60 dB, but will increase the threshold of a 300 Hz tone by only about 35 dB.

Notice also that the function relating masking effectiveness to frequency of the test stimulus is asymmetrical; the amount of masking decreases much faster as the test stimulus becomes lower in

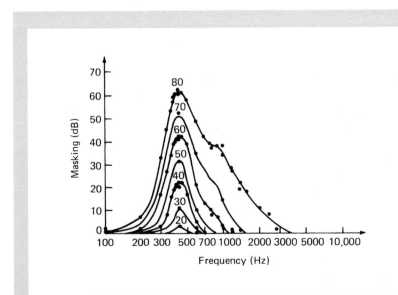

Fig. 17.11 Amount of masking plotted as a function of frequency, for seven different masking intensities. Masking stimulus was a narrow-band stimulus centered at 410 Hz. From Egan, J. P., and H. W. Hake (1950) On the masking pattern of a simple auditory stimulus. *J. Acoust. Soc. Am.* 22: 622–630. Reprinted by permission.

frequency than the masking stimulus, as opposed to when the test stimulus becomes higher in frequency. In other words, a masking stimulus is better at masking tones that are of higher frequency than the mask than those that are of lower frequency than the mask. This asymmetry makes intuitive sense when you consider how the basilar membrane responds to sounds of various frequencies. Figure 17.12 shows the response of the basilar membrane to a 1600 Hz tone; as noted in the last chapter, the response on the low-frequency side of the point of maximum vibration (toward the apex) decays much more rapidly with distance along the membrane than the response on the high-frequency side (toward the base). If masking effects are related to interactions of responses on the basilar membrane, it is reasonable to expect that a stimulus on the high side of the masking stimulus would be more affected by the mask than a stimulus on the low-frequency side.

The asymmetry of the masking functions in Fig. 17.11 also seems to become more pronounced as the intensity of the masking stimulus is increased. In other words, the slope of the masking decay on the high-frequency side becomes much shallower with increasing masking intensity, while the shape of the function on the low-frequency side remains much the same. This change in the shape of the masking curve with masking intensity provides an explanation for some everyday perceptual effects. For example, if a spoken sentence is recorded and then played back at a higher inten-

sity, it generally becomes much less intelligible. This is because as loudness of the total stimulus is increased, the low-frequency components of speech tend to mask the higher components more and more. As important information is carried by these higher components, decreasing their audibility will make speech less understandable (Moore, 1977). Speech perception is discussed further in Chapter 18.

Auditory space perception

In addition to the information you receive regarding the loudness, pitch, and timbre of an auditory stimulus, you are remarkably good at locating the position from which a sound originates. In order to do this, you depend in part on differences in stimulation at the two ears, just as binocular disparity is a cue for visual depth perception. As you will see, however, information from only one ear (monaural cues) can also aid in deciding the direction from which a sound is coming. In this section, you will see psychophysical data that quantitatively describe human localization abilities, as well as physiological data showing how individual cells in the auditory system respond to sounds from different locations. Then you will look at some of the cues used in making decisions about the location of a sound, and see what hap-

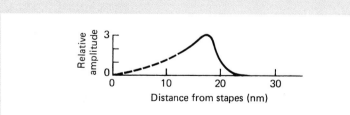

Fig. 17.12 Shape of the response pattern along the basilar membrane in response to a pure tone of moderately high frequency (bottom curve in Fig. 16. 2, p. 354).

pens when those cues are removed from the auditory environment.

Psychophysical data

In one early study, Stevens & Newman (1934) investigated how accurately subjects could localize the direction of pure tones that were gradually turned on and off. They found that subjects were good at distinguishing sounds originating on their left sides from sounds originating on their right sides but that the subjects often could not tell the difference between a sound in front of them and its mirror image behind them. They excluded front–back errors, and plotted the amount of uncertainty of direction localization as a function of the frequency of the stimulus. The results are shown in Fig. 17.13; localization is quite accurate for both low- and high-frequency sounds, but stimuli in the region of 3000 Hz are often localized inaccurately. When this experiment was repeated using more modern techniques (Sandel *et al.* 1955), the same type of function was again obtained, although the frequency for which localization was worst was about 1500 Hz. As you will see, the shape of this function is directly related to the physical nature of the cues used by the auditory system to localize the position of a sound source.

Neural systems

In recent years, investigators have begun to look at how the responses of single cells within the auditory system change as the position of a stimulus in space is varied. In the owl, an animal that relies greatly on its ability to identify the location of noise sources, cells have been found in the midbrain and in the primary auditory cortex that respond only to sounds in very specific locations. Knudsen *et al.* (1977) recorded from cells in the auditory cortex of the owl and found cells with spatial receptive fields like the one shown in Fig. 17.14; for this cell, responses are only obtained when the stimulus is within a restricted region just to the right of center. As is usually the case for auditory receptive fields, the vertical dimensions of the field are considerably broader than the lateral dimensions; in other words, the cell is more specifically tuned to lateral position than to vertical position.

Within an auditory nucleus of the owl's midbrain, Knudsen & Konishi (1978) found other cells that were sensitive to stimulus position. Unlike the

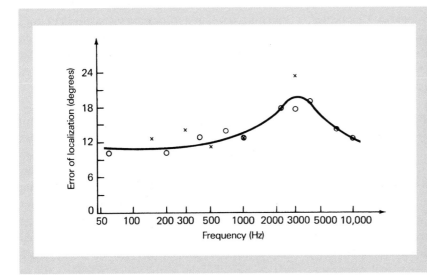

Fig. 17.13 Sound localization errors as a function of frequency. From Stevens, S. S. and E. B. Newman (1934) The localization of pure tones. *Proc. Natl. Acad. Sci.* 20: 593–596.

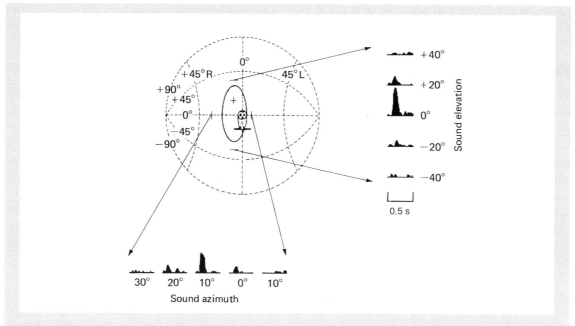

Fig. 17.14 Receptive field of an owl auditory neuron. Stimuli located within the oval will result in responses, while those outside will not. The cell's responses to stimuli moved vertically and horizontally across the receptive field are shown along the right and lower portions of the figure, respectively. From Knudsen, E. I., M. Konishi and J. D. Pettigrew (1977) Receptive fields of auditory neurons in the owl. *Science* 198: 1278–1280. Copyright 1977 by the AAAS. Reprinted by permission of the publisher and author.

cortical cells discussed in the previous paragraph, however, the receptive fields of midbrain cells had both excitatory and inhibitory regions. That is, if a stimulus was located within a central area, the cell responded with excitation; however, if the stimulus was placed just outside this region, the response of the cell was to suppress the maintained activity. The receptive field of such a cell is shown in Fig. 17.15; in many ways, the receptive fields of these cells seem to be auditory analogs to the spatially antagonistic receptive fields of retinal ganglion cells. BOX 17.5

Cortical cells with receptive fields that are specific to the position of the stimulus have also been found in the cat. Morrell (1972) has found cells in association areas of the cortex that respond to both visual and auditory stimuli. For such bimodal cells, the receptive field within which visual responses are evoked completely overlaps the auditory receptive field. The response of such a cell would be maximized when appropriate visual and auditory stimuli that originate from the same location in space are presented simultaneously. A similar human visual/auditory area has been located (Regan *et al.*, 1995).

Humans also have an alignment of visual, auditory, and somatosensory maps. Since we (like owls) are visual animals, the visual map generally guides the alignment of the other sensory maps. When the visual field is disrupted by a stroke, the other maps are affected—*if* the visual sense is still being used. Làdavas & Pavani (1998) reported a patient who had a stroke that blinded her for everything to her left. She showed a form of blindness called 'visual neglect'—she virtually denied the existence of the left half of the world! When asked to point to

Box 17.5 The consistency of auditory and visual space

The auditory maps in the tectum of the midbrain are aligned with visual maps. (Note that the owl cannot turn its eyes in its head, so the retinotopic and auditory maps do not get thrown out of register by eye movements.) Eric Knudsen has studied the ways in which the two maps develop in register, and how they depend upon each other.

In one experiment, Knudsen (1983) plugged one ear in baby barn owls, so that the auditory cues to position would be shifted (see the discussion of 'intensity differences' in the next section). When the birds matured, the auditory and visual maps in the tectum were in agreement; that is, the cells had overlapping visual and auditory fields. He then removed the earplugs, restoring a normal intensity balance (abnormal for the particular owl, who had grown up with an earplug). The visual map was unaffected, but the auditory map was significantly misaligned. These results were interpreted to indicate that the alignment of the two maps depends on experience in the two sensory systems.

In a later experiment, Knudsen (1988) did the converse operation: he raised owls with normal hearing but with their eyes closed. After 60 days, the eyes were opened, and the visual and auditory fields of cells in the tectum were analyzed. Although the owls had had no visual experience, their visual fields were essentially normal. Apparently, the visual system in birds does not require experience to maintain its function and mapping. The auditory maps, however, were crude and degraded, even though the birds had had normal auditory experience. The visual map apparently is essentially innate (in owls), and the auditory map gets actively aligned with it. The visual system must be active to guide the fine-tuning of the auditory map.

Later, Knudsen and his coworkers used prisms to shift the visual fields of owl chicks while leaving the auditory fields unaffected. The auditory map was distorted to match the new visual fields (Knudsen & Brainard, 1991, 1995). A similar result was found in guinea pigs (Withington-Wray *et al.*, 1990). When the prisms were removed from the owls, the auditory fields of *young* owls shifted back to the visual fields; in older animals, the visual and auditory fields became separated. Interestingly, if the owls had had normal experience before wearing the prisms and getting shifted, they could recover normal function again when the prisms were removed even when they were quite old (Knudsen, 1998).

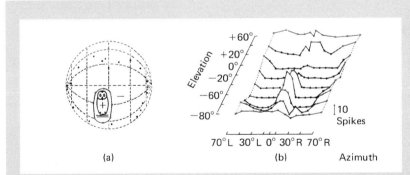

Fig. 17.15 Center/surround receptive field of an auditory neuron in the owl. (a) The receptive field; the area within the oval is excitatory, while the shaded area is inhibitory. (b) The responses of this cell to stimuli placed in different locations within the receptive field. From Knudsen, E. I. and M. Konishi (1978) Center-surround organization of auditory receptive fields in the owl. *Science* 202: 778–790. Copyright 1978 by the AAAS. Reprinted by permission of the publisher and author.

the source of a tone on the left, she pointed well to the right of the correct position. But when she was blindfolded, her pointing to a sound source was as accurate as a normal person's.

Although the neural circuit that is involved in the ability of animals to localize objects in space is unknown, at the very least an intact auditory cortex is necessary for animals to perform tasks that require object localization. Neff & Casseday (1977) destroyed the cochlea of one ear in each of a number of cats, and then trained the cats to perform a task involving auditory localization. After the animals had learned the task, the experimenters produced a lesion in the auditory cortex either ipsilateral or contralateral to the functioning ear. They found that when the auditory cortex contralateral to the good ear was destroyed, cats were unable to localize objects, although they were able to perform the task when only the ipsilateral auditory cortex was destroyed. There is no auditory space map known on the cortex, but spatial information may still be derived from the firing of cells.

It is possible that a pattern code (see Box 7.8, p. 132) carries the spatial information (Middlebrooks *et al.*, 1994). Cells in the inferior colliculus have also been implicated in localization of sounds in space (Kuwada *et al.*, 1979).

Cues for auditory space localization

This section considers what kinds of information available in the auditory signal can be used to allow us to determine where the signal is coming from. Binaural cues, or cues that require the presence of two ears, will be considered first.

Intensity differences Figure 17.16 shows a sound source positioned at an *azimuth* (lateral position) of 30° left, relative to the observer. That means that the left ear is directly in the path of the sound waves, but the right ear is somewhat blocked by the subject's head. There are two ways that the sound can reach the subject's right ear: it can bend around the head, or it can pass through the skull on the way

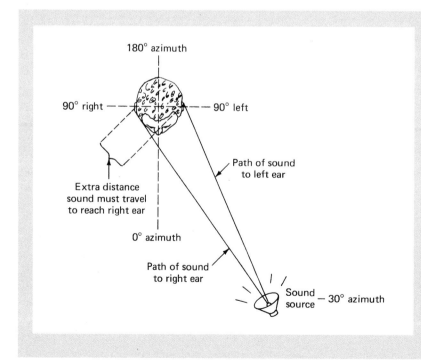

Fig. 17.16 Different paths that must be taken by sounds located off-center to reach the two ears.

to the ear. Low-frequency (long-wavelength) sounds have little trouble bending around an object the size of a skull and will therefore reach the right ear without being significantly blocked by the head. High-frequency sounds, however, will not bend around the skull, with the result that the head acts to cast an 'auditory shadow' in which the right ear lies. The only way that a high-frequency sound is able to get to the right ear is by passing through the head itself; in doing this, the head acts as a filter and reduces the amount of the sound reaching that ear. A high-frequency sound coming from the left side will therefore sound softer at the right ear than at the left ear. This difference in intensity between the two ears can serve as a cue for perceiving the azimuth of the stimulus. A sound originating exactly in front of or behind a subject produces sounds of equal intensities at the two ears, with the intensity difference increasing as the sound source moves to either side.

Now reconsider Fig. 17.13, which shows the uncertainty that people have in localizing sounds as a function of frequency. As the frequency increases from moderate (1500–3000 Hz) to high (>5000 Hz), the errors in localizing sounds decrease. This improvement in the ability to localize sounds is easily understood if intensity differences between the two ears are used as cues, as it is at this frequency range that the differences become apparent. The fact that accuracy also increases for low-frequency tones implies that other cues are more important in the low-frequency end of the auditory spectrum. There is also a non-linearity at the tectum that explains some of the difference between performance and the differences in the physical stimuli (Spitzer & Semple, 1991).

Timing differences The sounds received by the two ears of the subject in Fig. 17.16 differ in more than just their relative intensities. The ears, each being at different distances from the noise source, will receive the stimulus at slightly different times. For a pure tone, this means that the stimuli are somewhat out of phase at the two ears; that is, the signals at the two ears will look much the same ex-

cept that one signal will appear to lag behind the other by a certain fixed fraction of a cycle. The amount that one signal lags behind the other depends on the difference in path length of the sound to each ear; the farther the stimulus is from being equidistant from the two ears, the greater the path difference. For example, if the sound source in Fig. 17.16 were 45° left instead of 30° left in its azimuth, the path difference between the ears would be greater.

The difference in phase between the two ears for a pure tone input can only give useful information about the position of the sound if the wavelength of the tone is longer than about one-half of the distance of the path that the sound must travel around the head to go from one ear to the other. For shorter wavelengths, a given phase difference could be produced by a stimulus at a number of different locations in space. As the maximum distance (90° azimuth) is the distance between the ears (about 23 cm), a wavelength of 11.5 cm is about the shortest wavelength that provides useful information about sound location. This corresponds to a frequency of about 1500 Hz as the highest frequency tone for which phase information is useful. <u>**BOX 17.6**</u>

Information about the location of a pure tone is available from phase differences between the two ears for frequencies below 1500 Hz and from intensity differences at frequencies above this level. In the region between 1500 and 3000 Hz, however, neither cue provides unambiguous information, so that judgments of stimulus location are least accurate at these frequencies. This is the explanation for the bulge in the localization curve shown in Fig. 17.13.

So far this discussion has been about how pure tones that were turned on and off gradually are localized in space; however, more complicated stimuli provide other cues that may be used by the auditory system. For sounds that are continuously changing in intensity (most everyday sounds), there will be small timing differences between the arrivals of the transient changes in intensity at the two ears, and these transients seem to play

---

Box 17.6 Two mechanisms fit two ranges

Notice how well matched your neural mechanisms are to the constraints of the physical world. Phase information is useful only to about 1500 Hz. How would phase information be encoded? Presumably in the timing of the volleys of action potentials hypothesized by the volley theory (see Chapter 16), which is effective for frequencies up to about 2000 Hz. Information about higher frequencies is encoded mainly by the place theory, which would not be expected to retain phase information. However, phase is less useful at these higher frequencies, where relative intensity is a more potent indicator of position.

---

an important role in our localization abilities. Experiments have been designed to evaluate this factor in the absence of other cues such as head movements or intensity differences; this has been accomplished by presenting the signal through headphones so that intensity differences are eliminated and head movements are irrelevant. The signal going to one of the ears can be delayed by some particular amount of time to produce any timing difference between the two ears that the experimenter desires.

In order to assess how good people are at perceiving timing differences between the two ears, Klumpp & Eady (1956) presented various types of stimuli through headphones and determined the minimum perceivable timing difference for each. They found that this minimum perceivable difference was smallest when the stimulus was band-limited white noise, which changes continuously over time. When the stimulus was a 1000 Hz pure tone, a slightly greater time difference was required, while an even greater difference was necessary for a 1 ms click stimulus.

The minimum perceivable difference for the white noise was about 9 ms, which is clearly short enough to be of use in the detection of timing differences due to differences in path length. (For example, the time difference caused by a sound at 90° azimuth is about 700 ms. A 9 ms difference in a distant source under optimal conditions means you could detect a displacement from straight ahead of less than a degree—a movement somewhat greater than from one edge of the moon to the other!) It seems therefore that transients that occur within a stimulus reaching the two ears at slightly different times can aid in the perception of location of an acoustic stimulus.

A difference of 9 ms is incredibly small, and seems beyond the capabilities of a noisy nervous system. In fact, the ability of the human observer is apparently better than that of neurons in the early stages of the auditory pathway, implying that a code involving a number of neurons must be used (Fitzpatrick *et al.*, 1997). The number of cells required seems to be less at higher levels in the system, as these cells extract the details from the lower cells.

Head movements If your ears were just holes on either side of your head, the cues of intensity and timing differences just discussed would still provide useful information about the location of an auditory stimulus. You could not have an unambiguous idea of where a stimulus was, however. Rather, there would be a whole range of locations that would produce identical timing and intensity differences. Figure 17.17 shows such a 'cone of confusion'; the difference in path length between the stimulus and the subject's two ears is the same everywhere on the surface of this cone. The timing differences between the ears therefore also remain the same, and, assuming that the head is perfectly spherical, the intensity differences do not change either. You should therefore not be able to distinguish changes of position of the stimulus as it moves from one point to another on the surface of the cone. You would be able to tell that sounds at locations 1 and 2 in Fig. 17.17 were both on the left

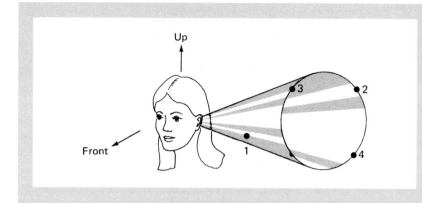

Fig. 17.17 A cone of confusion. Adapted from Mills (1972). In *Foundations of modern auditory theory*, Vol. 11, J. V. Tobias (ed.). Academic Press, Florida. Reprinted by permission.

side, but might not be able to say that one point was toward the front while the other was toward the back.

One way that you obtain information regarding the position of a stimulus on your cone of confusion is through the use of head movements. For example, by moving your head forward slightly, the stimulus should become slightly louder if it is at location 3, but softer if it is at location 2. Similarly, tilting your head in one direction or the other will help distinguish between sound locations 2 and 4 on the figure, which differ only in the vertical dimension. Head movements also result in changes in the relative loudness between the two ears, providing an additional cue to the position of the stimulus.

Monaural space perception   All of the cues in the previous section involve slightly different auditory information reaching the two ears. Even with only one ear, however, you are still able to make discriminations about the location of a sound source. Head movements are one way of obtaining information about the position of a stimulus using one ear. Another factor that also seems to be important is the shape of the pinna, the external auditory structure.

Batteau (1967) made plaster casts of human pinnas, and inserted a microphone where the eardrum would be. Sounds picked up by the microphone were presented to a subject through ear-

phones. Using this 'artificial ear', subjects could make some discriminations about the position of a stimulus relative to the plaster pinna; however, if the microphone was taken out of the cast and placed in open space, the subject no longer had any impression regarding the position of the noise source. This experiment shows, therefore, that the pinna can aid the perception of location of a sound source, even if only one ear is being used.

Harris & Sergeant (1971) attempted to measure the abilities of subjects to make localization discriminations monaurally in the absence of head movements. Subjects were told to keep their heads as still as possible, and were presented with white noise and pure tone stimuli both monaurally and binaurally. The measure used was the *minimum audible angle* (MAA), or the smallest angle of movement of the source that was necessary for the subject to detect a change. The experimenters found that the MAAs for binaural and monaural presentations of white noise were equal, although the binaural condition was superior to monaural when pure tone stimuli were used. It thus appears that monaural cues are dominant in discriminating differences in the locations of many sound sources.

The perception of movement of a sound source is detectable through other monaural cues. As a moving audible object comes close, it naturally tends to sound louder. This change in intensity may act as a cue for the movement of that object.

Another cue for detecting a moving object is called the *Doppler shift*; it provides information about movement when a high-velocity sound source moves past. The Doppler shift is a change in the perceived pitch of a sound, depending on whether it is moving toward you or away from you. A pure tone source emits sound waves at a constant frequency. As it moves toward you, however, the origin of each cycle is constantly moving, so that every successive cycle is produced at a location closer to you than the preceding cycle. This causes the waves to pile up in front of the source, so that they are closer together than they would be if the source were stationary. The fact that the cycles are closer together means that the frequency of the sound is higher (shorter wavelength). Just the opposite occurs as the sound passes you and heads away; each cycle of the sound wave reaches you slightly later than it would if the source were stationary, resulting in a lowering of the perceived frequency. The Doppler shift is the reason that a train whistle sounds high-pitched as the train comes toward you, but sounds much lower as it trails away.

Suggested readings

B. C. J. Moore's *Introduction to the psychology of hearing* (University Park Press, 1977) has good chapters on both auditory space perception and the perception of loudness. A somewhat more detailed look at the topic of space perception can be found in A. W. Mills's chapter in *Foundations of modern auditory theory*, Vol. 11, edited by J V. Tobias (Academic Press, 1972). These topics are also covered in Chapters 12 and 13 of *Hearing: physiological acoustics, neural coding, and psychoacoustics*, by W. L. Gulick, G. A. Gescheider, and R. D. Frisina (Oxford University Press, Oxford, 1989)

Scientific American articles relevant to the topics discussed in this chapter include M. R. Rosenzweig's 'Auditory localization' (October 1961; offprint #501) and G. Oster's 'Auditory beats in the brain' (October 1973; offprint #1282). The Rosenzweig article is reprinted in Held and Richards's *Perception: mechanisms and models* (W. H. Freeman, 1972), and the Oster article in Held and Richards's *Recent progress in perception* (W. H. Freeman, 1976).

Chapter 18
Speech perception

THE discussion of vision progressed from the sensory aspects to the perceptual, from physiology and psychophysics to pattern recognition. Similarly, the preceding chapters on audition have moved from the physiological to the psychophysical; this chapter addresses one of the most important pattern recognition problems faced by the auditory system.

Like the visual system, the auditory system recognizes particular patterns in the incoming stimuli. It does so without conscious intervention, working from cues that lead to perceptual hypotheses. Just as the visual system recognizes spatial shapes and objects and reconstructs a visual scene with objects corresponding to the proximal stimuli, the auditory system recognizes particular things in the environment: bells, sirens, voices, thunder, slamming sounds, music, and so forth.

Visual pattern recognition could be considered in terms of the locations of features (edges, borders) in a two-dimensional space, the frontal plane. At each point in a visual stimulus, there is some amount of radiance. In audition, the relevant features are sound waves of particular frequencies. They lie along a one-dimensional line, the sound frequency range. In fact, frequencies are actually physiologically arranged along a line—the tonotopic map on the auditory cortex (see Chapter 16) which is analogous to the retinotopic maps on the visual cortex (see Chapter 8). The auditory stimulus consists of a pattern of intensity at each frequency.

This might lead you to think of the auditory recognition problem as a one-dimensional version of the two-dimensional visual recognition problem, except that there is an essential second dimension to sound analysis: time. Sound patterns consist of frequency components shifting in time; freezing a sound into an unchanging tonal pattern would completely destroy its identity (unlike freezing a visual pattern, say, by taking a photograph, which does not make it unrecognizable). Of course, visual patterns can also be in motion, and sometimes depend on motion to be seen (remember the bar in 'Macro and micro fields', a motion demonstration associated with Chapter 13 on the CD, or the spinning sphere in 'Dot pattern' of the 'Equiluminant demonstrations' for Chapter 8). The discussion of pattern recognition has tended to ignore visual patterns that change because there is a wealth of interesting material in static patterns, which are less complicated.

Of all the pattern recognition problems faced by the auditory system, perhaps the most interesting and complex is the problem of recognizing the words spoken by our fellow human beings (many a musician would argue with that statement!). This is where much of the research in auditory pattern recognition has been done, and it is the only problem to be considered in this chapter. **BOX 18.1**

Box 18.1 The special task of speech perception

Although it is clear that the perception of speech is a form of perception that is auditory, it is really distinct from other forms of auditory perception. The perception of doors slamming, dogs barking, or sirens wailing is analogous to visual perception in that the perceptual system analyzes features of the world to determine what is 'out there'. In speech perception, however, the listener is charged with getting the semantic message that another person has encoded in a very stylized way, reflecting the peculiarities of the human vocal apparatus (see Liberman & Mattingly, 1989). The distal stimulus is not really the mouthings and sounds produced, it is the words and their meaning that the speaker wishes to convey.

Several kinds of evidence indicate that the perception of speech invokes a special mode of auditory perception, called the phonetic mode (Liberman & Studdert-Kennedy, 1978; Liberman, 1982). Sounds that are heard as speech when embedded in a stream of speech sound like chirps,

whistles, or clicks when they are isolated (Liberman *et al.*, 1952; Mattingly *et al.*, 1971; Whalen & Liberman, 1987). Compare the sound of 'Noise alone' to the other sounds in the frame marked 'Burst of noise as plosive' in the 'Speech sounds' demonstration associated with this chapter in the CD accompanying this book.

The way in which speech is analyzed in the brain bears a strong relationship to the way it is produced (Liberman *et al.*, 1967; Dorman *et al.*, 1979), even to the extent of sharing some of the same parts of the brain (Geschwind, 1972, 1979; Ojemann & Mateer, 1979; Zurif, 1980). Moreover, as you will learn at the end of this chapter, much of speech production and perception are functions of the left half of the brain (Studdert-Kennedy & Shankweiler, 1970; Geschwind, 1972; Kimura, 1973; Zatorre *et al.*, 1992). It may therefore be distinct from auditory perception in general, even though the initial processing is handled by the same sensory system.

Speech sounds

The first thing you need to know about the perception of speech is the nature of the stimuli that are being perceived. A large part of this chapter will be devoted to defining the units of speech, in both cognitive and acoustical terms. In fact, a large part of the study of speech perception is the study of speech itself.

It might seem that the sounds of speech are obvious. If you speak a phrase such as 'to catch pink salmon', you may think you are producing a sequence of discrete sounds, just as the written phrase is made up of a sequence of individual letters. You might think that in saying 'to catch pink salmon' you first made a 't' sound, then 'oo', then 'k', and so forth, as you might do if speaking absurdly slowly. As you will see later in this chapter, however, the sounds of speech come in a continu-

ous and indivisible stream. You cannot take a tape recording of the phrase 'to catch pink salmon' and chop it into letter-sized pieces that you can resplice into a different phrase; neither can you play the tape backwards and expect it to sound like 'nahmass knip chtak oot'. The apparent units of speech will occupy the first part of this discussion, but you will find later that these units do not actually stand alone.

Classification of speech sounds

The basic units of speech that correspond roughly to letters are the *phonemes*. Phonemes are those sound units that, by their differences, convey differences in meaning. Within a given phonemic class are sounds that are easily perceived as different but convey the same significance; differences in the perceived sound are called phonetic differences. For example, the sound of the 'A' in the word 'bad' is not the same when spoken normally, when whispered, or when spoken by someone who has a stuffed nose. Nonetheless, these phonetically different sounds are all part of the same phonemic class. The phonemes in this chapter refer only to their normally spoken phonetic versions.

Now a word about notation. The International Phonetic Association (IPA) devised an alphabet by which sounds may be transcribed into writing. (If you recall the way Professor Higgins transcribed Eliza's speech into apparently meaningless hieroglyphics in Shaw's *Pygmalion*—or *My Fair Lady*—he was presumably using the IPA notation.) If you read further in linguistics or speech perception, you will find that this notation is used throughout. But learning IPA notation for the sake of reading this one chapter is more effort than it is worth. It will also hamper your understanding, because you will probably have to keep looking back to decipher the notation. Therefore, this book uses the following, more cumbersome notation: letters representing the sound in question appear in boldface within a word (otherwise in italic) that tells you how to pronounce it. Thus '*b**A**d*' should be read as 'the sound of the "a" in the word "bad" ' (the IPA symbol for the phoneme *b**A**d* is **æ**). If you do further reading in speech perception you will have to deal with the IPA notation, which is summarized in many secondary sources (for example, Liberman, 1977)

The phonemes of English are generally divided into two classes: vowels and consonants. It is hard to explain the phonetic difference between them, although you undoubtedly already have a feeling for what is meant by vowels and what is meant by consonants. BOX 18.2

Vowels are classified according to the way they are produced. Vowels are *voiced* in normal speech; that is, the vocal cords vibrate while the vowel sound is being produced. The differences among the vowels are produced by the way in which the articulatory apparatus (particularly the tongue and lips) is positioned. Hold your mouth slightly open and make the prolonged sound *a-a-a-a-a* (*s**O**d*). While doing this, bring your lips back into a broad, smile (your mouth should be slightly open, and your tongue fairly high). The sound will change into a prolonged *eeeee* (*b**EA**d*); relax the smile and lower your tongue slightly and you get *ehhhhh* (*b**E**d*). Go back to the relaxed position (*s**O**d*), then purse your lips as if for a kiss; the sound changes to *ooooo* (*t**OO**th*). In all of these manipulations, you have changed the vowel sound by changing the position of your lips and tongue, without any particular change in what your vocal cords were doing. In fact, if you hold a vibrating instrument (such as an electric shaver) to your throat and silently perform the manipulations suggested above, you will hear the razor 'saying' the vowels. (That's how they used to make train whistles 'talk' in the ads or cartoons.)

The vowels of English can be classified according to the position the tongue takes when they are

---

Box 18.2 Vowels and consonants

It is difficult to state a rule for determining which sounds are vowels and which are consonants (Studdert-Kennedy, 1976). The one difference that is generally valid is that vowels contain more sound energy than consonants (Lieberman, 1977). Nevertheless, the consonants convey the bulk of the meaning in a sentence. Consider, for example, the following sentence with all its consonants omitted: 'A_oo_ _e_ _e_ _ei_ _a_ _ _o _i_ _, a_ _ _a_ _e_ _o _a_ _e' Quite a puzzle. The same sentence, however, with the vowels omitted and consonants included is not impossible to read: '_ g_ _d s_nt_nc_ _s h_rd t_ f_nd, _nd h_rd_r t_ p_rs_'. It seems odd that the main energy is going into the least informative parts of the speech. Quite possibly, the vowels convey other information, such as the stress, tone, or emotional content of the utterance (Lehiste, 1976). Box 18.8 (p.415) deals further with this possibility.

made. Most (not all) of the vowels fall along a continuum from tongue forward in the mouth and high (*b*EE), through tongue low in the mouth and far back (as if being swallowed) (*s*O*d*), then higher again though far back (and with the lips pursed) as one goes from *j*A*w* to *t*OO*th*. A plot of some of these sounds on a graph in which tongue position (high or low in the mouth) is the ordinate and the point where the passage is narrowed the most (near the front or back of the mouth) is the abscissa (Fig. 18.1) reveals a shape called the IPA vowel 'quadrilateral'.

This method of classifying vowel sounds was pioneered in the 19th century by Melville Bell. It is a valid classification in that the maneuvers described do produce the appropriate sounds, although modern X-ray studies of the vocal apparatus during speech have shown that these maneuvers are not necessarily the way the sounds are normally produced (Ladefoged *et al.*, 1972). The same sounds can be produced in different ways, and different speakers may use different strategies for generating the same phonemes. Even though

the classification scheme is based on maneuvers that may not in fact be performed, it provides a good framework for classifying speech sounds.

The consonants are somewhat more complicated than vowels, as they vary along more articulatory dimensions. Like the vowels, consonants may be produced with the major constriction of the articulatory pathways near the front, middle, or back of the mouth. There are a number of places where the constriction can be: the lips as in **P***it*, **B***it*, **M***e*, or **W***e*; the lips and teeth as in **F***an* or **V***an*; tongue and teeth, as in **T***ip*, **N***ip*, or **TH***in*; teeth alone, as in **S***in* or **Z***oo*; tongue near the middle of the mouth, as in **G***em*, **T***op*, **CH***urch*, or **D***ay*; or tongue near the back of the mouth, as in **G***et* or **C***ow*; or without any particular constriction, as in **H***at*.

In addition to the position of the constriction, consonants differ in how they are formed. A major distinction is between those made with the vocal cords vibrating and those made without vocal cords vibrating; the former are *voiced* and the latter *unvoiced*. For example, the difference between **F***an* and **V***an* or between **S***in* and **Z***oo* is that in the first

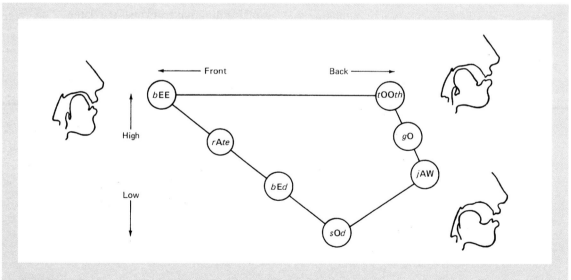

Fig. 18.1 The vowel 'quadrilateral', showing how the different vowel sounds depend on tongue position. After Lieberman, P. (1977) *Speech physiology and acoustic phonetics*. Macmillan, New York. Reprinted by permission of the author.

member of each pair the consonant is unvoiced, in the second it is voiced.

Another distinction is between the consonants that are *plosive* and those that are not. A plosive consonant is one in which the air from the lungs is bottled up by a restriction and suddenly released in a little puff. If the lips provide the restriction, we hear **P**it (unvoiced) or **B**it (voiced); if the tip of the tongue provides the block, we get **T**ip (unvoiced) or **D**ay (voiced); if the back of the tongue stops the passage, we hear **C**ow (unvoiced) or **G**et (voiced).

Another possible way to make consonants is by restricting the airway so that air gets out in a sort of hiss, rather than being completely stopped and then released. Sounds made in this way are called *fricatives*. As the point of constriction moves from the lips to farther back in the mouth we have a progression of unvoiced fricatives: **F**an, **TH**in, **S**in, and **SH**ow. The equivalent progression with voicing is: **V**an, **TH**en, **Z**oo, and *bei***G**e.

There are a number of other consonant types. *Nasals* are made by restricting the mouth and allowing the sound to come through the nose, as in **M**an (lips closed) or **N**ose (tongue to palate). *Laterals* are made by restricting one side of the mouth more than the other, as in **R**oad. *Glides* involve a relatively slow change from one sound to another, as in **Y**ell or **WH**at.

Acoustics of speech

The previous section outlined the nature of speech sounds in terms of the articulatory actions required to produce them. Now, what are the characteristics of the sound waves conveying speech to the ears? In the course of an utterance, many different sounds are emitted in rapid order; the stimulus for speech is a pattern of sound frequencies that changes with time. Before you can consider the acoustic characteristics of speech sounds, there must be a way of representing these stimuli graphically on the pages of this book. The graphi-

cal representations of speech sounds that you will see are called *spectrograms*; they are produced by a machine called the *sound spectrograph* (Koenig *et al.*, 1946). The next section is intended to explain what a spectrogram is, so that you can interpret the spectrograms in the remainder of the chapter.

The spectrogram

To understand what a spectrogram is, consider what it is intended to display. It is a representation that shows the component frequencies of a sound—this, of course, is a spectrum of the sound. You have already encountered spectra of spatial frequencies in visual displays (Chapter 9), and of continuous sounds (Chapter 15), so the idea of representing component frequencies should not be disconcerting. The special problem here is that the spectra of speech sounds are not steady in time, but are in constant flux. A tone generated by an oscillator is unchanging; you can look at its spectrum at any time and see the same picture as at any other time. But speech spectra are changing—the spectrum a moment after the sound starts can look different from those a few moments later, which can look different from ones still later.

For example, consider the sound made by a single ring of a telephone (an old-fashioned, black phone with a bell, not a chirping wireless phone). A spectrum of the sound just as the ring begins is shown in Fig. 18.2(a). This is an ordinary spectrum, just like those in Chapters 9 and 15, showing the energy in each band of frequencies as a function of frequency. There is considerable energy in the region below 1000 Hz, and a smear of energy (noise) in the region above about 1100 Hz. There is a tendency for there to be somewhat more energy in the regions of 1200, 2400, and 3600 Hz.

Fig 18.2(b) shows the spectrum of the sound about halfway through the ring. Now a great concentration of energy is in the region of 1200 Hz; most of the general noise has died and the spectrum shows four distinct bands of energy (four harmonics). Figure 18.2(c) shows the spectrum after the actual ring has ended. All that remains is the

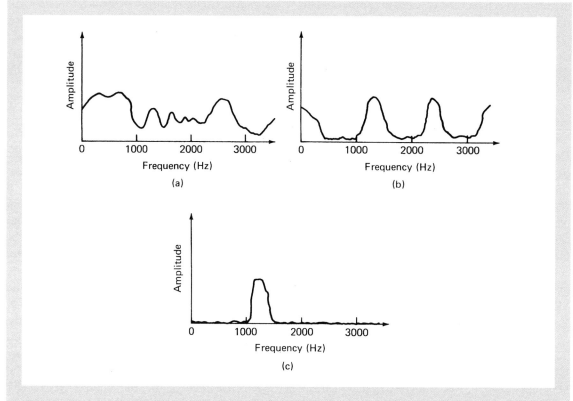

Fig. 18.2 Sound spectra of the ringing of an old bell-type telephone: (a) just after the ring begins; (b) near the middle of the ring; (c) after the ring has ended and the vibration is dying down.

relatively pure tone of the gradually fading vibrations of the bell, at about 1200 Hz.

If you took sample spectrograms every few milliseconds and leafed rapidly through them, you would have a movie of the spectrogram as it shifted and changed in time. This would be a fine representation of the spectrum in time, but it would be impossible to print in a book, and difficult to quantify or describe. There must be a better way of representing these successive pictures.

Suppose you took each spectrum and cut it out of heavy cardboard. You could then paste the cardboard spectra together to make a three-dimensional model of the sound. Figure 18.3 shows a sketch of this kind of model, with the three frames of Fig. 18.2 drawn in heavier lines. Each slice is the spectrum at a given moment. As

you move your attention along the time axis (toward you, out of the page) you scan from earlier to later spectra. You thus see the spectra evolving in time. Each of the four major harmonics (<500, 1200, 2500 and 3400 Hz) can be traced from the time it first appears until it disappears at the end of the ring.

Figure 18.3 is a sketch of a three-dimensional graph. Instead of using time as the third dimension (as in showing the successive spectra as a movie), the third axis is represented as if it were coming out of the paper. The problem is that three-dimensional graphs are hard to draw and not that easy to interpret. What you want is a two-dimensional picture like all the other graphs in this book.

A function plotted on a three-dimensional graph is a surface, rather than a curve. In Fig. 18.3 there is

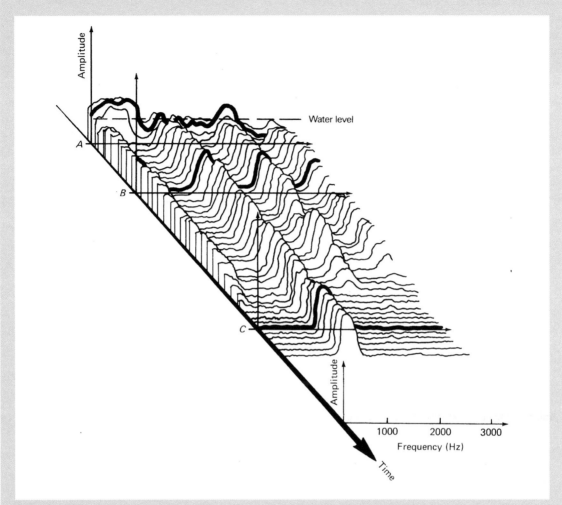

Fig. 18.3 Three-dimensional graph of the sound of the telephone ringing. The three spectra in Fig. 18.2 are indicated by heavier curves.

a surface representing the amplitude of sound energy (the height or elevation) at any point specified by its frequency (left–right direction) and the time (into or out of the paper direction). This surface is like a surface of land—ridges of mountains that happen to run parallel to the direction into and out of the paper. The problem is how to represent this mountain range on a flat piece of paper.

You can collapse a three-dimensional graph into a two-dimensional graph by sighting along one of the axes. If you sighted along the amplitude axis—looked down from above in Fig. 18.3—you would see the layout of the mountain range. In effect, you would be looking at a map, only the compass directions would be frequency (instead of north) and time (instead of east). How can you represent the elevation of the mountains at each point on this map? You can do this by using a *gray scale*. Make the map darker when the elevation is higher; for the sound make the paper darker when there is sound energy at that frequency and time. The dark parts of this picture, which is the spectrogram, show the locations of the components of the sound. It is as if you flooded the mountain range in Fig. 18.3 to the level indicated by the dashed line on the rearmost spectrum. The spectrogram becomes a map of the mountain peaks (islands, in black) in the newly flooded sea (white)

The spectrogram of a telephone ringing is shown in Fig. 18.4. In fact, Figs 18.2 and 18.3 were based on this spectrogram, and it should be easy to see how each of them follows from the spectrogram. (The times at which the three spectra shown in Fig. 18.2 were taken are indicated by the letters

A, B, and C in Fig. 18.4.) This spectrogram, a plot of frequency versus time, shows the location and history of each of the components. You can see the 1200 Hz component, for example, starting rather weakly (a faint gray line with gaps) but growing to become the strongest component (darkest) and eventually outlasting the other three. You can also see that this 'component' is really a range of frequencies (a single frequency would be a narrow line, not a band) and that it becomes louder and softer (the band gets quite light at points), presumably because of beats among the individual frequencies in the band (see Chapter 16). **BOX 18.3**

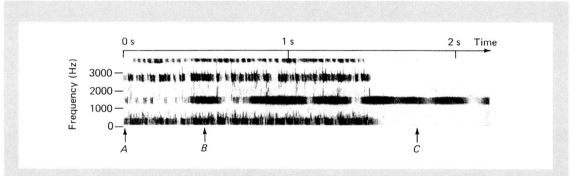

Fig. 18.4 Spectrogram of the sound of the telephone ringing. The times of the three spectra in Fig. 18.2 are indicated by arrows. From Koenig, W., H. K. Dunn and L. Y. Lacy (1946) The sound spectrograph. *J. Acoust. Soc. Am.* 17: 19. Reprinted courtesy of Bell Laboratories.

Box 18.3 The sound spectrograph

How is a spectrogram created? The original machine that did it, the *spectrograph*, performed what amounts to a continuous spectral analysis. Sound entered through a microphone and was converted to an electrical signal. In effect, the electrical signal was fed to a bank of filters—electronic devices that select specific narrow-frequency bands, somewhat like the spatial frequency channels in Chapter 9, but more selective. If the sound contained the frequencies a particular filter was tuned to, the signal came through the filter. If it did not contain the right frequency, nothing came out of the filter.

An electronic 'gate' looked at the output of each filter; if it found a signal, it sent an instruction to a pen corresponding to that filter to make a mark on the spectrograph paper as it moved through the machine. It is as if there were a bank of pens, each placed at a position corresponding to the frequency of the filter feeding it, writing on the moving paper. Therefore the position of each mark on the paper corresponded to a frequency and a time: the frequency of the filter associated with the pen and the time that part of the paper was under the pen. The darkness of the mark indicated the amount of energy (amplitude) in that frequency band at that moment. Of course, computers can do this task more efficiently today.

Physical characteristics of speech sounds

Now consider what physical stimuli correspond to each of the speech sounds in a phrase by seeing what its spectrogram looks like. The top part of Fig. 18.5 shows the spectrogram corresponding to the spoken phrase 'to catch pink salmon'. You probably think it looks like a bunch of blobs, but those who are accustomed to reading spectrograms can point out its very specific patterns. An idealized version of this one is shown below it. You can probably see where most of the dark patches in the ideal version correspond to blotches in the actual spectrogram, although the emphasis may not be exactly what you would have come up with

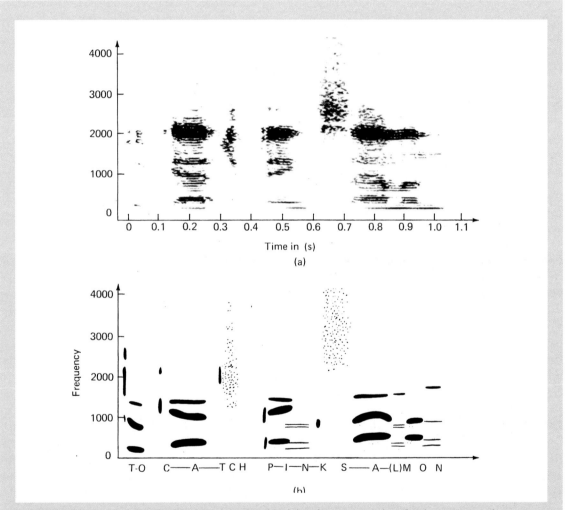

Fig. 18.5 Actual spectrogram (a) and ideal version (b) of the phrase 'to catch pink salmon'. From Liberman, A. M., P C. Delattre and F. S. Cooper (1952) Perception of the unvoiced stop consonants. *Am. J. Psychol.* 65: 497–509. Reprinted by permission.

Box 18.4 Features of the spectrogram *not* needed for speech perception

The idealization of the spectrogram in Fig. 18.5 has removed a feature that can be seen in the original. That feature is the horizontal banding evident in the vowel portions of the records. These are caused by the harmonics of the vibrations of the vocal cords. The vocal cords vibrate at a rate determined by the air flow through the pharynx, size of the vocal cords, and tension placed on the cords (this last is how you vary the pitch when you sing). The vibration of vocal cords, however, at least in the lower frequencies used in speech, is not sinusoidal. In fact, the waveform of the sound waves produced by the vocal cords is more nearly a triangle wave, containing energy at various higher harmonics of the fundamental frequency (you saw the spectrum of a triangular waveform in the demonstration 'Fourier components' for Chapter 9). The remainder of the vocal tract (lips, tongue, teeth) emphasize some of these harmonics while attenuating others, but the basic pattern of fundamental and harmonics remains (see Lieberman, 1977). Because the production of speech depends more on the articulation of the vocal tract than on actual shifts in the frequency of the vocal cord vibrations, these are the more interesting features, and you can ignore the 'stripes' caused by the harmonics of the vocal cord vibrations. You

are more interested in which stripes are emphasized, and which are absent.

As an analogy, consider someone singing a particular note; the sound emitted is complex. Now consider the difference in how the singer would sound at the end of a long cave; the sound is the same, but which of its components reach you will depend on the properties of the cave. The cave will act like an organ pipe to amplify frequencies whose wavelengths are integer multiples of the cave's dimensions; other frequencies will be absorbed within the cave. If you want to know something about the cave, you have to analyze which frequency regions are enhanced and which attenuated—not the pattern of harmonics that tells you it is a soprano and not a violin in the cave. Similarly, when you wish to see what the articulatory apparatus has done to the sound made by the vocal cords, you are not interested in the fact that the original sound came from vocal cords and not from one of the artificial vibrators used by people who have lost their vocal cords to disease. You therefore ignore the stripes and look for the frequency regions that are emphasized in the spectrograms of speech.

---

had you been asked to idealize the spectrogram. Nevertheless, the ideal version is easier to deal with, so consider the features in it. <u>BOX 18.4</u>

For the moment, consider only the vowels. Notice that for each vowel in Fig. 18.5 there is a pattern consisting of three component frequency bands. These components are called *formants*, and are numbered first, second, and third starting from the bottom (lowest frequency). Peterson & Barney (1952), in a classic study of the formants of English vowels, found that the first two formants contain enough information to allow identification of the vowel sounds. (The third formant has a smaller amplitude than the other two, and seems not to change as much from vowel to vowel.) Speech can be understood when the formants are replaced by bands of noise (Shannon *et al.*, 1995).

Ideal spectrograms of some of the vowels, including those shown in Fig. 18.1, are given in Fig. 18.6: plot (a) shows the spectrograms averaged

from 33 adult male speakers in the Peterson & Barney study, while plot (b) shows the average spectrograms of 15 children speaking the same vowels. The widths of the lines indicate the relative strengths of the formants (not the range of frequencies in each, as a real spectrogram would).

Each vertical slice of Fig. 18.6 represents a single-vowel spectrogram. On the left, corresponding to the 'high tongue near the front' in Fig. 18.1, is the sound *b***EE**. As you progress around the quadrilateral to *s***O***d*, the first and second formants approach each other. Having approached, they then move downward together as you follow the quadrilateral upward from *j***AW** to *t***OO***th*. Notice that the changes in the way the two formants progress occur at the same phonemes as the corners of the quadrilateral.

If you compare Figs 18.6 (a) and (b), you can see the differences between adult males and children. Not surprisingly, the children's voices are higher

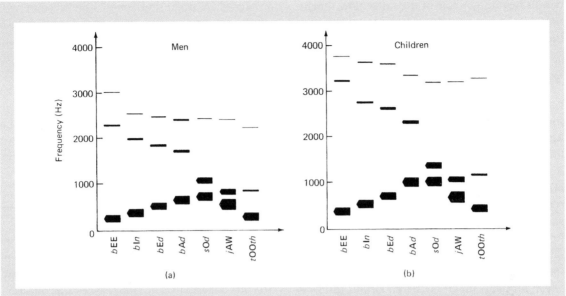

Fig. 18.6 First three formants of vowels spoken by men (a) and children (b). The width of each formant indicates the relative energy it contains (*not* its bandwidth). Based on data of Peterson, G. E. & H. L. Barney (1952). Control methods used in a study of the vowels. *J. Acoust. Soc. Am.* 24: 175–184. Reprinted by permission.

in pitch, although the increase in frequency is not the same for all formants. A child's voice is not exactly the same as a man's voice with all the components shifted upward in frequency; speeding up a tape (which would increase the frequencies of all sounds equally) gives a 'chipmunk' voice, not a child's. The vowels at the extremes of the range (high tongue positions on the quadrilateral—that is, *b***EE** and *t***OO***th*) show the greatest differences between the second formants of man and child;

Box 18.5 The importance of high frequencies

This section is supposed to deal with vowels, but before Fig. 18.5 is too far behind, here is a comment about consonants. Notice that the consonants in 'to catch pink salmon', particularly the **T**o, **CH**eck, and **S**in, are encoded by higher frequencies than the vowels. Since the third formant seems unimportant for identification of vowels, most of the useful vowel energy is below about 1200 Hz. Many of the consonants, on the other hand, depend on frequencies upward of 2000 Hz.

The fact that many consonants are signaled by high frequencies has an interesting consequence. You may recall from Chapter 17 that as we age we lose our sensitivities to the higher frequencies (presbycusis). As a result, older people may develop difficulty in hearing consonants, even though they can still hear. But consonants carry a large part of the information in speech (see Box 18.1). Older people may therefore have trouble understanding speech, simply because they miss many of the consonants. Unfortunately, this is sometimes interpreted as a mental decline with age, and can lead to psychological problems (Zimbardo *et al.*, 1981).

vowels near the middle of the range (low tongue, as *sOd* or *bAd*) show approximately equal shifts in the first two formants. BOX 18.5

Synthesized speech

Looking at spectrograms is a good way to see what the components of a speech sound are, but it has its limitations. One difficulty is that spectrograms are limited to the sounds that speakers actually make. If a speaker cannot make a sound part way between *bEE* and *bIt*, you cannot tell how it would be perceived; nor can you tell what would happen if there were some slight perturbation of only one of the formants. The second problem is that it is hard to say how realistic the idealizations based on the spectrograms are. For all we know, the gray stuff between formants might be the important things to the ear, and the formants just a big artifact.

Fortunately, there is a way to work the spectrograph backwards, to take a pattern painted on paper and generate the sound corresponding to it. The machine that does this is called the *pattern playback*, or *vocoder* (Liberman *et al.*, 1952). A large body of what is known about the perception of speech was derived by experiments performed at the Haskins Laboratories using this device (Cooper *et al.*, 1952; Liberman *et al.*, 1952, 1959). This work was done before computers made it relatively easy to produce any arbitrary sound you might want.

The pattern playback is effectively a reverse spectrograph. An idealized spectrogram painted on paper can be fed into the machine, and the sound corresponding to that spectrogram gets produced. A single horizontal line of paint will produce a single continuous tone. A small splash will cause a short burst of sound. A pattern like the one in Fig. 18.5 (b) will cause the machine to say, distinctly, 'to catch pink salmon'.

Peterson & Barney (1952) had surmised that the first two formants would be sufficient for the identification of vowels. This in fact proved to be the case; ideal 'vowels' consisting of the first two formants were readily recognized as the appropriate vowels (Liberman *et al.*, 1952). BOX 18.6

Consonants

So far so good: distinct patterns of formants uniquely determine the vowel phonemes they represent. The next question is what makes the consonants. Liberman *et al.* (1952) asked this question for the consonants **P**it, **T**ip, and **C**ow (the unvoiced plosives made with lips, tip of the tongue, and back of the tongue, respectively). They found that these consonants, when preceding a vowel, could be generated by a brief burst of relatively narrow band sound. Played alone, such bursts sound like clicks or plops, but in conjunction with a succeeding vowel they sound like the plosive consonants. Here you can see a hint of what is to come: the same sound in two different contexts may be perceived either as the (non-speech) sound of a plop, or as a consonant.

Figure 18.7 shows a typical stimulus used by Liberman *et al.* (1952). In this pattern, the noise burst was centered at about 1440 Hz and lasted 15 ms. It was followed by the first two formants of the vowel *sOd*. This particular stimulus would give

---

Box 18.6 Two-formant speech sounds

You can see the spectrograms and hear the corresponding sounds of these 'vowels' by playing the demonstration 'Speech sounds' on the CD accompanying this book. The spectrograms of the vowels are arrayed across the top of the screen. When you click on any one of them (or its dot), you will hear that sound while a cursor runs across the picture as it plays in time. Two clean formants don't sound much like a person speaking, but you should be able to tell which vowel is being 'said'.

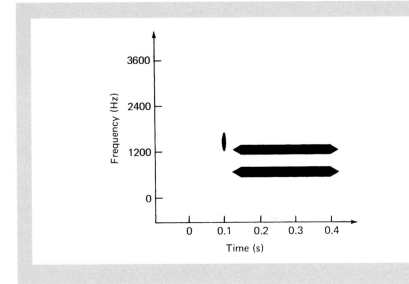

Fig. 18.7 Ideal spectrogram used in the pattern playback to produce the syllable **CO**p. Typical of the stimuli used by Liberman, A. M., P. C. Delattre and F. S. Cooper (1952) The role of selected stimulus variables in the perception of the unvoiced stop consonants. *Am. J. Psychol.* 65: 497–516. Reprinted by permission.

the sound of the plosive **C**ow followed by the vowel s**O**d, so the sound heard should be identified as the nonsense syllable **CO**p.

A noise burst of the same width and duration could be positioned at several different frequencies in front of any of seven different vowels (first two formants). For each stimulus, subjects were asked to identify the nonsense syllable they heard. Figure 18.8 shows a map of which plosives were perceived, as a function of which vowel patterns ensued. The *x*-axis lists the vowel phonemes, as in Fig. 18.6; the ordinate is frequency. The black bars show the locations of the vowel formants, as if each slice were a short piece of spectrogram. Superimposed on this picture are the regions in which a particular consonant was perceived when the noise burst placed at that frequency preceded that vowel. Open circles represent the consonant **T**ip, solid dots represent **P**it, and diagonal lines represent **C**ow. Larger symbols mean the judgments were more firm and reliable; smaller symbols (or blank area) mean the stimuli were ambiguous.

You can see that the **T**ip sound always resulted when the noise burst was at a high frequency, regardless of the following vowel. Bursts above about

3000 Hz were almost invariably perceived as **T**ip. The **P**it sound was not as constant: **P**it was heard when there was a medium-frequency burst followed by one of the high tongue vowels, but required a low-frequency burst when the burst was followed by a low tongue vowel. **C**ow was also very dependent on the following vowel: the further to the back of the mouth the constriction was in generating the vowel, the lower the frequency of the burst that was heard as **C**ow. The **C**ow part of the syllables **CA**pe or **KE**pt was generated by a burst centered at about 2600 Hz: the **C**ow part of **CO**de or **COO**p was generated by a burst centered at 800 Hz. If noise bursts of increasing frequency are placed before the formants of the vowel r**A**te, you would hear the progression of syllables **PA**in, **CA**ne, **PA**in, **CA**ne, and **TA**le (follow vertically above r**A**te in Fig. 18.8).

Now look at this another way. The same physical stimulus, a tone burst at, say, 1400 Hz, is heard as different consonants depending on the vowel by which it is followed. If you trace from left to right in the figure, you would hear the same burst generate the series **PEA**t, **PA**te, **PE**t, **CO**p (this is the stimulus in Fig. 18.7), **CA**ught, **PO**ny and **POO**l. The

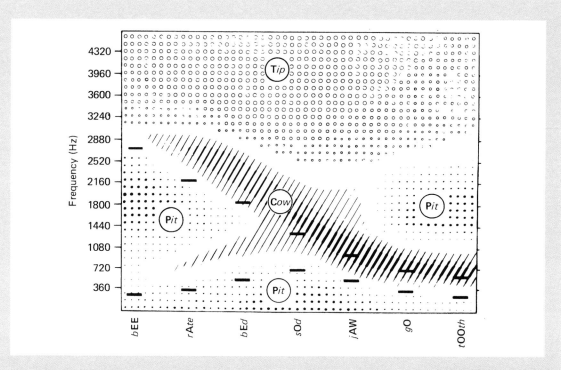

Fig. 18.8 Map of the areas in which the judgment of the phonemes **P**it, **T**ip, or **C**ow prevailed when a noise burst preceded vowel formants. Vowel formants are shown as horizontal bars, and indicated below the abscissa. From Liberman, Delattre, and Cooper (1952). Reprinted by permission.

perception of the sound depends on the context in which it is heard. This effect is demonstrated for a noise burst near 1800 Hz in the left center portion of the 'Speech sounds' demonstration on the CD. The same burst can be played alone (it sounds like a 'plunk' of a dripping faucet), or preceding *b***EE** (to make **PEE***p*), or preceding *s***O***d* (to make **CO***p*).
BOX 18.7

The plosive consonants are perceived in context; there is a dependency on the ensuing vowel. Other consonants also depend on the vowels with which they are associated, in ways that are even more revealing of the kinds of relationships involved. For example, Liberman *et al.* (1956) studied rapid-frequency shifts in the second formant that were the cues to certain consonants. These shifts, which would be heard as rapid glissandos or

chirps if they were not imbedded in speech, are called *transitions*.

Consider the series of spectrograms in Fig. 18.9. The same two formants are present (the vowel is *y***E***t*), but each is approached from a lower frequency with an abrupt rise in frequency. The low point at which each pattern starts is the same, and is called the *locus* of the transition. What differs in these three patterns is the time it takes to get from the locus to the position of the vowel formants. When the transition is brief, as in the left most spectrogram, the consonant heard is **B***ed*. When the transition lasts longer, the consonant becomes **W***et*; at the longest durations, it changes into a shifting vowel (the subjects heard two vowels shading into each other). This series would be heard as **BE***d*, **WE***t*, *cr***UE***t*. This series may be heard

Box 18.7 Is artificial speech different from real speech?

The importance of succeeding sounds does not depend on the fact that these are artificially produced speech sounds. Schatz (1954) cut up tapes of speakers saying words like *keep*, *cop*, *coop*, or *heap*, *hop*, *hoop*, and spliced the leading consonants from the first three words onto the vowels from the last three. This caused no change in the **C***ow* sound, but if the **SK***ip* of *ski*, *skate*, or *school* was used, the perceptions were dependent on the following vowel to which they were spliced. In fact, the pattern of perceived consonants as a function of the following vowel in the spliced tape (not the vowel originally used when the **SK***ip* was recorded) was reminiscent of the map in Fig. 18.8. The reason the experiment worked with the **SK***ip* sound is that there is a brief silence following this sound and preceding the vowel; the tapes could be cut during this (unperceived) silence. In the first series (*keep*, *cop*, *coop*) there is no such silence; the consonant included enough of a cue to the following vowel that subjects could correctly identify the consonant despite the ensuing splice.

in the 'Speech sounds' demonstration on the CD (lower left section of the screen). A similar series is shown in Fig. 18.10; in this case, the three sounds would be heard as **GE***t*, **YE***t*, and *v***IE***t*.

The locus of the transitions is constant, regardless of the following vowel. The second formant transition for **BE***d*, for example, starts at a locus near 1000 Hz; the transition proceeds to about 1800 Hz, the second formant of *b***E***d*. The optimal duration of **B***ed* was about 20 ms, so the rate of change of frequency was about 40 Hz/ms. Had the vowel been *b***EE**, whose second formant is about 2700 Hz, the rate of transition would have to be more than twice as rapid—about 85 Hz/ms—to get from 1000 to 2700 Hz in 20 ms. Nevertheless, the significant factor seems to be the duration of the shift, not the rate of change of frequency. The locus and duration of the second formant transitions were the same when **B***ed* was perceived before any vowel.

The locus of the second formant transition is the necessary cue for a number of consonants (Delattre *et al.*, 1955); however, this can manifest itself in somewhat unusual ways. Consider, for example, how **D***ig* is generated in front of various vowels. The locus for the second formant transition for **D***ig* is at about 1800 Hz; this can be seen in Fig. 18.11, which shows the series: **DEE***d*, **DA***te*,

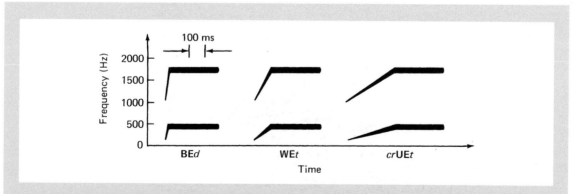

Fig. 18.9 Series of syllables in which the duration of the second formant transition varies. The three would be perceived as **BE***d*; **WE***t*, and *cr***UE***t*. After Liberman, Delattre, Gerstman, and Cooper (1956). These sounds are available in 'Speech sounds' on the CD.

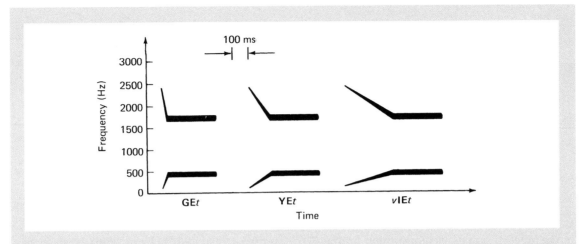

Fig. 18.10 Series of syllables of varying second formant transition duration. The three would be heard as **GE***t*, **YE***t* and **vIE***t*. After Liberman, Delattre, Gerstman, and Cooper (1956).

DE*nt*, **DO***g*, **DO***pe*, **DO**. Notice that in **DE***nt* there is no transition to the second formant, for the second formant is itself at about 1800 Hz, which is the locus. In **DEE***d* and **DA***te* the second formants are above the locus, so there is an upward transition; in the remainder of the syllables the second formant is below the locus and the transition is downward. What all these transitions have in common is that they originate at the same locus. The sounds

DEE*d*, **DE***nt*, and **DO** are in the right middle part of the 'Speech sounds' demonstration.

The transitions do not always start at the locus, however; they just point toward it. In fact, if the entire transition, starting from the locus, were given, the consonant would sometimes not sound like **D***ig* at all. This is shown in Fig. 18.12(a). The transitions actually tested are shown, all originating from 1800 Hz. When the transition was ex-

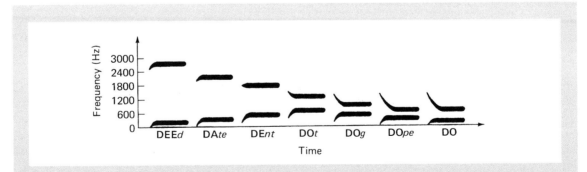

Fig. 18.11 Series of syllables in which the initial consonant is perceived as **D***ig*. Second formant transitions point to a locus at 1800 Hz. From Delattre, P. C., A. M. Liberman, and F. S. Cooper (1955) Acoustic loci and transitional cues. *J. Acoust. Soc. Am.* 27: 769–772. Reprinted by permission of the publisher and author. Also available in 'Speech sounds' on the CD.

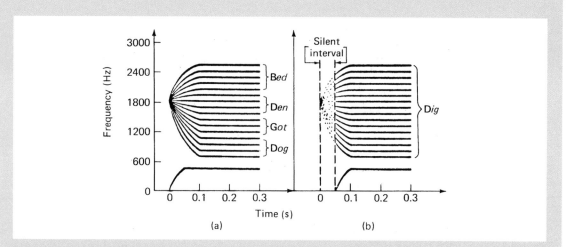

Fig. 18.12 Demonstration of the importance of the time of onset of second formant transitions. The series in (a) have second formant transitions starting at 1800 Hz but may variously be heard as **B**ed, **D**en, or **G**ot. The series in (b) have the identical second formants, except that the first 50 ms of each transition has been deleted; the first formant has been shifted 50 ms to start simultaneously with the second formant. All the stimuli to the right are perceived as having the same initial consonant **D**ig. From Delattre, Liberman, and Cooper (1955). Reprinted by permission.

treme upward, the consonant was perceived as **B**ed; when it was moderate downward, the consonant was **G**ot. If the first 50 ms of the transitions were silenced, however, as shown on the right, the consonant **D**ig, was always perceived. The dotted portions of the transitions show how they point at, but do not reach, the locus at 1800 Hz.

The units of speech

In the previous few pages, the phoneme was treated as the unit of speech. On the other hand, you have seen that the consonant simply cannot stand without an attached vowel. You also know that you cannot chop a tape into phoneme-sized pieces and splice them together to make words.

The size of the basic acoustic unit of speech perception is approximately that of a syllable (Studdert-Kennedy, 1976). There are a number of arguments indicating that this is probably the case, but one of the most convincing was given by

Huggins (1964), based on an observation made by Cherry (1953). A subject was asked to follow a stream of speech played through headphones. At a regular rate, the stream of speech switched back and forth from ear to ear. If the alternation was very fast (say, 20 switchovers per second) or very slow (one per second), the subjects had little difficulty following the gist of the speech. But at intermediate rates, comprehension became poor; the alternation from ear to ear made it nearly impossible to hear what was being said.

The relevance of this study can be understood by borrowing an analogy from Neisser (1967). Consider the effect of alternation on the written word. If a line of text were chopped up and alternate segments displaced downward, it would look like one of the patterns in Fig. 18.13. The top pattern has been cut at a 'slow rate'—relatively large chunks stay together before the next alternation. The bottom row shows text cut at a 'high rate'; part of each letter is on the original line and part on the displaced line. Neither of these forms is illegible.

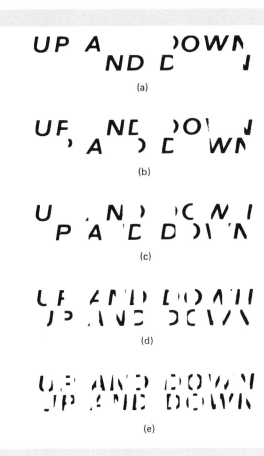

(a)

(b)

(c)

(d)

(e)

Fig. 18.13 Relation between the rate of chopping of text and the disruption of legibility, an analogy to the alternation of speech from ear to ear. See text. From Neisser, U. *Cognitive psychology* © 1967, p. 186. Reprinted by permission of Prentice Hall. Inc., Englewood Cliffs, New Jersey.

Consider, however, the texts chopped at 'medium rates'. The rate of alternation is very nearly the same as the size of the basic units of the text, the letters. Each letter is fractured, and the line is difficult or impossible to read.

The rate of alternation of speech in headphones that was most disruptive, therefore, would be the rate at which the segments were somewhat smaller than the perceptual units. In fact, the most disruptive rate corresponded to a size about 60% of the length of the average syllable; the syllable would appear to be about the right size for the acoustic unit of speech.

There is also evidence that speech perception involves larger units as well. Miller *et al.* (1951) found that the intelligibility of syllables masked by noise was greatly improved by embedding the syllables in meaningful words or sentences. Fodor & Bever (1965) asked subjects to identify where within a spoken text a click was superimposed. Not only was the click always perceived as occurring between syllables (even when it actually was superimposed on an unperceived silence within a syllable), but the reported position of the click was often shifted more than 100 ms to fall between meaningful elements of the speech. This is evidence for top-down processing in the speech system (Pennisi, 1996). <u>BOX 18.8</u>

In order to be able to analyze these larger units of speech, information about the speech signal must be stored over a period of time, for the parts of an utterance are not present simultaneously.

Box 18.8 Vowels and the *Gestalt* of speech

Aspects of speech that are encoded in pieces larger than a syllable are called the *prosodic* elements, also known as *suprasegmental features*. These refer to qualities such as intonation, stress, emphasis, and 'punctuation' (the spoken equivalents of periods, commas, and question marks). These important aspects of understanding spoken words are conveyed by patterns that extend across syllables, words, and phrases (Darwin, 1975).

As an example, stress does not correspond to any single acoustic feature. Stressed words are judged as louder, but physical measurements do not show this to be so. The physical correlate of stress seems to be the *effort* put into the word by the speaker—not some particular attribute of the sound produced (Lehiste, 1976). When you read the section on the motor theory of speech perception (p.

418), you will see other examples of cases in which the percept corresponds to a motor activity of the speaker rather than to a single acoustic feature of the utterance.

In natural English sentences, the fundamental frequency of voicing (rate of vocal cord vibration—see Box 18.2, p.399) falls toward the end of the sentence. Questions are distinguished from statements by the fact that the fundamental frequency does not fall at the end of the utterance. The decline in frequency is a result of the drop in pressure of the air being expelled from the lungs as the speaker prepares to inhale and renew the air supply for the next sentence. Note that the suprasegmental features are apparently conveyed by the vowels, which carry most of the voicing energy (see Box 18.2).

Just as visual pattern recognition depends on the net effect of a large number of features distributed in space (see Chapter 10), speech perception depends on features distributed in time. At least two types of memory have been postulated specifically for the immediate storage of the continuously arriving features in an utterance (Studdert-Kennedy, 1976). <u>**BOX 18.9**</u>

Box 18.9 A demonstration of the importance of context

Although phonemes and syllables seem to be the units of speech, normal conversational speech arrives in a continuous stream in which whole phrases run together. The division of this continuum into individual words is the responsibility of the listener; in doing this, perceptual hypotheses are made that are guided by the context of the conversation.

A striking demonstration of the way in which context influences speech perception was given by Prof. Ronald Cole of the Carnegie-Mellon Institute. The demonstration is on the CD under the name 'Mystery phrase', one of the choices for this chapter. Listen to the phrase (click 'Play the phrase') several times; the chances are that you will be unable to discern the words, and it will sound like gibberish. Now click the 'Give me a hint' button (which only appears after you play the phrase at least once). The hint gives the context of the phrase—you may now know what the phrase said just from your memory of the sounds. If

not, click 'Play the phrase' again, and see whether it makes sense. If it still does not, click 'Give me the answer' (which replaces 'Give me a hint' once you get the hint). Now that you know what the phrase is, play it again; you should hear it distinctly, even though the acoustic signal is just as poor as when you were unable to make head or tail of it.

This is a case in which there is clear perception of a stimulus that defied decoding until some guidance was given as to how to make a perceptual hypothesis; it is exactly like the perception of the hidden faces in the 'Motion from form' demonstration for Chapter 10 on the CD. When you first saw those figures, each looked like some abstract blobs, but once you were shown what they really were, they made sense. If you look back at that demonstration now, you will probably see the faces with little trouble—it may even be hard to imagine why the figures made no sense before you had clicked 'Reveal actual picture'. Just so, the 'mystery phrase' is perfectly intelligible once you

➤

(Box 18.9 continued)

know how to make the right perceptual hypotheses about the acoustic signal; it is hard to believe I didn't pull a fast one and play a more distinctly pronounced version after you saw the answer. But try it again next time you start the demonstrations; you will still be able to understand the phrase, just as you can still see the 'motion from form' faces.

Speech perception

How do you actually do the analysis implied by the discussion of all the acoustic features of speech? What are the neurophysiological and cognitive mechanisms involved?

To begin with, you should note that your ability to perceive spoken words is quite extraordinary. There is no sound equivalent of an alphabet (as you have seen); there is an intricately encoded signal to decode. Despite the intricacy of the code, it is so deeply ingrained that you can recognize and correctly categorize speech sounds that are drastically different from the norm.

When you identify a sound generated on the pattern-playback machine as one phoneme or another, you are merely categorizing it. Is your ability to discriminate these sounds somehow related to the categories into which you place them? Apparently so, for people are far poorer at discriminating sounds that are categorized as the same phoneme than at discriminating between sounds that are categorized as different phonemes—even though the pair of different phonemes may be acoustically more similar (Liberman *et al.*, 1957, 1961; Lieberman, 1977).

As an example of better discrimination of stimuli that are acoustically more similar than those not discriminated, consider Fig. 18.12(a). The four stimuli with the lowest frequency second formants lead to perception of the consonant sound **D**og (the syllable is probably something like **DO**g). The fifth stimulus leads to a consonant perceived as **G**et; subjects are better at discriminating be-

tween the fourth and fifth stimuli than between the first and fourth, even though the first and fourth are physically more disparate.

You might think of these discriminations as a matter of learning, but infants can also make some of these distinctions (Cutting & Eimas, 1975). Interestingly, when only the second formant is presented the distinctions are *not* sharpest at the phonemic boundary (the frequency at which the second formant would begin to signal a different phoneme). Infants presented with second formants without first formants are no better at discriminating the transition associated with **D**og from that associated with **B**it than any other equally different pair within the one category or the other. The effect of a boundary is only found when a first formant (that is the same between stimuli) is present as well (Cutting & Eimas, 1975). The same is true for adult listeners (Mattingly *et al.*, 1971). Apparently then, the phoneme boundaries are not specified by inherent preferences of the auditory system, but they are specific to the perception of speech.

You might have guessed that the definition of the boundaries was not innate, for they vary somewhat from language to language (see Lieberman, 1977). In fact, some of the pronunciation difficulties encountered when speaking a non-native language may be because the phonemic boundaries can be slightly different. Two sounds distinguished as different phonemes in one language may be categorized as the same phoneme in another language, and so not be differentiated by a person raised in the second language who attempts to speak the first. For example, if you make a continuous 'zzzzz' sound, and bring the tip of your tongue close to your front teeth, the sound will change into a prolonged **TH**en (a demonstration best not done in public). The distinction between **Z**oo and **TH**en is in the tongue position; the exact locus at which the sound changes from **Z**oo to **TH**en (the boundary) can be different in different languages. Thus native speakers of French make sounds that to their ears have crossed the boundary into **TH**en, but which to the ears of native speakers of English remain on the **Z**oo side; the French say they will ride in 'ze car'.

In short, categorization seems to be affected by learning, but either the learning begins very early in infancy, or it modifies a biological predisposition. Categorization of this kind is apparently not confined to the perception of speech (Cutting & Rosner, 1974; Pastore *et al.*, 1977). It is also not confined to spoken language (Poizner, 1981), or even human languages (Nelson & Marler, 1989; Wyttenbach *et al.*, 1996). <u>**BOX 18.10**</u>

Finally, how might the nervous system analyze the acoustic signals presented to it during a speech pattern? You have seen the various features that might be extracted: patterns of formants, transitions, and noise bursts. How do neurons respond to these?

Recordings have been made in the auditory cortex of monkeys while playing various acoustic signals (Wollberg & Newman, 1972). Many cells responded to a wide range of stimuli, but there were some cells that seemed highly specific to certain monkey vocalizations. Similarly, quite specific cells were found in cat cortex (Whitefield & Evans, 1965), bullfrog (Frishkopf & Goldstein, 1965), and bat (Suga *et al.*, 1979). Selective cells (for human speech sounds) have even been found in trained mynah birds, which mimic speech (Langer *et al.*, 1981). These feature-specific cells are somewhat reminiscent of the 'bug detectors' in frog retina (Chapter 5); it is hard to say how seriously to take

---

Box 18.10 Development of phonemic boundaries

One possible way that experience could modify biological predisposition is by pruning away those categorizations that are not used. As you saw, very young infants make phonemic distinctions, with boundaries similar to those found for adults. Some boundaries can be demonstrated in infants as young as 6 months (Kuhl *et al.*, 1992). Surprisingly, not only do infants make the distinctions their parents make, but they also 'recognize' boundaries that are used in foreign languages to which they have never been exposed (Werker, 1989). As children mature, they lose the ability to make distinctions across those phonemic boundaries they do not encounter, so that by about 1 year of age (roughly the time children begin to understand spoken language) they make discriminations only across those boundaries that are appropriate for their native language (Harnad, 1987; Werker, 1989).

If this interpretation of how categorization arises is correct, we can conclude that there are a number of possible phonemic boundaries inherent in our nervous systems. This does not mean that there are predispositions specifically 'designed' for language; the boundaries could be accidental arrangements that arise as the complicated brain self-organizes itself. The 'boundaries' would then really be the unstable cusps between neural attractor basins (Kelso, 1995). Either way, each human language draws on a subset of these boundaries, grouping all sounds within any boundary that is used as a particular phoneme. A newborn infant has the capability of making any of the phonemic discriminations, but only those that are exercised are retained.

'Exercised' does not mean necessarily by producing speech. Infants start segmenting speech into statistical units at a very early age (Saffran *et al.*, 1996), and can recognize words by 8 months (Jusczyk & Hohne, 1997)—well before they begin to say their first words. They recognize phonemic boundaries even earlier (Kuhl *et al.*, 1992). Apparently they are trained by the baby talk they hear. Baby talk, silly as it sounds to adults, is actually a pretty effective training set, because it exaggerates the separation of the sounds on the vowel quadrilateral, so the infant can learn more clearly to categorize the sounds (Kuhl *et al.*, 1992).

the claim that they are truly detecting the specific features claimed.

An interesting demonstration of feature detection in the auditory system comes from studies of the adaptation of the presumed detectors. Just as spatial frequency detection channels were demonstrated by adapting to specific frequencies and thus desensitizing the channels selective for those frequencies (see Chapter 9), Eimas & Corbit (1973) showed that listening to a long series of syllables within a phonemic category could affect the identification of a syllable near the boundary (see also Miller & Eimas, 1977). For example, the voiced plosive made by the lips (**B**it) and the unvoiced plosive (**P**it) differ in the duration of the transition from locus to vowel second formant. If the entire transition is used, **B**it is heard; if most of the transition is silent, **P**it is heard. With a moderate length of transition, a subject might hear either consonant. Consider a transition that tends to favor **B**it, but is ambiguous. After a subject listens to a series of repetitions of the syllable **BO**nd, the same slightly ambiguous **B**it can be tested; it will more likely sound like **P**it. The boundary has apparently shifted closer to the 'ideal' **B**it, because of fatigue of the **B**it detector.

In addition, the adaptation effect is apparently central and not caused by simple fatigue in the auditory periphery, for adaptation to syllables played in one ear can affect categorization of syllables played into the other ear (Eimas *et al.*, 1973). Note also that these feature detectors are not simply linked to a single aspect of the acoustic signal (such as the duration of the transition), for changing other cues to the identity of the phonemes (such as the rate at which the sounds are produced) affects the positions of the boundaries (Repp *et al.*, 1978). The feature detectors seem to be specific to complex auditory cues that might be associated with phonemic features; however, non-speech sounds can also affect these detectors (Samuel & Newport, 1979).

The motor theory of speech perception

Speech sounds might be recognized by feature detectors that pick out specific patterns in an auditory signal. And herein lies the same problem faced in visual perception: how can there be enough feature detectors to recognize all the possible speech sounds and their variants? Despite differences in emphasis, voicing, and differences among speakers, you can quickly and effectively interpret the sounds of speech, arriving at the awesome rate of 30 phonemes/s (Liberman *et al.*, 1967)

You have already encountered a hint of a further difficulty: the acoustic features associated with certain sounds can be specified in terms of transition locus, onset delay, and so forth, but these do not seem to be 'natural' things to use as cues. The series of transitions perceived as the sound **D**ig in Fig. 18.11 (and the demonstration) shows a definite tendency for all second formant transitions to point at the 1800 Hz locus; however, the truncated initial segment makes it hard to imagine how you could recognize this as the locus being pointed at in **DEE**d or **DO**.

An even more glaring example was presented by Delattre *et al.*, (1955) in a figure showing the second formant transitions responsible for the sound **G**et. Liberman (1957) emphasized the significance of the problem: there is a change in locus between the sounds **GO**t and **GAU**ze (Fig. 18.14). In the progression from **GEE**se to **GO**t, there is an ever-increasing second formant transition, pointing to a locus near 3000 Hz. But the next sound, **GAU**ze, has a minimal transition, and the subsequent series through **GOO** show small transitions from a locus near 1200 Hz. Three of these sounds (**GEE**se, **GO**t, and **GAU**ze) are available for you to listen to in the lower right portion of the 'Speech sounds' demonstration. There is an abrupt change in locus that has no corresponding shift in the phonetic value of the sound heard: the **G**et sound is the same in all of these syllables.

There is, however, a 'dimension' in which there

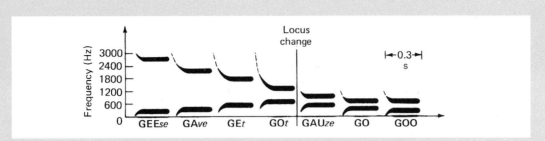

Fig. 18.14 Series of syllables in which the initial consonant is always perceived as **G**e*t*. Note the change of second formant transition locus between the syllables **GO***t* and **GAU***ze*. From Liberman, A. M. (1957) Results of research on speech perception. *J. Acoust. Soc. Am.* 29: 117–123. Reprinted by permission of the publisher and author. Also available in 'Speech sounds' on the CD.

is no change between the sounds **GO***t* and **GAU***ze*. There is no difference in the articulatory maneuvers a person makes to produce the **G**e*t* in each case. We perceive as being the same those phonemes that were made by the same motor activity (a voiced plosive from the rear of the mouth), even though the physical sounds seem to be in different classes. Evidence of this kind led Liberman *et al.*, (1967) to formulate a *motor theory of speech perception*. According to this theory, the acoustic cues are taken in syllable-sized chunks, and these chunks are 'decoded' by determining what motor behavior must have been necessary to produce such a sound. In effect, the listener 'knows' the motor behaviors that produce the various phonemes in conjunction with each other; when a syllable arrives in the ears, the listener builds a model of it based on the motor activity that would be made to produce that sound. (Of course, the listener does not actually make the sound, but just determines the motor action that would make it.)

This model should remind you of the analysis-by-synthesis models of visual perception. In fact, a somewhat more explicit version of a motor theory called analysis by synthesis was proposed (Halle & Stevens, 1959; Stevens, 1973). In this model, feature analyzers perform a preliminary analysis of the speech sounds and pass the digested version to a central processor. The central processor may find that the features presented (including the context, or other sounds previously presented to it) are sufficient for classification. If classification is ambiguous, a 'guess' (perceptual hypothesis) is made, and a synthesizer generates an internal model of the sound corresponding to the guess. This is compared with the memory of the features of the actual sound, and if it matches satisfactorily, the guess is taken to be correct. The point of all this is to generate an internal model of the articulatory gestures that would have led to the sound pattern received; this model then represents the utterance made by the speaker. It is analogous to the internal model in visual perception (Chapter 10) that is presumably built by making perceptual hypotheses about what distal stimulus could have been responsible for the proximal stimulus on your retinas. In speech, the distal stimulus is the articulation of the speaker, and the proximal stimulus is the acoustic pattern. <u>BOX 18.11</u>

One possible difficulty with a motor theory of speech perception is that it might imply that the ability to speak is needed for one to be able to perceive speech. But you would not expect a person who was speechless from birth because of a defective vocal tract to be unable to comprehend speech. Moreover, speechless animals are capable of discriminating the sounds of human speech; this is true for monkeys (Morse & Snowden, 1975) and even for a rodent, the chinchilla (Burdick & Miller, 1975; Kuhl & Miller, 1975).

Box 18.11 More relationships between vocal capabilities and speech perception

The motor theory was devised to explain how disparate acoustic stimuli could represent the same phoneme. The discontinuity in the acoustic stimuli for **GO**t and **GAU**ze provides a striking example in which the percepts are in accord with the articulatory maneuvers that made the sounds, rather than the acoustics of the sounds emitted. Another example is found in the interposition of brief silences in a spoken sentence. If a tape is made of the sentence 'please say shop', and a silence of about 50 ms is inserted after 'say', the sentence becomes 'please say chop' (Dorman et al., 1979). This makes sense given the articulatory gestures required to say 'please say chop': to produce the sudden burst of sound for **CH**op requires closing the airway briefly, thereby creating a brief silence.

Dorman et al. carried this one step further: they made a tape in which a female voice said 'please say' to which was spliced a male voice saying the word 'shop'. In this case, a silence between 'say' and 'shop' made no difference to the percept—the final word was always (correctly) heard as 'shop'. The perception of the acoustic stimulus for 'shop' depended in a very complex way on the perceived capabilities of the human vocal tract; when there were two different speakers, the silence was treated as irrelevant. From this and a number of other observations on the perception of speech with interposed silences, Dorman et al. concluded that speech perception is closely related to the perceiver's knowledge of the capabilities of the human vocal apparatus (also Repp & Liberman, 1987).

These objections are not as problematic as they might seem. Animals can learn to discriminate speech sounds, but we cannot say that they therefore perceive speech in the same way as humans do. They might simply be learning a set of auditory cues, just as you could learn to make various responses to different tones in a set of signal whistles but would not say the whistles were 'speaking'. As for the speechless human, the important thing might be the biological capability for speech, even in the absence of experience with a functioning vocal apparatus. In this regard, it is interesting that electrical stimulation of certain sites in the human brain leads to the facial gestures of speech and also affects the perception of phonemes (Ojemann & Mateer, 1979). There is a relationship between speech-perceiving and speech-producing in the brain; this relationship would not necessarily be disrupted by damage to the vocal tract.

It also appears that the development of the ability to speak is intimately associated with the perception of speech. Human infants who are born deaf do not learn to speak when normal infants would; they babble appropriately for about 6 months, then gradually stop vocalizing (Mavilya, 1972). Similarly (perhaps), certain species of songbirds fail to develop their species-specific songs unless allowed

to hear an adult version of the song during a critical period in their development (Marler, 1975). In the absence of appropriate role models, inappropriate songs develop, although there are certain features that remain. Marler (1975) suggested that the critical thing needed for the development of speech is a set of 'modifiable auditory templates' that serve both for categorical recognition of speech sounds and for motor control of the production of speech. Studdert-Kennedy (1976) took this idea further by suggesting that there are both auditory and articulatory (motor) templates that develop hand-in-glove as the individual learns to speak and understand a language. **BOX 18.12**

A motor theory of speech implies a bimodal process, for the auditory and motor systems must be linked. There is also a linkage to the visual system, for speech is easier to understand when you can watch the speaker's face. (Many hearing-impaired people make use of this fact, partly lip-reading what they cannot quite hear.) The link between the facial expression and the sound is, of course, the articulatory maneuver by which the speech is produced. You can infer this maneuver from the sound (motor theory) or by direct observation. When both kinds of information are available, you can 'hear' better than with only one. If the two

Box 18.12 Linkage between perception and the motor system

In many ways, the arguments about motor theory are like the old question of whether the chicken or the egg came first. Do infants babble because they have inborn templates, or are they imitating what they hear? Evidence for the latter is that infants exposed to sign language 'babble' in sign language; that is, they make sign-like gestures that mean nothing (Petitto & Marentette, 1991). There are cells in premotor cortex of monkeys that respond to specific hand movements—whether made by the monkey or by an experimenter the monkey is watching; a similar sys-

tem seems to exist in Broca's area (speech center) of humans (Rizzolatti & Arbib, 1998).

Further evidence that the sound being heard guides the motor system is found by giving distorted auditory feedback. Speakers who heard their own voices through a system that changed the ratios of the first two formants as they spoke soon adapted, and made speech sounds that provided the appropriate feedback through the system (Houde & Jordan, 1998).

are inconsistent (as in watching a dubbed movie), confusion may arise (McGurk & MacDonald, 1976).

The correspondence between sight and sound is also made by infants. If an 18- to 20-week-old infant is simultaneously shown two videos of the same face saying two different syllables, and hears one of the syllables through a loudspeaker placed directly between the video screens, the child gazes at the video face corresponding to the audible signal (Kuhl & Meltzoff, 1982). <u>**BOX 18.13**</u>

A final tantalizing link between sight, sound, and motor activity is found in gestures. Watch someone speak; the chances are that her hands will be waving about, even if she is speaking on the phone and knows the listener can't see her. Try explaining something while you are sitting on your hands—it's harder than you think. Even congenitally blind children make gestures, although they have never seen anyone gesture (and even when

they know the listener is also blind). Speech production may also activate other motor areas, and the entire larger network is involved in communication (Iverson & Goldin-Meadow, 1997, 1998).

The motor theory of speech perception has closed a circle, for now you see that the feature detectors of speech correspond to the speech sounds with which this chapter began. The features in speech perception are aspects such as voiced versus unvoiced, plosive versus non-plosive, fricative versus non-fricative, front, middle, or back of mouth, and so on. These features are constant when the perceptions are of the same phoneme, even though there are discontinuities in the acoustic properties of the sounds representing them. This means that the features of speech are very complicated in their acoustic definitions, although there are relatively few of them. In vision, such features as edges, lines, and so on, are easy to

Box 18.13 Lip-reading

Lip-reading is more important than you may think. As noted above, disparate audio and visual information can lead to confusion, a phenomenon known as the McGurk effect. When subjects are shown a clip of someone saying one thing while the sound track says something else, they often hear an 'intermediate' sound that is somewhat acceptable for each modality (Massaro & Stork, 1998). Interestingly, this mishearing caused by inconsistent vi-

sual input causes a shift in the pattern of activation in the auditory cortex (Sams et al., 1991). For that matter, the auditory cortex is activated during silent lip-reading (Calvert et al., 1997). All of these phenomena provide evidence of a top-down influence upon the auditory system during speech perception; the perception of the words is a high-level process drawing on audition, vision, and, of course, memory.

define but do little to explain perception, while such higher-order percepts as 'jack o'lantern' or 'mother-standing-at-the-door' are not only complicated but far too numerous to be represented by specific 'detectors'. In speech perception, there are a limited number of complex features to be detected, for the features of speech are limited by the capabilities of the human vocal apparatus.

Speech areas of the brain

This discussion of the perception of speech has made little reference to the brain or specific neural mechanisms that may be involved. However, scientists have been studying the anatomical basis of speech and speech comprehension for more than 130 years, and more is known about the neurology of language than about most other brain processes.

For the vast majority of people, language is largely a function of the left hemisphere of the brain. This is true for virtually all right-handed people, and for the majority of left-handed people as well (Kolb & Whishaw, 1985). For most of us, virtually the entire right half of the brain could be removed without causing any significant deficit in language abilities. A similar segregation of language specialization has been observed in monkeys (Heffner & Heffner, 1984), for the perception of species-specific vocalizations.

Within the left hemisphere, there is a specific circuit that must be intact for normal speech and language comprehension. Figure 18.15 shows the locations of the two major cortical components of this circuit. The first brain area found to be crucial for normal language is in the lower part of the frontal lobe. This area is called *Broca's area*, after the French

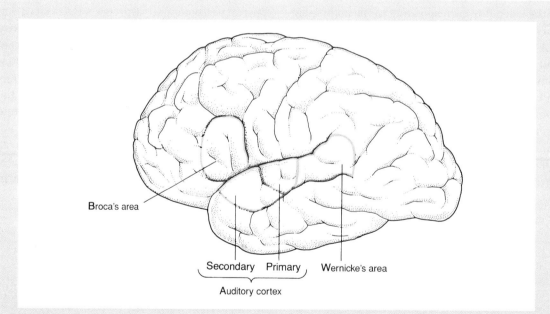

Fig. 18.15 View *of* the left side *of* the human brain, showing cortical areas important for hearing and speech. After A. C. Guyton, *Basic neuroscience: anatomy and physiology* W. B. Saunders, 1987. Reprinted by permission.

Box 18.14 Aphasia

Damage to Broca's area produces a clinical syndrome called *Broca's aphasia*. Patients with Broca's aphasia have a severely reduced speech output. The words produced are usually correct and meaningful, but they are produced with great effort, often at a maximum rate of only 10 words per minute. The problem is not simply in the forming of sounds, for grammatically important words that link the concepts together are noticeably lacking. In contrast, comprehension seems to be only mildly impaired. The defect appears to be in the output of meaningful speech, not in its perception.

Damage to Wernicke's area produces a spectrum of language defects that are quite different from Broca's aphasia. Wernicke's aphasics are quite fluent in their speech output, often producing words at a normal rate. Their grammar may be correct, and the inflection and flow are like normal speech. But the words make no sense when put together, and may even be nonsense words. The patient speaks fluent gibberish, such as 'Mother is away

here working her work to get her better, but when she's looking the two boys looking in the other part' (Geschwind, 1979, p. 111). In marked contrast to Broca's aphasia, comprehension in *Wernicke's aphasia* is grossly abnormal; patients are often unable to understand even simple, one-step instructions. Not surprisingly, both reading and writing are impossible for a patient with Wernicke's aphasia.

Another interesting speech deficit is known as *anomic aphasia*. Patients with this syndrome speak fluently, and have normal comprehension of speech; however, when they are asked to name objects, they perform poorly. They are exquisitely aware of their problem, and often try to hide it with phrases such as 'that thing', or 'whatever it's called'. They often exclaim 'it's on the tip of my tongue' (as we all do sometimes!). Anomic aphasia may be associated with Alzheimer's disease or any diffuse damage in the left hemisphere, but may also result from local damage near the top of Wernicke's area.

physician Paul Broca, who noted in 1861 that patients with markedly decreased speech output proved (on autopsy) to have damage in this area. Broca's area is connected by a fiber tract (the *arcuate fasciculus*) to *Wernicke's area* in the temporal lobe. Damage anywhere in the pathway, including Broca's and Wernicke's areas, produces speech defects characteristic of where the damage is. These speech deficits are collectively known as *aphasias*. **BOX 18.14**

Suggested readings

A very readable paperback account of the production and perception of speech is *The speech chain*, by P. B. Denes and E. N. Pinson (Anchor Books, 1973). It includes chapters on physics and psychophysics of sound, neurophysiology of hearing, physiology of speech production, acoustic characteristics of speech, speech recognition, and linguistics. Each chapter stands as a complete account of a topic,

with little cross-referencing between chapters, so you can read any part as desired.

A considerably more technical, but very readable, account is given by P. Lieberman in *Speech physiology and acoustic phonetics: an introduction* (Macmillan, 1977). This book spends considerable effort introducing the basic physics needed to understand the nature of the sounds produced in speech, and the spectral analyses of them. There is a detailed discussion of the principles of the spectrograph, with practical information on how to use it and interpret spectrograms. There is also a good discussion of the perception of speech. A newer examination of speech may be found in the book *Categorical perception* edited by Stevan Harnad (Cambridge University Press, Cambridge, 1987).

Arguments against the motor theory of speech are given by Carol Fowler (interestingly, of the Haskins Laboratories where the theory was born) in 'Auditory "objects": the role of motor activity in auditory perception and speech perception' in *Origins: brain & self organization* (K. Pribram, ed., Lawrence Erlbaum, Hillsdale, NJ, 1994, pp. 593–603).

Chapter 19

Somatosensory sensation and pain

PRECEDING chapters have gone into considerable detail about how your visual and auditory systems provide you with information about the world around you. Of course, you have other ways of receiving data regarding both your internal and external environments. Your chemical senses of smell and taste provide you with very important information about the outside world. Similarly, the somatic senses of touch and proprioception allow you to gauge the positions of your limbs in space and to perceive stimuli that directly contact your body. In this chapter and Chapter 20, you will learn how the somatic and chemical senses are organized and how they extract the relevant features you perceive as touch, taste, and smell.

Note that, like audition, touch and the chemical senses are sequential. Smell and taste do not produce a spatial map, as the visual sense does. Even in the somatic sense, a blind person recognizes objects by touch, but must feel around it *in a sequence*. The simultaneous 'wholeness' is not developed as it is for a sighted person (Sacks, 1995).

Somatic sensation

The first task in discussing the somatic senses is to describe the set of primary modalities. The sense of touch is obviously not unitary; the feeling of a feather tickling your skin is clearly different from the scratch of a cat's claws. Similarly, although a pinprick, a hot iron, a headache, and a punch on the nose can all be classified as painful, they are by no means the same sensations. However, by correlating anatomical and psychophysical studies, four primary somatic submodalities have emerged:

- *proprioception*: the sense of position of your body and limbs in space;
- *tactile sensation*: the sense elicited by non-painful stimuli placed against your body surface;
- *nociception (pain)*: the sense elicited by noxious stimuli applied to your body;
- *temperature*: the sense elicited by stimuli that are either warmer or colder than your body surface.

Although there is some overlap, these four submodalities are subserved by essentially different populations of receptors and follow one of two major pathways from the periphery to the brain.

Receptors

Many different types of receptors provide input into the somatic sensory system. Except for temperature receptors and one type of *nociceptor* (pain receptor), however, they are all mechanoreceptors; that is, their activity changes in response to mechanical deflection of their cell membranes. In this sense, they are similar to the hair cells of the auditory system, which become depolarized when their external cilia, or hairs, are moved by sound waves. The actual mechanism by which membrane deflection results in membrane depolarization is not completely understood. However, in response to mechanical stimulation, ion channels selective for sodium and potassium are opened, resulting in a graded local depolarization called a *receptor potential*.

The receptor potential generally begins in a *free nerve ending*, which refers to a dendrite-like projection of the cell. Instead of other cells synapsing on this projection, however, the free nerve ending responds to stimulation, just like a rod, cone, or hair cell. The response is typically a depolarization, which is propagated in decremental fashion within the cell to an area capable of generating action potentials. This area, called the trigger zone, is where action potentials are produced with a frequency that depends on the size of the receptor potential (see Appendix). As will be discussed in detail in this chapter, different receptor types are connected to axons of varying conduction velocities, which project to the spinal cord and then, by well defined pathways, to the brain.

Proprioception One could conceive of at least four different ways that the somatic sensory system could get information about the position of the body and limbs in space. One way does not require the use of peripheral receptors at all. Since the position of the body is determined by muscle contractions, which are in turn controlled by the motor system of the brain, perception of movement and position could derive from the motor system itself. In other words, motor commands for voluntary movement could be directly sent to proprioceptive centers elsewhere in the brain. According to this view, proprioception would be the result of one part of the brain monitoring the commands issued by another part, rather than arising from the activity of peripheral receptors.

This hypothesis, known as the outflow theory, was proposed by the German physiologist Hermann Helmholtz, in the last part of the 19th century (see Kandel & Schwartz, 1985). You read about it in Chapter 13 as a means of determining visual motion. However, if this mechanism were important in the perception of limb perception, one would expect that a limb moving passively without a motor command would be perceived poorly or not at all. In fact, passive movement can be perceived with exquisite sensitivity; passive movement at the ankle joint can be estimated to within 2–3° (Berenberg *et al.*, 1987). **BOX 19.1**

If the sense of position is usually not a direct result of the proprioceptive system monitoring commands issued by the motor system, then there must be peripheral receptors specialized to gather information about joint position. Cutaneous receptors located in the skin around joints could signal joint position by responding to changes in skin stretch. Such receptors do exist, and probably do provide important information about joint position. If the major nerves to the hand are

Box 19.1 The phantom limb

A phenomenon that does seems to be well explained by the outflow theory is phantom limb movement. Very often, after someone has had a limb amputated, that person will report a very striking feeling of the limb not only being present, but being in active motion. While initially disturbing, this sensation evoked by the phantom limb is probably very useful when a patient tries to incorporate a limb prosthesis into a complex activity like walking. It is easy to see how Helmholtz's idea that motor commands from the brain provide proprioceptive input could explain how someone could perceive movement in a limb that no longer exists.

inactivated with a local anesthetic, the forearm muscles that control hand movement are still functional, but sensation in the hand is abolished. Under these conditions, subjects report that they cannot tell whether or not their fingers are moving. Moreover, when their fingers are moved for them, position is correctly estimated only at the extremes of joint position (Moberg, 1983).

Under local anesthesia, both cutaneous sensation and any possible sensation from joint receptors is abolished. Receptors located within joints are called *tendon organs*; they are found in the tendons that tie the muscles to the bones. Tendon organs respond in direct proportion to tendon tension and are therefore good candidates to mediate joint position sense. However, when tendon organ response characteristics were carefully studied, it was found that they respond almost exclu-

sively to extremes of movement and are very insensitive to changes in position within most of the normal range of motion of an individual joint (Burgess *et al.*, 1982). Moreover, when they are completely removed, as happens when artificial joints are surgically implanted in the knee or hip, position sense in the artificial joint is nearly normal (Grigg *et al.*, 1973). Thus, cutaneous receptors are probably important for the perception of joint position, and joint receptors probably do not play a major role.

Another class of peripheral receptors important for detecting joint position are the muscle spindles. These receptors are composed of two types of specialized muscle fibers: the nuclear bag and the nuclear chain. Free nerve endings are wrapped around both types of fibers (see Fig. 19.1). When a muscle is stretched, the muscle spindle is also

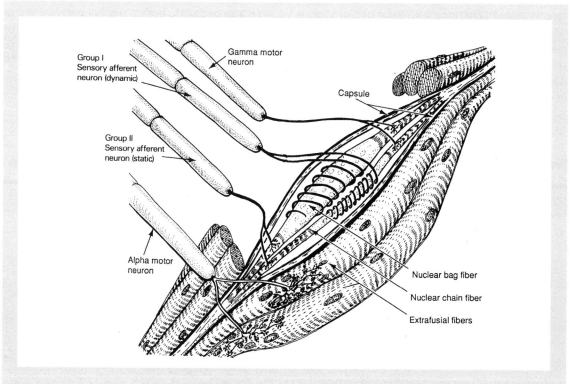

Fig. 19.1 Drawing of a muscle spindle, including a nuclear bag fiber and a nuclear chain fiber.

stretched; the mechanical deflection causes a change in membrane potential in the free nerve endings. This in turn results in an increase in the rate of firing of action potentials in the sensory fibers to which it is attached. Muscle spindles are sensitive to changes in joint position over the entire range of motion for an individual joint. Some of the sensory fibers that are excited by muscle spindle stretching fire in direct proportion to the actual length to which the muscle spindle is stretched; the responses of these fibers is said to be *static*, because they do not depend on how fast the muscle is stretched. Other fibers respond in a *dynamic* fashion; that is, they respond preferentially to change in the stretch of the muscle, and little or not at all when the length of the muscle remains constant. Thus, the brain receives information about actual joint position from the static fibers, and information about joint movement from the dynamic fibers. This should remind you of the sustained and transient fibers in the visual system. **BOX 19.2**

Tactile receptors The sense of touch comprises all the sensations caused by stimulation of the skin that are not painful or temperature specific. *Glabrous* skin—the hairless skin found on the palm and fingertips—contains the four types of receptors shown in Fig. 19.2. *Meissner corpuscles* and *Merkel cells* are located in the superficial layers, while *Pacinian corpuscles* and *Ruffini endings* lie more deeply in the skin.

Each of these receptors has a specialized terminal process that helps to determine its response properties. The Pacinian corpuscle consists of a free nerve ending encapsulated by concentric layers of non-neural connective tissue. When pressure is applied to the skin over a Pacinian corpuscle, this outer capsule is deformed and the free nerve ending is excited. However, the concentric layers of tissue accommodate to the pressure and so reduce the stimulation of the nerve ending as the stimulus continues. The response to a steady stimulus is thus a burst of initial activity, which

---

Box 19.2 The muscle spindle

Figure 19.1 shows the locations of the static and dynamic afferents from the muscle spindle. (A muscle unit contains both sensory and motor components, with sensory nerves (or *afferents*) and motor nerves (*efferents*) connecting them with the spinal cord. (Just *try* not to confuse 'afferent' with 'efferent'!) The sensory muscle spindles are called *intrafusal fibers*, as opposed to the workhorse *extrafusal fibers* that contract to produce the force that moves the limb. Group I axons emanate from the central region of the spindles, at a free nerve ending called the *annulospiral ending* because of the way it wraps around the nuclei. They project to the dorsal spinal cord. The group I fibers are fast conducting and are thought to be dynamic fibers, responding preferentially to change in stretch. Group II fibers arising in secondary endings along the periphery of the spindle extend more slowly, conducting axons to the spinal cord, and are thought to be static fibers.

Muscle spindles receive signals from the spinal cord via neurons called *gamma motor neurons*. These are a separate population of neurons from the *alpha motor neurons* that innervate the extrafusal fibers. Activation of gamma

fibers causes an increase in tension of the muscle fibers within the muscle spindle. This, in turn, causes a change in the baseline level of activity of the group I and II afferent fibers, thus changing the response characteristics of these nerve endings to external stretch. By increasing the activity of the gamma system, therefore, the brain can alter the sensitivity of the muscle spindle to different types of movements. This is another excellent example of feedback in a sensory system.

A simplified simulation of this system is presented in 'Muscle spindle feedback' associated with this chapter on the CD accompanying this book. Only the muscle spindle, extrafusal fiber, group I afferent, and the alpha and gamma efferents are included. When you 'stimulate' the gamma system, the intrafusal fiber stretches, stimulating the afferent and initiating contraction of the extrafusal fiber. When you drop a virtual weight on the muscle, the stretch initiates a similar sequence and the position is restored.

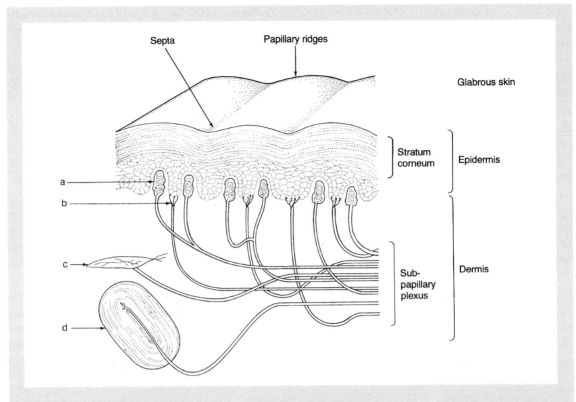

Fig. 19.2 Drawing of a section of hairless skin, with different types of mechanoreceptors. Near the surface are Meissner corpuscles (a) and Merkel cells (b), while Ruffini endings (c) and Pacinian corpuscles (d) lie more deeply in the dermis. From Light, A. R. and E. R. Perl (1984) Peripheral sensory systems. In *Peripheral neuropathy*, Dyck, P. J., P. K. Thomas, E. H. Lambert and R. Bunge (eds) W. B. Saunders, Philadelphia, p. 216. Reprinted by permission.

rapidly decays. If the connective tissue layers are somehow removed, the remaining free nerve ending responds to a steady stimulus with a sustained level of activity (Lowenstein & Mendelson, 1965). Thus, the Pacinian corpuscle is a fast adapting (transient) receptor by virtue of its non-neural accessory structure.

The other rapidly adapting receptor in the skin is the Meissner corpuscle, which lies closer to the surface of the skin than the Pacinian corpuscle. Perhaps due to this, the receptive fields of Meissner corpuscles are considerably smaller than those of Pacinian corpuscles (Johansson & Vallbo, 1983). With a smaller receptive field, the

Meissner cell provides information that can be used in making finer spatial discriminations. Not surprisingly, these receptors tend to be located in areas such as the fingertips where spatial discrimination is best.

The two other kinds of tactile receptors tend to give sustained responses to steady stimuli, and are called slowly adapting receptors. The Merkel receptors lie peripherally in the skin, like the Meissner corpuscle, and thus have smaller receptive fields than the deeply placed Ruffini endings. The receptive fields of Merkel receptors are relatively round, while those of the Ruffini endings are longer in one dimension than the other, and re-

Box 19.3 Functions of tactile receptors

By carefully considering the response properties of the receptors just described, you can make some good guesses about the specific functions they subserve. You have encountered the distinction between tonic and phasic cells in the visual system (X and Y retinal ganglion cells). You saw that these two types of cells provided the input for distinct systems, one of which may have been responsible for providing detailed spatial information, and the other for alerting you to new stimuli.

In the somatic sensory system, a similar division of labor may also take place. There are some tactile stimuli, such as vibration, that are predominantly phasic in nature. The rapidly adapting receptors are particularly well suited to respond to this kind of stimulus. Conversely, in order to hold a delicate glass, you need information about the steady-state level of force you are exerting against the glass. Slowly adapting receptors would be particularly important in providing that kind of tonic information.

spond differentially to skin stretch in one direction (Johansson & Vallbo, 1983). A good account of how the mechanoreceptors work and how they evolved from single cells is given by Hamill & McBride (1995). <u>BOX 19.3</u>

Pain receptors From a consideration of your personal experiences with painful stimuli, it might not seem obvious that pain is mediated by different receptors from those that process touch and temperature. Pain often seems simply to be an excess amount of a stimulus. For example, a blunt object placed against the skin becomes painful only when the pressure it is exerting against the skin exceeds a certain level. Similarly, a warm stimulus becomes painful when a certain threshold temperature is exceeded (or when it remains in place for a long enough time). However, when it became possible to record from single afferent fibers in peripheral nerves, individual fibers were found that responded only to noxious (painful) stimuli (Burgess & Perl, 1973).

Cutaneous receptors that respond selectively to noxious stimuli do not have distinctive terminal specializations as do the receptors for touch. Instead, they are simply free nerve endings located at varying levels within the skin. Some, responsive preferentially to painful mechanical stimuli, are called nociceptors. Others respond best to hot stimuli, while a separate group is multimodal, responding to both noxious mechanical and thermal stimuli (LaMotte *et al.*, 1982).

Temperature receptors Anatomically, receptors sensitive to thermal stimuli are free nerve endings, like nociceptors. Their response properties, however, are quite selective. There are separate receptors for heat and cold, with receptive fields each about 1 mm in diameter (Kenshalo & Duclaux, 1977; Duclaux & Kenshalo, 1980). The hot and cold receptive fields are non-overlapping, creating punctate hot and cold spots on the skin. You can demonstrate cold spots on yourself by gently poking the back of your hand with a pencil point; at certain locations, the point will feel cold.

An illusion that illustrates the presence of localized cold spots is that of paradoxical cold. If a very hot stimulus is applied to a cold spot, the stimulus is not experienced as hot, but as cold. This is because cold receptors have two response ranges, one between temperatures of 10° and 30°C (body temperature is 37°C), and another at temperatures above 45° (Long, 1977). At the high temperatures, cold receptors respond with increased activity, and the stimulus is interpreted as cold. The reverse phenomenon also exists: subjects occasionally report a paradoxically hot sensation when presented with a stimulus that rapidly changes from warm to cold (Hamalainen *et al.*, 1982). <u>BOX 19.4</u>

Box 19.4 The 'Grill' illusion

A curious illusion results when warm and cool are intermixed: the resultant seems burning hot. Of course, if you mix warm and cool water you just get tepid water—you have to keep them separated. This can be done by twisting thin copper tubes around each other, and running the warm water through one and the cool through the other. Because they are so close, hot and cold receptors in the same region are stimulated, and the impression is that it is painfully hot. Because the two tubes are wrapped, the apparatus looks like a grill, hence the name.

It was originally thought that the reason for this sensation is that both kinds of receptor (hot and cold) are stimulated. As noted above, this happens for hot stimuli, which affect the high range of the cold receptors. It now appears that the reason is somewhat different; this combination disinhibits the pain system, and it is the pain you react to (Craig & Bushnell, 1994). This is consistent with the finding that this illusion affects the activity of the anterior cingulate, a pain region of the brain (Vogel, 1996).

Primary afferent fibers

The different classes of receptors just discussed transmit their information to the spinal cord by way of primary afferent fibers. (Recall that 'afferent' refers to the sensory fibers, which project to the central nervous system from the periphery.) In most cases these are simply the axons of the receptor cells themselves; however, at least one receptor type appears to have a peripheral synapse onto a separate primary afferent fiber. Different types of primary afferent fibers carry signals from specific receptor types to specific locations in the spinal cord, with each type transmitting action potentials at a characteristic conduction velocity. As discussed in the Appendix, axons conduct action potentials at speeds that are determined by their diameters. When anatomists looked at the distribution of diameters of primary afferent fibers, they found that four distinct groups of fibers could be isolated (see Table 19.1). The smallest axons are named C fibers—they are unmyelinated and conduct action potentials slowly, at a rate of about 1 m/s. A-delta fibers are the next smallest; they are thinly myelinated and conduct at a rate of about 5–30 m/s. A-beta and A-alpha fibers are also myelinated, and their larger diameters allow them to conduct action potentials at rates of 35–75 m/s and 80–120 m/s, respectively.

The large variation in primary afferent fiber conduction velocities means that information from peripheral receptors can arrive at the spinal cord at significantly different times. For example, if your toe is pinched and the information is carried along C-fibers, it would take about a second for the signal to reach your spinal cord. However, if A-alpha fibers were to carry the signal, the information would reach your spinal cord in about 10 ms, which is 1/100th of the time required for the C-fibers.

As might be expected, different receptor types do not randomly transmit signals along all fiber types; instead there is an orderly relationship between receptor and type of primary afferent fiber. The receptors of proprioception—muscle spindles and joint receptors—need to send their information to the spinal cord as quickly as possible, so that movements can be coordinated. Accordingly, their signals are transmitted along A-alpha and A-beta fibers. All of the tactile receptors are connected to A-beta fibers as well. In contrast, the free nerve endings that mediate temperature and pain have axons that are either C-fibers or A-delta fibers.

The fact that pain fibers transmit action potentials slower than tactile fibers should correspond to your own personal experience. Have you ever stubbed your toe? If so, your first sensation will have been a non-painful sense that your foot had struck something. After a noticeable delay, you will have started to feel a distinct sense of pain, which far outlasted the specific feeling of something touching your toe. The delay in the sensation

Table 19.1 Spatial afferent fibers

Fiber	Name	Myelin	Conduction velocity (m/s)	Functions
Aa	A-alpha	Yes	80–120	Proprioception
Ab	A-beta	Yes	35–75	Proprioception, tactile
Ad	A-delta	Thin	5–30	Temperature, sharp pain
C	C	No	~1	Temperature, burning pain

of pain is a direct result of the slow conduction velocities of the C-fibers transmitting the information. The persistence of pain long after the actual stimulus has ceased is due in part to the fact that, in addition to external stimuli, pain receptors also respond to chemical substances released locally into tissues in response to a noxious stimulus. These substances may remain in the area around the pain receptor long after the actual physical stimulus has been removed.

If you have ever stuck yourself with a pin, you are likely to have noticed that different types of pain reach your awareness at different rates. The first pain sensation in response to a pinprick is a quite sharp and well-localized feeling that is easily recognized as pain. This sensation is transmitted to the spinal cord along A-delta fibers. Shortly thereafter, a less well-localized sensation, perhaps best characterized as burning pain, becomes apparent. One reason that the sensation of burning pain comes later than sharp pain is that receptors mediating this feeling transmit information along C-fibers, the slowest conducting primary afferents. As you will see later, however, this is not the whole story, as the central pathway for burning pain is slower and more circuitous than that for sharp pain.

Central pathways for somatic sensation

So far you have seen that there are different receptor types that selectively respond to different somatic sensations, and that the axons of these receptors can have distinctly different fiber diameters and thus conduction velocities. As you follow the pathways of somatic sensation from the spinal cord to the brain, you will see that the pathways for different kinds of sensations remain distinct. Before studying these pathways, however, you must first know something about the general organization of the spinal cord.

The spinal cord is divided into 29 distinct segments. Each segment receives sensory information via a single pair of sensory roots, one from the right side and one from the left side of the body. A pair of motor roots goes out from each spinal segment as well. As shown in Fig. 19.3, the sensory roots enter the spinal cord on the dorsal side of the cord (closest to your back). Each sensory root is composed of a large number of primary afferent fibers, the cell bodies of which lie outside of the spinal cord in the *dorsal root ganglion*. The cell bodies located here belong to the peripheral receptors that you encountered earlier in this chapter. Note that even though the motor fibers from the ventral root also pass near the area of the dorsal root ganglion, their cell bodies are in the spinal cord, not in the ganglion.

A single primary afferent fiber may follow a rather involved route to reach the spinal cord. First, it joins a peripheral nerve, containing both motor and sensory fibers. This peripheral nerve contains primary afferent fibers that will eventually enter the spinal cord at different segments. As a peripheral nerve gets close to the spinal cord, the sensory and motor fibers separate, and the distinct spinal roots are formed.

Each spinal root contains sensory fibers from a certain area of the body. An area of the body that is innervated by a single spinal root is called a *dermatome*. Figure 19.4 shows a map of the

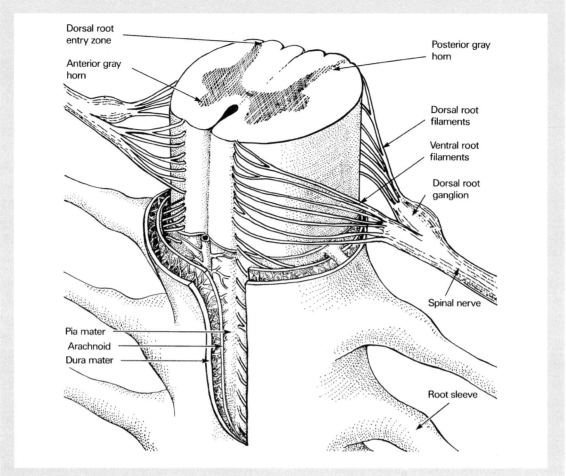

Fig. 19.3 Drawing of the spinal cord and roots.

dermatomes of the human body. There are 29 dermatomes on each side of the body, one for each pair of spinal roots that enter each segment of the spinal cord. The letters associated with each dermatome refer to the level of the spinal column from which the associated nerve root exits: 'C' stands for cervical (neck), 'T' for thoracic (chest), 'L' for lumbar (middle back), and 'S' for sacral (lower back). BOX 19.5

Once entering the spinal cord in the dorsal root, primary afferent fibers may follow a number of different routes. As is shown in Fig. 19.5, fibers can either synapse with spinal cord neurons within the

gray matter of the spinal cord, or they can join one of a number of fiber tracts that form the white matter of the cord. Some primary afferent fibers do both; that is, they divide into collateral fibers, one of which synapses in the gray matter, while the other joins a fiber tract and ascends to the brain.

It is convenient to divide the white matter of the spinal cord into two regions. The *posterior columns* consist of the fiber tracts that lie between the two dorsal horns of gray matter, as shown in Fig. 19.5. The fibers that lie in this region are mostly those that mediate proprioception and tactile sense. The *anterolateral columns*, which lie mostly along the lat-

Box 19.5 Mapping the spinal roots with a virus

You might wonder how a map such as that shown in Fig. 19.4 could be produced. One way is to examine a large number of patients with a disease called shingles, caused by the same virus that causes chickenpox. This virus lies dormant in cell bodies of primary afferent fibers, often just in one dorsal root ganglion. For unknown reasons, at certain times the virus becomes activated and travels down the primary afferent fibers to the periphery. The area of skin in the region around the affected receptors erupts in the rash known as shingles. The distribution of the rash is precisely the dermatome of the spinal segment from which the virus came. Maps such as the one in Fig. 19.4 are generated by looking at the rashes of a large number of patients with shingles.

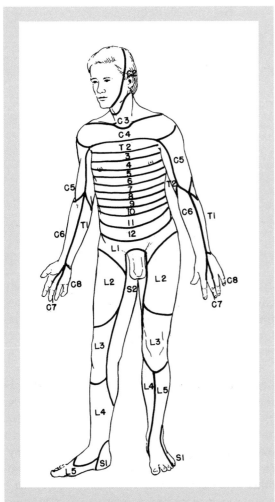

Fig. 19.4 A dermatome map.

eral side of the cord, contain fibers that mediate pain and temperature. (The white matter not shaded in the figure consists mostly of motor fibers from the brain to the motor neurons in the ventral horns of the spinal cord.)

So you see that sensory input to the spinal cord is exceedingly orderly. Fibers are separated into dermatomes according to their origin on the body surface. Within the cord itself, primary afferent fibers are separated into distinct fiber tracts according to the types of stimuli to which they respond. Armed with this basic information, you can now consider the pathways of somatic sensation.

Pathways for proprioception and tactile sensation

As you saw, the ascending tracts of the spinal cord can be divided into two major systems: the *posterior columns* and the *anterolateral columns*. Fibers that derive from receptors sensitive to tactile sensation and proprioception travel within the spinal cord in the dorsal columns. Fig. 19.6 outlines the path that such fibers follow. Primary A-alpha and A-beta fibers enter the spinal cord; they then branch, with one collateral synapsing in the gray matter of the spinal cord, and the other entering the posterior column. Fibers carrying information from the legs comprise the medial part of the column, called the

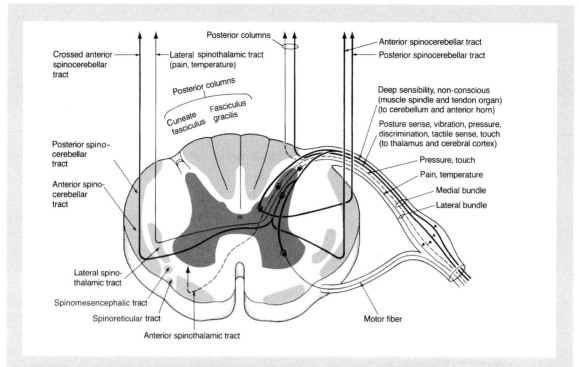

Fig. 19.5 A cross-section of the spinal cord, showing the course of sensory fibers entering the cord at the dorsal horn. Fibers are shown entering the spinal cord through the dorsal root and either synapsing in the gray matter of the spinal cord and/or passing directly into an ascending tract. From Duus, P., *Topical diagnosis in neurology*, 2nd edn. Georg Thieme Verlag, Stuttgart, 1989. Reprinted by permission.

fasciculus gracilis (see Fig. 19.5). Fibers from the chest and arms are more laterally placed in the posterior columns and form the *cuneate fasciculus*. Both groups of posterior column fibers ascend to the medulla, the part of the brain closest to the spinal cord, where they synapse on secondary neurons in the *gracile* and *cuneate* nuclei.

Axons of these neurons ascend to the thalamus in a fiber tract called the *medial lemniscus*. In doing so, they cross from one side of the brain to the other, so that fibers from the left side of the body synapse on neurons in the right thalamus. You should recall that both the lateral and medial geniculate thalamic nuclei, the relay stations for the visual and auditory systems, also receive information from the contralateral side of the body. The thalamic nucleus receiving tactile and proprioceptive information via the medial lemniscus is called the *ventral posterior lateral nucleus*, or VPL. Tactile information from the face is processed in the nearby *ventral posterior medial nucleus*, or VPM. BOX 19.6

Thalamic fibers from VPL and VPM travel in a fiber tract called the *internal capsule* to the *primary sensory cortex* (S1), located in the *parietal lobe*. Fig. 19.7 shows the location of primary sensory cortex on the lateral surface of the brain (it is also marked on the brain pictures in 'Brain anatomy' for Chapter 7 on the CD). Just posterior to S1 is another area that responds to somatic sensory stimuli, the secondary sensory cortex (S2). This area does not receive direct thalamic input, but instead receives the output of cells from S1. S2 is con-

Box 19.6 Diseases of the spinal cord

There are a number of diseases that selectively involve the posterior columns. Although the late complications of syphilis are much less common than in the days before antibiotics (fortunately!), central nervous system involvement is still seen in patients who have not been adequately treated. *Tabes dorsalis* is a form of neurosyphilis characterized by atrophy of the dorsal roots and posterior columns. In its advanced stages, patients with this disease have a markedly unsteady gait because of loss of position sense in the lower extremities. Patients may be able to stand with their eyes open, but, when they close their eyes, they tend to topple over because of their loss of position sense. Similarly, they may be able to reach for

an object fairly accurately under visual guidance, but make wild flinging movements when their eyes are closed.

Vitamin B$_{12}$ deficiency is another disease that damages the spinal cord, and peripheral nerves as well. The first sign may be progressive numbness, starting in the toes and fingertips and progressing toward the trunk. Loss of coordination due to lack of position sense occurs slightly later and is more prominent in the legs than in the arms. Although the damage in the spinal cord is not completely limited to the dorsal columns, many of the early symptoms of this disease are due to damage of the spinal tracts.

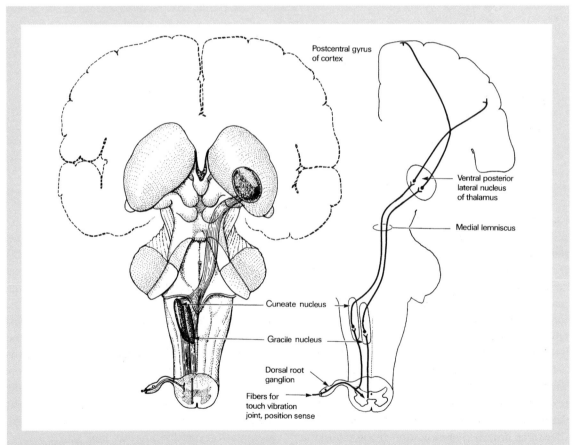

Fig. 19.6 The course of the dorsal column–medial lemniscus sensory pathway, from receptors to the brain.

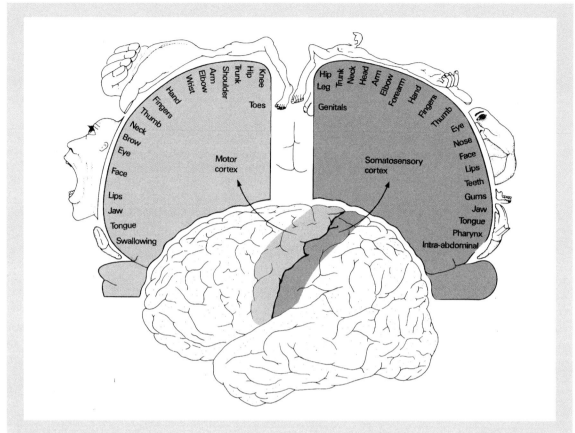

Fig. 19.7 Human primary sensory cortex. A view of the surface of the brain, showing the location of motor and sensory cortices.

cerned with more complicated aspects of somatic perception, and lesions in this area have been shown to interfere with learning new tactile discriminations (Randolph & Semmes, 1974). You may recall that behind this area in the parietal lobe lie the visual areas of the dorsal stream, which is involved in visually guided movements (see Chapter 8).

Primary sensory cortex has much in common with both primary auditory and primary visual cortex. First, tactile sense from the contralateral side of the body is represented in sensory cortex. Second, there is an orderly representation of one side of the body onto the surface of the brain. This projection of the body onto sensory cortex is called a *somato-*

topic map, and it presents a picture called the *homunculus*, meaning 'little man'. The homunculus is sketched in Fig. 19.7. The first thing you will probably notice about the homunculus is that it looks like no human body you have ever seen. The face, lips, and hands are huge compared with the feet, legs, and trunk. This increased size of certain parts of the body corresponds to the increased tactile sensitivity of those areas as compared with other parts represented on smaller areas of cortex. You can make much finer sensory discriminations with your fingertips and lips than you can when stimuli are presented on your belly or legs. **BOX 19.7**

We humans use our fingertips and hands to make most fine discriminations, so it makes sense

Box 19.7 The shape of the homunculus

The experimental data used to construct the homunculus in Fig. 19.7 were obtained in a very interesting way. Wilder Penfield, a Canadian neurosurgeon, was a pioneer in surgical removal of epileptic foci in the brain as a treatment for intractable epilepsy. He performed surgery on patients who were anesthetized only with local anesthetic. Local anesthesia was used so that the patient could communicate and move voluntarily, allowing Penfield to avoid damaging brain areas crucial for movement and speech. Since the brain itself has no specialized pain receptors, this was not unduly unpleasant for the patient.

Before removing a part of the brain he believed might be responsible for the patient's epileptic seizures, Penfield would gently stimulate that area with a mild electric shock. When he did this in areas of S1, patients would report various tactile sensations in particular areas on the contralateral side of the body. By stimulating systematically throughout S1, Penfield was able to generate a map of the projection of various parts of the body onto the brain.

that human sensory cortex should selectively emphasize sensory input from that part of the body. What about the somatotopic maps from other animals for whom tactile information from the forelimbs is not so important? Fig. 19.8 displays what the homunculi look like for a rabbit, a cat, a monkey, and a human. The most striking difference between the cat or rabbit and the monkey or human is the lack of magnification of the sensory input from the forelimb in the two lower animals. Instead, sensory input from the face—especially the whiskers—is emphasized much more than in primate cortex. The homunculus for the monkey much more closely approximates that of humans, except that the hands still receive rather less magnification and the feet somewhat more.

The responses of single cells in primary sensory cortex have been studied in much the same way that Hubel and Wiesel studied single cells in the visual system. In fact, recordings from single cortical neurons were made from sensory cortex considerably before single cells were studied in the visual cortex. Such recordings have in general verified the somatotopic organization that Penfield described. However, more detailed studies have shown that, instead of one homunculus, there are four distinct somatotopic maps in primary sensory cortex (Kaas et al., 1983). These maps correspond well to four areas of S1 that have been identified by anatomical methods. The areas were creatively

named 1, 2, 3a, and 3b by an anatomist named Brodmann, who divided the entire cortex into more than 40 separate areas (Brodmann, 1909). The maps are parallel to one another, which explains why Penfield (see Box 19.7) found only a single representation.

The four somatotopic maps differ from one another in the kind of stimuli that produce the best responses (Kaas et al., 1983). Cells in area 1 seem primarily sensitive to stimulation of rapidly adapting skin receptors, while those in area 2 respond best to deep pressure. Area 3a receives most of its input from muscle stretch receptors, while 3b responds to cutaneous stimulation of both transient and sustained types. This selectivity of different parts of cortex is not absolute; within any one map, cells can be found that respond to all modalities. However, it does demonstrate that the stimulus selectively of different receptor types is maintained throughout the somatic pathway.

The different functions of the four somatotopic maps in S1 were illustrated in an interesting way by Randolph & Semmes (1974). They made precise lesions in the cortices of monkeys, waited for the animals to recover, and then studied how the differently placed lesions affected their behavior. Lesions in area 1 interfered with an animal's ability to make discriminations based on the texture of objects. In contrast, animals with lesions in area 2 could not accurately assess the sizes and shapes of

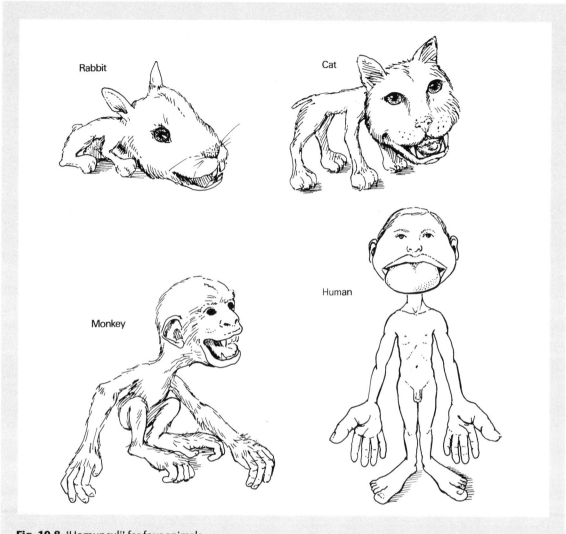

Fig. 19.8 'Homunculi' for four animals.

objects. Lesions in area 3 prevented the monkeys from discriminating size, shape, or texture.

In addition to demonstrating the multiplicity of somatotopic maps in S1, single-cell recording techniques have provided more precise information about the response properties of individual cells. Cells in sensory cortex have receptive fields that are similar in many ways to those of cells in the visual system. They have well-defined receptive fields; that is, a given cell will respond only to stim-

ulation of a circumscribed area of the body. They also exhibit spatial antagonism; stimulation of the central area of a cell's receptive field will result in excitation, while stimulation of the surrounding area will cause inhibition of the response (Mountcastle, 1957; Mountcastle & Darien-Smith, 1968). This center/surround organization is precisely analogous to that seen in retinal ganglion cells. Lateral antagonism in the somatic sensory system has the same function that it does in the visual system; it allows for enhanced discrimination between neighboring stimuli.

Receptive fields of cells in primary sensory cortex vary greatly in size. Cells that respond to stimulation of the legs and trunk have receptive fields that are several square centimeters in area. In contrast, cells that respond to stimulation of the fingertips have receptive fields that are as much as 100 times smaller. This variation in receptive field size correlates quite well with the relative magnification of the face and fingers on the homunculus in Fig. 19.7; that is, cortical cells with the smallest receptive fields are those located in areas of the brain where the body surface is most magnified. Thus, both cortical magnification and variation in receptive field size combine to produce greater discriminative ability in the face and hands than in other parts of the body. This should remind you of the magnification of the fovea in the retinotopic representation of the world in visual cortex.

Some cells have more complicated receptive fields than simple center/surround antagonism. Several groups of experimenters (Hyvarinen & Poranen, 1978; Costanzo & Gardner, 1980) have described cells that respond when an object is swept in a certain direction across the skin. However, when the object is moved in another direction, the cell either responds with inhibition or fails to respond at all. Fig. 19.9 shows examples of responses of direction-specific neurons. The behavior of such cells should remind you of complex cells in visual cortex.

Another way in which visual and primary sensory cortices are similar is the overall way in which neurons are organized. Recall from Chapter 8 that visual cells are organized into columns; when Hubel and Wiesel advanced their electrodes through the cortex, they found that successive cells they encountered were similar both in their ocular dominance and in their preferred orientation. Similarly, S1 is also organized into discrete columns (Mountcastle, 1957; Kaas *et al.*, 1979). In

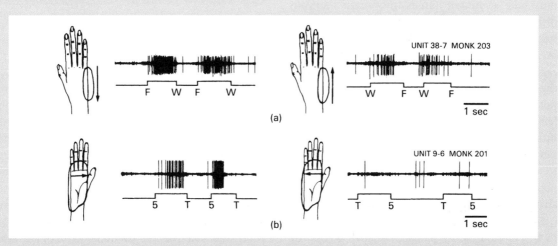

(a)

(b)

Fig. 19.9 The direction sensitivity of two different neurons in primary sensory cortex. In (a), the receptive field of the cell is along the side of the hand; movement in either longitudinal direction evokes a response. The cell in (b) responds to movement in only one direction. From Costanzo, R. M. and E. P Gardner (1980) A quantitative analysis of responses of direction sensitive neurons in somatosensory cortex of awake monkeys. *J. Neurophysiol.* 43: 1319–1341. Copyright 1980 by the American Physiological Society. Reprinted by permission.

fact, it was Mountcastle's work that inspired Hubel and Wiesel to look for columns in visual cortex. If a given cortical cell close to the surface of the brain responds best to stimulation of rapidly adapting receptors, then the cells directly underneath will show the same selectivity. As one moves from one somatotopic map to another, the relative widths of columns vary. For example, in area 1, columns of cells responsive to rapidly adapting receptors predominate, while in area 3a, columns of cells that respond to muscle stretch are relatively larger.

Perception of palpated shapes

So far, it may have seemed as if feeling were a matter of passively allowing things to press against your skin. But feeling is an active process, in which your fingers move across the object, much as your eyes scan a visual scene. Just as your visual system must take account of your eye movements, so your proprioceptive system must 'know' about (and perhaps make use of) your limb and finger movements.

Not coincidentally, it was one of the foremost theorists of visual perception, J. J. Gibson, who first noted the difference between passive and active feeling (Gibson, 1962). He asked subjects to determine the shapes of cookie cutters that were felt but not seen. The subjects did very well if allowed to run their hands across the shapes, but did poorly when the experimenter simply pressed the shapes against their hands.

Note, however, that this difference may be due to the motion of the palpated shapes across the skin (Schwartz *et al.*, 1975). Just as visual stimuli fade if they do not change (see Chapter 6), pressure stimuli undergo adaptation (Nafe & Wagoner, 1941; Hamill & McBride, 1995). If the stimulus does not change, it eventually ceases to be sensed.

If you place your hand in a bowl of water, you will experience another example of somatosensory adaptation. Very quickly, you will lose the awareness of your hand being surrounded by water that is likely to be at a very different temperature from the air. The only place you will sense the difference is at the interface between air and water, perhaps because of small movements that continually change the location of the interface on your skin. Take it from someone who sometimes swims in Lake Michigan: the water always seems coldest when you first get in!

It is not surprising that there are interactions between proprioception and kinesthesis. There are also interactions between proprioception and vision. If you pick up two weights, you can judge that they weigh the same, or that one is heavier, with reasonable accuracy (remember Weber's law, discussed in Chapter 2). However, if the two weights are of different sizes, your judgment will be affected. In general, you will judge the physically smaller of two equal weights to be heavier (Stevens & Rubin, 1970).

Pain

The anterolateral system

You have already seen that the receptors that respond to pain and temperature are distinct from those mediating other somatic sensations. This segregation is maintained within the spinal cord. The free nerve endings that are the receptors for pain and/or temperature transmit their responses to the cord along the smallest diameter primary afferent fibers, A-delta and C-fibers. These fibers enter the spinal cord via the dorsal root, and synapse on neurons within the gray matter of the spinal cord. Most of these second-order neurons send their axons across to the other side of the spinal cord, where they ascend to the brain as the anterolateral system. About 15% of these second-order neurons do not cross the midline but join the anterolateral system on the ipsilateral side.

Already, two important differences should be apparent between the dorsal column system and the anterolateral system. First, the axons in the dorsal columns are branches of primary afferent fibers themselves, while fibers in the anterolateral system are axons of second-order neurons. Second, while the dorsal columns consist of fibers that have not crossed the midline, most fibers in the anterolateral system have already crossed. **BOX 19.8**

One other difference between the two major somatic sensory systems is that while the dorsal columns consist of one large fiber bundle, the anterolateral system is composed of three distinct tracts. These different tracts mediate quite different types of pain perception. Remember what happens when you accidentally stick yourself with a pin. The first feeling that you get is a sensation of sharpness, or stinging. If you thought about it, you would probably classify that sensation as painful, but not particularly emotionally disturbing or even very unpleasant. Immediately thereafter, however, comes a more poorly localized burning pain that is much more disturbing than the initial sensation.

The first sensation is called 'fast pain' and is mediated by the *lateral spinothalamic tract*, the largest fiber tract within the anterolateral system (see Fig. 19.5). This tract receives its input from the relatively rapidly conducting A-delta fibers. Most spinothalamic fibers cross the midline of the spinal cord, and ascend to the thalamus

(Fig. 19.10). There they synapse in the same nucleus as did fibers from the posterior column system, the VPL nucleus. However, cells from the VPL that receive their input from the spinothalamic tract do not also respond to stimulation of the dorsal columns; the segregation of painful and tactile sensation is maintained within the VPL of the thalamus. It is also maintained in S1, where the axons of VPL neurons project.

The other two fiber tracts within the anterolateral system are called the *spinoreticular* and *spinomesencephalic tracts*. Together, they mediate the sensations of temperature and burning pain previously described. They seem to be adrenergic systems; that is, they use the neurotransmitter (and sometime neuromodulator) norepinephrine (Sato & Perl, 1991). Their primary input is from the much slower conducting C-fibers. While some second-order neurons cross the midline like the spinothalamic tract, a much larger percentage remain on the ipsilateral side of the spinal cord during their ascent to the brainstem. Upon reaching the brainstem, rather than synapsing directly in the thalamus, most fibers from the spinoreticular and spinomesencephalic tracts synapse in a region called the *reticular formation*. This is a large area in the center of the brainstem extending from the medulla all the way to the thalamus. Within the reticular formation, many synapses are made; eventually, information about burning pain reaches the *central lateral* (CL) nucleus, an area of

Box 19.8 Results of damage to crossed and uncrossed systems

This second difference between the anterolateral and posterior column tracts is illustrated by a clinical picture seen after some types of spinal cord injuries. If either the right or left side of the spinal cord is damaged by trauma, a combination of deficits known as a *Brown–Sequard syndrome* results. If, for example, the right side of the spinal cord is damaged, the right posterior columns are obviously affected. This produces a loss of touch and position sense on the right side of the body below the level of the injury. The anterolateral system on

the right side of the cord is also damaged; however, since this system has predominantly crossed, pain and temperature sensations are reduced on the left side of the body, starting several spinal dermatomes below the site of the injury. This loss of pain and temperature on one side of the body, with loss of position sense and touch on the other side of the body, is an unfortunate but striking demonstration of the difference in spinal cord organization of the two somatic sensory pathways.

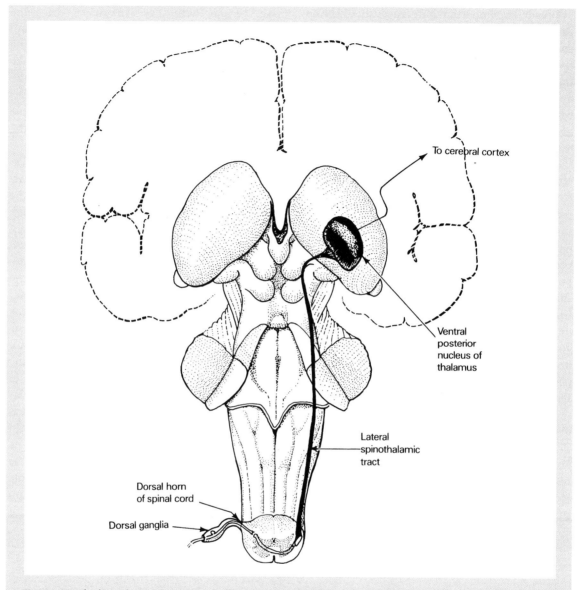

Fig. 19.10 The lateral spinothalamic tract, from receptor to brain.

the thalamus that seems selectively pain-sensitive (Giesler *et al.*, 1981). Axons of CL neurons project diffusely throughout the cortex, as well as to many areas of the brainstem. BOX 19.9

When electrical recordings are made from single fibers in the anterolateral system, a number of classes of cells can be distinguished. Within the spinothalamic tract, the majority of fibers respond briskly to noxious thermal or mechanical stimuli, but not at all to non-painful stimuli. These cells have been named 'high threshold' (HT) cells. Another group responds to both innocuous and painful stimuli, and are called 'wide dynamic range' (WDR) cells (Willis, 1981). Fig. 19.11 shows a

Box 19.9 Two pain systems

The fact that there are two pain pathways that may use different neurotransmitters allow for manipulation of these systems. The slow, burning pain is the one we are more concerned with, because this is the intractable chronic pain that can so debilitate those who suffer from it. Some hope comes from work that shows that this pathway also depends on substance P, a protein that serves as a neurotransmitter and neuromodulator (and is related to the systems that respond to opium and other narcotics; it also is involved in control of food intake, among other things). In particular, manipulations that destroy the brain's receptors for substance P can eliminate chronic pain without affecting acute pain (Mantyh *et al.*, 1997). That is, the chronic suffering can be eliminated without making the person less sensitive to the sudden pain of an injury—a pain message that could be important to alert the person that there is some harm being done and that action should be taken. Similar results have been reported with other chemical manipulations (Malmberg *et al.*, 1997).

comparison of the responses of WDR and HT cells to a range of stimuli.

Cells in the spinothalamic tract can also be distinguished according to the size of their receptive fields. While most cells have quite discrete receptive fields, some cells in the spinothalamic tract have been found to have receptive fields that extend to virtually the entire body surface (Giesler *et al.*, 1981). An example of one such cell is shown in Fig. 19.12. Most of these cells respond only to noxious stimuli, and therefore can be classified as HT cells.

Within the VPL nucleus of the thalamus, the majority of cells seem to respond to tactile stimuli rather than nociceptive stimuli. However, some cells can be found that have responses similar to cells of the spinothalamic tract (Kenshalo *et al.*, 1980). Both WDR and HT cells have been found, with receptive field sizes that are quite similar to those of spinothalamic tract cells.

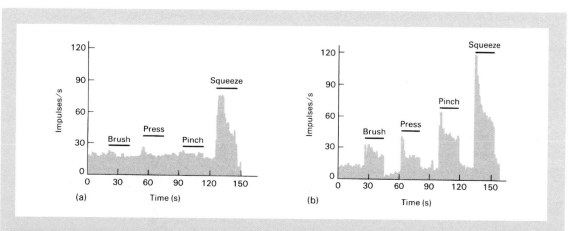

Fig. 19.11 Responses of an HT (a) and a WDR (b) cell to different types of stimuli. The HT cell responds only minimally to all stimuli except a strong squeeze, to which it briskly reacts. The WDR cell responds with graded excitation to all stimuli, with response level increasing as strength of stimulation increases. From Willis, W. D. (1981) Ascending pathways from the dorsal horn. In *Spinal cord sensation: sensory processing in the dorsal horn*, Brown, A. A. and M. Rethelyi (eds) Scottish Academic Press, Edinburgh. Reprinted by permission.

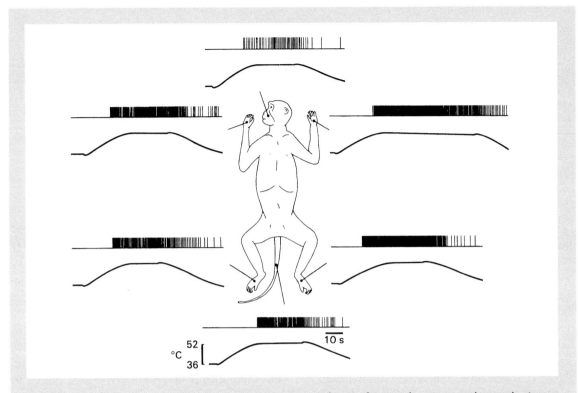

Fig. 19.12 Responses of a spinothalamic tract neuron to stimulation of various locations on the monkey's body. A brisk response is generated by stimulation almost anywhere on the body surface. From Giesler, G. J., R. P. Yezierski, K. K. Gerhart and W. D. Willis (1981) Spinothalamic tract neurons that project to medial and/or lateral thalamic nuclei: evidence for a physiologically novel population of spinal cord neurons. *J. Neurophysiol.* 46: 1285–1308. Copyright 1981 by the American Physiological Society. Reprinted by permission.

Nociceptive-specific cells have also been found in primary somatosensory cortex. Just as there are distinct columns of cells that respond to stimulation of rapidly adapting and slowly adapting tactile receptors, so there are columns of cells that respond selectively to nociceptive input (Lamour *et al.*, 1983). Within the nociceptive columns, the majority of cells have response properties that are quite similar to nociceptive cells in the thalamus (Kenshalo & Isensee, 1983).

However, in addition to cells with discrete, contralateral receptive fields, some cells have been found that have large, often bilateral receptive fields. It is interesting to consider what function such cells might have in the perception of pain. They are not likely to be useful in discriminating the precise location of the painful stimulus — cells with smaller receptive fields would do that job much better. Most of the cells with large receptive fields are WDR cells, so they are also not likely to help in determining the actual nature of a painful stimulus. Instead, these cells, as well as cells with large receptive fields in the thalamus, may be important in determining the affective or emotional response to painful stimuli, as well as in the central control of pain perception. The actual coding of pain more likely takes place in the cingulate cortex, which is folded deep inside the very center of the brain (Rainville *et al.*, 1997). Like other senses, pain has multiple representations (Talbot *et al.*, 1991). In addition, as you will see in the next section, descending pathways play a considerable role in the perception of pain.

Central inhibition of pain perception

As you have seen throughout this book, a general rule for perceptual systems is that one's perception of a given stimulus is not a direct copy of the stimulus. Instead, there is an often complex interaction between the response of the peripheral receptors to a specific stimulus, the state of activation of neighboring receptors, and one's state of arousal or attention that determines the final percept. The color of a visual stimulus depends not only on the wavelength of the stimulus itself, but also on the background.

Similarly, a stimulus that is normally perceived as painful may feel quite different if other cutaneous receptors are stimulated simultaneously. This fact has been known for many years and underlies a number of methods, both ancient and modern, for reducing pain. The expression 'bite the bullet' is a familiar one; it refers to times past when patients in a field hospital would bite on a bullet while surgery was being performed without anesthesia. People realized that the perception of pain could be dulled, if only slightly, by the presence of a strong second stimulus. But you know

this; after all, you rub yourself when you get bruised, and scratch when you itch. BOX 19.10

In 1965, Melzack & Wall proposed a theory of analgesia to account for these kinds of phenomena (*analgesia* means the removal of pain.) In their model, both myelinated non-nociceptive fibers and unmyelinated C-fibers directly excite second-order transmission cells. However, myelinated fibers also excite an interneuron within the dorsal horn, while unmyelinated pain fibers inhibit this same interneuron. Activity of the interneuron inhibits activity of the transmission cell. Thus, activity of the pain fiber alone excites the transmission cell directly, and also acts to inhibit the interneuron, thereby indirectly resulting in excitation of the transmission cell. If the myelinated fiber is simultaneously stimulated, output of the transmission cell is reduced through stimulation of the inhibitory interneuron. Thus, non-painful stimulation reduces the response of the transmission cell to nociceptive input. This theory has been dubbed the *gate control theory* of analgesia.

The gate control theory easily explains the reduction in perceived pain produced by simultaneous, non-painful cutaneous stimulation, such as that produced by TENS units (see Box 19.10). More support for the theory comes from studies in which myelinated sensory fibers are selectively inactivated. Under these conditions, noxious stimuli are perceived as more painful than when the myelinated fibers (A-alpha and A-beta) are

Box 19.10 Pain relief by stimulation

The use of stimulation to block pain may be part of the explanation for the effects of acupuncture. In this ancient art, needles are placed in specific positions to treat various ailments, including pain. While there are several theories about why these particular placements work, it is not unreasonable to expect that the stimulation by the acupuncture needle serves to divert the pain messages.

A more high-tech example of how pain can be lessened by extraneous stimuli is the use of transcutaneous electrical stimulation in the treatment of chronic pain syndromes. A machine called a transepidermal nerve stimulation unit (TENS) provides low-level electrical current to the skin, usually close to the site of chronic pain. A number of studies have demonstrated that such stimulation significantly reduces the level of perceived pain (Hansson & Ekblom, 1983; Warfield *et al.*, 1985). This reduction in pain level often persists for hours after the TENS unit is turned off.

functioning normally (Price *et al.*, 1977). The most direct explanation of this phenomenon is that activity of myelinated fibers exerts an inhibitory effect on pain transmission.

In addition to peripheral mechanisms of altering pain perception, the brain also exerts powerful descending influences to reduce pain under certain circumstances. This descending system can be demonstrated in a number of different ways. For example, electrical stimulation of particular areas within the brainstem produces an analgesic effect (Hosobuchi *et al.*, 1977; Richardson & Akil, 1977). This phenomenon is called stimulation-produced analgesia (SPA), and has proved to be useful in the treatment of patients with severe, intractable pain. Electrodes are surgically implanted into patients with this sort of pain, and small electric impulses are provided periodically throughout the day. Patients report a slow fading of their pain over several minutes after the onset of SPA, sometimes associated with a feeling of relaxation or well-being. Reactivity to non-painful stimuli is preserved, and patients are able to perform normal intellectual functions.

The areas in the brain where SPA can be produced constitute a system for the central control of pain. Many experiments have been performed to map this system, which begins in the center of the brainstem just below the thalamus and extends downward to the medulla (Fields, 1987). The areas in which SPA is most effective have neurons whose axons project downward in the spinal cord and synapse in the dorsal horn onto or near to nociceptive primary afferents. Thus, it appears that SPA works by activating a pre-existing system for pain control.

Another way in which scientists have studied the brain's ability to modulate the level of pain perception has been through the study of opiate analgesics. Drugs such as morphine have been known for years to possess powerful analgesic properties. Over the last 30 years, a growing body of evidence has accumulated supporting the idea that this class of analgesics (called opiate analgesics because they are derived from the opium poppy) acts by exerting a specific excitatory effect on a class of brain receptors. It was hypothesized that some neurons within the brain possessed receptors that were specifically sensitive to opioids. In fact, opioid receptors have been isolated, and have been found to be distributed in the brain in the very areas where electric stimulation produces analgesia (Simon *et al.*, 1973; Snyder, 1980). Injecting very small amounts of morphine into these brain areas produces a striking degree of analgesia (Yaksh, 1978). Both the analgesia produced by morphine and that produced by electrical stimulation can be abolished by pretreatment with naloxone, a drug with a chemical structure related to morphine (Akil *et al.*, 1976). The ability of naloxone to inhibit the effects of morphine was found to be due to the fact that naloxone binds to opiate receptors without exciting them, thus rendering them inexcitable by opiate drugs. Thus, the

---

Box 19.11 Why should pain be blocked?

If pain makes sense because it forces you to deal with dangerous stimuli, why have an elaborate system to block it? Perhaps it is because the pain would interfere with other important activities even after you did all you could do about the danger.

When an animal is stressed, it becomes less sensitive to painful stimuli. Maier *et al.* (1982) showed that this effect was greater when rats were subjected to painful shocks that they could not avoid than when they were subjected to pain that could be avoided (by running in a wheel). This makes sense—if the pain can be avoided, let it hurt so the animal will do whatever it can to get away from it. But if the pain cannot be avoided, hurting serves no purpose, so stop the pain and get on with other activities. This kind of pain alleviation is mediated by the opiate system.

Box 19.12 Opioids and the 'placebo effect'

There are a number of situations in which this descending system can be demonstrated. You have probably heard of the placebo effect, where a subject is given an inert 'sugar pill' with some specific function ascribed to it, and subjectively experiences an improvement in symptoms. If such a placebo is given for the purpose of pain relief, subjects often report that their pain is decreased. However, if subjects are either pretreated with naloxone or given naloxone after the placebo, they report an increase in their level of pain (Grevert *et al.*, 1983). Since naloxone's only known effect is to block the activity of the endogenous opiate system, the experiments just described suggest that placebos work by causing increased release of endogenous opiates within the brain to activate the brain's descending system of analgesia.

analgesia produced by either stimulus seems to result from stimulation of the opioid system in the brain.

Why should the brain possess receptors specifically for a class of drugs related to the opium poppy? The answer turns out to be quite simple; within the brain, there are endogenous substances, chemically related to opiate drugs, whose functions are to activate the brain's system for analgesia. The reason that opiate drugs are effective is that they are so similar to these endogenous chemicals. The first endogenous opiates to be discovered were called enkephalins (Hughes *et al.*, 1975). Shortly thereafter, a different class of chemical, beta-endorphin, derived from the hormone propiomelanocortin, was also found to stimulate opiate receptors (Herbert *et al.*, 1983). More recently, over 20 different protein-like substances that are active at opiate receptor sites have been isolated from brain tissue. Different subclasses of opiate receptors have also been isolated, each with slightly different actions when activated (Martin, 1984). <u>BOX 19.11</u>

To summarize, these data suggest that the brain possesses a descending system for modulating the perception of pain. This system can be directly activated by electrical stimulation of the central areas of the brainstem, or by use of morphine-like substances. The brain itself activates this system through a class of neurotransmitters called endogenous opiates. <u>BOX 19.12</u>

Suggested readings

An excellent in-depth treatment of the sensory systems for touch and pain can be found in *Principles of neural science*, edited by E. R. Kandel and J. H. Schwartz (Elsevier, 1986). Chapters 23 through 26 discuss the structure and function of the somatosensory system from receptor to brain. The same authors have a well-respected text on basic neural science called *Essentials of neural science and behavior* by E.R. Kandel, J.H. Schwartz, and T. M. Jessell (Appleton & Lange, Norwalks, 1995). Chapter 18 includes the somatosensory representation; chapter 20 compares the common features of all the sensory systems. A good review of mechanoreceptors and their functioning can be found in the article by Hamill & McBride (1995) 'Mechanoreceptive membrane channels' in *American Scientist* (83: 30–37).

Chapter 20

The chemical senses : taste and smell

Introduction

The senses of taste and smell provide a slightly different perspective on how the brain processes sensory information. The sensory systems you have read about so far can be examined without necessarily having to refer to parts of the brain involved with non-sensory processing. While the information you receive from other senses certainly affects your behavior, each sense could be discussed in relative isolation. In contrast, both the gustatory and olfactory systems are intimately related to parts of the brain that mediate learning, as well as the primary drives of hunger and sex. As a consequence, a discussion of how chemical stimuli are processed must also consider their effects on specific behaviors. These two senses are also intimately related to each other.

Another difference between the chemical senses of taste and smell and the other sensory systems is that, in the former, it is more difficult to describe the components of the stimulus that are important for its perception. The relevant aspects of a visual stimulus are its luminance, color, and spatial distribution—not surprising when a little bit about the physics of light is known. In contrast, philosophers and scientists have argued for centuries about what constitutes the primary qualities of smell and taste. The difficulty in defining what it is

about the stimulus that is important for sensation has had a great effect on how the chemical senses have been studied through the years.

Taste (gustation)

Anatomy of the gustatory pathway

Taste receptors are located primarily on the tongue, but are also found on the soft palate and other structures in the back of the throat. They lie within a sensory organ called a *taste bud*, which consists of about 50–150 receptor cells in close association with two other cell types, the *supporting cells* and *basal cells*. Figure 20.1 shows a view of a taste bud—all three cell types are tightly arranged in a flask-like structure with a pore (the *taste pore*) that opens onto the surface of the tongue; the receptor cells tend to be at the center of the taste bud while the supporting cells lie peripherally (McLaughlin & Margolskee, 1994). At the tip of each receptor are small processes called microvilli extending through the opening pore and directly contacting the saliva in the mouth. Substances that produce taste stimulate the taste receptors by contacting the microvilli at the taste bud pore.

Taste receptors have a life span of about 10 days; they are constantly being replaced by new recep-

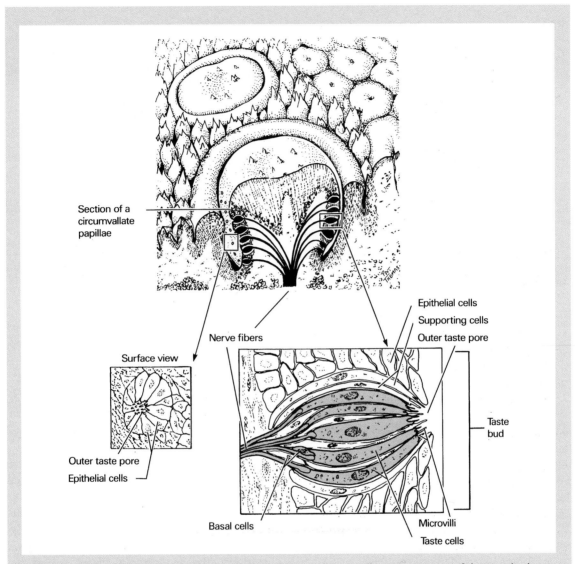

Section of a circumvallate papillae

Nerve fibers

Epithelial cells
Supporting cells
Outer taste pore

Surface view

Taste bud

Outer taste pore
Epithelial cells

Basal cells

Microvilli

Taste cells

Fig. 20.1 Schematic drawing of a taste bud within a circumvallate papillae. *Top*: Location of the taste buds within the papillae. *Bottom*: The taste bud itself.

tors generated by mitotic division of the supporting cells (Pfaffmann, 1978b) that migrate inward toward the center of the taste bud. Since taste receptors are derived from specialized epithelial cells (the supporting cells), they are not considered true neurons.

If you look at your own tongue in the mirror, you will notice that there are many small protuberances distributed along the edge. These are called papillae, and contain clusters of taste buds (see Fig. 20.2). Fungiform papillae are the most numerous, and are found all along the edge of the tongue. Foliate and circumvallate papillae are found at the back of the tongue; the taste buds found in these

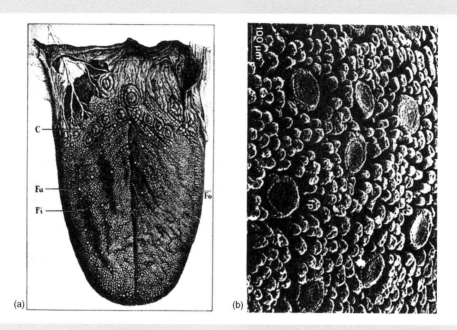

Fig. 20.2 (a) Drawing of human tongue with different types of papillae: C, circumvallate; Fu, fungiform; Fi, filiform; Fo, foliate. From Warren, H. C. and L. Carmichael, (1930) *Elements of human psychology*. Houghton Mifflin, Boston. (b) Scanning electron micrograph of the surface of a frog tongue with filiform papillae. From Graziadei, P. and R. S. Dehan (1971) The ultrastructure of frogs taste organs. *Acta Anat.* 80: 563–603. New York: S. Karger AG, Basel. Reprinted by permission.

papillae probably respond to different kinds of taste stimuli from the taste buds located in the fungiform papillae. However, as you will learn later in this chapter, the differential distribution of sensitivities is not as clear as it was once believed to be (McLaughlin & Margolskee, 1994).

The receptor cells do not have axons of their own to carry taste information to the brain. Instead, they make synapses at the bottom of the taste bud with nerve fibers that project into the brainstem. A single nerve fiber synapses with many individual taste receptors from an average of two taste buds (Beidler, 1978). The taste fibers extend from the tongue and mouth areas to the brain as components of three large nerves: the *facial, glossopharyngeal,* and *vagus* nerves. These are three of the 12 cranial nerves that enter the brainstem; the

optic nerve and auditory nerve are also cranial nerves.

Fibers from all three nerves synapse in a part of the brainstem called the *solitary nucleus* (see Fig. 20.3). From there, taste fibers travel in one of two directions. The majority of fibers ascend the brainstem to the *ventral posterior medial nucleus* (VPM) of the thalamus. Remember that the thalamus is the primary sensory relay station for the sensory systems. You may also recall that the VPM nucleus is also the sensory relay station for fibers from the somatosensory system that carry touch, pain, and temperature information from the face and mouth (see Chapter 19). Like the fibers carrying somatosensory information, the fibers carrying taste information travel from VPM to primary sensory cortex (S1). Not surprisingly,

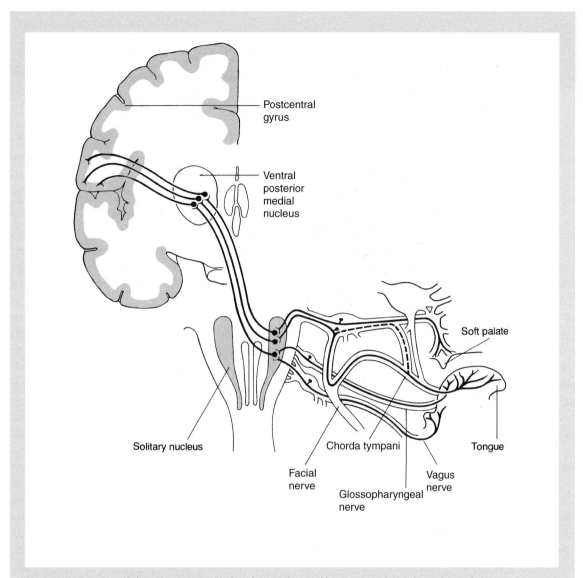

Fig. 20.3 Diagram of the neuroanatomical pathway of taste fibers. Heavy lines show the paths most commonly seen. Most fibers travel from the chorda tympani to the facial nerve; other fibers travel in the vagus and glossopharyngeal nerves. From Brodal, A. (1981) *Neurological anatomy*, 3rd edn. Oxford University Press, New York. Reprinted by permission.

the area of sensory cortex sensitive to taste stimuli lies close to the area subserving touch, pain, and temperature sensations from the mouth and tongue. <u>BOX 20.1</u>

Psychophysics of taste

For the other sensory systems, it was possible to describe the basic qualities of the sensory stimulus that determined how the stimulus was perceived.

Box 20.1 Comparison of the taste pathway to other sensory pathways

The pathway just described is similar in many respects to the sensory pathways of the visual, auditory, and somatosensory systems. There is the obligatory synapse at the thalamus, and from there, a monosynaptic relay to S1. However, some taste fibers from the solitary nucleus take an alternate route to the *amygdala* and *hypothalamus*, both of which are part of the *limbic system* (Ricardo & Koh, 1978). This part of the brain has many complicated functions, but is particularly important for emotional

responses and reward systems. One of the major differences between the chemical senses and the other sensory systems is the strong emotional responses that can be associated with gustatory and olfactory stimuli, so the fact that the sensory system for taste has a direct projection into this area is notable. You may recall from Chapter 8 that the ventral visual pathway also has connections with the amygdala, but the visual connection is from higher cortical areas, not the primary input.

For example, once you know the frequency and intensity of a given auditory stimulus, the subjective perception can be fairly well predicted. What are the primary qualities for a gustatory stimulus? This question has been discussed since the time of Aristotle (384–322 BC), who proposed that there were seven basic taste qualities: sweet, bitter, sour, salty, astringent, pungent, and harsh (Bartoshuk, 1978). He felt that all other tastes could be produced by appropriate combinations of these qualities. The idea that combinations of primary sensory qualities could evoke seemingly different perceptions should be a familiar one; it is analogous to the theory of visual trichromacy discussed in Chapter 14.

The assumption that all tastes could be produced by a combination of a limited number of primary taste sensations has been accepted with little challenge since then, with arguments on this subject being devoted to what the primary taste qualities might actually be. There has been consistent agreement that the qualities of sweet, sour, bitter, and salty represent primary modalities; however, the number and nature of other primary tastes have been vigorously debated. For example, Haller (1786) proposed that seven other qualities also required inclusion: rough, urinous, spirituous, aromatic, acrid, putrid, and insipid. Two more 'primaries' have since been added: *metallic* and *umami* (the taste of monosodium glutamate, or MSG, the meat tenderizer in oriental cooking that gives some people headaches).

One of the first people to propose that all tastes could be produced by combinations of just four primaries was Kiesow (1896), a student of Wilhelm Wundt. He used sodium chloride (table salt), weak hydrochloric acid, sucrose (sugar), and quinine as the stimuli that would produce 'pure' sensations of salty, sour, sweet, and bitter, respectively. With combinations of these substances, he was able to produce a wide variety of different taste sensations. These observations were confirmed and extended by Henning (1927).

The hypothesis that taste quality is determined by the combined activity of four different channels that are each tuned to one of the four primary taste modalities is still accepted today. This hypothesis is supported by the observation that different areas of the tongue are selectively sensitive to different taste qualities. The tip of the tongue is quite sensitive to sweet stimuli, but relatively insensitive to bitter and sour. The sides of the front part of the tongue are most responsive to salty stimuli (Pfaffmann, 1978a), while the sensitivity to sour is best along the sides of the back part of the tongue. Bitter stimuli are tasted best on the back of the tongue and on the soft palate (Yamamoto & Kawamura, 1972). Most of the top surface of the tongue responds poorly to taste stimuli; this corresponds to the fact that there are very few taste buds on this part of the tongue.

Although there is considerable overlap, the different types of papillae seem to be preferentially sensitive to different stimuli. Figure 20.2 (a) shows the approximate distribution of the different papillae on the human tongue. The fungiform papillae predominate along the circumference of the front part of the tongue. In this region are areas of sensitivity to sweet, salty, and sour stimuli, but bitter stimuli are not tasted well. The area along the surface of the back of the tongue, where bitter stimuli such as quinine are tasted best, is also the area where the circumvallate papillae predominate. Sour stimuli are tasted well over areas of the tongue that have a high density of any kind of papillae. Since the receptor cells of a given taste bud all have similar response characteristics, these data would suggest that different types of taste buds predominate in different types of papillae.

More evidence that taste is processed by four independent channels comes from experiments demonstrating that each of the four primary tastes adapts separately from the others. For example, subjects presented with a strong acid stimulus (for example, sour) for 2 min become less sensitive to the taste of sour substances (Abrahams *et al.*, 1937; Krakauer & Dallenbach, 1937; McBurney *et al.*, 1972). Similarly, adaptation to sugar reduces the sweetness of other sweet substances (McBurney, 1972), and chronic presentation of sodium chloride makes other salty stimuli seem less so (Smith & McBurney, 1969).

This phenomenon is exactly analogous to adaptation in the visual system. For example, staring at a green object for several minutes lowers your sensitivity to that color; because of the opponent processing in the visual system, you see a red afterimage after the object is removed (remember the 'Afterimages' demonstrations for Chapter 6 on the CD). In the case of adaptation to a sour stimulus, the subject's taste threshold is raised both for stimulation by the same sour substance and to other sour tastes. Similar arguments were made for spatial frequency channels (see Chapter 9). **BOX 20.2**

Another dramatic demonstration that different taste qualities are processed through independent channels comes from the use of taste-altering substances. If you treat your tongue with gymnemic acid (an extract from the plant *Gymnema sylvestre*), you temporarily lose the capacity to appreciate sweet tastes. This is true whether sweetness is tested with sucrose or with an artificial sweetener such as saccharin. It is as if the activity from receptors sensitive to sweet tastes were completely abolished.

This effect can also be demonstrated physiologically. Fig. 20.4 shows the combined responses of many taste-sensitive nerve fibers to stimulation by the different primary tastes and the artificial sweetener saccharin. Before the administration of gymnemic acid, there are responses to all the substances tested; however, after the extract is painted on the tongue, the response to both sugar and saccharin is eliminated while the responses to sour, bitter, and salty stimuli are unchanged. This study demonstrates that the

---

Box 20.2 The taste of water

A similar phenomenon to taste adaptation is the taste of pure water. By appropriately combining primary taste stimuli, any of the four primary tastes can be perceived simply by drinking water (McBurney & Gent, 1979). After adaptation to a sweet stimulus, water tastes sour or bitter. Adapting to sour or bitter stimuli produces a sweet water taste. However, the taste of water is not as predictable as taste adaptation; for example, eating artichokes also makes water taste sweet, even though there

is no obvious bitter adapting taste (Bartoshuk *et al.*, 1972).

Although the water tastes produced by adaptation to specific gustatory stimuli seem idiosyncratic, the evoked tastes combine additively with directly evoked tastes. Thus, water tastes sweet after sour or bitter adapting stimuli, and sweetened water tastes even sweeter than without adaptation (McBurney & Bartoshuk, 1973).

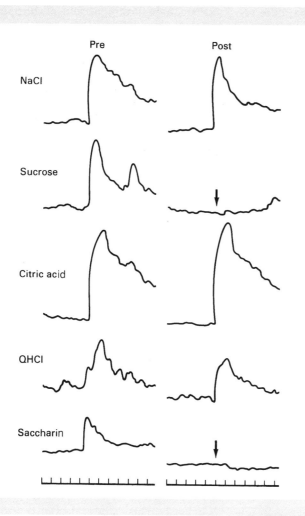

Pre   Post

NaCl

Sucrose

Citric acid

QHCl

Saccharin

Fig. 20.4 Summed responses of the chorda tympani to different taste stimuli, before and after administration of gymnemic acid. From Diamant, H., B. Oakley, L. Strom, C. Wells and Y. Zotterman (1965) A comparison of neural and psychophysical responses to taste stimuli in man. *Acta Physiol. Scand.* 64: 67–74. Reprinted by permission.

quality of sweet taste is processed independently from other taste qualities at an early point in the gustatory system. In addition, it shows that artificial sweet-tasting substances such as saccharin work by mimicking the effect of sugar at or near the level of the receptor.

The physiology of taste

The taste receptor, like all the other sensory receptor cells you have studied, has a negatively charged membrane potential in the resting state. When it is stimulated with the appropriate substance, it re-

sponds with a graded change in its level of polarization. Most commonly, receptor cells depolarize in response to a taste stimulus, but on occasion they can show a hyperpolarizing response (Ozeki & Sato, 1972). When the response of the receptor cell is depolarization, neurotransmitter substance within synaptic vesicles is released into the cleft between the receptor cell and the afferent sensory nerve fiber carrying taste information from the tongue to the brainstem.

The response of the receptor cell to taste stimulation is called a generator potential, and is analogous to the generator potentials produced by hair cells in the cochlea or by rods and cones in the retina. As is true with the other receptors just mentioned, taste receptors do not generate action potentials; the strength of a response to a given stimulus is signaled by the amount of depolarization rather than by the frequency of action potentials being fired. In contrast, the afferent nerve fiber does fire action potentials, with the frequency of firing being related to the total amount of depolarization of all the receptor cells with which it synapses. Remember, the afferent nerve fiber receives transmitter from many taste receptors within a given taste bud, as well as in neighboring taste buds. <u>BOX 20.3</u>

Given all the psychophysical evidence suggesting that the four primary taste groups are processed in independent channels, you might expect that a given taste receptor would respond well to only one taste stimulus. However, when Kimura & Beidler (1961) first recorded from single taste receptor cells, they were surprised to find that most taste receptors were stimulated by at least two (and often more) of the basic taste qualities. Figure 20.5 shows the electrical responses of three taste receptor cells in the rat tongue to stimulation by salt, sugar, quinine, and acid. The first cell responds best to quinine, but also responds well to salt. The second cell responds almost equally to sugar, quinine, and acid, but does not respond to salt. Sato (1973) studied the response properties of 109 taste receptor cells, and found that cells could respond to between one and four of the primary taste qualities.

Box 20.3 Mechanisms of taste receptors

The different taste receptors have somewhat different mechanisms for producing changes in polarization of the cell membrane. Saltiness, of course, depends on sodium chloride (NaCl), or salt. Sodium causes depolarization by a relatively straightforward mechanism: sodium ions (Na^+) enter the cell and depolarize it. Other salts (sodium can be combined with different negative ions) have different amounts of saltiness, even though the sodium content is the same. This is apparently because the negative ions (for example, Cl^- in NaCl) cross the membrane with more or less difficulty; the amount of these ions that cross change the internal polarization of the cell and therefore the force causing sodium to enter (Ye *et al.*, 1991).

The other 'basic' flavors each have their own mechanism. Sour is associated with acid, an excess of hydrogen ions (H^+). Acidity apparently closes a potassium pore, slowing the efflux of potassium and thus depolarizing the neuron.

Sweet tastes have a more complicated mechanism involving a G-protein cascade (similar to the cascade in visual receptors; see Box 4.6, p. 57). In one cascade, G-protein activates a kinase that destroys the ATP that normally closes potassium channels. Potassium leaves the cell, resulting in hyperpolarization. In other cells that respond to sweetness, sweet substances cause an increase in cyclic AMP, which in turn activates a protein enzyme

that acts to inactivate channels in the membrane permeable to potassium (Avenet *et al.*, 1988a,b). The decrease in potassium conductance causes the cell to depolarize. To make things even more complicated, other investigators found that sweet stimuli caused depolarization of dog taste receptors by increasing membrane conductance to sodium (Simon *et al.*, 1989). A single receptor cell may even use different ionic mechanisms to respond to each particular type of stimulus.

Bitter tastes also activate a G-protein, which through a different cascade releases calcium ions that in turn open a potassium channel. This also results in hyperpolarization (McLaughlin & Margolskee, 1994). Other receptors sensitive to bitter stimuli use an entirely different method of taste transduction. A subpopulation of rat taste receptor cells was found for which bitter stimuli caused an increase in intracellular calcium (Akabas *et al.*, 1988). Stimulation with sweet stimuli did not cause this increase, which appeared to be a result of calcium release from endogenous storage sites rather than entry across the membrane. As a rise in intracellular calcium can produce transmitter release in the presynaptic terminals of axons, it is possible that in these cells, the critical factor for stimulus transduction is the change in calcium concentration rather than membrane depolarization.

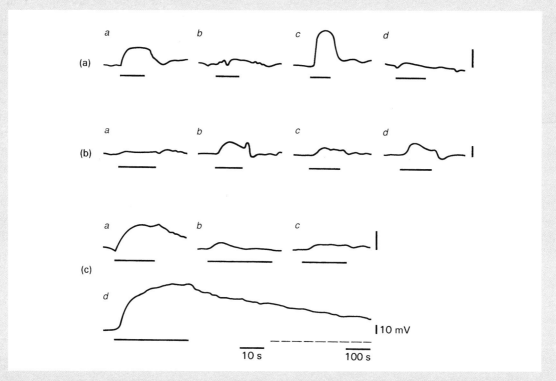

Fig. 20.5 Intracellular responses of three gustatory cells in rat tongue to four different taste stimuli. For cells (a), (b), and (c), *a* represents the response to NaCl, *b* the response to sucrose, *c* the response to quinine, and *d* the response to HCl. From Ozeki, M. and M. Sato (1972) Responses of gustatory cells in the tongue of rat to stimuli representing four taste qualities. *Comp. Biochem. Physiol.* 41A: 391–407. Copyright 1972 by Pergamon Press, Inc. Reprinted by permission.

The fact that most taste receptors respond to more than one taste quality raises problems for the contention that the four primary tastes are processed independently. For example, if a cell responds well to both sweet and salty stimuli, how can the brain know which is present?

One possibility would be that it is the ensemble response of a large number of taste receptors that determines the resulting perception. Such a system would only work if sensitivity to the different taste qualities were distributed independently over the population of receptors. If, for example, salty and sweet were always linked together at the level of the receptor, there would be no way for the brain to somehow differentiate between them.

However, if some cells responded to both salty and sweet tastes, but other cells responded only to sweet, the brain would be able to differentiate between the two stimuli.

Ozeki & Sato (1972) studied this question for rat taste receptor cells. They recorded from a large number of receptors, and determined the taste qualities to which each receptor responded. They found that the distribution of sensitivities to different taste types was independent; that is, there was no tendency for sensitivity to one primary taste quality to be linked to another. From these data, it seems most likely that there are individual taste receptor sites for each of the four primary taste qualities, and that these receptor sites are distributed randomly on the surface of taste receptor cells (Sato, 1980). Therefore, the hypothesis that there are four independent taste channels is after all consistent with the data just described.

The response characteristics of the nerve fibers onto which the receptor cells synapse are significantly more complicated than those of the receptors themselves. Like the receptor cells, single nerve fibers respond to more than one taste quality. Pfaffman (1941, 1955) was the first to record from single fibers in the *chorda tympani*, a segment of the cranial nerve that runs from the receptors in the tongue to the brainstem. He found that a given nerve fiber responded best to one of the four primary taste qualities, but would usually respond to at least one other kind of taste stimulus. For a given stimulus type, the neuron would show an increased response as the concentration of the stimulus was increased. Fig. 20.6 shows the responses to a single chorda tym-

pani fiber that was most sensitive to salt in a wide variety of salt concentrations.

Pfaffman found that an individual nerve fiber was usually most sensitive to a single stimulus type, and he identified neurons as salt-best, sugar-best, and so on. He found that some cells responded almost solely to the stimulus type for which it was most sensitive, while others were more widely responsive. Fig. 20.7 shows the concentration/response curves for two cells to different concentrations of all four stimulus types. The cell in the left half of the figure responds best to salt, but also responds well to increasing concentrations of both acid and sugar. In contrast, the cell on the right responds best to sugar, only slightly to salt, and virtually not at all to bitter or sour stimuli.

Fibers coming from different parts of the tongue were also found to have different sensitivity profiles: not surprising since different parts of the tongue are differentially able to detect different

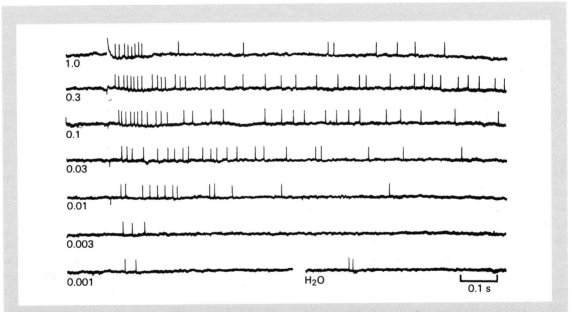

Fig. 20.6 Responses of a single fiber in the rat gustatory nerve to NaCl solutions of increasing concentration. From Pfaffman, C. (1955) Gustatory nerve impulses in rat, cat, and rabbit. *J. Neurophysiol.* 18: 429–440. Copyright 1955 by the American Physiological Society. Reprinted by permission.

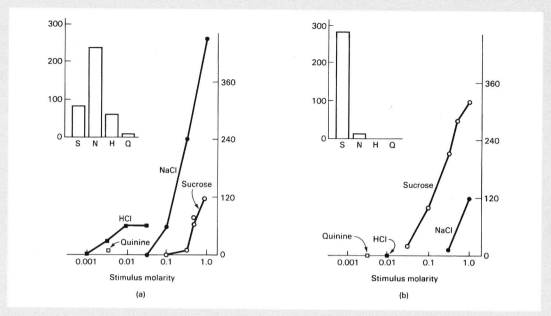

Fig. 20.7 Responses of two different gustatory nerve fibers in the squirrel monkey to increasing concentrations of different stimuli. The relative responsivity to different stimulus classes are shown in the histograms: S, sncrose; N, NaCl; H, HCl; Q, quinine. From Pfaffman, C., M. Frank, L. Bartoshuk and T. C. Snell (1976) Coding gustatory information in the squirrel monkey chorda tympani. In *Progress in psychobiology and physiological psychology*, J. M. Sprague and A. N. Epstein (eds) Academic Press, New York. Reprinted by permission.

taste qualities. Quinine-best neurons are rarely found coming from fungiform papillae on the front of the tongue, but are plentiful in the regions with foliate or circumvallate papillae (Frank, 1975). In the rat, sugar-best cells are rare coming from fungiform or circumvallate papillae, but are more common coming from foliate papillae. After recording from a range of nerve fibers coming from different areas of the tongue, Nowlis & Frank (1977) were able to determine stimulus profiles for four different cell types (see Fig. 20.8). From the figure, it is clear that, when the four prototypic stimuli are used, it is possible to group the response characteristics of nerve fibers into four discrete groups.

The afferent nerve fibers just discussed have their synapses in the solitary nucleus of the brain-stem. The cells in this region can also be characterized according to the primary taste quality to which they respond best. Scott *et al.* (1986) recorded from solitary nucleus cells in awake monkeys. They found that taste was *chemotopically* organized at this level of the brain, in the same way that touch is somatotopically organized, sound is tonotopically organized, and vision is retinotopically organized. In other words, certain areas were selectively sensitive to particular tastes. Posteriorly (in the region within the nucleus closest to the spinal cord), cells were most responsive to sour stimuli. More anteriorly, sugar- and salt sensitive cells predominated. Cells most sensitive to bitter tastes seemed to be distributed more generally.

Although Scott and others have been able to

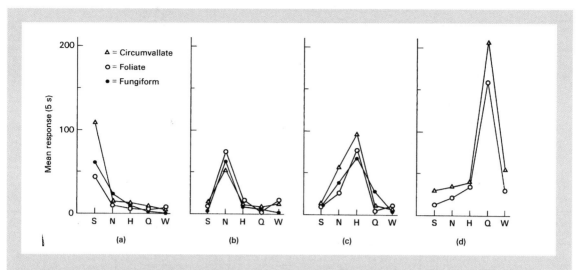

Fig. 20.8 Response profiles of four different types of taste fibers in the hamster glossopharyngeal nerve. Responses to sucrose (S), salt (N), acid (H), and quinine (Q) are shown; within each class, nerve fibers have consistent response properties. From Nowlis, G. H. and M. Frank (1977) Qualities in hamster taste: behavioral and neural evidence. In *Sixth International Symposium on Olfaction and Taste*. J. LeMagnen and P. Macleod, (eds) Information Retrieval, London, pp. 241–248.

group cells in the brainstem into discrete types according to which stimulus type they responded to best, there seems to be much variability in the response patterns of these cells. Smith *et al.* (1983) recorded from cells in the hamster *parabrachial nucleus*, the relay station in the brainstem just after the solitary nucleus. They presented cells with an array of 18 different taste stimuli. Although they could group cells according to the primary stimulus to which they were most sensitive, there was much variability within a group. Fig. 20.9 shows the responses of 10 salt sensitive cells to the 18 different stimuli; although there is a similarity to the general pattern of the responses, the variability between individual cells is quite prominent. Instead of trying to simply group cells by which single stimulus caused the best response, Smith and colleagues performed a statistical analysis that grouped cells by overall similarity of their responses across the entire array of stimuli. They found that cells could be grouped into three main clusters that could be roughly characterized as

being most responsive to sweet, sour, and salty stimuli. Responsivity to bitter stimuli was present in many individual cells, but no clear group could be identified as being predominantly sensitive to bitter.

In summary, many taste phenomena can be accounted for by the hypothesis that taste is processed through four independent channels representing the four primary taste qualities. Cross adaptation studies, the differing taste sensitivities over different tongue areas, and the results of studies in which different combinations of the primary taste stimuli are used to reproduce other tastes all provide support for this idea. Physiological studies are also roughly consistent, but show that single cells at many levels of the gustatory system respond to more than one taste quality. The fact that taste-sensitive neurons are so widely tuned means that the taste of a given stimulus cannot be signaled by the response of a single neuron or even an entire class of neurons. Rather, it is determined by comparing the

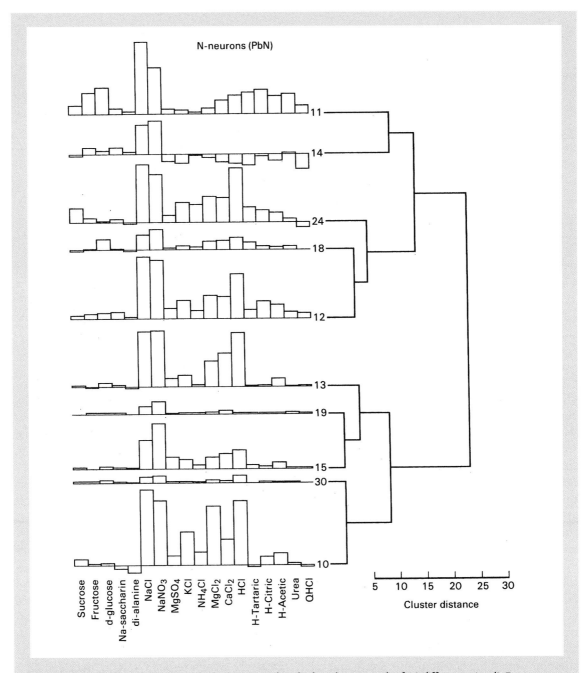

Fig. 20.9 Responses of 10 cells in the hamster parabrachial nucleus to each of 18 different stimuli. From Smith, DN., R. L. Van Buskirk, J. B. Travers and S. L. Bieber (1983) Gustatory neuron types in hamster brainstem. *J. Neurophysiol.* 50: 922–54(0). Copyright 1983 by the American Physiological Society. Reprinted by permission.

responses of all classes of neurons to the same stimulus (Castellucci, 1985).

Taste and feeding

One of the differences between the gustatory system and the other sensory systems we have previously discussed is the close relationship between taste and behavior. Animals and humans modify their diets preferentially to include substances in which they are deficient. A good example of this is salt hunger—when salt-depleted, animals select a diet high in sodium, although this diet might not be selected when the animal is salt-replete. This change in preferred diet results from the increased hedonistic value of salt in the deprived state (Scott & Mark, 1986); that is, a high- salt diet tastes better when you are salt-depleted. You can verify this phenomenon for yourself; after you have been exercising on a hot day, you may notice that you are using much more salt on your food than you would otherwise, and that salty foods such as potato chips are particularly tasty.

This effect has a physiological correlate at the level of the afferent taste fiber. Contreras & Frank (1979) recorded from single fibers of the chorda tympani of the rat under conditions of salt deprivation and repletion. They found that the fibers that were most salt-sensitive under baseline conditions became significantly more sensitive to salt when the animal was deprived. Thus the increased tendency to eat a diet high in sodium may result from a change in the response properties of the receptors themselves.

Another example of how the gustatory system interacts with behavior is the phenomenon called conditioned taste aversion. If a novel taste stimulus is presented with a substance that produces significant gastrointestinal distress (that is, nausea and vomiting), the novel taste acquires a strong negative association such that the animal actively avoids foods with that taste (Garcia *et al.*, 1955). This effect is so strong that a single pairing of the novel taste with nausea can cause an animal to avoid that taste indefinitely. Taste aversion is another phenomenon about which you may have a subjective familiarity. Many people can recall a food that they avoid because of a single episode of stomach upset, possibly just because of overeating! In this type of situation, the pleasurable associations to the taste of the food are replaced by negative associations. <u>BOX 20.4</u>

Is the conditioned taste aversion phenomenon a product of reinforcement systems outside the realm of the gustatory system, or do taste fibers themselves actually change their response characteristics to account for the change in hedonistic value of the stimulus? Chang & Scott (1984) asked

---

Box 20.4 Conditioned taste aversion at a gut level

Conditioned taste aversion occurs when a distinctive flavor is followed a while later (often an hour or more) by illness. The illness need not be induced by the food—in rats, it can be caused by X-ray treatment, which the rats can actually sense. Do people show the effect when they know the illness is actually not food-related? The evidence here is mostly anecdotal, so here is an anecdote.

On the evening my wife had her first labor contractions with our first child, we expected that it would be some time before the actual delivery, so we went ahead with dinner. We had a rare treat, a flounder prepared in a new way. About half an hour after dinner, hard labor commenced, and the baby was born within about 3 hours.

About a month later, we decided to try that hastily-eaten flounder dish again. I thought it was great, but my wife complained that it had a bad taste. I tried her portion, and it was fine. Then we realized: she had eaten flounder and then suffered abdominal pain—she had conditioned taste aversion. Mind you, she knew full well that the baby was not linked to flounders, but the aversion persisted for many years.

this question by recording from neurons in the solitary nucleus of rats who had either been conditioned by the pairing of saccharin and nausea, or exposed to saccharin without subsequent gastrointestinal distress. They found that the response characteristics of the sweet sensitive cells over a wide range of stimuli was altered so the response to saccharin more closely resembled the response to quinine (bitter) than to other sweet stimuli. Thus, the mechanism of conditioned taste aversion may be that the response of the gustatory system to the conditioned stimulus is altered so that it is more similar to the response of a naturally aversive stimulus. This is similar to the top-down processing you have encountered in other sensory systems.

The fact that single fibers in the gustatory system change their response properties under conditions of specific hungers or conditioned taste aversions implies that taste and mechanisms of reinforcement are intimately related in the brain. In fact, as you have seen, there is a direct connection between the gustatory system and the limbic system. Many experiments have been performed in which various components of limbic system have been surgically ablated and the effects of acquisition and retention of conditioned taste aversions and specific hungers have been studied. The integrity of both the hypothalamus and the amygdala appears to be necessary for the occurrence of conditioned taste aversion and specific hunger (Arthur, 1975; Nachman & Ashe, 1974; Mikulka *et al.* 1977).

Flavor

All of this has been about taste—but the perception is of flavor. Flavor depends not only on taste as determined by the responses of taste receptors, but on odor, color, texture, and other factors relating to general appearance. Texture is a somesthetic sensation, dependent on the feel as the tongue touches the food, as well as on the pressure against the teeth and palate. Pity those who must have all their food homogenized in a blender!

You will probably not be surprised to learn that odor contributes to flavor. Your ability to identify flavors is dramatically handicapped by eliminating odor perception (Mozell *et al.*, 1969). You know that you cannot really enjoy the flavor of food when you have a stuffed nose. You have probably also heard that with your nose pinched (and eyes shut) you can be given a piece of onion and think it is an apple. You can evaluate the contribution of odor in a less antisocial way by pinching your nose shut before a meal, and opening it part way through. Notice that when you open your nose it is not the odor that increases, it is the flavor. Adding an odorant to food generally seems to enhance its flavor, not its odor (Sekuler & Blake, 1985). **BOX 20.5**

Box 20.5 'Looks good' is part of flavor

There is also a visual component to flavor. 'Do you like green eggs and ham?' is a valid question asked in the children's classic by Dr Seuss. Before white chocolate was familiar, a psychophysical taste test was done to compare its flavor with that of ordinary brown chocolate. Blindfolded people found the samples of brown chocolate and white chocolate equally tasty, but without the blindfolds they rated the white samples less chocolatey—although these were the same white chocolate samples that tasted fine when they were rated while wearing the blindfold (Duncker, 1939).

It is a bit tricky to provide demonstrations of this effect in a book or on a computer. You may have experienced something like it if a practical joker has colored your food in an odd way. The demonstration 'Taste and appearance' on the CD accompanying this book attempts to reproduce this effect. Decide whether each of the foods pictured is most appetizing when the color is normal, desaturated, or distorted.

Smell (Olfaction)

While not as exquisitely sensitive as in some other animals, our sense of smell is nonetheless quite well developed. Smell is the phylogenetically oldest sensory system, and as such has some distinctive structural and functional characteristics. It is the only sensory system in which information reaches the neocortex without first passing through the thalamus—an obligate sensory relay station for all the other senses. This primitive sense seems to offend our highly developed sensibilities, and we sanitize and perfume our world so that we rarely deal with odors as informative stimuli. Nevertheless, you may be surprised at how much of a role this sense plays, and not just in the flavors of food. BOX 20.6

Probably the most distinctive aspect of the olfactory system—at least for lower animals—is the relationship between odor and general physiology and behavior. Odors act as stimuli for changes in hormone production, and as such have an effect on the timing of puberty, as well as the estrus cycle in rats and other rodents. In addition, certain odors are required for behaviors as diverse as sexual activity, suckling behavior in newborns, and selection of appropriate shelter (Halpern, 1987). The close relationship between odors and specific behaviors is a consequence of the connections the olfactory system makes with phylogenetically primitive portions of the brain.

The search for primary odor qualities

As was true for the sense of taste, the aspect of olfaction that most concerned early philosophers and scientists was how to describe and classify olfactory quality. Aristotle used exactly the same scheme for odors as he did for taste, except for the addition of an olfactory quality he called fetid (Cain, 1978). Although his actual classifications of taste and smell qualities were almost identical, Aristotle felt that taste was a sense much more amenable to logical description than was smell.

Linnaeus (1752), whose major scientific contribution was in the classification of animal and plant species, also attempted to describe primary taste qualities (Cain, 1978). He grouped odors into seven classes: (1) aromatic, (2) fragrant, (3) ambrosial (musky), (4) alliaceous (garlicky), (5) hircine (goaty), (6) repulsive, and (7) nauseous. The Dutch physiologist Zwaardemaker (1895) proposed an updated version of this classification that was accepted until well into the 20th century.

While these classification attempts were useful in that they provided a structure by which to discuss olfactory phenomena, they were based on introspection and personal experience rather than on experimental data. Henning (1916) was the first

---

Box 20.6 How good is your sense of smell?

There are many examples that demonstrate that your sense of smell is more sensitive than you might think. One study demonstrated the ability of humans to recognize gender from odors. A group of subjects was each asked to wear an undershirt for 24 h (and to forgo deodorant, soap, and perfume for both the day of the experiment and the day before). The shirts were then placed in bags, and the subjects were each presented with three bags to smell. First, each was asked which of the three shirts was his or her own—75% chose correctly. They were then asked to pick which of two shirts was worn by a male—again 75% were correct (Russell, 1976).

In a related study, 6-week-old infants were able to recognize a pad worn against its own mother's breast, rather than one worn by a stranger. This is apparently not inborn, for the performances of 2-week-old babies were random (Russell, 1976).

to try to define primary odors experimentally, and to use different combinations of primary stimuli to produce other odors. He created an odor prism, with primary odors located at the corners (Fig. 20.10). He proposed that all the odors lying along the edge between two corners resembled only the primaries located at those corners, while odors that were on a surface of the prism resembled more than two primary odors. This type of theory is similar in many ways to the trichromatic theory of color vision, as well as the theory of four primary taste stimuli. However, when experimental subjects were presented with a large variety of different odors, there was great variation in where on the prism each odor was placed, and Henning's theory eventually fell out of favor.

More recently, attempts continue to be made to define primary odors. Amoore (1964) proposed that there were seven primary odor qualities, based on physiocochemical properties of the stimuli. He suggested that there are olfactory receptors corresponding to these seven primaries, with each receptor responding to a specific stimulus in proportion to how similar the physical structure of the stimulus molecule was to the primary for

which the receptor was specifically tuned. Amoore presented subjects with a wide variety of different stimuli, and concluded that all stimuli could be accounted for by appropriate combinations of his primaries. However, further studies showed that molecules with very similar structures generated quite different odors; in addition, different stimulus combinations produced odors that could not be predicted by combinations of the primary odors (Schiffman, 1974). Other attempts have concentrated on the vibration pattern of the molecules (Wright, 1966, 1977; Cain, 1978).

There is currently no accepted scheme for dividing odors into primary qualities, and it may be that the olfactory system is simply not designed in a way that allows for classification of odors in this manner. However, another line of research has recently revitalized the idea that there are indeed primary olfactory qualities. Studies of disorders of the sense of smell have led to the discovery of *specific anosmias*—that is, inability to smell very specific and restricted types of stimuli. These disorders are probably genetically based, with several dozen being demonstrated so far in humans (Amoore, 1971, 1982). The fact that some people

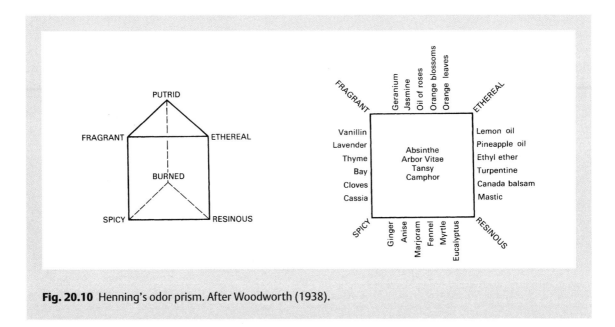

Fig. 20.10 Henning's odor prism. After Woodworth (1938).

are unable to smell a restricted range of stimuli suggests the possibility that they have an underlying abnormality in the receptor type specifically tuned to that stimulus type. With several dozen specific anosmias so far described, it may be that the number of primary taste qualities to which specific receptor types are tuned is far greater than what has been proposed in the theories of olfaction previously described.

Structure of the olfactory system

Olfactory receptors are embedded in a portion of the nasal cavity called the *olfactory neuroepithelium*. Within this 2–5 cm² area, there are about 6 000 000 receptors. Figure 20.11 schematically displays a portion of the neuroepithelial cell layer. The receptors are oriented perpendicularly to the epithelial surface, which is coated with a layer of mucus. Within the mucus are long cilia, connecting with the receptor tips. As is the case with taste

receptors, the actual interaction between the sensory stimulus and the receptor occurs along the surface membrane of the terminal cilia. (Recall that visual rods and cones and auditory hair cells also have modified cilia that serve as their sensitive regions.) At the other end of the receptor, a thin non-myelinated axon emerges, which joins with other fibers to form the olfactory nerve leading into the brain.

Also residing within the olfactory neuroepithelium are two other cell types: supporting cells and basal cells. Supporting cells are oriented in the same direction as the receptors, but do not have cilia or axons. The basal cells lie close to the region of the receptor axons. Receptor cells have a normal life span of about 60 days, and new receptors are constantly being produced through differentiation of the basal cells.

In many ways, this process is similar to that in the gustatory system; however, olfactory receptors are different from taste receptors in two important

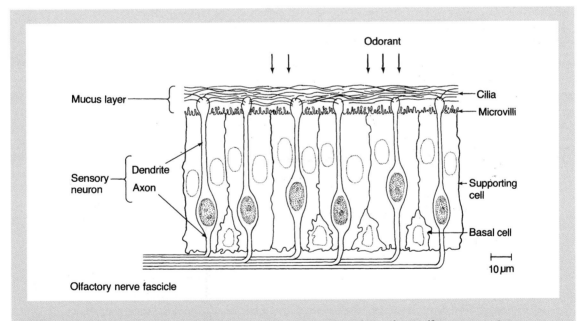

Fig. 20.11 The olfactory neuroepithelial layer. From Lancet, D. (1986) Vertebrate olfactory reception. Reproduced, with permission, from the *Annual Review of Neuroscience*, Volume 9, © 1986 by Annual Reviews Inc.

Box 20.7 Cells of the olfactory bulb

The axons of the olfactory receptors extend only a short distance, and synapse in the olfactory bulb (Fig. 20.12). The anatomy of this structure has been extensively studied, and is remarkably similar in different species of animals. In many ways, it is analogous to the retina, with structural opportunities for convergence of information as well as lateral antagonism.

Closest to the surface of the olfactory bulb, the axons of the olfactory receptors synapse in discrete areas called *glomeruli*. The dendrites of *mitral cells, tufted cells,*

and *periglomerular cells* lie within the glomeruli; mitral and tufted cell axons extend out of the olfactory bulb while the periglomerular cells extend only from one glomerulus to another. Thus the periglomerular cells apparently mediate lateral interactions between glomeruli. Deeper within the olfactory bulb, another class of non-projection neurons called *granule cells* also appear to provide an opportunity for interactions between the output cells of neighboring glomeruli.

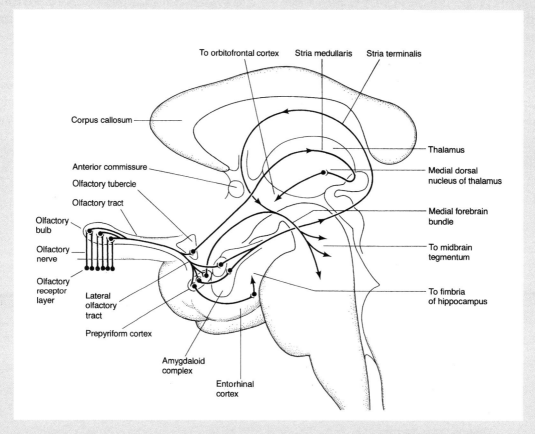

Fig. 20.12 Schematic representation of the central olfactory pathways. Reprinted by permission of the publisher from 'The chemical senses: taste and smell' by Castellucci, V. G. In E. R. Kandel and J. H. Schwartz (eds) *Principles of neural science*, 2nd edn, pp. 409–425. Copyright 1985 by Elsevier Science Publishing Co., Inc.

ways. While taste receptors are modified epithelial cells without specialized neural structures, olfactory receptors are true neurons that possess axons projecting into the brain. In addition, as you will soon see, olfactory receptors respond to appropriate stimuli by generating action potentials, while taste receptors can only generate graded electrical potentials.

From the olfactory bulb, axons project to a number of different areas of the brain, including the amygdala, the *olfactory tubercle*, and the *prepyriform cortex*. These areas are part of the limbic system, which is also intimately associated with the gustatory system. It is a phylogenetically old part of the brain concerned with reinforcement systems and primary drives, as well as many other things. From the limbic system, taste fibers finally project to the *medial dorsal nucleus* of the thalamus, and then to neocortex. This system is unique among the sensory systems in that the thalamus is not an obligate relay station before taste information reaches cortex, but instead receives information that has already been processed within the limbic system.

Physiology of olfaction

At the receptor level, the processes involved in the initiation of olfaction are very similar to taste reception. Molecules that act as stimuli for smell become absorbed in the mucus layer just above the olfactory neuroepithelium (Cometto-Muniz & Cain, 1990; Cometto-Muniz *et al.*, 1998). A molecule

that excites a given receptor attaches to the membrane of the cilia of that receptor. The point of attachment is a receptor protein, whose specific shape and electrical charge make it able to bind molecules of some shapes but not others. Through a complex sequence of events within the receptor cell, binding of the stimulus molecule causes ion channels in the membrane to open, allowing sodium and potassium ions to flow into the cell (Lancet, 1986). The flow of positively charged ions into the receptor causes it to depolarize slightly— this is the generator potential seen in all receptors. As in other sensory systems, the generator potential is graded: the higher the concentration of stimulus molecules present in the mucus layer, the more molecules will bind with the receptor proteins on the receptor cell surface and the larger the generator potential will be.

At the other end of the receptor cell, the axon hillock is the area of the receptor where action potentials are produced. The number of action potentials generated in response to a specific stimulus depends on the size of the generator potential produced by that stimulus. In addition, the latency, or time from presentation of the stimulus to the observed response, depends on the concentration of the stimulus. A stimulus that produces a moderate-sized response in the receptor axon may do so with a latency of about 1 s; however, if the stimulus is presented at a concentration 100 times less than the original stimulus, the response latency may increase to 30 s or more (Gesteland, 1978). **BOX 20.8**

Box 20.8 Transduction in the olfactory system

The process by which olfactory receptors depolarize in response to odorants is similar in many ways to taste transduction in taste receptor cells (see Box 20.3, p. 455). Olfactory cells also make use of second messengers; when the appropriate stimulus binds to the receptor membrane, a specific enzyme—guanosine triphosphate (GTP) binding protein—is activated (Pace *et al.*, 1985; Sklar *et al.*, 1986). As in gustation, this results in an increase in intracellular

cyclic AMP. Cyclic AMP in turn activates another protein that is responsible for opening ionic channels within the receptor membrane and causing depolarization (Nakamura & Gold, 1987; Baraniga, 1996). Using the techniques of molecular biology, the actual DNA sequence of the gene that produces the olfactory GTP binding protein has been determined (Jones & Reed, 1989).

An individual olfactory receptor responds to a wide range of stimuli. Sicard & Holley (1984) recorded action potentials from a large number of receptor cell axons, in response to a standard set of 20 odors. They found that the responses to certain clusters of similar stimuli, such as camphors and aromatic compounds, seemed to be grouped within certain cells. However, the response characteristics of most cells were quite broad, and they were unable to define specific groups of receptors. The results therefore do not support the idea that there are a relatively small number of receptor types, but instead suggest that the population of receptor types is significantly larger than in other sensory systems. The implication is that odor is coded peripherally by arrays of receptor cells with odor preferences that are heavily overlapped.

Cloning of the receptor genes indicates there may be 100–300 different olfactory receptors; if two different types are paired in each cell there could be 10 000 combinations available to form fully 'labelled' lines (Baraniga, 1991; Johnston, 1992). Interestingly, the sensitivity of olfactory receptors to different odors can change with exposure (training) to these odorants (Wang et al., 1993).

Recordings of cells in the olfactory bulb also demonstrate a number of interesting properties. Cells in the olfactory bulb respond to a wide range of different stimuli, but have certain odors to which they respond better than others. There is also a variety of responses that cells may make; some cells respond with a burst of action potentials at stimulus onset, some at stimulus removal, and some at both (Shibuya et al., 1962). Inhibition also plays a role in the responses seen at this level; while most responses to stimuli involve an increase in the number of action potentials produced, some cells inhibit their firing in response to certain odors (Mathews, 1972). In a manner suggestive of the response properties of retinal ganglion cells, cochlear nucleus cells, and somatosensory cortical cells, some olfactory bulb neurons respond with excitation to some odors and inhibition to others (Mancia et al., 1962).

Within the olfactory bulb, different odors seem to stimulate different populations of glomeruli (Shepherd, 1985). Benson et al. (1985) stimulated rats with specific odors, using an anatomical technique in which activated neurons could be labeled with a radioactive dye. They found that an entire glomerulus could be uniformly activated by certain stimuli, although a neighboring glomerulus might not be excited at all. Thus, cells within a given glomerulus all have the same response characteristics to different odors.

If you recall the structure of the olfactory bulb, you may remember that the periglomerular cells provide the potential for communication between glomeruli. The fact that neighboring glomeruli have distinctly different responses to different olfactory stimuli raises the question of whether there is a lateral inhibitory network between the glomeruli that acts to sharpen the response properties of the different glomeruli. To test this, Wilson & Leon (1987) recorded from cells within the olfactory bulb in the rat, marking the position of each cell from which they recorded. They found that, if a given cell was strongly excited by a certain olfactory stimulus, they could predict that other surrounding cells at distances that would place them in neighboring glomeruli would be inhibited by that stimulus. From these data, they concluded that there is an inhibitory network between glomeruli.

There is also the possibility that the odors are represented by patterns of oscillatory responses (MacLeod & Laurent, 1996). Synchronization of the firing of neural assemblies may be the key to the recognition of odors, much as synchronization in the visual cortex was suggested as a means of binding the features that comprise a visual object (see Chapter 10).

From the olfactory bulb, fibers enter the complicated circuitry of the limbic system, and from there to the medial thalamus and frontal cortex. The responses of cells to olfactory stimuli in these areas vary greatly; cells in the limbic system respond to olfactory stimuli as well to many other stimuli that are not smell-related.

The segment of the olfactory pathway projecting

to medial thalamus and then to cortex may be specifically involved in learning behaviors based on olfactory cues. Slotnick & Kaneko (1981) trained rats to perform a discrimination task based on either a visual or olfactory cue. After the rats had learned the task, a small lesion was placed in either the medial dorsal nucleus of the thalamus or the amygdala. Neither lesion affected performance in the task based on visual discrimination. However, destruction of the medial thalamus severely disrupted performance in the olfactory discrimination task, while a lesion in the amygdala did not affect this task. Thus, the thalamocortical portion of the olfactory system seems to have a function in olfactory learning not shared by the limbic system.

Pheromones

One consequence of the olfactory system's close interconnections with the limbic system is the role that odors have in modulating sexual behavior and other primary drives such as aggression and shelter-seeking. It has been known for many years that animals secrete or excrete substances whose odor affects the behavior of other members of the same species. These substances are called *pheromones*.

Two kinds of pheromones have been described. *Primary pheromones* act by altering the release of specific hormones within the target animal, and so affect behavior by inducing estrus, stimulating the occurrence of puberty, and so on. *Releasing* or *signaling pheromones* probably provide a method of chemical communication to affect behaviors relating to aggression, maternal infant interactions, aggregation, and other social behaviors (Halpern, 1987). As they do not act via hormonal manipulation, the response to releasing pheromones is much faster than to primary pheromones.

Some examples may help to illustrate the action of primary and releasing pheromones. If female rats are housed in a group, none of them will go into estrus (the time in their reproductive cycle when they are fertile and receptive to sexual advances by a male). This is called the Lee–Boot effect, and is due to an increase in circulating prolactin blood levels. But female rats whose estrus cycles are suppressed by female group housing will go into estrus if a male rat is introduced into the group. That this is mediated by an olfactory stimulus is demonstrated by the fact that the induction of estrus can also be produced by odors from male urine. When various female hormones are measured, it is found that male urine odors stimulate a surge in luteinizing hormone, which in turn induces estrus (Halpern, 1987). **BOX 20.9**

Releasing pheromones act as clues that allow the initiation of certain behaviors. Odors from female hamsters are necessary for the male to initiate mating behavior. Specific substances are necessary for specific behaviors to occur. For example, female hamster vaginal secretions have both a volatile and a non-volatile component. The volatile component seems to contain the pheromone responsible for attracting the male hamster to the vicinity of the female, while the non-volatile component is associated with the

---

Box 20.9 Pheromones in college women

Similar effects can be demonstrated in human beings. McClintock (1971) asked young women in a dormitory to record the dates of their menstrual cycles over a period of 1 year. By the end of the year, roommates were very likely to be having their periods at the same time. Women who did not live in such close proximity with each other were less likely to have their menstrual cycles linked. Although the specific chemical was not isolated in this study, it is very likely that this effect is mediated by a primary pheromone.

pheromone that stimulates mounting behavior (O'Connell & Meredith, 1984). If the volatile component of the vaginal secretions is eliminated or the olfactory response to it is reduced by damaging the olfactory system, male hamsters become less proficient at locating a responsive female by chemical cues; however, mounting behavior is not abolished if the non-volatile component is still present. The scent affects the 'attractability' of the female, and varies with the female estrus cycle (Holden, 1996).

Not all effects of pheromones are excitatory. Just as foul odors inhibit your appetite, some pheromones can inhibit behavior. For example, the queen honey bee chemically inhibits her female subjects from becoming fertile (Holden, 1996).

Many of the effects of pheromones are mediated by the structures of the olfactory system that we have just discussed. However, olfactory stimuli are also processed in the closely related parallel *vomeronasal system*. About 100 genes encode this organ, indicating a huge potential for recognizing different stimuli (Hines, 1997). Receptors of the vomeronasal system lie in a separate part of the nasal cavity called *Jacobson's organ*, and their axons synapse within the *accessory olfactory bulb*, which lies quite close to the primary olfactory bulb. From the accessory olfactory bulb, fibers extend to the same limbic structures as do primary olfactory bulb fibers.

Damage to the vomeronasal system may cause specific alterations in the response of animals to specific pheromones, without affecting response to other olfactory stimuli. For example, damage to the vomeronasal system does not affect the attraction of male hamsters by the pheromone in volatile vaginal secretions, but the response to the non-volatile secretions (initiation of mounting behavior) is reduced (O'Connell & Meredith, 1984). Similarly, an intact vomeronasal system is required both for the suppression of estrus in group-housed rats and for the induction of estrus by male odor (Johns *et al.* 1978; Reynolds & Keverne, 1979; Halpern 1987).

Suggested readings

An excellent detailed discussion about the mechanism underlying taste and learned taste aversions can be found in a review by T. R. Scott and G. P. Mark called 'Feeding and taste' in *Progress in Neurobiology* (27: 293–317; 1986). More information about pheromones and the anatomic substrate for pheromone action is offered in a review by M. Halpern, 'The organization and function of the vomeronasal system', in *Annual Review of Neuroscience* (10: 325–362; 1987).

Chapter 32 in E. R. Kandel and J. H. Schwartz' *Principles of neural science* (Elsevier, 1986) provides a very readable discussion about the anatomy and physiology of the gustatory and olfactory systems.

Appendix

PERCEPTION and sensation are a part of the branch of psychology known as experimental psychology—they are vulnerable to research by the experimental method. The data are often presented graphically and sometimes mathematically. At times, a point in this book can only be understood through the graphical or mathematical presentation of data.

You may have gotten a little rusty in these areas, so this appendix reviews the basic ideas necessary to understand graphs and equations. There is also material on logarithms and trigonometric functions, which may not be familiar, but which may be useful to read over when they are encountered in the text. Finally, there is a brief overview of the basic neurophysiology and physiological methods referred to in the book.

Graphs and equations

When there is a relation between two things, it is best to express it so that others may understand what it is. In this book, there are many such relationships; there are those between the energy of a stimulus and how bright or loud it seems, between the energy of a stimulus and how much effect it has on a particular nerve cell, between the size of a stimulus and how far away it seems to be, and so forth.

Consider another more familiar relation. There is a relation between how much you drink in a club

and how much you owe at the end of the evening. This can serve as an illustration for how to express relations between two things.

Suppose that you go to a club where the drinks are delivered by a metered pump at your table (like the pumps in a gas station that read out exactly how much gas they delivered). Suppose there is a cover charge of $1 to go in, and you fill your glass from the pump at your table as often as you like. The drinks cost 10¢ per ounce; when you leave, they read the pump to see how much you took, multiply by 10¢, add the dollar cover charge, and that is your bill.

You could draw a picture of what your bill would be depending on how much you drink (Fig. A.1). Such a picture is called a *graph*. There are two axes: the horizontal axis (called the *x*-axis) represents the amount consumed, the vertical axis (called the *y*-axis) represents how much you pay. The farther to the right you go, the more you have consumed; the higher up you go (on the graph), the more you pay. Of course, there is a relationship between the two (the more you drink, the more you pay), which we can represent by a line or curve on the graph.

Suppose you are not thirsty. You drink nothing and pay only the $1 cover; on the graph in Fig. A.1, your evening plots as the triangle (0 oz consumed, $1 charge). If you drank 10 oz, you would pay $2 (10 times 10¢ is $1, plus $1 cover); you would plot the circle on Fig. A.1 (10 oz, $2; in graphspeak, the abscissa is 10, and the ordinate is 2). If you drank 20 oz, your bill would be $3 (cross), and so on. The points corresponding to every possible amount consumed would all fall on

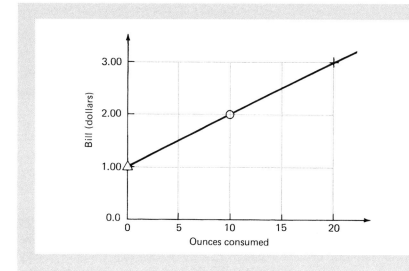

Fig. A.1 Graphical representation of the bill in a club versus the number of ounces of fluid consumed. The three symbols represent the three cases discussed; the line corresponds to eqn (A.1).

the solid line drawn through the three symbols. That line represents the relationship between amount consumed and amount paid. If arithmetic had never been invented, the club could post a graph like Fig. A.1 as a price list. You would go to the x-axis, find the amount you drank, move up to the line, and read off the amount of the bill as the ordinate.

Restaurants don't post graphs of their rate of charging, because it is simpler to spell out the charges. In fact, that's what was done to tell you how to compute a bill, but in a wordy way. There is another way to express this relation: write an equation. An equation is a shorthand way of stating the rule that was spelled out in words. It uses symbols to represent longer phrases. For example, '+' and '–', which you know from arithmetic, stand for the words 'added to' and 'reduced by'. Letters are assigned the roles of the things being related; in this example, x represents the amount drunk and y represents the bill. There is one more essential symbol: '=' is read 'equals', and it means that the stuff to the left of it is equal to (or worth as much as) the stuff on the right. Now the equation for charges in the club reads:

$$y = 1.00 + 0.10\, x \tag{A.1}$$

(the 0.10 written next to the x means multiply x by 0.10). Equation (A.1) can be read as 'the bill (in dollars) is equal to $1 plus $0.10 times the number of ounces consumed.'

Equation (A.1) is the equation of the line in Fig. A.1; both the equation and the graph say the same thing. The equation is neater in that it takes less room and can be used with as much precision as you wish. The graph cannot be read to great accuracy, but it gives a good overall picture of what is going on. You can see at a glance that you pay more the more you drink, that the minimum bill is $1, and that your total bill is less per ounce if you drink more.

Equations are easy to manipulate once you get the hang of it, giving results that are equivalent but look different. As long as you do the same thing to both sides, the statement remains true. For example,

$$10\, y = 10.0 + x \tag{A.2}$$

is also true. Ten times your bill is $10 plus $1 per oz. You can also rearrange terms without affecting the truth:

$$y = 0.1\,x + 1.00 \qquad (A.3)$$

(you pay 10 ¢ an oz plus $1).

Equation (A.3) is in a standard form for the equation of a straight line:

$$y = mx + b \qquad (A.4)$$

(in eqn A.3, $m = 0.1$ and $b = 1.00$). In this form, m is the slope of the line ($ per ounce) and b is the y-intercept ($1 is the value where the line hits the y-axis, which is where $x = 0$). Any straight line on a graph can be represented in this form.

Of course, not all lines are straight, and not all equations are so simple. There is, however, a correspondence between equations and curves on graphs: every equation can be drawn on a graph, and every curve on a graph can be represented (at least approximately) by an equation.

Consider a slightly harder equation:

$$y = x^2 \qquad (A.5)$$

This equation says that y is given by the square of x.

This equation is plotted as a curve on the graph in Fig. A.2. If $x = 0$, $x^2 = 0$, so y is 0; this point is where the two axes meet, which is called the *origin*. It is shown as a triangle in Fig. A.2. If $x = 1$, 1^2 also is 1 ($1 \times 1 = 1$), so $y = 1$; the point where $x = 1$ and $y = 1$ is plotted with a circle. When $x = 2$, $y = 2^2 = 2 \times 2 = 4$. The point at which $x = 2$ and $y = 4$ is shown by a cross. When $x = 3$, $y = x^2 = 3^2 = 3 \times 3 = 9$ (tilted triangle), which is nearly off the top of the picture. Although there is no more space for larger values, you can indicate what y would be for any small value of x; the solid curve is the one that corresponds to eqn (A.5).

Logarithms

The plot in Fig. A.2 ran out of space before getting very far into the graph. You could help things by shrinking the y-axis so that fewer inches would be

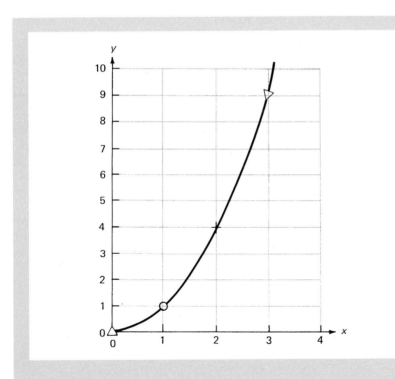

Fig. A.2 Graphic representation of the equation $y = x^2$ (eqn A.5). The four symbols correspond to points discussed.

eaten up by large numbers, but then you would squeeze down all the details in the small numbers. For example, the ordinate in Fig. A.3 is 1/10 the scale of that in Fig. A.2, which lets you get about three times as far out on the x-axis, but makes it hard to see what is happening when x takes the small values seen in Fig. A.2. Another way to handle the problem of rapidly growing numbers is to use a logarithmic scale. Many of the figures in this book are on logarithmic scales.

First, what is a *logarithm*? A logarithm is the exponent to which 10 must be raised to give a particular number (10 is only one of many possible bases for logarithms, but it is the only one used in this book). The equation

$$y = \log(x) \tag{A.6}$$

reads 'y is (or equals) the power to which 10 must be raised to give x' (The short form 'log' means logarithm and will be used from here on.) This can be said another way:

$$10^y = x \tag{A.7}$$

or

$$10^{\log(x)} = x \tag{A.8}$$

Equation (A.8) tells you how to take the 'antilog': to find the number given its logarithm, take 10 to the power $\log(x)$.

Now consider some properties of exponents of 10 (or of any number, for that matter). An exponent tells how many times to multiply a number by itself:

$$10^1 = 10 \tag{A.9}$$

$$10^2 = 10 \times 10 = 100 \tag{A.10}$$

$$10^3 = 10 \times 10 \times 10 = 1000 \tag{A.11}$$

$$10^4 = 10 \times 10 \times 10 \times 10 = 10\,000. \tag{A.12}$$

This gives you a way to prepare a table of logs. Look at eqn (A.9), and compare it to (A.8); it is the same equation with numbers written in. So $\log(x)$ is 1 when x is 10; that is, $\log(10) = 1$. Similarly, eqn (A.10) tells you that $\log(100) = 2$, and you can write a table based on eqns (A.8)–(A.12):

$$\log 10 = 1$$

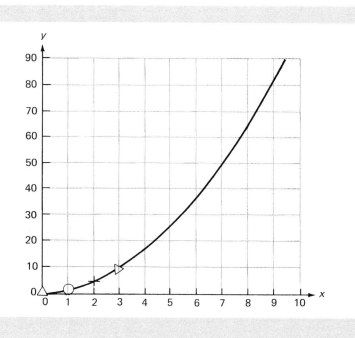

Fig. A.3 Another graph of the equation $y = x^2$, on a compressed vertical scale.

log 100 = 2

log 1000 = 3

log 10 000 = 4

and so forth. Notice how slowly the logs grow as compared with the increase in the sizes of the numbers. **BOX A.1**

Box A.1 Manipulating powers and logarithms

Now consider what happens when you multiply powers of 10. Look at eqns (A.9) and (A.10); multiply them — you get

$$10^1 \times 10^2 = (10 \times 10 \times 10) = 10^3 = 10^{1+2} \qquad (A.13)$$

In fact, it is a general rule that when you multiply 10^a times 10^b you get 10 raised to the sum of the two powers:

$$10^a \times 10^b = 10^{a+b} \qquad (A.14)$$

Now consider what that means for logs. If $x = 10^a$, $a = \log (x)$; also if $y = 10^b$, then $b = \log (y)$. Now set $z = 10^{a+b}$ so that $a + b = \log (z)$. You can substitute x, y, and z for the things they represent in eqn (A.14) and get

$$xy = z \qquad (A.15)$$

You are allowed to do the same thing to both sides of an equation, and it will still be true. So, take the log of both sides of eqn (A.15), and you get

$$\log (xy) = \log (z) \qquad (A.16)$$

Log $(z) = a + b$, which is log (x) + log (y); putting this in place of log (z) on the right side of (A.16) gives a very important result:

$$\log (xy) = \log (x) + \log (y) \qquad (A.17)$$

In words, the log of the product of two numbers is the sum of the log of each. Adding logs is equivalent to multiplication.

If adding logs is equivalent to multiplication, subtracting must be equivalent to division. You can see this from eqn (A.17). Subtract log(y) from both sides of the equation (you are allowed to do the same thing to both sides of any equation):

$$\log (xy) - \log (y) = \log (x) + \log (y) - \log (y)$$

$$\log (xy) - \log (y) = \log (x) \qquad (A.18)$$

If log (x) = log (xy) - log (y), it must be equivalent to log $(x y/y)$ which is log (x).

This fact lets you expand the log table. Log (10) = 1; if

you subtract log (10) from log (10) you get 0, which is equivalent to dividing 10 by 10 (=1):

$$\log (10) - \log (10) = 1 - 1$$

$$\log (10/10) = 0$$

so

$$\log (1) = 0.$$

Now go further:

$$\log (1) - \log (10) = 0 - 1$$

$$\log (1/10) = -1.$$

You can see that negative logs correspond to fractions:

$$\log (1/100) = -2$$

$$\log (1/1000) = -3$$

So far, all the logs you have seen have been integers (whole numbers). How can you deal with logs that are fractions? What would be the power to which 10 would need to be raised to give, say, 2? To understand this, you must delve further into the rules for powers of numbers.

Suppose you multiply a log by some number. For example, what is 2 times the log of x?

$$2 \log (x) = \log (x) + \log (x). \qquad (A.19)$$

Addition of logs is equivalent to multiplication (eqn A.17):

$$\log (x) + \log (x) = \log (xx) = \log (x^2). \qquad (A.20)$$

Similarly,

$$3 \log (x) = \log (xxx) = \log (x^3). \qquad (A.21)$$

In short, multiplication of a log is equivalent to raising a number to a power:

$$n \log (x) = \log (x^n). \qquad (A.22)$$

But suppose n is not a whole number. Say n is a fraction:

$$n = 1/m. \qquad (A.23)$$

Then

➡

(Box A.1 continued)

$$(1/m) \log (x) = \log (x^{1/m}). \tag{A.24}$$

Furthermore

$$m(1/m) \log (x) = m \log (x^{(1/m)}) = \log (x). \tag{A.25}$$

In other words:

$$(x^{1/m})^m = x, \tag{A.26}$$

so $x^{1/m}$ must be the mth root of x. For example, if m is $1/2$, that means square root, for the square root squared is the original number.

This result lets you find values for fractional logarithms. For example, take the square root:

$$10^{1/2} = \sqrt{10} = 3.16228$$

so

$$\log (3.16228) = 0.5.$$

You can multiply by 10 by adding 1 (if you don't see why, review the table based on eqn A.8 and the result in eqn A.17):

$$\log (31.6228) = 1.5$$

and so forth.

It turns out that

$$10^{0.3} = 2$$

or

$$\log (2) = 0.3.$$

Then you know that log(4) must be 0.6, either by doubling log 2 ($2^2 = 4$) or by adding log(2) to log(2) (because $2 \times 2 = 4$). With no further information, you should be able to find that

$$\log (8) = 0.9$$

$$\log (80) = 1.9$$

$$\log (400) = 2.6$$

$$\log (0.2) = -0.7$$

and a large number of other results.

Summary of logarithms

You could summarize the rules for manipulating logs (derived in the preceding box) with two statements:

1. *Addition of logs corresponds to multiplication of numbers* (eqn A.17). You can find the product of two numbers by finding the log of each (from a log table), adding the two logs, and finding the number corresponding to the sum (in the table). Similarly, subtraction corresponds to division. We actually used to do this before hand calculators!
2. *Multiplying a log by a number corresponds to raising to a power* (eqn A.22). Twice the log of a number is the sum of the log and itself; from rule 1 above, that corresponds to the number times itself, or the number squared (raised to the power 2).

Now that you 'know' what logs are, and have some idea of the values they take, you can draw the picture corresponding to them. Figure A.4 shows the function 'log (x)' versus x (that is, it shows $y = \log(x)$. As you now know, the log of 1 is 0, so the curve crosses the x-axis at $x = 1$ ($y = \log 1 = 0$).

For values of x less than 1 (fractions), $\log(x)$ is negative; it is below the x-axis. As x becomes larger than 1, $\log(x)$ also increases. It does not, however, increase nearly as rapidly as x. When x is 10, $\log(x)$ is 1—but $\log(x)$ does not reach a value of 2 until x is 100. The value of $\log(x)$ increases by the same amount (same difference) for constant ratios of x; there is the same 0.3 difference in height of the curve when x changes by a factor of 2 whether x goes from 1 to 2, from 2 to 4, or from 6 to 12 (indicated on the figure). The same 0.3 difference in height would be found where x goes from 100 to 200, from 1024 to 2048, or from 79 020 to 158 040.

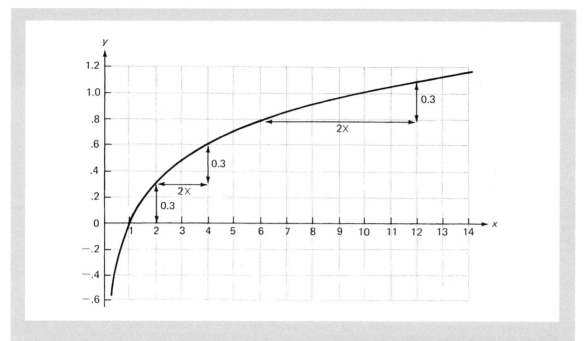

Fig. A.4 A graph of the function $y = \log(x)$. The vertical arrows indicate a difference in the vertical direction of 0.3, which occurs for each doubling of the x-axis.

Log axes

The point of learning about logarithms is that log scales are the axes of many graphs. A log scale simply means the numbers along the axis are placed in positions corresponding to their logs. In Figs A.1–A.4, the numbers along all the scales were placed in the same way as the inches are marked on a ruler; this is called a *linear* scale. Each number is placed at a position as far from the origin as the number itself says it is. You could simply place a ruler along a line and use its scale (inches or mm) instead of buying graph paper; there is the same distance between 0 and 1 as between 1 and 2, or 2 and 3, or 100 and 101.

A log scale is one in which the distance from the origin to a number is the log of that number. Thus 10 is one unit farther from the origin than 1, 100 is one unit farther than 10, and so forth. Graph paper can be purchased already ruled in this way; it is called *log paper*.

Figure A.5 shows a sheet of log paper in which only the x-axis is ruled as a log scale. Notice the wide space between 1 and 2 and the progressively narrower spaces between 2 and 3, 3 and 4, and so on until the space between 9 and 10 is small. In fact, the space between 10 and 20 is as small as the space between 1 and 2, because they are in the same ratio and therefore the same distance apart on a log scale. The y-axis on this paper is the same linear scale you are already familiar with. Graph paper of this type, on which one axis is logarithmic and one is linear, is called *semilog paper*.

The function $y = \log(x)$ has been plotted on the semilog paper of Fig. A.5; this is the same function plotted on linear paper in Fig. A.4. You can verify that the same points appear: $\log(x)$ is 0 at $x = 1$, $\log(x)$ is 1 at $x = 10$, $\log(x)$ is negative for x less than 1, and so on. The curve you saw in Fig. A.4 plots a straight line on semilog paper, however. Plotting on a log scale squeezed it to the left and straightened it out.

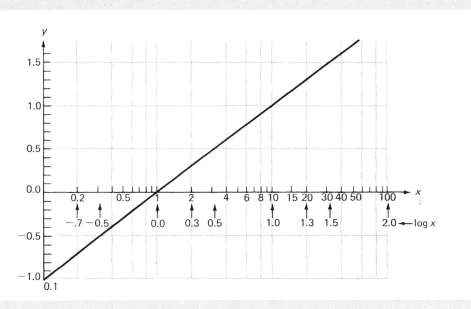

Fig. A.5 The function $y = \log(x)$ plotted on semilog paper. Numbers on the x-axis are spaced according to their logs. Logs of the numbers on the x-axis are indicated beneath them, showing regular spacing.

To see why the function $y = \log(x)$ plots as a straight line on semilog paper, think about what the log axis is doing. The numbers on the x-axis are placed according to their logs; when you find a number (x) on the x-axis, it is at the position $\log(x)$. You are really plotting versus $\log(x)$—and what are you plotting versus $\log(x)$? Why, $\log(x)$! Figure A.5 shows $\log(x)$ versus $\log(x)$—naturally the two are always equal, and you get the straight line $y = x$. To make this point clearer, the values of $\log(x)$ are written under some of the x values on the x-axis; these numbers line up in the ordinary linear (ruler) scale way. If you look only at the log (x) scale, you can easily see that each number is plotted versus itself.

An even more interesting thing happens when you use graph paper on which both axes are ruled as log scales. Such paper, available in the campus bookstore, is called log–log paper (also known as double-log paper, or full-log paper). A sample is shown in Fig. A.6. The scales on log–log paper are just like the log scale on semilog paper—it is just that both of them are that way. Now when you find a point y corresponding to x, you are plotting $\log(y)$ versus $\log(x)$.

What happens if you plot an equation such as eqn (A.5) on log–log paper? (Equation A.5 said $y = x^2$.) This has been done in Fig. A.6. When x is 1, y is also 1 (circle). When x is 2, y is 4 (cross); when x is 3, y is 9 (triangle). These points, which fell on an upward curve in Figs A.2 and A.3, fall on a straight line on the log–log plot. In fact, eqn (A.5) is the straight line on this plot shown by the solid line.

You can understand why this equation gives a straight line by reviewing what you learned about logs. If you take logs of both sides of eqn (A.5) (which does not change its validity),

$$\log(y) = \log(x^2). \tag{A.27}$$

Equation (A.22) says you can rewrite (A.27) as

$$\log(y) = 2\log(x). \tag{A.28}$$

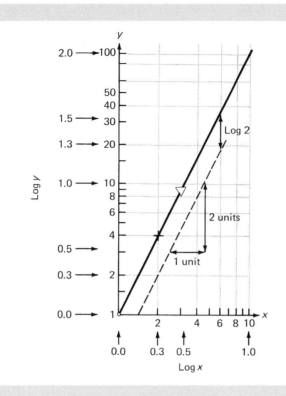

Fig. A.6 The function $y = x^2$ (*solid line*) and $y = 1\,\tfrac{1}{2}x^2$ (*dashed line*) on log–log coordinates. Three of the points plotted in Fig. A.2 are indicated by the same symbols as in that figure. Logs of numbers along the y-axis and x-axis are indicated.

Now remember that log(y) is the thing you plot on the y-axis (using the linear scale to the left), and log(x) is what you are plotting linearly on the x-axis (linear scale below). If you call log $(y) = Y$ and let $X = $ log(x), eqn (A.27) reads

$$Y = 2\,X \tag{A.29}$$

which is the equation of a straight line on the actual linear scales. In fact, it is a straight line with a slope of 2; there is a 2-log unit increase in height for every log unit across.

This result is quite general: if an equation of the form

$$y = a\,x^n \tag{A.30}$$

is plotted on log–log coordinates, it plots as a straight line with a slope of n. This is true whether n is larger than 1 or fractional, positive or negative. (A negative n, as in the case of a negative power of 10, means 1 divided by the number to that power.)

Equation (A.30) introduced another quantity: a. Now, a is a multiplier, which was unity (1) in eqn (A.5). If a is not 1, it will change the position of the line. For example, if $a = 1/2$, eqn (A.5) would read

$$y = 1/2x^2 \tag{A.31}$$

and every y would be half as large as it was. In an equation such as (A.4), plotted on linear paper, a would represent a change in slope—here you are plotting on log paper, and the effect is quite different. In Fig. A.6, eqn (A.31) is plotted with a dashed line. When $x = 1$, $y = 1/2$; when $x = 2$, $y = 4/2 = 2$; when $x = 3$, $y = 9/2 = 4.5$. (You should find and verify these points on the figure.) The effect is that the line has shifted down a constant amount—that amount is the log of 2. You have divided every value of y by 2, and therefore you subtract the log of 2. This idea can be put a bit more mathematically by taking logs of both sides of eqn (A.31):

$$\log(y) = \log(1/2x^2). \tag{A.32}$$

The log of a product is the sum of the logs, so

$$\log(y) = \log(x^2) + \log(1/2). \tag{A.33}$$

You may also note that the log of 1 divided by a number is minus the log of number (if you prefer, you could have started by saying $\log(y) = \log(x^2/2)$ and noting that the log of a ratio is the difference of the logs):

$$\log(y) = \log(x^2) - \log(2) \tag{A.34}$$

and with the exponentiation rule (A.22)

$$\log(y) = 2\log(x) - \log(2). \tag{A.35}$$

On the linear scale, with $X = \log(x)$ and $Y = \log(y)$:

$$Y = 2X - \log 2 \tag{A.36}$$

which is the equation of a straight line just like eqn (A.4). The y intercept, $-\log(2)$, represents a shift downward of the curve by $\log(2)$ (which is 0.3).

The important point to gain from the preceding discussion is this: multiplication (or division) on a log axis has the effect of shifting the curve by a constant amount. Multiplication of x shifts the curve to the left or right; multiplication of y shifts it up or down. (With a straight line, you cannot say whether it shifted down or to the right—other functions are less forgiving.) The shifting of a curve along a logarithmic axis when the parameter plotted on that axis is multiplied by some factor is quite general. It is also true on semilogarithmic

plots, a useful fact to remember when looking at plots of response versus log(intensity).

Normal probability axes

Other axes have been designed to convert specific non-linear functions into straight lines, just as log axes convert power functions into straight lines. Of particular value in the study of sensory and perceptual systems is *normal probability paper*. On this paper, the probability axis is spaced so that equal standard deviations (z scores) are equally spaced. As a result, a cumulative normal distribution (the integral of the normal distribution) plots as a straight line.

Probability axes are often used when plotting psychometric functions. As explained in Box 2.1, a probability of detection curve (such as in Fig. 2.1b) can be considered as the integral of an underlying normal distribution representing the probability of the threshold taking any particular value. On linear paper, such as in Fig. 2.1(b), the function is an ogive. Replotted on probability paper, it becomes a straight line, as shown in Fig. A.7. BOX A.2

The value of using probability paper is that it is far easier to draw a straight line than a curve. The exact curve in Fig. 2.1(b) would be hard to determine or to draw, but the straight line in Fig. A.7 is easily drawn with just a ruler. It is pretty easy to see how to place a straight line among a spattering

---

Box A.2 Normal probability graph paper

Notice that only three of the 'data' points in Table 2.1 and Fig. 2.1(b) appear in the plot in Fig. A.7. That is because 0 and 100% are an infinite number of standard deviations below and above the mean, respectively, and so are off the bottom and top of the paper. The axes shown range from 1 to 99.99%. To obtain 99.99% would require one 'no' and 9999 'yesses'! With a finite number of trials, you can only estimate the percentages. For example, with only four trials, you can obtain 50% (2 'yesses') or 75% (3 'yesses'). There is no way to obtain 90% even if that is the 'true' value, for you cannot have 3.6 'yesses'. If all four responses were 'yes', you would not know that the next was not going to be a 'no', or whether the 'true' value is 75.0001%, 90%, or 99.999%. Thus, perfect scores (all 'yes' or all 'no') cannot be plotted on probability axes.

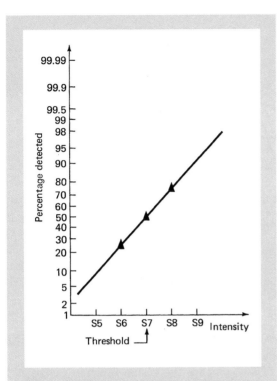

Fig. A.7 Data of Table 2.1 plotted on normal probability paper. The ogive of Fig. 2.1(b) appears as a straight line. Notice that the stimuli for which the subject scores 100% (or 0%) cannot be plotted on this figure, as they are off the paper.

2AFC experiment, the raw 'correct' responses must be corrected for guessing before plotting on the probability coordinates; click the '?' box at the upper right corner of the normal probability graph for a further explanation.)

Normal probability paper is also useful for receiver operatic characteristic (ROC) curves, like that in Fig. 2.9 and the upper right graph of the 'Signal detection theory' demonstration on the CD. Since the underlying distributions of noise and signal + noise are assumed to be normal distributions (Figs 2.8 and 2.9 and the upper left graph in 'Signal detection theory'), the use of normal probability axes makes sense. In this application, both the x-axis and the y-axis are probability axes. Plotted this way, ROC curves become straight lines. If the standard deviations of the noise and the signal + noise distributions are equal (as in the example in Figs 2.8 and 2.9), the line has a slope of unity (parallel to the diagonal), and d' can be determined from the line's distance from the diagonal. If the standard deviations are not equal, the ROC curve will still be a straight line, but its slope will not be unity. This is a simple way to demonstrate that the assumption of equal standard deviations is not valid in a particular case.

of points. If more precision or objectivity is desired, it is straightforward to perform a simple linear regression (on the coordinates of the probability plot, not the raw numbers). The threshold can then be determined by where the line intersects 50% detection.

The psychometric functions in the 'Threshold experiment' associated with Chapter 2 on the CD accompanying this book are shown on both linear (top left) and normal probability coordinates (bottom left). Only points that have a mixture of 'yesses' and 'no's' appear on the probability plot; when at least three points (with a positive slope) are plotted, the best line is shown and replotted as an ogive on the linear graph. (Note that for the

Sines and cosines

The sinusoids and sine functions in this book are the same ones that plagued you in trigonometry. The trigonometric relationship is shown by Fig. A.8. Consider a clock with only one hand, and say that hand is 1.0 unit long. What is the height of the pointer end of the hand (relative to the pivot) as a function of the angular position of the hand? Start at 0° (12 o'clock); the pointer is vertical, as high as it can be, at a height of 1.0 (its length) above the pivot. As time passes, the angle θ increases and the pointer gets lower and lower. At 3 o'clock the hand is horizontal, having moved 90°, and the height is 0.0. Then the pointer drops below the pivot, and

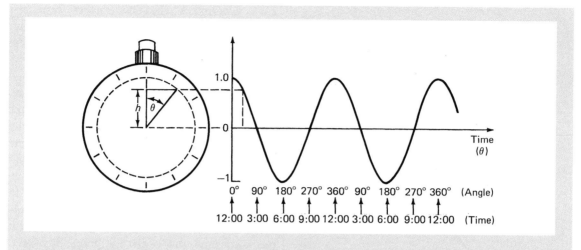

Fig. A.8 One-handed clock, showing how the height of the pointer end of the hand traces a cosine function in time. Cosine function shown to the right.

the height becomes increasingly negative, until 6 o'clock when the hand is again vertical (180°). This time the pointer is as far below the pivot as it can be, at –1.0. As the hand moves around to the left, it again rises, until at 9 o'clock (270°) it is horizontal, and the height is again 0.0. The height then becomes more positive as the hand returns to its starting point (12 o'clock, which is both 360° and 0°). The same sequence repeats as many times as the hand goes around. The figure traces just over 2 cycles of sinusoid, as a function of the angle, θ; if the hand rotates at a constant speed (as clocks are supposed to), you could just as well label the x-axis with the time at which that angle was achieved.

The particular sinusoidal function traced in Fig. A.8 is a *cosine*; that this is the same kind of cosine encountered in trigonometry may be seen from the small triangle sketched in the clock face. This triangle shows how to find the height (h) when the hand is at the angle θ shown. It is a right triangle; the hypotenuse is the hand, and the height is the side adjacent to the angle θ. The definition of a cosine is that it is the ratio of the adjacent side of a right triangle to the hypotenuse, or

$$\cos \theta = h \,/\, \text{hypotenuse}.$$

As the hypotenuse is 1.0, $h = \cos \theta$ is the function shown.

Now compare the cosine function in Fig. A.8 with the sine function at the top of Fig. A.9. The only difference between them is that they start at different places. If you place the 0° point of the cosine at the leftmost measurement point for the wavelength λ in Fig. A.9, the two would superimpose perfectly. This shift is called a difference in *phase*; there is a 90° phase shift between the sine wave and the cosine wave. That is,

$$\cos \theta = \sin (\theta + 90°).$$

In fact, you could derive the sine wave (rather than cosine) directly from the clock by asking for the excursion of the pointer along the direction at 90° to vertical (that is, horizontal). At 0° (12 o'clock) the horizontal excursion is 0.0—the pointer is neither right nor left of center. At 90° it is at the maximum rightmost (positive) excursion; at 180° it is back to zero, and so forth. The horizontal excursion is given by the unlabeled side of the triangle drawn into the clock, the side opposite the angle θ. Recall that the sine is defined as the ratio of the opposite side of a right triangle to the hypotenuse.

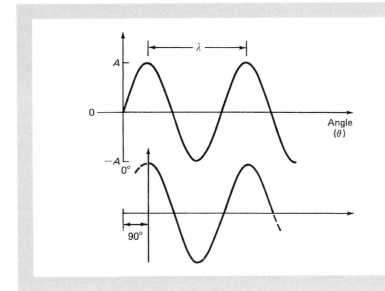

Fig. A.9 Sine function (*top*), indicating that it is the same as the cosine function (*below*) shifted by 90°.

Basic neurophysiology

One of the premises of this book is that the functioning of the sensory/perceptual systems will (someday) be best understood in terms of the physiological machinery that is actually responsible for these phenomena. As a consequence, you will encounter data and descriptions in terms of basic neurophysiology, terms that may be unfamiliar to you. The purpose of this part of the Appendix is to help you understand these phenomena at a level sufficient to understand the references to them in the text. But don't expect to be an expert in neurophysiology after reading this section.

Glia and neurons

Glia The nervous system, which includes the sensory systems, consists of two basic cell types: glia and neurons. Glia are the basic support cells of the nervous system (the word is derived from the Greek word for 'glue'). Support—that includes the physical structure originally envisioned as its func-

tion, but quite a lot more. Glia also help nourish the neurons, and maintain the correct extracellular environment that neurons require to function properly. In fact, by altering that environment, glia may even participate in the signaling and processing done by neurons. Glia also guide the development of the nervous system.

Neurons Nevertheless, neurons are considered the main players in the nervous system. In most cases, specialized neurons called *receptor cells* receive the information from the environment and *transduce* it (change its form) to the signals nerve cells can use. Other neurons receive the information about the environment from the receptor cells, and pass it to other neurons. Neurons receive information from many other neurons, integrate it, process it, and pass it along. Ultimately, information is passed to muscle cells, causing us to move in response to the stimuli we receive. Somewhere, somehow, in the midst of all this processing, a conscious perception of the world arises in our brains. You see a tasty-looking morsel; you reach your hand to it, take it and place it on your tongue; your senses of taste and smell report that it is indeed good; you chew and swallow, you take more. And inside, you feel pleased, and know that this was a delicious slice of pizza.

The neurons that are responsible are cells, much like most other cells in the body. They consist of a 'skin' called the *cell membrane*. The membrane is made of only two layers of fatty molecules; inside that delicate bag is a watery solution with other, smaller specialized bags called organelles that are like cells within cells performing special functions. Some of these contain genetic material, the instructions for making the chemicals the cell uses to function and to repair itself. Others manufacture these chemicals, or metabolize sugar with oxygen to produce the chemical 'fuel' that supplies the energy needs of the neuron.

There are some specializations in the shape, or *morphology*, of neurons that deserve mention. Some neurons are small and compact, acting locally, while others are long and stringy, carrying information to and from distant parts of the nervous system. While neurons all have a main container-like body (called variously the *cell body* or *soma*), most have at least some branching extensions. Most neurons have some that branch relatively close to the soma and seem to be mainly receiving antennae for signals from other neurons; these branches are called *dendrites* (from the Greek word for tree). Traditionally, dendrites are considered the receivers, but many also send messages (for instance, the dendrites of horizontal cells and amacrine cells in the retina; see Chapter 4).

The other special outgrowth is called the *axon*, which is typically a long string-like extension with branches at its ending, or *terminal*. Complementary to the dendrites, the axon is considered the output, or sending, structure. But like dendrites, axons may receive information from other neurons as well as send information. Some axons are short; these are for neurons that only affect other neurons local to them. Other axons are extremely long; for example, when you stub your toe, the signal travels along an axon that extends from your toe to your spinal cord, about 1 m away, and another axon extends from the lower part of your spine to your brain. Most neurons have a single axon, but some have several, or have an axon that sends branches to different targets; these branches are called *collaterals*.

Functions of neurons

How do neurons do everything they do? To answer this, you need to know a little about the physical chemistry of neurons. Then you can understand how that is applied to the specific information-handling functions of neurons.

Neural potentials   A neuron lives in an environment of slightly salty water, and contains fluid that is also slightly salty. But the particular salts inside and outside the cells are different, and because the fluids are separated by a membrane that almost, but not quite, keeps them from mixing, the neurons become tiny batteries.

You don't want to get too concerned by the physical chemistry here. Outside the cell, the *extracellular fluid* (which is just filtered blood) is mainly sodium chloride—that's right, table salt in water. There are very important traces of other elements, but the key thing is sodium chloride. Inside the cell is a salt solution of the same concentration, but it is mainly *potassium* chloride. So there is a relatively high potassium concentration inside the cell, and a high sodium concentration outside. Both sodium and potassium form positively charged particles (*ions*), and they are balanced by the negative chloride ions.

The potassium locked inside wants out, and the sodium wants in. And that is where the membrane is important; it is relatively easy for potassium to leak out, but difficult for sodium to get in. So a tiny bit of potassium leaves, leaving some (negative) chloride ions unescorted—the inside of the cell becomes negative. That tends to pull the oppositely charged potassium back in, until a point is reached at which the negativity inside is just enough to balance the push of crowded potassium to leave (and allow for the attraction of sodium from the crowded outside, despite the difficulty for sodium to get in). That is effectively a battery, making the inside of each neuron negative.

The battery makes the inside negative by about 70 mV (*millivolts* are thousandths of a volt, so 70 mV = 0.07 volts). Voltage is potential energy, a potential to do work. The voltage is small (about 1/20th of a flashlight battery), but it is strong enough to do the work of the neuron. This –70 mV (the remainder of the body is usually considered as neutral, so the inside is considered negative) is referred to as the cell's *resting potential*.

Slow potentials How is the battery used? The potential controls processes that release chemicals from the neuron. These chemicals then affect other neurons (you will learn about this process later, in the section on the synapse). As a rule, the negative potential inside seems to disallow release; when that potential is reduced (the term for reducing it is *depolarization*), making it less negative (which is to say, more positive), the chemicals are extruded at a faster rate. To prevent extrusion, the cell can be made even more negative than resting potential; such a change is called *hyperpolarization*, meaning even more polarized.

The simplest way to change potential is to change the ability of sodium or potassium (or chloride or some other ion) to cross the membrane. This can be done by opening specialized pores, or channels, that let something through—kind of like opening the airport gate for 'first class passengers and families with children only'. Let sodium through and it rushes in, depolarizing the neuron. Let chloride through, and it also rushes in, but, being negative, it hyperpolarizes the neuron.

When something like this changes, the potential changes locally. But when there is a difference between potentials at two places, Nature tries to even things out. A local potential is like a pile of water. Electrical currents flow, making a smoother pattern of potential across the surface of the cell. There's resistance to electrical flow, so it doesn't all find the same level like water; it is more like piling thick gravy. Unlike watching the gravy-pile droop, however, the electrical currents are instan-

taneous, so the final spread forms instantly. This spreading out, with less effect the further from the original point you look, is called *decremental conduction*. Since the pile lasts for as long as the situation stays the same, these changes from resting potential are called *slow potentials*.

The currents that sustain these electrical patterns add. Thus, the potential at any given point on the neuron is the sum of the influences from all other points on the cell membrane. This is the way the neuron computes its electrical state from all the influences upon it.

Action potentials Slow potentials spreading across the neuron are fine for influencing parts of the cell that are nearby. But the other end of a long axon is far from an influence near the soma. The potential gets smaller and smaller the further away from the source you look. It is like communicating by sending energy from your mouth (speaking, not spitting). If you want to talk to someone in the same room, you just talk. But if the person is at the other end of a football stadium, you need to do some really exceptional shouting. And across town—well, you need to use a telephone.

Neurons apply a similar logic. If a neuron is small, so the message goes only a short distance, slow potentials are adequate. When the neuron has a long axon and the message has to travel a great distance, some form of amplifier (like a telephone) is needed. The axon is specialized to carry messages by an active process that uses the membrane battery for power.

The method used is to produce an amplified signal called an *action potential*, which is a brief, all-or-none event (sometimes called a *nerve impulse*, or *spike*). Action potentials are all alike; they are the same size and last the same amount of time. They start when the membrane is depolarized enough ('enough' is typically about 15 mV, a level called *threshold*). Then, because the currents associated with the massive depolarization of an action potential inevitably spread, the nearby axon also depolarizes, and it, too, produces an action potential. In this way, the action potential propagates down the axon, much the way a flame spreads along a fuse by heating the neighboring regions.

Fast as it is, the spread of an action potential takes some time for the action potential to develop at each point along the axon; it is not instantaneous like the spread of a slow potential. The trade-off is that while it takes longer to reach the end, it is still full-size at the far end. A slight transmission delay is the penalty paid for successful transmission. But that penalty can be important:

imagine if you couldn't move a muscle until several seconds after you willed it!

To speed up the transmission, the axon is usually set up like a relay chain. There are points at which action potentials occur; the relatively short distances between these points transmit the action potential by decremental conduction. Axons that support this method are called *myelinated*, because the decremental conduction segments are electrically insulated with a fatty sheath called *myelin*

Box A.3 Mechanism of the action potential

Our understanding of the action potential is based on a classical set of experiments at the Physiological Laboratory in Cambridge, England, in the early 1950s (Hodgkin & Huxley, 1952). To explain their data, these workers hypothesized that depolarization opens pores that allow sodium into the cell. The influx of sodium further depolarizes the cell, opening more of the sodium pores, further depolarizing the axon, and so forth. This would simply change the axon to a state of complete depolarization, except the pores are like revolving doors that do a half turn and then lock. That is, the pores open and

then close—in fact, it is depolarization that makes them close. Meanwhile, slower-responding potassium pores open in response to depolarization, letting potassium flood out, hyperpolarizing the neuron. The result is that once the threshold depolarization is reached, there is a massive, rapid depolarization (actually a slight repolarization in the other direction, inside positive), followed by a slight, longer-lasting hyperpolarization. The whole event lasts less than a thousandth of a second. It is sketched in Fig. A.10. Later work showed that these hypothetical explanations of the phenomena were correct.

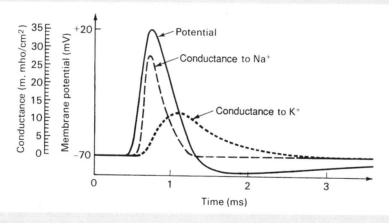

Fig. A.10 Graph showing the voltage changes that occur at a point along the nerve membrane during an action potential. Changes in the membrane's conductance for sodium and potassium ions are also shown. Conductance is the physical property that can be measured when electrical current crosses a membrane; it is a result of the opening of ionic pores that is presumed to occur. From Hodgkin, A. L. and A. F. Huxley (1952) A quantitative description of membrane current and its application to conduction and excitation in nerve. *J. Physiol.* 117: 500–544. Reprinted by permission.

(which is actually formed by wrappings of certain glia cells). Not all axons are myelinated; of course, those that support action potentials are myelinated, but there are also some small unmyelinated axons that transmit action potentials. No axons in invertebrates have myelin. __BOX A.3__

Coding by action potentials   If all action potentials are alike, it is easy to see how they can be used to send a simple 'now' message, but how can they send messages about how much stimulus there is, or what it is like? The answer is that neurons usually fire action potentials in a series, or train, and code information by the frequency at which the action potentials occur.

Consider a neuron undergoing a steady depolarizing influence. As it slowly depolarizes, it reaches threshold and fires an impulse. Following the impulse, it is slightly hyperpolarized, and slowly depolarizes until finally it reaches threshold and fires another impulse. The time between successive impulses depends on the strength of the depolarizing current. If the current is weak and the depolarization occurs slowly, there are long intervals between impulses; the firing is at a low rate. If the current is strong and the depolarization occurs

rapidly, there are very short intervals between impulses; the firing is at a rapid rate. This simple scheme suggests a *rate coding* for impulse trains.

Since each impulse is tiny and brief, it is common to amplify them, view them on an oscilloscope, listen to them through an audio amplifier and speaker, and record their times of occurrence with a computer. The stored list of times can be used to create later displays for analyses and publication. __BOX A.4__

The displays used in the lab are simulated in four of the demonstrations on the CD accompanying this book: 'Retinal cells responding to light' (Chapter 4), 'Ganglion cells responding to light' (Chapter 5), 'Cortical cell responses' (Chapter 7), and 'Opponent cells' (Chapter 14). Each of these simulations shows responses of spiking cells to various stimuli (presented in a window at the upper left). An oscilloscope-like display of each response appears in a window at the upper right, with the accompanying clicks as if there were an audio monitor. In two of these (Chapters 5 and 14), a peristimulus time histogram (see below) is presented in a window at the lower right. For this discussion, please follow along on the Chapter 5 demonstration.

Box A.4 Visualizing impulses

The direct 'viewing' of action potentials is on the oscilloscope. An oscilloscope is just a device that can rapidly draw a graph of voltage against time. It is rapid because it 'draws' with a beam of electrons on a screen like a computer monitor or TV. Modern oscilloscopes have built-in computers that let them remember previous displays, hold a display long after the event is over, or change the parameters of the picture for better viewing. But basically, they are graphing voltage *versus* time. When a train of impulses provides the voltage, the graph is a series of spikes (hence the other word for action potentials) sticking up and down from a noisy horizontal line.

Feeding an impulse to an audio system (amplifier and speaker) produces an audible click. A train of impulses then produces a series of clicks; if the impulses follow fast

enough, it sounds more like a sharp tone. Experimenters familiar with this kind of 'display' can tell better what a neuron is doing by hearing the impulses than by any other display short of extensive computer analyses.

While these displays are useful for letting the experimenters see what is happening during the experiment, the data are also stored in a computer. Since action potentials are all-or-none, the only important thing to save is the times at which each occurred. These lists of times of occurrence are then used to reconstruct the data in as much detail as desired. They are also used 'on-line' (that is, at the time of the experiment) to create displays of rate *versus* time that are synchronized with the stimulus presentations.

The 'default' setting of the demonstration is an ON-center X-cell, stimulated with a strong, white spot centered on its receptive field. Watch the 'scope' (short for oscilloscope) at the upper right. This is a representation of voltage *versus* time. Each time there is an impulse, the trace jumps vertically and a click is heard from the audio monitor. To present a stimulus, click the 'Present stimulus' button just below the middle of the screen. This initiates the scope sweep. When the stimulus comes on, about one-third of the way across (you can see it on the map at the left out of the corner of your eye), a red bar underlines the trace. (A real oscilloscope has no other colors, but might have a second trace that deflects to indicate the presence of the stimulus.) The firing becomes more rapid, as you see by the closer spacing of the spikes and hear by the more urgent clicking. The spot is extinguished at a point about two-thirds of the way across; the red underline ends, and the impulse rate drops to below what it was in the dark before the spot first appeared.

The idea of the rate code is that higher firing rates imply more excitation. The ON-center X-cell must have been excited by the onset of the spot, and anti-excited (inhibited) when it went away. What if the spot were less intense? Select a weak strength (choice buttons at the bottom, just left of center), and watch again. There is still an increase in rate when the spot appears, but it is less dramatic. (The previous trial shifts down a step, so you can still see it below the current trial.)

If you present the same stimulus again and again, you will notice that the responses are similar but not identical. There is a certain amount of variability in the responses. To characterize the response, you would like to see an average of some kind. It would also be nice to see the response in terms of firing rate, rather than as a train of impulses. These goals are accomplished by forming a peristimulus time histogram (PSTH). The PSTH for the responses you have just generated is in the window at the bottom right. To make a PSTH, the time in the trace is divided into short 'bins'—in this case, each bin was 67 ms in duration, providing 15 bins/s. Each bin counts the number of impulses falling within it; this can be converted to rate by dividing by bin duration (0.067 s). As further trials are run, impulses add to the bins, and a PSTH is developed. In the demonstration, the PSTH is cumulated when a stimulus is repeated at least twice; as you continue to repeat the same stimulus, you will see the PSTH becoming smoother as the statistics are based on larger numbers of impulses. <u>BOX A.5</u>

Synaptic transmission The transmission from neuron to neuron is usually achieved by a chemical messenger, called a *transmitter*. This happens at an almost-union of the two neurons, called a *synapse* (from the Greek for 'coming together'). The operation of the 'standard' chemical synapse was described in an elegant series of papers by B. Katz and his coworkers at the Physiological Laboratory of Cambridge University (Fatt & Katz, 1952, 1954; Katz & Miledi, 1967a,b).

The transmitter is manufactured and stored by the 'sending' neuron (the *presynaptic neuron*). It is

---

Box A.5 Other possible impulse codes

The PSTH provides a convenient way to visualize the firing rate as a function of time, but it may lose some information by averaging. Not only does it average across trials, but because the bins are of finite width, it loses the time resolution inherent in individual impulses. In fact, there may be important information in the patterning of the impulse trains, information that is lost when only the mean firing rate is considered (Richmond & Optican, 1990; Richmond *et al.*, 1990, 1997). The methods for examining these possibilities are beyond the scope of this book, but you should be aware that these possibilities exist (see Box 7.8, p.132).

usually stored in tiny, bubble-like containers within the cell (*vesicles*). When the presynaptic cell depolarizes, pores open that allow calcium into it; the calcium enables vesicles to move to the cell membrane and fuse with it. Like bubbles breaking at the top of a glass of soda, the vesicles 'pop', releasing their transmitter into the space outside the cell (the *synaptic cleft*). The transmitter molecules diffuse across the cleft to the 'receiving' cell (*postsynaptic neuron*). There, it binds to special molecules in the membrane (*receptor sites*). The receptor molecules are like the pores responsible for the action potential, except that instead of opening because of depolarization, they open because transmitter is bound to them. Think of the transmitter molecules as tiny keys that work the 'locks' to open the pores. <u>BOX A.6</u>

The mechanism of lock and key varies at different synapses. Sometimes, the transmitter is like a mechanical key that directly opens the pore. Sometimes, the transmitter–receptor complex acts like an enzyme, forming another active chemical that (often several steps away) operates the pore. This is more like the remote 'buzz your guest in' at an apartment, or a keycard opener. (An example of a long chain of this type, initiated by light rather than a transmitter, is the activation of visual receptors described in Box 4.6, p. 57.)

Depending on the nature of the pore, different ions may be allowed to enter or leave the neuron. If positive ions (like sodium or calcium) enter, the postsynaptic cell depolarizes. That is, it becomes excited—it is nearer the threshold for action potentials if it fires any, in any case releasing transmitter of its own. The slow potential that results is called an *excitatory postsynaptic potential*, or *EPSP*. Since the postsynaptic cell copies what the presynaptic cell did (depolarizing and releasing transmitter because the presynaptic cell depolarized and released transmitter), this is sometimes called a *sign-conserving* synapse.

If the pore allows the flow of positive potassium ions out of the cell, or of negative chloride ions into it, the postsynaptic cell hyperpolarizes. That is, it is inhibited—it is further from the threshold for action potentials if it fires any, in any case releasing less transmitter of its own. The slow potential that results is called an *inhibitory postsynaptic potential*, or *IPSP*. Since the postsynaptic cell does the opposite of what the presynaptic cell did (hyperpolarizing and stopping the release of transmitter because the presynaptic cell depolarized and released transmitter), this is sometimes called a *sign-inverting* synapse.

If some synapses are excitatory and some are inhibitory, there must be chemical differences among them. Indeed, there are a large number of different transmitters that have been identified, and most of them are found in the sensory systems (as well as throughout the brain). In addition, most of the known transmitters have associated with them several different postsynaptic receptor

---

Box A.6 Synapses that are exceptions

Before going further into the mechanisms of chemical synapses, it is worth a reminder that this is not the only way cells communicate at synapses. While most chemical synapses have a calcium-dependent vesicle release system, some neurons release their transmitter by 'pumping' it directly across the membrane. While these membrane pumps usually depend on voltage, they do not involve the intermediary step of calcium entering the cell. Some convenient tricks, like poisoning the calcium mechanism to turn off synapses, don't work on these.

Another important kind of synapse doesn't use chemical transmission at all. These are called *electrical synapses*, or (morphologically) *gap junctions* (see Box 4.7, p. 61). At gap junctions, the two cells come in close apposition, like two people holding hands. Aligned pores connect the two cells, and electrical currents can pass between them. Thus, electronic spread can extend beyond the boundary of a single neuron.

Box A.7 Other chemical interactions at synapses

In the 'classical' chemical synapse, the transmitter opens channels for particular ions, causing an EPSP or an IPSP. But sometimes, the effects are more subtle. For example, a chemical can attach to a part of the receptor molecule (or complex of molecules) without directly affecting the ion channel; what it does is to change the efficacy of the transmitter that normally opens the channel. Such a chemical is called a *neuromodulator*—it modulates the transmission at the synapse. Thus, the transmitter opens a channel, but opens it wider (or for longer) if the modulator is present than if it is absent. Note that modulator alone (absent transmitter) has no effect. Neuromodulators are usually released in a general region, rather than confined to specific synapses. Neuromodulation can also affect the efficiency of electrical synapses (see Box A.6).

There are a number of other interactions found at specific types of synapses. One that has attracted considerable interest is called the NMDA receptor (it responds to a chemical whose initials are NMDA). The NMDA receptor is found in synapses that use the monoamine transmitter *glutamate* (an amino acid). It is not the only type of glutamate receptor; others respond to a chemical called kainate, and still others to a chemical whose initials are AMPA.

The NMDA receptors display an interesting property: when they are stimulated repeatedly, or stimulated while the postsynaptic cell is relatively depolarized, they increase the ability for the synapse to respond to glutamate in the future. That is, repeated use, or use in association with other synapses on the same cell, strengthens the synapse for future stimuli. This process is called *long-term potentiation* (LTP), and seems to be the basis for various kinds of learning. That such receptors, and LTP, are found in visual cortex indicates that how we learn to perceive may be a very primitive process.

---

molecules, with different ion pores operated by each. You will not need to know the pharmacology of these synapses for this book, but you should be aware that considerable research has gone into finding which transmitters (and receptor subtypes) are involved at each of the synapses in the sensory systems. BOX A.7

Experimental techniques

Now that you have seen what trains of impulses look like, and read about synapses and transmitters, you may be wondering how anyone can detect such tiny events from microscopic cells, or know what is going on inside a brain. This section will indicate some of the answers to these questions.

Chemical techniques

In this text, you will not encounter much discussion of the specific chemical transmitters used by the systems under study, so this section will be a brief overview. Three kinds of chemical technique will be mentioned: staining particular cells, detecting transmitters, and manipulating cells that use a particular transmitter.

Staining particular cells Certain cells are distinctive for various reasons. They may have a surplus of some enzyme or material, such as a particular transmitter or the enzymes for making it. They may be derived from a particular germ cell type that has a distinctive genetic marker. They may be especially active, or made active by a particular stimulus. By taking advantage of this, these cells can be stained, or marked, so they can be picked out under a microscope. Their location and morphological type can then be determined.

Cells with an excess of the metabolism enzyme cytochrome oxidase can be stained with a chemical that makes cytochrome oxidase visible. The animal is sacrificed (usually by an overdose of anesthetic, so it is put into a fatal coma), and the brain removed. The brain is 'fixed' in formaldehyde or some other preservative that prevents deterioration (and usually toughens the tissue), and sliced. The stain is applied, and the stained sections can be viewed (see Chapter 8 for the importance of the cytochrome oxidase stain).

Some cells are already marked by having some genetic quirk that represents their history in the evolution of the sensory system. These can be identified by making antibodies to the distinctive chemicals in their membranes. The markers are called *monoclonal antibodies*, and attach themselves to cells containing the chemical, just as your immune system attacks invaders. Cells with the attached antibodies can then be stained and visualized. Similarly, cells that make a particular transmitter can be marked by staining them with stains that attach to the enzymes used for the manufacture of these transmitters.

Cells that are active during a particular stimulus can be marked by causing them to take in a chemical because of their activity. The usual chemical is called 2-deoxyglucose, or 2-DG. This stuff is a lot like glucose (the simplest sugar). Cells that are active gobble up glucose, and are fooled into taking in 2-DG if it is injected into the bloodstream. The cells may be active because the animal is looking at a particular pattern (see Chapter 8). Glucose is metabolized, but 2-DG is not, so it accumulates inside the cells that took it in (Sokoloff, 1975). After the session, the animal is sacrificed, and the 2-DG is visualized in the brain sections. Those cells involved in the task will be the most stained.

Detecting transmitter   Sometimes it is possible to detect the transmitter released by active synapses. Not all the transmitter manages to find (or stick to) a postsynaptic receptor; some of it leaks away. Much of the leaking or used-up transmitter is taken back by the cell that released it, but some gets away. By collecting fluid from around the tissue, the experimenter can perform chemical analyses that detect the transmitter. The amount detected during different stimuli gives a clue as to what stimuli the cells releasing that transmitter are most 'interested' in. Sometimes, it is possible to place a microscopic tube (a *microcannula*) into the

tissue in question, and only collect fluid from the local region of interest (how such a tube might be placed is discussed below. There are also cannulae that have a special membrane that produces an electrical response to the transmitter, so the amount released can be recorded in real time. This technique is called *microiontophoresis*.

Manipulating cells that use a particular transmitter
If the transmitter is known, various drugs may be available to affect the operation of the system. Some of these drugs, called *agonists*, enhance the operation of the system; some of these, called *mimetics*, duplicate the action of the transmitter even if it is not there. Other drugs are called *antagonists*; these oppose the operation of the transmitter. The antagonists known as *blockers*, for example, gum up the receptors (often of a particular subtype) so the transmitter has less or no effect. It is like sticking chewing gum in a lock so that the key is useless.

Electrophysiological recordings

Recordings from single cells   To record from a single neuron requires four things: a way to find the cell; a means of holding the recording device steady enough that the cell is not lost; a device capable of intercepting the electrical currents produced by the cell; and a means of amplifying the minute currents into a signal you can work with.

Finding the cell is not too difficult in an isolated structure like the retina; it is there, you can see the retina (at least with a microscope), and you just keep poking until you get a cell. If you are recording inside the cell (*intracellularly*, see below), you know you have entered the cell because the potential drops to resting potential. Of course, you don't know *which* cell you have entered. That you must find out later, by injecting dye into the cell and looking at the fixed tissue under a microscope.

In the brain itself, you can't see where you're going. You have to find the right structure in the same way that a pilot finds an airport in fog: navigate to the coordinates. There are detailed drawings, called *atlases*, of the brains of various species. These atlases show a cross-section every millimeter, with all the important structures labeled. In addition, there is a grid superimposed, giving the distances from a known, fixed point. That point is usually the midpoint of the line between the two ear canals; the reference for horizontal is the line forward to the teeth. The distances are then given in millimeters anterior (forward of the line between the ears), horizontal (above or below that line), and lateral (to the left or right of center).

These distances are directly readable, because the animal's head is held in a firm support in a known position. Of course, the animal is under full surgical anesthesia, and monitored to ensure it is completely unconscious and pain-free. The head is typically held by two bars, one inserted into each ear canal, providing the ear-to-ear line; the upper front teeth rest on another bar, establishing the horizontal axis. The electrode or cannula is held steady by a device that has readings corresponding to the grid on the atlas. The fine micrometer that reads the position allows adjusting in the forward/aft, left/right, and up/down directions. This setup is known as a *stereotactic frame*, or simply *stereotax*.

What device is held by the stereotax depends on the task at hand. It could be a cannula for injecting or removing fluids (for detecting or affecting transmitter systems). It could be a knife or electrode for cutting or burning a bit of brain tissue to examine the effect of loss of that region on the functioning of the system.

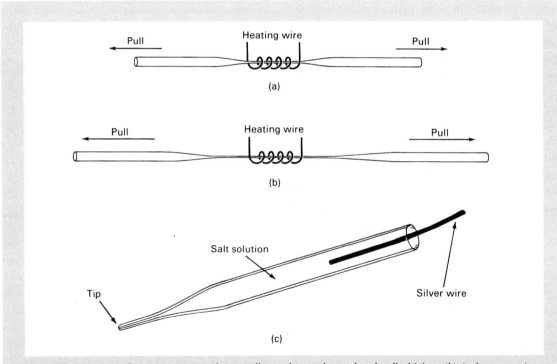

Fig. A.11 Anatomy of a micropipette. Glass capillary tubing is heated and pulled (a) until it is drawn out into a fine filament (b). The filament breaks in the center to form the tip. Sometimes the tip is polished in a stream of water containing fine jeweler's rouge. The pipette is filled with a salt solution, and a silver wire inserted into the wide end to provide electrical contact (c).

Recordings from single cells (intracellular) are typically made with *micropipettes*. A micropipette is made from a fine glass tube (it starts about 1 mm in diameter—about the diameter of the glass straws used to absorb a drop of blood from the tip of your finger in a 'stab' blood test). The tube is placed in a device (*puller*) that applies controlled heat and pull, stretching the middle to microscopic proportions (see Fig. A.11). If you have ever played with chemistry lab tubing and a bunsen burner, you know that heating the glass makes it soft; if you stretch it out, it becomes a thin fiber—but the lumen (opening) through the center stays open the whole way. The glass breaks in the middle, forming two micropipettes. The tip of each is so small that it cannot be seen in an ordinary light microscope because it is on the same order as the wavelength of light!

The micropipette is filled with concentrated salt solution (usually potassium chloride to match the stuff inside the cell), so it makes electrical contact with the inside of the cell. A silver wire in the end makes contact to connect to a high-gain amplifier. Often, the pipette also has a dye inside it; passing a bit of current after the recording is over ejects the dye and stains the cell so it can be identified under a microscope.

Electrodes for recording action potentials don't have to be so fine, because the currents from an action potential are large enough to detect from outside the cell (*extracellular* recording). Since only the time of occurrence is of interest, there is no premium on accurate measuring of voltage. Sometimes, extracellular electrodes can be made from metal wire that has been etched to a fine point and insulated at all but the very tip with glass or varnish. Of course, these electrodes cannot eject a dye to mark the cell, although they can sometimes pass a large enough current to make a small burn that marks the location of the recording.

Multi-cell recordings Recently, the techniques used in manufacturing integrated circuits have made it possible to build arrays of over 100 metal extracellular electrodes. Computers are now fast enough to compare the signals recorded by these arrays, and reconstruct the patterns of firings of several cells (even dozens) at once. With this technique, it is becoming possible to monitor a small chunk of nervous tissue, and discern the relationships among the various neurons. BOX A.8

Brain imaging

In recent years, tremendous strides have been made in visualizing the brain inside a living being without having to cut through the skin. You may be familiar with the CAT scan (CAT stands for computer-aided tomography), which is really an X-ray technique in which a slim beam of X-rays passes through the head (or any other part of the body) from a large number of directions, and a computer reconstructs the shape of the structures it has passed through. Like an ordinary X-ray, this gives a picture of what lies within.

Of more interest for perceptual processes, there are techniques that allow one to see the patterns of activity deep inside the brain. The first technique that did this was called a PET scan (which stands for positron emission tomography). Instead of X-rays, the detectors in this technique record positrons released from a minute amount of radioactive material in the blood. Brain regions that are active have more blood flow and release more positrons; the computer recreates the spatial patterns of activity. Of course, one must accept the assumption that the active regions will use more oxygen at the time they are being active.

Another problem with PET scans is that the spatial localization is poor. This problem led to the development of a technique that detects shifts in the magnetic states of chemicals in the brain when in a magnetic field. The slight changes in the field give a rapid and relatively precise indication of where the activity is. The technique is called MRI (magnetic resonance imaging), or fMRI (functional MRI). With this technique, a person can watch a display or solve a puzzle while researchers observe which parts of the brain are being active ('lighting up') and in what order.

There are some older techniques that allow us to

Box A.8 Gross potentials

Before there were single- and multiple-cell recordings, coarser electrodes allowed the recording of *gross potentials*. What this refers to is recording the combined currents from many cells in a region of brain. You may be familiar with the EEG, a recording of general brain activity made with electrodes pasted to the scalp. The obvious advantage is that these kinds of recordings are *non-invasive*; that is, they can be made without cutting into the subject. This makes them especially useful for exploring the workings of the human nervous system without disrupting the person under study. It also makes them convenient tools for clinical diagnoses.

A convenient gross potential of the eye is called the *electroretinogram*, or *ERG*. This is a potential that develops across the retina, due to currents that run radially (through the retina) as the retinal cells respond. It can be recorded with an electrode (often built into a special contact lens) placed on the cornea of the eye (see Chapter 3). Component waves of the ERG have been identified that correspond to activity in the receptors, the bipolar cell layer, and the ganglion cell layer (see Chapter 4). It is a very

useful diagnostic for many retinal disorders. (For a review of the ERG and its components, see Steinberg *et al.*, 1991).

Although they do not get mentioned elsewhere in this book, you may be interested to know of some other gross potentials. One is called the *evoked response*; it is found in the EEG when recording from the scalp. When a stimulus is repeated many times, the EEG as a function of time since the stimulus can be averaged; the waves that survive averaging are time-locked to the stimulus and represent the brain's processing of the stimulus. Waves that follow immediately after the stimulus represent the sensory effect. These are a good demonstration that the peripheral organs (eyes, ears, or whatever) are functional and that a patient's inability to see, hear, or whatever is due to a more central problem. Later waves represent the cognitive processing of the stimulus.

A potential comparable to the ERG can be recorded from the ear. It is called the *cochlear microphonic*, and represents the responses of the auditory receptors in the ear (see Chapter 15). It is also possible to record receptor-related potentials from the other sensory systems.

see the activity in a brain with some precision—but at the cost of sacrificing the subject. The 2-DG technique discussed above is a good way to see which areas were active, but it is not well localized. There are also techniques that allow one to view a small section of cortex and see the activity directly. A voltage-sensitive dye is placed on the exposed cortex; when the cells change their polarization (say, by firing action potentials), the dye molecules change their states. When they are illuminated by ultraviolet light, this state change shows clearly as a glow of emitted light. The beauty of this technique is that the same area in the same animal can be observed with different stimuli (unlike 2-DG, which only allows a single 'snapshot' from an animal). For example, an animal is shown horizontal lines and the active areas are videotaped; then the animal is shown vertical lines and a new image is obtained, and so forth. In this way, the microstructure of responses to different stimuli can be compared (using

a 'false color' reconstruction, like the radar images on the TV weather maps) in the same area of the same animal. You can see examples of visual cortex in this false color imagery in the 'Cortical columns' demonstration associated with Chapter 8 on the CD.

Suggested readings

Material related to this appendix, particularly the biophysics of the action potential, may be found by searching the Internet. One particularly nice site allows simulations of the action potential and the Hodgkin–Huxley experiments that lead to our understanding of it. The site is authored by F. Bezanilla, and may be found at <http://pb010.anes.ucla.edu/—a JAVA browser is required. There is a general textbook available, along with several easy-to-use simulations.

References

Abraham, M. H. *see* Cometto-Muniz

Abrahams, H., Krakauer, D., & Dallenbach, K. (1937) Gustatory adaptation to salt. *Am. J. Psychol., 49,* 462–469. {20}

Abramov, I. (1968) Further analyses of the responses of LGN cells. *J. Opt. Soc. Am., 58,* 574–579. {14}

Abramov, I., & Gordon, J. (1994) Color appearance: on seeing red—or yellow, or green, or blue. *Annu. Rev. Psychol., 45,* 451–485. {14}

Abramov, I. *see also* DeValois; Gordon; Levine

Acuña, C. *see* Alonso

Adams, A. J., & Afanador, A. J. (1971) Ganglion cell receptive field organization at different levels of light adaptation. *Am. J. Optom., 48,* 889–896. {6}

Adams, J. E. *see* Hosobuchi

Adelson, E. H. (1993) Perceptual organization and the judgment of brightness. *Science, 262,* 2042–2044. {12}

Adelson, E. H. *see also* Bergen; Emerson

Adey, W. R., & Noda, H. (1973) Influence of eye movements on geniculo-striate excitability in the cat. *J. Physiol. 235,* 805–821. {13}

Aertsen A. *see* Neven

Afanador, A. J. *see* Adams

Aglioti, S., DeSouza, J. F. X., & Goodale, M. A. (1995) Size-contrast illusions deceive the eye but not the hand. *Curr. Biol., 5,* 679–685. {7, 12}

Aguilar, M., & Stiles, W. S. (1954) Saturation of the rod mechanism of the retina at high levels of stimulation. *Optica Acta, 1,* 59–65. {6}

Ahissar, M., & Hochstein, S. (1997) Task difficulty and the specificity of perceptual learning. *Nature, 387,* 401–406. {10}

Ahroon, W. A. *see* Pastore

Ai, N. *see* Shibuya

Aicardi, G. *see* Galletti

Akabas, M. H., Dodd, J., & Al-Awqati, Q. (1988) A bitter substance induces a rise in intracellular calcium in a subpopulation of rat taste cells. *Science, 242,* 1047–1050. {20}

Akil, H., Mayer, D. J., & Liebeskind, J. C. (1976) Antagonism of stimulation produced analgesia by naloxone, a narcotic antagonist. *Science, 191,* 961–962. {19}

Akil, H. *see also* Richardson

Akopian, A. *see* Weiler

Akutsu, H., & Legge, G. E. (1995) Discrimination of compound gratings: spatial frequency channels or local features? *Vision Res. 35,* 2685–2695. {9}

Alais, D., Burke, D., & Wenderoth, P. (1996) Further evidence for monocular determinants of perceived plaid direction. *Vision Res., 36,* 1247–1253. {9}

Al-Awqati, Q. *see* Akabas

Albee, G. W. *see* Bruell

Albert, L. H. *see* Grevert

Albrecht, D. G., & DeValois, R. L. (1981) Striate cortex responses to periodic patterns with and without the fundamental harmonics. *J. Physiol., 319,* 497–514. {9}

Albrecht, D. G., DeValois, R. L., & Thorell, L. G. (1980) Visual cortical neurons: Are bars or gratings the optimal stimuli?, *Science. 207,* 88–90. {9}

Albrecht, D. G., & Geisler, W. S. (1991) Motion selectivity and the contrast-response function of simple cells in the visual cortex. *Visual Neurosci., 7,* 531–546. {7}

Albrecht, D. G. *see also* DeValois

Albright, T. D. *see* Rodman; Stoner

Allen, B. J. *see* Mantyh

Allison, J. D., & Bonds, A. B. (1994) Inactivation of the infragranular striate cortex broadens orientation tuning of supragranular visual neurons in the cat. *Exp. Brain Res., 101,* 415–426. {7}

Allman, J. M. *see* Dobbins

Aloimonos, Y., & Rosenfeld, A. (1991) Computer vision. *Science, 253,* 1249–1254. {11}

Alonso, J. M., Cudeiro, J., Pérez, R., Gonzalez, F., & Acuña, C. (1993) Orientational influences of layer V of visual area 18 upon cells in layer V of area 17 in the cat cortex. *Exp. Brain Res., 96*, 212–220. {7}

Alonso, J.-M., Usrey, W. M., & Reid, R. C. (1996) Precisely correlated firing iun the cells of the lateral geniculate nucleus. *Nature, 383*, 815–819. {7}

Alonso, J.-M. *see also* Reid

Ammermüller, J. *see* Perlman

Amoore, J. E. (1964) Current status of the steric theory of odor. *Ann. N. Y. Acad. Sci., 116*, 457–476. {20}

Amoore, J. E. (1971) Olfactory genetics and anosmia. In L. M. Beidler (Ed.), *Handbook of Sensory Physiology. Vol. 4: Chemical Senses: Olfaction* (pp. 245–256). Berlin: Springer-Verlag. {20}

Amoore, J. E. (1982) Odor theory and odor classification. In F. Theimer (Ed.), *Fragrance Chemistry—The Science of the Sense of Smell* (pp. 27–76). New York: Academic Press. {20}

Andersen, R. A., Essick, G. K., & Siegel, R. M. (1985) Encoding of spatial location by posterior parietal neurons, *Science, 230*, 456–458. {8}

Andersen, R. A. *see also* Geesaman

Andersen, S. M. *see* Zimbardo

Anderson, D. J. *see* Rose

Anderson, N. H. *see* Massaro

Andrews, B. W. *see* Pollen

Anholt, R. R. *see* Sklar

Antonini, A., & Stryker, M. P. (1998) Effect of sensory disuse on geniculate afferents to cat visual cortex. *Visual Neurosci., 15*, 401–409. {8}

Archie, K. A. *see* Mel

Arend, L. E., & Goldstein, R. (1987) Simultaneous constancy, lightness, and brightness. *J. Opt. Soc. Amer. A, 4*, 2281–2285. {12}

Arezzo, J. C. *see* Schroeder

Assad, J. A., & Maunsell, J. H. R. (1995) Neuronal correlates of inferred motion in primate posterior parietal cortex. *Nature, 373*, 518–521. {13}

Arbib, M. A. *see* Rizzolatti

Arthur, J. B. (1975) Taste aversion learning is impaired by interpolated amygdaloid stimulation but not by post training amygdaloid stimulation. *Behav. Biol., 13*, 369–376. {20}

Ashe, J. *see* Nachman

Aslin, R. N. *see* Saffran

Atkinson, J., & Campbell, F. W. (1974) The effect of

phase on the perception of compound gratings. *Vision Res., 14*, 159–162. {9}

Attneave, F. (1954) Some informational aspects of visual perception. *Psych. Rev., 61*, 183–193. {10}

Attneave, F. (1957) Physical determinants of the judged complexity of shapes. *J. Exper. Psychol., 53*. 221–227. {10}

Attneave, F. (1962) Perception and related areas. In S. Koch (Ed.), *Psychology: A Study of a Science, Vol. 4* (pp. 619–659). New York: McGraw-Hill. {2}

Atteneave, F. (1971) Multistability in perception. *Sci. Am., 225*. 62–72. {10, **10.19**}

Attwell, D., & Wilson, M. (1980) Behaviour of the rod network in the tiger salamander retina mediated by membrane properties of individuals rods. *J. Physiol., 309*, 287–315. {4}

Aubert, H. (1886) Die bewegungsemp-findung. *Arch. ges. Physiol., 39*, 347–370. {13}

Aulanko, R. *see* Sams

Ault, S. J. *see* Leventhal

Austin, P. *see* Wallach

Avenet, P., Hofmann, F., & Lindemann, B. (1988a) Signalling in taste receptor cells: cAMP dependent protein kinase causes depolarization by closure of 44 pS k-channels. *Comp. Biochem. Physiol. (A), 90*, 681–685. {20}

Avenet, P., Hofmann, F., & Lindemann, B. (1988b) Transduction in taste receptor cells requires cAMP dependent protein kinase. *Nature, 331*, 351–354. {20}

Azulay, A. *see* Schwartz

Azzopardi, P. *see* Tovee

Badcock, D. R. (1984a) Spatial phase or luminance profile discrimination? *Vision Res., 24*, 613–623. {9}

Badcock, D. R. (1984b) How do we discriminate relative spatial phase? *Vision Res., 24*, 1847–1854. {9}

Badcock, D. R. *see also* Derrington

Bader, C. R. *see* Brownell

Baffrito, K. J. *see* Pastore

Baker, C. L. *see* Boulton; Mullen

Bakus, A. S. *see* Kiang

Balkema, G. W., & Bunt-Milam, A. H. (1982) Cone outer segment shedding in the goldfish retina characterized with the ^{3}H-fucose technique. *Investig. Ophthal. & Vis. Sci., 23*, 319–331. {4}

Bannister, N. J. *see* Stratford

Baraniga, M. (1991) How the nose knows: olfactory receptor cloned. *Science, 252*, 209–210. {20}

Baraniga, M. (1992) Neuroscience fantasia in an appropriate setting: Tuning our hearing. *Science, 258,* 889. {15}

Baraniga, M. (1996) Mutant mice and worms help solve mysteries of olfaction. *Science, 274,* 500–501. {20}

Baratz, S. S. *see* Epstein

Barlow, H. B. (1953) Summation and inhibition in the frog's retina. *J. Physiol., 119,* 69–88. {5}

Barlow, H. B. (1964) Dark adaptation: a new hypothesis. *Vision Res., 4,* 47–58. {6}

Barlow, H. B. (1997a) The knowledge used in vision and where it comes from. *Phil. Trans. R. Soc. Lond. B, 352,* 1141–1147. {5, 8, 10, 11, 13}

Barlow, H. B. (1997b) Performance, perception, dark-light, and gain boxes. *Neurosci. Res. Program Bull., 15,* 394–397. {6}

Barlow, H. B., Blakemore, C., & Pettigrew, J. D. (1967) The neural mechanisms of binocular depth discrimination. *J. Physiol., 193,* 327–342. {11}

Barlow, H. B., FitzHugh, R., & Kuffler, S. W. (1957) Dark adaptation, absolute threshold, and purkinje shift in single units of the cat's retina. *J. Physiol., 137,* 327–337. {6}

Barlow, H. B., & Hill, R. M. (1963) Selective sensitivity to direction of movement in ganglion cells of the rabbit retina. *Science, 139,* 412–414. {5}

Barlow, H. B., Hill, R. M., & Levick, W. R. (1964) Retinal ganglion cells responding selectively to direction and speed of image motion in the rabbit. *J. Physiol., 173,* 377–407. {**5.9**}

Barlow, H. B., & Levick, W. R. (1969) Changes in the maintained discharge with adaptation level in the cat retina. *J. Physiol., 202,* 699–718. {5}

Barlow, H. B., Narasimhan, R., & Rosenfeld, A. (1972) Visual pattern analysis in machine and animals. *Science, 177,* 567–574. {10}

Barlow, H. B., & Reeves, B. C. (1979) The versatility and absolute efficiency of detecting mirror symmetry in random dot displays. *Vision Res., 19,* 783–793. {10}

Barlow, H. B. *see also* Pelah

Barnes, S. *see* Eliasof

Barney, H. L. *see* Peterson

Baro, J. A. *see* Lehmkuhle

Bartlett, N. R. *see* Graham

Bartley, S. H. (1938) Subjective brightness in relation to flash rate and the light-dark ratio. *J. Exp. Psychol., 23,* 313–319. {12}

Bartley, S. H. *see also* Miller; Nelson

Bartoshuk, L. M. (1978). History of taste research. In E. G. Carterette & M. P. Friedman (Eds.), *Handbook of Perception, Vol. VIA: Tasting and Smelling,* (pp. 3–18). New York: Academic Press. {20}

Bartoshuk, L. M., Lee, C.-H., & Scarpolino, R. (1972) Sweet taste of water induced by artichoke. *Science, 178,* 988–990. {20}

Bartoshuk, L. M. *see also* McBurney

Basbaum, A. I. *see* Malmberg

Bassi, C. J., & Powers, M. K. (1990) Rod outer segment length and visual sensitivity. *Investig. Ophthal. & Vis. Sci., 31,* 2320–2325. {4}

Bastian, J. *see* Liberman

Batra, R. *see* Fitzpatrick

Battaglini, P. P., Galletti, C., & Fattori, P. (1996) Cortical mechanisms for visual perception of object motion and position in space. *Behav. Brain Res., 76,* 143–154. {11}

Battaglini, P. P. *see also* Galletti

Batteau, D. W. (1967) The role of the pinna in human localization. *Proc. R. Soc. Lond. Ser. B, 168,* 158–180. {15, 17}

Bauer, R. *see* Eckhorn

von Baumgarten, R. *see* Mancia

Baumgartner, G. *see* von der Heydt

Baxter, W. T., & Dow, B. M. (1989) Horizontal organization of orientation-sensitive cells in primate visual cortex. *Biol. Cybern., 61,* 171–182. {8}

Baylor, D. A., & Hodgkin, A. L. (1974) Changes in time scale and sensitivity in turtle photoreceptors. *J. Physiol., 242,* 729–758. {6}

Baylor, D. A., Fuortes, M. G. F., & O'Bryan, P. M. (1971) Receptive fields of cones in the retina of the turtle. *J. Physiol., 214,* 265–294. {4}

Baylor, D. A., Nunn, B. J., & Schnapf, J. L. (1984) The photocurrent, noise and spectral sensitivity of rods of the monkey *Macaca Fascicularis. J. Physiol., 357,* 575–607. {6}

Baylor, D. A. *see also* DeVries; Schnapf

Bean, B. P. *see* Feigenspan

Beatty, J. *see* Kahneman

Beck, J. (1966) Effect of orientation and of shape similarity on perceptual grouping. *Percept. Psychophys., 1,* 300–302. {**10.5**}

Beck, J. (1972) Similarity, groupings and peripheral discriminability under uncertainty. *Am. J. Psychol., 85,* 1–20. {10}

Beck, J., & Gibson, J. J. (1955) The relation of apparent shape to apparent slant in the perception of objects. *J. Exp. Psychol., 50*, 125–133. {12}

Beck, J. *see also* Hochberg

Beck, P. D. *see* DeBruyn

Becker, J. D. *see* Krüger

Beidler, L. M. (1978) Biophysics and chemistry of taste. In E. C. Carterette & M. P Friedman (Eds.), *Handbook of Perception, Vol. VIA: Tasting and Smelling* (pp. 21–49). New York: Academic Press. {20}

Beidler, L. M. *see also* Kimura

von Békésy, G. (1928) Zur theorie des horens; die schwingungsform der basilarmembran. *Phys. Z., 29*, 793–810. {16}

von Békésy, G. (1942) Über die schwingungen der schneckentrennwand beim praparet und obrenmodell. *Akust. Z, 7*, 173–186. {16}

von Békésy, G. (1947) The variation of phase along the basilar membrane with sinusoidal vibrations. *J. Acoust. Soc. Am., 19*, 452–460. {16, **16.1**}

von Békésy, G. (1960), *Experiments in Hearing.* New York: McGraw-Hill. {15, **16.2**, **16.3**}

Belin, P., McAdams, S., Smith, B., Savel, S., Thivard, L., Samson, S., & Samson, Y. (1998) The functional anatomy of sound intensity discrimination. *J. Neurosci., 18*, 6388–6394. {17}

Benardete, E. A., Kaplan, E., & Knight, B. W. (1992) Contrast gain control in the primate retina: P cells and not X-like, some M cells are. *Visual Neurosci., 8*, 483–486. {7}

Benevento, L. A. *see* Lysakowski

Benimoff, N. I., Schneider, S., & Hood, D. C. (1982) Interactions between rod and cone channels above threshold: a test of various models. *Vision Res., 22*, 1133–1140. {6}

Benson, T. E., Burd, G. D., Green, C. A., Pedersen, P. E., Landis, D. M. D., & Shepherd, G. M. (1985) High resolution 2-deoxyglucose autoradiography in quick-frozen slabs of neonatal rat olfactory bulb. *Brain Res., 339*, 67–78. {20}

Benton, A. L. *see* Damasio

Berardi, N. *see* Fiorentini

Berbaum, K. *see* Weisstein

Berenberg, R. A., Shefner, J. M., & Sabol, J. (1987) Quantitative assessment of position sense at the ankle: a functional approach. *Neurology, 37*, 89–94. {19}

Bergen, J. R., & Adelson, E. H. (1988) Early vision and texture perception. *Nature, 333*, 363–364. {10}

Bergen, J. R. *see also* Emerson

Berlin, B., & Kay, P. (1969) *Basic Color Terms, their Universality and Evolution.* Berkeley, CA: University of California Press. {14}

Berman, N., & Cynader, M. (1972) Comparison of receptive-field organization of the superior colliculus in siamese and normal cats. *J. Physiol., 224*, 363–389. {7}

Berman, N. *see also* Cynader

Berman, P. W., & Leibowitz, H. W. (1965) Some effects of contour on simultaneous brightness contrast. *J. Exp. Psychol., 69*, 251–256. {12}

Bernstein, I. H., Fisicaro, S. A., & Fox, J. A. (1976) Metacontrast suppression and criterion content: a discriminant function analysis. *Percept. Psychophys., 20*, 198–204. {9}

Berntson, G. G. *see* Burkhardt

Berrien, F. K. (1946) The effects of noise. *Psych. Bull., 43*, 141–161. {**17.3**}

Berti, A., & Rizzolatti, G. (1992) Visual processing without awareness: evidence from unilateral neglect. *J. Cognit. Neurosci., 4*, 345–351. {7}

Bertrand, D. *see* Brownell

Bertrand, O. *see* Tallon-Baudry

Bever, T. G. *see* Fodor

Bhatia, B. (1975) Minimum separable as a function of speed of a moving object. *Vision Res., 15*, 23–33. {13}

Bieber, S. L. *see* Smith

Bien, B. (1988) The promise of neural networks. *Amer. Scientist, 776*, 561–564. {10}

Bienfang, D. C. *see* Vaina

Billone, M., & Raynor, S. (1973) Transmission of radial shear forces to cochlear hair cells. *J. Acoust. Soc. Am., 54*, 1143–1156. {15}

Bilotta, J., DeMarco, P. J., & Powers, M. K. (1995) The contributions of ON- and OFF-pathways to contrast sensitivity and spatial resolution in goldfish. *Vision Res., 35*, 103–108. {4}

Binns, K. E. *see* Withington-Wray

Birch, D. G. *see* Hood

Birdsall, T. G. *see* Swets

Bischoff, W. F., & Di Lollo, V. (1990) Perception of directional sampled motion in relation to displacement and spatial frequency: Evidence for a unitary motion system. *Vision Res., 30*, 1341–1362. {13}

Bishop, P. O. *see* Nelson; Sanderson

Bisti, S., Maffei, L., & Piccolino, M. (1974)

Visuovestibular interactions in the cat superior colliculus. *J. Neurophysiol., 37*, 146–155. {7}

Bisti, S. *see also* Usai

Blake, R., & Camisa, J. (1978) Is binocular vision always monocular? *Science, 200*, 1497–1499 {11}

Blake, R., & Cormack, R. H. (1979) Psychophysical evidence for a monocular visual cortex in stereo-blind humans. *Science, 203*, 274–275. {11}

Blake, R., & Hirsch, H. V. B. (1975) Deficits in binocular depth perception in cats after alternating monocular deprivation. *Science, 190*, 1114–1116. {8, 11}

Blake, R. *see also* Nawrot; Schall; Sekuler; Wiesenfelder

Blakemore, C., & Campbell, F. W. (1969) On the existence of neurones in the human visual system selectively sensitive to the orientation and size of retinal images. *J. Physiol., 203*, 237–260. {9, **9.8**, **9.9**}

Blakemore, C., & Cooper, G. F. (1970) Development of the brain depends on the visual environment. *Nature, 228*, 477–478. {8}

Blakemore, C., & Sutton, P. (1969) Size adaptation: a new aftereffect. *Science, 166*, 245–247. {9, **9.12**}

Blakemore, C. *see also* Barlow

Blamey, P. J. *see* Tong

Blanco, R., Vaquero, C. F., & de la Villa, P. (1996) The effects of GABA and glycine on horizontal cells of the rabbit retina. *Vision Res., 36*, 3987–3995. {5}

Blasdel, G. G. (1992a) Differential imaging of ocular dominance and orientation selectivity in monkey striate cortex. *J. Neurosci., 12*, 3115–3138. {8}

Blasdel, G. G. (1992b) Orientation selectivity, preference, and continuity in monkey striate cortex. *J. Neurosci., 12*, 3139–3161. {8}

Blasdel, G. G., & Salama, G. (1986) Voltage-sensitive dyes reveal a modular organization in monkey striate cortex. *Nature, 321*, 579–585. {8}

Blasdel, G. G. *see also* Obermayer

Blommaert, F. J. J., & Martens, J.-B. (1990) An object-oriented model for brightness perception. *Spat. Vision, 5*, 15–41. {12}

Bloomfield, S. A. (1991) Two types of orientation-sensitive responses of amacrine cells in the mammalian retina. *Nature, 350*, 347–350. {4}

Bloomfield, S. A. (1996) Effect of spike blockade on the receptive field size of amacrine and ganglion cells in the rabbit retina. *J. Neurophysiol., 75*, 1878–1893. {4, 5}

Bloomfield, S. A., Xin, D., & Persky, S. E. (1995) A comparison of receptive field and tracer coupling size of horizontal cells in the rabbit retina. *Visual Neurosci., 12*, 985–999. {4}

Blough, D. S. (1955) Method for tracing dark adaptation in the pigeon. *Science, 121*, 703–704. {2}

Blume, H. *see* Seeck

Bok, D. (1985) Retinal photoreceptor-pigment epithelium interactions. *Investig. Ophthal. & Vis. Sci., 26*, 1659–1694. {4}

Bonds, A. B. (1989) Role of inhibition in the specification of orientation selectivity of cells in the cat striate cortex. *Visual Neurosci. 2*, 41–55. {7}

Bonds, A. B. *see also* Allison; DeBruyn

Bonhoeffer, T., & Grinvald, A. (1991) Iso-orientation domains in cat visual cortex are arranged in pinwheel-like patterns. *Nature, 353*, 429–431. {8}

Bonhoeffer, T., & Grinvald, A. (1993) The layout of iso-orientation domains in area 18 of cat visual cortex: optical imaging reveals a pinwheel-like organization. *J. Neurosci., 13*, 4157–4180. {8}

Bonhoeffer, T. *see also* Hübener

Bonke, D. *see* Langner

Boothe, R. *see* Makous

Boring, E. G. (1930) A new ambiguous figure. *Am. J. Psychol., 42*, 444–445. {10, **10.25**}

Boring, E. G. (1942) *Sensation and Perception in the History of Experimental Psychology.* New York: Appleton-Century-Crofts. {12}

Boring, E. G. *see also* Holway; Purkinje

Born, R. T., & Tootell, R. B. H. (1991) Spatial frequency tuning of single units in macaque supragranular striate cortex. *Proc. Natl Acad. Sci., 88*, 7066–7070. {8}

Borresen, C. R., & Lichte, W. H. (1962) Shape constancy: dependence upon stimulus familiarity. *J. Exp. Psychol., 63*, 91–97. {12}

Borst, J. M. *see* Cooper

Bossomaier, T. R. J. *see* Osorio

Boulton, J. C., & Baker, C. L. (1993a) Different parameters control motion perception above and below a critical density. *Vision Res., 33*, 1803–1811. {13}

Boulton, J. C., & Baker, C. L. (1993b) Dependence on stimulus onset asynchrony in apparent motion: evidence for two mechanisms. *Vision Res., 33*, 2013–2019. {13}

Bourassa, C. *see* Nelson

Boussaoud, D. *see* Tanné

Bowling, D. B., & Wieniawa-Narkiewicz, F. (1986) The distribution of on- and off-centre X- and Y-like cells in the A layers of the cat's lateral geniculate nucleus. *J. Physiol., 375,* 561–572. {7}

Bowling, D. B. *see also* Thurlow

Bowmaker, J. K. (1998) Visual pigments ond molecular genetics of color blindness. *News Physiol. Sci., 13,* 63–69. {4}

Bowmaker, J. K. *see also* Hunt; Shyue

Bownds, D. *see* Woodruff

Boycott, B. B., & Dowling, J. E. (1969) Organization of the primate retina: light microscopy. *Philos. Trans. R. Soc. Lond., 255,* 109–184. {**4.1**}

Boycott, B. B., Dowling, J. E., Fisher, S. K., Kolb, H., & Laties, A. M. (1975) Interplexiform cells of the mammalian retina and their comparison with catecholamine-containing retinal cells. *Proc. R. Soc. Lond., 191,* 353–368. {4}

Boycott, B. B., & Hopkins, J. M. (1991) Cone bipolar cells and cone synapses in the primate retina. *Visual Neurosci., 7,* 49–60. {4}

Boycott, B. B., & Hopkins, J. M. (1993) Cone synapses of a flat diffuse cone bipolar cell in the primate retina. *J. Neurocyt., 22,* 765–778. {4}

Boycott, B. B., & Wässle, H. (1974) The morphological types of ganglion cells of the domestic cat's retina. *J. Physiol., 240,* 397–419. {5}

Boycott, B. B. *see also* Dowling; Hopkins; Wässle

Boyer-Zeller, N. *see* Tanné

Boyle, A. J. *see* Johnstone

Boynton, R. M. (1988) Color vision. *Ann. Rev. Psychol., 39,* 69–100. {14}

Boynton, R. M., & Gordon, J. (1965) Bezold-Brücke hue shift measured by color-naming technique. *J. Opt. Soc. Am., 55,* 78–86. {14}

Boynton, R. M., & Montag, E. (1988) Categorical color names. *Proc. Int. Soc. for Eye Res., 5,* 154. {14}

Boynton, R. M., & Olson, C. X. (1990) Salience of chromatic basic color terms confirmed by three measures. *Vision Res., 30,* 1311–1317. {14}

Boynton, R. M. *see also* Uchikawa

Braddick, O. (1988) Contours revealed by concealment. *Nature, 333,* 803–804. {10, **10–13**}

Braddick, O. (1993) Segmentation versus integration in visual motion processing. *Trends in Neurosci., 16,* 263–268. {13}

Braddick, O. J. *see also* Snowden

Bradley, A., Switkes, E., & DeValois, K. (1988) Orientation and spatial frequency selectivity of adaptation to color and luminance gratings. *Vision Res., 28,* 841–856. {9}

Brainard, M. S. *see* Knudsen

Braje, W. L., Tjan, B. S., & Legge, G. E. (1995) Human efficiency for recognizing and detecting low-pass filtered objects. *Vision Res., 35,* 2955–2966. {10}

Braje, W. L. *see also* Tjan

Brammer, M. J. *see* Calvert; Howard

Brauner, J. D., & Lit, A. (1976) The Pulfrich effect, simple reaction time, and intensity discrimination. *Am J. Psychol., 89,* 105–114. {13}

Bray, C. W. *see* Wever

Breitmeyer, B. G., & Ganz, L. (1976) Implications of sustained and transient channels for theories of visual pattern masking. saccadic suppression. and information processing. *Psychol. Rev., 83,* 1–36. {5}

Breitmeyer, B. G. *see also* Williams

Brenner, E. *see* Foster

Bridgeman, B., Van der Heijden, A. H. C., & Velichkovsky, B. M. (1994) A theory of visual stability across saccadic eye movements. *Behav. Brain Sci., 17,* 247–292. {13}

Brigell, M., & Uhlarik, J. (1980) Bending the parallels of the Poggendorff figure. *Bull. Psychonom. Soc., 16,* 1–4. {12}

Brill, M. H., & West, G. (1986) Chromatic adaptation and color constancy: a possible dichotomy. *COLOR Res. and Applic., 11,* 196–204. {14}

Bringuier, V. *see* Frégnac

Britten, K. H., Newsome, W. T., Shadlen, M. N., Celebrini, S., & Movshon, J. A. (1996) A relationship between behavioral choice and the visual responses of neurons in macaque MT. *Visual Neurosci., 13,* 87–100. {13}

Britten, K. H., Shadlen, M. N., Newsome, W. T., & Movshon, J. A. (1992) The analysis of visual motion: a comparison of neuronal amd psychophysical performance. *J. Neurosci., 12,* 4745–4765. {13}

Brivanlou, I. H., Warland, D. K., & Meister, M. (1998) Mechanisms of concerted firing among retinal ganglion cells. *Neuron, 20,* 527–539. {5}

Brodal, A. (1981) Neurological Anatomy. 3rd edn New York: Oxford University Press. {**20.3**}

Brodmann, K. (1909) *Verglelehende Lokalisationslehre der Grosshirnrinde in ihren Prinzipien Dargestellt auf Grund des Zellenbaues.* Leipzig: Barth. {19}

Brooke, R. N. L., Downer, J. C., & Powell, T. P. S. (1965) Centrifugal fibres to the retina in the monkey and cat. *Nature, 207*, 1365–1367. {15}

Brosch, M. *see* Eckhorn

Brosgole, L., & Whalen, P. (1967) The effect of meaning on the allocation of visually induced movement. *Percept. Psychophys., 2*, 275–277. {13}

Brosgole, L. *see also* Rock

Brown, B. M. *see* Farber

Brown, C. M. (1984) Computer vision and natural constraints. *Science, 224*, 1299–1305. {11}

Brown, D. R. *see* McMahon

Brown, J. E., & Pinto, L. H. (1974) Ionic mechanism for the photoreceptor potential of the retina of *Bufo marinus. J. Physiol., 236*, 575–591. {4}

Brown, J. F. (1931) The visual perception of velocity. *Psychologische forschung, 14*, 199–232. Reprinted in *Readings in the Study of Visually Perceived Movement*, I. M. Spigel (Ed.). New York: Harper and Row, 1965. {**13.7**}

Brown, J. L. (1965) The structure of the visual system. In C. H. Graham (Ed.), *Vision and Visual Perception*, (pp. 39–59). New York: Wiley. {3}

Brown, K. T., Watanabe, K., & Murakami, M. (1965) The early and late receptor potentials of monkey cones and rods. *Cold Spring Harbor Symp. Quant. Biol., 30*, 457–482. {**4.2**}

Brown, K. T. *see also* Flaming; Whitten

Brown, P. K., & Wald, G. (1964) Visual pigment in single rods and cones of the human retina. *Science, 144*, 45–52. {14}

Brown, P. K. *see also* Pepperberg; Wald

Brownell, W. E., Bader, C. R., Bertrand, D., & Ribaupierre, Y. de (1985) Evoked mechanical responses of isolated cochlear outer hair cells. *Science, 227*, 194–196. {16}

Bruce, C., Desimone, R., & Gross, C. G. (1981) Visual properties of neurons in a polysensory area in superior temporal sulcus of the macaque. *J. Neurophysiol., 46*, 369–384. {8}

Bruell, J. H., & Albee, G. W. (1955) Notes toward a motor theory of visual egocentric localization. *Psychol. Rev., 62*, 391–399. {13}

Brugge, J. F., & Merzenich, M. M. (1973) Responses of neurones in auditory cortex of macaque monkey to monaural and binaural stimulation. *J. Neurophysiol., 36*, 1138–1158. {15, 16}

Brugge, J. F. *see also* Imig; Rose

Buchsbaum, G. *see* Courtney; Rao-Mirotznik

Buckley, D., & Frisby, J. P. (1993) Interaction of stereo, texture and outline cues in the shape perception of three-dimensional ridges. *Vision Res., 33*, 919–933. {11}

Buckley, D., Frisby, J. P., & Mayhew, J. E. W. (1989) Integration of stereo and texture cues in the formation of discontinuities during three-dimensional surface interpolation. *Percept., 18*, 563–588. {11}

Bullier, J. *see* Girard; Salin

Bullmore, E. T. *see* Calvert; Howard

Bunt-Milam, A. H. *see* Balkema

Burbeck, C. A. (1987) Position and spatial frequency in large-scale localization judgments. *Vision Res, 27*, 417–427. {9}

Burd, G. D. *see* Benson

Burdick, C. K., & Miller, J. D. (1975) Speech perception by the chinchilla: discrimination of sustained /a/ and /i/. *J. Acoust. Soc. Am., 58*, 415–427. {18}

Burgess, P. R., & Perl, E. R. (1973) Cutaneous mechanoreceptors and nociceptors. In A. Iggo (Ed.), *Handbook of Sensory Physiology, Vol. 2. Somatosensory System.* Heidelberg: Springer-Verlag. {19}

Burgess, P. R., Wei, J. Y., Clark, F. J., & Simon, J. (1982) Signalling of kinesthetic information by peripheral sensory receptors. *Ann Rev. Neurosci., 5*, 171–187. {19}

Burke, D. *see* Alais

Burke, W., & Sefton, A. J. (1966) Discharge patterns of principal cells and inhibitory interneurons in lateral geniculate nucleus of rat. *J. Physiol., 187*, 201–212. {7}

Burke, W. *see also* Wang

Burkhardt, D. A., & Berntson, G. G. (1972) Light adaptation and excitation: lateral spread of signals within frog retina. *Vision Res., 12*, 1095–1111. {6}

Burr, D. C. (1987) Implications of the Craik-O'Brien illusion for brightness perception. *Vision Res., 27*, 1903–1913. {9}

Burr, D. C., & Morrone, M. C. (1996) Temporal impulse response functions for luminance and colour during saccades. *Vision Res., 36*, 2069–2078. {7}

Burr, D. C., Morrone, M. C., & Ross, J. (1994) Selective suppression of the magnocellular visual pathway during saccadic eye movements. *Nature, 371*, 511–513. {7}

Bushnell, M. C., Goldberg, M. E., & Robinson, D. L. (1981) Behavioral enhancement of visual responses in monkey cerebral cortex. I. Modulation in posterior parietal cortex related to selective visual attention. *J. Neurophysiol., 46*, 755–772. {8}

Bushnell, M. C. *see also* Craig; Rainville; Talbot

Butcher, J. *see* Fillenbaum

Butler, S. R. *see* Walsh

Caan, W. *see* Perrett

Cain, W. S. (1978) History of research on smell. In E. C. Carterette & M. P. Friedman (Eds.), *Handbook of Perception. Vol. VIA: Tasting and Smelling* (pp. 197–243). New York: Academic Press. {20}

Cain, W. S. *see also* Cometto-Muniz

Calkins, D. J., Tsukamoto, Y., & Sterling, P. (1998) Microcircuitry and mosaic of a blue-yellow ganglion cell in the primate retina. *J. Neurosci., 18*, 3373–3385. {14}

Callaway, E. M., & Wiser, A. K. (1996) Contributions of individual layer 2–5 spiny neurons to local circuits in macaque primary visual cortex. *Visual Neurosci., 13*, 907–922. {8}

Callaway, E. M. *see also* Katz

Caltagirone, C. *see* Carlesimo

Calvert, G. A., Bullmore, E. T., Brammer, M. J., Campbell, R., Williams, S. C. R., McGuire, P. K., Woodruff, P. W. R., Iverson, S. D., & David, A. S. (1997) Activation of the auditory cortex during silent lipreading. *Science, 276*, 593–596. {18}

Camisa, J. *see* Blake

Campbell, D. T. *see* Segall

Campbell, F. W., & Robson, J. G. (1968) Application of Fourier analysis to the visibility of gratings. *J. Physiol., 197*, 551–566. {9, **9.5**}

Campbell, F. W., & Wurtz, R. H. (1978) Saccadic omission: Why we do not see a grey-out during a saccadic eye movement. *Vision Res., 18*, 1297–1303. {13}

Campbell, F. W., Howell, E. R., & Johnstone, J. R. (1978) A comparison of threshold and suprathreshold appearance of gratings with components in the low and high spatial frequency range. *J. Physiol., 284*, 193–201. {9}

Campbell, F. W. *see also* Atkinson; Blakemore

Campbell, R. *see* Calvert

Cannon, M. W., & Fullenkamp, S. C. (1991) Spatial interactions in apparent contrast: inhibitory effects among grating patterns of different spatial frequencies, spatial positions and orientations. *Vision Res., 31*, 1985–1998. {9}

Carandini, M., & Ferster, D. (1997) A tonic hyperpolar-

ization underlying contrast adaptation in cat visual cortex. *Science, 276*, 949–952. {6}

Carandini, M., Movshon, J. A., & Ferster, D. (1998) Pattern adaptation and cross-orientation interactions in the primary visual cortex. *Neuropharmacol., 37*, 501–511. {9}

Cardozo, B. L. *see* Schouten

Carey, D. P. *see* Goodale

Carl, J. W., & Hall, C. F. (1972) The application of filtered transforms to the general classification problem. *IEEE Trans. on Computers, C-21*, 785–790. {9}

Carlesimo, G. A., & Caltagirone, C. (1995) Components in the visual processing of known and unknown faces. *J. Clin. & Exp. Neuropsychol., 17*, 691–705. {8}

Carmichael, L. *see* Warren

Carrier, B. *see* Rainville

de Carvalho, L. A. V., & Roitman, V. L. (1995) A computational model for the neurobiological substrates of visual attention. *Int. J. Bio-Med. Comput., 38*, 33–45. {10}

Casagrande, V. A. *see* DeBruyn; Ding; Lachica

Casco, C. *see* Morgan

Casseday, J. H. *see* Neff

Castellucci, V. F. (1985) The chemical senses: taste and smell. In E. R. Kandel, & J. H. Schwartz (Eds.), *Principles of Neural Science*, 2nd edn (pp. 409–428). New York: Elsevier. {20, **20-12**}

Cavanagh, P. (1991a) Short-range vs long-range motion: not a valid distinction. *Spatial Vis., 5*, 303–309. {13}

Cavanagh, P. (1991b) What's up in top-down processing? In A. Gonea (Ed.), *Representations of Vision* (pp. 295–304). Cambridge: Cambridge University Press. {10}

Cavanagh, P., Tyler, C. W., & Favreau, O. E. (1984) Perceived velocity of moving chromatic gratings. *J. Opt. Soc. Amer. A, 1*, 893–899. {13}

Cavanagh, P. *see also* He; Tyler

Celebrini, S., & Newsome, W. T. (1994) Neuronal and psychophysical sensitivity to motion signals in extrastriate area MST of the macaque monkey. *J. Neurosci., 14*, 4109–4124. {13}

Celebrini, S. *see also* Britten

Cerf, J. A. *see* Otis

Chader, G. J. *see* Crouch

Chalupa, L. M., & Rhoades, R. W. (1977) Responses of visual. somatosensory and auditory neurones in the golden hamster's superior colliculus. *J. Physiol., 270*, 595–626. {7}

Chan, R. Y., & Naka, K.-I. (1976) The amacrine cell. *Vision Res., 16*, 1119–1129. {4}

Chang, F.-C. T., & Scott, T. R. (1984) Conditioned taste aversions modify neural responses in the rat nucleus tractus solitarius. *J. Neurosci., 4*, 1850–1862. {20}

Chaparro, A., Stromeyer, C. F., Chen, G., & Kronauer, R. E. (1995) Human cones appear to adapt at low light levels: measurements on the red-green detection mechanism. *Vision Res., 35*, 3103–3118. {6}

Chappell, R. L., & Naka, K.-I. (1991) Sensitivity transformation for vertebrate vision. *Visual Neurosci., 6*, 371–374. {6}

Chase, A. M. *see* Hecht

Chase, R., & Kalil, R. E. (1972) Suppression of visual evoked responses to flashes and pattern shifting during voluntary saccades. *Vision Res., 12*, 215–220. {13}

Chaudhuri, A. (1990) A motion illusion generated by afternystagmus suppression. *Neurosci. Lett., 118*, 91–95. {13}

Chavane, F. *see* Frégnac

Chelazzi, L., Miller, E. K., Duncan, J., & Desimone, R. (1993) A neural basis for visual search in inferior temporal cortex. *Nature, 363*, 345–347. {8}

Chen, C. *see* Malmberg

Chen, G. *see* Chaparro

Chen, H.-W. *see* Jacobson

Cheng, H. *see* Chino; Hamamoto

Chernenko, G. *see* Cynader

Cherry, C. (1953) Some experiments on the recognition of speech. with one and with two ears. *J. Acoust. Soc. Am., 25*, 975–979. {18}

Chichilnisky, E. J., & Wandell, B. A. (1996) Seeing gray through the ON and OFF pathways. *Visual Neurosci., 13*, 591–596. {4}

Chino, Y. M. (1997) Receptive-field plasticity in the adult visual cortex: dynamic signal rerouting or experience-dependent plasticity. *Sem. in Neurosci., 9*, 34–46. {8}

Chino, Y. M., Smith, E. L., Kaas, J. H., Sasaki, Y., & Cheng, H. (1995) Receptive-field properties of deafferentated visual cortical neurons after topographic map reorganization in adult cats. *J. Neurosci., 15*, 2417–2433. {8}

Chino, Y. M., Smith, E. L., Yoshida, K., Cheng, H., & Hamamoto, J. (1994) Binocular interactions in striate cortical neurons of cats reared with discordant visual inputs. *J. Neurosci., 14*, 5050–5067. {8}

Chino, Y. M. *see also* Hamamoto

Choi, A. V. *see* Vaina

Chubb, C., & Sperling, G. (1988) Drift-balanced random stimili: a general basis for studying non-Fourier motion perception. *J. Opt. Soc. Am. A, 5*, 1986–2007. {9}

Chubb, C., & Sperling, G. (1989) Two motion perception mechanisms revealed through distance-driven reversal of apparernt motion. *Proc. Natl Acad. Sci., 86*, 2985–2989. {13}

Chun, M.-H., & Wässle, H. (1993) Some horizontal cells of the bovine retina receive input synapses in the iner plexiform layer. *Cell Tis. Res., 272*, 447–457. {4}

Chun, M.-H., Grünert, U., Martin, P. R., & Wässle, H. (1996) The synaptic complex of cones in the fovea and in the periphery of the macaque monkey retina. *Vision Res., 36*, 3383–3395. {4}

Churchland, P. S., & Sejnowski, T. J. (1988) Perspectives on cognitive neuroscience. *Science, 242*, 741–745. {14}

Churchland, P. S. *see also* Sejnowski

Cicerone, C. M., & Green, D. G. (1980) Dark adaptation within the receptive field centre of rat retinal ganglion cells. *J. Physiol., 301*, 535–548. {6}

Cicerone, C. M., Hayhoe, M. M., & MacLeod, D. I. A. (1990) The spread of adaptation in human foveal and parafoveal cone vision. *Vision Res., 30*, 1603–1615. {6}

Cinerman, G. A. *see* Grigg

Clark, F. J. *see* Burgess

Clark, G. M. *see* Tong

Clark, L. F. *see* Kiang

Clarke, P. G. H., Donaldson, I. M. L., & Whitteridge, D. (1976) Binocular mechanisms in cortical areas I and II of the sheep. *J. Physiol., 256*, 509–526. {11}

Cleland, B. G., & Enroth-Cugell, C. (1968) Quantitative aspects of sensitivity and summation in the cat retina. *J. Physiol., 198*, 17–38. {6}

Cleland, B. G., Dubin, M. W., & Levick, W. R. (1971) Sustained and transient neurones in the cat's retina and lateral geniculate nucleus. *J. Physiol., 217*, 473–496. {7}

Cleland, B. G., & Lee, B. B. (1985) A comparison of visual responses of cat lateral geniculate nucleus neurones with those of ganglion cells afferent to them. *J. Physiol., 369*, 249–268. {7}

Cleland, B. G., & Levick, W. R. (1974) Brisk and sluggish concentrically organized ganglion cells in the cat's retina. *J. Physiol., 240*, 421–456. {5}

Cleland, B. G., Levick, W. R., & Sanderson, K. J. (1973) Properties of sustained and transient ganglion cells in the cat retina. *J. Physiol., 228*, 649–680. {7}

Cleland, B. G., Levick, W. R., & Wässle, H. (1975) Physiological identification of a morphological class of cat retinal ganglion cells. *J. Physiol., 248*, 151–171. {5}

Cleland, B. G. *see also* Dubin; Levine

Clock, A. E. *see* Middlebrooks

Clymer, A. B. *see* Matin

Colby, C. L., Duhamel, J.-R., & Goldberg, M. E. (1995) Oculocentric spatial representation in parietal cortex. *Cerebr. Cort., 5*, 470–481. {8}

Colby, C. L. *see also* Duhamel

Coleman, P. D., Flood, D. G., Whitehead, M. C., & Emerson, R. C. (1981) Spatial sampling by dendritic trees in visual cortex. *Brain Res., 214*, 1–21. {8}

Comb, M. *see* Herbert

Cometto-Muniz, J. E., & Cain, W. S. (1990) Thresholds for odor and nasal pungency. *Physiol. & Behav., 48*, 719–725. {20}

Cometto-Muniz, J. E., Cain, W. S., & Abraham, M. H. (1998) Nasal pungency and odor of homologous aldehydes and carboxylic acids. *Exp. Brain Res., 118*, 180–188. {20}

Comis, S. D. *see* Pickles

Conradi, N. *see* Sjöstrand

Constantinidis, C. *see* Steinmetz

Conte, M. M. *see* Victor

Contreras, R., & Frank, M. (1979) Sodium deprivation alters neural responses to gustatory stimuli. *J. Gen. Physiol., 73*, 569–594. {20}

Cook, C. A. *see* Koretz

Cooper, F. S., Delattre, P. C., Liberman, A. M., Borst, J. M., & Gerstman, L. J. (1952) Some experiments on the perception of synthetic speech sounds. *J. Acoust. Soc. Am., 24*, 597–606. {18}

Cooper, F. S. *see also* Delattre; Liberman

Cooper, G. F. *see* Blakemore

Cooper, R. M. *see* Thurlow

Cooper, W. E. *see* Eimas

Cooperman, A. M. *see* Glezer

Copenhagen, D. R., & Owen, W. G. (1980) Current-voltage relations in the rod photoreceptor network of the turtle retina. *J. Physiol., 308*, 159–184. {4}

Corbetta, M. (1998) Frontoparietal cortical networks for directing attention and the eye to visual locations: identical, independent, or overlapping neural systems? *Proc. Natl Acad. Sci., 95*, 831–838. {8}

Corbit, J. D. *see* Eimas

Coren, S. (1972) Subjective contours and apparent depth. *Psychol. Rev., 79*, 359–367. {**10.12**}

Coren, S., & Girgus, J. S. (1973) Visual spatial illusions: many explanations. *Science, 179*, 503–504. {12}

Coren, S., & Komoda, M. K. (1973) Apparent lightness as a function of perceived direction of incident illumination. *Am. J. Psychol., 86*, 345–349. {12}

Coren, S., Porac, C., & Ward, L. M. (1979) *Sensation and Perception.* New York: Academic Press. {12, **12.5**, **12.25**}

Corey, D. P., & Hudspeth, A. J. (1979) Ionic basis of the receptor potential in a vertebrate hair cell. *Nature, 281*, 675–677. {15}

Corey, D. P., & Hudspeth, A. J. (1983) Kinetics of the receptor current in bullfrog saccular hair cells. *J. Neurosci., 3*, 962–976. {15}

Cormack, R. H. *see* Blake

Cornelissen, P. L., Hansen, P. C., Hutton, J. L., Evangelinou, V., & Stein, J. F. (1998) Magnocellular visual function and childrens single word reading. *Vision Res., 38*, 471–482.

Cornelissen, F. W. *see also* Foster

Cornsweet, T. N. (1970) *Visual Perception.* New York: Academic Press. {14}

Cornwell, P. *see* Lomber

Corwin, T. *see* Green

Cosgrove, R. *see* Seeck

Costanzo, R. M., & Gardner, E. P. (1980) A quantitative analysis of responses of direction sensitive neurons in somatosensory cortex of awake monkeys. *J. Neurophysiol., 43*, 1319–1341. {19, **19.9**}

Courtney, S. M., & Buchsbaum, G. (1991) Temporal differences between color pathways within the retina as a possible origin of subjective colors. *Vision Res., 31*, 1541–1548. {14}

Courtney, S. M., Ungerleider, L. G., Keil, K., & Haxby, J. V. (1996) Object and spatial visual working memory activate separate neural systems in human cortex. *Cerebr. Cort., 6*, 39–49. {8}

Cowan, J. D. *see* Williams

Cowan, W. M. *see* Dowling

Cowey, A. (1996) Visual awareness: still at sea with seeing? *Curr. Biol., 6*, 45–47. {7}

Cowey, A. *see also* Gulyás

Cowey, A., & Wilkinson, F. (1991) The role of the corpus callosum and extra striate visual areas in stereoacuity in macaque monkeys. *Neuropsychol., 29*, 465–479. {11}

Cox, J. F. *see* Rowe

Craig, A. D., & Bushnell, M. C. (1994) The thermal grill illusion: unmasking the burn of pain. *Science, 265*, 252–255. {19}

Cramer, R. P. *see* Wilson

Craven, B. J. *see* Foster

Craver-Lemley, C., & Reeves, A. (1992) How visual imagery interferes with vision. *Psychol. Rev., 99*, 633–649. {8}

Crawford, B. H. *see* Stiles

Creutzfeldt, O. D., Crook, J. M., Kastner, S., Li, C.-Y., & Pei, X. (1991a) The neurophysiological correlates of colour and brightness contrast in lateral geniculate neurons. I. Population analysis. *Exp. Brain Res., 87*, 3–21. {14}

Creutzfeldt, O. D., Kastner, S., Pei, X., & Valberg, A. (1991b) The neurophysiological correlates of colour and brightness contrast in lateral geniculate neurons. II. Adaptation and surround effects. *Exp. Brain Res., 87*, 22–45. {14}

Creutzfeldt, O. *see also* Grüsser; Volgushev

Croner, L. J., & Kaplan, E. (1995) Receptive fields of P and M ganglion cells across the primate retina. *Vision Res., 35*, 7–24. {7}

Crook, J. M., & Eysel, U. T. (1992) GABA-induced inactivation of functionally characterized sites in cat visual cortex (area 18): effects on orientation tuning. *J. Neurosci., 12*, 1816–1825. {7}

Crook, J. M., Kisvárday, Z. F., & Eysel, U. T. (1997) GABA-induced inactivation of functionally characterized sites in cat striate cortex: effects on orientation tuning and direction selectivity. *Visual Neurosci., 14*, 141–158. {7}

Crook, J. M., Kisvárday, Z. F., & Eysel, U. T. (1998) Evidence for a contribution of lateral inhibition to orientation tuning and direction selectivity in cat visual cortex: reversible inactivation of functionally characterized sites combined with neuroanatomical tracing techniques. *Eur. J. Neurosci., 10*, 2056–2075. {7}

Crook, J. M. *see also* Creutzfeldt

Crouch, J. F., & McClintic, J. R. (1971) *Human Anatomy and Physiology.* New York: Wiley. {3.10}

Crouch, R. K., Chader, G. J., Wiggert, B., &

Pepperberg, D. R. (1996) Retinoids and the visual process. *Photochem. & Photobiol., 64*, 613–621. {4}

Cudeiro, J., & Sillito, A. M. (1996) Spatial frequency tuning of orientation-discontinuity-sensitive cortigofugal feedback to the cat lateral geniculate nucleus. *J. Physiol., 490*, 481–492. {7}

Cudeiro, J. *see also* Alonso

Cuenca, N. *see* Kolb

Cunningham, J. R. *see* Neal

Cultan, R. *see* Wong-Riley

Cutting, J. E., & Eimas, P. D. (1975) Phonetic feature analyzers and the processing of speech in infants. In: J. F. Kavanagh & J. E. Cutting (Eds.), *The Role of Speech in Language* (pp. 127–148) Cambridge, MA: MIT Press. {18}

Cutting, J. E., & Rosner, B. S. (1974) Categories and boundaries in speech and music. *Percept. Psychophys., 20*, 55–60. {18}

Cynader, M., Berman, N., & Hein, A. (1973) Cats reared in stroboscopic illumination: effects on receptive fields in visual cortex. *Proc. Natl Acad. Sci., 70*, 1353–1354. {8}

Cynader, M., & Chernenko, G. (1976) Abolition of directional sensitivity in the visual cortex of the cat. *Science, 193*, 504–505. {8}

Cynader, M., & Regan, D. (1982) Neurons in cat visual cortex tuned to the direction of motion in depth: effect of positional disparity. *Vision Res., 22*, 967–982. {8}

Cynader, M. *see also* Berman; Giaschi

Dacey, D. M. (1990) The dopaminergic amacrine cell. *J. Comp. Neurol., 301*, 461–489. {6}

Dacey, D. M. (1996) Circuitry for color coding in the primate retina. *Proc. Natl Acad. Sci., 93*, 582–588. {14}

Dacey, D. M. *see also* Stafford

Dacheux, R. F., & Miller, R. F. (1976) Photoreceptor-bipolar cell transmission in the perfused retina eyecup of the mudpuppy. *Science, 191*, 963–964. {4}

Dacheux, R. F. *see also* Miller

Dallenbach, K. *see* Abrahams; Krakauer

Dallos, P. (1996) Overview: cochlear neurobiology. In: P. Dallos, A. N. Popper, & R. R. Fay (Eds.), *The Cochlea* (pp. 1–43) New York: Springer. {16}

Dallos, P., & Evans, B. N. (1995) High-frequency motility of outer hair cells and the cochlear amplifier. *Science, 267*, 2006–2009. [also: High-frequency outer hair cell motility: corrections and addendum. (1995) *Science, 268*, 1420–1421.] {16}

Dallos, P., & Harris, D. (1978) Properties of auditory nerve responses in absence of outer hair cells. *J. Neurophysiol., 41*, 365–383. {16}

Dallos, P., Santos-Sacchi, J., & Flock, A. (1982) Intracellular recordings from cochlear outer hair cells. *Science, 218*, 582–584. {15, 16}

Damasio, A. R. (1981) Central achromatopsia. *Neurology, 31*, 920–921. {8}

Damasio, A. R. (1985) Disorders of complex visual processing: agnosias, achromatopsia, Balint's Syndrome, and related difficulties of orientation and construction. In M. M. Mesulam (Ed.), *Principles of Behavioral Neurology*. Philadelphia: F. A. Davis. {8}

Damasio, A. R., & Benton, A. L. (1979) Impairment of hand movements under visual guidance. *Neurology, 29*, 170–178. {8}

Daniel, P. M., & Whitteridge, D. (1961) The representation of the visual field on the cerebral cortex of monkeys. *J. Physiol., 159*, 203–221. {7}

Darien-Smith, I. *see* Mountcastle; Sanderson

Darling, W. G., & Hondzinski, J. M. (1997) Visual perceptions of vertical and intrinsic longitudinal axes. *Exp. Brain Res., 116*, 485–492. {10}

Darwin, C. J. (1975) On the dynamic use of prosody in speech perception. In A. Cohen and S. G. Nooteboom (Eds.), *Structure and Process in Speech Perception* (pp. 178–193). New York: Springer-Verlag. {18}

Daughters, R. S. *see* Mantyh

Daugman, J. G. (1984) Spatial visual channels in the Fourier plane. *Vision Res., 24*, 891–910. {9}

David, A. S. *see* Calvert

Davis, G., & Driver, J. (1994) Parallel detection of Kanizsa subjective figures in the human visual system. *Nature, 371*, 791–793. {10}

Davis, H. *see* Stevens

Daw, N. W. (1968) Colour coded ganglion cells in the goldfish retina: extension of their receptive field properties by means of new stimuli. *J. Physiol., 197*, 567–592. {14}

Daw, N. W., & Wyatt, H. J. (1976) Kittens reared in a unidirectional environment: evidence for a critical period. *J. Physiol., 257*, 155–170. {8}

Dawson, W. W., & Perez, J. M. (1973) Unusual retinal cells in the dolphin eye. *Science, 181*, 747–749. {4}

Day, R. H. (1965) Inappropriate constancy explanation of spatial distortions. *Nature, 207*, 891–893. {12}

DeAngelis, G. C., Ohzawa, I., & Freeman, R. D. (1993) Spatiotemporal organization of simple-cell receptive fields in the cat's striate cortex. II. Linearity of temporal and spatial summation. *J. Neurophysiol., 69*, 1118–1135. {7}

DeAngelis, G. C. *see also* Ohzawa

Debanne, D., Shulz, D. E., & Frégnac, Y. (1998) Activity-dependent regulation of 'on' and 'off' responses in cat visual cortical receptive fields. *J. Physiol., 508. 2*, 523–548. {7}

DeBruyn, E. J., Casagrande, V. A., Beck, P. D., & Bonds, A. B. (1993) Visual resolution and sensitivity of single cells in the primary visual cortex (V1) of a nocturnal primate (bush baby): correlations with cortical layers and cytochrome oxidase patterns. *J. Neurophysiol., 69*, 3–18. {7}

DeClerk, J. *see* Ladefoged

Dehan, R. S. *see* Graziadei

Dekorver, L. *see* Kolb

Delattre, P. C., Liberman, A. M., & Cooper, F. S. (1955) Acoustic loci and transitional cues for consonants. *J. Acoust. Soc. Am., 27*, 769–773. {18, **18.11, 18.12**}

Delattre, P. C. *see also* Cooper; Liberman

Delpuech, C. *see* Tallon-Baudry

DeMarco, P. J. *see* Bilotta

DeMonasterio, F. M., Gouras, P., & Tolhurst, D. J. (1975) Trichromatic colour opponency in ganglion cells of the rhesus monkey retina. *J. Physiol., 251*, 197–216. {14}

Derrington, A. M. (1990) Mechanisms for coding luminance patterns: are they really linear? In: C. Blakemore (Ed.), *Vision: Coding and Efficiency* (pp. 175–184). Cambridge: Cambridge University Press. {4}

Derrington, A. M., & Badcock, D. R. (1985) The low level motion system has both chromatic and luminance inputs. *Vision Res., 25*, 1879–1884. {13}

Derrington, A. M., & Henning, G. B. (1993) Linear and non-linear mechanisms in pattern vision. *Curr. Biol., 3*, 800–803. {9}

Derrington, A. M., & Suero, M. (1991) Motion of complex patterns is computed from the perceived motions of their components. *Vision Res., 31*, 139–149. {13}

DeSimone, J. A. *see* Ye

Desimone, R., Schein, S. J., Moran, J., & Ungerleider, L. G. (1985) Contour, color and shape analysis beyond the striate cortex. *Vision Res., 25*, 441–452. {8}

Desimone, R. *see also* Bruce; Chelazzi; Lehky; Lueschow; Spitzer

Desmedt, J. E. (1960) Neurophysiological mechanisms controlling acoustic input. In G. L. Rasmussen and W. F. Windle (Eds.), *Neural Mechanisms of the Auditory and Vestibular Systems.* Springfield, IL: Charles C Thomas. {15}

DeSouza, J. F. X. *see* Aglioti

DeValois, K. (1977) Independence of black and white: phase-specific adaptation. *Vision Res., 17*, 209–215. {9}

DeValois, K. K., & Tootell, R. B. H. (1983) Spatial frequency-specific inhibition in cat striate cortex cells. *J. Physiol., 336*, 359–376. {9}

DeValois, K. (K.) *see also* Bradley

DeValois, R. L. (1978) Spatial processing of luminance and color information. *Invest. Ophthalmol., 17*, 834–835. {9}

DeValois, R. L., Abramov, I., & Jacobs, G. H. (1966) Analysis of response patterns of LGN cells. *J. Opt. Soc. Am., 56*, 966–977 {14, 14.19}

DeValois, R. L., Albrecht, D. G., & Thorell, L. G. (1982) Spatial frequency selectivity of cells in macaque visual cortex. *Vision Res., 22*, 545–559. {7, 9}

DeValois, R. L., Morgan, H. C., Polson, M. C., Mead, W. R., & Hull, E. M. (1974) Psychophysical studies of monkey vision. I: Macaque luminosity and color vision tests. *Vision Res., 14*, 53–67. {2, 14}

DeValois, R. L., Yund, E. W., & Hepler, N. (1982) The orientation and direction selectivity of cells in macaque visual cortex. *Vision Res., 22*, 531–544. {7}@references:DeValois, R. L. *see also* Albrecht; Tootell

DeVries, S. H., & Baylor, D. A. (1995) An alternative pathway for signal flow from rod photoreceptors to ganglion cells in mammalian retina. *Proc. Natl. Acad. Sci., 92*, 10 658–10 662. {4}

DeYoe, E. A., Felleman, D. J., Van Essen, D. C., & McClendon, E. (1994) Multiple processing streams in occipitotemporal visual cortex. *Nature, 371*, 151–154. {8}

DeYoe, E. A., Trusk, T. C., & Wong-Riley, M. T. T. (1995) Activity correlates of cytochrome oxidase-defined compartments in granular and supragranular layers of primary visual cortex of the macaque monkey. *Visual Neurosci., 12*, 629–639. {8}

DeYoe, E. A., & Van Essen, D. C. (1988) Concurrent processing streams in monkey visual cortex. *Trends in Neurosci., 11*, 219–226. {8, 8.6}

Diamant, H., Oakley, B., Strom, L., Wells, C., & Zotterman, Y. (1965) A comparison of neural and psychophysical responses to taste stimuli in man. *Acta Physiol. Scand., 64*, 67–74. {20.4}

van Dijk, B. W. *see* Lamme

Dill, M., & Fahle, M. (1997) The role of visual field position in pattern-discrimination learning. *Proc. Roy. Soc. Lond. B, 264*, 1031–1036. {10}

Di Lollo, V. *see* Bischoff

Ding, Y., & Casagrande, V. A. (1997) The distribution and morphology of LGN K pathway axons within the layers and CO blobs of owl monkey V1. *Visual Neurosci., 14*, 691–704. {8}

Djamgoz, M. B. A., Reynolds, S. H., Rowe, J. S., & Ruddock, K. H. (1981) Control of retinal S-potentials in dark adapted and bleached retina. *Vision Res., 21*, 1581–1584. {6}

Dobbins, A. C., Jeo, R. M., Fiser, J., & Allman, J. M. (1998) Distance modulation of neural activity in the visual cortex. *Science, 281*, 552–555. {11, 12}

Dobelle, W. H. *see* Marks

Dodd, J. *see* Akabas

Dodwell, P. C., & O'Shea, R. P. (1987) Global factors generate the McCollough effect. *Vision Res., 27*, 569–580. {9}

Donaldson, I. M. L. *see* Clarke

Dong, C.-J., & McReynolds, J. S. (1991) The relationship between light, dopamine release, and horizontal cell coupling in the mudpuppy retina. *J. Physiol., 440*, 291–309. {6}

Dong, C.-J., & McReynolds, J. S. (1992) Comparison of the effects of flickering and steady light on dopamine release and horizontal cell coupling in the mudpuppy retina. *J. Neurophysiol., 67*, 364–372. {6}

van Doorn, A. J. *see* van de Grind

Dorman, M. F., Raphael, L. J., & Liberman, A. M. (1979) Some experiments on the sound of silence in phonetic perception. *J. Acoust. Soc. Am., 65*, 1518–1532. {18}

Douglas, R. *see* Giaschi

Dow, B. M. *see* Baxter

Dowell, R. C. *see* Tong

Dowling, J. E. (1965) Foveal receptors of the monkey retina: Fine structure. *Science, 147*, 57–59. {4.7}

Dowling, J. E. (1967) The organization of vertebrate visual receptors. In J. M. Allen (Ed.), *Molecular*

Organization and Biological Function (pp. 186–210) New York: Harper & Row. {**4.4**}

Dowling, J. E. (1968) Synaptic organization of the frog retina: an electron microscopic analysis comparing the retinas of frogs and primates. *Proc. R. Soc. Lond. Ser. B., 170*, 205–228. {4}

Dowling, J. E. (1970) Organization of vertebrate retinas. *Invest. Ophthalmol., 9*, 655–680. {4, **4.10**}

Dowling, J. E. (1977) Receptoral and network mechanisms of visual adaptation. *Neurosci. Res. Prog. Bull., 15*, 397–407. {6}

Dowling, J. E. (1978) How the retina 'sees.' *Invest. Ophthalmol., 17*, 832–834. {4}

Dowling, J. E. (1979) A new retinal neurone – the interplexiform cell. *Trends in Neurosci., 2*, 189–191. {6}

Dowling, J. E. (1989) Neuromodulation in the retina: the role of dopamine. *Seminars in Neurosci., 1*, 35–43. {6}

Dowling, J. E., & Boycott, B. B. (1965) Neural connections of the retina: fine structure of the inner plexiform layer. *Cold Spring Harbor Symp. Quant. Biol., 30*, 393–402. {**4.9**}

Dowling, J. E., & Boycott, B. B. (1966) Organization of the primate retina: electron microscopy. *Proc. R. Soc. Lond. Ser. B., 166*, 80–111. {4}

Dowling, J. E., & Cowan, W. M. (1966) An electron microscopic study of normal and degenerating centrifugal fiber terminals in the pigeon retina. *Z. Zellforsch. Mikrosk. Anat., 71*, 14–28. {4, 15}

Dowling, J. E., & Ehinger, B. (1975) Synaptic organization of the amine-containing interplexiform cells of the goldfish and cebus monkey retinas. *Science, 188*, 270–273. {4}

Dowling, J. E., & Ehinger, B. (1978a) The interplexiform cell system. I. Synapses of the dopaminergic neurons of the goldfish retina. *Proc. R. Soc. Lond. Ser. B., 201*, 7–26. {4}

Dowling, J. E., & Ehinger, B. (1978b) Synaptic organization of the dopaminergic neurons in the rabbit retina. *J. Comp. Neurol., 180*, 203–220. {4}

Dowling, J. E., & Ripps, H. (1976) Potassium and retinal sensitivity. *Brain Res. 107*, 617–622. {6}

Dowling, J. E. *see also* Boycott; Gold; Hedden; Kleinschmidt; Pepperberg; Werblin

Downer, J. C. *see* Brooke

Draper, S. W. (1978) The Penrose triangle and a family of related figures. *Perception, 7*, 283–296. {10, **10.36**}

Dreher, B. (1972) Hypercomplex cells in the cat's visual cortex. *Invest. Ophthalmol., 11*, 355–356. {7}

Dreher, B., Fukada, Y., & Rodieck, R. W. (1976) Identification, classification and anatomical segregation of cells with X-like and Y-like properties in the lateral geniculate nucleus of old-world primates. *J. Physiol., 258*, 433–452. {7}

Dreher, B. *see also* Leventhal; Stone; Wang

Drexler, W., Findl, O., Schmetterer, L., Hitzenberger, C. K., & Fercher, A. F. (1998) Eye elongation during accommodation in humans: differences between emmetropes and myopes. *Investig. Ophthal. & Vis. Sci., 39*, 2140–2147. {3}

Driver, J. *see* Davis

Drugan, R. C. *see* Maier

Drum, B. (1982) Summation of rod and cone responses at absolute threshold. *Vision Res., 22*, 823–826. {6}

Dubin, M. W. (1970) The inner plexiform layer of the vertebrate retina: a quantitative and comparative electron microscopic analysis. *J. Comp. Neurol., 140*, 479–506. {4}

Dubin, M. W., & Cleland, B. G. (1977) Organization of visual inputs to interneurons of the lateral geniculate nucleus of the cat. *J. Neurophysiol., 40*, 410–427. {7}

Dubin, M. W. *see also* Cleland

Dubner, R. *see* Price

Dubuisson, D. *see* Seeck

Duclaux, R., & Kenshalo, D. R. (1980) Response characteristics of cutaneous warm receptors in the monkey. *J. Neurophysiol., 43*, 1–15. {19}

Duclaux, R. *see also* Kenshalo

Duhamel, J.-R., Colby, C. L., & Goldberg, M. E. (1992) The updating of the representation of visual space in parietal cortex by intended eye movements. *Science, 255*, 90–92. {8}

Duhamel, J.-R. *see also* Colby

Dulai, K. S. *see* Hunt

Duncan, G. H. *see* Rainville; Talbot

Duncan, J. *see* Chelazzi

Duncker, K. (1939) The influence of past experience upon perceptual properties. *Am. J. Psychol., 52*, 255–265. {20}

Dunn, H. K. *see* Koenig

Dürsteler, M. R., & Wurtz, R. H. (1988) Pursuit and optokinetic deficits following chemical lesions of cortical areas MT and MST. *J. Neurophysiol., 60*, 940–965. {8}

Dürsteler, M. R. *see also* von der Heydt

Duus, P. (1989) *Topical Diagnosis in Neurology* 2nd edn Stuttgart: Georg Thieme Verlag. {**19.5**}

D'Zmura, M. *see* Lennie

Eady, H. R. *see* Klumpp

Earnest, M. *see* Wong-Riley

Easland, G. S. *see* Wasserman

Easter, S. S. (1968a) Excitation in the goldfish retina: evidence for a non-linear intensity code. *J. Physiol., 195,* 253–271. {2, 12}

Easter, S. S. (1968b) Adaptation in the goldfish retina. *J. Physiol., 195,* 273–281. {6}

Easton, A. M. *see* Festinger

Ebrey, T. G., & Honig, B. (1977) New wavelength-dependent visual pigment nomograms. *Vision Res., 17,* 147–151. {14, **4.6, 14.10**}

Eccardt, T. *see* Repp

Eckhorn, R., Bauer, R., Jordan, W., Brosch, M., Kruse, W., Munk, M., & Reitboeck, H. J. (1988) Cherent oscillations: a mechanism of feature linking in the visual cortex? *Biol. Cybern., 60,* 121–130. {10}

Eckhorn, R., & Obermueller, A. (1993) Single neurons are differently involved in stimulus specific oscillations in cat visual cortex. *Exp. Brain Res., 95,* 177–182. {7, 10}

Eddy, R. L. *see* Nathans

Edelman, G. M. (1987) *Neural Darwinism: The Theory of Neuronal Group Selection.* New York: Basic Books. {10}

Edelman, G. M. *see also* Tononi; Wray

Edelman, I. *see also* Simon

Edelman, S., & Weinshall, D. (1991) A self-organizing multiple-view representation of 3D objects. *Biol. Cybern., 64,* 209–219. {10}

Edelstyn, N. M. J., & Hammond, P. (1988) Relationship between cortical lamination and texture sensitivity in complex neurones of the striate cortex in cats. *J. Comp. Neurol., 278,* 397–404. {10}

Edwards, M. W. *see* Matin

Egan, J. P., & Hake, H. W. (1950) On the masking pattern of a simple auditory stimulus. *J. Acoust. Soc. Am., 22,* 622–630. {17, **17.11**}

Egan, J. P. *see also* Postman

Egan, R. *see* Wong-Riley

Ehinger, B., Falck, B., & Laties, A. M. (1969) Adrenergic neurons in teleost retina. *Z. Zellforsch., 97,* 285–297. {4}

Ehinger, B. *see also* Dowling

Eimas, P. D., & Corbit, J. D. (1973) Selective adaptation of linguistic feature detectors. *Cognit. Psychol., 4,* 99–109. {18}

Eimas, P. D., Cooper, W. E., & Corbit, J. D. (1973) Some properties of linguistic feature detectors. *Percept. Psychophys., 13,* 247–252. {18}

Eimas, P. D. *see also* Cutting; Liberman; Miller

Ejima, Y. *see* Ohtani

Ekblom, A. *see* Hansson

Ekelid, M. *see* Shannon

Ekman, G. (1964) Is the power law a special case of Fechner's law? *Perceptual and Motor Skills, 19,* 730. {2}

Elepfandt, A. *see* Lee

Eliasof, S., Barnes, S., & Werblin, F. (1987) The interaction of ionic currents mediating single spike activity in retinal amacrine cells of the tiger salamander. *J. Neurosci., 7,* 3512–3524. {4}

Elston, G. N., & Rosa, M. G. P. (1998) Morphological variation of layer III pyramidal neurones in the occipitotemporal pathway of the macaque monkey visual cortex. *Cerebr. Cortex, 8,* 278–294. {8}

Emerson, R. C., Bergen, J. R., & Adelson, E. H. (1992) Directionally selective complex cells and the computation of motion energy in cat visual cortex. *Vision Res., 32,* 203–218. {7}

Emerson, R. C. *see also* Coleman; Stevens

Engel, A. K., König, P., Kreiter, A. K., Schillen, T. B., & Singer, W. (1992) Temporal coding in the visual cortex: new vistas on integration in the nervous system. *Trends in Neurosci., 15,* 218–226. {7, 10}

Engel, A. K. *see also* Fries

Enoch, J. M. (1963) Optical properties of the retinal receptors. *J. Opt. Soc. Am., 53,* 71–85. {6}

Enright, J. T. (1991) Exploring the third dimension with eye movements: better than stereopsis. *Vision Res., 31,* 1549–1562. {11}

Enroth, C. (1952) The mechanism of flicker and fusion studied on single retinal elements in the dark-adapted eye of the cat. *Acta. Physiol. Scand., 27* (Suppl. 100), 1–67. {12}

Enroth-Cugell, C., & Pinto, L. H. (1970) Algebraic summation of centre and surround inputs to retinal ganglion cells of the cat. *Nature, 226,* 458–459. {12}

Enroth-Cugell, C., & Robson, J. G. (1966) The contrast sensitivity of retinal ganglion cells of the cat. *J. Physiol., 187,* 517–552. {5, **5.12, 5.13**}

Enroth-Cugell, C., & Shapley, R. M. (1973) Flux, not retinal illumination, is what cat retinal ganglion cells really care about. *J. Physiol. 233*, 311–326. {6}

Enroth-Cugell, C. *see also* Cleland; Jakiela; Levine; Shapley; Troy

Epstein, W., & Baratz, S. S. (1964) Relative size in isolation as a stimulus for relative perceived distance. *J. Exp. Psychol., 67*, 507–513. {11}

Erickson, R. G., & Thier, P. (1991) A neuronal correlate of spatial stability during periods of self-induced visual motion. *Exp. Brain Res., 86*, 608–616. {13}

Erickson, R. G. *see also* Thier

Erwin, E., Obermayer, K., & Schulten, K. (1995) Models of orientation and ocular dominance columns in the visual cortex: a critical comparison. *Neural Comput., 7*, 425–468. {8}

Eskandar, E. N., Richmond, B. J., & Optican, L. M. (1992) Role of inferior temporal neurons in visual memory I. Temporal encoding of information about visual images, recalled images, and behavioral context. *J. Neurophysiol., 68*, 1277–1295. {10}

Essick, G. K. *see* Andersen

Evangelinou, V. *see* Cornelissen

Evans, A. C. *see* Talbot; Zatorre

Evans, B. N. *see* Dallos

Evans, E. F. *see* Whitfield

Evans, J. A., Hood, D. C., & Holtzman, E. (1978) Differential effects of cobalt ions on rod and cone synaptic activity in the isolated frog retina. *Vision Res., 18*, 145–151. {4}

Eyding, D. *see* Eysel

Eysel, U. T., Eyding, D., & Schweigart, G. (1998) Repetitive optical stimulation elicits fast receptive field changes in mature visual cortex. *NeuroRep., 9*, 949–954. {10}

Eysel, U. T., Muche, T., & Wörgötter, F. (1988) Lateral interactions at direction-selective striate neurones in the cat demonstrated by local cortical inactivation. *J. Physiol. 399*, 657–675. {7}

Eysel, U. T. *see also* Crook; Wörgötter

Fahle, M. (1982) Binocular rivalry: suppression depends on orientation and spatial frequency. *Vision Res., 22*, 787–800. {11}

Fahle, M. *see also* Dill

Fain, G. L. (1975) Quantum sensitivity of rods in the toad retina. *Science, 187*, 838–841. {4}

Fain, G. L. *see also* Matthews

Falck, B. *see* Ehinger

Famiglietti, E. V., & Kolb, H. (1976) Structural basis for ON- and OFF-center responses in retinal ganglion cells. *Science, 194*, 193–195. {4}

Farber, D. B., Brown, B. M., & Lolley, R. N. (1978) Cyclic GMP: proposed role in visual cell function. *Vision Res., 18*, 497–499. {4}

Fattori, P. *see* Battaglini

Fatt, P., & Katz, B. (1952) Spontaneous subthreshold activity at motor nerve endings. *J. Physiol., 117*, 109–128. {A}

Fatt, P., & Katz, B. (1954) Quantal components of the end-plate potential. *J. Physiol., 124*, 560–573. {A}

Favreau, O. E. *see* Cavanagh

Fedderson, W. E. *see* Sandel

Feder, H. H. *see* Johns

Feeser, H. R. *see* McCormick

Feigenspan, A., Gustincich, S., Bean, B. P., & Raviola, E. (1998) Spontaneous activity of solitary dopaminergic cells of the retina, *J. Neurosci., 18*, 6776–6789. {4, 5}

Feldon, S. E. *see* Pollen

Feldtkeller, R. *see* Zwicker

Felleman, D. J. *see* DeYoe

Felsten, G. *see* Wasserman

Fender, D. H. *see* Lu

Fendrich, R., Wessinger, C. M., & Gazzaniga, M. S. (1992) Residual vision in a scotoma: implications for blindsight. *Science, 258*, 1489–1491. {7}

Fenstemaker, S. B. *see* Kiper

Fercher, A. F. *see* Drexler

Ferguson, G. A. *see* Mooney

Ferster, D. (1988) Spatially opponent excitation and inhibition in simple cells of the cat visual cortex. *J. Neurosci., 8*, 1172–1180. {7}

Ferster, D., & Koch, C. (1987) Neuronal connections underlying orientation selectivity in cat visual cortex. *Trends in Neurosci., 10*, 487–492. {7}

Ferster, D. *see also* Carandini; Jagadeesh

Fertig, E. *see* Stark

Fesenko, E. E., Kolesnikov, S. S., & Lyubarsky, A. L. (1985) Induction by cyclic GMP of cationic conductance in plasma membrane of retinal rod outer segment. *Nature, 313*, 310–313. {4}

Festinger, L., & Easton, A. M. (1974) Inferences about

the efferent system based on a perceptual illusion produced by eye movements. *Psychol. Rev., 18*, 44–58. {13, **13.5**}

Fetter, M. *see* Tweed

Fetz, E. E. *see* Komatsu

Fields, H. L. (1987) *Pain.* New York: McGraw Hill. {19}

Fillenbaum, S., Schiffman, H. R., & Butcher, J. (1965) Perceptions of off-size versions of a familiar object under conditions of rich information. *J. Exp. Psychol., 69*, 298–303. {11}

Findl, O. *see* Drexler

Fink, E. A. *see* Pastore

Finlay, B. L. *see* Schiller

Fiorani, M., Rosa, M. G. P., Gattass, R., & Rocha-Mirand, C. E. (1992) Dynamic surrounds of receptive fields in primate striate cortex: a physiological basic for perceptual completion? *Proc. Natl Acad. Sci., 89*, 8547–8551. {8}

Fiorentini, A., & Berardi, N. (1997) Visual perceptual learning: a sign of neural plasticity at early stages of visual processing. *Arch. Ital. Biol., 135*, 157–167. {10}

Fiorentini, A. *see also* Maffei

Fischler, H., Frei, E., Spira, D., & Rubinstein, M. (1967) Dynamic response of middle ear structures. *J. Acoust. Soc. Am., 41*, 1220–1231. {15}

Fiser, J. *see* Dobbins

Fisher, G. H. (1970) An experimental and theoretical appraisal of the perspective and size-constancy theories of illusions. *Quart. J. Exp. Psychol., 22*, 631–652. {12}

Fisher, H. G. *see* Freedman

Fisher, L. J. (1979) Interplexiform cell of the mouse retina: a Golgi demonstration. *Invest. Ophthalmol., 18*, 521–523. {4}

Fisher, S. K. *see* Boycott; Kolb

Fisicaro, S. A. *see* Bernstein

Fitzgerald, H. E. (1968) Autonomic pupillary reflex activity during early infancy and its relation to social and non-social visual stimuli. *Dissertation Abstracts, 28*, 3896–3897B. {3}

FitzHugh, R. *see* Barlow

Fitzpatrick, D. C., Batra, R., Stanford, T. R., & Kuwada, S. (1997) A neuronal population code for sound localization. *Nature, 388*, 871–874. {17}

Fize, D. *see* Thorpe

Flaming, D. G., & Brown, K. T. (1979) Effects of calcium on the intensity-response curve of toad rods. *Nature, 278*, 852–853. {4}

Flock, A. *see* Dallos; Gibson

Flood, D. G. *see* Coleman

Flottorp, G. *see* Zwicker

Fodor, J. A., & Bever, T. G. (1965) The psychological reality' of linguistic segments. *J. Verb. Learn. Verb. Behav., 4*, 414–420. {18}

Forestner, D. M. *see* Wilson

Foster, D. H., Nascimento, S. M. C., Craven, B. J., Linnell, K. J., Cornelissen, F. W., & Brenner, E. (1997) Four issues concerning colour constancy and relational colour constancy. *Vision Res., 37*, 1341–1345. {14}

Fothergill, L. A. *see* Hughes

Fox, C. R. *see* Matin

Fox, J. A. *see* Bernstein

Fox, R. *see* Lehmkuhle

Frank, H. A. *see* Warfield

Frank, M. (1975) Response patterns of rat glossopharyn-geal taste neurons. In D. A. Denton & J. P. Coghlan (Eds.), *Olfaction and Taste V* (pp. 59–64. (New York: Academic Press). {20}

Frank, M. *see also* Contreras; Nowlis

Freed, M. A., Smith, R. G., & Sterling, P. (1987) Rod bipolar array in the cat retina: pattern of input from rods and GABA-accumulating amacrine cells. *J. Comp. Neurol., 266*, 445–455. {4}

Freed, M. A. *see also* Smith

Freedman, S. J., & Fisher, H. G. (1968) The role of the pinna in auditory localization. In S. J. Freedman (Ed.), *Neuropsychology of Spatially Oriented Behavior* (pp. 135–152). Pacific Grove, CA.: Brooks/Cole. {15}

Freeman, F. G. *see* Mikulka

Freeman, R. D. *see* DeAngelis; Ghose; Ohzawa; Robson; Stone

Frégnac, Y., Bringuier, V., & Chavane, F. (1996a) Synaptic integration fields and associative plasticity of visual; cortical cells *in vivo. J. Physiol. (Paris), 90*, 367–372. {7, 10}

Frégnac, Y., Bringuier, V., & Chavane, F., Glaeser, L., & Lorenceau, J. (1996b) An intracellular study of space and time representation in primary visual cortical receptive fields. *J. Physiol. (Paris), 90*, 189–197. {7}

Frégnac, Y. *see also* Debanne

Frei, E. *see* Fischler

Friedman, C. *see* Pastore

Fries, P., Roelfsema, P. R., Engel, A. K., König, P., & Singer, W. (1997) Synchronization of oscillatory responses in visual cortex correlates with perception of interocular rivalry. *Proc. Natl Acad. Sci., 94*, 12 699–12 704. {10, 11}

Frisby, J. P. *see* Buckley

Frishkopf, L. S., & Goldstein, M. H. (1963) Responses to acoustic stimuli from single units in the eighth nerve of the bullfrog. *J. Acoust. Soc. Am., 35*, 1219–1228. {18}

Frishman, L. J., & Levine, M. W. (1983) Statistics of the maintained discharge of cat retinal ganglion cells. *J. Physiol., 339*, 475–494. {5}

Frishman, L. J., Reddy, M. G., & Robson, J. G. (1996) Effects of background light on the human dark-adapted electroetinogram and psychophysical threshold. *J. Opt. Soc. Am. A, 13*, 601–612. {6}

Frishman, L. J., Schweitzer-Tong, D. E., & Goldstein, E. B. (1983) Velocity tuning of cells in dorsal lateral geniculate nucleus and retina of the cat. *J. Neurophysiol., 50*, 1393–1414. {7}

Frishman, L. J., & Sieving, P. A. (1995) Evidence for two sites of adaptation affecting the dark-adapted ERG of cats and primates. *Vision Res., 35*, 435–442. {6}

Frishman, L. J., Sieving, P. A., & Steinberg, R. H. (1988) Contributions to the electroretinogram of currents originating in proximal retina. *Visual Neurosci., 1*, 307–315. {6}

Frishman, L. J. *see also* Levine; Robson; Sieving; Steinberg; Viswanathan

Frisina, R. D. *see* Gulick

Frost, B. J., & Nakayama, K. (1983) Single visual neurons code opposing motion independent of direction. *Science, 220*, 744–745. {13}

Frost, B. J. *see also* von Grunau

Frost, D. O. *see* Métin

Frost, J. *see* Wong-Riley

Frumkes, T. E., & Temme, L. A. (1977) Rod-cone interaction in human scotopic vision. II. Cones influence rod increment thresholds. *Vision Res., 17*, 673–679. {6}

Fukada, Y. (1971) Receptive field organization of cat optic nerve fibers with special reference to conduction velocity. *Vision Res., 11*, 209–226. {5}

Fukada, Y., & Saito, H. (1972) Phasic and tonic cells in the cat's lateral geniculate nucleus. *Tohoku J. Exp. Med., 106*, 209–210. {7}

Fukada, Y. *see also* Dreher; Saito

Fukuda, Y., & Stone, J. (1974) Retinal distribution and central projections of Y-, X-, and W-cells of the cat's retina. *J. Neurophysiol., 37*, 749–772. {7}

Fukuda, Y. *see* Stone

Fullenkamp, S. C. *see* Cannon

Fuller, J. H. *see* Miles

Funke, K., & Wörgötter, F. (1997) On the significance of temporally structured activity in the dorsal lateral geniculate nucleus (LGN). *Prog. in Neurobiol., 53*, 67–119. {7, 8, 10}

Fuortes, M. G. F. *see* Baylor

Furness, D. N. *see* Meyer

Fuster, J. M., & Jervey, J. P. (1981) Inferotemporal neurons distinguish and retain behaviorally relevant features of visual stimuli. *Science, 212*, 952–955. {8}

Galambos, R. *see* Rose

Gallego, A. (1971) Horizontal and amacrine cells in the mammal's retina. *Vision Res. Suppl., 3*, 33–50. {4}

Galletti, C., Battaglini, P. P., & Aicardi, G. (1988) 'Real motion' cells in visual area V2 of behaving macaque monkeys. *Exp. Brain Res., 69*, 279–288. {8}

Galletti, C., Battaglini, P. P., & Fattori, P. (1990) 'Real-motion' cells in area V3A of macaque visual cortex. *Exp. Brain Res., 82*, 67–76. {8}

Galletti, C. *see also* Battaglini

Ganz, L. (1966) Mechanism of figural after-effects. *Psychol. Bull., 73*, 128–150. {9}

Ganz, L. *see also* Breitmeyer; Stromeyer

Garcia, J., Kimmeldorf, D. J., & Koelling, F. A. (1955) Conditional aversion to saccharin resulting from exposure to gamma radiation. *Science, 122*, 157–158. {20}

Gardner, E. P. *see* Costanzo

Garzia, R. P. *see* Lehmkuhle

Garner, W. R. (1947) The effect of frequency spectrum on temporal integration of energy in the ear. *J. Acoust. Soc. Am., 19*, 808–815. {2}

Garraghty, P. E. *see* Roe; Sur

Gaska, J. P. *see* Jacobson; Liu; Pollen

Gässler, G. (1954) Über die hörschwelle für schallereignisse mit verschieden breitem frequenzspektrum. *Acustica, 4*, 408–414. {17}

Gattass, R. *see* Fiorani

Gaudiano, P. (1994) Simulations of X and Y retinal ganglion cell behavior with a nonlinear push-pull model of spatiotemporal retinal processing. *Vision Res.,* 34, 1767–1784. {5}

Gawne, T. J., Kjaer, T. W., & Richmond, B. J. (1996) Latency: another potential code for feature binding in striate cortex. *J. Neurophysiol.,* 76, 1356–1360. {10}

Gawne, T. J., Richmond, B. J., & Optican, L. M. (1991) Interactive effects among several stimulus parameters on the responses of striate cortical complex cells. *J. Neurophysiol.,* 66, 379–389. {7}

Gawne, T. J. *see also* Kjaer; Richmond

Gazzaniga, M. S. *see* Fendrich

Geesaman, B. J., & Andersen, R. A. (1996) The analysis of complex motion patterns by form/cue invariant MSTd neurons. *J. Neurosci.,* 16, 4716–4732. {13}

Gegenfurtner, K. R. *see* Kiper

Geisler, W. S. *see* Albrecht

Gelb, A. (1929) Die 'Farbenkonstanz' der Sehdinge. *Handb. Norm. Pathol. Physiol.,* 12, 594–678. {12}

Geldard, F. A. (1972) *The Human Senses,* 2nd edn. New York: Wiley. {16, 17}

Gent, J. F. *see also* McBurney

Georgeson, M. A., & Harris, M. G. (1990) The tempral range of motion sensing and motion perception. *Vision Res.,* 30, 615–619. {13}

Georgopoulos, A. P., Lurito, J. T., Petrides, M., Schwartz, A. B., & Massey, J. T. (1989) Mental rotation of the neuronal population vector. *Science,* 243, 234–236. {10}

Georgopoulos, A. P., Taira, M., & Lukashin, A. (1993) Cognitive neurophysiology of the motor cortex. *Science,* 260, 47–52. {10}

Georgopoulos, A. P. *see also* Pellizzer

Gerhart, K. K. *see* Giesler

Gerstein, G. L. *see* Stevens

Gerstman, L. J. *see* Cooper; Liberman

Gescheider, G. A. *see* Gulick

Geschwind, N. (1972) Language and the brain. *Sci. Am.,* 226, 76–83. {18}

Geschwind, N. (1979) Specializations of the human brain. In: *The Brain* (pp. 108–117). San Francisco: W. H. Freeman. {18}

Gesteland, R. C. (1978) The neural code: integration neural mechanisms. In E. C. Carterette & M. P. Friedman (Eds.), *Handbook of Perception, Vol. VIA: Tasting and Smelling* (pp. 259–276). New York: Academic Press. {20}

Ghilardi, J. R. *see* Mantyh

Ghose, G. M., & Freeman, R. D. (1992) Oscillatory discharge in the visual system: does it have a functional role? *J. Neurophysiol.,* 68, 1558–1574. {10}

Ghose, G. M., Ohzawa, I., & Freeman, R. D. (1994) Receptive-field maps of correlated discharge between pairs of neurons in the cat's visual cortex. *J. Neurophysiol.,* 71, 330–346. {10}

Giaschi, D., Douglas, R., Marlin, S., & Cynader, M. (1933) The time course of direction-selective adaptation in simple and complex cells in cat striate cortex. *J. Neurophysiol.,* 70, 2024–2034. {13}

Gibson, E. J., Gibson, J. J., Smith, O. W., & Flock, H. (1959) Motor parallax as a determinant of perceived depth. *J. Exp. Psychol,* 58, 40–51. {11, **11.12**}

Gibson, J. J. (1937) Adaptation, after-effect and contrast in the perception of tilted lines. II. Simultaneous contrast and the areal restriction of the aftereffect. *J. Exp. Psychol,* 20, 553–569. {9}

Gibson, J. J. (1950) *The Perception of the Visual World.* Boston: Houghton Mifflin. {11, **11.11**}

Gibson, J. J. (1962) Observations on active touch. *Psych. Rev.,* 69, 477–491. {19}

Gibson, J. J. (1966) *The Senses as Perceptual Systems.* Boston: Houghton Mifflin. {13}

Gibson, J. J. (1968) What gives rise to the perception of motion? *Psycho. Rev.,* 75, 335–346. {13}

Gibson, J. J. *see also* Beck; Gibson

Giesler, G. J., Yezierski, R. P., Gerhart, K. K., & Willis, W. D. (1981) Spinothalamic tract neurons that project to medial and/or lateral thalamic nuclei: evidence for a physiologically novel population of spinal cord neurons. *J. Neurophysiol.,* 46, 1285–1308. {19, **19.12**}

Giesler, G. J. *see also* Kenshalo

Gilbert, C. D. (1977) Laminar differences in receptive field properties of cells in cat primary visual cortex. *J. Physiol.,* 268, 391–421. {7}

Gilbert, C. D. (1983) Microcircuitry of the visual cortex. *Ann. Rev. Neurosci.,* 6, 217–247. {7}

Gilbert, C. D., & Wiesel, T. N. (1985) Intrinsic connectivity and receptive field properties in visual cortex. *Vision Res.,* 25, 365–374. {7}

Gilbert, C. D., & Wiesel, T. N. (1992) Receptive field dynamics in adult primary visual cortex. *Nature,* 356, 150–152. {10}

Gilbert, C. D. *see also* Ts'o

Gilchrist, A. L. (1977) Perceived lightness depends on perceived spatial arrangement. *Science, 195,* 185–187. {12}

Ginsburg, A. P. (1975) Is the illusory triangle physical or imaginary? *Nature, 257,* 219–220. {10}

Girard, P., Salin, P. A., & Bullier, J. (1992) Response selectivity of neurons in area MT of the macaque monkey during reversible inactivation of area VI. *J. Neurophysiol., 67,* 1437–1446. {7}

Girard, P. *see also* Salin

Girgus, J. S. *see* Coren

Gjedde, A. *see* Zatorre

Glaeser, L. *see* Frégnac

Glezer, V. D., Cooperman, A. M., Ivanov, V. A., & Tsherbach, T. A. (1976) An investigation of spatial frequency characteristics of the complex receptive fields in the visual cortex of the cat. *Vision Res., 16,* 789–797. {9}

Goede, P. *see* Kolb

Gogel, W. C. (1970) The adjacency principle and three-dimensional visual illusions. *Psychon. Monogr. Suppl., 3,* 153–169. {10}

Gogel, W. C., & Sturm, R. D. (1972) A comparison of accommodative and fusional convergence as cues to distnace. *Percept. Psychophys., 11,* 166–168. {11}

Gogel, W. C. *see also* Mershon

Gold, G. H., & Dowling, J. E. (1979) Photoreceptor coupling in retina of the toad, *Bufo Marinus*. I. Anatomy. *J. Neurophysiol., 42,* 292–310. {4}

Gold, G. H. *see also* Nakamura; Wang

Goldberg, M. E. *see* Bushnell; Colby; Duhamel; Robinson; Wurtz

Goldin-Meadow, S. *see* Iverson

Goldstein, A. *see* Grevert

Goldstein, E. B. (1979) Rotation of objects in pictures viewed at an angle: evidence for different properties of two types of pictorial space. *J. Exp. Psychol.: Human Percept. & Perf, 5,* 78–87. {12}

Goldstein, E. B. *see also* Frishman

Goldstein, M. H. (1974) The auditory periphery. In V. B. Mountcastle (Ed.), *Medical Physiology,* 13th, edn. St Louis: C. V. Mosby. {15}

Goldstein, M. H. *see also* Frishkopf

Goldstein, R. *see* Arend

Goldwater, B. C. (1972) Psychological significance of pupillary movements. *Psychol. Bull., 77,* 340–355. {3}

Gombrich, E. H. (1961) *Art and Illusion,* 2nd edn. Princeton, NJ: Princeton University Press. {10}

Gonzalez, F. *see* Alonso; Poggio

Goodale, M. A. (1993) Visual pathways supporting perception and action in the primate cerebral cortex. *Curr. Opin. in Neurobiol., 3,* 578–585. {8}

Goodale, M. A. (1998) Where does vision end and action begin? *Curr. Biol., 8,* R489–491. {8}

Goodale, M. A., & Haffenden, A. (1998) Frames of reference for perception and action in the human visual system. *Neurosci. & Behav. Rev., 22,* 161–172. {8}

Goodale, M. A., Milner, A. D., Jakobson, L. S., & Carey, D. P. (1991) A neurological dissociation between perceiving objects and grasping them. *Nature, 349,* 154–156. {7}

Goodale, M. A. *see also* Aglioti; Servos

Goodchild, A. K. *see* Martin

Gordon, J., & Abramov, I. (1977) Color vision in the peripheral retina. II. Hue and saturation. *J. Opt. Soc. Am., 67,* 202–207. {4}

Gordon, J. *see also* Abramov; Boynton

Gorea, A. *see* Papathomas

Gosline, C. J., MacLeod, D. I. A., & Rushton, W. A. H. (1973) Rod dark-adaptation measured above the cone threshold. *J. Physiol., 234,* 27–28P. {6}

Gouras, P. (1968) Identification of cone mechanisms in monkey ganglion cells. *J. Physiol., 199,* 533–547. {14}

Gouras, P. *see also* DeMonasterio; Kolb; Nelson

Grabowski, S. R., & Pak, W. L. (1975) Intracellular recordings of rod responses during dark adaptation. *J. Physiol., 247,* 363–391. {6}

Gracely, R. H. *see* Price

Graf, W. *see* Simpson

Grafman, J. *see* Stark

Graham, C. H. (1965) Some fundamental data. In C. H. Graham (Ed.), *Vision and Visual Perception* (pp. 68–80). New York: Wiley. {2}

Graham, C. H., & Bartlett, N. R. (1939) The relation of size of stimulus and intensity in the human eye. II. Intensity thresholds for red and violet light. *J. Exp. Psychol., 24,* 574–587. {**2.6**}

Graham, N. (1979) Does the brain perform a Fourier analysis of the visual scene? *Trends Neurosci., 2,* 207–208. {9}

Graham, N., & Nachmias, J. (1971) Detection of grating patterns containing two spatial frequencies: a comparison of single-channel and multiple-channel models. *Vision Res., 11*, 251–259. {9}

Graham, N. *see also* Ratliff

Granit, R. (1977) *The Purposive Brain.* Cambridge, Mass.: MIT Press. {12}

Granit, R., Holmberg, T., & Zewi, M. (1938) On the mode of action of visual purple on the rod cell. *J. Physiol., 94*, 430–440. {6}

Grau, J. W. *see* Maier

Gray, C. M., & Singer, W. (1989) Stimulus-specific neuronal oscillations in orientation columns of cat visual cortex. *Proc. Natl Acad. Sci., 86*, 1698–1702. {10}

Gray, C. M. *see also* Maldonado; Singer

Graziadei, P., & Dehan, R. S. (1971) The ultrastructure of frogs taste organs. *Acta Anat., 80*, 563–603. {**20.2**}

Green, C. A. *see* Benson

Green, D. G. *see* Cicerone; Tong

Green, D. M. *see* Middlebrooks

Green, J. D. *see* Mancia

Green, M., Corwin, T., & Zemon, V. (1976) A comparison of Fourier analysis and feature analysis in pattern-specific color aftereffects. *Science, 192*, 147–148. {9}

Green, M., & Odom, J. V. (1986) Correspondence matching in apparent motion: evidence for three-dimensional spatial representation. *Science, 233*, 1427–1429. {13}

Green, S. H. *see* Woodruff

Greenberg, D. P. (1989) Light reflection models for computer graphics. *Science, 244*, 166–173. {11}

Greene, E., & Verloop, M. (1994) Anomalous and luminance contours produce similar angular induction effects. *Percept., 23*, 147–156. {10}

Greenlee, M. W., & Magnussen, S. (1988) Interactions among spatial-frequency and orientation channels adapted concurrently. *Vision Res. 28*, 1303–1309. {9}

Greenwood, D. D., & Maruyama, N. (1965) Excitatory and inhibitory response areas of auditory neurons in the cochlear nucleus. *J. Neurophysiol., 28*, 863–892. {16, **16.8**}

Gregory, R. L. (1970) *The Intelligent Eye.* New York: McGraw-Hill. {12}

Gregory, R. L. (1978) *Eye and Brain*, 3rd edn. New York: McGraw-Hill. {10, 12, 13, **13.1, 13.4**}

Gregory, R. L. (1995) Visual perception. Seeing backwards in time. *Nature, 373*, 21–22. {10}

Gregory, R. L., & Harris, J. P. (1975) Illusion destruction by appropriate scaling. *Perception, 4*, 203–220. {12}

Gregory, R. L., & Harris, J. P. (1984) Real and apparent movement nulled. *Nature, 307*, 729–730. {13}

Gregory, R. L., & Wallace, J. G. (1963) Recovery from early blindness: a case study. *Quart. J. Exper. Psychol.* Monograph suppl. 2. Cambridge: Heffers. {10}

Grevert, P., Albert, L. H., & Goldstein, A. (1983) Partial antagonism of placebo analgesia by naloxone. *Pain, 14*, 129–143. {19}

Griffith, B. C. *see* Liberman

Grigg, P., Cinerman, G. A., & Riley, L. H. (1973) Joint position sense after total hip replacement. *J. Bone and Joint Surgery, 55A*, 1016–1025. {19}

van de Grind, W. A., Koenderink, J. J., & van Doorn, A. J. (1992) Viewing-distance invariance of movement detection. *Exp. Brain Res., 91*, 135–150. {13}

van de Grind, W. A. *see also* Pennartz

Grinvald, A. *see* Bonhoeffer; Hübener

Grosof, D. H., Shapley, R. M., & Hawken, M. J. (1993) Macaque V1 neurons can signal 'illusory' contours. *Nature, 365*, 550–552. {8}

Gross, C. G. *see* Bruce; Rodman

Grossberg, S. (1992) Cortical dynamics of visual motion perception: short-range and long-range apparent motion. *Psych. Rev., 99*, 78–121. {13}

von Grunau, M., & Frost, B. J. (1983) Double opponent-process mechanism underlying RF-structure of directionally specific cells of cat lateral suprasylvian visual area. *Exp. Brain Res., 49*, 84–92. {13}

von Grünau, M. *see also* Kolers

Grünert, U. *see* Chun; Wässle

Grunfeld, E. D., & Spitzer, H. (1995) Spatio-temporal model for subjective colours based on colour coded ganglion cells. *Vision Res., 35*, 275–283. {14}

Grüsser, O. J., & Creutzfeldt, O. (1957) Eme neurophysiologische Grundlage des Brücke-Bartley-Effektes: Maxima der Impulsfrequenz retinaler und corticaler Neurone bei Flimmerlicht mittlerer Frequenzen. *Pfluegers Arch., 263*, 668–681. {12}

Guido, W. *see* Lu

Guilbark, G. *see* Lamour

Gulick, W. L. (1971) *Hearing: Physiology and Psychophysics.* New York: Oxford University Press. {15, 16}

Gulick, W. L., Gescheider, G. A., & Frisina, R. D.

(1989) *Hearing: Physiological Acoustics Neural Coding, and Psychoacoustics.* New York: Oxford University Press. {15, **15.8, 15.9, 16.8**}

Gulyás, B., Roland, P. E., Heywood, C. A., Popplewell, D. A., & Cowey, A. (1994) Visual form discrimination from luminance or disparity cues: functional anatomy by PET. *Neuro. Rep., 5,* 2367–2371. {11}

Gummer, A. W. *see* Meyer

Gur, M., & Snodderly, D. M. (1997) Visual receptive fields of neurons in primary visual cortex (V1) move in space with the eye movements of fixation. *Vision Res., 37,* 257–265. {7}

Gustincich, S. *see* Feigenspan

Gutierrez, C. *see* Williams

Guyton, A. C. (1987) *Basic Neuroscience: Anatomy and Physiology.* Philadelphia: Saunders. {**18.15**}

Gynder, I. C. *see* Vaney

Hackney, C. M. *see* Meyer

Haffenden, A. *see* Goodale

Hagihara, K. *see* Hata

Hagins, W. A. *see* Penn; Yoshikami

Hahm, J.-O. *see* Roe

Hahn, S. *see* Paradiso

Hansen, P. C. *see* Cornelissen

Haig, C. *see* Hecht

Hake, H. W. *see* Egan

Hall, C. F. *see* Carl

Halle, M., & Stevens, K. N. (1959) Analysis by synthesis. In W. Wathen-Dunn and L. E. Woods (Eds.), *Proceedings of the Seminar on Speech Compression and Processing.* AFCRC-TR-59-198. Vol. 11. Washington, DC: US Air Force. {18}

Halpern, M. (1987) The organization and function of the vomeronasal system. *Ann. Rev. Neurosci., 10,* 325–362. {20}

Halwes, T. *see* Mattingly

Hamalainen, H., Vartiamen, M., Karvanen, L., & Jarvilehto, T. (1982) Paradoxical heat sensations during moderate cooling of the skin. *Brain Res., 251,* 77–81. {19}

Hämäläinen, M. *see* Sams

Hamamoto, J., Cheng, H., Yoshida, K., Smith, E. L., & Chino, Y. M. (1994) Transfer characteristics of lateral geniculate nucleus X-neurons in the cat: effects of temporal frequency. *Exp. Brain Res., 98,* 191–199. {7}

Hamamoto, J. *see also* Chino

Hamill, O. P., & McBride, D. W. (1995) Mechanoreceptive membrane channels. *Am. Scientist, 83,* 30–37. {19}

Hamilton, C. R. *see* Sugishita

Hamilton, S. L. *see* Tootell

Hammond, P., & Kim, J.-N. (1996) Role of suppression in shaping orientation and direction selectivity of complex neurons in cat striate cortex. *J. Neurophysiol., 75,* 1163–1176. {7}

Hammond, P., & Mouat, G. S. V. (1988) Neural correlates of motion after-effects in cat striate cortical neurones: interocular transfer. *Exp. Brain Res., 72,* 21–28. {13}

Hammond, P., Mouat, G. S. V., & Smith, A. T. (1988) Neural correlates of motion after-effects in cat striate cortical neurones: monocular adaptation. *Exp. Brain Res., 72,* 1–20. {13}

Hammond, P. *see also* Edelstyn

Hampson, E. C. G. M., Vaney, D. I., & Weiler, R. (1992) Dopaminergic modulation of gap junction permeability between amacrine cells in mammalian retina. *J. Neurosci., 12,* 4911–4922. {6}

Hanski, E. *see* Pace

Hansson, P., & Ekblom, A. (1983) Transcutaneous electrical nerve stimulation (TENS) as compared to placebo TENS for the relief of acute oro-facial pain. *Pain, 15,* 157–165. {19}

Hari, R., Salmelin, R., Tissari, S. O., Kajola, M., & Virsu, V. (1994) Visual stability during eyeblinks. *Nature, 367,* 121–122. {7}

Hari, R. *see also* Sams

Harkins, A. B. *see* Rao-Mirotznik

Harmon, L. D., & Julesz, B. (1973) Masking in visual recognition: effects of two-dimensional filtered noise. *Science, 180,* 1194–1197. {9, **9.11**}

Harnad, S. (1987) Psychophysical and cognitive aspects of categorical perception: a critical overview. In: S. Harnad, (Ed.), *Categorical Perception; the Groundwork of Cognition* (pp. 1–25). Cambridge: Cambridge University Press. {18}

Harris, C. S. *see* Weisstein

Harris, D. *see* Dallos

Harris, J. D. (1952) Pitch discrimination. *J. Acoust. Soc. Am., 24,* 750–755. {**16.13**}

Harris, J. D., Sergeant, R. L. (1971) Monaural/binaural

minimum audible angles for a moving sound source. *J. Speech Hear. Res., 14*, 618–629. {17}

Harris, J. P. *see* Gregory

Harris, K. S. *see* Liberman

Harris, L. R., Morgan, M. J., & Still, A. W. (1981) Moving and the motion after-effect. *Nature, 293*, 139–141. {13}

Harris, M. G. *see* Georgeson

Harsanyi, K., & Mangel, S. C. (1992) Activation of a D_2 receptor increases electrical coupling between retinal horizontal cells by inhibiting dopamine release. *Proc. Natl. Acad. Sci., 89*, 9220–9224. {6}

Hartline, H. K. (1938) The response of single optic nerve fibers of the vertebrate eye to illumination of the retina. *Am. J. Physiol., 121*, 400–415. {5}

Hartline, H. K. (1949) Inhibition of activity of visual receptors by illuminating nearby retinal areas in the *Limulus* eye. *Fed. Proc. 8*, 69. {5}

Hartline, H. K., & Ratliff, F. (1957) Inhibitory interaction of receptor units in the eye of *Limulus. J. Gen. Physiol., 40*, 357–376. {5}

Hartline, H. K., Wagner, H. G., & MacNichol, E. F. (1952) The peripheral origin of nervous activity in the visual system. *Cold Spring Harbor Symp. Quant. Biol., 17*, 125–141. {3}

Hartline, H. K., Wagner, H. G., & Ratliff, F. (1956) Inhibition in the eye of *Limulus. J. Gen. Physiol., 39*, 651–673. {3, 5}

Harvey, L. O., & Michon, J. A. (1974) Detectability of relative motion as a function of exposure duration, angular separation, and background. *J. Exp. Psychol., 103*, 317–325. {13}

Harwerth, R. S. *see* Viswanathan; Walters

Hash, T. *see* Lehmkuhle

Hashimoto, H. *see* Kaneko; Toyoda

Haslwanter, T. *see* Tweed

Hastorf, A. H., & Way, K. S. (1952) Apparent size with and without distance cues. *J. Gen. Psychol., 47*, 181–188. {12}

Hata, Y., & Stryker, M. P. (1994) Control of thalamocortical afferent rearrangement by postsynaptic activity in developing visual cortex. *Science, 265*, 1732–1735. {8}

Hata, Y., Tsumoto, T., Sato, H., Hagihara, K., & Tamura, H. (1988) Inhibition contributes to orientation selectivity in visual cortex of cat. *Nature, 336*, 815–817. {7}

Hata, Y. *see also* Sato

Hawken, M. J. *see* Grosof

Hayhoe, M. M. *see* Cicerone

Haynes, L. W., & Yau, K.-W. (1985) Cyclic GMP-sensitive conductance in outer segment membranes of catfish cones. *Nature, 317*, 61–64. {4}

Haxby, J. V. *see* Courtney

He, P. *see* Regan

He, S., Cavanagh, P., & Intrilligator, J. (1996) Attentional resolution and the locus of visual awareness. *Nature, 383*, 334–337. {10}

Hebb, D. O. (1949) *The Organization of Behavior.* New York: Wiley. {10}

Hecht, S. (1937) Rods, cones, and the chemical basis of vision. *Physiol. Rev., 17*, 239–290. {6}

Hecht, S., Haig, C., & Chase, A. M. (1937) The influence of light adaptation on subsequent dark adaptation of the eye. *J. Gen. Physiol., 20*, 831–850. {6, **6.3, 6.4**}

Hecht, S., Shlaer, S., & Pirenne, M. H. (1942) Energy, quanta, and vision. *J. Gen. Physiol., 25*, 819–840. {6}

Heck, G. L. *see* Ye

Heeger, D. J. (1992) Normalization of cell responses in cat striate cortex. *Visual Neurosci., 9*, 181–197. {7}

Heeger, D. J., Simoncelli, E. P., & Movshon, J. A. (1996) Computational models of cortical visual processing. *Proc. Natl. Acad. Sci., 93*, 623–627. {7}

Hedden, W. L., & Dowling, J. E. (1978) The interplexiform cell system. II. Effects of dopamine on goldfish retinal neurons. *Proc. R. Soc. Lond. Ser. B., 201*, 27–55. {6}

Heffner, H. E., & Heffner, R. S. (1984) Temporal lobe lesions and perception of species-specific vocalizations by macaques. *Science, 226*, 75–76. {18}

Heffner, R. S. *see* Heffner

Heggelund, P. (1981) Receptive field organization of complex cells in cat striate cortex. *Exp. Brain Res., 42*, 99–107. {7}

Hein, A. *see* Cynader

Heinemann, E. G. (1955) Simultaneous brightness induction as a function of inducing and test field luminance. *J. Exp. Psychol., 50*, 89–96. {12}

Heinemann, E. G., Tulving, E., & Nachmias, J. (1959) The effect of oculomotor adjustments on apparent size. *Am. J. Psychol., 72*, 32–45. {11}

Heise, G. A. *see* Miller

von Helmholtz, H. C. F. (1924) *Physiological Optics, Vol. 11* (trans. J. Southall). Rochester, N: Optical Society of America.

von Helmholtz, H. (1866) *Treatise on Physiological Optics, Vol. III*, Ed: J. PC. Southall (translated from the 3rd German edition). New York: Dover, 1962. {13}

Helson, H. (1948) Adaptation level as a basis for a quantitative theory of frames of reference. *Psychol. Rev., 55*, 297–313. {12}

Helson, H. (1964) Current trends and issues in adaptation level theory. *Am. Psychol., 19*, 26–28. {12}

Hemila, S. (1977) Background adaptation in the rods of the frog's retina. *J. Physiol., 265*, 721–741. {6}

Hemmi, I. *see* Sugishita

Hendry, S. H. C., & Yoshioka, T. (1994) A neurochemically distinct third channel in the macaque dorsal lateral geniculate nucleus. *Science, 262*, 575–577. {8}

Henneman, R. H. (1935) A photometric study of the perception of object color. *Arch. Psychol., 27*, 5–88. {12}

Henning, G. B. *see* Derrington

von Henning, H. (1916) *Der Geruch.* Leipzig: Barth. {20}

von Henning, H. (1927) Psychologische Studien am Geshmackssinn. In: E. Abderhalden (Ed.), *Handbuch der Biologischen Arbeitsmethoden.* Berlin: Urban and Schwarzenberg. {20}

Hepler, N. *see* DeValois

Herbert, E., Oates, E., Martens, G., Comb, M. & Rosen, M. (1983) Generation of diversity and evolution of opioid peptides. *Cold Spring Harbor Symp. Quant. Biol., 48, pt. 1*, 375–384. {19}

Herskovits, M. J. *see* Segall

Hertz, J. A. *see* Kjaer

Hess, C., & Pretori, H. (1894) Messende Untersuchungen über die Gesetzmassigkeit des sumultanen Heligkeits-Contrastes. *Arch. Ophthalmol., 40*, 1–24. {12}

Hess, E. H. (1965) Attitude and pupil size. *Sci. Am., 212*, 46–54. {3}

Hess, E. H., & Polt, J. M. (1960) Pupil size as related to interest value of visual stimuli. *Science, 132*, 349–350. {3}

Hess, E. H., & Polt, J. M. (1964) Pupil size in relation to mental activity during simple problem-solving. *Science, 140*, 1190–1192. {3}

Hevner, R. F. *see* Wong-Riley

Hewett-Emmett, D. *see* Shyue

Heywood, C. A. *see* Gulyás

Hietanen, J. K., & Perrett, D. I. (1996) Motion sensitive cells in the macaque superior temporal polysensory area: response discrimination between self-generated and externally generated pattern motion. *Behav. Brain Res., 76*, 155–167. {13}

Hill, R. M. *see* Barlow

Hiller, J. M. *see* Simon

Hillman, P. *see* Shechter

Hind, J. E. *see* Rose

Hines, P. J. (1997) Unconscious odors. *Science, 278*, 79. {20}

Hirano, A. A. & MacLeish, P. R. (1991) Glutamate and 2-amino-4-phosphonobutyrate evoke an increase in potassium conductance in retinal bipolar cells. *Proc. Natl Acad. Sci., 88*, 805–809. {4}

Hirsch, H. V. B., & Spinelli, D. N. (1970) Visual experience modifies distribution of horizontally and vertically oriented receptive fields in cats. *Science, 168*, 869–871. {8}

Hirsch, H. V. B. *see also* Blake

Hitzenberger, C. K. *see* Drexler

Hochberg, J. E. (1971a) Perception. I. Color and shape. In J. W. Kling & L. A. Riggs (Eds.), *Woodworth and Schlosberg's Experimental Psychology*, 3rd edn. (pp. 395–474). New York: Holt, Rinehart & Winston. {10, 12, 13}

Hochberg, J. E. (1971b) Perception. II. Space and movement. In: J. W. Kling & L. A. Riggs (Eds.), *Woodworth and Schlosberg's Experimental Psychology*, 3rd edn. (pp. 475–530). New York: Holt, Rinehart, and Winston. {11}

Hochberg, J. E., & Beck, J. (1954) Apparent spatial arrangement and perceived brightness. *J. Exp. Psychol., 47*, 263–266. {12}

Hochberg, J. E., & McAlister, E. (1953) A quantitative approach to figural 'goodness.' *J. Exp. Psychol., 46*, 361–364. {10}

Hochberg, J. E., & Silverstein, A. (1956) A quantitative index of stimulus similarity: proximity vs. difference in brightness. *Am. J. Psychol., 69*, 456–458. {10}

Hochstein, S., & Shapley, R. M. (1976) Linear and nonlinear spatial subunits in Y cat retinal ganglion cells. *J. Physiol., 262*, 265–284. {5,7}

Hochstein, S. *see also* Ahissar; Rubin; Shapley; Shechter; Spitzer

Hocking, D. R. *see* Horton

Hodgkin, A. L., & Huxley, A. F. (1952) A quantitative

description of membrane current and its application to conduction and excitation in nerve. *J. Physiol., 117*, 500–544. {A, **A.10**}

Hodgkin, A. L. *see also* Baylor

Hoffman, H. S. *see* Liberman

Hoffmann, K.-P., & Stone, J. (1971) Conduction velocity of afferents to cat visual cortex: a correlation with cortical receptive field properties. *Brain Res., 32*, 460–466. {7}

Hoffman, K.-P. *see also* I1g; Stone

Hofmann, F. *see* Avenet

Hogness, D. S. *see* Nathans

Hohne, E. A. *see* Jusczyk

Hoke, M. *see* Pantev

Holden, C. (1996) Sex and olfaction. *Science, 273*, 313. {20}

Holden, C. (1997) A special place for faces in the brain. *Science, 278*, 41. {8}

Holley, A. *see* Sicard

Holmberg, T. *see* Granit

Holtzman, E. *see* Evans

Holway, A. H., & Boring, E. G. (1940) The moon illusion and the angle of regard. *Am. J. Psychol., 53*, 509–516. {12}

Holway, A. H., & Boring, E. G. (1941) Determinants of apparent visual size with distance variant. *Am. J. Psychol., 54*, 21–37. {12, **12.8**}

Hondzinski, J. M. *see* Darling

Honig, B. *see* Ebrey

Honore, P. *see* Mantyh

Hood, D. C., & Birch, D. G. (1993) Light adaptation of human rod receptors: the leading edge of the human *a*-wave and models of rod receptor activity. *Vision Res., 33*, 1605–1618. {6}

Hood, D. C. *see also* Benimoff; Evans

Hood, J. D. (1972) Fundamentals of identification of sensorineural hearing loss. *Sound, 6*, 21–26. {17}

Hopfield, J. J. (1982) Neural networks and physical systems with emergent collective computational abilities. *Proc. Natl Acad. Sci., 79*, 2554–2558. {10}

Hopfield, J. J. (1995) Pattern recognition computation using action potential timing for stimulus representation. *Nature, 376*, 33–36. {10}

Hopkins, J. M. & Boycott, B. B. (1995) Synapses between cones and diffuse biplar cells of a primate retina. *J. Neurocytol., 24*, 680–694. {4}

Hopkins, J. M. *see also* Boycott

Horton, J. C., & Hocking, D. R. (1996) An adult-like pattern of ocular dominance columns in striate cortex of newborn monkeys prior to visual experience. *J. Neurosci., 16*, 1791–1807. {8}

Hosobuchi, Y., Adams, J. E., & Linchitz, R. (1977) Pain relief by electrical stimulation of the central grey matter in humans and its reversal by naloxone. *Science, 197*, 183–186. {19}

Houde, J. F., & Jordan, M. I. (1998) Sensorimotor adaptation in speech production. *Science, 279*, 1213–1216. {18}

Howard, I. P., & Templeton, W. B., (1966) *Human Spatial Orientation.* New York: Wiley. {13}

Howard, R. J., Brammer, M., Wright, I., Woodruff, P. W., Bullmore, E. T., & Zeki, S. (1996) A direct demonstration of functional specialization within motion-related visual and auditory cortex of the human brain. *Curr. Biol., 6*, 1015–1019. {13}

Howell, E. R. *see* Campbell

Hoy, R. R. *see* Wyttenbach

Hu, J. W. *see* Price

Hubbard, A. E., & Mountain, D. C. (1983) Alternating current delivered into the scala media alters sound pressure at the eardrum. *Science, 222*, 510–512. {16}

Hubel, D. H., & Livingstone, M. S. (1983) Blobs and color vision. *Can. J. Physiol. Pharmacol., 61*, 1433–1441. {7, 8}

Hubel, D. H., & Livingstone, M. S. (1987) Segregation of form, color, and stereopsis in primate area 18. *J. Neurosci., 7*, 3378–3415. {8, 14}

Hubel, D. H., & Wiesel, T. N. (1959) Receptive fields of single neurones in the cat's striate cortex. *J. Physiol., 148*, 574–591. {7, **7.7**}

Hubel, D. H., & Wiesel, T. N. (1961) Integrative action in the cat's lateral geniculate body. *J. Physiol., 155*, 385–398. {7}

Hubel, D. H., & Wiesel, T. N. (1962) Receptive fields, binocular interaction and functional architecture in the cat's visual cortex. *J. Physiol., 160*, 106–154. {7, **7.8, 7.9, 8.1**}

Hubel, D. H., & Wiesel, T. N. (1963) Receptive fields of cells in striate cortex of very young visually inexperienced kittens. *J. Neurophysiol., 26*, 994–1002. {8}

Hubel, D. H., & Wiesel, T. N. (1965a) Receptive fields and functional architecture in two non-striate visual areas (18 and 19) of the cat. *J. Neurophysiol., 28*, 229–289. {7, **7.10**}

Hubel, D. H., & Wiesel, T. N. (1965b) Binocular interaction in striate cortex of kittens reared with artificial squint. *J. Neurophysiol., 28*, 1041–1059. {8}

Hubel, D. H., & Wiesel, T. N. (1968) Receptive fields and functional architecture of monkey striate cortex. *J. Physiol., 195*, 215–243. {7, 8}

Hubel, D. H., & Wiesel, T. N. (1970) Stereoscopic vision in macaque monkey. *Nature, 225*, 41–42. {11}

Hubel, D. H., & Wiesel, T. N. (1974a) Sequence regularity and geometry of orientation columns in the monkey striate cortex. *J. Comp. Neurol., 158*, 267–294. {8, **8.2**}

Hubel, D. H., & Wiesel, T. N. (1974b) Uniformity of monkey striate cortex: a parallel relationship between field size, scatter, and magnification factor. *J. Comp. Neurol., 158*, 295–306. {7,8}

Hubel, D. H., & Wiesel, T. N. (1977) Functional architecture of macaque monkey visual cortex. *Proc. R. Soc. Lond. Ser. B., 198*, 1–59. {7, 8, **7.3, 7.6**}

Hubel, D. H., Wiesel, T. N., & Stryker, M. P. (1978) Anatomical demonstration of orientation columns in macaque monkey. *J. Comp. Neurol., 177*, 361–380. {8, **8.3**}

Hubel, D. H. *see also* Livingstone; Wiesel

Hübener, M., Shoham, D., Grinvald, A., & Bonhoeffer, T. (1997) Spatial relationships among three columnar systems in cat area 17. *J. Neurosci., 17*, 9270–9284. {8}

Hudspeth, A. J. (1982) Extracellular current flow and the site of transduction by vertebrate hair cells. *J. Neurosci., 2*, 1–10. {15}

Hudspeth, A. J. (1985) The cellular basis of hearing: the biophysics of hair cells. *Science, 230*, 745–752. {15}

Hudspeth, A. J. *see also* Corey

Huggins, A. W. F. (1964) Distortion of the temporal pattern of speech: interruption and alternation. *J. Acoust. Soc. Am., 36*, 1055–1064. {18}

Hughes, G. W., & Maffei, L. (1965) On the origin of the dark discharge of retinal ganglion cells. *Arch. Ital. Biol., 103*, 45–59. {5}

Hughes, G. W., & Maffei, L. (1966) Retinal ganglion cell response to sinusoidal light stimulation. *J. Neurophysiol., 29*, 333–352. {12}

Hughes, J., Smith, T. W., Kosterlitz, H. W., Fothergill, L. A., Morgan, B. A., & Morris, H. R. (1975) Identification of two related pentapeptides from the brain with potent agonist activity. *Nature, 258*, 577–579. {19}

Hughes, J. R. *see* Rose

Hull, E. M. *see* DeValois

Hunt, D. M., Dulai, K. S., Bowmaker, J. K., & Mollon, J. D. (1995) The chemistry of John Dalton's color blindness. *Science, 267*, 984–988. {14}

Hunt, D. M. *see also* Shyue

Hurlbert, A. (1991) Deciphering the colour code. *Nature, 349*, 191–193. {14}

Hurlbert, A. (1997) Colour vision. *Curr. Biol., 7*, R400–402. {14}

Hurvich, L. M., & Jameson, D. (1957) An opponent-process theory of color vision. *Psychol. Rev., 64*, 384–404. {14, **14.18**}

Hurvich, L. M. *see also* Jameson

Hutton, J. L. *see* Cornelissen

Huxley, A. F. *see* Hodgkin

Hyvarinen, J., & Poranen, A. (1978) Movement sensitive and direction and orientation selective cutaneous receptive fields in the hand area of the post central gyrus in monkeys. *J. Physiol. (Lond.), 283*, 523–537. {19}

Ideura, Y. *see* Komatsu

Ilg, U. J., & Hoffmann, K.-P. (1993) Motion perception during saccades. *Vision Res., 33*, 211–220. {13}

Illing, R. B. *see* Wässle

Imig, T. J., Ruggero, M. A., Kitzes, L. M., Javel, E., & Brugge, J. F. (1977) Organization of auditory cortex in the owl monkey (*Aotus trivirgatus*). *J. Comp. Neurol., 171*, 111–128. {**15.10**}

Ingemann, F. *see* Liberman

Ingle, D. (1985) The goldfish is a retinex animal. *Science, 227*, 651–654. {14}

Ingling, C. R. (1977) The spectral sensitivity of the opponent-color channels. *Vision Res., 17*, 1083–1090. {14}

Ingling, C. R., Lewis, A. L., Loose, D. R., & Myers, K. J. (1977) Cones change rod sensitivity. *Vision Res., 17*, 555–563. {6}

International Commission on Illumination. (1932) *Proceedings of the Eighth Session.* Cambridge: Cambridge University Press. {14}

Intriligator, J. *see* He

Isabelle, E. *see* Leibowitz

Isensee, O. *see* Kenshalo

Ishida, A. T. *see* Stell

Ittelson, W. H. (1968) *The Ames Demonstrations in Perception.* New York: Hefner. {**10.33**}

Ittelson, W. H., & Kilpatrick, F. P. (1951) Experiments in perception. *Sci. Am., 185,* 50–55. {11}

Ivanov, V. A. *see* Glezer

Iverson, J. M., & Goldin-Meadow, S. (1997) What's communication got to do with it? Gesture i children blind from birth. *Dev. Psychol., 33,* 453–467. {18}

Iverson, J. M., & Goldin-Meadow, S. (1998) Why people gesture when they speak. *Nature, 396,* 228. {18}

Iverson, S. D. *see* Calvert

Ives, J. *see* Seeck

Iwai, E. (1985) Neuropsychological basis of pattern vision in macaque monkeys. *Vision Res., 25,* 425–439. {8}

Jack, J. J. B. *see* Stratford

Jacobs, G. H. *see* DeValois; Neitz

Jacobson, L. D., Gaska, J. P., Chen, H.-W., & Pollen, D. A. (1993) Structural testing of multi-input linear-nonlinear cascade models for cells in macaque striate cortex. *Vision Res., 33,* 609–626. {7}

Jacobson, L. D. *see also* Liu; Pollen

Jagadeesh, B., Wheat, H. S., & Ferster, D. (1994) Linearity of summation of synaptic potentials underlying direction selectivity in simple cells of the cat visual cortex. *Science, 262,* 1901–1904. {7}

Jagadeesh, B., Wheat, H. S., Kontsevich, L. L., Tyler, C. W., & Ferster, D. (1997) Direction selectivity of synaptic potentials in simple cells of the cat visual cortex. *J. Neurophysiol., 78,* 2772–2789. {7}

Jahoda, G. (1966) Geometric illusions and environment: a study in Ghana. *Br. J. Psychol., 57,* 193–199. {10}

Jakiela, H. G., Enroth-Cugell, C., & Shapley, R. (1976) Adaptation and dynamics in X-cells and Y-cells of the cat retina. *Exp. Brain Res., 24,* 335–342. {5}

Jakobson, L. S. *see* Goodale

Jameson, D., & Hurvich, L. M. (1961) Complexities of perceived brightness. *Science, 133,* 174–179. {12}

Jameson, D. *see also* Hurvich

Jáñez, L. (1984) Visual grouping without low spatial frequencies. *Vision Res., 24,* 271–274. {10}

Jarvilehto, T. *see* Hamalainen

Javel, E. *see* Imig

Jeffress, L. A. *see* Sandel

Jenness, J. W., & Shevell, S. K. (1995) Color appear-ance with sparse chromatic context. *Vision Res., 35,* 797–805. {14}

Jepson, A. *see* Schneider

Jerger, J. F. (1957) Auditory adaptation. *J. Acoust. Soc. Am., 29,* 357–363. {17}

Jervey, J. P. *see* Fuster

Jin, G.-X. *see* Richmond

Johansson, R. S., & Vallbo, A. B. (1983) Tactile sensory coding in the glabrous skin of the human hand. *Trends Neurosci., 6,* 27–32. {19}

Johns, M. A., Feder, H. H., Komisaruk, B. R., & Mayer, A. D. (1978) Urine-induced reflex ovulation in anovulatory rats may be a vomeronasal effect. *Nature, 272,* 446–448. {20}

Johnson, C. A. *see* Leibowitz

Johnston, J. (1992) Why are we able to smell? *Brain Work, Fall-Winter, 5.* {20}

Johnston, J. C., & McClelland, J. L. (1974) Perception of letters in words: seek not and ye shall find. *Science, 184,* 1192–1194. {10}

Johnstone, B. M., Taylor, K. J., & Boyle, A. J. (1970) Mechanics of guinea pig cochlea. *J. Acoust. Soc. Am., 47,* 504–509. {16}

Johnstone, J. R. *see* Campbell

Jonas, J. B., Schneider, U., & Naumann, G. O. H. (1992) Count and density of human retinal photorecep-tors. *Graefe Arch. Clin. Exp. Ophthalmol., 230,* 505–510. {4}

Jones, D. T., & Reed, R. R. (1989) Golf: an olfactory neuron specific G protein involved in odorant signal transduction. *Science, 244,* 790–795. {20}

Jones, H. E. *see* Sillito

Jones, J. P., & Palmer, L. A. (1987) An evaluation of the two-dimensional Gabor filter model of simple receptive fields in cat cortex. *J. Neurophysiol., 58,* 1233–1258. {9}

Jordan, M. I. *see* Houde

Jordan, W. *see* Eckhorn

Judd, D. B. (1951) Basic correlates of the visual stimulus. In: S. S. Stevens (Ed.), *Handbook of Experimental Psychology.* (pp. 811–867). New York: Wiley. {14}

Julesz, B. (1964) Binocular depth perception without familiarity cues. *Science, 145,* 356–362. {11}

Julesz, B. (1971) *Foundations of Cyclopean Perception.* Chicago: University of Chicago Press. {11}

Julesz, B. (1974) Cooperative phenomena in binocular depth perception. *Amer. Scientist, 62,* 32–43. {11}

Julesz, B. (1981) Textons, the elements of texture

perception, and their interactions. *Nature, 290,* 91–97. {10}

Julesz, B., & Krose, B. (1988) Visual texture perception: features and spatial filters. *Nature, 333,* 302–303. {10}

Julesz, B. *see also* Harmon; Papathomas; Sagi

Jusczyk, P. W., & Hohne, E. A. (1997) Infants' memory for spoken words. *Science, 277,* 1984–1986. {18}

Kaas, J. H., Merzenich, M. M., & Killackey, H. P. (1983) The reorganization of somatic sensory cortex following peripheral nerve damage in adult and developing mammals. *Ann. Rev. Neurosci., 6,* 325–336. {19}

Kaas, J. H., Nelson, R. J., Sur, M., Lin, C.-S., & Merzenich, M. M. (1979) Multiple representations of the body within the primary somatosensory cortex of primates. *Science, 204,* 521–523. {19}

Kaas, J. H. *see also* Chino; Krubitzer; Sherman

Kabat, L. G. *see* Zimbardo

Kahneman, D., & Beatty, J. (1967) Pupillary responses in a pitch discrimination task. *Percept. Psychophys., 2,* 101–105. {3}

Kahneman, D., & Pearler, W. S. (1969) Incentive effects and pupillary changes in association learning. *J. Exp. Psychol., 79,* 312–318. {3}

Kainz, P. M. *see* Neitz

Kaiser, P. K. (1967) Perceived shape and its dependency on perceived slant. *J. Exper. Psychol., 75,* 345–353. {12}

Kaiser, P. K. *see also* Valberg

Kaji, S. *see* Komatsu

Kajola, M. *see* Hari

Kalil, R. E. *see* Chase

Kallos, T. *see* Stevens

Kamath, V. *see* Shannon

Kandel, E. R., & Schwartz, J. H. (1985) *Principles of Neural Science.* New York: Elsevier. {19}

Kaneko, A. (1971) Electrical connections between horizontal cells in the dogfish retina. *J. Physiol., 213,* 95–105. {4}

Kaneko, A., & Hashimoto, H. (1969) Electrophysiological study of single neurons in the inner nuclear layer of the carp retina. *Vision Res., 9,* 37–55. {4}

Kaneko, A., & Shimazaki, H. (1975) Effects of external ions on the synaptic transmission from photoreceptors to horizontal cells in the carp retina. *J. Physiol., 252,* 509–522. {4}

Kaneko, A., de la Villa, P., Kurahashi, T., & Sasaki,

T. (1994) Role of L-glutamate for formation of on- and off-responses in the retina. *Biomed. Res., 15, suppl. 1,* 41–45. {4}

Kaneko, A. *see also* Tachibana; Tomita

Kaneko, N. *see* Slotnik

Kanow, G. *see* Schneider

Kaplan, E., Marcus, S., & So, Y. T. (1979) Effects of dark adaptation on spatial and temporal properties of receptive fields in cat lateral geniculate nucleus. *J. Physiol., 294,* 561–580. {7}

Kaplan, E., & Shapley, R. M. (1982) X and Y cells in the lateral geniculate nucleus of macaque monkeys. *J. Physiol., 330,* 125–143. {7}

Kaplan, E., & Shapley, R. M. (1986) The primate retina contains two types of ganglion cells, with high and low contrast sensitivity. *Proc. Natl Acad. Sci., 83,* 2755–2757. {**7.4**}

Kaplan, E. *see also* Benardete; Croner; Levine

Kardos, L. (1934) Ding und Schatten. *Z. Psychol. Ergebnisse, 23.* {12}

Karni, A., & Sagi, D. (1991) Where practice makes perfect in texture discrimination: evidence for primary visual cortex plasticity. *Proc. Natl Acad. Sci., 88,* 4966–4970. {9}

Karvanen, L. *see* Hamalainen

Kastner, S. *see* Creutzfeldt

Kato, H. *see* Nelson

Katsuyama, N. *see* Sato

Katz, B. & Miledi, R. (1967a) The release of acetyl-choline from nerve endings by graded elctric pulses. *Proc. Roy. Soc. B, 167,* 23–38. {A}

Katz, B. & Miledi, R. (1967b) The timing of calcium action during neuromuscular transmission *J. Physiol., 189,* 535–544. {A}

Katz, B. *see also* Fatt

Katz, L. C., & Callaway, E. M. (1992) Development of local circuits in mammalian visual cortex. *Ann. Rev. Neurosci., 15,* 31–56. {7}

Kay, P. *see* Berlin

Kaufman, L. (1974) *Sight and Mind.* New York: Oxford University Press. {10, **10.4**, 12}

Kaufman, L., & Rock, I. (1962) The moon illusion. I. *Science, 136,* 953–961. {12, **12.22**}

Kaufman, L. *see also* Pitblado; Rock

Kaufman, P. L. *see* Koretz

Kawamura, Y. *see* Yamamoto

Kawano, K. *see* Sakata

Keating, M. J. *see* Withington-Wray

Keil, K. *see* Courtney

Kelly, D. H. (1976) Pattern detection and the two-dimensional Fourier transform: flickering checkerboards and chromatic mechanisms. *Vision Res., 16,* 277–287. {9}

Kelso, J. A. S. (1995) *Dynamic Patterns: The Self-Organization of Brain and Behavior.* Cambridge: MIT Press. {18}

Kemp, J. A. *see* Sillito

Kennedy, H. *see* Salin

Kenkel, F. (1913) Untersuchungen über den Zusammenhang Zwischen Erscheinungsgrösse und Erscheinungsbewegung bei einigen sogenannten optischen Täuschungen. *Z. Psychol., 67,* 358–449. {13}

Kennedy, J. M. (1980) Blind people recognizing and making haptic pictures. In W. Schiff and F. Foulke (Eds), *The Perception of Pictures* (pp. 305–331). Cambridge: Cambridge University Press. {**12.24**}

Kenshalo, D. R., & Duclaux, R. (1977) Response properties of cutaneous cold receptors in the monkey. *J. Neurophysiol., 40,* 319–332. {19}

Kenshalo, D. R., Giesler, G. J., Leonard, R. B., & Willis, B. D. (1980) Responses of neurons in primate ventral posterior lateral nucleus to noxious stimuli. *J. Neurophysiol., 43,* 1594–1614. {19}

Kenshalo, D. R., & Isensee, O. (1983) Responses of primate S1 cortical neurons to noxious stimuli. *J. Neurophysiol., 50,* 1479–1496. {19}

Kenshalo, D. R. *see also* Duclaux

Kersten, D. *see* Knill; Tjan

Keverne, E. B. *see* Reynolds

Khanna, S. M., & Leonard, D. G. B. (1982) Basilar membrane tuning in the cat cochlea. *Science, 215,* 303–304. {16}

Khanna, S. M. *see also* Tonndorf

Kiang, N. Y-S. (1968) A survey of recent developments in the study of auditory physiology. *Ann. Otol. Rhinol. Laryngol., 77,* 656–675. {17, **17.5**}

Kiang, N. Y.-S., Moxon, E. C., & Levine, R. A. (1970) Auditory nerve activity in cats with normal and abnormal cochleas. In: G. F. Wostenholme and J. Knight (Eds), *Sensorineural Hearing Loss* (pp. 241–273). London: Churchill. {16}

Kiang, N. Y.-S., Pfeiffer, R. R., Warr, W. B., & Bakus, **A. S.** (1965) Stimulus coding in the cochlear nucleus. *Ann. Otol. Rhinol. Laryngol, 74,* 463–485. {16}

Kiang, N. Y.-S., Rho, J. M., Northrop, C. C., Liberman, M. C., & Ryugo, D. K. (1982) Hair-cell innervation by spiral ganglion cells in adult cats. *Science, 217,* 175–177. {15}

Kiang, N. Y.-S., Watanabe, T., Thomas, E. C., & Clark, L. F. (1962) Stimulus coding in the cat's auditory nerve. *Ann. Otol. Rhinol. Laryngol., 71,* 1009–1026. {**16.6**}

Kiesow, F. (1896) Beitrage zur physiologischen psychologie des geschmackssinnes. *Philosophische Studien., 12,* 255–278. {20}

Killackey, H. P. *see* Kaas

Kilpatrick, F. P. *see* Ittelson

Kim, D.-S. *see* Toth

Kim, J.-N. *see* Hammond

Kimmeldorf, D. J. *see* Garcia

Kimura, D. (1973) The asymmetry of the human brain. *Sci. Am., 228,* 70–78. {18}

Kimura, K., & Beidler, L. M. (1961) Microelectrode study of taste receptors of rat and hamster. *J. Cell. Comp. Physiol., 187,* 131–140. {20}

Kiper, D. C., Gegenfurtner, K. R., & Movshon, J. A. (1996) Cortical oscillatory responses do not affect visual segmentation. *Vision Res., 36,* 539–544. {10}

Kiper, D. C., Fenstemaker, S. B., & Gegenfurtner, K. R. (1997) Chromatic properties of neurons in macaque area V2. *Visual Neurosci., 14,* 1061–1072. {14}

Kirk, D. L. *see* Levick

Kisvárday, Z. F. *see* Crook

Kitzes, L. M. *see* Imig

Kjaer, T. W., Gawne, T. J., Hertz, J. A., & Richmond, B. J. (1997) Insensitivity of V1 complex cell responses to small shifts in the retinal image of complex patterns. *J. Neurophysiol., 78,* 3187–3197. {7}

Kjaer, T. W. *see also* Gawne

Klarén, L. *see* Sjöstrand

Klein, A. B. (1936) *Colour Cinematography.* London: Chapman & Hall. {14}

Klein, B. E. K. *see* Wang

Klein, R. *see* Wang

Klein, S. *see* Stromeyer

Kleinschmidt, J., & Dowling, J. E. (1975) Intracellular recordings from gecko photoreceptors during light and dark adaptation. *J. Gen. Physiol., 66,* 617–648. {6}

Klumpp, R. G., & Eady, H. R. (1956) Some measurements of interaural time difference thresholds. *J. Acoust. Soc. Amer., 28,* 859-860. {17}

Knight, B. W. *see* Benardete; Ratliff

Knight, P. L. *see* Merzenich

Knill, D. C., & Kersten, D. (1991) Apparent surface curvature affects lightness perception. *Nature, 351,* 228-230. {12}

Knudsen, E. I. (1983) Early auditory experience aligns the auditory map of space in the optic tectum of the barn owl *Science, 222,* 939-942. {17}

Knudsen, E. I. (1988a) Early blindness results in a degraded auditory map of space in the optic tectum of the barn owl. *Proc. Natl. Acad. Sci., 85,* 6211-6214. {17}

Knudsen, E. I. (1998b) Capacity for plasticity in the adult owl auditory system expanded by juvenile experience. *Science, 279,* 1531-1533. {17}

Knudsen, E. I., & Brainard, M. S. (1991) Visual instruction of the neural map of auditory space in the developing optic tectum. *Science, 253,* 85-87. {17}

Knudsen, E. I., & Brainard, M. S. (1995) Creating a unified representation of visual and auditory space in the brain. *Annu. Rev. Neurosci., 18,* 19-43. {17}

Knudsen, E. I., & Konishi, M. (1978) Center-surround organization of auditory receptive fields in the owl. *Science, 202,* 778-780. {17, **17.15**}

Knudsen, E. I., Konishi, M., & Pettigrew, J. D. (1977) Receptive fields of auditory neurons in the owl. *Science, 198,* 1278-1280. {17, **17.14**}

Koch, C. *see* Ferster; Sejnowski

Koelling, F. A. *see* Garcia

Koenderink, J. J. *see* van de Grind

Koenig, W., Dunn, H. K., & Lacy, L. Y. (1946) The sound spectrograph. *J. Acoust. Soc. Am., 17,* 19-49. {18, **18.4**}

Koffka, K. (1935) *Principles of Gestalt Psychology.* New York: Harcourt Brace. {12}

Koga, K. *see* Rossetti

Koh, E. T. *see* Ricardo

Köhler, W., & Wallach, H. (1944) Figural aftereffect, an investigation of visual processes. *Proc. Am. Philos. Soc., 88,* 269-357. {9, **9.14**}

Kolata, G. (1985) What causes nearsightedness? *Science, 229,* 1249-1250. {3}

Kolb, B., & Whishaw, I. Q. (1985) *Fundamentals of Human Neuropsychology,* 2nd edn. New York: Freeman. {18}

Kolb, H. (1974) The connections between horizontal cells and photoreceptors in the retina of the cat: electron microscopy of Golgi preparations. *J. Comp. Neurol., 155,* 1-14. {4}

Kolb, H., Cuenca, N., Wang, H.-H., & Dekorver, L. (1990) The synaptic organization of the dopaminergic amacrine cell in the cat retina. *J. Neurocytol., 19,* 343-366. {6}

Kolb, H., Goede, P., Roberts, S., Mcdermott, R., & Gouras, P. (1997) Uniqueness of the S-cone pedicle in the human retina and consequences for color processing. *J. Comp. Neurol., 386,* 443-460. {14}

Kolb, H., Linberg, K. A., & Fisher, S. K. (1992) Neurons of the human retina: a Golgi study. *J. comp. Neurol., 318,* 147-187. {4}

Kolb, H., & Nelson, R. (1981) Amacrine cells of the cat retina. *Vision Res., 21,* 1625-1633. {4}

Kolb, H., & Nelson, R. (1983) Rod pathways in the retina of the cat. *Vision Res., 23,* 301-312. {4}

Kolb, H., Nelson, R., & Mariani, A. (1981) Amacrine cells, bipolar cells and ganglion cells of the cat retina: a Golgi study. *Vision Res., 21,* 1081-1114. {4}

Kolb, H. *see also* Boycott; Famiglietti; Nelson

Kolers, P. A., & von Grünau, M. (1975) Visual construction of color is digital. *Science, 187,* 757-759. {13}

Kolers, P. A., & von Grünau, M. (1976) Shape and color in apparent motion. *Vision Res., 16,* 329-335. {13}

Kolers, P. A., & Pomerantz, J. R. (1971) Figural change in apparent motion. *J. Exp. Psychol., 87,* 99-108. {13}

Kolesnikov, S. S. *see* Fesenko

Komatsu, H., Ideura, Y., Kaji, S., & Yamane, S. (1992) Color selectivity of neurons in the inferior temporal cortex of the awake macaque monkey. *J. Neurosci., 12,* 408-424. {14}

Komatsu, Y., Nakajima, S., Toyama, K., & Fetz, E. E. (1988) Intracortical connectivity revealed by spike-triggered averaging in slice preparations of cat visual cortex. *Brain Res., 442,* 359-362. {7}

Komatsu, H., & Wurtz, R. H. (1988a) Relation of cortical areas MT and MST to pursuit eye movements. I. Localization and visual properties of neurons. *J. Neurophysiol., 60,* 580-603. {13}

Komatsu, H., & Wurtz, R. H. (1988b) Relation of cortical areas MT and MST to pursuit eye movements. III. Interaction with full-field visual stimulation. *J. Neurophysiol., 60,* 621-643. {13}

Komatsu, H. *see also* Newsome

Komisaruk, B. R. *see* Johns

Komoda, M. K., & Ono, H. (1974) Oculomotor adjustments and size-distance perception. *Percept. Psychophys., 15,* 353-360. {11}

Komoda, M. K. *see also* Coren

König, P. *see* Engel; Fries

Konishi, M. *see* Knudsen; Pettigrew

Kontsevich, L. L. *see* Jagadeesh

Koretz, J. F., Cook, C. A., & Kaufman, P. L. (1997) Accommodation and presbyopia in the human eye. *Investing. Ophthal. & Vis. Sci., 38,* 569-578. {3}

Korte, A. (1915) Kinematoskopische Untersuchungen. *Z. Psychol., 72,* 193-296. {13}

Kosterlitz, H. W. *see* Hughes

Koutalos, Y. & Yau, K.-W. (1996) Regulation of sensitivity in vertebrate rod photoreceptors by calcium. *Trends in Neurosci., 19,* 73-81. {4, 6}

Kovács, G., Vogels, R., & Orban, G. A. (1995) Selectivity of macaque inerior temporal neurons for partially occluded shapes. *J. Neurosci., 15,* 1984-1997. {10}

Kraft, T. W., Schneeweis, D. M., & Schnapf, J. L. (1993) Visual transduction in human rod photoreceptors. *J. Physiol., 464,* 747-765. {6}

Kraft, T. W. *see also* Schnapf

Krakauer, D., & Dallenbach, K. (1937) Gustatory adaptation to sweet, sour and bitter. *Am. J. Psychol., 49,* 469-475. {20}

Krakauer, D. *see* Abrahams

Krause, F. *see* Poggio

Kreiter, A. K. *see* Engel

Kremers, J., Lee, B. B., Pokorny, J., & Smith, V. C. (1993) Responses of macaque ganglion cells and human observers to compound periodic waveforms. *Vision Res., 33,* 1997-2011. {4}

Kremers, J. *see also* Valberg

Kronauer, R. E. *see* Chaparro

Krose, B. *see* Julesz

Krubitzer, L. A., & Kaas, J. H. (1989) Cortical integration of parallel pathways in the visual system of primates. *Brain Res., 478,* 161-165. {8}

Krüger, J., & Becker, J. D. (1991) Recognizing the visual stimulus from neuronal discharges. *Trends in Neurosci., 14,* 282-285. {7}

Kruger, L. *see* Stein

Kruse, W. *see* Eckhorn

Kuba, M. *see* Kubová

Kubová, Z., Kuba, M., Peregrin, J., & Nováková, V. (1995) Visual evoked potential evidence for magnocellular system deficit in dyslexia. *Physiol. Res., 44,* 87-89. {8}

Kuffler, S. W. (1953) Discharge patterns and functional organization of mammalian retina. *J. Neurophysiol., 16,* 37-68. {5, **5.2**}

Kuffler, S. W. *see also* Barlow

Kuhl, P. K., & Meltzoff, A. N. (1982) The bimodal perception of speech in infancy. *Science, 218,* 1138-1140. {18}

Kuhl, P. K., & Miller, J. D. (1975) Speech perception by the chinchilla: voiced-voiceless distinction in alveolar plosive consonants. *Science, 190,* 69-72. {18}

Kuhl, P. K., Williams, K. A., Lacerda, F., Stevens, K. N., & Lindblom, B. (1992) Linguistic experience alters phonetic perception in infants by 6 months of age. *Science, 255,* 606-608. {18}

Kujiraoka, T. *see* Saito; Toyoda

Kurahashi, T. *see* Kaneko

Kuwada, S., Yin, T. C. T., & Wickesberg, R. E. (1979) Response of cat inferior colliculus neurons to binaural beat stimuli: possible mechanisms for sound localization. *Science, 206,* 586-588. {17}

Kuwada, S. *see also* Fitzpatrick

Kwon, Y. H. *see* Roe

Jeo, R. M. *see* Dobbins

Labarca, P. *see* Simon

Lacerda, F. *see* Kuhl

Lachica, E. A., & Casagrande, V. A. (1993) The morphology of collicular and retinal axons ending on small relay (W-like) cells of the primate lateral geniculate nucleus. *Visual Neurosci., 10,* 403-418. {7}

Lacy, L. Y. *see* Koenig

Làdavas, E., & Pavani, F. (1998) Neuropsychological evidence of the functional integration of visual, auditory, and proprioceptive spatial maps. *NeuroReport, 9,* 1195-1200. {17}

Ladefoged, P., DeClerk, J., Lindau, M., & Papcun, G. (1972) An auditory motor theory of speech production. *UCLA Phonetics Lab. Working Papers in Phonetics, 22,* 48-76. {18}

Lagae, L., Maes, H., Raiguel, S., Xiao, D.-K., & Orban, G. A. (1994) Responses of macaque STS neurons to optic flow components: a comparison of areas MT and MST. *J. Neurophysiol., 71,* 1597-1626. {13}

Lagnado, L. *see* Sagoo

Lam, D. M. K. *see* Lasater

Lamb, T. (1986) Transduction in vertebrate photoreceptors: the roles of cyclic GMP and calcium. *Trends in Neurosci., May 1986*, 224–228. {4}

Lamb, T. D. (1990) The role of photoreceptors in light-adaptation and dark-adaptation of the visual system. In C. Blakemore (Ed.), *Vision: Coding and Efficiency* (pp. 161–168). Cambridge: Cambridge University Press. {6}

Lamb, T. D., McNaughton, P. A., & Yau, K.-W. (1981) Spatial spread of activation and background desensitization in toad rod outer segments. *J. Physiol., 319*, 463–496. {6}

Lamb, T. D. *see also* Matthews; Pugh

Lamme, V. A. F., van Dijk, B. W., & Spekreijse, H. (1992) Texture segregation is processed by primary visual cortex in man and monkey. Evidence from VEP experiments. *Vision Res., 32*, 797–807. {9}

Lamme, V. A. F., van Dijk, B. W., & Spekreijse, H. (1993) Contour from motion processing occurs in primary visual cortex. *Nature, 363*, 541–543. {13}

Lamme, V. A. F., Zipser, K., & Spekreijse, H. (1998) Figure-ground activity in primary visual cortex is suppressed by anesthesia. *Proc. Natl Acad. Sci., 95*, 3263–3268. {8}

LaMotte, R. H., Thalhammer, J. G., Torebjork, H. E., & Robinson, C. J. (1982) Peripheral neural mechanisms of cutaneous hyperalgesia following mild injury by heat. *J. Neurosci., 2*, 765–781. {19}

Lamour, Y., Guilbark, G., & Willer, J. C. (1983) Rat somatosensory (Sm 1) cortex: II. Laminar and columnar organization of noxious and non-noxious inputs. *Exp. Brain Res., 49*, 46–54. {19}

Lancet, D. (1986) Vertebrate olfactory reception. *Ann. Rev. Neurosci., 9*, 329–355. {20}

Lancet, D. *see also* Pace

Land, E. H. (1986) Recent advances in retinex theory. *Vision Res., 26*, 7–21. {14}

Land, E. H., & McCann, J. J. (1971) Lightness and retinex theory. *J. Opt. Soc. Amer., 61*, 1–11. {12}

Landis, D. M. D. *see* Benson

Landis, T. *see* Rentschler

Langdon, J. (1951) The perception of a changing shape. *Q. J. Exp. Psychol., 3*, 157–165. {12}

Lange, A. F. *see* Stromeyer

Langner, G., Bonke, D., & Scheich, H. (1981) Neuronal

discrimination of natural and synthetic vowels in field L of trained mynah birds. *Exp. Brain Res., 43*, 11–24. {18}

Lappi, D. A. *see* Mantyh

Lasater, E. M. (1991) Membrane properties of distal retinal neurons. In: N. N. Osborne & G. J. Chader (Eds.), *Progress in Retinal Research, Vol. 11.* (pp. 215–246). NY: Pergamon. {4}

Lasater, E. M., & Lam, D. M. K. (1984) The identification and some functions of GABAergic neurons in the distal catfish retina. *Vision Res., 24*, 497–506. {4}

Laties, A. M., & Liebman, P. A. (1970) Cones of living amphibian eye: selective staining. *Science, 168*, 1475–1477. {4}

Laties, A. M. *see also* Boycott; Ehinger

Laughlin, S. B. (1990) Coding efficiency and visual processing. In C. Blakemore (Ed.), *Vision: Coding and Efficiency* (pp. 25–31). Cambridge: Cambridge University Press. {5}

Laurent, G. *see* MacLeod

Lawrence, M. *see* Wever

Lee, B. B., Elepfandt, A., & Virsu, V. (1981) Phase of responses to sinusoidal gratings of simple cells in cat striate cortex. *J. Neurophysiol., 45*, 818–828. {9}

Lee, B. B. *see also* Cleland; Kremers; Nothdurft; Smith; Valberg

Lee, C. *see* Lee

Lee, C.-H. *see* Bartoshuk

Lee, D., Lee, C., & Malpeli, J. G. (1992) Acuity-sensitivity trade-offs of X and Y cells in the cat lateral geniculate complex: role of the medial interlaminar nucleus in scotopic vision. *J. Neurophysiol., 68*, 1235–1247. {6}

Leeper, R. W. (1935) A study of a neglected portion of the field of learning: the development of sensory organization. *J. Genet. Psychol., 46*, 41–75. {10}

Legge, G. E. *see* Akutsu; Braje

Le Grand, T. (1957) *Light, Colour, and Vision*, trans. R. Hunt, T. Walsh, & F. Hunt. New York: Wiley. {**14.16**}

Lehiste, I. (1976) Suprasegmental features of speech. In N. J. Lass (Ed.), *Contemporary Issues in Experimental Phonetics* (pp. 225–239). New York: Academic Press. {18}

Lehky, S. R., & Sejnowski, T. J. (1988) Network model of shape-from-shading: neural function arises from both receptive and projective fields. *Nature, 333*, 452–454. {8, 10, 11}

Lehky, S. R., Sejnowski, T. J., & Desimone, R. (1992) Predicting responses of nonlinear neurons in monkey striate cortex to complex patterns. *J. Neurosci., 12,* 3568–3581. {7}

Lehmkuhle, S., & Fox, R. (1980) Effect of depth separation on metacontrast masking. *J. Exper. Psychol.: Human Percept. & Perform., 6,* 605–621. {10}

Lehmkuhle, S., Garzia, R. P., Turner, L., Hash, T., & Baro, J. A. (1993) A defective visual pathway in children with reading disability. *New Eng. J. Med., 328,* 989–996. {8}

Lehmkuhle, S. W. *see also* Spoehr; Steinman

Lehnertz, K. *see* Pantev

Leibovic, K. N. & Moreno-Diaz, R. (1992) Rod outer segments are designed for optimum photon detection. *Biol. Cybern., 66,* 301–306. {4}

Leibowitz, H. W. (1955) The relation between rate threshold for the perception of movement and luminance for various durations of exposure. *J. Exp. Psychol., 49,* 209–214. {13}

Leibowitz, H. W. (1971) Sensory, learned, and cognitive mechanisms of size perception. *Ann. N. Y. Acad. Sci., 188,* 47–62. {11}

Leibowitz, H. W., Johnson, C. A., & Isabelle, E. (1972) Peripheral motion detection and refractive error. *Science, 177,* 1207–1208. {13, **13.2**}

LeMay, M. *see* Vaina

Lennie, P. (1980) Parallel visual pathways: a review. *Vision Res., 20,* 561–594. {7}

Lennie, P., & D'Zmura, M. (1988) Mechanisms of color vision. *CRC Critical Rev. in Neurobiol., 3,* 333–401. {14}

Lennie, P. *see also* Shapley

Leon, M. *see* Wilson

Leonard, D. G. B. *see* Khanna

Leonard, R. B. *see* Kenshalo

Leonards, U., & Singer, W. (1997) Selective temporal interactions between processing streams with differential sensitivity for colour and luminance contrast. *Vision Res., 37,* 1129–1140. {8}

Leopold, D. A., & Logothetis, N. K. (1996) Activity changes in early visual cortex reflect monkeys' percepts during binocular rivalry, *Nature, 379,* 549–553. {11}

Lettvin, J. Y., Maturana, H. R., McCulloch, W. S., & Pitts, W. H. (1959) What the frog's eye tells the frog's brain. *Proc. Inst. Radio Engineers, 47,* 1940–1951. {5}

Leventhal, A. G., Rodieck, R. W., & Dreher, B. (1981) Retinal ganglion cell classes in the old world monkey: morphology and central projections. *Science, 213,* 1139–1142. {7}

Leventhal, A. G., Thompson, K. G., Liu, D., Zhou, Y., & Ault, S. J. (1995) Concomitant sensitivity to orientation, direction, and color of cells in layers 2, 3, and 4 of monkey striate cortex. *J. Neurosci., 15,* 1808–1818. {8}

Leventhal, A. *see also* Stone; Thompson

Levick, W. R. (1967) Receptive fields and trigger features of ganglion cells of the rabbit's retina. *J. Physiol., 188,* 285–307. {5, **5.10**}

Levick, W. R., Kirk, D. L., & Wagner, H. G. (1981) Neurophysiological tracing of a projection from temporal retina to contralateral visual cortex of the cat. *Vision Res., 21,* 1677–1679. {7}

Levick, W. R. *see also* Barlow; Cleland

Levine, M. W., & Abramov, I. (1975) An analysis of spatial summation in the receptive fields of goldfish retinal ganglion cells. *Vision Res., 15,* 777–789. {2, 12}

Levine, M. W., Cleland, B. G., Mukherjee, P., & Kaplan, E. (1996) Tailoring of variability in the lateral geniculate nucleus of the cat. *Biol. Cybern., 75,* 219–227. {7}

Levine, M. W., & Frishman, L. J. (1984) Interactions between rod and cone channels: a model that includes inhibition. *Vision Res., 24,* 513–516. {6}

Levine, M. W., Frishman, L. J., & Enroth-Cugell, C. (1987) Interactions between the rod and the cone pathways in the cat retina. *Vision Res., 27,* 1093–1104. {6}

Levine, M. W., Saleh, E. J., & Yarnold, P. R. (1988) Statistical properties of the maintained discharge of chemically isolated ganglion cells in goldfish retina. *Visual Neurosci., 1,* 31–46. {5}

Levine, M. W., & Shefner, J. M. (1975) Independence of 'on' and 'off' responses of retinal ganglion cells. *Science, 190,* 1215–1217. {4, 5}

Levine, M. W., & Shefner, J. M. (1977) Variability in ganglion cell firing patterns; implications for separate 'on' and 'off' processes. *Vision Res., 17,* 765–777. {4, 5}

Levine, M. W., & Troy, J. B. (1986) The variability of the maintained discharge of cat dorsal lateral geniculate cells. *J. Physiol., 375,* 339–359. {7}

Levine, M. W., & Zimmerman, R. P. (1988) Evidence for local circuits within the receptive fields of retinal ganglion cells in goldfish. *Visual Neurosci., 1,* 377–385. {5}

Levine, M. W. *see also* Frishman; Shefner

Levine, R. A. *see* Kiang

Levinson, E., & Sekuler, R. (1975) The independence of channels in human vision selective for direction of movement. *J. Physiol., 250,* 347–366. {13}

Levitt, J. B. *see* Yoshioka

Lewis, A. L. *see* Ingling

Li, C.-Y. *see* Creutzfeldt

Li, J. *see* Mantyh

Li, R. H. *see* Marrocco

Li, W., & Matin, L. (1998) Change in visually perceived eye level without change in perceived pitch. *Percept., 27,* 553–572. {10}

Li, W. *see also* Matin

Li, W.-H. *see* Shyue

Liberman, A. M. (1957) Some results of research on speech perception. *J. Acoust. Soc. Am., 29,* 117–123. {10, 18, **18.14**}

Liberman, A. M. (1982) On finding that speech is special. *Amer. Psychol., 37,* 148–167. {18}

Liberman, A. M., Cooper, F. S., Shankweiler, D. S., & Studdert-Kennedy, M. (1967) Perception of the speech code. *Psychol. Rev., 74,* 431–461. {18}

Liberman, A. M., Delattre, P. C., & Cooper, F. S. (1952) The role of selected stimulus variables in the perception of the unvoiced stop consonants. *Am. J. Psychol., 65,* 497–516. {18, **18.5, 18.7, 18.8**}

Liberman, A. M., Delattre, P. C., Gerstman, L. J., & Cooper, F. S. (1956) Tempo of frequency change as a cue for distinguishing classes of speech sounds. *J. Exp. Psychol., 52,* 127–137. {18, **18.9, 18.10**}

Liberman, A. M., Harris, K. S., Eimas, P. D., Lisker, L., & Bastian, J. (1961) An effect of learning on speech perception: discrimination of durations of silence with and without phonemic significance. *Lang. Speech, 4,* 175–195. {18}

Liberman, A. M., Harris, K. S., Hoffman, H. S., & Griffith, B. C. (1957) Discrimination of speech sounds within and across phoneme boundaries. *J. Exp. Psychol., 54,* 358–368. {18}

Liberman, A. M., Ingemann, F., Lisker, L., Delattre, P., & Cooper, F. S. (1959) Minimal rules for synthesizing speech. *J. Acoust. Soc. Am., 31,* 1490–1499. {18}

Liberman, A. M., & Mattingly, I. G. (1989) A specialization for speech perception. *Science, 243,* 489–494. {18}

Liberman, A. M., & Studdert-Kennedy, M. (1978) Phonetic perception. In R. Held, H. W. Liebowitz, & H

L. Teuber (Eds.), *Handbook of Sensory Physiology Vol. VIII.* (pp. 143–178) Berlin: Springer-Verlag. {18}

Liberman, A. M. *see also* Cooper; Delattre; Dorman; Mattingly; Repp; Whalen

Liberman, M. C. *see* Kiang

Lichte, W. H. *see* Borresen

Lichten, W., & Lurie, S. (1950) A new technique for the study of perceived size. *Am. J. Psychol., 63,* 280–282. {12}

Lichten, W. *see also* Miller

Licklider, J. C. R. (1956) Auditory frequency analysis. In C. Cherry (Ed.), *Information Theory.* New York: Academic Press. {16}

Lidstrom, P. *see* Mikulka

Lieberman, P. (1977) *Speech Physiology and Acoustic Phonetics: An Introduction.* New York: Macmillan. {18, **18.1**}

Liebeskind, J. C. *see* Akil

Liebman, P. A., & Pugh, E. N. (1979) The control of phosphodiesterase in rod disk membranes: kinetics, possible mechanisms and significance for vision. *Vision Res., 19,* 375–380. {4}

Liebman, P. A. *see also* Laties

Leibowitz, H. W. *see* Berman; Zeigler

Light, A. R., & Perl, E. R. (1984) Peripheral sensory systems. In: P. J. Dyck, P. K. Thomas, E. H. Lambert & R. Bunge (Eds.), *Peripheral Neuropathy.* Philadelphia: W. B. Saunders. {**19.2**}

Lightfoot, D. O. *see* Stell

Lin, C.-S. *see* Kaas

Linberg, K. A. *see* Kolb

Linchitz, R. *see* Hosobuchi

Lindau, M. *see* Ladefoged

Lindblom, B. *see* Kuhl

Lindemann, B. *see* Avenet

Lindsay, P. H., & Norman, D. A. (1977) *Human Information Processing: An Introduction to Psychology.* New York: Academic Press. {**17.4**}

Linnell, K. J. *see* Foster

Lisker, L. *see* Liberman

Lit, A. *see* Brauner

Liu, D. *see* Leventhal; Thompson

Liu, Z., Gaska, J. P., Jacobson, L. D., & Pollen, D. A. (1992) Interneuronal inteaction between members of quadrature phase and anti-phase pairs in the cat's visual cortex. *Vision Res., 32,* 1193–1198. {7}

Livingstone, M. S., & Hubel, D. H. (1987a) Connections between layer 4B of area 17 and the thick cytochrome oxidase stripes of area 18 in the squirrel monkey. *J. Neurosci., 7,* 3371–3377. {8}

Livingstone, M. S., & Hubel, D. H. (1987b) Psychophysical evidence for separate channels for the perception of form, color, movement, and depth. *J. Neurosci., 7,* 3461–3468. {8, 11, 12}

Livingstone, M. S., & Hubel, D. H. (1988) Segregation of form, color, movement, and depth: anatomy, physiology and perception. *Science, 240,* 740–749. {8, **8.4**}

Livingstone, M. S. *see also* Hubel

Loewenfeld, I. E. (1968) Comment on Hess' findings. *Sur. Opthathalmol., 11,* 293–294. {3}

Logothetis, N. K., & Pauls, J. (1995) Psychophysical and physiological evidence for viewer centered object representations in the primate. *Cerebr. Cort., 3,* 270–288. {12}

Logothetis, N. K. *see also* Leopold

Lolley, R. N. *see* Farber

Lomber, S. G., Payne, B. R., Cornwell, P., & Long, K. D. (1996) Perceptual and cognitive visual functions of parietal and temporal cortices in the cat. *Cerebr. Cort., 6,* 673–695. {8}

Long, K. D. *see* Lomber

Long, R. R. (1977) Sensitivity of cutaneous cold fibers to noxious heat: paradoxical cold discharge. *J. Neurophysiol., 40,* 489–502. {19}

Loose, D. R. *see* Ingling

Lorenceau, J. *see* Frégnac

Lounasmaa, O. V. *see* Sams

Lovegrove, W. J. *see* Williams

Lowenstein, W. R., & Mendelson, M. (1965) Components of receptor adaptation in a Pacinian Corpuscle. *J. Physiol., 177,* 377–397. {19}

Lu, C., & Fender, D. H. (1972) The interaction of color and luminance in stereoscopic vision. *Investig. Ophthal., 11,* 482–490. {11}

Lu, S.-M., Guido, W., & Sherman, S. M. (1992) Effects of membrane voltage on receptive field properties of lateral geniculate neurons in the cat: contributions of the low-threshold Ca^{2+} conductance. *J. Neurophysiol., 68,* 2185–2198. {7}

Lu, S.-M., Guido, W., & Sherman, S. M. (1993) The brain-stem parabrachial region controls mode of response to visual stimulation of neurons in the cat's lateral geniculate nucleus. *Visual Neurosci., 10,* 631–642. {7}

Lu, S.-T. *see* Sams

Lu, Z.-L., & Sperling, G. (1996) Second-order illusions: Mach bands, Chevreul, and Craik-O'Brien-Cornsweet. *Vision Res., 36,* 559–572. {5}

Lueschow, A., Miller, E. K., & Desimone, R. (1994) Inferior temporal mechanisms for invariant object recognition. *Cerebr. Cort., 5,* 523–531. {12}

Lukashin, A. *see* Georgopoulos

Lukasiewicz, P. *see* Maguire

Lund, J. S. *see* Yoshioka

Lund, N. J., & MacKay, D. M. (1983) Sleep and the McCollough effect. *Vision Res., 23,* 903–906. {9}

Lurie, M. *see* Pepperberg

Lurie, S. *see* Lichten

Lurito, J. T. *see* Georgopoulos

Lütkenhöner, B. *see* Pantev

Lützow, A. V. *see* Nelson

Lynch, J. C., Mountcastle, V. B., Talbot, W. H., & Yin, T. C. T. (1977) Parietal lobe mechanisms for directed visual attention. *J. Neurophysiol., 40,* 362–389. {8}

Lysakowski, A., Standage, G. P., & Benevento, L. A. (1988) An investigation of collateral projections of the dorsal lateral geniculate nucleus and other subcortical structures to cortical areas V1 and V4 in the macaque monkey: a double label retrograde tracer study. *Exp. Brain Res., 69,* 651–661. {8}

Lythgoe, J. N., & Partridge, J. C. (1991) The modelling of optimal visual pigments of dichromatic teleosts in green coastal waters. *Vision Res., 31,* 361–371. {4}

Lyubarsky, A., Nikonov, S., & Pugh, E. N. (1996) The kinetics of inactivation of the rod phototransduction cascade with constant Ca^{2+}. *J. Gen. Physiol., 107,* 19–34. {4}

Lyubarsky, A. L. *see also* Fesenko

Maes, H. *see* Lagae

MacArthur, R. *see* Matin

MacDonald, J. *see* McGurk

MacKay, D. M. (1967) Ways of looking at perception. In W. Watheu-Dunn (Ed.), *Models for the Perception of Speech and Visual Form.* Cambridge, Mass.: MIT Press. {10}

MacKay, D. M. *see also* Lund

MacKenzie, C. L. *see* Sivak

MacKinnon, G. E. *see* Matin

MacLeish, P. R. *see* Hirano

MacLeod, D. I. A. *see* Cicerone; Gosline; Williams

MacLeod, K., & Laurent, G. (1996) Distinct mechanisms for synchronization and temporal patterning of odor-encoding neural assemblies. *Science, 274,* 976–979. {20}

MacNeil, M. A. & Masland, R. H. (1998) Extreme diversity among amacrine cells: implications for function. *Neuron, 20,* 971–982. {4}

MacNichol, E. F. *see* Hartline; Marks

Maffei, L., & Fiorentini, A. (1973) The visual cortex as a spatial frequency analyzer. *Vision Res., 13,* 1255–1267. {9}

Maffei, L., & Fiorentini, A. (1976) The unresponsive regions of visual cortical receptive fields. *Vision Res., 16,* 1131–1139. {9}

Maffei, L. *see also* Bisti; Hughes

Magalhães-Castro, B. *see* Stein

Magnussen, S. *see* Greenlee

Maguire, G., Lukasiewicz, P., & Werblin, F. (1989) Amacrine cell interactions underlying the response to change in the tiger salamander retina. *J. Neurosci., 9,* 726–735. {4}

Maguire, W. *see* Weisstein

Maier, S. F., Drugan, R. C., & Grau, J. W. (1982) Controllability, coping behavior, and stress-induced analgesia in the rat. *Pain, 12,* 47–56. {19}

Mainwaring, N. *see* Seeck

Makous, W., & Boothe, R. (1974) Cones block signals from rods. *Vision Res., 14,* 285–294. {6}

Malchow, R. P., & Yazulla, S. (1986) Separation and light adaptation of rod and cone signals in the retina of the goldfish. *Vision Res., 26,* 1655–1666. {6}

Maldonado, P. E., & Gray, C. M. (1996) Heterogeneity in local distributions of orientation-selective neurons in the cat primary visual cortex. *Visual Neurosci., 13,* 509–516. {8}

Malmberg, A. B., Chen, C., Tonegawa, S., & Basbaum, A. I. (1997) Preserved acute pain and reduced neuropathic pain in mice lacking PKCγ. *Science, 278,* 279–283. {19}

Malpeli, J. G. *see* Lee; Mignard; Schiller

Manabe, T. *see* Suga

Mangel, S. C. *see* Harsanyi

Mano, T. *see* Rossetti

Mancia, M., von Baumgarten, R., & Green, J. D. (1962) Response patterns of olfactory bulb neurons. *Arch. Ital. Biol., 100,* 449–462. {20}

Mantyh, P. W., Rogers, S. D., Honore, P., Allen, B. J., Ghilardi, J. R., Li, J., Daughters, R. S., Lappi, D. A., Wiley, R. G., & Simone, D. A. (1997) Inhibition of hyperalgesia by ablation of Lamina I spinal neurons expressing the Substance P receptor. *Science, 278,* 275–279. {19}

Maple, B. R. & Wu, S. M. (1996) Synaptic imputs mediating bipolar cell responses in the tiger salamander retina. *Vision Res., 36,* 4015–4023. {4}

Marchiafava, P. L., & Torre, V. (1978) The responses of amacrine cells to light and intracellularly applied currents. *J. Physiol., 276,* 83–102. {4}

Marchiafava, P. L. *see also* Weiler

Marcus, S. *see* Kaplan

Marentette, P. F. *see* Petitto

Margolskee, R. F. *see* McLaughlin

Mariani, A. P. (1990) Amacrine cells of the rhesus monkey. *J. Comp. Neurol., 301,* 382–400. {4}

Mariani, A. *see also* Kolb

Mark, G. P. *see* Scott

Marks, W. B. (1965) Visual pigments of single goldfish cones. *J. Physiol., 178,* 14–32. {4, 14, **14.14**}

Marks, W. B., Dobelle, W. H., & MacNichol, E. F. (1964) Visual pigments of single primate cones. *Science, 143,* 1181–1183. {4}

Marler, P. (1975) On the origin of speech from animal sounds. In J. F. Kavanagh & J. F. Cutting (Eds.), *The Role of Speech in Language* (pp. 11–37) Cambridge, MA: MIT Press. {18}

Marler, P. *see also* Nelson

Marlin, S. *see* Giaschi

Marr, D. (1976) Early processing of visual information. *Phil. Trans. Roy. Soc. Lond. B, 275,* 483–524. {10}

Marr, D. (1982) *Vision.* San Francisco: W. H. Freeman. {5, 10, **10.5, 10.6,** 11, **11.22**}

Marrett, S. *see* Talbot

Marrocco, R. T., & Li, R. H. (1977) Monkey superior colliculus: properties of single cells and their afferent inputs. *J. Neurophysiol., 40,* 844–860. {7}

Marrocco, R. T. *see also* McClurkin

Martens, G. *see* Herbert

Martens, J.-B. *see* Blommaert

Martin, K. A. C. (1988a) The lateral geniculate nucleus strikes back. *Trends in Neurosci., 11,* 192–194. {7}

Martin, K. A. C. (1988b) From enzymes to visual perception: A bridge too far? *Trends in Neurosci., 11,* 380–387. {8}

Martin, K. A. C. *see also* Stratford

Martin, P. R., White, A. J. R., Goodchild, A. K., Wilder, H. D., & Sefton, A. E. (1997) Evidence that blue-on cells are part of the third geniculocortical pathway in primaters. *Eur. J. Neurosci., 9,* 1536–1541. {8}

Martin, P. R. *see also* Chun; Smith

Martin, W. R. (1984) Pharmacology of opioids. *Pharmacol. Rev., 35,* 283–323. {19}

Maruyama, N. *see* Greenwood

Masarachia, P. *see* Tsukamoto

Masland, R. H., & Tauchi, M. (1986) The cholinergic amacrine cell. *Trends in Neurosci., May. 1986,* 218–223. {4}

Masland, R. H. *see also MacNeil*

Massaro, D. W., & Anderson, N. H. (1970) A test of a perspective theory of geometrical illusions. *Am. J. Psychol., 83,* 567–575. {12}

Massaro, D. W., & Stork, D. G. (1998) Speech recognition and sensory integration. *Am. Scient., 86,* 236–244. {18}

Massaro, D. W. *see also* Waite

Massey, J. T. *see* Georgopoulos

Massey, S. C., & Redburn, D. A. (1987) Transmitter circuits in the vertebrate retina. *Progress in Neurobiol., 28,* 55–96. {4}

Mast, R. *see* Wilson

Mateer, C. *see* Ojemann

Mathews, D. F. (1972) Response patterns of single neurons in the tortoise olfactory epithelium and olfactory bulb. *J. Gen. Physiol., 60,* 166–180. {20}

Mathies, R. A. *see* Schoenlein; Wang

Matin, E., Clymer, A. B., & Matin, L. (1972) Metacontrast and saccadic suppression. *Science, 178,* 179–181. {13}

Matin, L., & Fox, C. R. (1989) Visually perceived eye level and perceived elevation of objects: linearly additive influences from visual field pitch and from gravity. *Vision Res., 29,* 315–324. {10}

Matin, L., & Li, W. (1994) The influence of a stationary single line in darkness on the visual perception of eye level. *Vision Res., 34,* 311–330. {10}

Matin, L., & MacKinnon, G. E. (1964) Autokinetic movement: selective manipulation of directional components by image stabilization. *Science, 143,* 147–148. {13}

Matin, L., Picoult, E., Stevens, J. K., Edwards, M. W., Young, D., & MacArthur, R. (1982) Oculoparalytic illusion: visual-field dependent spatial mislocalizations by humans partially paralyzed with curare. *Science, 216,* 198–201. {13}

Matin, L. *see also* Li; Matin; Servos

Matteson, H. H. *see* May

Matthews, G., & Watanable, S.-I. (1987) Properties of ion channels closed by light and opened by guanosine 3′, 5′-cyclic monophosphate in toad retinal rods. *J. Physiol., 389,* 691–715. {4}

Matthews, H. R., Murphy, R. L. W., Fain, G. L., & Lamb, T. D. (1988) Photoreceptor light adaptation is mediated by cytoplasmic calcium concentration. *Nature, 334,* 67–69. {4}

Mattingly, I. G., Liberman, A. M., Syrdal, A. K., & Halwes, T. (1971) Discrimination in speech and nonspeech modes. *Cognit. Psychol., 2,* 131–157. {18}

Mattingly, I. G. *see also* Liberman

Maturana, H. R. *see* Lettvin

Maunsell, J. H. R., & Newsome, W. T. (1987) Visual processing in monkey extrastriate cortex. *Ann. Rev. Neurosci., 10,* 363–401. {8}

Maunsell, J. H. R. *see also* Assad; Merigan

Mavilya, M. (1972) Spontaneous vocalization and babbling in hearing-impaired infants. In: C. G. M. Fant (Ed.), *International Symposium in Speech Communication Ability and Profound Deafness,* (pp. 163–171). Washington, DC: Alexander Graham Bell Association for the Deaf. {18}

May, J. G., & Matteson, H. H. (1976) Spatial frequency-contingent color aftereffects. *Science, 192,* 145–147. {9}

May, M. L. *see* Wyttenbach

Mayer, A. D. *see* Johns

Mayer, D. J. *see* Akil

Mayhew, J. E. W. *see* Buckley

McAdams, S. *see* Belin

McAlister, E. *see* Hochberg

McBride, D. W. *see* Hamill

McBurney, D. H. (1972) Gustatory cross-adaptation between sweet tasting compounds. *Perception and Psychophysics, 11,* 225–227. {20}

McBurney, D. H., & Bartoshuk, L. M. (1973) Interactions between stimuli with different taste qualities. *Physiology and Behavior, 10,* 249–252. {20}

McBurney, D. H., & Gent, J. F. (1979) On the nature of taste qualities. *Psych. Bull., 86,* 151–167. {20}

McBurney, D. H., Smith, D. V., & Shick, T. R. (1972)

Gustatory cross-adaptation: sourness and bitterness. *Perception and Psychophysics, 11*, 228–232. {20}

McBurney, D. H. *see also* Smith

McCann, J. J. *see* Land

McClelland, J. L. *see* Johnston

McClendon, E. *see* DeYoe

McClintic, J. R. *see* Crouch

McClintock, M. K. (1971) Menstrual synchrony and suppression. *Nature, 229*, 244–245. {20}

McClurkin, J. W., & Marrocco, R. T. (1984) Visual cortical input alters spatial tuning in monkey lateral geniculate nucleus cells. *J. Physiol., 348*, 135–152. {7}

McClurkin, J. W., & Optican, L. M. (1996) Primate striate and prestriate cortical neurons during discrimination I. Simultaneous temporal encoding of information about color and pattern. *J. Neurophysiol., 75*, 481–495. {8}

McCollough, C. (1965) Color adaptation of edge detectors in the human visual system. *Science, 149*, 1115–1116. {9}

McCormick, D. A., & Feeser, H. R. (1990) Functional implications of burst firing and single spike activity in lateral geniculate relay neurons. *Neurosci., 39*, 103–113. {7}

McCulloch, W. S. *see* Lettvin

McDermott, R. *see* Kolb

McDermott, W. *see* Rock

McFarlane, D. K. *see* Wilson

McGuire, B. A., Stevens, J. K., & Sterling, P. (1986) Microcircuitry of beta ganglion cells in cat retina. *J. Neurosci., 6*, 907–918. {5}

McGuire, P. K. *see* Calvert

McGurk, H., & MacDonald, J. (1976) Hearing lips and seeing voices. *Nature, 264*, 746–748. {18}

McIlwain, J. T. (1995) Lateral geniculate lamination and the corticogeniculate projection: a potential role in binocular vision in the quadrants. *J. Theor. Biol., 172*, 329–333. {7}

McKee, S. P., & Smallman, H. S. (1998) Size and speed constancy. In V. Walsh & J. Kulikowski (Eds.), *Perceptual Constancy: Why Things Look as They Do*, (pp. 373–408). Cambridge: Cambridge University Press. {12}

McLaughlin, J. P. *see* Pearler

McLaughlin, S., & Margolskee, R. F. (1994) The sense of taste. *Am. Scientist, 82*, 538–545. {20}

McMahon, D. G., & Brown, D. R. (1994) Modulation of gap-junction channel gating at zebrafish retinal electrical synapses. *J. Neurophysiol., 72*, 2257–2268. {6}

McNaughton, P. A. (1990) The light response of photoreceptors. In: C. Blakemore (Ed.), *Vision: Coding and Efficiency* (pp. 65–73). Cambridge: Cambridge University Press. {6}

McNaughton, P. A. *see also* Lamb

McReynolds, J. S. *see* Dong

McShane, R. C. *see* Petry

Mead, W. R. *see* DeValois

Meister, M. *see* Brivanlou; Nirenberg; Warland

Mel, B. W. (1997) SEEMORE: combining color, shape, and texture histogramming in a neurally inspired approach to visual object recognition. *Neural. Comput., 9*, 777–804. {10}

Mel, B. W., Ruderman, D. L., & Archie, K. A. (1998) Translation-invariant orientation tuning in visual 'complex' cells could derive from intradendritic computations. *J. Neurosci., 18*, 4325–4334. {7}

Meltzoff, A. N. *see* Kuhl

Melzack, R., & Wall, P. D. (1965) Pain mechanisms: a new theory. *Science, 150*, 971–979. {19}

Mendelson, M. *see* Lowenstein

Merbs, S. L., & Nathans, J. (1992) Absorption spectra of the hybrid pigments responsible for anomalous color vision. *Science, 258*, 464–466. {**14.13**}

Meredith, M. *see* O'Connell

Meredith, M. A. *see* Wallace

Merigan, W. H. (1996) Basic visual capacities and shape discrimination after lesions of extrastriate area V4 in macaques. *Visual Neurosci., 13*, 51–60. {8}

Merigan, W. H., & Maunsell, J. H. R. (1993) How parallel are the primate visual pathways? *Annu. Rev. Neurosci., 16*, 369–402. {8}

Merigan, W. H., & Pham, H. A. (1998) V4 lesions in macaques affect both single- and multiple-viewpoint shape discriminations. *Visual Neurosci., 15*, 359–367. {8}

Merlot, C. *see* Thorpe

Mershon, D. H., & Gogel, W. C. (1970) Effect of stereoscopic cues on perceived whiteness. *Am. J. Psychol., 83*, 55–67. {12}

Merton, D. A. *see* Riggs

Merzenich, M. M., Knight, P. L., & Roth, G. L. (1975) Representation of cochlea within primary auditory cortex in the cat. *J. Neurophysiol., 38*, 231–249. {16}

Merzenich, M. M. *see also* Brugge; Kaas

Mesulam, M.-M. *see* Seeck

Métin, C., & Frost, D. O. (1989) Visual responses of neurons in somatosensory cortex of hamsters with experimentally induced retinal projections to somatosensory thalamus. *Proc. Natl. Acad. Sci., 86,* 357–361. {8}

Metzler, J. *see* Shepard

Meyer, E. *see* Talbot; Zatorre

Meyer, G. E. (1987) Subjective contour humor. *Perception, 16,* 412. {**10.15**}

Meyer, J., Furness, D. N., Zenner, H.-P., Hackney, C. M., & Gummer, A. W. (1998) Evidence for opening of hair-cell transducer channels after tip-link loss. *J. Neurosci., 18,* 6748–6756. {15}

Michael, C. R. (1972) Functional organization of cells in superior colliculus of the ground squirrel. *J. Neurophysiol., 35,* 833–846. {7}

Michael, C. R. (1973) Opponent-color and opponent-contrast cells in the lateral geniculate nucleus of the ground squirrel. *J. Neurophysiol., 36,* 536–550. {14}

Michael, C. R. (1979) Color-sensitive hypercomplex cells in monkey striate cortex. *Neurophysiol., 42,* 726–744. {14}

Michael, C. R. (1981) Columnar organization of color cells in monkey's striate cortex. *J. Neurophysiol., 46,* 587–604. {7, 14}

Michael, C. R. (1985) Laminar segregation of color cells in the monkey's striate cortex. *Vision Res., 25,* 415–423. {14}

Michael, C. R. (1988) Retinal afferent arborization patterns, dendritic field orientations, and the segregation of function in the lateral geniculate nucleus of the monkey. *Proc. Natl. Acad. Sci., 85,* 4914–4918. {7}

Michon, J. A. *see* Harvey

Middlebrooks, J. C., Clock, A. E., Xu, L., & Green, D. M. (1994) A panoramic code for sound localization by cortical neurons. *Science, 264,* 842–844. {17}

Mignard, M., & Malpeli, J. G. (1991) Paths of information flow through visual cortex. *Science, 251,* 1249–1251. {8}

Mikami, A. (1992) Spatiotemporal characteristics of direction-selective neurons in the middle temporal visual area of the macaque monkeys. *Exp. Brain Res., 90,* 40–46. {5, 13}

Mikulka, P. J., Freeman, F. G., & Lidstrom, P. (1977) The effect of training technique and amygdala lesions on the acquisition and retention of taste aversion. *Behav. Biol., 19,* 509–517. {20}

Miledi, R. *see* Katz

Miles, F. A., & Fuller, J. H. (1975) Visual tracking and the primate flocculus. *Science, 189,* 1000–1002. {13}

Miller, E. K. *see* Chelazzi; Lueschow; Rao

Miller, G. A., Heise, G. A., & Lichten, W. (1951) The intelligibility of speech as a function of the context of the test materials. *J. Exp. Psychol., 41,* 329–335. {18}

Miller, J. L., & Eimas, P. D. (1977) Studies on the perception of place and manner of articulation: a comparison of the labial-alveolar and nasal-stop distinctions. *J. Acoust. Soc. Am. 61,* 835–845. {18}

Miller, J. D. *see* Burdick; Kuhl

Miller, J. W., & Bartley, S. H. (1954) A study of object shape as influenced by instrumental magnification. *J. Gen. Psychol., 50,* 141–146. {12}

Miller, R. F., & Dacheux, R. F. (1976) Synaptic organization and ionic basis of on and off channels in mudpuppy retina. I. Intracellular analysis of chloride-sensitive electrogenic properties of receptors, horizontal cells, bipolar cells, and amacrine cells. *J. Gen. Physiol., 67,* 639–659. {4}

Miller, R. F., & Slaughter, M. M. (1986) Excitatory amino acid receptors of the retina: diversity of subtypes and conductance mechanisms. *Trends in Neurosci.,* May, 1986, 211–218. {4}

Miller, R. F. *see also* Dacheux

Mills, A. W. (1972) Auditory localization. In J. V. Tobias (Ed.), *Foundations of Modern Auditory theory. Vol. 11,* New York: Academic Press. {**17.17**}

Milner, A. D. (1997) Vision without knowledge. *Phil. Trans. Roy. Soc. Lond. B, 352,* 1249–1256. {8}

Milner, A. D. *see also* Goodale

Mingolla, E., Todd, J. T., & Norman, J. F. (1992) The perception of globally coherent motion. *Vision Res., 32,* 1015–1031. {13}

Mingolla, E. *see also* Pessoa

Minsky, M., & Papert, S. (1969) *Perceptrons.* Cambridge, MA: MIT Press. {10}

Mishkin, M. *see* Murray; Ungerleider

Mitchell, D. E., Reardon, J., & Muir, D. W. (1975) Interocular transfer of the motion after-effect in normal and stereoblind observers. *Exp. Brain Res., 22,* 163–173. {13}

Moberg, E. (1983) The role of cutaneous afferents in

position sense, kinesthesia, and motor function of the hand. *Brain, 106*, 1-19. {19}

Mohler, C. W., & Wurtz, R. H. (1977) Role of striate cortex and superior colliculus in visual guidance of saccadic eye movements in monkeys. *J. Neurophysiol., 40*, 74-94. {7}

Mohler, C. W. *see also* Wurtz

Mollon, J. D. *see* Hunt; Shyue

Montag, E. *see* Boynton

Mooney, C. M., & Ferguson, G. A. (1951) A new test of closure. *Can. J. Psychol., 5*, 129-133. {10}

Moore, B. C. J. (1977) *Psychology of Hearing.* Baltimore: University Park Press. {15, 16, 17, **17.6**}

Moraglia, G. *see* Schneider

Moran, J. *see* Desimone; Spitzer

Moreno-Diaz, R. *see* Leibovic

Morgan, B. A. *see* Hughes

Morgan, H. C. *see* DeValois

Morgan, I. G. (1991) What do amacrine cells do? *Prog. Ret. Res., Vol. 11.* Eds.: N. N. Osborne & G. J. Chader. (New York: Pergamon) pp. 193-214. {4}

Morgan, M. J. & Casco, C. (1990) Spatial filtering and spatial primitives in early vision: an explanation of the Zöllner-Judd class of geometrical illusion. *Proc. Roy. Soc. Lond. B., 242*, 1-10. {12}

Morgan, M. J. *see also* Harris; Watt

Mornsey, J. L. *see* Woodruff

Morrell, F. (1972) Integrative properties of parastriate neurons. In A. G. Karczmar & J. C. Eccles (Eds.), *Brain and Human Behavior* (pp. 259-289) Heidelberg: Springer-Verlag. {17}

Morris, H. R. *see* Hughes

Morrone, M. C. *see* Burr

Morse, P. A., & Snowden, C. T. (1975) An investigation of categorical speech discrimination by rhesus monkeys. *Percept. Psychophys., 17*, 9-16. {18}

Morton, H. B. *see* Riggs

Moss, S. E. *see* Wang

Motter, B. C. (1994a) Neural correlates of attentive selection for color or luminance in extrastriate area V4. *J. Neurosci., 14*, 2178-2189. {8}

Motter, B. C. (1994b) Neural correlates of feature selective memory and pop-out in extrastriate area V4. *J. Neurosci., 14*, 2190-2199. {8}

Mouat, G. S. V. *see* Hammond

Mountain, D. C. *see* Hubbard

Mountcastle, V. B. (1957) Modality and topographic properties of single neurons of cat's somatic sensory cortex. *J. Neurophysiol., 20*, 408-434. {19}

Mountcastle, V. B., & Darien-Smith, I. (1968) Neural mechanisms in somesthesia. In V. B. Mountcastle (Ed.) *Medical Physiology: Vol. II.* (pp. 1372-1423) St. Louis: Mosby) {19}

Mountcastle, V. B. *see also* Lynch

Movshon, J. A. (1975) The velocity tuning of single units in cat striate cortex. *J. Physiol., 249*, 445-468. {7}

Movshon, J. A., Thompson, I. D., & Tolhurst, D. J. (1978a) Spatial summation in the receptive fields of simple cells in the cat's striate cortex. *J. Physiol., 283*, 53-77. {7}

Movshon, J. A., Thompson, I. D., & Tolhurst, D. J. (1987b) Receptive field organization of complex cells in the cat's striate cortex. *J. Physiol., 283*, 79-99. {7}

Movshon, J. A. *see also* Britten; Carandini; Heeger; Kiper

Moxon, E. C. *see* Kiang

Mozell, M. M., Smith, B. P., Smith, P. E., Sullivan, R. L., & Swender, P. (1969) Nasal chemoreception in flavor identification. *Arch. Otolaryng., 90*, 367-373. {20}

Muche, T. *see* Eysel

Muir, D. W. *see* Mitchell

Mukherjee, P. *see* Levine

Mullen, K. T., & Baker, C. L. (1985) A motion aftereffect from an isoluminant stimulus. *Vision Res., 25*, 685-688. {13}

Mullen, K. T. *see also* Sankeralli

Müller, F., Wässle, H., & Voigt, T. (1988) Pharmacological modulation of the rod pathway in the cat retina. *J. Neurophysiol., 59*, 1657-1672. {4}

Munk, M. *see* Eckhorn

Muntz, W. R. A. *see* Northmore

Murakami, I. (1995) Motion aftereffect after monocular adaptation to filled-in motion at the blind spot. *Vision Res., 35*, 1041-1045. {13}

Murakami, M., & Shimoda, Y. (1977) Identification of amacrine and ganglion cells in the carp retina. *J. Physiol., 264*, 801-818. {4}

Murakami, M. *see also* Brown; Tomita

Murch, G. M. (1976) Classical conditioning of the McCollough effect: temporal parameters. *Vision Res., 16*, 615-619. {9}

Murphy, P., & Sillito, A. (1996) Functional morphology

of the feedback pathway from area 17 of the cat visual cortex to the lateral geniculate nucleus. *J. Neurosci., 16*, 1180–1192. {7}

Murphy, R. L. W. *see* Matthews

Murray, E. A., & Mishkin, M. (1998) Object recognition and location memory in monkeys with excitotoxic lesions of the amygdala and hippocampus. *J. Neurosci., 18*, 6568–6582. {8}

Myers, K. J. *see* Ingling

Nachman, M., & Ashe, J. (1974) Effects of basolateral amygdala lesions on neophobia, learned taste aversions, and sodium appetite in rats. *J. Comp. Physiol. Psychol., 87*, 622–643. {20}

Nachmias, J. *see* Graham; Heinemann

Nafe, J. P., & Wagoner, K. S. (1941) The nature of sensory adaptation. *J. Gen. Psych., 25*, 295–321. {19}

Naka, K.-I. (1977) Functional organization of catfish retina. *J. Neurophysiol., 40*, 26–43. {4}

Naka, K.-I., & Rushton, W. A. H. (1966) S-potentials from colour units in the retina of fish (*Cyprinidae*). *J. Physiol., 185*, 536–555. {6, 12, 14}

Naka, K.-I. *see also* Chan; Chappell

Nakajima, S. *see* Komatsu

Nakamura, T., & Gold, G. H. (1987) A cyclic nucleotide gated conductance in olfactory receptory cilia. *Nature, 325*, 442–444. {20}

Nakatani, K., & Yau, K.-W. (1988) Calcium and light adaptation in retinal rods and cones. *Nature, 334*, 69–72. {4}

Nakatani, K. *see also* Yau

Nakayama, K., Shimojo, S., & Silverman, G. H. (1989) Stereoscopic depth: its relation to image segmentation, grouping, and the recognition of occluded objects. *Perception, 18*, 55–68. {**10.13**}

Nakayama, K. *see also* Frost; Rubin; Vaina

Narasimhan, R. *see* Barlow

Narayan, S. S., Temchin, A. N., Recio, A., & Ruggero, M. A. (1998) Frequency tuning of basilar membrane and auditory nerve fibers in the same cochleae. *Science, 282*, 1882–1884. {16}

Nascimento, S. M. C. *see* Foster

Nathans, J., Piantanida, T. P., Eddy, R. L., Shows, T. B., & Hogness, D. S. (1986a) Molecular genetics of inherited variation in human color vision. *Science, 232*, 203–210. {14}

Nathans, J., Thomas, D., & Hogness, D. S. (1986b) Molecular genetics of human color vision: The genes encoding blue, green, and red pigments. *Science, 232*, 193–202. {14}

Nathans, J. *see also* Merbs

Naumann, G. O. H. *see* Jonas

Nawrot, M., & Blake, R. (1989) Neural integration of information specifying structure from stereopsis and motion. *Science, 244*, 716–718. {13}

Nawrot, M. *see also* Schall

Nayar, S. K., & Oren, M. (1995) Visual appearance of matte surfaces. *Science, 267*, 1153–1156. {11}

Neal, M. J. & Cunningham, J. R. (1995) Baclofen enhancement of acetylcholine release from amacrine cells in the rabbit retina by reduction of glycinergic inhibition. *J. Physiol., 482. 2*, 363–372. {4}

Neff, W. D. (1961) Neural mechanisms of auditory discrimination. In: W. A. Rosenblith (Ed.), *Sensory Communication* (pp. 259–275) Cambridge, MA: MIT Press. {15}

Neff, W. D., & Casseday, J. H. (1977) Effects of unilateral ablation of auditory cortex on monaural cat's ability to localize sound. *J. Neurophysiol., 40*, 44–52. {17}

Neisser, U. (1967) *Cognitive Psychology*. New York: Appleton-Century-Crofts. {10, 18, **18.13**}

Neisser, U. *see also* Selfridge; Wallach

Neitz, M. (1998) Society and colorblindness: a view in need of correction. *Res. To Prev. Blindness Sci. Writers Sem.*, 64–66. {14}

Neitz, M., Neitz, J., & Jacobs, G. H. (1991) Spectral tuning of pigments underlying red-green color vision. *Science, 252*, 971–974. {14}

Neitz, M., Neitz, J., & Jacobs, G. H. (1995) Genetic basis of photopigment variations in human dichromats. *Vision Res., 35*, 2095–2103. {14}

Neitz, M. *see also* Neitz

Neitz, J., Neitz, M., & Kainz, P. M. (1996) Visual pigment gene structure and the severity of color vision defects. *Science, 274*, 801–804. {14}

Neitz, J. *see also* Neitz

Nelson, D. A., & Marler, P. (1989) Categorical perception of a natural stimulus continuum: birdsong. *Science, 244*, 976–978. {18}

Nelson, J. I., Kato, H., & Bishop, P. O. (1977) Discrimination of orientation and position disparities by binocularly activated neurons in cat striate cortex. *J. Neurophysiol., 40*, 260–283. {11}

Nelson, R. (1982) AII amacrine cells quicken time

course of rod signals in the cat retina. *J. Neurophysiol., 47*, 928–947. {4}

Nelson, R., & Kolb, H. (1983) Synaptic patterns and response properties of bipolar and ganglion cells in the cat retina. *Vision Res., 23*, 1183–1195. {4}

Nelson, R., Lützow, A. V., Kolb, H., & Gouras, P. (1975) Horizontal cells in cat retina with independent dendritic systems. *Science, 189*, 137–139. {4}

Nelson, R. *see also* Kolb

Nelson, R. J. *see* Kaas

Nelson, S. B. *see* Somers

Nelson, T. M., & Bartley, S. H. (1956) The perception of form in an unstructured field. *J. Gen. Psychol., 54*, 57–63. {12}

Nelson, T. M., Bartley, S. H., & Bourassa, C. (1961) The effect of areal characteristics of targets upon shape-slant invariance. *J. Psychol., 52*, 479–490. {12}

Neufeld, G. R. *see* Stevens

Neumann, H. *see* Pessoa

Neven H., & Aertsen A. (1992) Rate coherence and event coherence in the visual cortex: a neuronal model of object recognition. *Biol. Cybern., 67*, 309–322. {8, 10}

Newman, E. B. *see* Stevens

Newman, J. D. *see* Wollberg

Newport, E. L. *see* Saffran; Samuel

Newsome, W. T., & Pare, F. B. (1988) A selective impairment of motion perception following lesions of the middle temporal visual area (MT). *Neurosci., 8*, 2201–2211. {8}

Newsome, W. T., Wurtz, R. H., & Komatsu, H. (1988) Relation of cortical areas MT and MST to pursuit eye movements. II. Differentiation of retinal from extraretinal inputs. *J. Neurophysiol., 60*, 604–619. {13}

Newsome, W. T. *see also* Britten; Celebrini; Maunsell

Newton, I. (1704) *Optics*, 1st edn. London: W. Innys. {14}

Nguyen, T. *see* Wong-Riley

Nguyen-Legros, J. (1991) Les cellules interplexiformes de la rètine des mammifères. *Ann. Sci. Naturelles, Zool., 12*, 71–88. {4}

Nichols, C. W. *see* Stevens

Nikonov, S. *see* Lyubarsky

Nirenberg, S. & Meister, M. (1997) The light response of retinal ganglion cells is truncated by a displaced amacrine circuit. *Neuron, 18*, 637–650. {4}

Nishida, S.-Y. *see* Ohtani

Noda, H. (1975) Discharges in relay cells of the lateral geniculate nucleus of the cat during spontaneous eye movements in light and darkness. *J. Physiol., 250*, 579–595. {7}

Noda, H. *see also* Adey

Norcia, A. M., Sutter, F. E., & Tyler, C. W. (1985) Electrophysiological evidence for the existence of coarse and fine disparity mechanisms in human. *Vision Res., 25*, 1603–1611. {11}

Norman, D. A. *see* Lindsay

Norman, J. F. *see* Mingolla

Normann, R. A., & Werblin, F. S. (1974) Control of retinal sensitivity I. Light and dark adaptation of vertebrate rods and cones. *J. Gen. Physiol., 63*, 37–61. {**6.2**}

Normann, R. A. *see also* Perlman

Northmore, D. P. M., & Muntz, W. R. A. (1974) Effects of stimulus size on spectral sensitivity in a fish. *(Scardinus erythrophthalmus)*, measured with a classical conditioning paradigm. *Vision Res., 14*, 503–514. {2}

Northrop, C. C. *see* Kiang

Norton, T. T. (1974) Receptive field properties of superior colliculus cells and development of visual behavior in kittens. *J. Neurophysiol., 37*, 674–689. {7}

Nothdurft, H. C. (1990) Texture discrimination by cells in the cat lateral geniculate nucleus. *Exp. Brain Res., 82*, 48–66. {10}

Nothdurft, H. C., & Lee, B. B. (1982) Responses to coloured patterns in the macaque lateral geniculate nucleus: pattern processing in single neurones. *Exp. Brain Res., 48*, 43–54. {14}

Nováková, V. *see* Kubová

Nowlis, G. H., & Frank, M. (1977) Qualities in hamster taste: behavioral and neural evidence. In J. LeMagnen & P. MacLeod (Eds.), *Sixth International Symposium on Olfaction and Taste* (pp. 241–248). London: Information Retrieval LTD. {20, **20.8**}

Nunn, B. J. *see* Baylor; Schnapf

Oakley, B. *see* Diamant

Oates, E. *see* Herbert

Obata, S. *see* Usukara

Obermayer, K., & Blasdel, G. G. (1993) Geometry of orientation and ocular dominance columns in monkey striate cortex. *J. Neurosci., 13*, 4114–4129. {8}

Obermayer, K. *see also* Erwin

Obermueller, A. *see* Eckhorn

O'Bryan, P. M. *see* Baylor

Ochs, A. L. (1979) Is Fourier analysis performed by the visual system or by the visual investigator? *J. Opt. Soc. Am.*, *69*, 95–98. {9}

O'Connell, D. N. *see* Wallach

O'Connell, R. J., & Meredith, M. (1984) Effects of volatile and nonvolatile chemical signals on male sex behaviors mediated by the main and accessory olfactory system. *Behav. Neurosci.*, *98*, 1083–1093. {20}

Odom, J. V. *see* Green

Ohtani, Y., Ejima, Y., & Nishida, S.-Y. Contribution of transient and sustained responses to the perception of apparent motion. *Vision Res.*, *31*, 999–1012. {13}

Ohtsu, K. *see* Toyoda

Ohzawa, I., DeAngelis, G. C., & Freeman, R. D. (1996) Encoding of binocular disparity by simple cells in the cat's visual cortex. *J. Neurophysiol.*, *75*, 1779–1805. {7}

Ohzawa, I., DeAngelis, G. C., & Freeman, R. D. (1997) Encoding of binocular disparity by complex cells in the cat's visual cortex. *J. Neurophysiol.*, *77*, 2879–2909. {11}

Ohzawa, I. *see also* DeAngelis; Ghose; Robson

Ojemann, G., & Mateer, C. (1979) Human language cortex: localization of memory, syntax, and sequential motor-phoneme identification systems. *Science*, *205*, 1401–1403. {18}

Olavarria, J. F., & Van Essen, D. C. (1997) The global pattern of cytochrome oxidase stripes in visual area V2 of the macaque monkey. *Cerbr. Cort.*, *7*, 395–404. {8}

Olson, C. X. *see* Boynton

Olzak, L. A., & Thomas, J. P. (1991) When orthogonal orientations are not processed independently. *Vision Res.*, *31*, 51–57. {9}

O'Neill, W. E. *see* Suga

Ono, H. *see* Komoda

Optican, L. M. *see* Eskandar; Gawne; McClurkin; Richmond

Orban, G. A. *see* Kovács; Lagae

Oren. M. *see* Nayar

Osborne, M. P. *see* Pickles

O'Shea, R. P. *see* Dodwell

Osorio, D., & Bossomaier, T. R. J. (1992) Human cone-pigment spectral sensitivities and the reflectances of natural surfaces. *Biol. Cybern.*, *67*, 217–222. {4}

Osorio, D., & Vorobyev, M. (1996) Colour vision as an adaptation to frugivory in primates. *Proc. Roy. Soc. Lond. B*, *263*, 593–599. {14}

Osterberg, G. (1935) Topography of the layer of rods and cones in the human retina. *Acta Ophthalmol. Suppl.*, *6*, 1–103. {**4.3**}

Ostrosky, D. *see* Schneider

Otis, C. S., Cerf, J. A., & Thomas, G. (1957) Conditioned inhibition of respiration and heartrate in the goldfish. *Science*, *126*, 263–264. {2}

Owen, W. G. *see* Copenhagen

Owens, D. A., & Reed, E. S. (1994) Seeing where we look: fixation as extraretinal information. *Behav. & Brain Sci.*, *17*, 271–272. {13}

Ozeki, M., & Sato, M. (1972) Responses of gustatory cells in the tongue of rat to stimuli representing four taste qualities. *Comp. Biochem. Physiol.*, *41A*, 391–407. {20}

Pace, U., Hanski, E., Salomon, Y., & Lancet, D. (1985) Odorant-sensitive adenylate cyclase may mediate olfactory reception. *Nature*, *316*, 255–258. {20}

Pak, W. L. *see* Grabowski

Pallas, S. L. *see* Roe

Palmer, L. A. *see* Jones

Pan, Z.-H., & Slaughter, M. M. (1991) Control of retinal information coding by $GABA_B$ receptors. *J. Neuroscience*, *11*, 1810–1821. {5}

Pantev, C., Hoke, M., Lütkenhöner, B., & Lehnertz, K. (1989) Tonotopic organization of the auditory cortex: pitch versus frequency representation. *Science*, *246*, 486–488. {16}

Pantle, A. (1970) Adaptation to pattern spatial frequency; effects on visual movement sensitivity in humans. *J. Opt. Soc. Am.*, *60*, 1120–1124. {9}

Pantle, A., & Sekuler, R. (1969) Contrast response of human visual mechanisms sensitive to orientation and direction of motion. *Vision Res.*, *9*, 397–406. {9}

Papathomas, T. V., Gorea, A., & Julesz, B. (1991) Two carriers for motion perception: color and luminance. *Vision Res.*, *31*, 1883–1891. {13}

Papcun, G. *see* Ladefoged

Papert, S. *see* Minsky

Paradiso, M. A., & Hahn, S. (1996) Filling-in percepts produced by luminance modulation. *Vision Res.*, *36*, 2657–2663. {5}

Pare, F. B. *see also* Newsome

Parker, S. *see* Schneider

Partridge, J. C. *see* Lythgoe

Pasik, P. *see* Solomon

Pasik, T. *see* Solomon

Pastore, R. F., Ahroon, W. A., Baffrito, K. J., Friedman, C., Pulea, J. S., & Fink, E. A. (1977) Common factor model of categorical perception. *J. Exp. Psych.: Hum. Percept. Perf, 3,* 686–696. {18}

Pauls, J. *see* Logothetis

Pautler, E. L. *see* Tomita

Pavani, F. *see* Làdavas

Payne, B. R. *see* Lomber

Pearler, W. S., & McLaughlin, J. P. (1967) The question of stimulus content and pupil size. *Psychonomic Science, 8,* 505–506. {3}

Pearler, W. S. *see also* Kahneman

Pedersen, P. E. *see* Benson

Pei, X. *see* Creutzfeldt; Volgushev

Peichl, L. (1991) Alpha ganglion cells in mammalian retinae: common properties, species differences, and some comments on other ganglion cells. *Visual Neurosci., 7,* 155–169. {5, 7}

Peichl, L., & Wässle, H. (1981) Morphological identification of on- and off-centre brisk transient (Y) cells in cat retina. *Proc. Roy. Soc. Lond. B, 212,* 139–156. {5}

Peichl, L., & Wässle, H. (1983) The structural correlate of the receptive field centre of β ganglion cells in the cat retina. *J. Physiol., 341,* 309–324. {5}

Peichl, L. *see also* Wässle

Pelah, A., & Barlow, H. B. (1996) Visual illusion from running. *Nature, 381,* 283. {13}

Pellizzer, G., & Georgopoulos, A. P. (1993) Common processing constraints for visuomotor and visual mental rotations. *Exp. Brain Res., 93,* 165–172. {10}

Penn, R., & Hagins, W. A. (1972) Kinetics of the photocurrent of retinal rods. *Biophysics J., 12,* 1073–1094. {6}

Pennartz, C. M. A., and van de Grind, W. A. (1990) Simulation of movement detection by direction-selective ganglion cells in the rabbit and squirrel retina. *Vision Res., 30,* 1223-1234. {5}

Pennisi, E. (1996) How the songbird makes his song. *Science, 273,* 1801–1802. {18}

Penrose, L. S., & Penrose, R. (1958) Impossible objects: a special type of illusion. *Br. J. Psychol., 49,* 31–33. {10, **10.35**}

Penrose, R. *see* Penrose

Pepperberg, D. R., Brown, P. K., Lurie, M., & Dowling, J. E. (1978) Visual pigment and photoreceptor sensitivity in the isolated skate retina. *J. Gen. Physiol., 71,* 369–396. {4}

Pepperberg, D. R. *see also* Crouch

Peregrin, J. *see* Kubová

Perey, A. J. *see* Schwartz

Perez, J. M. *see* Dawson

Pérez, R. *see* Alonso

Perl, E. R. *see* Burgess; Light; Sato

Perlman, I., & Ammermüller, J. (1994) Receptive-field size of L1 horizontal cells in the turtle retina: effects of dopamine and background light. *J. Neurophysiol., 72,* 2786–2795. {6}

Perlman, I., & Normann, R. A. (1998) Light adaptation and sensitivity controlling mechanisms in vertebrate photoreceptors. *Prog. Retinal & Eye Res., 17,* 523–563. {6}

Pernier, J. *see* Tallon-Baudry

Persky, S. E. *see* Bloomfield

Perrett, D. I., Rolls, E. T., & Caan, W. (1982) Visual neurones responsive to faces in the monkey temporal cortex. *Exp. Brain Res., 47,* 329–342. {8}

Perrett, D. I. *see also* Hietanen

Perry, V. H. *see* Shapley; Silveira

Pesetsky, D. *see* Repp

Pessoa, L., Mingolla, E., & Neumann, H. (1995) A contrast-and luminance-driven multiscale network model of brightness perception. *Vision Res., 15,* 2201–2223. {12}

Peteanu, L. A. *see* Schoenlein; Wang

Peterhans, E., & von der Heydt, R. (1989) Mechanisms of contour perception in monkey visual cortex. II. Contours bridging gaps. *J. Neurosci., 9,* 1749–1763. {8}

Peterhans, E. *see also* von der Heydt

Peterson, G. E., & Barney, H. L. (1952) Control methods used in a study of the vowels. *J. Acoust. Soc. Am., 24,* 175–184. {18, **18.6**}

Petitto, L. A., & Marentette, P. F. (1991) Babbling in the manual mode: evidence for the ontogeny of language. *Science, 251,* 1493–1496. {18}

Petrides, M. *see* Georgopoulos

Petry, S., & McShane, R. C. (1988) Subjective contours to the second power. *Investig. Ophthal. Visual Sci., 29 (Suppl.),* 401. {**10.14**}

Petry, S., & Siegel, S. (1989) Parametric analysis of subjective contours. *Investig. Ophthal. Visual Sci., 30 (Suppl.),* 254. {10}

Pettigrew, J. D. (1990) Is there a single, most-efficient algorithm for stereopsis? In: C. Blakemore (Ed.), *Vision:*

coding and Efficiency (pp. 283–290) Cambridge: Cambridge University Press. {11}

Pettigrew, J. D., & Konishi, M. (1976) Neurons selective for orientation and binocular disparity in the visual walst of the barn owl *(Tyto alba) Science, 193,* 675–678. {11}

Pettigrew, J. D. *see also* Barlow; Knudsen

Pfaffmann, C. (1941) Gustatory afferent impulses. *J. Cell. Comp. Physiol., 17,* 243–258. {20}

Pfaffmann, C. (1955) Gustatory nerve impulses in rat, cat, and rabbit. *J. Neurophysiol., 18,* 429–440. {20, **20.6**}

Pfaffmann, C. (1978a) Neurophysiological mechanisms of taste. *Am. J. Clin. Nutr., 31,* 1058–1067. {20}

Pfaffmann, C. (1978b) The vertebrate phylogeny, neural code, and integrative processes of taste. In E. C. Carterette & M. P. Friedman (Eds.) *Handbook of Perception, Vol. 6A: Tasting and Smelling* (pp. 51–123) New York: Academic Press. {20}

Pfeiffer, R. R. *see* Kiang

Pham, H. A. *see* Merigan

Phillips, G. C. *see* Wilson

Piantanida, T. (1988) The molecular genetics of color vision and color blindness. *Trends in Genet., 4,* 319–323. {14}

Piantanida, T. P. *see also* Nathans

Piccolino, M. *see* Bisti

Pickles, J. O., Comis, S. D., & Osborne, M. P. (1984) Cross-links between stereocilia in the guinea pig organ of Corti, and their possible relation to sensory transduction. *Hearing Res., 15,* 103–112. {15]

Picoult, E. *see* Matin

Pinto, L. H. *see* Brown; Enroth-Cugell

Pirenne, M. H. *see* Hecht

Pitblado, C. B., & Kaufman, L. (1967) On classifying the visual illusions. In L. Kaufman (Ed.), *Contour Descriptor Properties of Visual Shape.* Sperry Rand Research Center Report SRRC-CR 67-43, pp. 32–53. Cited by L. Kaufman (1974) *Sight and Mind.* New York: Oxford University Press. {12}

Pitts, W. H. *see* Lettvin

Pizlo, Z. (1994) A theory of shape constancy based on perspective invariants. *Vision Res., 34,* 1637–1658. {12}

Plug, C. *see* Ross

Poggio, G. F., Gonzalez, F., & Krause, F. (1988) Stereoscopic mechanisms in monkey visual cortex: binocular correlation and disparity selectivity. *J. Neurosci., 8,* 4531–4550. {11}

Poggio, G. F., & Talbot, W. H. (1981) Mechanisms of static and dynamic stereopsis in foveal cortex of the rhesus monkey. *J. Physiol., 315,* 469–492. {11}

Poizner, H. (1981) Visual and 'phonetic' coding of movement: evidence from American sign language. *Science, 212,* 691–693. {18}

Pokorny, J. *see* Kremers; Smith

Polat, U., & Sagi, D. (1993) Lateral interactions between spatial channels: suppression and facilitation revealed by lateral masking experiments. *Vision Res., 33,* 993–999. {9}

Pollen, D. A., Andrews, B. W., & Feldon, S. E. (1978) Spatial frequency selectivity of periodic complex cells in the visual cortex of the cat. *Vision Res., 18,* 665–682. {9}

Pollen, D. A., Gaska, J. P., & Jacobson, L. D. (1988) Responses of simple and complex cells to compound sine-wave gratings. *Vision Res., 28,* 25–39. {9}

Pollen, D. A., & Ronner, S. F. (1975) Periodic excitability changes across the receptive fields of complex cells in the striate and parastriate cortex of the cat. *J. Physiol., 245,* 667–697. {9}

Pollen, D. A., & Ronner, S. F. (1981) Phase relationships between adjacent simple cells in visual cortex. *Science, 212,* 1409–1411. {9}

Pollen, D. A., & Ronner, S. F. (1982) Spatial computation performed by simple and complex cells in the visual cortex of the cat. *Vision Res., 22,* 101–118. {9}

Pollen, D. A. *see also* Jacobson; Liu

Polson, M. C. *see* DeValois

Polt, J. M. *see* Hess

Pomerantz, J. R. *see* Kolers

Popplewell, D. A. *see* Gulyás

Pourcho, R. G. (1996) Neurotransmitters in the retina. *Curr. Eye Res., 15,* 797–803. {4}

Porac, C. *see* Coren

Poranen, A. *see* Hyvarinen

Porat, M., & Zeevi, Y. Y. (1989) Localized texture processing in vision: analysis and synthesis in Gaborian space. *IEEE Trans. Biomed. Engineering, 36,* 115–128. {9}

Porter, J. D. *see* Sparks

Postman, L., & Egan, J. P. (1949) *Experimental Psychology.* New York: Harper & Row. {17, **17.7**}

Powell, T. P. S. *see* Brooke

Powers, M. K. *see* Bassi; Bilotta

Pretori, H. *see* Hess

Price, D. D., Hu, J. W., Dubner, R., & Gracely, R. H. (1977) Peripheral suppression of first pain and central summation of second pain evoked by noxious heat pulses. *Pain, 3*, 57–68. {19}

Price, D. D. *see also* Rainville

Priestly, J. (1772) *The History and Present State of Discoveries Relating to Vision, Light, and Colours.* London: J. Johnson. {3}

Przybyszewski, A. W. (1998) Vision: does top-down processing help us to see? *Curr. Biol., 8*, R135–139. {10}

Puckett, J. de W., & Steinman, R. M. (1969) Tracking eye movements with and without saccadic correction. *Vision Res., 9*, 295–303. {13}

Pugh, E. N., & Lamb, T. D. (1990) Cyclic GMP and calcium: the internal messengers of excitation and adaptation in vertebrate photoreceptors. *Vision Res., 30*, 1923–1948. {4}

Pugh, E. N. *see also* Liebman; Lyubarsky

Pulea, J. S. *see* Pastore

Purkinje, J. E. (1825) *Neue Beiträge zur Kenntniss des Sehens in Subjectiver Hinsicht.* 108–110. Cited by E. G. Boring (1942) *Sensation and Perception in the History of Experimental Psychology.* (pp. 177–178. New York: Appleton-Century-Crofts). {6}

Raiguel, S. *see* Lagae

Rainer, G. *see* Rao

Rainville, P., Duncan, G. H., Price, D. D., Carrier, B., & Bushnell, M. C. (1997) Pain affect encoded in human anterior cingulate but not somatosensory cortex. *Science, 277*, 968–971. {19}

Randolph, M., & Semmes, J. (1974) Behavioral consequences of selective subtotal ablations in the post central gyrus of Maccaca mulatta. *Brain Res., 70*, 55–70. {19}

Ransil, B. J. *see* Seeck

Rao, S. C., Rainer, G., & Miller, E. K. (1997) Integration of what and where in the primate prefrontal cortex. *Science, 276*, 821–824. {8}

Rao, S. C. *see also* Toth

Rao-Mirotznik, R., Harkins, A. B., Buchsbaum, G., & Sterling, P. (1995) Mammalian rod terminal: architecture of a binary synapse. *Neuron, 14*, 561–569. {4}

Raphael, L. J. *see* Dorman

Ratliff, F. (1976) On the psychophysiological bases of universal color terms. *Proc. Am. Philos. Soc., 120*, 311–330. {14}

Ratliff, F. (1984) Why Mach bands are not seen at the edges of a step. *Vision Res., 24*, 163–165. {5}

Ratliff, F., & Sirovich, L. (1978) Equivalence classes of visual stimuli. *Vision Res., 18*, 845–851. {9}

Ratliff, F., Knight, B. W., & Graham, N. (1969) On tuning and amplification by lateral inhibition. *Proc. Natl. Acad. Sci., 62*, 733–740. {12}

Ratliff, F. *see also* Hartline

Ratto, G. M. *see* Usai

Raviola, E. *see* Feigenspan

Raynor, S. *see* Billone

Read, H. L. *see* Siegel

Reardon, J. *see* Mitchell

Recio, A. *see* Narayan

Redburn, D. A. *see* Massey

Reddy, M. G. *see* Frishman

Reed, E. S. *see* Owens

Reed, R. R. *see* Jones

Reeves, A. *see* Craver-Lemley

Reeves, B. C. *see* Barlow

Regan, D. *see* Cynader; Regan

Regan, M. P., He, P., & Regan, D. (1995) An audio-visual convergence area in the human brain. *Exp. Brain Res., 106*, 485–487. {17}

Reger, S. N. (1960) Effect of middle ear muscle action on certain psychological measurements. *Ann. Otol. Rhinol. Laryngol., 69*, 1179–1198. {15}

Reid, R. C., & Alonso, J.-M. (1995) Specificity of monosynaptic connections from thalamus to visual cortex. *Nature, 378*, 281–284. {7}

Reid, R. C., & Alonso, J.-M. (1996) The processing and encoding of information in the visual cortex. *Curr. Opin. In Biol., 6*, 475–480. {7}

Reid, R. C., Soodak, R. E., & Shapley, R. M. (1991) Direction selectivity and spatiotemporal structure of receptive fields of simple cells in cat striate cortex. *J. Neurophysiol., 66*, 505–529. {7}

Reid, R. C. *see also* Alonso; Usrey

Reinagel, P. *see* Warland

Reitboeck, H. J. *see* Eckhorn

Reitner, A., Sharpe, L. T., & Zrenner, E. (1991) Is colour vision possible with only rods and blue-sensitive cones? *Nature, 352*, 798–800. {14}

Rentschler, I., Treutwein, B., & Landis, T. (1994) Dissociation of local and global processing in visual agnosia. *Vision Res., 34*, 963–971. {8}

Repp, B. H., & Liberman, A. M. (1987) Phonetic category boundaries are flexible. In S. Harnad (Ed.), *Categorical Perception; the Groundwork of Cognition* (pp. 89–112). Cambridge: Cambridge University Press). {18}

Repp, B. H., Liberman, A. M., Eccardt, T., & Pesetsky, D. (1978) Perceptual integration of acoustic cues for stop, fricative, and affricative manner. *J. Exp. Psychol., Hum. Percept. Perform., 4,* 621–637. {18}

Reppas, J. B. *see* Usrey

Restle, F. (1970) Moon illusion explained on the basis of relative size. *Science, 167,* 1092–1096. {12}

Reynolds, G. S., & Stevens, S. S. (1960) Binaural summation of loudness. *J. Acoust. Soc. Am., 32,* 1337–1344. {17}

Reynolds, J., & Keverne, E. B. (1979) The accessory olfactory system and its role in the pheromonally mediated suppression of oestrus in grouped mice. *J. Reprod. Fert., 57,* 31–35. {20}

Reynolds, S. H. *see* Djamgoz

Rho, J. M. *see* Kiang

Rhoades, R. W. *see* Chalupa

Ribaupierre, Y. de *see* Brownell

Ricardo, J. A., & Koh, E. T. (1978) Anatomical evidence of direct projections from the nucleus of the solitary tract to the hypothalamus, amygdala, and other forebrain structures in the rat. *Brain Res., 153,* 1–26. {20}

Richards, W. (1973) Visual processing in scotomata. *Exp. Brain Res., 17,* 333–347. {7}

Richardson, D. E., & Akil, H. (1977) Pain reduction by electrical brain stimulation in man. *J. Neurosurg., 47,* 178–183. {19}

Richmond, B. J., & Optican, L. M. (1990) Temporal encoding of two-dimensional patterns by single units in primate primary visual cortex. II. Information transmission. *J. Neurophysiol., 64,* 370–380. {7, A}

Richmond, B. J., Gawne, T. J., & Jin, G.-X. (1997) Neuronal codes: reading them and learning how their structure influences network organization. *BioSystems, 40,* 149–157. {A}

Richmond, B. J., Optican, L. M., & Spitzer, H. (1990) Temporal encoding of two dimensional patterns by single units in primate primary visual cortex. I. stimulus-response relationships. *J. Neurophysiol., 64,* 351–369. {A}

Richmond, B. J. *see also* Eskandar; Gawne; Kjaer

Richter, A., & Simon, E. J. (1974) Electrical responses of double cones in the turtle retina. *J. Physiol., 242,* 673–683. {4}

Riggs, L. A., Merton, D. A., & Morton, H. B. (1974) Suppression of visual phosphenes during saccadic eye movements. *Vision Res., 14,* 997–1011. {13}

Riley, L. H. *see* Grigg

Ringach, D. L., & Shapley, R. (1996) Spatial and temporal properties of illusory contours and amodal boundary completion. *Vision Res., 36,* 3037–3050. {10}

Ripps, H. *see* Dowling

Ritsma, R. J. *see* Schouten

Ritter, M. (1977) Effect of disparity and viewing distance on perceived depth. *Percept. Psychophys., 22,* 400–407. {11}

Rizzolatti, G., & Arbib, M. A. (1998) Language within our grasp. *Trends in Neurosci., 21,* 188–194. {18}

Rizzolatti, G. *see also* Berti

Robb, R. *see* Simon

Roberts, S. *see* Kolb

Robinson, C. J. *see* LaMotte

Robinson, D. L., Goldberg, M. E., & Stanson, G. B. (1978) Parietal association cortex in the primate: sensory mechanisms and behavioral modulations. *J. Neurophysiol., 41,* 910–932. {8}

Robinson, D. L. *see also* Bushnell

Robinson, W. E. *see* Yoshikami

Robson, J. G., & Frishman, L. J. (1995) Response linearity and kinetics of the cat retina: the bipolar cell component of the dark-adapted electroretinogram. *Visual Neurosci., 12,* 837–850. {6}

Robson, J. G., Tolhurst, D. J., Freeman, R. D., & Ohzawa, I. (1988) Simple cells in the visual cortex of the cat can be narrowly tuned for spatial frequency. *Visual Neurosci., 1,* 415–419. {9}

Robson, J. G. *see also* Campbell; Enroth-Cugell; Frishman; Viswanathan; Watson

Rocha-Mirand, C. E. *see* Fiorani

Rock, I. (1974) The perception of disoriented figures. *Sci. Am., 230,* 78–85. {10, 10.20}

Rock, I., & Brosgole, L. (1964) Grouping based on phenomenal proximity. *J. Exp. Psychol., 67,* 531–538. {10}

Rock, I., & Kaufman, L. (1962) The moon illusion. II. *Science, 136,* 1023–1031. {12}

Rock, I., & McDermott, W. (1964) The perception of visual angle. *Acta Psychol., 22,* 119–134. {12}

Rock, I. *see also* Kaufman

Rodieck, R. W. (1967) Maintained activity in cat retinal ganglion cells. *J. Neurophysiol., 30*, 1043–1071. {5}

Rodieck, R. W. (1973) *The Vertebrate Retina*. San Francisco: W. H. Freeman. {4, 15}

Rodieck, R. W. (1979) Visual pathways. *Ann. Rev. Neurosci., 2*, 193–225. {5, 7}

Rodieck, R. W., & Stone, J. (1965) Analysis of receptive fields of cat retinal ganglion cells. *J. Neurophysiol., 28*, 833–849. {5, 12}

Rodieck, R. W. *see also* Dreher; Leventhal

Rodman, H. R., & Albright, T. D. (1989) Single-unit analysis of pattern-motion selective properties in the middle temporal visual area (MT). *Exp. Brain Res., 75*, 53–64. {8}

Rodman, H. R., Scalaidhe, S. P. Ó., & Gross, C. G. (1993) Response properties of neurons in temporal cortical visual areas of infant monkeys. *J. Neurophysiol., 70*, 1115–1136. {8}

Roe, A. W., Garraghty, P. E., & Sur, M. (1989) Terminal arbors of single ON-center and OFF-center X and Y retinal ganglion cell axons within the ferret's lateral geniculate nucleus. *J. Comp. Neurol., 288*, 208–242. {8}

Roe, A. W., Pallas, S. L., Hahm, J.-O., & Sur, M. (1990) A map of visual space induced in primary auditory cortex. *Science, 250*, 818–820. {15, 17}

Roe, A. W., Pallas, S. L., Kwon, Y. H., & Sur, M. (1992) Visual projections routed to the auditory pathway in ferrets: receptive fields of visual neurons in primary auditory cortex. *J. Neurosci., 12*, 3651–3664. {8, 16}

Roe, A. W. *see also* Sur

Roelfsema, P. R. *see* Fries

Rogers, S. D. *see* Mantyh

Röhrenbeck, J. *see* Wässle

Roitman, V. L. *see* de Carvalho

Roland, P. E. *see* Gulyás

Rolls, E. T. *see* Perrett; Scott; Tovee

Ronner, S. F. *see* Pollen

Rosa, M. G. P. *see* Elston; Fiorani

Rose, J. E., Brugge, J. F., Anderson, D. J., & Hind, J. E. (1968) Patterns of activity in single auditory nerve fibers of the squirrel monkey. In: A. V. S. deReuck & J. Knight (Eds.), *Hearing Mechanisms in Vertebrates*. (pp. 144–157 London: Churchill). {16}

Rose, J. E., Galambos, R., & Hughes, J. R. (1959) Microelectrode studies of the cochlear nuclei of the cat. *Johns Hopkins Hosp. Bull., 104*, 211–251. {16, **16.7**}

Rose, J. E., Hind, J. E., Anderson, D. J., & Brugge, J. F. (1971) Some effects of stimulus intensity on response of auditory nerve fibers in the squirrel monkey. *J. Neurophysiol., 34*, 685–699. {16, **16.5, 16.11**}

Rosen, M. *see* Herbert

Rosenfeld, A. *see* Aloimonos; Barlow

Rosenquist, A. C. *see* Stevens

Rosner, B. S. *see* Cutting

Ross, H. E., & Plug, C. (1998) The history of size constancy and size illusions. In V-Walsh & J. Kulikowski (Eds.), *Perceptual Constancy: Why Things Look as They Do* (pp. 499–519). (Cambridge: Cambridge University Press. {12}

Ross, J., & Speed, H. D. (1991) Contrast adaptation and contrast masking in human vision. *Proc. Roy. Soc. B, 246*, 61–69. {9}

Ross, J. *see also* Burr

Rossetti, Y., Koga, K., & Mano, T. (1993) Prismatic displacement of vision induces transient changes in the timing of eye-hand coordination. *Percept. & Psychophys., 54*, 355–364. {3}

Roth, G. L. *see* Merzenich

Rouiller, E. M. *see* Tanné

Rowe, J. S. *see* Djamgoz

Rowe, M. H., & Cox, J. F. (1993) Spatial receptive-field structure of cat retinal W cells. *Visual Neurosci., 10*, 765–779. {5}

Rubin, L. L. *see* Stevens

Rubin, N., Nakayama, K., & Shapley, R. (1996) Enhanced perception of illusory contours in the lower versus upper visual hemifields. *Science, 271*, 651–653. {10, **10.16**}

Rubin, N., Solomon, S., & Hochstein, S. (1995) Restricted ability to recover three-dimensional global motion from one-dimensional local signals: theoretical observations. *Vision Res., 35*, 569–578. {13}

Rubinstein, M. *see* Fischler

Ruddock, K. H. *see* Djamgoz

Ruderman, D. L. *see* Mel

Ruggero, M. A. *see* Imig; Narayan

Rushton, W. A. H. (1961a) Rhodopsin measurement and dark adaptation in a subject deficient in cone vision. *J. Physiol., 156*, 193–205. {6}

Rushton, W. A. H. (1961b) Peripheral coding in the nervous system. In W. R. Rosenblith (Ed.). *Sensory Communication* (pp. 169–181). Cambridge: MIT Press). {2}

Rushton, W. A. H. (1965) The Ferrier Lecture, 1962. Visual adaptation. *Proc. Soc. Lond. Ser. B., 162,* 20–46. {6}

Rushton, W. A. H., & Westheimer, G. (1962) The effect upon the rod threshold of bleaching neighbouring rods. *J. Physiol., 164,* 318–329. {6}

Rushton, W. A. H. *see also* Gosline; Naka

Russell, M. J. (1976) Human olfactory communication. *Nature, 260,* 520–522. {20}

Ryugo, D. K. *see* Kiang

Sabol, J. *see* Berenberg

Sachtler, W. L., & Zaidi, Q. (1992) Chromatic and luminance signals in visual memory. *J. Opt. Soc. Am. A, 9,* 877–894. {14}

Sacks, O. (1995) To see and not see. In *An Anthropologist on Mars* (pp. 108–152). New York: Alfred A. Knopf. {14, 15, 19}

Saffran, J. R., Aslin, R. N., & Newport, E. L. (1996) Statistical learning by 8-month-old infants. *Science, 274,* 1926–1928. {18}

Sagi, D., & Julesz, B. (1985) 'Where' and 'what' in vision. *Science, 228,* 1217–1219. {10}

Sagi, D. *see also* Karni; Polat

Sagoo, M. S., & Lagnado, L. (1996) The action of cytoplasmic calcium on the cGMP-activated channel in salamander rod photoreceptors. *J. Physiol., 497,* 309–319. {4}

Saito, T., Kujiraoka, T., & Yonaha, T. (1983) Connections between photoreceptors and horseradish peroxidase-injected bipolar cells in the carp retina. *Vision Res., 23,* 353–362. {4}

Saito, H.-A., Shimahara, T., & Fukada, Y. (1970) Four types of responses to light and dark spot stimuli on the cat optic nerve. *Tohoku J. Exp. Med., 102,* 127–133. {5}

Saito, H. *see also* Fukada

Sakata, H., Shibutani, H., & Kawano, K. (1980) Spatial properties of visual fixation neurons in posterior parietal association cortex of the monkey. *J. Neurophysiol., 43,* 1654–1672. {8}

Sakuma, I. *see* Sugishita

Salama, G. *see* Blasdel

Saleh, E. J. *see* Levine

Salin, P. A., Girard, P., Kennedy, H., & Bullier, J. (1992) Visuotopic organization of corticocortical connections in the visual system of the cat. *J. Comp. Neurol., 320,* 415–434. {8}

Salin, P. A. *see also* Girard

Salmelin, R. *see* Hari

Salomon, Y. *see* Pace

Salt, T. E. *see* Sillito

Sams, M., Aulanko, R., Hämäläinen, M., Hari, R., Lounasmaa, O. V., Lu, S.-T., & Simola, J. (1991) Seeing speech: visual information from lip movements modifies activity in the human auditory cortex. *Neurosci. Lett., 127,* 141–145. {18}

Samson, S. *see* Belin

Samson, Y. *see* Belin

Samuel, A. G., & Newport, E. L. (1979) Adaptation of speech by nonspeech: evidence for complex acoustic cue detectors. *J. Exp. Psychol. Hum. Percept. Perform., 5,* 563–578. {18}

Sandell, J. H., & Schiller, P. H. (1982) Effect of cooling area 18 on striate cortex cells in the squirrel monkey. *J. Neurophysiol., 48,* 38–48. {7}

Sandel, T. T., Teas, D. C., Fedderson, W. E., & Jeffress, L. A. (1955) Localization of sound from single and paired sources. *J. Acoust. Soc. Am., 27,* 842–852. {17}

Sanderson, K. J., Bishop, P. O., & Darien-Smith, I. (1971) The properties of the binocular receptive fields of lateral geniculate neurons. *Exp. Brian Res., 13,* 178–207. {7}

Sankeralli, M. J., & Mullen, K. T. (1996) Estimation of the L-, M-, and S-cone weights of the postreceptoral detection mechanisms. *J. Opt. Soc. Am. A., 13,* 906–915. {14}

Santos-Sacchi, J. *see* Dallos

Sasaki, T. *see* Kaneko

Sasaki, Y. *see* Chino

Sato, H., Katsuyama, N., Tamura, H., Hata, Y., & Tsumoto, T. (1996) Mechanisms underlying orientation selectivity of neurons in the primary visual cortex of the macaque. *J. Physiol., 494. 3,* 757–771. {7}

Sato, H. *see also* Hata

Sato, J., & Perl, E. R. (1991) Adrenergic excitation of cutaneous pain receptors induced by peripheral nerve injury. *Science, 251,* 1608–1610. {19}

Sato, M. (1973) Gustatory receptor mechanism in mammals. *Adv. Biophys., 4,* 103–152. {20}

Sato, M. *see also* Ozeki

Sato, T. (1980) Recent advances in the physiology of taste cells. *Prog. Neurobiol., 14,* 25–67. {20}

Savel, S. *see* Belin

Scarpolino, R. *see* Bartoshuk

Scalaidhe, S. P. Ó. *see* Rodman

Schaeffel, F. *see* Wagner

Schall, J. D., Nawrot, M., Blake, R., & Yu, K. (1993) Visually guided attention is neutralized when informative cues are visible but unperceived. *Vision Res., 33,* 2057–2064. {11}

Scharf, B. (1961) Complex sounds and critical bands. *Psychol. Bull., 58,* 205–217. {17}

Scharf, B. (1970) Critical bands. In J. V. Tobias (Ed.), *Foundations of Modern Auditory Theory,* Vol. 1 (pp. 157–202) New York: Academic Press). {17}

Schatz, C. (1954) The role of context in the perception of stops. *Language, 30,* 47–56. {18}

Scheich, H. *see* Langner

Schein, S. J. *see* Desimone; Tsukamoto

Schellart, N. A. M., & Spekreijse, H. (1973) Origin of the stochastic nature of ganglion cell activity in isolated goldfish retina. *Vision Res., 13,* 337–347. {5}

Schiffman, H. R. (1967) Size estimation of familiar objects under informative and reduced conditions of viewing. *Am. J. Psychol., 80,* 229–235. {11}

Schiffman, H. R. *see also* Fillenbaum

Schiffman, S. S. (1974) Physicochemical correlates of olfactory quality. *Science, 185,* 112–117. {20}

Schillen, T. B. *see* Engel

Schiller, P. H. (1995) The ON and OFF channels of the mammalian visual system. *Prog. Ret. Eye Res., 15,* 173–195. {4}

Schiller, P. H. (1996) On the specificity of neurons and visual areas. *Behav. Brain Res., 76,* 21–35. {8}

Schiller, P. H., Finlay, B. L., & Volman, S. F. (1976a). Quantitative studies of single-cell properties in monkey striate cortex. I. Spatiotemporal organization of receptive fields. *J. Neurophysiol., 39,* 1288–1319. {9}

Schiller, P. H., Finlay, B. L., & Volman, S. F. (1976b) Quantitative studies of single-cell properties in monkey striate cortex. III. Spatial frequency. *J. Neurophysiol., 39,* 1334–1351. {7, 9}

Schiller, P. H., & Malpeli, J. G. (1978) Functional specificity of lateral geniculate nucleus laminae of the rhesus monkey. *J. Neurophysiol., 41,* 788–797. {7}

Schiller, P. H. *see also* Sandell

Schmetterer, L. *see* Drexler

Schnapf, J. L., Kraft, T. W., Nunn, B. J., & Baylor, D. A. (1988) Spectral sensitivity of primate photoreceptors. *Visual Neurosci., 1,* 255–261. {14}

Schnapf, J. L. *see also* Baylor; Kraft

Schneeweis, D. M. *see* Kraft

Schneider, B., Moraglia, G., & Jepson, A. (1989). Binocular unmasking: an analog to binaural unmasking? *Science, 243,* 1479–1481. {10}

Schneider, B., Parker, S., Ostrosky, D., Stein, D., & Kanow, G. (1974). A scale for the psychological magnitude of number. *Percept. Psychophys., 16,* 43–46. {2}

Schneider, G. E. (1969) Two visual systems. *Science, 163,* 895–902. {7}

Schneider, S. *see* Benimoff

Schneider, U. *see* Jonas

Schoenlein, R. W., Peteanu, L. A., Mathies, R. A., & Shank, C. V. (1991). The first step in vision: femtosecond isomerization of rhodopsin. *Science, 254,* 412–415. {4}

Schoenlein, R. W. *see also* Wang

Scholes, J. H. (1975) Colour receptors, and their connexions in the retina of a cyprinid fish. *Phil. Trans. R. Soc. Lond. Ser. B., 270,* 61–118. {4}

Schomer, D. *see* Seeck

Schouten, J. F., Ritsma, R. J., & Cardozo, B. L. (1962). Pitch of the residue. *J. Acoust. Soc. Am., 34,* 1418–1424. {16}

Schroeder, C. E., Tenke, C. E., Arezzo, J. C., & Vaughan, H. G. (1990) Binocularity in the lateral geniculate nucleus of the alert macaque. *Brain Res., 521,* 303–310. {7}

Schulten, K. *see* Erwin

Schumann, F. (1904) Emige Beobachtungen über die Zusammenfassung von Gesichlseindrücken zu Einheiten. *Psychol. Studies, 1,* 1–32. {10}

Schwartz, A. B. *see* Georgopoulos

Schwartz, A. S., Perey, A. J., & Azulay, A. (1975) Further analysis of active and passive touch in pattern discrimination. *Bull. Psychon. Soc., 6,* 7–9. {19}

Schwartz, E. A. (1975) Cones excite rods in the retina of the turtle. *J. Physiol., 246,* 639–651. {4}

Schwartz, E. A. (1976) Electrical properties of the rod syncytium in the retina of the turtle. *J. Physiol., 257,* 379–406. {4}

Schwartz, J. H. *see* Kandel

Schweigart, G. *see* Eysel

Schweitzer-Tong, D. E. *see* Frishman

Scott, T. R., & Mark, G. P. (1986) Feeding and taste. *Prog. Neurobiol., 27,* 293–331. {20}

Scott, T. R., Yaxley, S., Sienkiewicz, Z. J., & Rolls, E. T. (1986) Gustatory responses in the nucleus tractus solitarius of the alert cynomolgus monkey. *J. Neurophysiol., 55*, 182–200. {20}

Scott, T. R. *see also* Chang

Seashore, C. E. (1938) *Psychology of Music.* New York: McGraw-Hill. {**15.4**}

Seeck, M., Schomer, D., Mainwaring, N., Ives, J., Dubuisson, D., Blume, H., Cosgrove, R., Ransil, B. J., Mesulam, M.-M. (1995) Selectively distributed processing of visual object recognition in the temporal and frontal lobes of the human brain. *Ann. Neurol., 37,* 538–545. {8}

Sefton, A. J. *see* Burke; Martin

Segall, M. H., Campbell, D. T., & Herskovits, M. J. (1963) Cultural differences in the perception of geometric illusions. *Science, 139,* 769–771. {10}

Sejnowski, T. J., Koch, C., & Churchland, P. S. (1988) Computational neuroscience. *Science, 241,* 1299–1306. {7, 11}

Sejnowski, T. J. *see also* Churchland; Lehky; Zemel

Sekuler, R., & Blake, R. (1985) *Perception.* New York: Knopf. {20}

Sekuler, R. *see also* Levinson; Pantle; Tynan

Selfridge, O. G. (1959) Pandemonium: a paradigm for learning. In D. V. Blake & A. M. Uttley (Eds.) *Symposium on the Mechanization of Thought Processes* (pp. 511–529). London: HMSO. {10}

Selfridge, O. G., & Neisser, U. (1960) Pattern recognition by machine. *Sci. Am., 203(2),* 60–68. {10}

Semmes, J. *see* Randolph

Semple, M. N. *see* Spitzer

Sengpiel, F. (1997) Binocular rivalry: ambiguities resolved. *Curr. Biol., 7,* R447–450. {11}

Sergeant, R. L. *see* Harris

Servos, P., Matin, L., & Goodale, M. A. (1995) Dissociation between two modes of spatial processing by a visual form agnosic. *NeuroReport, 6,* 1893–1896. {10}

Shank, C. V. *see* Schoenlein; Wang

Shannon, R. V., Zeng, F.-G., Kamath, V., Wygonski, J., & Ekelid, M. (1995) Speech recognition with primarily temporal cues. *Science, 270,* 303–304. {18}

Shapley, R. (1986) The importance of contrast for the activity of single neurons, the VEP and perception. *Vision Res., 26,* 45–61. {12, **12.3, 12.4**}

Shadlen, M. N. *see* Britten

Shankweiler, D. S. *see* Liberman; Studdert-Kennedy

Shannon, R. V. *see* Zeng

Shapley, R. (1998) Visual cortex: pushing the envelope. *Nature Neurosci., 1,* 95–96. {8}

Shapley, R., & Enroth-Cugell, C. (1984) Visual adaptation and retinal gain controls. *Prog. Retinal Res., 3,* 263–346. {6}

Shapley, R., & Hochstein, S. (1975) Visual spatial summation in two classes of geniculate cells. *Nature, 256,* 411–413. {7}

Shapley, R., & Lennie, P. (1985) Spatial frequency analysis in the visual system. *Ann. Rev. Neurosci., 8,* 547–583. {9}

Shapley, R., & Perry, V. H. (1986). Cat and monkey retinal ganglion cells and their visual functional roles. *Trends in Neurosci.,* May, 1986, 229–235. {7}

Shapley, R. M., & Victor, J. D. (1979) Nonlinear spatial summation and the contrast gain control of cat retinal ganglion cells. *J. Physiol., 290,* 141–161. {5}

Shapley, R. M. *see also* Enroth-Cugell; Grosof; Hochstein; Jakiela; Kaplan; Reid; Ringach; Rubin; So

Sharpe, L. T. *see* Reitner

Shechter, S., Hochstein, S., & Hillman, P. (1988) Shape similarity and distance disparity as apparent motion correspondence cues. *Vision Res., 28,* 1013–1021. {13}

Shedlovsky, A. *see* Woodruff

Shefner, J. M., & Levine, M. W. (1976) A psychophysical demonstration of goldfish trichromacy. *Vision Res., 16,* 671–673. {2}

Shefner, J. M., & Levine, M. W. (1977) Interactions between rod and cone systems in the goldfish retina. *Science, 198,* 750–753. {6}

Shefner, J. M., & Levine, M. W. (1981) Distance-dependent interactions between the rod and the cone systems in goldfish retina. *Exp. Rain Res., 44,* 353–361. {6}

Shefner, J. M. *see also* Berenberg; Levine

Shepard, R. N. (1964) Circularity in judgments of relative pitch. *J. Acoust. Soc. Am. 36,* 2346–2353. {10}

Shepard, R. N., & Metzler, J. (1971) Mental rotation of three-dimensional objects. *Science, 171,* 701–703. {10}

Shepherd, G. M. (1985) The olfactory system: the uses of neural space for a nonspatial modality. *Prog. Clin. Biol. Res., 176,* 99–114. {20}

Shepherd, G. M. *see also* Benson

Sherman, S. M. (1979) The functional significance of X and Y cells in normal and visually deprived cats. *Trends Neurosci., 2,* 192–195. {5}

Sherman, S. M., Wilson, J. R., Kaas, J. H., & Webb, S. V. (1976) X- and Y-cells in the dorsal lateral geniculate nucleus of the owl monkey (*Aotus trivirgatus*). *Science, 192,* 475–477. {7}

Sherman, S. M. *see also* Lu; Sur

Sherrington, C. S. (1918) Observations on the sensual role of the proprioceptive nerve supply of the extrinsic ocular muscles. *Brain, 41,* 332–343. {13}

Shevell, S. K. *see* Jenness

Shibutani, H. *see* Sakata

Shibuya, T., Ai, N., & Takagi, S. (1962) Response types of single cells in the olfactory bulb. *Proc. Japan Acad., 38,* 231–233. {20}

Shick, T. R. *see* McBurney

Shimahara, T. *see* Saito

Shimazaki, H. *see* Kaneko

Shimoda, Y. *see* Murakami

Shimojo, S. *see* Nakayama

Shipp, S. *see* Zeki

Shlaer, S. *see* Hecht

Shoham, D. *see* Hübener

Shows, T. B. *see* Nathans

Shulz, D. E. *see* Debanne

Shyue, S.-K., Hewett-Emmett, D., Sperling, H. G., Hunt, D. M., Bowmaker, J. K., Mollon, J. D., & Li, W.-H. (1995) Adaptive evolution of color vision genes in higher primates. *Science, 269,* 1265–1267. {14}

Sicard, G., & Holley, A. (1984) Receptor cell responses to odorants: similarities and differences among odorants. *Brain Res., 292,* 283–296. {20}

Siegel, R. M., & Read, H. L. (1997) Analysis of optic flow in the monkey parietal area 7a. *Cerebr. Cort., 7,* 327–346. {13}

Siegel, R. M. *see also* Andersen

Siegel, S. *see* Petry

Sienkiewicz, Z. J. *see* Scott

Sieving, P. A., Frishman, L. J., & Steinberg, R. H. (1986) M-wave of proximal retina in cat. *J. Neurophysiol., 56,* 1039–1048. {6}

Sieving, P. A. *see also* Frishman; Steinberg

Sillito, A. M., & Jones, H. E. (1996) Context-dependent interactions and visual processing in V1. *J. Physiol. (Paris), 90,* 205–209. {7}

Sillito, A. M., Salt, T. E., & Kemp, J. A. (1985) Modulatory and inhibitory processes in the visual cortex. *Vision Res., 25,* 375–381. {7}

Sillito, A. M., & Versiani, V. (1977) The contribution of excitatory and inhibitory inputs to the length preference of hypercomplex cells in layers II and III of the cats striate cortex. *J. Physiol., 273,* 775–790. {7}

Sillito, A. M. *see also* Cudeiro; Murphy

Silveira, L. C. L., & Perry, V. H. (1991) The topography of magnocellular projecting ganglion cells (M-ganglion cells) in the primate retina. *Neurosci., 40,* 217–237. {7}

Silverman, G. H. *see* Nakayama

Silverman, M. S. *see* Tootell

Silverstein, A. *see* Hochberg

Simola, J. *see* Sams

Simon, E. J., Hiller, J. M., & Edelman, I. (1973) Stereospecific binding of the potent narcotic analgesic (3H) etorphine to rat-brain homogenate. *Proc. Natl Acad. Sci. (USA), 70,* 1947–1949. {19}

Simon, J. *see* Burgess; Richter

Simon, S. A., Labarca, P., Robb, R. (1989) Activation by saccharides of a cation selective pathway on canine lingual epithelium. *Am. J. Physiol., 256,* R394–402. {20}

Simoncelli, E. P. *see* Heeger

Simone, D. A. *see* Mantyh

Simpson, J. J., & Graf, W. (1985) The selection of reference frames by nature and its investigators. In: B. Jones & M. Jones (Eds.) *Adaptive Mechanisms in Gaze Control: Facts and Theories* (pp. 3–16). Amsterdam: Elsevier Science Publishers. {3}

Singer, W. (1977) Control of thalamic transmission by corticofugal and ascending reticular pathways in the visual system. *Physiol. Rev., 57,* 386–420. {7}

Singer, W., & Gray, C. M. (1995) Visual feature integration and the temporal correlation hypothesis. *Annu. Rev. Neurosci., 18,* 555–586. {8, 10}

Singer, W. *see also* Engel; Fries; Gray; Leonards

Sirovich, L. *see* Ratliff

Sivak, B., & MacKenzie, C. L. (1990) Integration of visual information and motor output in reaching and grasping: the contributions of peripheral and central vision. *Neuropsychol., 28,* 1095–1116. {8}

Sivian, L. J., & White, S. D. (1933) On minimum audible sound fields. *J. Acoust. Soc. Am., 4,* 288–321. {**17.1**}

Sjöstrand, J., Conradi, N., & Klarén, L. (1994) How many ganglion cells are there to a foveal cone? *Graefe's Arch. Clin. & Exp. Ophthal., 232,* 432–437. {4}

Sklar, P. B., Anholt, R. R., & Snyder, S. H. (1986). The odorant sensitive adenylate cyclase of olfactory receptor cells. *J. Biol. Chem., 261*, 15 538–15 543. {20}

Slaughter, M. M. *see* Miller; Pan

Slotnik, B. M., & Kaneko, N. (1981). Role of mediodorsal thalamus nucleus in olfactory discrimination in rats. *Science, 214*, 91–92. {20}

Smallman, H. S. *see* McKee

Smith, A. T. *see* Hammond

Smith, B. *see* Belin

Smith, B. P. *see* Mozell

Smith, D. V., & McBurney, D. H. (1969). Gustatory cross adaptation: does a single mechanism code the salty taste? *J. Exper. Psychol., 80*, 101–105. {20}

Smith, D. V., Van Buskirk, R. L., Travers, J. B., & Bieber, S. L. (1983). Gustatory neuron types in hamster brainstem. *J. Neurophysiol., 50*, 522–540. {20, **20.9**}

Smith, D. V. *see also* McBurney

Smith, E. L. *see* Chino; Hamamoto; Viswanathan

Smith, O. W. *see* Gibson

Smith, P. E. *see* Mozell

Smith, P. H. *see* Wald

Smith, R. G., Freed, M. A., & Sterling, P. (1986). Microcircuitry of the dark-adapted cat retina: functional architecture of the rod-cone network. *J. Neurosci., 6*, 3505–3517. {4}

Smith, R. G. *see also* Freed

Smith, T. W. *see* Hughes

Smith, V. C., Lee, B. B., Pokorny, J., Martin, P. R., & Valberg, A. (1992). Responses of macaque ganglion cells to the relative phase of heterochromatically modulated lights. *J. Physiol., 458*, 191–221. {14}

Smith, V. C., Pokorny, J., & Starr, S. J. (1976). Variability of color mixture data – I. Interobserver variability in the unit coordinates. *Vision Res., 16*, 1087–1094. {**14.12**}

Smith, V. C. *see also* Kremers

Snodderly, D. M. *see* Gur

Snowden, C. T. *see* Morse

Snowden, R. J., & Braddick, O. J. (1990). Differences in the processing of short-range apparent motion at small and large displacements. *Vision Res., 30*, 1211–1222. {13}

Snyder, S. H. (1980). Brain peptides as neurotransmitters. *Science, 209*, 976–983. {19}

Snyder, S. H. *see also* Sklar

So, Y. T., & Shapley, R. M. (1981). Spatial tuning of cells in and around lateral geniculate nucleus of the cat: X and Y relay cells and perigeniculate interneurons. *J. Neurophysiol., 45*, 107–120. {7}

So, Y. T. *see also* Kaplan

Sokoloff, L. (1975). Influence of functional activity on local cerebral utilization. In D. H. Ingvar & N. A. Lassen (Eds.), *Brain Work. The Coupling of Function, Metabolism and Blood Flow in the Brain* (pp. 385–388). New York: Academic Press. {A}

Solomon, J. A., & Sperling, G. (1994). Full-wave and half-wave rectification in second-order motion perception. *Vision Res., 34*, 2239–2257. {9}

Solomon, S. J., Pasik, T., & Pasik, P. (1981). Extrageniculostriate vision in the monkey. VIII. Critical structures for spatial localization. *Exp. Brain Res., 44*, 259–270. {7}

Solomon, S. *see also* Rubin

Somers, D. C., Nelson, S. B., & Sur, M. (1995). An emergent model of orientation selectivity in cat visual cortical simple cells. *J. Neurosci., 15*, 5448–5465. {7}

Soodak, R. E. *see* Reid

Sparks, D. L., & Porter, J. D. (1983). Spatial localization of saccade targets. II. Activity of superior colliculus neurons preceding compensatory saccades. *J. Neurophysiol., 49*, 64–74. {7}

Speed, H. D. *see* Ross

Spekreijse, H. *see* Lamme; Schellart

Sperling, G. *see* Chubb; Lu; Solomon

Sperling, H. G. *see* Shyue

Spinelli, D. N. *see* Hirsch

Spira, D. *see* Fischler

Spitzer, H., Desimone, R., & Moran, J. (1988). Increased attention enhances both behavioral and neuronal performance. *Science, 240*, 338–340. {8}

Spitzer, H., & Hochstein, S. (1985). A complex-cell receptive-field model. *J. Neurophysiol., 53*, 1266–1286. {7}

Spitzer, H. *see also* Grunfeld; Richmond

Spitzer, M. W., & Semple, M. N. (1991). Interaural phase coding in auditory midbrain: influence of dynamic stimulus features. *Science, 254*, 721–724. {**17**}

Spiwoks-Becker, I. *see* Vollrath

Spoehr, K. T., & Lehmkuhle, S. W. (1982) *Visual*

Information Processing. San Francisco: W. H. Freeman. {**10.2**}

Spoendlin, H. (1970). Structural basis of peripheral frequency analysis. In R. Plomp & G. F. Smoorenburg (Eds.) *Frequency Analysis and Periodicity Detection in Hearing* (pp 2–36). Leiden: Sijthoff. {15}

Stafford, D. K., & Dacey, D. M. (1997). Physiology of the A1 amacrine: a spiking, axon-bearing interneuron of the macaque monkey retina. *Vis. Neurosci., 14,* 507–522. {4}

Standage, G. P. *see* Lysakowski

Stanford, L. R. (1987). X-cells in the cat retina: relationships between the morphology and physiology of a class of cat retinal ganglion cells. *J. Neurophysiol., 58,* 940–964. {5}

Stanford, T. R. *see* Fitzpatrick

Stanson, G. B. *see* Robinson

Stark, M. E., Grafman, J., & Fertig, E. (1997) A restricted 'spotlight' of attention in visual object recognition. *Neuropsychol., 35,* 1233–1249. {8}

Starr, S. J. *see* Smith

Stein, B. E., Magalhães-Castro, B., & Kruger, L. (1975) Superior colliculus: visuotopic-somatic overlap. *Science, 189,* 224–226. {**7**}

Stein, B. E. *see also* Wallace

Stein, D. *see* Schneider

Stein, J. F. *see* Cornelissen

Stein, J. M. *see also* Warfield

Steinberg, R. H., Frishman, L. J. and Sieving, P. A. (1991) Negative components of the electroretinogram from proximal retina and photoreceptor. In N. N. Osborne & G. J. Chader (Edn.), *Progress in Retinal Research, vol. 10,* (pp. 121–160). Oxford, UK: Permagon. {A}

Steinberg, R. H. *see also* Frishman; Sieving

Steinman, B. A., Steinman, S. B., & Lehmkuhle, S. (1997) Transient visual attention is dominated by the magnocellular stream. *Vision Res., 37,* 17–23. {8}

Steinman, R. M. *see* Puckett

Steinman, S. B. *see* Steinman

Steinmetz, M. A., & Constantinidis, C. (1995) Neurophysiological evidence for a role of posterior parietal cortex in redirecting visual attention. *Cerebr. Cort., 5,* 448–456. {8}

Stell, W. K. (1967) The structure and relationships of horizontal cells and photoreceptor-bipolar synaptic complexes in goldfish retina. *Am. J. Anat., 121,* 401–424. {4}

Stell, W. K. (1975) Horizontal cell axons and axon terminals in goldfish retina. *J. Comp. Neurol., 159,* 503–520. {4}

Stell, W. K., Ishida, A. T., & Lightfoot, D. O. (1977) Structural basis for on- and off-center responses in retinal bipolar cells. *Science, 198,* 1269–1271. {4}

Stenson, H. H. (1966). The physical factor structure of random forms and their judged complexity. *Percept. Psychophys., 1,* 303–310. {10}

Sterling, P. (1983). Microcircuitry of the cat retina. *Ann. Rev. Neurosci., 6,* 149–185. {4}

Sterling, P. *see also* Calkins; Freed; McGuire; Rao-Mirotznik; Smith; Tsukamoto

Stevens, J. C., & Rubin, L. L. (1970) Psychophysical scales of apparent heaviness and the size weight illusion. *Percept. and Psychophys., 8,* 225–230. {19}

Stevens, J. K., Emerson, R. C., Gerstein, G. L., Kallos, T., Neufeld, G. R., Nichols, C. W., & Rosenquist, A. C. (1976) Paralysis of the awake human: visual perceptions. *Vision Res., 16,* 93–98. {13}

Stevens, J. K. *see also* Matin; McGuire

Stevens, K. N. (1973) Potential role of property detectors in the perception of consonants. *Q. Prog. Rep. Res. Lab. Electronics MIT 110,* 155–168. {18}

Stevens, K. N. *see also* Halle; Kuhl

Stevens, S. S. (1956) The direct estimation of sensory magnitudes: Loudness. *Am. J. Psychol., 69,* 1–25. {2}

Stevens, S. S. (1957) On the psychophysical law. *Psychol. Rev., 64,* 153–181. {2}

Stevens, S. S. (1962) The surprising simplicity of sensory metrics. *Am. Psychol., 17,* 29–39. {2}

Stevens, S. S. (1972). Perceived level of noise by Mark VII and decibels (E). *J. Acoust. Soc. Am., 51,* 575–601. {17}

Stevens, S. S., & Davis, H. (1938) *Hearing.* New York: Wiley. {17}

Stevens, S. S., & Newman, E. B. (1934). The localization of pure tones. *Proc. Natl. Acad. Sci., 20,* 593–596. {17, **17.12**}

Stevens, S. S., & Volkmann, J. (1940). The relation of pitch to frequency, a revised scale. *Am. J. Psychol., 53,* 329–353. {16}

Stevens, S. S. *see also* Reynolds; Zwicker

Stiles, W. S., & Crawford, B. H. (1933). The luminous efficiency of rays entering the eye pupil at different points. *Proc. R. Soc. Lond. Ser. B., 112,* 428–450. {6}

Stiles, W. S. *see also* Aguilar

Still, A. W. *see* Harris

Stone, J., Dreher, B., & Leventhal, A. (1979). Hierarchical and parallel mechanisms in the organization of visual cortex. *Brain Res. Rev., 1,* 345–394. {7}

Stone, J., & Freeman, R. B. (1971). Conduction velocity groups in the cat's optic nerve classified according to their retinal origin. *Exp. Brain Res., 13,* 489–497. {5}

Stone, J., & Fukuda, Y. (1974). Properties of cat retinal ganglion cells: a comparison of W-cells with X- and Y-cells. *J. Neurophysiol., 37,* 722–748. {5}

Stone, J., & Hoffmann, K.-P. (1971). Conduction velocity as a parameter in the organisation of the afferent relay in the cat's lateral geniculate nucleus. *Brain Res., 32,* 454–459. {7}

Stone, J., & Hoffmann, K.-P. (1972). Very slow-conducting ganglion cells in the cat's retina: a major, new functional type? *Brain Res., 43,* 610–616. {5}

Stone, J. *see also* Fukuda; Hoffmann; Rodieck

Stoner, G. R., & Albright, T. D. (1992). Neural correlates of perceptual motion coherence. *Nature, 358,* 412–414. {10, 13}

Stork, D. G., & Wilson, H. R. (1990). Do Gabor functions provide appropriate descriptions of visual cortical receptive fields? *J. Opt. Soc. Am. A, 7,* 1362–1373. {9}

Stork, D. G. *see also* Massaro

Straforini, M. *see* Verri

Stratford, K. J., Tarczy-Hornoch, K., Martin, K. A. C., Bannister, N. J., & Jack, J. J. B. (1996). Excitatory synaptic imputs to spiny stellate cells in cat visual cortex. *Nature, 382,* 258–261. {7}

Strom, L. *see* Diamant

Stromeyer, C. F., Lange, A. F., & Ganz, L. (1973). Spatial frequency phase effects in human vision. *Vision Res., 13,* 2345–2360. {9}

Stromeyer, C. F., & Klein, S. (1974). Spatial frequency channels in human vision as asymmetric (edge) mechanisms. *Vision Res., 14,* 1409–1420. {**9.17**}

Stromeyer, C. F. *see also* Chaparro

Stryker, M. P. *see* Antonini; Hata; Hubel; Zahs

Studdert-Kennedy, M. (1976). Speech perception. In N. J. Lass (Ed.), *Contemporary Issues in Experimental Phonetics* (pp. 243–293). New York: Academic Press. {18}

Studdert-Kennedy, M., & Shankweiler, D. (1970) Hemispheric specialization for speech perception. *J. Acoust. Soc. Am., 48,* 579–594. {18}

Studdert-Kennedy, M. *see also* Liberman

Sturm, R. D. *see* Gogel

Suga, N., & Manabe, T. (1982). Neural basis of amplitude-spectrum representation in auditory cortex of the mustached bat. *J. Neurophysiol., 47,* 225–255. {15}

Suga, N., O'Neill, W. E., & Manabe, T. (1979). Harmonic-sensitive neurons in the auditory cortex of the mustache bat. *Science, 203,* 270–274. {18}

Suero, M. *see* Derrington

Sugishita, M., Hamilton, C. R., Sakuma, I., & Hemmi, I. (1994). Hemispheric representation of the central retina of commissurotomized subjects. *Neuropsychologia, 32,* 399–415. {7}

Sugita, Y. (1996) Global plasticity in adult visual cortex following reversal of visual input. *Nature, 380,* 523–526. {3}

Sullivan, R. *see* Mozell

Sur, M., Garraghty, P. E., & Roe, A. W. (1988) Experimentally induced visual projections into auditory thalamus and cortex. *Science, 242,* 1437–1441. {8}

Sur, M., & Sherman, S. M. (1982) Linear and non-linear W-cells in C-laminae of the cat's lateral geniculate nucleus. *J. Neurophysiol., 47,* 869–884. {5}

Sur, M. *see also* Kaas; Roe; Somers; Toth

Sutherland, N. S. (1973) Object recognition. In E. C. Carterette & M. P. Friedman (Eds.), *Handbook of Perception, Volume III: Biology of Perceptual Systems.* pp. 157–185. (New York: Academic Press). {10}

Sutter, F. E. *see* Norcia

Sutton, P. *see* Blakemore

Syrdal, A. K. *see* Mattingly

Swender, P. *see* Mozell

Swets, J. A., Tanner, W. P., & Birdsall, T. G. (1961) Decision processes in perception. *Psychol. Rev., 68,* 301–340. {2}

Switkes, E. *see* Bradley; Tootell

Szpir, M. (1992) Accustomed to your face. *Am. Scient., 80,* 537–539. {8}

Tachibana, M., & Kaneko, A. (1988) Retinal bipolar cells receive negative feedback input from GABAergic amacrine cells. *Visual Neurosci., 1,* 297–305. {4}

Tadmor, Y., & Tolhurst, D. J. (1993) Both the phase and the amplitude spectrum may determine the appearance of natural images. *Vision Res., 33,* 141–145. {9}

Taira, M. *see* Georgopoulos

Takagi, S. *see* Shibuya

Talbot, J. D., Marrett, S., Evans, A. C., Meyer, E., Bushnell, M. C., & Duncan, G. H. (1991) Multiple representations of pain in human cerebral cortex. *Science, 251,* 1355–1358. {19}

Talbot, W. H. *see* Lynch; Poggio

Tallon-Baudry, C., Bertrand, O., Delpuech, C., & Pernier, J. (1997) Oscillatory γ-band (30–70 Hz) activity induced by a visual search task in humans. *J. Neurosci., 17,* 722–734. {10}

Tamura, H. *see* Hata; Sato

Tanaka, K. (1985) Organization of geniculate inputs to visual cortical cells in the cat. *Vision Res., 25,* 357–364. {7}

Tanaka, K. (1996) Inferotemporal cortex and object vision. *Annu. Rev. Neurosci., 19,* 109–139. {8}

Tanné, J., Boussaoud, D., Boyer-Zeller, N., & Rouiller, E. M. (1995) Direct visual pathways for reaching movements in the macaque monkey. *NeuroRep., 7,* 267–272. {8}

Tanner, W. P. *see* Swets

Tarczy-Hornoch, K. *see* Stratford

Tauchi, M. *see* Masland

Taylor, K. J. *see* Johnstone

Taylor, W. R., & Wässle, H. (1995) Receptive field properties of starburst cholinergic amacrine cells in the rabbit retina. *Eur. J. Neurosci., 7,* 2308–2321. {4}

Teas, D. C. *see* Sandel

Teller, D. Y. (1984) Linking propositions. *Vision Res., 24,* 1233–1246. {5}

Temchin, A. N. *see* Narayan

Temme, L. A. *see* Frumkes

Templeton, W. B. *see* Howard

Tenke, C. E. *see* Schroeder

Thalhammer, J. G. *see* LaMotte

Thier, P., & Erickson, R. G. (1992) Responses of visual-tracking neurons from cortical area MST-I to visual, eye and head motion. *Eur. J. Neurosci., 4,* 539–553. {8}

Thier, P. *see also* Erickson

Thivard, L. *see* Belin

Thomas, D. *see* Nathans

Thomas, E. C. *see* Kiang

Thomas, G. *see* Otis

Thomas, J. P. *see* Olzak

Thompson, I. D. *see* Movshon

Thompson, K. G., Leventhal, A. G., Zhou, Y., & Liu, D. (1994a) Stimulus dependence of orientation and direction sensitivity of cat LGNd relay cells without cortical inputs: a comparison with area 17 cells. *Visual Neurosci., 11,* 939–951. {7}

Thompson, K. G., Zhou, Y., & Leventhal, A. G. (1994b) Direction-sensitive X and Y cells within the A laminae of the cat's LGNd. *Visual Neurosci., 11,* 927–938. {7}

Thompson, K. G. *see also* Leventhal

Thorell, L. G. *see* Albrecht; DeValois

Thorpe, S., Fize, D., & Merlot, C. (1996) Speed of processing in the human visual system. *Nature, 381,* 520–522. {10}

Thouless, R. H. (1931) Phenomenal regression to the real object. *Br. J. Psychol., 21,* 339–359. {12}

Thurlow, G. A., Bowling, D. B., & Cooper, R. M. (1993) ON and OFF activity gradients in the lateral geniculate nucleus of the cat: a combined ^{14}C 2-deoxyglucose and D,L-2-amino-4-phosphobutyric acid study. *Visual Neurosci., 10,* 1027–1033. {7}

Tissari, S. O. *see* Hari

Tjan, B. S., Braje, W. L., Legge, G. E., & Kersten, D. (1995) Human efficiency for recognizing 3-D objects in luminance noise. *Vision Res., 35,* 3053–3069. {10}

Tjan, B. S. *see also* Braje

Todd, J. T. *see* Mingolla

Todd, T. C. *see* Vitz

Tolhurst, D. J. (1973) Separate channels for the analysis of the shape and the movement of a moving visual stimulus. *J. Physiol., 231,* 385–402. {5}

Tolhurst, D. J. *see also* DeMonasterio; Movshon; Robson; Tadmor

Tomita, T. (1970) Electrical activity of vertebrate photoreceptors. *Q. Rev. Biophys., 3,* 179–222. {4}

Tomita, T., Kaneko, A., Murakami, M., & Pautler, E. L. (1967) Spectral response curves of single cones in the carp. *Vision Res., 7,* 519–531. {4, 14, **14.14**}

Tonegawa, S. *see* Malmberg

Tong, L., & Green, D. G. (1977) Adaptation pools and excitation receptive fields of rat retinal ganglion cells. *Vision Res., 17,* 1233–1236. {6}

Tong, Y. C., Dowell, R. C., Blamey, P. J., & Clark, G. M. (1983) Two-component hearing sensations produced by two-electrode stimulation in the cochlea of a deaf patient. *Science, 219,* 993–994. {16}

Tonndorf, J., & Khanna, S. M. (1970) The role of the tympanic membrane in middle ear transmission. *Ann. Otol. Rhinol. Laryngol., 79,* 743–753. {15}

Tononi, G., & Edelman, G. M. (1998) Consciousness and complexity. *Science, 282,* 1846–1851. {10}

Tootell, R. B. H., Hamilton, S. L., & Switkes, E. (1988a) Functional anatomy of macaque striate cortex. IV. Contrast and magno-parvo streams. *J. Neurosci., 8,* 1594–1609. {7, 8}

Tootell, R. B. H. *see also* Born; DeValois

Tootell, R. B. H., Silverman, M. S., Hamilton, S. L., DeValois, R. L., & Switkes, E. (1988b) Functional anatomy of macaque striate cortex. III. Color. *J. Neurosci., 8,* 1569–1593. {7, 8}

Torebjork, H. E. *see* LaMotte

Torre, V. *see* Marchiafava; Verri

Toth, L. J., Kim, D.-S., Rao, S. C., & Sur, M. (1997) Integration of local inputs in visual cortex. *Cerebr. Cort., 7,* 703–710. {7}

Tovee, M. J., Rolls, E. T., & Azzopardi, P. (1994) Translation invariance in the responses to faces of single neurons in the temporal visual cortical areas of the alert macaque. *J. Neurophysiol., 72,* 1049–1060. {8}

Toyama, K. *see* Komatsu

Toyoda, J.-I. (1973) Membrane resistance changes underlying the bipolar cell response in the carp retina. *Vision Res., 13,* 283–294. {4}

Toyoda, J.-I., Hashimoto, H., & Ohtsu, K. (1973) Bipolar-amacrine transmission in the carp retina. *Vision Res., 13,* 295–307. {4}

Toyoda, J.-I., Kujiraoka, T. (1982) Analyses of bioplar cells responses elicited by polarization of horizontal cells. *J. Gen. Physiol., 79,* 131–145. {4}

Travers, J. B. *see* Smith

Treutwein, B. *see* Rentschler

Trezona, P. W. (1970) Rod participation in the 'blue' mechanism and its effect upon colour matching. *Vision Res., 10,* 317–332. {6}

Tritsch, M. F. (1992) Fourier analysis of the stimuli for pattern-induced flicker colors. *Vision Res., 32,* 1461–1470. {14}

Troy, J. B., & Enroth-Cugell, C. (1993) X and Y ganglion cells inform the cat's brain about contrast in the retinal image. *Exp. Brain Res., 93,* 383–390. {5}

Troy, J. B. *see also* Levine

Trusk, T. C. *see* DeYoe

Tsherbach, T. A. *see* Glezer

Ts'o, D. Y., & Gilbert, C. D. (1988) The organization of chromatic and spatial interactions in the primate striate cortex. *J. Neurosci., 8,* 1712–1727. {7, 8, 14}

Tsukamoto, Y., Masarachia, P., Schein, S. J., & Sterling, P. (1992) Gap junctions between the pedicles of macaque foveal cones. *Vision Res., 32,* 1809–1815. {4}

Tsumoto, T. *see* Hata; Sato

Tsukamoto, Y. *see also* Calkins

Tulving, E. *see* Heinemann

Turner, L. *see* Lehmkuhle

Tweed, D., Haslwanter, T., & Fetter, M. (1988) Optimizing gaze control in three dimensions. *Science, 281,* 1363–1366. {3}

Tyler, C. W. (1990) A stereoscopic view of visual processing streams. *Vision Res., 30,* 1877–1895. {11}

Tyler, C. W., & Cavanagh, P. (1991) Purely chromatic perception of motion in depth: two eyes as sensitive as one. *Percept. & Psychophys., 49,* 53–61. {13}

Tyler, C. W. *see also* Cavanagh; Jagadeesh; Norcia

Tynan, P., & Sekuler, R. (1975) Moving visual phantoms: a new contour completion effect. *Science, 188,* 951–952. {13, **13.3**}

Uchikawa, K., & Boynton, R. M. (1987) Categorical color perception of Japanese observers: comparison with that of Americans. *Vision Res., 27,* 1825–1833. {14}

Uhlarik, J. *see* Brigell

Uhr, L. (1973) *Pattern Recognition, Learning, and Thought.* Englewood Cliffs, NJ.: Prentice Hall. {10}

Ullman, S. (1986) Artificial intelligence and the brain: computational studies of the visual system. *Ann. Rev. Neurosci., 9,* 1–26. {9, 10}

Ungerleider, L. G., & Mishkin, M. (1982) Two cortical visual systems. D Ingle, M. A. Goodale, & R. J. W. Mansfield In (Eds.), *Analysis of Visual Behavior.* (pp. 549–586. Cambridge: MIT). {8}

Ungerleider, L. G. *see also* Courtney; Desimone

Updyke, B. V. (1974) Characteristics of unit responses in superior colliculus of the Cebus monkey. *J. Neurophysiol., 37,* 896–909. {7}

Usai, C., Ratto, G. M., & Bisti, S. (1991) Two systems of branching axons in monkey's retina. *J. Comp. Neurol., 308,* 149–161. {4}

Usrey, W. M., Reppas, J. B., & Reid, R. C. (1998) Paired-spike interactions and synaptic efficacy of retinal inputs to the thalamus. *Nature, 395,* 384–387. {7}

Usrey, W. M. *see also* Alonso

Usukara, J. & Obata, S. (1995) Morphogenesis of photoreceptor outer segments in retinal development. *Prog. Ret. Eye Res., 15*, 113–125. {4}

Vaina, L. M., LeMay, M., Bienfang, D. C., Choi, A. V., & Nakayama, K. (1990) Intact 'biological motion' and 'structure from motion' perception in a patient with impaired motion mechanisms: a case study. *Visual Neurosci., 5*, 353–369. {13}

Valberg, A., Lee, B. B., Kaiser, P. K., & Kremers, J. (1992) Responses of macaque ganglion cells to movement of chromatic borders. *J. Physiol., 458*, 579–602. {14}

Valberg, A. *see also* Creutzfeldt; Smith

Vallbo, A. B. *see* Johansson

Van Buskirk, R. L. *see* Smith

Van der Heijden, A. H. C. *see* Bridgeman

Van Essen, D. C. (1979) Visual areas of the mammalian cerebral cortex. *Ann. Rev. Neurosci., 2*, 227–263. {7}

Van Essen, D. C. *see also* DeYoe; Olavarria

Vaney, D. I. (1986) Morphological identification of serotonin-accumulating neurons in the living retina. *Science, 233*, 444–446. {4}

Vaney, D. I. (1994) Patterns of neuronal coupling in the retina. *Prog. Ret. Eye Res., 13*, 301–355. {4}

Vaney, D. I., Young, H. M., & Gynder, I. C. (1991) The rod circuit in the rabbit retina. *Vis. Neurosci., 7*, 141–154. {4}

Vaney, D. I. *see also* Hampson

Vaquero, C. F. *see* Blanco

Vartiamen, M. *see* Hamalainen

Vaughan, H. G. *see* Schroeder

Velichkovsky, B. M. *see* Bridgeman

Verloop, M. *see* Greene

Verri, A., Straforini, M., & Torre, V. (1992) Computational aspects of motion perception in natural and artificial vision systems. *Phil. Trans. Roy. Soc. Lond. B, 337*, 429–443. {13}

Versiani, V. *see* Sillito

Victor, J. D., & Conte, M. M. (1991) Spatial organization of nonlinear interactions in form perception. *Vision Res., 31*, 1457–1488. {10}

Victor, J. D. *see also* Shapley

Vidyasagar, T. R. *see* Volgushev

de la Villa, P. *see* Blanco; Kaneko

Virsu, V. *see* Hari; Lee

Viswanathan, S., Frishman, L. J., Robson, J. G., Harwerth, R. S., & Smith, E. L. (1999) The photopic negative response of the macaque electroretinogram: reduction by experimental glaucoma. *Investig. Ophthalmol & Vis. Sci., 40*, 1124–1136.

Vitz, P. C., & Todd, T. C. (1971) A model of the perception of simple geometric figures. *Psychol. Rev., 78*, 207–228. {10}

Vogel, G. (1996) Illusion reveals pain locus in brain. *Science, 274*, 1301. {19}

Vogels, R. *see* Kovács

Voigt, T. *see* Müller

Volgushev, M., Pei, X., Vidyasagar, T. R., & Creutzfeldt, O. D. (1993) Excitation and inhibition in orientation selectivity of cat visual cortex neurons revealed by whole-cell recordings in vivo. *Visual Neurosci., 10*, 1151–1155. {7}

Volkmann, J. *see* Stevens

Vollrath, L. & Spiwoks-Becker, I. (1996) Plasticity of retinal ribbon synapses. *Micros. Res. Tech., 35*, 472–487. {4}

Volman, S. F. *see* Schiller

von der Heydt, R., & Peterhans, E. (1989) Mechanisms of contour perception in monkey visual cortex. I. Lines of pattern discontinuity. *J. Neurosci., 9*, 1731–1748. {8}

von der Heydt, R., Peterhans, E., & Baumgartner, G. (1984) Illusory contours and cortical neuron responses. *Science, 224*, 1260–1262. {8, **8.7**}

von der Heydt, R., Peterhans, E., & Dürsteler, M. R. (1992) Periodic-pattern-selective cells in monkey visual cortex. *J. Neurosci., 12*, 1416–1434. {9}

Von der Heydt, R. *see also* Peterhans

Vorobyev, M. *see* Osorio

Wagner, H., & Schaeffel, F. (1991) Barn owls (*Tyto alba*) use accommodation as a distance cue. *J. Comp. Physiol. A, 169*, 515–521. {11}

Wagner, H. G. *see* Hartline; Levick

Wagoner, K. S. *see* Nafe

Waite, H., & Massaro, D. W. (1970) Test of Gregory's constancy scaling explanation of the Müller-Lyer illusion. *Nature, 227*, 733–734. {12}

Wald, G. (1945) Human vision and the spectrum. *Science, 101*, 653–658. {**6.5**}

Wald, G., Brown, P. K., & Smith, P. H. (1955) Iodopsin. *J. Gen. Physiol., 38*, 623–681. {4}

Wald, G. *see also* Brown

Wall, P. D. *see* Melzack

Wallace, J. G. *see* Gregory

Wallace, M. T., Meredith, M. A., & Stein, B. E. (1993) Converging influences from visual, auditory, and somatosensory cortices only output neurons of the superior colliculus. *J. Neurophysiol., 69,* 1797–1809. {7}

Wallach, H. (1948) Brightness constancy and the nature of achromatic colors. *J. Exp. Psychol., 38,* 310–324. {12}

Wallach, H. (1959) The perception of motion. *Sci. Am., 201,* 55–60. {13}

Wallach, H. (1963) The perception of neutral colors. *Sci. Am., 208,* 107–116. {12}

Wallach, H. (1987) Perceiving a stable environment when one moves. *Ann. Rev. Psychol., 38,* 1–27. {3, 12}

Wallach, H., & Austin, P. (1954) Recognition and the localization of visual traces. *Am. J. Psychol., 57,* 338–340. {10}

Wallach, H., & O'Connell, D. N. (1953) The kinetic depth effect. *J. Exp. Psychol., 45,* 205–217. {11}

Wallach, H., O'Connell, D. N., & Neisser, U. (1953) The memory effect of visual perception of three-dimensional form. *J. Exp. Psychol., 45,* 360–368. {11}

Wallach, H. *see also* Köhler

Walls, G. L. (1967) *The Vertebrate Eye and its Adaptive Radiation.* New York: Hafner. {**3.7, 3.12**}

Walsh, V. (1995) Adapting to change. *Curr. Biol., 5,* 703–705. {14}

Walsh, V., & Butler, S. R. (1996) Different ways of looking at seeing. *Beh. Brain Res., 76,* 1–3. {8}

Walters, J. W., & Harwerth, R. S. (1978) The mechanism of brightness enhancement. *Vision Res., 18,* 777–779. {12}

Wandell, B. A. *see* Chichilnisky

Wang, C., Dreher, B., & Burke, W. (1994) Non-dominant suppression in the dorsal lateral geniculate nucleus of the cat: laminar differences and class specificity *Exp. Brain Res., 97,* 451–465. {7}

Wang, H.-H. *see* Kolb

Wang, H.-W., Wysocki, C. J., & Gold, G. H. (1993) Induction of olfactory receptor sensitivity in mice. *Science, 260,* 998–1000. {20}

Wang, Q., Klein, B. E. K., Klein, R., & Moss, S. E. (1994) Refractive status in the Beaver Dam eye study. *Investig. Ophthalmol. & Vis. Sci., 35,* 4344–4347. {3}

Wang, Q., Schoenlein, R. W., Peteanu, L. A.,

Mathies, R. A., & Shank, C. V. (1994) Vibrationally coherent photochemistry in the femtosecond primary event of vision. *Science, 266,* 422–424. {4}

Ward, L. M. *see* Coren

Warfield, C. A., Stein, J. M., & Frank, H. A. (1985) The effect of transcutaneous electrical nerve stimulation on pain after thoracotomy. *Ann. Thorac. Surg., 39,* 462–465. {19}

Warland, D. K., Reinagel, P., & Meister, M. (1997) Decoding visual information from a population of retinal ganglion cells. *J. Neurosphysiol., 78,* 2336–2350. {5}

Warland, D. K. *see also* Brivanlou

Warr, W. B. *see* Kiang

Warren, H. C., & Carmichael, L. (1930) *Elements of Human Psychology.* Boston: Houghton Mifflin. {**20.2**}

Warren, R. M. (1970) Elimination of biases in loudness judgments for tones. *J. Acoust. Soc. Am., 48,* 1397–1403. {17}

Wasserman, G. S. (1990) Artificial neuroreceptor interfaced to natural brain: real-time portable version. *Int. Neural Network Conf., 1,* 459–462. {16}

Wasserman, G. S., Felsten, G., & Easland, G. S. (1979) The psychophysical function: harmonizing Fechner and Stevens. *Science, 204,* 85–87. {2}

Wässle, H., & Boycott, B. B. (1991) Functional architecture of the mammalian retina. *Physiol. Rev., 71,* 447–470. {5, 7}

Wässle, H., Boycott, B. B., & Illing, R. B. (1981a) Morphology and mosaic of on- and off-beta cells in the cat retina and some functional considerations. *Proc. Roy. Soc. Lond. B., 212,* 177–195. {5}

Wässle, H., Grünert, U., Röhrenbeck, J., & Boycott, B. B. (1990) Retinal ganglion cell density and cortical magnification factor in the primate. *Vision Res., 30,* 1897–1911. {4, 7}

Wässle, H., Peichl, L., & Boycott, B. B. (1981b) Morphology and topology of on- and off-alpha cells in the cat retina. *Proc. Roy. Soc. Lond. B, 212,* 157–175. {5}

Wässle, H. *see also* Boycott; Chun; Cleland; Müller; Peichl; Taylor

Watanabe, K. *see* Brown

Watanabe, M. (1992) Frontal units of the monkey coding the assiative significance of visual and auditory stimuli. *Exp. Brain Res., 89,* 233–247. {8}

Watanabe, S.-I. *see* Matthews

Watanabe, T. *see* Kiang

Watson, A. B., & Robson, J. G. (1981) Discrimination at threshold: labelled detectors in human vision. *Vision Res., 21*, 1115–1122. {9}

Watt, R. J., & Morgan, M. J. (1983) The recognition and representation of edge blur: evidence for spatial primitives in human vision. *Vision Res., 23*, 1465–1477. {5}

Way, K. S. *see* Hastorf

Webb, S. V. *see* Sherman

Wei, J. Y. *see* Burgess

Weiler, R., & Akopian, A. (1992) Effects of background illuminations on the receptive field size of horizontal cells in the turtle retinal are mediated by dopamine. *Neurosci. Lett., 140*, 121–124. {6}

Weiler, R., & Marchiafava, P. L. (1981) Physiological and morphological study of the inner plexiform layer in the turtle retina. *Vision Res., 21*, 1635–1638. {4}

Weiler, R. *see also* Hampson

Weinberger, N. M. (1995) Dynamic regulation of receptive fields and maps in the adult sensory cortex. *Annu. Rev. Neurosci., 18*, 129–158. {10}

Weinshall, D. *see* Edelman

Weiss, A. D. (1963) Auditory perception in relation to age. In J. E. Birren, R. N. Butler, S. W. Greenhouse, L. Sokoloff, & M. Tarrow (Eds.), *Human Aging*. PHS Publ. No. 986. Washington, DC: US Department of Health, Education. and Welfare. {**17.2**}

Weiss, T. F. (1964) A model for firing patterns at auditory nerve fibers. *Research Laboratory in Electronics Technical Report No. 418*. Cambridge, MA: MIT Press. {16}

Weiss, T. F. (1982) Bidirectional transduction in vertebrate hair cells: a mechanism for coupling mechanical and electrical processes. *Hearing Res., 7*, 353–360. {16}

Weisstein, N. (1968) A Rashevsky-Landahl neural net: simulation of metacontrast. *Psychol. Rev. 75*, 494–521. {9}

Weisstein, N., & Harris, C. S. (1974) Visual detection of line segments: an object superiority effect. *Science, 186*, 752–755. {10}

Weisstein, N., Maguire, W., & Berbaum, K. (1977) A phantom-motion after-effect. *Science, 198*, 955–957. {13}

Weisstein, N. *see also* Wong

Weiten, W. (1989) *Psychology: Themes and Variations*. Pacific Grove, CA: Brooks/Cole. {**12.13**}

Wells, C. *see* Diamant

Wenderoth, P. *see* Alais; van der Zwan

Werblin, F. S. (1971) Adaptation in a vertebrate retina. Intracellular recordings in *Necturus. J. Neurophysiol., 34*, 228–241. {6}

Werblin, F. S. (1974) Control of retinal sensitivity. II. Lateral interactions at the outer plexiform layer. *J. Gen. Physiol., 63*, 62–87. {6}

Werblin, F. S. (1977) Regenerative amacrine cell depolarization and formation of on-off ganglion cell response. *J. Physiol., 264*, 767–785. {4}

Werblin, F. S., & Dowling, J. E. (1969) Organization of the retina of the mudpuppy, *Necturus maculosus*. II. Intracellular recording. *J. Neurophysiol., 32*, 339–355. {4, **4.8**}

Werblin, F. *see also* Eliasof; Maguire; Normann

Werker, J. F. (1989) Becoming a native listener. *Amer. Scient., 77*, 54–59. {18}

Werner, H. (1935) Studies on contour. *Am. J. Psychol., 47*, 40–64. {**10.24**}

Werner, J. S. *see* Wooten

Wertheimer, M. (1912) Experimentelle studien über des Sehen von Bewegung. *Z. Psychol., 61*, 161–265. {13}

Wertheimer, M. (1923) Untersuchungen zur Lehre von der Gestalt. II. *Psychol. Forsch., 5*, 301–350. Abridged and translated by M. Wertheimer in *Readings in Perception*, Beardsley & Wertheimer (Eds.) New York: Van Nostrand, 1958. {10}

Wessinger, C. M. *see* Fendrich

West, G. *see* Brill

Westheimer, G. H. (1975) The eye. In V. B. Mountcastle (Ed.), *Medical Physiology, Vol. 1*, 13th edn (pp. 440–457) St Louis: C. V. Mosby. {3}

Westheimer, G. *see also* Rushton

Wever, E. G. (1949) *Theory of Hearing*. New York: Wiley. {16, **16.10**}

Wever, E. G., & Bray, C. W. (1930) Present possibilities for auditory theory. *Psychol. Rev., 37*, 365–380. {16}

Wever, E. G., & Bray, C. W. (1937) The perception of low tones and the resonance-volley theory. *J. Psychol., 3*, 101–114. {16}

Wever, E. G., & Lawrence, M. (1954) *Physiological Acoustics*. Princeton, NJ: Princeton University Press. {15}

Whalen, D. H., & Liberman, A. M. (1987) Speech perception takes precedence over nonspeech perception. *Science, 237*, 169–171. {18}

Whalen, P. *see* Brosgole

Wheat, H. S. *see* Jagadeesh

Whishaw, I. Q. *see* Kolb

White, A. J. R. *see* Martin

White, S. D. *see* Sivian

Whitehead, M. C. *see* Coleman

Whitfield, I. C., & Evans, E. F. (1965) Responses of auditory cortical neurons to stimuli of changing frequency. *J. Neurophysiol., 28*, 655–672. {18}

Whitten, D. N., & Brown, K. T. (1973) Photopic suppression of monkeys' rod receptor potential, apparently by a cone-initiated lateral inhibition. *Vision Res., 13*, 1629–1658. {6}

Whitteridge, D. *see* Clarke; Daniel

Wickesberg, R. E. *see* Kuwada

Wieniawa-Narkiewicz, F. *see* Bowling

Wiesel, T. N., & Hubel, D. H. (1963) Single-cell responses in striate cortex of kittens deprived of vision in one eye. *J. Neurophysiol., 26*, 1003–1017. {8, 11}

Wiesel, T. N., & Hubel, D. H. (1965) Comparison of the effects of unilateral and bilateral eye closure on cortical unit responses in kittens. *J. Neurophysiol., 28*, 1029–1040. {8}

Wiesel, T. N., & Hubel, D. H. (1966) Spatial and chromatic interactions in the lateral geniculate body of the rhesus monkey. *J. Neurophysiol., 29*, 1115–1156. {7, 14}

Wiesel, T. N., & Hubel, D. H. (1974) Ordered arrangement of orientation columns in monkeys lacking visual experience. *J. Comp. Neurol., 158*, 307–318. {8}

Wiesel, T. N. *see also* Gilbert; Hubel

Wiesenfelder, H., & Blake, R. (1991) Apparent motion can survive binocular rivalry suppression. *Vision Res., 31*, 1589–1599. {11}

Wiggert, B. *see* Crouch

Wilder, H. D. *see* Martin

Wiley, R. G. *see* Mantyh

Wilkinson, F. *see* Cowey

Willer, J. C. *see* Lamour

Williams, D. R., & MacLeod, D. I. A. (1979) Interchangeable backgrounds for cone after-images. *Vision Res., 19*, 867–877. {6}

Williams, D. W., Wilson, H. R., & Cowan, J. D. (1982) Localized effects of spatial-frequency adaptation. *J. Opt. Soc. Amer., 72*, 878–887. {9}

Williams, K. A. *see* Kuhl

Williams, M. C., Breitmeyer, B. G., Lovegrove, W. J., & Gutierrez, C. (1991) Metacontrast with masks varying in spatial frequency and wavelength. *Vision Res., 31*, 2017, 2023. {5}

Williams, S. C. R. *see* Calvert

Willis, B. D. *see* Kenshalo

Willis, W. D. (1981) Ascending pathways from the dorsal horn. In A. B. Brown & M. Rethely (Eds.) *Spinal Cord Sensation: Sensory Processing in the Dorsal Horn.* Edinburgh: Scottish Academic Press. {19, **19.11**}

Willis, W. D. *see also* Giesler

Wilson, D. A., & Leon, M. (1987) Evidence of lateral synaptic interactions in olfactory bulb output cell responses to odors. *Brain Res., 417*, 175–180. {20}

Wilson, H. R., & Mast, R. (1993) Illusory motion of texture boundaries. *Vision Res., 33*, 1437–1446. {9}

Wilson, H. R., McFarlane, D. K., & Phillips, G. C. (1983) Spatial frequency tuning of orientation selective units estimated by oblique masking. *Vision Res., 23*, 873–882. {9}

Wilson, H. R. *see also* Stork; Williams

Wilson, J. R. Forestner, D. M., & Cramer, R. P. (1996) Quantitative analyses of synaptic contacts of interneurons in the dorsal lateral geniculate nucleus of the squirrel monkey. *Visual Neurosci., 13*, 1129–1142. {7}

Wilson, J. R. *see also* Sherman

Wilson, M. *see* Attwell

Wiser, A. K. *see* Callaway

Withington-Wray, D. J., Binns, K. E., & Keating, M. J. (1990) The maturation of the superior collicular map of auditory space in the guinea pig is disrupted by developmental visual deprivation. *Eur. J. Neurosci., 2*, 682–692. {17}

Witkovsky, P. (1971) Synapses made by myelinated fibers running to teleost and elasmobranch retinas. *J. Comp. Neurol., 142*, 205–222. {4, 15}

Wollberg, Z., & Newman, J. D. (1972) Auditory cortex of squirrel monkey: response patterns of single cells to species-specific vocalizations. *Science, 175*, 212–214. {18}

Wong, E., & Weisstein, N. (1982) A new perceptual context-superiority effect: line segments are more visible against a figure than against a ground. *Science, 218*, 587–589. {10}

Wong-Riley, M. T. T. (1979) Changes in the visual system of monocularly sutured or enucleated cats demonstrable with cytochrome oxidase histochemistry. *Brain Res., 171*, 11–28. {8}

Wong-Riley, M. T. T., Hevner, R. F., Cutlan, R.,

Earnest, M., Egan, R., Frost, J., & Nguyen, T. (1993) Cytochrome oxidase in the human visual cortex: distribution in the developing and the adult brain. *Visual Neurosci., 10*, 41–58. {8}

Wong-Riley, M. T. T. *see also* DeYoe

Woodmansee, J. J. (1965) An evaluation of pupil response as a measure of attitude toward Negroes. *Doctoral dissertation.* University of Colorado. {3}

Woodruff, M. L., Bownds, D., Green, S. H., Mornsey, J. L., & Shedlovsky, A. (1977) Guanosine 3′, 5′-cyclic monophosphate and the *in vitro* physiology of frog photoreceptor membranes. *J. Gen. Physiol., 69*, 667–679. {4}

Woodruff, P. W. R. *see* Calvert; Howard

Woodworth, R. S. (1938) *Experimental Psychology.* New York: Holt. {**20.10**}

Wooten, B. R., & Werner, J. S. (1979) Short-wave cone input to the red-green opponent channel. *Vision Res., 19*, 1053–1054. {14}

Wörgötter, F., & Eysel, U. T. (1991) Topographical aspects of intracortical excitation and inhibition contributing to orientation specificity in area 17 of the cat visual cortex. *Eur. J. Neurosci., 3*, 1232–1244. {7}

Wörgötter, F. *see also* Eysel; Funke

Wray, J., & Edelman, G. M. (1996) A model of color vision based on cortical reentry. *Cerebr. Cort., 6*, 701–716. {10}

Wright, I. *see* Howard

Wright, R. H. (1966) Why is an odour? *Nature, 209*, 551–554. {20}

Wright, R. H. (1977) Odor and molecular vibration: neural coding of olfactory information. *J. Theor. Biol., 64*, 473–502. {20}

Wu, S. M. (1994) Synaptic transmission in the outer retina. *Annu. Rev. Physiol., 56*, 141–168. {6}

Wu, S. M. *see also* Maple

Wurtz, R. H., & Goldberg, M. E. (1971) Superior colliculus cell responses related to eye movements in awake monkeys. *Science, 171*, 82–84. {7}

Wurtz, R. H., & Mohler, C. W. (1976). Organization of monkey superior colliculus: enhanced visual response of superficial cell layers. *J. Neurophysiol., 39*, 74–765. {7}

Wurtz, R. H. *see also* Campbell; Dürsteler; Komatsu; Mohler; Newsome

Wyatt, H. J. *see* Daw

Wygonski, J. *see* Shannon

Wysocki, C. J. *see* Wang

Wyttenbach, R. A., May, M. L., & Hoy, R. R. (1996) Categorical perception of sound frequency by crickets. *Science, 273*, 1542–1544. {18}

Xiao, D.-K. *see* Lagae

Xin, D. *see* Bloomfield

Xu, L. *see* Middlebrooks

Xu, L. (1998) Effects of light adaptation on the activities of rod-driven bipolar cells in the cat electroretinogram. *Masters thesis.* College of Optometry, University of Houston. {**6.8**}

Yaksh, T. L. (1978) Narcotic analgesics: CNS sites and mechanisms of action as revealed by intracerebral injection techniques. *Pain, 4*, 299–359. {19}

Yamamoto, T., & Kawamura, Y. (1972) Gustatory responses from circumvallate and foliate papillae of the rat. *J. Physiol. Soc. Japan, 34*, 83–84. {20}

Yamane, S. *see* Komatsu

Yarnold, P. R. *see* Levine

Yau, K.-W. (1994) Phototransduction mechanism in retinal rods and cones. *Invest. Ophthal. & Vis. Sci., 35*, 9–32. {4}

Yau, K.-W., & Nakatani, K. (1984) Cation selectivity of light-sensitive conductance in retinal rods. *Nature, 309*, 352–354. {4}

Yau, K.-W. *see also* Haynes; Koutalos; Lamb; Nakatani

Yaxley, S. *see* Scott

Yazulla, S. *see* Malchow

Ye, Q., Heck, G. L., & DeSimone, J. A. (1991) The anion paradox in sodium taste reception: resolution by voltage-clamp studies. *Science, 254*, 724–726. {20}

Yezierski, R. P. *see* Giesler

Yin, T. C. T. *see* Kuwada; Lynch

Yonaha, T. *see* Saito

Yoshida, K. *see* Chino; Hamamoto

Yoshikami, S., & Hagins, W. A. (1971) Ionic basis of dark current and photocurrent of retinal rods. *Biophys. J., 10*, 60a. {4}

Yoshikami, S., Robinson, W. E., & Hagins, W. A. (1974) Topology of the outer segment membranes of retinal rods and cones revealed by fluorescent probe. *Science, 185*, 1176–1179. {4}

Yoshioka, T., Levitt, J. B., & Lund, J. S. (1994) Independence and merger of thalamocortical channels within macaque monkey primary visual cortex: anatomy of interlaminar projections. *Visual. Neurosci., 11*, 467–489. {8}

Yoshioka, T. *see also* Hendry

Yost, W. A. (1992) Auditory perception and sound source determination. *Curr. Dir. In Psychol. Sci., 1,* 179–184. {17}

Young, D. *see* Matin

Young, H. M. *see* Vaney

Young, M. P. (1992) Objective analysis of the topological organization of the primate cortical visual system. *Nature, 358,* 152–155. {8}

Young, R. W. (1978) The daily rhythm of shedding and degradation of rod and cone outer segment membranes in the chick retina. *Invest. Ophthalmol., 17,* 105–116. {4}

Yu, K. *see* Schall

Yund, E. W. *see* DeValois

Zahs, K. R., & Stryker, M. P. (1988) Segregation of ON and OFF afferents to ferret visual cortex. *J. Neurophysiol., 59,* 1410–1429. {7}

Zaidi, Q. *see* Sachtler

Zatorre, R. J., Evans, A. C., Meyer, E., & Gjedde, A. (1992) Lateralization of phonetic and pitch discrimination in speech processing. *Science, 256,* 846–849. {18}

Zeevi, Y. Y. *see* Porat

Zeigler, H. P., & Leibowitz, H. (1957) Apparent visual size as a function of distance for children and adults. *Am. J. Psychol., 70,* 106–109. {12}

Zeki, S. (1973) Color coding in rhesus monkey prestriate cortex. *Brain Res., 53,* 422–427. {14}

Zeki, S. M. (1974) Functional organization of a visual area in the posterior bank of the superior temporal sulcus of the rhesus monkey. *J. Physiol., 236,* 549–573. {8}

Zeki, S. (1983a) The distribution of wavelength and orientation selective cells in different areas of monkey visual cortex. *Proc. Roy. Soc. B, 217,* 449–470. {8}

Zeki, S. (1983b) Colour coding in the cerebral cortex: the responses of wavelength-selective and colour-coded cells in monkey visual cortex to changes in wavelength composition. *Neurosci., 9,* 767–781. {14}

Zeki, S., & Shipp, S. (1988) The functional logic of cortical connections. *Nature, 335,* 311–317. {8}

Zeki, S. *see also* Howard

Zemel, R. S., & Sejnowski, T. (1998) A model for encoding multiple object motions and self-motion in area MST of primate visual cortex. *J. Neurosci., 18,* 531–547. {13}

Zemon, V. *see* Green

Zeng, F. -G., & Shannon, R. V. (1994) Loudness-coding mechanisms inferred from electric stimulation of the human auditory system. *Science, 264,* 564–566. {2, 17}

Zeng, F. -G. *see also* Shannon

Zenner, H. -P. *see* Meyer

Zewi, M. *see* Granit

Zhou, Y. *see* Leventhal; Thompson

Zimbardo, P. G., Andersen, S. M., & Kabat, L. G. (1981) Induced hearing deficit generates experimental paranoia. *Science, 212,* 1529–1531. {18}

Zimmerman, R. P. *see* Levine

Zipser, K. *see* Lamme

Zotterman, Y. *see* Diamant

Zrenner, E. *see* Reitner

Zurif, E. B. (1980) Language mechanisms: a neuropsychological perspective. *Amer. Scient., 68,* 305–311. {18}

Zwaardemaker, H. (1895) *Die Physiologie des Geruchs.* Leipzig: Engelmann. {20}

van der Zwan, R., & Wenderoth, P. (1994) Psychophysical evidence for area V2 involvement in the reduction of subjective contour tilt aftereffects by binocular rivalry. *Visual Neurosci., 11,* 823–830. {13}

Zwicker, E., & Feldtkeller, R. (1956) *Das Ohr als Nachrichtenempfänger.* Stuttgart: S. Hirzel Verlag. {17, **17.9**}

Zwicker, E., Flottorp, G., & Stevens, S. S. (1957) Critical bandwidth in loudness summation. *J. Acoust. Soc. Am., 29,* 548–557. {17, **17.10**}

Glossdex

2AFC *See* Two alternative forced choice

4AFC *See* Four alternative forced choice

2½D sketch Hypothetical viewer-centered representation of space generated as input for the full three-dimensional representation, **243**

AII Amacrine cell Amacrine cell in the rod pathway, **68**, 69. *See also* Amacrine cell

Abscissa Horizontal position on a graph, **471**

Absolute threshold Minimum detectable amount of stimulation, **5**–12, 19–21. *See also* Dark adaptation, Spectral sensitivity, Threshold

Absorbance spectrum Curve relating percentage of light absorbed by a pigment to the wavelength of the light (also called *absorption spectrum or percentage absorption*), **95**–6, 310–12, 314–16

Accommodation Process of focusing the eye on objects at varying distances, **39**–42, 231. *See also* Ciliary muscles, Lens

Achromatopsia Inability to see colors, due to damage in higher cortex, **149**, 319

Acoustic reflex Reflex protecting the ear from intense sounds by contraction of the stapedius and tensor tympani muscles, 342, **343**

Action potential Electrical event by which a neuron can transmit information for long distances along its axon, 74, 198, **485**–488, 493

Acuity Ability to discern fine details, **37**, 42, 53, 54, 82, 92, 102, 103, 116, 138, 162, 197, 319

Adaptation Changing sensitivity to accommodate different levels of stimulation, 58, 77, 94, **98**–110, 168, 170, 173, 177, 179–81, 261, 281–3, 322, 324, 329–30, 345, 381–3, 418, 422, 440, 453. *See also* Dark adaptation, Light adaptation; Auditory fatigue

Adaptation level Theory that perceived lightness is judged relative to mean luminance in the entire scene, **250**–1, 329

Adapting pool Local region of retina in which all neurons adapt as a unit, **106**

Additive color mixture Superposition of two or more colored lights, **299**–302. *See also* Metameric match

Afferent Nerve fiber carrying sensory information to the central nervous system, **427**, 429, 430–3, 440–1, 446, 454–9

Aftereffect Altered perception due to previously presented stimuli, **176**–7, 200, 280–5, 322. *See also* Figural aftereffect, McCullough effect, Movement aftereffect

Afterimages Images of a stimulus seen after the physical stimulus is extinguished, **106**–10, 179–80, 261, 270, 320, 322, 324. *See also* Emmert's law; negative, 109–10; positive, 108–9

Albedo *See* Reflectance

Alexia Inability to read, 149

Amacrine cell Laterally connecting cells of the inner plexiform layer of the retina, **51**, 66–70. *See also* AII Amacrine cell

Ambiguous figure A pattern that can be interpreted in either of two ways, **210**, 212–15. *See also* Reversible figure

Ames demonstrations Stimuli that require unusual perceptual hypotheses to be seen veridicially, 216–19, 262–4. *See also* Illusion, Trapezoidal window

Analgesia The reduction of pain, **445**–7

Analysis-by-synthesis Model of perception in which an internal representation is built by making perceptual hypotheses, **208**, 419

Anamorphic art Pictures that can be seen 'correctly' only if viewed with a specific distortion, **275**–7

Annulus Ring-shaped visual stimulus, **62**

Anomalous trichromat Trichromat with an abnormal visual pigment in one cone type, **317**

Anosmia Inability to sense odors, **464**–5

Anterior chamber Front chamber of the eye, between cornea and iris, **35**

Anterolateral columns Columns at the sides of the spinal cord, mediating pain sensations, **432**–3, 440–5. *See also* Spinomesencephalic tract, Spinothalamic tract

Anvil   Incus; *see* Ossicles

Aperture problem   Ambiguity about direction of motion of a line passing behind a window, **285**, 292

Apex   Top of the cochlea, farthest from the oval window, **343**, **351**

Aphasia   Inability to produce speech, **423**

Apparent movement   Impression of movement given by stationary stimuli, 282, 290, 291. *See also* Autokinetic effect, Movement aftereffect, Pulfrich effect, Stroboscopic movement

Apraxia   Impaired ability to perform complex motions, **150**

Aqueous humor   Fluid in the anterior chamber of the eye, **35**

Articulation   Formation of speech sounds by the vocal apparatus, **399**–401, 406, 419

Artificial intelligence   Computer models of perceptual systems, 187–90. *See also* Parallel distributed processing

Ascending series   Method of limits in which threshold is approached from below, **8**

Astigmatism   Defect of the eye in which focus is different for stimuli of different orientations, **42**

Ataxia   Difficulty reaching under visual control, **150**

Attention   Process of 'spotlighting' particular areas or aspects of the visual field, 150–1, 199

Auditory cortex   Portion of temporal lobe devoted to the auditory sense, 347–9, 361, 363, 381, 389–92, 397, 417, 421

Auditory fatigue   Loss in sensitivity following an intense auditory stimulus, **381**–3

Auditory localization   Ability to discern the position of a sound source in space, 388–96. *See also* Auditory receptive fields, Cone of confusion, Monaural cues

Auditory nerve   Fibers that convey information from the cochlea to the brainstem, 345–**347**, 348, 357–60, 363–7, 379–81

Auditory receptive field   Area of space to which an auditory neuron is tuned, **389**–91

Autokinetic effect   Apparent random motion of a small stimulus in a large, blank field, **289**

Axon   Long neural extension that carries output information from a neuron, **484**

Axon terminal   End of the axon where it is presynaptic to other cells, **484**

Azimuth   Lateral position, **392**

Balint's syndrome   Disorder of perception in which a patient has difficulty localizing and integrating parts of the visual scene, **150**, 219

Bandwidth   Range of frequencies represented in a stimulus (can also refer to range to which a system is sensitive), **382**, **383**–5

Base   Part of cochlea nearest the oval window, **351**

Basilar membrane   Major membrane of the cochlea, separating the cochlear duct from the scala tympani, **344**, 350–60, 375–6, 379, 381, 386–8. *See also* Envelope, Place theory, Resonance curve, Telephone theory

Beats   Periodic changes in loudness of a sound consisting of two tones of similar frequency, **370–1**, 387

Benham's top   Black-and-white circular pattern that, when spun, gives an appearance of colors, **325**–6

Beta movement   Stroboscopic movement of a stimulus from one position to another (also *optimal movement*), **292**. *See also* Stroboscopic movement

Bezold–Brücke hue shift   Change in hue of a light as its intensity is changed, **21**, 299

Binaural cues   Cues to the location of a sound source requiring the use of both ears, 392–5; head movements, 394–5; intensity differences, 392–3; timing differences, 393–4

Binding   Problem of determining which features should be associated into single objects, 153, 195, **198**, 206

Binocular cues   Cues to depth or distance based on binocular disparity, **235**–43, 267. *See also* Binocular disparity, Convergence

Binocular disparity   Difference between the images on the two retinas due to differences in depth, **148**, **237**–44, 295

Binocular interaction   Combination of signals from both eyes, 117, 130–1, 135–8, 141–2

Binocular rivalry   Condition in which dichoptic stimuli conflict so only one may be seen at a time, 198, **242**–4, 283

Bipolar cells   Retinal cells that conduct signals from the outer plexiform layer to the inner plexiform layer, **49**–50, 64–6, 69–70, 87, 106

Blind spot   The optic disc, where there are no receptors, 37–**38**, 53

Blink suppression   Temporary insensitivity of the visual system during eye blinks, **117**

Blobs   Areas of dark cytochrome oxidase staining in V1, where cells sensitive to wavelength are found (also called *puffs*), **138**–40, 325

Bloch's law   Trade-off between intensity and duration of equally detectable lights, **20**

Blocker Drug that prevents a transmitter from having its effect at a synapse, **491**

Bottom-up processing *see* Top-down processing

Brightness Apparent amount of light emanating from an object, **248**, 255–7

Brightness enhancement Increased brightness of a flickering light, **256**

Broca's area Region in frontal cortex of the left hemisphere of the brain that is essential for the production of speech, **422**–3

CFF *See* Critical fusion frequency

CIE See Commission Internationale de l'Éclairage

CIE color diagram Color space defined by the CIE, **307**–10, 317–20

CL *See* Central lateral nucleus

CSF *See* Contrast sensitivity function

Camouflage *See* Masking, simultaneous

Cataract Condition in which the lens of the eye becomes opaque, **36**, 209

Cell assembly Groupings of neurons hypothesized to 'learn' by strengthening synaptic connections, **209**–10. *See also* Parallel distributed processing

Central lateral nucleus (CL) Nucleus of the thalamus that serves as a pain relay, **441**–2

Centrifugal fibers Efferent fibers from the central nervous system to the peripheral sense organs, **51**, 144. *See also* Feedback

Channels Hypothetical visual detectors of different spatial frequencies and/or orientations, **166**–70, 180–1

Characteristic frequency Frequency to which an auditory nerve fiber is most sensitive, **351**, **358**–60

Charpentier illusion *See* size-weight illusion

Choroid Layer of the eye that lies between the sclera and pigment epithelium, **36**

Chromophore Vitamin A aldehyde (retinal) portion of a visual pigment, **55**–9

Ciliary muscles Eye muscles that control state of visual accommodation, **36**, 40, 42, 231. *See also* Accommodation

Clarity Cue depth to atmospheric degradation, **225**–6

Closure Gestalt principle stating that people tend to see figures as enclosed wholes, **195**, 197, 199, 206, 219

Cochlea Spiral structure of the inner ear containing the organ of Corti, **343**–6. *See also* Basilar membrane, Hair cells, Organ of Corti

Cochlear duct Middle chamber of the cochlea, containing the endolymph (also call *scala media*), **343**

Cochlear microphonic Gross potential reflecting the activity of auditory hair cells, **493**

Cochlear nucleus First relay station for auditory nerve fibers entering the brainstem, **347**, 359–60, 379

Cognitive learning 209–10

Color aftereffect Apparent color produced in a black-and-white stimulus as a result of inspection of a colored pattern, 109, 179–80. *See also* McCullough effect

Color blindness Condition in which certain color discriminations cannot be made (more properly called *color defects*), 317–19. *See also* Achromatopsia, Anomalous trichromat, Dichromacy, Monochromacy

Color constancy Tendency for the color of an object to be perceived as the same regardless of the spectral composition of the light illuminating it, **328**–31. *See also* Lightness constancy

Color matching *See* Metameric match

Color naming Psychophysical technique in which the subject assigns names to lights of various wavelengths, **320**–1

Color perception. 328–31. *See also* Additive color mixture, Color naming, Metameric matching, Opponent process theory, Saturation, Subtractive color mixture, Surface color, Trichromatic theory

Color space Geometric representation of the facts of color mixing, 306–7. *See also* CIE color diagram

Columns, cortical Organization of cortex such that cells with similar properties are found in vertical columns, **134**–41, 148, 149, 349, 439–40, 444. *See also* Hypercolumns, Ocular dominance columns, Orientation columns

Columns, spinal Collections of axons running the length of the spinal cord, carrying information toward (or from) the brain. *See* Anterolateral columns, Posterior columns

Commission Internationale de l'Éclairage (CIE) International commission that defined standards of light and color, **308**. *See also* CIE color diagram

Common fate Gestalt principle stating that items moving in the same direction at the same speed are grouped together, **195**, 284

Complementary colors Pairs of lights that, when added together, yield white, **320**

Complex cells Type of cell in the visual cortex that does not select for position of a stimulus within its receptive field, **126**, 127–30, 143, 181, 194, 244

Complex sounds Sounds containing more than one frequency component, 369, 370–2, 377–8, 379, 383–6

dBC Sound intensity scale based on energy levels, **335**. *See also* Decibel

DL Difference limen. *See* Difference threshold

Dark adaptation Gradual lowering of visual threshold with time, **98**–103. *See also* Adaptation, photochromatic interval, Photopic system, Purkinje shift, Scotopic system

Decibel (dB) Logarithmic intensity scale, used particularly to express amplitude of sound waves, **335**–6, 337

Decremental conduction Passive spread of electrical signal within a cell, **485**

Demons Hypothetical detectors and decision-makers in pandemonium model. *See* Pandemonium

Dendrite Portion of a neuron specialized for receiving neural inputs, **484**

Depolarization For a nerve cell, becoming less polarized (more positive) inside, **485**

Depth of field Extent to which an object can move in distance from a lens and still be in reasonable focus, **43**–4

Depth perception Perception of the distances of objects from the observer, 223–43

Dermatome Area of the body innervated by a single spinal root, **431**–3

Descending pathways *See* Centrifugal fibers

Descending series Method of limits in which the threshold is approached from above, **8**. *See also* Method of limits

Deuteranope Dichromat lacking the medium-wave-length-sensitive pigment, **317**, 319

Development of cortical neurons 141–3. *See also* Phonemic boundaries

Dichoptic presentation Presentation of independent stimuli to each eye, **236**, 239–43

Dichromacy Form of color blindness in which only two color mechanisms are functional, **311**–14, 317–19. *See also* Deuteranope, Protanope, Tritanope

Difference threshold Smallest detectable difference between two stimuli, the just noticeable difference (also called jnd or DL), **12**–13

Diopter Measure of the strength of a lens, computed as one over the focal length in meters, **33**

Diplopia Double vision, **45**–6, 239

Direct scaling *See* Magnitude estimation

Direction-selective cells *See* Motion detectors

Discs Photopigment-rich membrane packets in outer segments of photoreceptors. *See* Outer segment, Shedding

Disjunctive eye movement Shift of gaze such that the eyes move in opposite directions, **45**

Disparity *See* Binocular disparity

Distal stimulus Actual object being observed, **208**, 257, 271–2, 398, 419

Doppler shift Change in pitch of a sound source moving relative to the observer, **396**

Dorsal root ganglion Collection of cell bodies of afferents to the spinal cord, **431**, 433

Dorsal stream Visual areas in the upper part of the brain having heavy magnocellular input, concerned with depth, location of objects, and visually guided behaviour, **146**, 150–2, 153, 199, 205, 245, 284–6, 295, 436

Double opponent field Type of visual receptive field in which the antagonistic center and surround each exhibit spectral opponency, **325**

Dyad Synaptic complex in the inner plexiform layer of the retina, **66**, 70

Dyslexia Reading disorder in which the order of letters is reversed, **150**

EPSP *See* Excitatory postsynaptic potential

ERG *See* Electroretinogram

Eardrum *See* Tympanic membrane

Efferent Fiber carrying information from the central nervous system to the periphery. *See* Centrifugal fibers, Gamma motorneurons

Ehrenstein illusion Illusion of shape, **266**. *See also* Illusion

Electromagnetic radiation Form of energy of which visible light is an example, **28**–9

Electroretinogram (ERG) Gross potential reflecting the activity of retinal neurons, 107–8, **493**

Electrotonic conduction *See* Decremental conduction

Emmert's law Relationship between apparent size of an afterimage and the distance to the surface against which it is seen, **261**

Emmetrope Person whose eye is correctly focused at infinity when unaccommodated, **41**

Endolymph Potassium-rich fluid in the cochlear duct, **344**, 345

End-stopped Cortical cell property of being selective for the length of a stimulus, **126**–7, 130, 131

Enkephalins Endogenous neurotransmitters chemically related to opioids, **447**

Envelope Maximum displacement of the basilar membrane during a sustained sound as a function of position along the membrane, 351, **354**–6

Equiluminant Differing in color but not in luminance

(also called *isoluminant*),**152**–3, 227, 230, 234, 243–4, 266, 294, 311, 324, 325, 328

Excitatory postsynaptic potential (EPSP) Depolarization caused by transmitter released from a presynaptic cell, **489**

Extracellular fluid (ECF) Fluid-filled space surrounding the cells, **484**

Extraocular muscles Muscles that move the eye, 44–5, 223, 286–7

Eye–head movement system System that follows a moving stimulus with eye and head movements, 286–90

Eye movements 44–6, 117, 122, 150, 151, 153, 235, 265–6, 279, 283, 286–90. *See also* Extraocular muscles, Inflow theory, Outflow theory, Saccadic movement, Smooth pursuit movement

Eyeshine Light reflected from the back of the eye that appears to come from the pupil, 48

FAE *See* Figural aftereffect

Face recognition 148–9, 190, 199, 205. *See also* Prosopagnosia

Fading *see* Troxler fading

Far point Most distant point for which a myopic eye can produce a sharp image on the retina, 40, **42**

Farsightedness *See* Hypermetropia

Feature detectors Cells sensitive to specific aspects of the stimulus display, 85–6, **131**–2, 188, 190, 418, 421

Feedback Process by which 'higher' centers affect their inputs. **66**, 70, 110, 117, 130, 132, 144, 148, 189, 190, 290, 331, 348, 421, 427. See also Recursion, Reentrant processing, Top-down processing

Field adaptation That component of visual adaptation due to neural processes, **105**, 110

Figural aftereffect (FAE) Change in perception of a figure caused by inspection of another pattern, **173**, 177. *See also* Movement aftereffect

Figure Central object attended to in a scene, **198**–9

Filling-in Effect of perceptual completion of a stimulus partly obscured by the blind spot or a scotoma, **38**

Flavor 462. *See also* Conditioned taste aversion

Flicker Rapid flashing of a light, 256, 301

Focal length Measure of the strength of a lens: the distance from lens to focal point, **32**–3

Focal point Point at which a lens focuses parallel light rays, **32**

Forced choice Psychophysical method in which a subject must decide which of several alternatives contained the stimulus, **10**–11, 27. *See also* Four alternative forced choice, Two alternative forced choice

Formant Frequency band emphasized by the vocal apparatus in voiced phonemes, **406**–8. *See also* Locus, Transition

Four alternative forced choice (4AFC) Psychophysical method in which the subject chooses which of four stimuli differs from the other three, **11**

Fourier transform Mathematical procedure for approximating a function as a sum of sinusoids, **156**–60, 162, 334–5, 338, 357

Fovea Region in central retina specialized for fine detail discrimination, 37–9, **53**–4, 68, 82, 98, 101–3, 116, 121, 138, 280. *See also* Acuity, Cones

Frame of reference Visual frame of orientation or position of a figure, 204–5, 280

Frequency Number of complete vibrations per unit time, 28–30, 256, 301, 333–4

Frontal plane projection Projection of a visual scene upon a plane in front of the eyes, like a photograph, **271**–3

Fundamental frequency Lowest frequency component of a complex waveform, **159**–60, 164–5, 168, 336–8, 367, 371–2, 406, 415

Fundus Inside back of the eye, **39**

Fuse Combine dichoptic views into a single, coherent image, **239**, 241, 242

Gabor filter Spatial filter that optimizes the trade-off between spatial frequency and position information, **170**, 181

Gabor patch Stimulus consisting of a sinusoid within a Gaussian (normal) window; *see* Gabor filter

Gamma motor neuron Fiber that causes contraction of the muscle spindle fibers, **427**

Ganglion cells Output cells of the retina whose axons form the optic nerve, **51**–3, 54, 66, 68–9, 73–7; direction selective, 86–7; M- and P-cells, 119–20; orientation selective, 87–8; special types of, 84–8; W-cells, 92–3, 122; X- and Y-cells, 89–92, 119–20, 122

Ganzfeld Completely uniform and featureless visual field

Gate control theory Theory that pain signals are modulated by other stimuli, **445**

Generator potential Slow potential produced within a receptor cell in response to a stimulus, **454**–5, 467

Generic recognition Recognition of the general class an object is in, rather than its specific identity, **149**

Inner ear   Fluid-filled part of the ear, **338**, 343–6. See *also* Basilar membrane, Cochlea, Hair cells, Organ of Corti

Inner nuclear layer   Layer of the retina containing cell bodies of horizontal cells, bipolar cells, amacrine cells, and interplexiform cells, **49**–51, 65

Interblob regions   Areas of the upper layers of V1 cortex between the cytochrome oxidase blobs, **138**, 144–5, 148, 325

Interlaminar cells   *See* Koniocellular system

Internal capsule   Fibers from thalamus to somatosensory cortex, **434**

International Phonetic Association (IPA)   Organization that devised an alphabet for representing speech sounds (phonetic alphabet), **399**. *See also* Vowel quadrilateral

Interplexiform cells   Cells in the retina that conduct signals from the inner plexiform layer to the outer plexiform layer, **51**, 68, 70, 73, 110

Interposition   Occlusion of a distant object by a nearer object, a cue to depth, **224**–5

Interspike interval histogram   Histogram of times between successive action potentials fired by a neuron, **365**–6

Intracellular   The fluid-filled volume inside a cell, **491**–3

Iodopsin   The first cone pigment to be isolated chemically, **60**

Ion   An atom with too few or too many electrons, giving it an electrical charge, **484**–6, 489; calcium = Ca^{++}; chloride = Cl^- potassium = K^+; sodium = Na^+

Ipsilateral   On the same side of the body, **114**

Iris   Smooth muscle ring controlling size of the pupil; the colored part of the eye, **35**, 42. *See also* Pupil

Irradiance   Radiometric measure of light striking a surface, **31**

Isochronal threshold   Threshold for motion measured with a constant duration stimulus, **280**

Iso-intensity contour   Plot of responses of an auditory nerve fiber to various frequencies, 357–**8**

Isoluminance   *See* Equiluminant

Isomerization   Change in configuration of a visual pigment chromophore after absorption of a photon of light, **56**–7

jnd   Just noticeable difference. *See* Difference threshold

Jastrow illusion   Illusion of size, **265**, 267. *See also* Illusion

KDE   *See* Kinetic depth effect

Kinetic depth effect (KDE)   Depth impression produced

by moving a two-dimensional stimulus, **234**, 282

Kinetic optical occlusion   Successive eclipsing of objects by a moving object, a cue to depth, **294**

Konicocellular system   Visual pathways that starts with the koniocellular (interlaminar LGN) cells, **120**, 143–4

Korte's laws   Relationships among intensity, timing, and spatial configuration of stimuli that produce stroboscopic motion, 292

LGN   *See* Lateral geniculate nucleus

Landolt C   Test of acuity, **197**

Lateral antagonism   Process by which responses in one region in a receptive field oppose the responses from another area (often called *lateral inhibition*), **77**–84, 117–18, 128, 163, 171, 177, 252, 328, 357, 438, 466. *See also* Craik–O'Brien illusion, Hermann grid, Lightness constancy, Mach bands, Simultaneous contrast, Staircase illusion

Lateral geniculate nucleus (LGN)   Part of the thalamus that relays visual signals to the cortex, **115**–20, 128, 132, 137, 146, 194, 323–5, 328, 330. *See also* Magnocellular system, Parvocellular system, Principal cells

Lateral inhibition   Older term for lateral antagonism, still generally used especially in sensory systems other than vision. *See* Lateral antagonism

Lateral spinothalamic tract   *See* Spinothalamic tract

Law of specific nerve energies   Principle that firing of sensory nerves is interpreted as a stimulus of the appropriate modality

Lee-Boot effect   Inhibition of estrus among female animals housed together, **469**

Lens   Optical component that produces an image of an object, **32**–5; of the eye, **36**. *See also* Accommodation, Cataract, Focal length

Lens equation   Relationship between focal length of a lens and object and image distances, **33**

Light adaptation   Decrease in sensitivity with increases in ambient light, 103–5. *See also* Adaptation, Photopic system, Weber's law

Lightness   Apparent whiteness or grayness of an object, **248**

Lightness constancy   Tendency to judge surface color as the same despite changes in illumination, 248–57

Limen   *See* Threshold

Limits, method of   *See* Method of limits

Limulus polyphemus   Horseshoe crab, 46–7, 84

Linear summation   Simple addition of influences that

allows cancellation of opposing effects, 91, 127–9, 138, 162, 182

Linking proposition   Theoretical assumption about how a physiological response gives rise to a perception; see Binding problem

Lip reading   420

Locus   Frequency defining one end of the transition of a formant in speech, **411**–13, 418–19

Logarithm   Exponent to which 10 is raised to give a particular number; usually referred to as a *log*, **474**–81

Log law   Fechner's logarithmic relationship between stimulus intensity and apparent magnitude: $S = c \times \log (I)$, 14–**15**, 18

Long range motion system   Motion system concerned with global features, 285

Loudness   Apparent magnitude of sound, 334, 336, 369; of complex sounds, 383–6; of pure tones, 376–81

Luminance   Photometric measure of light emitted or reflected by an area of surface, **31**

Luminous flux   Photometric measure of total light emitted by a source, **31**

MAA   *See* Minimum audible angle

MAE   *See* Movement aftereffect

MAF   *See* Minimum audible field

MAP   *See* Minimum audible pressure

MT   *See* Mediotemporal cortex

MTF   *See* Modulation transfer function

MTS   An area of mediotemporal cortex

Mach bands   Illusory light and dark bands produced at the transition from a uniformly illuminated area to a gradient, **78**–81

Macula lutea   Pigmented central region of the retina containing the fovea, **37**, 39

'Magic Eye'   241, *see also* Random dot stereogram

Magnification   Distortion of the retinotopic map upon the LGN or cortex, with the fovea represented by a disproportionately large area, 116, 121, 138. Also applies to the distortion of the homunculus in somatosensory cortex, 437, 439

Magnitude estimation   Psychophysical scaling method in which the subject assigns numbers according to the apparent magnitudes of the stimuli, **16**

Magnitude production   Psychophysical scaling method in which the subject sets a stimulus intensity so the apparent magnitude is at a preassigned level, **16**

Magnocellular system   Visual processing pathway that starts with the large cells of the ventral layers of the LGN, **117**, 118–21, 138, 140, 143–6, 150, 152–3, 175, 192, 202, 234, 243–4, 266, 285, 294, 311, 328

Maintained discharge   Ongoing activity of a sensory neuron in the absence of any change in stimulation, **74**–5, 90, 198, 357, 390

Malleus   First ossicle, which receives vibration from the tympanic membrane. *See* Ossicles

Masking   Obscuring a stimulus by presenting another stimulus, **170**–2, 177, 288; auditory, 386–8; backward, 170, 288; forward, 170, 288; simultaneous, 170, 203–6. *See also* Metacontrast, Camouflage

Maxwellian view system   Optical system in which stimulus is projected directly on the retina, **300**

McCullough effect   Color aftereffect, **179**–80

McGurk effect   Disrupted speech perception due to inconsistent visual cues, 218–19

Medial geniculate nucleus   Part of the thalamus that relays auditory signals to temporal cortex, **347**, 359

Medial lemniscus   Somatosensory tract from spinal cord to thalamus, **434**–5

Mediotemporal cortex (MT)   Visual area with mainly magnocellular input, also known as V5, 113, 145–**6**, 149–50, 286, 288–9, 294–5

Meissner corpuscle   Somatosensory receptor, **427**–8

Mel   A scale that measures pitch, **355**–6

Merkel cells   Somatosensory receptor cells, **427**–8

Metacontrast   Backward masking in which the mask is spatially separate from the test, **171**. *See also* Masking, backward

Metameric match   Two colored stimuli that look alike but have different spectra, **305**–6

Metathetic continuum   Variable for which a larger numerical value does not imply a greater quantity, **13**

Methods, psychophysical   *See* Constant stimuli, Forced choice, Method of limits, Magnitude estimation, Magnitude production, Signal detection theory

Method of adjustment   Method of limits in which the subject controls the stimulus intensity, **8**

Method of limits   Psychophysical method in which intensity is varied until threshold is reached, **6**. *See also* Ascending series, Descending series, Method of adjustment

Michelson contrast   *see* Rayleigh contrast

Microelectrode   Small electrode that can be placed inside or near single cells, 492–**93**

Micromanipulator   Device for the precise positioning of a microelectrode, *See* stereostatic instrument

Micropipette   A kind of microelectrode made of glass, **492**–93

Microspectrophotometer   Instrument that measures the absorption spectrum of single photoreceptors, **315**–16, 326

Middle ear   Air-filled chamber containing the ossicles, **338**, 341–3. *See also* Ossicles, Stapedius, Tensor tympani

Minimum audible angle (MAA)   Smallest detectable movement of a sound source in space, **395**

Minimum audible field (MAF)   Absolute auditory threshold measured using loudspeakers, **374**

Minimum audible pressure (MAP)   Absolute auditory threshold measured using headphones, **374**

Missing fundamental illusion   Illusion that the fundamental frequency is present when only its harmonics are presented, **165**, 181. *See also* Craik–O'Brien illusion; auditory, 371–2

Modulation   *see* Contrast

Modulation transfer function (MTF)   Plot of magnitude of responses of a system as a function of spatial frequency, **161**–2

Monaural cues   Cues to the location of a sound source that require only one ear, 395–6. *See also* Doppler shift

Mondrian   Abstract complex visual pattern used to examine color constancy, **253**–4, 330

Monochromacy   Condition of complete color blindness in which only one visual pigment is functional, 310–12, 319

Monochromatic light   Light consisting of only one wavelength, **297**

Monochromator   Instrument that delivers nearly monochromatic light, **300**

Monocular cues   Cues to depth that require only one eye, **223**–34. *See also* Movement cues, Pictorial cues

Moon Illusion   Illusion that the horizon moon is larger than the zenith moon, 267–71

Motion detectors   Cells that respond best to stimuli that are moving, often in a preferred direction, 86–7, 122, 126, 148, 149–50, 281–6, 294

Motion parallax   Relative movement of objects at different distances, a cue to depth, **231**–3

Motor theory of speech perception   Theory that speech sounds are perceived according to an analysis-by-synthesis model, **419**–22

Movement aftereffect (MAE)   Impression of motion resulting from previous inspection of a moving target, 281–3, 286, 294

Movement cues   Depth cues derived from motion, 231–4. *See also* Kinetic depth effect, Motion parallax

Müller–Lyer Illusion   Illusion of length of lines, **265**–9. *See also* Illusion

Muscle spindle   Stretch receptive organ in voluntary muscles, 426–7

Myelin   Part of a glial cell that wraps around axons, speeding conduction of action potentials, **486**–7

Myopia   Nearsightedness, **41**

Nanometer (nm)   Measure of length; 1 nm = 10^{-9} m

Nasal retina   Half of the retina nearest the nose, **114**

Near point   Closest distance at which the accommodated lens can project a focused image on the retina, **40**, 42

Nearsightedness   *See* Myopia

Necker cube   Reversible figure, 214–16

Necturus maculosus   A salamander, commonly called the mud puppy, **62**

Negative light   Use of a primary in a metameric match such that it is added to the light being matched, **306**

Nerve impulse   *See* Action potential

Nerve spike   *See* Action potential

Neuron   Cell that is the basic unit of the nervous system, **483**–4

Neurotransmitter   *See* Transmitter

Neutral point   Monochromatic light that a dichromat confuses with white, **313**–14, 317–18

Nociception   Sense of pain, **424**, 429, 440–5

Noise   Random variation in a sensory channel, 21–3, 54, 94, 117, 481; as a stimulus, 334–5, 382–7, 394–5, 408–10, 414, 417

Nonlinearity   Failure of linearity, 90, 127, 128, 194, 372

Normal probability paper   Axes on which the integral of a normal distribution plots as a straight line, 480–1

Nystagmus   Rapid back-and-forth eye movement, **45**

Oblique muscles   Extraocular muscles that rotate the eye in the socket, **44**

Occipital cortex   Part of the brain nearest the back of the head, containing mainly visual processing areas, **112**–13. *See also* Visual area 1, V2, V3

Ocular dominance   Classification of cortical cells according to how strongly they are driven by each eye, **135**, 141–2

Ocular dominance columns   Slab-like groups of cells in visual cortex that are all driven primarily by the same eye, 135–8

Odor prism   System for representing the classification of odorants, 464

OFF-center cell   Cell that produces an OFF response to the presentation of light in the center of its receptive field, **68**, 74–6

OFF response   Response in which increased activity or depolarization occurs at offset of the stimulus (and decreased activity or hyperpolarization usually occurs at onset), **75**

OFFSET response   Response to the termination of a stimulus, **67**, **75**

Ogive   Continuously increasing 'S'-shaped curve, **6**–7

Olfaction   The sense of smell, 463–5

Olfactory bulb   Part of the brain where olfactory receptors synapse, **466**–8, 470

Olfactory neuroepithelium   The olfactory sensory organ, **465**

Ommatidium   Single facet of a compound eye, 46–**7**, 84

ON–OFF response   Response in which there is increased activity or depolarization at both onset and offset of the stimulus, **68**, 74

ON-center cell   Cell that produces an ON response to the presentation of light in the center of its receptive field, **68**, **75**–6, 78–9, 84

ON response   Response in which increased activity or depolarization occurs at onset of the stimulus (and decreased activity or hyperpolarization usually occurs at offset), **75**

ONSET response   Response to the initiation of a stimulus, **67**, **75**

Opiate analgesics   Narcotics derived from the opium poppy, used as pain killers, 446–7

Opponent process theory   Theory stating that the three fundamental color processes represent trade-offs in red/green, yellow/blue, and black/white systems, **321**–5

Opsin   Large protein portion of a visual pigment molecule, **55**, 60

Optic ataxia   *see* ataxia

Optic apraxia   *see* apraxia

Optic chiasm   Intersection of the optic nerves, **113**–14

Optic disc   Region where the optic nerve fibers leave the eyeball, also called the *blind spot*, **37**–9, 53

Optic nerves   Bundles of ganglion cell axons between the eyes and optic chiasm, **37**, 52, 84, 93, 113–16

Optic radiation   Bundles of axons of LGN principal cells connecting the LGN to the visual cortex, 113, 115

Optic tracts   Bundles of ganglion cell axons between the optic chiasm and thalamus or brainstem, **113**

Optics   Study of the reflection and refraction of light, 31–5

Orbison illusion   Illusion of shape, **266**. *See also* Illusion

Ordinate   Vertical position (height) of a point on a graph, 471

Organ of Corti   Primary auditory receptor structure on the basilar membrane of the cochlea, **344**. *See also* Basilar membrane, Hair cells

Orientation columns   Groups of cells lying in a vertical column in the visual cortex, all of which possess the same optimal stimulus orientation preference, 134–5, 137, 139–41

Orientation of figures   Angle at which complex visual patterns are viewed, 203–5

Oscillations   Repeating patterns of activity that may be involved in linking features or recognizing stimuli, 132, 198, 206, 468

Oscilloscope   Device for displaying voltage as a function of time, 487

Ossicles   Three small bones in the inner ear: the malleus ('hammer'), incus ('anvil'), and stapes ('stirrup'), **341**–2

Outer ear   External sound-gathering portion of the ear, 339–41. *See also* Pinna, Tympanic membrane

Outer nuclear layer   Layer of the retina containing the cell bodies of rods and cones, **49**

Outer segment   Part of the visual receptors that contains the visual pigment, **52**, 54, 56–9, 101. *See also* Shedding

Outflow theory   Theory that positions (of eyes or limbs) are monitored by noting the signals sent to the muscles, 283, **287**–8, 289, **425**

Oval window   Soft opening through which the stapes affects the fluid of the cochlea, **341**–3

PDP   *See* Parallel distributed processing

PSTH   *See* Peristimulus time histogram

Pacinian corpuscle   Somatosensory receptor, **427**–8

Pain perception   *See also* Nociception

Pale stripes   Areas of minimal cytochrome oxidase staining in V2, part of the parvocellular pathway, **144**–5

Palpated shapes   Perception of shape by touching, 440

Pandemonium   Hierarchical, parallel-processing model for pattern recognition, 188–9

Ponzo illusion Illusion of size due to distance, **262**–3. *See also* Illusion

Porphyropsin Photopigment found in rods of certain cold-blooded animals, **60**

Posterior columns The cuneate fasciculus and fasciculus gracilis, columns of the spinal cord mediating proprioception and the tactile sense, **432**–5, 441

Posterior parietal cortex Cortex in parietal lobe of the brain; part of the dorsal stream, 113, 145–6, 150, 284

Postsynaptic potential Potential difference caused by release of a transmitter at a synapse, **489**. *See also* Excitatory postsynaptic potential, Inhibitory postsynaptic potential, Potential difference, Voltage difference

Power law Psychophysical relationship stating that apparent magnitude is proportional to stimulus magnitude raised to an exponent: $S = k I^n$, **16**–19

Pragnanz Gestalt principle stating that features group to form 'good' figures, **195**–8, 206, 225

Preattentive process A process that works automatically, without conscious effort, **191**, 194, 202

Presbycusis Loss of sensitivity for higher-frequency sounds with advancing age (also called presbyacusia), **375**, 382

Presbyopia Decrease in accommodative ability with advancing age, **40**–2 *See also* Accommodation

Primal sketch Basic internal 'sketch' made from features, 187

Primary colors, additive Three colored lights that can be added to match any other light; usually taken as red, green, and blue, 300, 305–7, 310. *See also* Metameric match

Principal cell Type of cell in the LGN that projects to the visual cortex (also called *relay cell*), **117**–18

Prisms, inverting Device to invert the visual image, 35

Propagation of action potentials 485–7

Proprioception Sense of position of the body and limbs, 425–7

Prosodic element Qualitative aspect of relatively large segments of speech (also called *suprasegmental features*), **415**

Prosopagnosia Condition in which patient is unable to perform fine visual distinctions, specifically recognizing faces, **149**

Protanope Dichromat lacking the long wavelength sensitive pigment, **317**–19

Proximity Gestalt principle stating that nearby items are grouped together, **191**–2, 195, 216, 244

Psychometric function Plot of percentage detection or score as a function of stimulus strength, **6**–8, 9–12, 480–1

Psychophysics Study of the capability of an organism to detect, quantify, or identify a stimulus, **5**–27. *See also* Constant stimuli, Forced choice, Method of limits, Signal detection theory

Pulfrich effect Apparent motion in depth of a moving object viewed with a filter placed before one eye, **295**

Pupil Central opening of the iris, **35**, 42–3

Purity, colorimetric Relative amount of monochromatic light in a mixture with white light, 299, 310

Purkinje shift Difference in spectral sensitivity between the photopic and scotopic states, **100**

Quantum of light *See* Photon

RL Reiz limen. *See* Absolute threshold

ROC curve *See* Receiver operating characteristic curve

Radiance Radiometric measure of light emitted or reflected by an area of surface, **30**

Radiant flux Radiometric measure of total light emitted by a source, **30**

Radiometric measures Measures of the energy of light, **30**

Random dot stereogram Stereogram in which each separate image is a jumble of randomly placed dots, **239**–41, 243. *See also* Stereogram

Rate code Principle that since all action potentials are the same size, information is encoded by the firing rate, 74–5, 198, **407**

Rayleigh contrast Ratio of modulation amplitude to mean light level, 157

Receiver operating characteristic curve (ROC curve) Plot of percentage 'hits' versus percentage 'false alarms' in a signal detection experiment, **24**–6

Receptive field Area in which stimulation leads to response of a particular sensory neuron; auditory, 389–92; somatosensory, 425–7, 438–9, 443–4; visual, **64**–5, 67, 68, 76–7, 85–8, 90–3, 116–18, 123–6, 130–1, 163–4, 244, 252, 285–6, 324–5

Receptors Cells sensitive to stimulus energy; auditory, *see* Hair cells; kinesthetic, 426–7; olfactory, 465–7; pain, 429; pheromone, 470; tactile, 427–9; taste, 448–50; temperature, 429; visual, *see* Cone, Rod

Recovered sight 209

Rectus muscles Type of extraocular muscles, **44**–5

Recursion Repeated steps of processing to approach a

448–50, 453, 455, 457–8, 462

Tonic response   *See* Sustained response

Tonotopic map   Systematic relationship between location of cells in the brain and the sound frequencies to which they are most sensitive, **348**–9. **358**–61

Top-down processing   Concept that 'higher' centers modulate and guide the processing done in the 'lower' centers, 190–1

Transient response   Type of response that is only present immediately following a change in the stimulus (also called a *phasic response*), **66**–8, 70, 90, 92, 106, 182, 280, 285, 428, 437. *See also* ON–OFF response

Transition   Rapid shift in the frequency of a formant, **410**–13

Transmission curve   Characteristic of a filter expressed by percentage transmission as a function of wavelength, **302**–5

Transmitter   Chemical substance used in neuronal communication at synapses, **488**–90

Trapezoidal window   Demonstration of shape constancy, 216–17. *See also* Ames demonstrations, Illusion

Travelling wave   Pattern of vibration of the basilar membrane in which waves move from base to apex, with a maximum amplitude at a position determined by the sound frequency, 350–2. *See also* Place theory

Triad   Synaptic complex in the receptor invaginations of the retina, **61**–2

Triangle wave   Pattern of a series of uniform increases and decreases, **160**

Trichromacy   Normal human condition of having three color systems, and thus requiring three primaries to match any light, 314–15

Trichromatic theory   Theory that the existence of three additive primary colors indicates three broad fundamental color systems, 315–17

Tritanope   Dichromat lacking the short-wavelength-sensitive pigment, **317**–18

Troxler fading   Loss of visual sensation in the absence of changes, **37** *See also* Stabilized image

Two alternative forced choice (2AFC)   Psychophysical method in which the subject chooses in which of two possibilities the stimulus lies, **11**

Tympanic membrane   Membrane at end of outer ear canal that vibrates in response to sound (also called the *eardrum*), **340**–1

Umbra   Dark central portion of a shadow. *See* Shadows

Unique colors   Colors that seem psychologically 'pure', specifically red, yellow, green, and blue, **320**

Univariance   Principle that individual receptors cannot signal the wavelength of the light they have absorbed, **311**–12

Unstructured field   Visual display lacking cues to size or distance, **260**

V1   Primary visual cortex. Also called *striate cortex*. *See* Visual area I

V2   Secondary visual cortex, 113, 144–8, 244–5, 259, 325, 330

V3   Area of visual cortex with mainly magnocellular input, 113, 144–6, 148

V4   Area of visual cortex in the ventral stream, 113, 144–6, 148, 201, 259, 272–3, 330

V5   *See* Mediotemporal cortex

V8   Color area in posterior inferotemporal cortex of humans, 330

VPL   *See* Ventral posterior lateral nucleus

VPM   *See* Ventral posterior medial nucleus

Ventral posterior lateral nucleus   Nucleus of the thalamus that relays tactile and proprioceptive information about the body to the cortex, **435**

Ventral posterior medial nucleus   Nucleus of the thalamus that relays taste information, as well as tactile and proprioceptive information about the face, to the cortex, **450**

Ventral stream   Visual areas on the lower part of the brain that get heavy parvocellular input, concerned largely with identification of objects, **146**, 148–9, 151–2, 205, 285

Vertebrate eye   35–9

Visual angle   Angle of view subtended by an object, 157, **257**–8, 260–1, 267

Visual area I   Primary visual cortex (also called *striate cortex, V1*), 113, 120–1, 130–41, 143, 146–8, 244–5, 259, 282, 325, 330. *See also* Complex cells, Hypercolumns, Concentric cells, Magnocellular system, Ocular dominance columns, Orientation columns, Parvocellular system, Simple cells

Visual pigment   *See* Chromophore, Cone pigment, Iodopsin, Porphyropsin, Retinal, Rhodopsin

Vitreous humor   Fluid in the major chamber of the eye, **36**

Vocal cords   Bands of muscle in the airway that vibrate to produce sound for speech, 399–400, 406, 415

Voiced sound   Speech sound made with the vocal cords vibrating. *See* Consonants, or; Vowels

Volley principle   Theory that individual auditory nerve fibers fire only at certain phases of the cycle of incoming sound waves, **364**–6, 393

Voltage   Potential difference (electrical potential)

Vomeronasal system   Receptive organ for pheromones, located in Jacobson's organ in the nose, **470**

Vowel quadrilateral   Representation of vowel sounds according to tongue, lips, and jaw positions, **400**, 417

Vowels   Speech sounds, generally voiced, with high energy, 399–401

Waterfall illusion   Example of a movement after effect, 281

Wavelength   Distance in space from the peak of one wave to the peak of the next; wavelengths of light generally correspond to hues or colors, **29**

Weber contrast   Ratio of magnitude of stimulus to background level, 103–4

Weber fraction   Constant of proportionality in Weber's law, 13

Weber's law   Principle that the jnd is a constant fraction of the comparison stimulus: $\Delta I/I_0 = k$, where k is the Weber fraction, **13**, 107

Wernicke's area   Area in left cortex involved in speech comprehension, 422–**3**

Wundt illusion   Illusion of shape, **265**–6. *See also* Illusion

Zollner illusion   Illusion of shape, **266**. *See also* Illusion

Zonule of Zinn   Fiber sac holding the lens in position behind the iris, **36**, 40

CD-ROM conditions of use

Please read these terms before proceeding with the CD installation. By installing the CD you agree to be bound by these terms.

The enclosed CD contains the program SensPerc, which runs on IBM PCs and their clones under Windows 95, Windows 98, Windows NT, and Windows 2000 operating systems.

The materials contained on this CD-ROM have been supplied by the author of this book. Whilst every effort has been made to check the software routines and the text, there is always the possibility of error and users are advised to confirm the information in this product through independent sources.

Michael Levine grants you a non-exclusive licence to use this CD to search, view and display the contents of this CD on a single computer at a single location and to print off multiple screens from the CD for your own private use or study. All rights not expressly granted to you are reserved to Michael Levine, and you shall not adapt, modify, translate, reverse engineer, decompile or disassemble any part of the software on this CD, except to the extent permitted by law.

These terms shall be subject to English laws and the English courts shall have jurisdiction.

THIS CD-ROM IS PROVIDED 'AS IS' WITHOUT WARRANTY OF ANY KIND, EXPRESS OR IMPLIED, INCLUDING BUT NOT LIMITED TO IMPLIED WARRANTIES OF SATISFACTORY QUALITY OR FITNESS FOR A PARTICULAR PURPOSE. IN NO EVENT SHALL ANYONE ASSOCIATED WITH THIS PRODUCT BE LIABLE FOR ANY DIRECT, INDIRECT, SPECIAL, CONSEQUENTIAL, OR ACCIDENTAL DAMAGES RESULTING FROM ITS USE.

THE SOFTWARE IS NOT SUPPORTED.

Instructions for installing the software are to be found in the Preface, pages ix–x.

SensPerc program contents

Chapter 1: Introduction
- General introduction and instructions
Layout and use of controls *(D)*

Chapter 2: Psychophysics
- Threshold experiment
Detection by Method of Constant Stimuli or by Method of Limits. Shows psychometric function on linear and probability coordinates *(D,T)*
- Signal detection theory (D)

Chapter 3: The Eye
- Three demonstrations: (1) Blind spot, (2) Peripheral vision, and (3) Foveal Acuity
Allows students to see effects of viewing with different retinal regions *(D)*
- The fundus
View of the fundus with landmarks indicated and explained *(D)*

Chapter 4: The Retina
- Retinal cells responding to light
Simulated retinal cells changing polarization when a stimulus is flashed *(D,I)*

Chapter 5: Ganglion cells
- Ganglion cells responding to light
Simulates responses of different classes of ganglion cell to spots and annuli. Generates PSTH for repeated stimuli. "Guessing game" for students to guess the cell from its responses. *(D, I, Q)*

Chapter 6: Adaption
- Afterimages
Three possible images that can be presented as positive or negative afterimages *(D)*

Chapter 7: Primary visual areas of the brain
- Brain anatomy
Images of the brain, with visual areas highlighted. Animation of response spread through visual areas *(D)*
- Blink suppression
Demonstration of the lack of the apparent dimming when the student blinks voluntarily *(D)*

- Responses of cortical cells
  Simulates responses of various types of cortical cells to bars and edges, some moving. Similar to 'ganglion cells', with guessing game *(D, I, Q)*

Chapter 8: Higher cortical areas
- Architecture of cortical columns
  Organization of orientation and ocular dominance columns *(D, I)*
- Equiluminant images
  Four photos, a line drawing, and a pattern of moving dots to demonstrate effects of images at equiluminance (no magnocellular response) *(D, T)*

Chapter 9: Fourier components
- Fourier components of gratings
  Shows sinusoidal, square, peaks-add, and triangle gratings and their components. Demonstrates summation of components. *(D, I)*
- See your own CSF
  Figure in which spatial frequency changes along abscissa and contrast along ordinate. *(D)*
- McCollough effect
  Inspection figure (color plate) for Figure 9–16. *(D)*

Chapter 10: Form perception
- Motion from form
  Two high contrast faces that look like blobs until revealed. Alternation between them is nonsensical until they have been seen as faces; alternation then looks like coherent motion
- Impossible figures
  Impossible drawing accompanied by impossible sound *(D)*

Chapter 11: Depth perception
- Three demonstrations of apparent depth from motion of randon dots
  Random dots produce flow fields for parallax, transparency, or approach *(D)*

Chapter 12: Constancies and illusions
- Six optical illusions of brightness, alignment, size, or shape.
  Student adjusts comparison figure, then sees how much error was made. Simultaneous contrast, apparent lightness, the Ponzo illusion, the Poggendorf illusion, the Muller–Lyer illusion, and shape constancy *(D, I, T)*

Chapter 13: Movement
- Motion past an aperture
  The aperture effect: lines seem to move at right angles to their orientation when viewed through an aperture *(D)*
- Motion aftereffect (waterfall illusion)
  Field of dots provides continuous motion for opposite aftereffect *(D)*

- Path of motion
  Path of moving spot seems distorted without reference frame *(D)*
- Macro and micro fields of random dots
  'Common fate' defines object in field of differently moving random dots. Motion of defined object is not in the direction of any motion *(D)*
- Relative movement # 1
  Motion induced in a stationary object by movement of a frame around it *(D)*
- Relative movement # 2
  A pigeon's head seems to move backward when it actually stops *(D)*

Chapter 14: Color vision
- Additive color mixing
  Sum of three primaries in additive mixing *(D, I)*
- Responses of opponent cells
  Simulates responses of various types of color opponent cells to lights of different colors, with different adapting backgrounds. Similar to 'ganglion cells' and 'Cortical cells', with guesing game and PSTH *(D, I, Q)*

Chapter 15: Structure of the Auditory system
- Animations of mechanics of the middle and inner ear
  Three animations: (1) motion of the ossicles, (2) bending of hair cell cilia by motion of the basilar membrane, and (3) mechanical opening of channels in cilia as they deflect *(D)*

Chapter 16: Perception of pitch
- Traveling waves on the basilar membrane
  Animation of the traveling waves and their envelopes for different frequencies of sound *(D)*

Chapter 17: Perception of pitch and loudness
- Pitch and loudness
  Plays tones of various amplitudes and frequencies, allowing appreciation of relationship between these physical attributes and pitch and loudness *(D, I)*

Chapter 18: Speech perception
- Speech sounds and their spectrograms
  Shows spectrograms and allows 'vocoder' playback for phonemes consisting of only two formats *(D, I)*
- Mystery phrase
  Plays a spoken phrase that is almost impossible to comprehend out of context; more comprehensible with clues *(D, T)*

Chapter 19: Somatosensory sensation
- Feedback in muscle length detection
  Animation of muscle spindle shows effect of feedback as muscle length is changed *(D, I)*

Chapter 20: Taste
> - Effect of vision on taste
>   Shows foods in true color, and with faded or distorted colors to demonstrate effect of vision on gustation *(D)*

D = demonstration, simulation, or animation
I = interaction: student controls what will be displayed or done
T = test: student data obtained
Q = quiz: student solves questions